A RIGHTEOUSLY AWESOME EIGHTIES CHRISTMAS

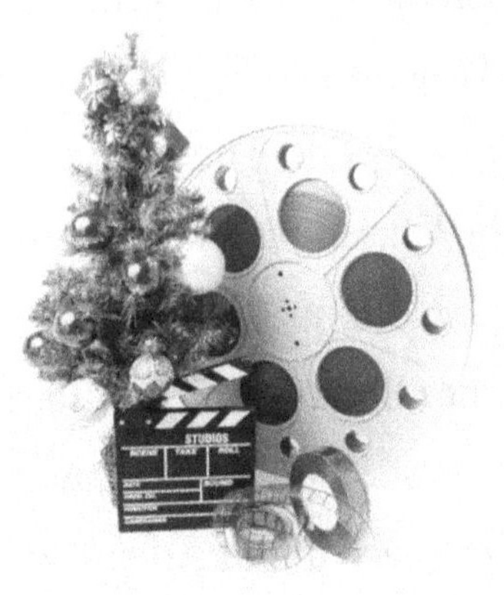

Thomas A. Christie

Other Books by
Thomas A. Christie

Liv Tyler: Star in Ascendance

The Cinema of Richard Linklater

John Hughes and Eighties Cinema

Ferris Bueller's Day Off: The Pocket Movie Guide

The Christmas Movie Book

Notional Identities

The James Bond Movies of the 1980s

Mel Brooks: Genius and Loving It!

The Spectrum of Adventure

A RIGHTEOUSLY AWESOME EIGHTIES CHRISTMAS

Festive Cinema of the 1980s

Thomas A. Christie

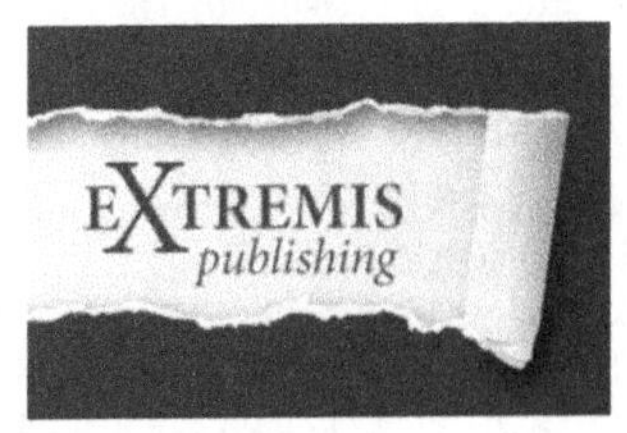

A Righteously Awesome Eighties Christmas: Festive Cinema of the 1980s by Thomas A. Christie.

First published in Great Britain in 2016 by Extremis Publishing Ltd.,
Suite 218, Castle House, 1 Baker Street, Stirling, FK8 1AL, United Kingdom.
www.extremispublishing.com

Extremis Publishing is a Private Limited Company registered in Scotland (SC509983) whose Registered Office is 47/51 Horsemarket, Kelso, Roxburghshire, TD5 7AA, United Kingdom.

A CIP catalogue record for this book is available from the British Library.

ISBN: 978-0-9934932-3-2

Typeset in Goudy Bookletter 1911, designed by The League of Moveable Type.

Printed and bound in Great Britain by IngramSpark, Chapter House, Pitfield, Kiln Farm, Milton Keynes, MK11 3LW, United Kingdom.

This book is dedicated to

The Invincible Amy Leitch

The best of friends, now and always.

Contents

A RIGHTEOUSLY AWESOME EIGHTIES CHRISTMAS

Festive Cinema of the 1980s

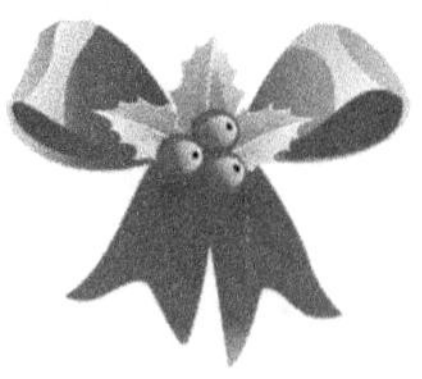

'Happy, happy Christmas, that can win us back to the delusions of our childhood days, recall to the old man the pleasures of his youth, and transport the traveller back to his own fireside and quiet home.'

Charles Dickens (1812–70)

Introduction

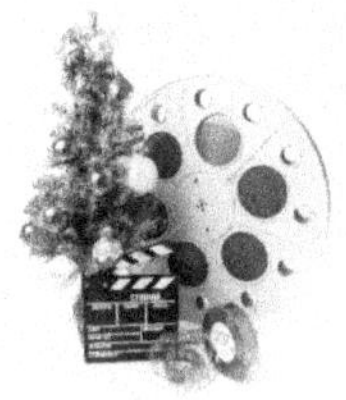

The 1980s were among the most exciting, innovative and often surprising of all decades in modern cinema, and the Christmas films of this period were no less varied or engaging. Following a golden age of festive movie-making throughout the 1940s and 50s, when the predominant tropes of the genre were established and the recognised stylistic conventions that are now associated with this category of film became acknowledged amongst audiences, the sixties and seventies would witness a long period where a relative paucity of Christmas features were to be found in cinemas. With films such as *It's a Wonderful Life* (Frank Capra, 1946), *Miracle on 34*th *Street* (George Seaton, 1947), *The Bishop's Wife* (Henry Koster, 1947), *Scrooge* (Brian Desmond Hurst, 1951) and *White Christmas* (Michael Curtiz, 1954) all having played their part in instituting the now-accepted precepts of festive cinema – celebrating the redemptive and transformative qualities of Christmas, commending the central importance of family and friends, and emphasising altruism over avarice – the following two decades would form a kind of wilderness period for the genre. While most prominent yuletide features of the 1960s and 70s were to be produced for television, including Kizo Nagashima and Larry Roemer's *Rudolph the Red-Nosed Reindeer* (1964), Bill

Melendez's *A Charlie Brown Christmas* (1965), Chuck Jones and Ben Washam's *How the Grinch Stole Christmas* (1966) and Jules Bass and Arthur Rankin Jr's *Frosty the Snowman* (1969), film theatres would prove to be largely devoid of festive fare throughout the course of the decade. The 1970s continued this trend with even fewer well-known movies in the genre appearing on the big screen during the course of the decade, though the Christmas film's torch was being carried by several made-for-television productions. Many high-quality features were broadcast in this period, such as *It Happened One Christmas* (Donald Wrye, 1977), with Orson Welles and Cloris Leachman; *The House Without a Christmas Tree* (Paul Bogart, 1972), which starred Jason Robards; *An American Christmas Carol* (Eric Till, 1979), which featured a compelling central performance from Henry Winkler, and *The Homecoming: A Christmas Story* (Fielder Cook, 1971), which was the precursor to the popular television series *The Waltons* (1972-81).

In spite of the prolific output of festive animations and TV movies, the sixties and seventies were far from having been vintage decades for Christmas films, but their peculiar blend of the traditional and the experimental marked them out as being a nonetheless intriguing period in the evolution of the genre. Some of the cinematic output would eventually achieve cult status, such as B-movie-style science fiction romps like *Santa Claus* (Rene Cardona, 1960) and the infamous *Santa Claus Conquers the Martians* (Nicholas Webster, 1964), whereas Ronald Neame's lavish *Scrooge* (1970) – a musical version of Charles Dickens's *A Christmas Carol*, starring Albert Finney – became a popular staple of the period in its own right. Yet if this era of festive film production is of specific interest to cinema historians, it is primarily on account of its less conventional entries in the genre: films such as Terence Young's evocative *The Christmas Tree* (1969), Milton H. Lehr's moving historical drama *The Juggler of Notre Dame* (1970), and most especially Bob Clark's pioneering and hugely influential hybrid of the horror movie and Christmas feature, *Black Christmas* (1974). These films had all challenged the sentimentalism and generic expectations that had been laid down throughout the golden age of the forties and fifties, exploring the boundaries of the format in energetic and frequently unanticipated ways.

With the arrival of the 1980s, the Christmas movie was abruptly back in vogue again: after two decades of relative obscurity on the big screen, festive film production was about to enter a period of major revival. The traditional themes of philanthropy, self-sacrifice and egalitarianism which had been established throughout the genre's golden age had swiftly attained new relevance in the era of high capitalism and conspicuous consumption. Over the course of the next ten years, the Christmas film would be dominated by depictions of the battle between the unselfish impartiality of the festive season and the emergent glorification of greed and materialism in the cultural environment of the time. The avaricious spirit of *It's a Wonderful Life*'s Mr Potter, it seemed, had returned with a vengeance, and a whole new generation of George Baileys would be required to counter its influence.

However, the complex ramifications of the generic experimentation that had been witnessed during the Christmas movie's long wilderness period could also be observed throughout the eighties in many ways. Never before had festive cinema seen such a plethora of different styles, with traditional family fare competing with lively teen comedies, yuletide-themed horror movies, contemplative dramas, high-octane action features, and many others besides. Suddenly the Christmas film was back in action, and its dynamic reinvention throughout the eighties would help to shape its continued development and sustained popularity throughout the decades that were to follow.

This book discusses seventeen prominent Christmas-themed movies which were released theatrically during the 1980s. Criss-crossing through many different subgenres, it will build a picture of the vibrant and rapidly-evolving field of festive film-making during one of the most socio-culturally turbulent decades in recent history, discussing the many ways in which the production teams of the time were addressing contemporary issues through the features they created. But the ongoing development of Christmas cinema itself is also explored, as the eighties were to see the tropes of the genre being challenged, subverted and reinterpreted as never before. While a distinctly postmodern approach to festive movie conventions has become commonplace from the 2000s onwards, the playful creative dexterity which underpinned the shift towards hybridisation and reconfiguration of genre characteristics arguably started to gain serious momentum from the eighties onwards, marking an era where audiences began to realise that their presumptions would need to be more adaptable than had been the case in decades past. Though the eighties would, of course, see their own share of traditional Christmas films which concentrate upon long-established themes of the genre, the period has generally become more markedly noted for the confrontation between traditional yuletide values and the prevailing ideologies of the time, exploring the innate incompatibility which lay between the joy and goodwill of the festive season and the cynicism and unchecked covetousness of the modern age.

As a number of the films under discussion have become somewhat obscure over the passing years, a detailed synopsis of each movie is included within every chapter for anyone unfamiliar with the plotline of any given feature. Because of its focus on cinematic output, this book does not discuss the abundant festive-themed TV features of the decade, which included domestic drama *A Christmas without Snow* (John Korty, 1980); *Mr Krueger's Christmas* (Kieth Merrill, 1980), a moving meditation on loneliness starring James Stewart; George C. Scott as a memorably commanding Ebenezer Scrooge in *A Christmas Carol* (Clive Donner, 1984), or whimsical fantasy *Babes in Toyland* (Clive Donner, 1986). Nor are documentary productions examined as part of the unfolding narrative, such as the captivating *The Store* (Frederick Wiseman, 1983) – a well-known feature which followed the staff and shoppers of the Neiman-Marcus department store in Dallas, Texas during the holiday season.

The 1980s were to be one of the most consistently engaging and inventive decades in Christmas cinema, and – as we will see – the films which would emerge during this tempestuous decade would cover just about every possible subject and subgenre, broadening and redefining the thematic scope of festive movie-making in ways that proved to be almost as profound as its formative golden age. In a period of rapid cultural and technological change, with the creative industry labouring to keep pace with a society that seemed to be in a perpetual state of flux, the comfortingly traditional would collide with the brashly contemporary to startling effect – sometimes startling, occasionally incongruous, but almost always imaginative and creatively fertile.

The Christmas film would never be quite the same again.

1

Christmas Evil (1980)

Edward R. Pressman Productions

Director: Lewis Jackson
Producers: Pete Kameron and Burt Kleiner
Screenwriter: Lewis Jackson

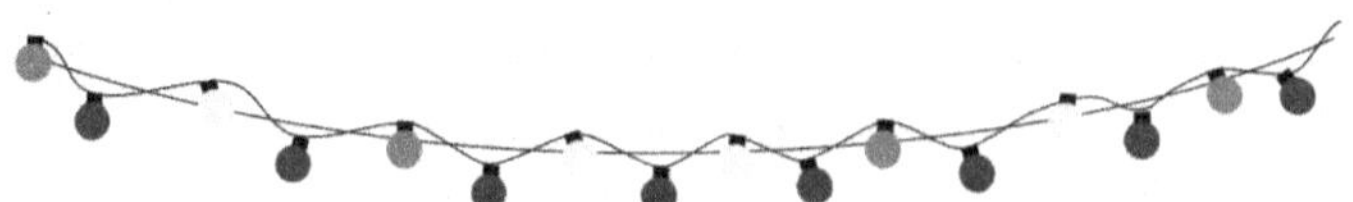

Christmas Evil was among the first festive films to be released in the 1980s, and it is a feature which also established what would become a popular creative engagement with the Christmas horror hybrid film throughout the early part of the decade. The yuletide horror movie had quickly cemented itself into the public consciousness with the arrival of Bob Clark's seminal slasher thriller *Black Christmas* in 1974. Helped in no small part by the scarcity of festive film production throughout the seventies, *Black Christmas* quickly gained cult notoriety amongst audiences, and the feature's tense atmosphere and suspenseful plot were influential not only to later Christmas cinema but also to horror film-making in general – popular movies such as *Halloween* (John Carpenter, 1978) and *Friday the 13th* (Sean S. Cunningham, 1980) exhibited many thematic and stylistic influences emanating from Clark's ground-breaking entry in the genre.

The early eighties have become synonymous with horror cinema ranging from the ground-breaking to the crude 'video nasty'; commercially successful horror franchises such as Wes Craven's long-running *A Nightmare on Elm Street* series would take up shelf-space in video stores along with many hack-and-slash titles ranging from the slickly produced to the gleefully cheap and cheerful. *Christmas Evil,* however, was to carve its own niche thanks to its part in commencing an entirely new subgenre of festive horror film: that of the appropriation of the benevolent figure of Santa Claus as a psychotic killer, a trope sometimes employed for comic effect but often heralding gore and suspense in abundance. Occasionally also known by the alternative titles *You Better Watch Out* and *Terror in Toyland, Christmas Evil* kicked off one of the most unconventional decades in festive film-making in a very distinctive (and highly entertaining) way, combining psychological terror with the darkest of humour to striking effect.

Christmas Evil was by no means a high-profile release at the time of its first appearance in cinemas, but the growing popularity of home entertainment formats such as **VHS** videotape throughout the early eighties meant that the film quickly found an audience amongst horror aficionados and Christmas movie buffs alike. The feature has become a career highlight in the filmography of director/screenwriter Lewis Jackson, who had been no stranger to the horror genre at the time of its production – in years past he had helmed other, smaller-scale films which had dexterously amalgamated dark humour with a sinister air of suspense, such as *The Deviates* (1970) and *The Transformation: A Sandwich of Nightmares* (1974). It is almost certainly *Christmas Evil* for which Jackson has become best known, however, and for good reason: while many later films focusing on Santa Claus as a murderous antagonist would largely rely upon gratuitous bloodletting and calculated shocks to supply their entertainment value, *Christmas Evil* was an altogether more cerebral affair, subtly contemplating the multifarious complexities of mental illness – and the malleable perception of reality that can sometimes result from particular psychological conditions – in ways that were far removed from most of the low-budget slasher features that would follow it.

The film opens with a shot of a cosy suburban home in America, one fateful Christmas Eve in 1947. As Clement Clark Moore's famous poem 'A Visit from St Nicholas' is read out, promising an annual visit from Father Christmas, two little boys and their mother (Ellen McElduff) watch in wonderment from the house's staircase as Santa Claus (Brian Hartigan) drops down the chimney into the fireplace and proceeds to enjoy the festive treats that have been left for him in the living room. The children watch in wonderment as Santa distributes presents under the tree and fills their stockings with gifts. But some time later, tucked up in their beds, the boys find themselves in disagreement over Santa's visit. Philip (Wally Moran) insists that the festive stopover was simply the work of their father, while Harry (Gus Salud) is equally certain that their yuletide guest was the genuine article. Upset at even the notion that Father Christmas's appearance was the work of an impostor, Harry creeps out of the bedroom... only to stumble upon the unwelcome sight of his parents enjoying an amorous tryst while his father remains dressed in the Santa Claus costume. Now thoroughly disillusioned by the deceit that he feels that he has been subjected to, Harry races to the house's attic and smashes a snowglobe containing a cheerful Christmas scene. Picking up a jagged shard of glass, he begins to self-harm by cutting deeply into the flesh of his hand.

More than thirty years later, Harry Stadling (Brandon Maggart) is now a somewhat ill-starred adult who leads a solitary life in New York, bereft of any loving companion and largely free from social contact with any friends. He has developed a lifelong obsession with Christmas, which has led him to transform his home into a kind of winter wonderland full of festive paraphernalia and kitschy toys. Seemingly neither able nor willing to leave childhood behind, he remains fanatical about Santa Claus and is constantly haunted by the heartbreak of his Christmas Eve disenchantment of thirty-three years previously.

Harry's behaviour proves to be considerably more psychologically disturbing than simply exhibiting the hallmarks of a man-child who cannot face the harsh realities of adulthood. He sneaks around his neighbourhood, covertly watching young children through binoculars to determine which are being 'good' and which are being 'bad'. Such is his unworldly innocence, Harry seems completely oblivious towards how sinister this behaviour is – or how it may be misconstrued by others. Keeping a list of who is naughty and nice, he spots a boy putting out the household garbage and a girl playing with a doll – pronouncing them both 'good' – before discovering another youngster, Moss Garcia (Peter Neuman), leafing through a copy of *Penthouse* magazine. Racing back to his apartment, Harry produces the latest in a series of leatherbound books containing his list of 'Bad Boys and Girls', adding Moss's perceived transgressions to an already lengthy register of past indiscretions. But he takes greater pleasure in adding to the list of 'Good Boys and Girls', noting their virtues too.

In keeping with his Christmas mania, Harry works at a toy factory owned by a company named Jolly Dreams. Unpopular with his colleagues, in no small part due to his utter fixation on providing the best-quality toys for children, he occupies a minor management role and seems incapable of buoying the flagging morale of the assembly line workers under his supervision. His colleagues resent Harry's recent promotion to a junior desk job, little realising (or caring) that he actually misses the hands-on approach to toy manufacturing and feels isolated by his modest career advancement. Adding to the unrelenting fusillade of disrespect and mockery, Harry is browbeaten into taking on the shift of one of his pushy assembly line workers, Frank Stoller (Joe Jamrog), leaving him looking even more ineffectual in the eyes of his team. Heading out to the factory floor, incipient rage at his treatment begins to bubble up inside of Harry, causing him to cut his hand on a partially-assembled toy – almost exactly as he had done as a child.

Though Stoller had called in sick, Harry sees him relaxing in a local bar with some colleagues when he makes his way home at night. Unaware that his comments are being overheard, Stoller laughs at how easy it was to hoodwink the ingenuous Harry into assuming his shift so that he could take it easy. Enraged at the way that he has been conned, Harry runs home and – unable to contain his anger – plucks a male figurine from his doll's house, breaking it apart as he frenziedly hums the tune to 'Santa Claus is Coming to Town'. Later, he visits the exterior of his now-adult brother Philip's (Jeffrey DeMunn) house and spies on his family through a window. But watching his sibling playing with his two young children offers no solace, and Harry grows even more uncomfortable when he sees Philip and his wife Jackie

(Dianne Hull) entering into a passionate embrace; the image brings back not only bad memories from Harry's childhood, but a painful reminder of his current singleton status.

The next morning, Harry watches a Thanksgiving Day Parade on television and eagerly awaits the traditional arrival of Santa Claus. He calls Philip and, still affected by the feelings encountered while snooping the previous night, tells his brother that he will be unable to join him for Thanksgiving dinner as he has made alternative arrangements. Philip is nonplussed at Harry's sudden change of plans, but the news brings him mixed emotions – he has a difficult relationship with his brother, and has often berated him for his purposeless life decisions. But Harry has little time to consider his sibling's feelings. Singularly preoccupied by the arrival of Jolly Old Saint Nick on his TV set, Harry retreats further into his apartment and sets to work on the development of a very exacting Santa Claus costume.

With the approach to the festive season now well underway, Harry carefully paints an image of a sleigh onto the side of his white van as he painstakingly runs through a list of all the local kids in his area and the gifts that he intends to bring them in his adopted guise as Santa Claus. Later that day, Harry is returning to his apartment with some groceries when he is greeted by a nearby group of boys and girls. The children are fond of the eccentric man, but an indecorous comment from Moss Garcia causes Harry to revisit the pages of his 'Bad Boys and Girls' book when he gets home. Creeping over to the youngster's home at night, Harry smears his hands and face in dirt and leaves their imprint on an external wall of the Garcia house – an ominous warning against further bad behaviour. He only barely manages to escape detection by diving for some shrubbery when Moss and his harried mother

(Patricia Richardson) unexpectedly leave the house to go on a car journey.

Back home, Harry's behaviour continues to gradually unravel. He begins using his basement-based smelting equipment to meticulously create an army of toy soldiers, bayonets drawn, and other militaristic playthings. Soon afterwards, at the toy factory, Harry attends a Christmas staff party that has been organised by the management. Remaining a solitary figure amongst his celebrating colleagues, he listens attentively to a video message recorded by the company's owner, where a promise is made to donate toys from Jolly Dreams to the nearby Willowy Springs State Hospital. However, as the owner emphasises, production will need to be stepped up on manufacturing output – the more toys that are fabricated by the company, the greater number that will be donated to the hospital.

Harry continues to be needled by his workmates, who provoke him with observations about how easily manipulated he is, but the once-docile junior supervisor intimates that the worm is about to turn. His reflections are interrupted by the introduction of a new employee – a youthful go-getter who has obvious ambitions to get ahead in the company. Oblivious to the office politics that are in play, Harry refuses to ingratiate himself and instead pushes for more information about the toys being donated to the hospital. When it becomes obvious that the entire scheme has been concocted as a cynical ploy to engender greater productivity from the workforce, with little concern about manufacturing enough toys to ensure that every child patient will receive a gift, Harry reacts in disgust and storms out of the party.

Leaving the revelry behind, Harry returns to the currently-deserted production line and starts stuffing bags full of brand new toys that have only just been manufactured. As dawn breaks, he arrives at a remote riverbank area and fills several sacks with loose earth. Now increasingly unhinged, Harry begins to transform himself into Santa Claus, gluing a fake beard onto his face and lapsing into hysterics in the process. He has now begun to associate himself so closely with the famous festive figure that he is on the cusp of losing his personal identity altogether.

Christmas Eve arrives, and a thoroughly deranged Harry – now dressed in full Santa Claus regalia – starts breaking into the homes of the local children, brandishing a steak knife. Jubilantly, he begins distributing a combination of home-made toys and stolen merchandise from the Jolly Dreams factory to the 'good' boys and girls, while dropping off a sack filled of dirt on the doorstep of Moss Garcia, thus cementing his 'bad' status. Determined to correct the moral vacuity that he detects in his company's attitudes, Harry then visits the Willowy Springs State Hospital in his sleigh-bedecked van with the intention of dropping off further bags of Christmas gifts for the unwell children staying within. His intentions are met with considerable scepticism by the hospital's crotchety security guard (William Robertson), but Harry manages to appeal to the man's spirit of goodwill. A doctor (Robert Ari) and nurse (Sheila Anderson) arrive at the door, and are amazed to discover that Harry has loaded his entire van with gifts; an army of their colleagues need to be called upon to bring the presents inside. Unsuspecting of Harry's disturbed mental state, the doctor quizzically asks who has donated all of these generous contributions, only for 'Santa' to reply that they have come from people who had never even guessed just how charitable they could be.

Harry considers his benevolent mission to have been successful, but subsequently remembers that the ambitious executive who had unfeelingly expounded on the donation drive at the party is planning to attend a Midnight Mass service at a nearby church. Arriving in his van, Harry holds a silent vigil at the base of the steps leading to the church doorway, patiently waiting for the service to end. A group of obnoxious, well-groomed attendees emerge and immediately start berating the toy-toting Santa Claus, ridiculing everything from his outfit to his mode of transport. Finally snapping, Harry attacks the ringleader, gouging his eye with a bayonet-holding toy soldier and then assaulting him – and the others – with a miniature axe. The scene of bloody carnage at the hands of 'Santa' causes mass horror amongst the other churchgoers, who watch in awestruck fear as he speeds off into the night in his van. At the top of the steps, Harry's senior colleagues are dumbstruck by the unexpected attack – not least as it has become clear, in the aftermath, that the slaughter has been caused entirely by weaponised toys.

Making a getaway, Harry stops at a safe distance from the crime scene in order to pull himself together. His singular Christmas fixation is once again roused, however, when he hears the sound of cheery festive music from a nearby Families and Friends Association. Throwing a sack of toys over his shoulder, Harry wanders up to a nearby window and glances balefully at the happy scenes of merriment taking place within. To his surprise, two of the partyers spot Harry lurking outside the building and decide to drag him in to the gathering – much to his discomfiture. He quickly overcomes his initial awkwardness when he discovers that their welcoming crowd are genuinely pleased to see him... not least a gaggle of adoring children. Reassuming his festive character,

Harry delights everyone by distributing toys to the expectant youngsters. None of the oblivious adults suspect his involvement in the recent homicidal actions, even as the onlookers at the church remain in a state of shock. Becoming the life and soul of the party, 'Santa' leads the partygoers in some yuletide dancing and enjoys their hospitality before reluctantly deciding to withdraw. Parting with a slightly-too-sincere warning to the children that they must behave well if they want to receive good gifts, lest they go in the 'Bad Boys and Girls' book and receive 'something horrible' instead, Harry makes a suitably theatrical exit (leaving some of the parents looking slightly uncomfortable in his wake).

Now increasingly unbalanced, Harry cries out to Santa's reindeer as he drives his van – convinced that he really is in control of an airborne sleigh. The fantasy is marred only by memory echoes of the bad treatment he has received at the hands of his workmates, which seems to plant the seed of a new idea. Grabbing a set of extendable stepladders from his van, Harry heads through the increasingly heavy snow until he reaches the roof of Frank Stoller's house. Attempting to clamber down the chimney with a bag of toys, he soon finds himself stuck tight – only with major effort is he able to pull free from the stack. Unwilling to admit defeat, he instead breaks into the house through a basement-level window. Stoller's children watch in wonder as Santa adds new gifts to the pile of presents beneath their Christmas tree. But they are unaware that this not-so-jolly figure then moves on to Frank's bedroom and tries to suffocate his slumbering nemesis with a bag of toys – an act of revenge due to his colleague's earlier selfish behaviour at work. When this strategy fails, Harry reaches for a decorative Christmas star and promptly slashes Frank's throat with it. With Stoller's wife (Marian Vitale) screaming in terror at the discovery of her dead spouse, Harry flees from the house before he can be apprehended.

Morning breaks on Christmas Day, and Philip's two sons are enjoying their gifts while their father worries about Harry's absence. As Harry always arrives promptly at their home when Christmas arrives, his non-appearance has left Philip feeling anxious and confused. While Jackie pleads with him to stop being concerned, reasoning that Harry is likely still upset at the sibling conflict that usually rages between his brother and himself, a newsflash interrupts their train of thought. The newscaster solemnly announces the murders outside the church and the mysterious slaying of Frank Stoller, explaining that the police are unaware of the killer's identity and recommending that the public avoid contact with anyone wearing a Santa Claus outfit. This pronouncement does nothing to allay Philip's nagging sense of unease.

Meanwhile, Harry is groggily emerging from his van – his costume now somewhat worse for its struggle with Stoller's chimney. He heads into the deserted Jolly Dreams factory floor and, on inspecting a new batch of toy aeroplanes, reacts with anger at what he perceives to be shortcomings in their production. Starting the assembly lines running, he watches with intense deliberation as toy after toy plummets off the end of the conveyor belt and smashes onto the ground. Little does he realise that, at a nearby police station, Detectives Grella (Sam Gray), Gottlieb (Bobby Lesser) and Gleason (Ray Barry) are conducting numerous identity parades of costumed Santas. However, their investigations have thus far brought them no closer to pinpointing the culprit behind the recent slayings; they are baffled and frustrated by the fact that there appears to be no connection between the deaths of the churchgoers and the later murder of Stoller.

As night falls, Harry phones up the increasingly jittery Philip from his office, entering into a surreal conversation where he confides in his brother the fact that he has finally hit on 'the right tune' after having searched so long for it. Philip, now deeply concerned for Harry's wellbeing, begs him to come over so that they can talk the situation through. But Harry refuses, instead issuing an ominous warning that soon everyone will hear his tune for themselves.

Heading off in his van once more, Harry is perturbed when the icy conditions cause his vehicle to skid off the road (accompanied by the imagined crack of sleigh reins), eventually leading it to become immobilised on a muddy embankment. He finds himself on a brightly illuminated street which is lined by a seemingly-endless array of Christmas lights and outdoor ornaments. At first he seems enchanted by the sight, but his fascination is short-lived – a group of children cluster around him, eager to thank 'Santa' for their recent gifts. As he produces yet more presents from his bag, much to the kids' delight, their parents react first with suspicion and then with outright hostility when they recognise Harry as the murderer from the recent news broadcasts. Harry tries to talk them out of violent action, explaining that children need someone like Santa to enforce moral decisions so that they will avoid confusion over what is right and wrong. However, the stand-off soon turns violent, and Harry is only just able to escape the confrontation with his life.

Tearing down the street, the parents quickly manage to assemble a growing mob to hunt Harry down before he can kill anyone else. Flaming torches burning in the night sky, the horde of outraged civilians pursue the errant Santa along various alleyways and darkened pathways. Now on the cusp of a complete mental breakdown, Harry only just manages to evade the rampaging throng, but they regain pursuit just as he returns to his van. To their fury, he manages to get the lethargic vehicle back on the road before the mob can catch up with him.

Harry manages to reach Philip's house, albeit in the dead of night. Upon seeing his brother's dishevelled costume, Philip immediately realises that Harry has been behind the recent spate of killings. Desperately, Philip tries to make Harry comprehend the fact that – far from being Santa Claus – he has lost control of his faculties. Harry slowly explains, upset though calm, that he has come to understand that the modern world no longer wants Santa Claus; he has been rejected simply because people don't believe in him. Relating it back to his childhood experiences, Harry tells his brother that because Philip refused to believe in the existence of Santa Claus, he had to do whatever it took to prove that this figure of Christmas comfort and joy was alive and well. Incensed that Harry would blame him for his misfortunes, and indeed that he is being held indirectly responsible for a series of murders based on a throwaway comment when he was six years old, Philip's temper finally boils over. He furiously throttles Harry until his brother collapses to the ground.

Shocked by the violence of his actions, Philip begins to panic. He picks up Harry's prone form and drags him out of the house, manoeuvring him back into the driver's seat of his van. His two sons watch the scene in horrified awe from their bedroom window. But Harry is not quite as dead as Philip had surmised. Taking a well-aimed punch at his brother, he makes yet another narrow getaway, accelerating away in spite of Philip's fevered protests. As Philip pursues him on foot,

Harry quickly encounters the mob that has been searching for him; such are their numbers that they force the van off the road, causing Harry to drive through the barrier of a bridge. Philip watches in shock as the van then flies through the air, as though levitated by magic in the manner of Santa's sleigh. Harry assumes an expression of delighted satisfaction as the van continues to soar into the night sky, gliding away as the narrator reads the closing lines of 'A Visit from St Nicholas'.

Although *Christmas Evil* has become most immediately recognised for its then-novel use of a Santa Claus figure in an antagonistic role, in truth the film is less of a horror film than it is a dark satire on society's relationship with traditional Christmas conventions. It is also a much more nuanced and contemplative feature than it is often given credit for. A bleak meditation on mental illness, the film is as foreboding as it is thought-provoking, and director/screenwriter Lewis Jackson takes his time in slowly building suspense. Great restraint is demonstrated in the fact that the first killings don't take place until nearly an hour of the film has passed, with far greater emphasis being placed on the slow-motion breakdown of a protagonist who catastrophically proved to be unable (or perhaps unwilling) to grow up.

In the highly capable hands of Brandon Maggart, Harry becomes a truly tragic figure; his downfall is delineated with pathos and tinged with despair throughout. As Shawn Macomber notes, *Christmas Evil* 'is a really intriguing mélange, like *The Santa Clause* meets *Henry: Portrait of a Serial Killer* or *Psycho* remade as an outré vigilante movie by John G. Avildsen during the early *Joe* (1970)/*Save the Tiger* (1973) man-out-of-time phase of his career – all with a pinch of Seventies style, jaded urban detective flick thrown in for good measure'.[1] Jackson requires his viewers to walk a fine line of moral judgement, on one hand empathising with Harry's ill treatment and downtrodden outsider status, yet clearly not expecting them to support or commiserate with the horror of his subsequent actions. While we see Harry being ridiculed by his workmates, treated condescendingly by his superiors and undermined by his brother, we also cannot ignore his increasingly bizarre behaviour as his breakdown unfolds: giggling uncontrollably at the appearance of the shaving-foam beard, the deadly serious way that he maintains his naughty and nice lists, and – perhaps most notably – his disturbing line in voyeurism. Harry's guilelessness is so profound that he genuinely appears unaware of the connotations which would inevitably be drawn if he were to be caught spying on the actions and behaviour of young children; certainly it is made clear that his interests start and end with their moral character, and that there is no more sinister aspect to his conduct (however alarming it may be). Yet the audience is never less than aware of Harry's doleful but unanswered need for companionship of his own; though a loner by nature, we see him looking longingly at his brother's (comparatively) happy domestic situation and similarly showing attraction for one of the women attending the Christmas party at the Families and Friends Association... and yet he demonstrates no concentrated motivation to correct this deficit in his life. Harry seems acutely aware of his lack of female company and dwindling chances of parenthood, and yet never seems able or willing to make the changes in his life necessary to pursue a relationship; rather, his idolisation of 'good' children appears to form a kind of proxy for a family he never had. But it could also be argued that Harry takes his role in promoting the values of Christmas so seriously that the added responsibility of domestic relationships would be an unneeded distraction from his self-imposed primary goals. Jim Knipfel notes that:

> The success of the film [...] is due in no small part to Brandon Maggart's brilliant performance. It's a rare thing to say about the lead in a grainy, low-budget horror movie, but despite all the insanity and the killing, he manages to turn Harry into an extremely sympathetic character. After all, he simply expects that people will behave with some common decency and a little selflessness – that they'll care about one another and be nice. Is that really too much to ask? Santa was someone, maybe the last one, who not only kept track of who was naughty and nice, but who doled out justice as well. Children needed to believe that someone in the world could promise them a little justice, right?[2]

Harry's moral motivations are at the very core of the film, which contrast the violence of his homicidal actions with the gradual erosion of his dignity and self-confidence at the hands of others – whether they be essentially well-meaning, such as his brother and sister-in-law, or unfeeling and dismissive, as in the case of his workmates. Though Anthony Nield is correct in his assertion that 'we're not quite dealing with a psychological portrait akin to [Martin Scorsese's] *Taxi Driver* here (a more pertinent comparison would be something like William Lustig's *Maniac*)',[3] nonetheless there is quiet power in Jackson's quiet indignation at the ill-treatment of an innocent who appears to sincerely want greater impartiality and mutual respect for all. The film's Christmas setting is, of course, crucially important given Harry's identification with Santa Claus as the *bona fide* arbiter of social justice, but there is further significance to the seasonal milieu in the sense that, as Bill Gracey has explained, 'the fact that Christmas can be a desperately sad and lonely time for many individuals is also rife throughout the narrative. The juxtaposition of Harry's isolated existence with that of his brother's family life is particularly effective, if somewhat under-explored'.[4] While we are not, of course, expected to countenance Harry's murderous spree on account of his isolation and abuse by others, the festive background makes his personal plight considerably more sympathetic and his actions all the more shocking because of the comparison it invites between comforting Christmas traditions and wanton terror and slaughter. Because Harry desperately wants to fit in, yet cannot bring himself to conform to expectation (or is incapable of doing so), his impasse makes him seem even more of a wretched character, but the fact that his mental breakdown plays out against the tinsel, snowflakes and gift-wrap of Christmas encourages the viewer to question whether the inequity doled out to the unworldly Harry appears even more callous during the festive season. Jim Harper observes that 'the moral points [the film] makes are actually fairly valid. Christmas isn't about money, and Harry's victims seem to genuinely deserve their treatment. It makes a far more effective case about Christmas commercialism than the droves of "family" movies released every year. It's not a happy film or a reassuring one, but it's worth seeing, if only as an antidote to films like *Santa Claus: The Movie*.[5] Though Harry's descent into madness is not by any means deliberate, meaning that his subsequent actions are not premeditated, he never wavers from his primary goal – that of ensuring that the virtues and principles of the festive season are upheld at all costs. Unfortunately, the gulf which lies between his worldview and the actual conduct of society is so vast that his resulting fury seems as inevitable as it is disastrous. As James

Dennis explains, Harry's behaviour may be demonstrably erratic or even outright deranged, but from his own point of view he is operating from a position of elevated ethical responsibility:

> As deluded and crazy as Harry is, he's fundamentally driven by a desire to keep the more traditional Christmas values alive. Travis Bickle in a stick-on beard if you like; a loner with a bent set of principles, not a lunatic killer out for revenge. Harry's growing disillusionment is pretty compelling, though marred by some ropey effects once he does get down to some knife work. What could have been some genuinely shocking moments are blighted by dodgy editing and ineffective gore.[6]

In a modest way, *Christmas Evil* was an early example of the way in which the festive movie was becoming more ideologically charged with the arrival of the 1980s. Although the concept of mass consumption being incompatible with the core values of Christmas – that is, the conflict between greed and altruism – had been expounded upon at length by classics of the genre such as George Seaton's *Miracle on 34th Street* (1947), the methodology and public perception of consumer culture had evolved significantly in the intervening decades, meaning that the topic was ripe for re-examination with the dawning of a new age of high capitalism. Macomber notes that 'Rather than pervert Christmas for shock value, [*Christmas Evil*] raises the holiday's best, most righteous aspects, aspirations, and traditions to a horrifying apotheosis. Which is perhaps why, despite the degradation and violence, so much of the film feels cathartic and cheer-worthy,' adding that 'Harry's rampage proves to be less about terrorizing children than avenging his own unshakable outsider status and seizing, by force, a respect the world hitherto has refused to give him'.[7] Indeed, the murderous outcome of Harry's pent-up frustrations may be disastrous, but it is also a cry for help against forces which he perceives to be eroding the innocence and generosity that underlies the festive season. Thus the film becomes, as Dennis elucidates, 'a grimy and intimate portrait of a man's nervous breakdown. Surprisingly light on slashing, it's heavy on psychological anguish and twisted ideology'.[8] Yet the film's central dichotomy, anomalous though it may seem, is that of a man whose outrage at the emasculation of Christmas goodwill leads him to engage in acts of outright bloodshed – surely the very antithesis of festive benevolence and mutual understanding. Certainly it is unsurprising that the film proved to be controversial at the time of its first appearance in 1980, provoking debate not just amongst audiences but also horror enthusiasts; as Jagd Slarek observes, rather than proving to be 'another in a line of masked stalk-and-slash killers, Harry walks an altogether less predictable path, one that apparently messed with the heads of those expecting a straight-up slasher on the film's initial release, including the film's backers. Instead of going on the expected killing spree, Harry divides his time between acts of altruistic kindness and brief explosions of furious anger'.[9] There is, of course, an obvious subtext in play concerning the moral imperative for adults to put aside childish things in the name of individual responsibility (consider Harry's supremely ironic comment to Frank Stoller that the latter is a child no more), which co-exists – if occasionally somewhat incongruously – with the major theme of society's willingness to jeopardise the artless virtues of Christmas in favour of the unfeeling pursuit of commercial goals. While the violent variation between the traditional compassion and gentleness typified by the character of Santa Claus and the brutal viciousness of a psychotic killer may have seemed jarring to some, its sheer unpredictability added considerable entertainment value for fans of the genre – especially at this nascent stage in the development of the Christmas horror film. The creative resourcefulness was just one reason for the enduring cult popularity of *Christmas Evil*, as Scott Clark has explained:

> Jackson's film has received flak over the years for being anti-Christmas but the film seems more focused on the commercialisation of Christmas as opposed to an attack on the holiday itself. A sharp eye for the trashy quality of Christmas imagery and the miserable, at times pointless, bizarre functions of the holiday push the film beyond the reach of a crappy B-film. This is a film at once ridiculing the Santa myth (Santa Clauses at [the] police line-up) and celebrating it, whilst dragging the whole Christmas ordeal into a sewer of madness and mayhem.[10]

The film has been noted by critics for its deeply dark vein of humour, which includes deft touches such as a long-winded philosophical discussion between police detectives regarding the role of Santa Claus in modern society while a killer remains on the loose, the festively-themed murder weapons, an attempted lynching which almost appears to be lifted straight from the frames of an old Universal horror movie (complete with burning torches), and most especially the craftily premeditated bite when the old Christmas favourite 'I Saw Mommy Kissing Santa Claus' plays over the action as Harry's breakdown gets underway in earnest (pointedly reminding the audience of the original cause of his sinister behaviour). Peter Normanton was not alone in describing the film's 'subversive comedic streak, which included the slapstick being-stuck-in-the-chimney routine, imagining his van is being pulled by reindeer and a police identity line-up of the most scurrilous looking Santas you are ever likely to see. This feature, however, can be looked upon as a psychological study of a man whose obsession becomes so twisted he can't help but lose his mind'.[11] While the actual psychological foundations for Harry's eventual mental disintegration are hazily demarcated at best – logic would suggest that he would actually resent Christmas and the figure of Santa Claus for the part they played in destroying his childhood innocence, rather than idolising them as an adult in early middle age – the sheer hopelessness and dreary monotony of Harry's life are such that we are expected to accept the transformation from diffident dogsbody into unstable lunatic in any respect. Scott Aaron Stine reflects that 'the reasoning behind our psychopath's impairment [...] is far from credible, but with this film's tongue-in-cheek approach, I doubt any other explanation would seem as sound',[12] and while Harry's headlong charge into insane savagery may be the inevitable payoff to the long-gestating personal collapse that Jackson slowly and patiently unveils, the approach is not without its occasional hitches. Dennis Schwartz, for instance, offers the opinion that 'the story is not helped when the filmmaker can't quite articulate what he's driving at (aiming for the theme of the [James Whale] *Frankenstein* film that society is the real monster, which becomes hard to carry off after all of the vicious murders by the psycho Santa)',[13] and while it is difficult not to feel some pity for the cruelties meted out to Harry in his personal and professional life, there is just as much repulsion to be experienced in his formative moments of unbalanced behaviour. These include the voodoo doll-like destruction of the figurine from his festively-decorated doll's house (following his unwelcome realisation of the sheer contempt that his workmates hold for him), the frankly worrying sight of framed photos of some of the neighbourhood kids in his apartment, and his fixation on altering his personal appearance, leading to various scenes in front of a mirror as he seeks to obscure and eventually eliminate his genuine self in favour of simulacra. As distorted and discordant Christmas carols are played following the church murders to genuinely creepy effect, the audience are prompted to ask themselves: in spite of the semantic cleverness of the title, is it only Harry's actions which are evil in this film, or do those around him share responsibility for the malevolence of his bloodied deeds?

Schwartz has described *Christmas Evil* as 'a black comedy cult favorite Yuletide psychological thriller that offers a pertinent character study on a grownup crushed by his brief disappointing childhood experience with Santa Claus and [who] is traumatized for life', though further stating that 'how one perceives it as a Christmas film depends on one's taste and values, as it seems more suited for the viewer who is not afraid to stray far afield from the traditional Christmas movie'.[14] Certainly there is no denying the film's cult credentials, its freshness and originality at the time of its release, or indeed its arrestingly enigmatic nature. Much commentary has been expended over its inscrutable closing sequence, raising questions over Harry's actual fate. While his escape from retribution in his van (reflecting the motion of Santa Claus's flying sleigh) is heavily suggested to be a figment of Harry's increasingly fecund imagination, the actual nature of his true destiny remains unclear. Does the muffled sound of an explosion which accompanies Philip's fruitless pursuit of the van suggest that Harry simply crashed through the bridge's barrier to his death? Or was Harry's earlier revival from Philip's attempt to throttle him actually a fantasy, meaning that everything he experiences from that point actually takes place following the end of his life? Ultimately only the viewer can decide upon their own interpretation. This conundrum is only one reason for the film's continuing appeal, as Knipfel suggests: 'At the film's end we know what happens – all the evidence is there if you pay close attention – but what we see on the screen is pure fantasy. It's a sharp bit of filmmaking from a director who turned [*Christmas Evil*] into much more than it could have been. 35 years later it's a film that still stands apart from and above that flood of killer Santa movies that followed'.[15] While there would be no shortage of films which would emerge over the coming years with a Santa Claus figure cast in a threatening or antagonistic role, very few could claim to be of such enduring interest to cineastes. Though *Christmas Evil* was by no means a significant commercial hit, its cult qualities are impeccable; Adam Tyner sagely notes that:

> Rather than being hammered out fast, cheap, and dirty, *Christmas Evil* genuinely is a well-crafted film. The cinematography by Ricardo Aronovich – who'd routinely worked with the likes of [Alain] Resnais and [Louis] Malle – is worlds removed from anything you'd expect to see unspooling in a dingy 42nd St. theater. The visuals are in every way outstanding, strengthened further by shooting on location wherever possible, drawing from a collection of strange Saint Nick-nacks that writer/director Lewis Jackson spent a decade amassing, filming in an actual toy factory, and a couple of particularly ambitious shots that far outstrip what *Christmas Evil* should've been able to accomplish on this budget.[16]

There is no doubt that Aronovich's cinematography, which is as well-judged as it is skilful, helps to elevate the film above many other competitors which would emerge in the years following its production. However, there are many other aspects of *Christmas Evil* which are worthy of note, from well-observed supporting performances (especially from Jeffrey DeMunn and Dianne Hull as Harry's concerned brother and sister-in-law) to the excellent, atmospheric original music score by Joel Harris, Julia Heyward and Don Christensen. For such a modestly-budgeted feature, *Christmas Evil* constantly punches above its weight: a testament to Jackson's sharp eye for detail in addition to his sheer dedication in getting the project off the ground. Clark reflects that 'for a film left in the side-lines, *Christmas Evil* is actually well-shot and directed; sure there's some crude editing and naff moments of action but on the whole the film has more rewards than flops. After style the story impresses with a much more toned down approach to carnage than expected. The film isn't a blood bath start to finish, [it's] collected and well-paced'.[17] Though overlooked by many in the critical community when first released, *Christmas Evil* has achieved and retained high regard amongst commentators in subsequent years. In many ways this is a triumph of the film's durability in the face of its subsequent competition; its reputation seemed initially in danger of being subsumed by the wave of festively-situated horror films which were to follow, as Brian Albright observes: 'Weird, melancholy, funny and whimsical, *Christmas Evil* stands as one of the finest films ever made for the exploitation market. Unfortunately it was overshadowed in the Santa-suited-killer genre by the more gruesome *Silent Night, Deadly Night* (1984), and its reputation was further eroded thanks to rampant bootlegging of substandard prints during the video era'.[18] Yet the film has somehow persisted nonetheless, remaining an offbeat, low-key alternative to more conventional holiday season output which manages to remain subversive even in the present day – due in no small part to its relentless challenging of the treacly sentimentalism that typified (and in many ways continues to characterise) many of the family-oriented Christmas films that have proven to be more commercially successful at the box-office. For others, the film's historical controversy has ensured that it remains a curio amongst fans of festive movie-making and horror feature connoisseurs alike; Bill Gibron remarks that:

> Initial audiences in the early '80s were stunned when they learned that this festive fright flick – re-titled with the far more lurid *Christmas Evil* label by financially strapped distributors – featured an unbalanced man who took the notion of 'being' Santa to painful, unwholesome extremes. Already angry at the mixing of the festive with the frightening in several celebrated slasher films, the seedy subtext involving children and bloodshed made even the most high-minded horror fan more than a little ill. And that's too bad really, since their ready dismissal prevented them from appreciating a truly remarkable movie.[19]

Ultimately, the success of *Christmas Evil* lies in its appealing craftsmanship; Jackson's film contains a heady mix of biting social satire and genuinely unexpected depth of character which allows the movie sufficient room to breathe amongst a surfeit of pale imitations. This is a feature where, as Tyner has commented, the protagonist is far from being simply 'some psychopath who makes a detour at a costume shop before slaughtering an hour and a half's worth of victims. Santa Claus isn't a suit he wears; it's who he *is*. [[...]] Just another slice of Xmasploitation it's not. *Christmas Evil* has proven to be deeply divisive for three and a half decades now, but I look at it as a truly outstanding film: one that's crafted with a great deal of thought, care, artistry, and subtlety'.[20] With its appearance right at the beginning of the 1980s, the quiet bellicosity of Jackson's creative approach sent out an influential message which would be further explored and developed as the decade continued: where earlier films had reacted to the corrosion of traditional Christmas values with moral messages and comforting truisms, the methodology of their defence throughout the eighties was to be considerably more direct – and significantly less passive than in years gone by.

REFERENCES

1. Shawn Macomber, '*Christmas Evil* (Vinegar Syndrome Blu-Ray Review)', in *Shock Till You Drop*, 24 December 2014.
   <http://www.shocktillyoudrop.com/news/371795-christmas-evil-vinegar-syndrome-blu-ray-review/>

2. Jim Knifpel, '*You Better Watch Out*: The *Taxi Driver* of Christmas Movies', in *Den of Geek*, 10 December 2015.
   <http://www.denofgeek.us/movies/you-better-watch-out/34766/you-better-watch-out-the-taxi-driver-of-christmas-movies>

3. Anthony Nield, '*Christmas Evil*, in *The Digital Fix*, 19 December 2012.
   <http://film.thedigitalfix.com/content/id/76149/christmas-evil.html>

4. Bill Gracey, '*Christmas Evil*, in *Behind the Couch*, 20 December 2012.
   <http://watchinghorrorfilmsfrombehindthecouch.blogspot.co.uk/2012/12/christmas-evil.html>

5. Jim Harper, *Legacy of Blood: A Comprehensive Guide to Slasher Movies* (Manchester: Headpress/Critical Vision, 2004), p.75.

6. James Dennis, 'DVD Review: *Christmas Evil* Isn't Quite What You'd Expect', in *Twitch*, 25 November 2012.
   <http://twitchfilm.com/2012/11/dvd-review-christmas-evil-isnt-quite-what-youd-expect.html>

7. Macomber, 2014.

8.   Dennis, 2012.

9.   Jagd Slarek, '*Christmas Evil* DVD Review', in *CineOutsider*, 22 December 2012.
        <*http://www.cineoutsider.com/reviews/dvd/c/christmas_evil.html*>

10.   Scott Clark, '*Christmas Evil* DVD Review', in *The People's Movies*, 12 November 2012.
        <*http://thepeoplesmovies.com/2012/11/christmas-evil-dvd-review/*>

11.   Peter Normanton, *The Mammoth Book of Slasher Movies* (London: Robinson, 2012), p.307.

12.   Scott Aaron Stine, *The Gorehound's Guide to Splatter Films of the 1980s* (Jefferson: McFarland, 2011), p.75.

13.   Dennis Schwartz, '*You Better Watch Out* (aka *Christmas Evil*)', in *Dennis Schwartz's Movie Reviews*, 21 December 2011.
        <*http://homepages.sover.net/~ozus/youbetterwatchout.html*>

14.   ibid.

15.   Knipfel, 2015.

16.   Adam Tyner, '*Christmas Evil* (Blu-Ray)', in *DVD Talk*, 18 November 2014.
        <*http://www.dvdtalk.com/reviews/66272/christmas-evil/*>

17.   Clark, 2012.

18.   Brian Albright, *Regional Horror Films, 1958-1990: A State-by-State Guide with Interviews* (Jefferson: McFarland, 2012), p.97.

19.   Bill Gibron, '*Christmas Evil*', in *DVD Talk*, 14 November 2006.
<http://www.dvdtalk.com/reviews/25047/christmas-evil/>

20.   Tyner, 2014.

2

To All a Goodnight (1980)

Four Features Partners/Intercontinental Releasing Corporation

Director: David Hess
Producers: Sandy Cobe and Jay Rasumny
Screenwriter: Alex Rebar

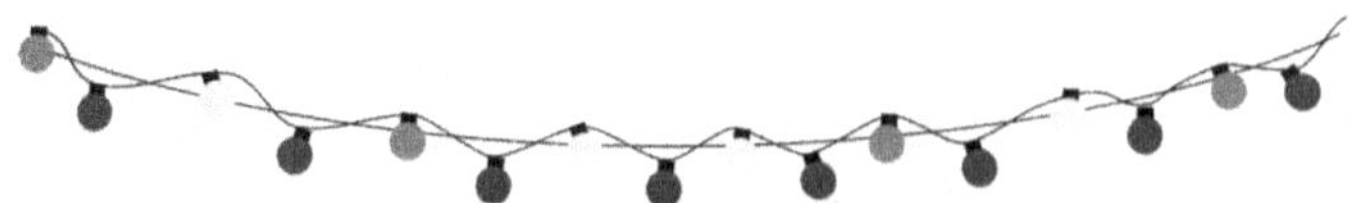

If *Christmas Evil* had been among the earliest horror films to feature an antagonist whose appearance was influenced by the legend of Santa Claus, *To All a Goodnight* – released in the same year – was to be less overtly influenced by psychological or ideological issues emanating from the festive season, instead owing more to the sombre style and narrative beats of Bob Clark's ground-breaking 1974 suspense thriller *Black Christmas*. Yet in spite of the sorority house setting and a festive ambience which was nominal at best, *To All a Goodnight* has all the hallmarks of a fairly standard campus slasher horror (albeit with a token scattering of Christmas trimmings) at an early point in this subgenre's development. Although actually released some months prior to the debut of *Christmas Evil, To All a Goodnight* has come to be regarded as the lesser of the two films in terms of critical opinion; its long-term reputation has become more closely aligned with that gore-drenched thrillers such as Sean S. Cunningham's popular *Friday the 13th* (1980) (which was in production at roughly the same time) than the Christmas-themed horror movies which preceded and succeeded it. In some ways this may largely be explained by the film's relatively muted engagement with Christmas motifs; whereas *Christmas Evil* would concern itself very directly with the altruistic methodology of Santa Claus, exploring the conflict between guileless philanthropy and materialistic cynicism via the protagonist's gradual mental breakdown, *To All a Goodnight* was instead to take a rather less subtle approach to the season of goodwill, employing it largely as a backdrop to its scenes of wholesale slaughter rather than a subject which was core to the film itself. If there was any social commentary at play in this movie at all, it certainly didn't linger too long on the traditions of the festive season.

To All a Goodnight was directed by David Hess, a popular songwriter and composer as well as an actor. His performances included the role of psychotic criminal Krug Stillo in Wes Craven's notorious horror *The Last House on the Left* (1972) (Hess also composed the film's score), and – many years later – the character of Ferret in Craven's slyly-crafted sci-fi movie *Swamp Thing* (1982). *To All a Goodnight* would be the only feature film that he would direct in the course of his long and eclectic career, though he would also helm a brief documentary film – *Steel Drums, No Guns* (2010) – shortly before his death in 2011. The screenplay for *To All a Goodnight* was penned by Alex Rebar, who had been active throughout the seventies and eighties both as an actor and scriptwriter. His other screenplays would include harrowing thriller *Demented* (Arthur Jeffreys, 1980) and suspenseful action drama *Nowhere to Hide* (Mario Azzopardi, 1987), though at the time he was considerably more recognisable to moviegoing audiences as Steve West, the unfortunate protagonist of William Sachs's sci-fi horror *The Incredible Melting Man* (1977).

To All a Goodnight begins during one fateful Christmas at the remote Calvin Finishing School for Girls. A brief pre-title sequence depicts a flashback of events from two years previously, when a young woman (Carrie Cobb) is killed due to an accidental fall from a balcony when chased by a group of her fellow classmates. Moving on from the aftermath of this disastrous prank, we revisit the school in the present day. With the holiday season fast approaching, many of the students are heading home to be with their families… but this is not true of all of them.

Some of the young women studying at the Calvin School are planning to remain on campus over Christmas, though their attitudes range from those who miss their families to others who would do anything to avoid returning home for the holidays. Kindly housekeeper Mrs Ruth Jensen (Katherine Herrington) does her best to keep their spirits up; the communal area has been brightly bedecked with festive decorations, and she prepares a comforting dinner of stew followed by cherry pie. Unknown to the young women staying at the school, however, a mysterious figure is pulling on a pair of gloves and removing a sharp knife from a desk drawer, pausing only to consider a framed photograph of the prank victim who had lost her life two years previously.

Over dinner, Mrs Jensen explains that headmistress Mrs Calvin has phoned to give notice that her return to the school will be delayed until after the weekend, due to her mother falling ill. Once the housekeeper has left the room, however, the students' reaction is anything but sympathetic. One of their number, Leia (Judith Bridges) has secretly arranged for her well-heeled boyfriend T.J. (William Lauer) to visit her at the school – and as he intends to arrive on his father's private jet, he is planning to bring along a number of his friends. The women react with excitement at the prospect of some male company, with the exception of the guileless Nancy (Jennifer Runyon) whose 'teacher's pet' attitude has led her classmates to keep her out of the plan.

Mrs Jensen, who is unaware of their scheme, asks why Cynthia (another of the students) is not present for dinner, only to be told that she is feeling unwell and has retired to her room. In actuality, Cynthia (Lisa Labowskie) has rather more diverting plans than attending an evening meal. Her boyfriend calls up to her room from the school courtyard outside, inviting her to get dressed so that they can head off for an evening together. While he waits around for her to leave the building, however, he is attacked from behind by a shadowy assailant – wielding a very familiar-looking blade. Moments later, Cynthia emerges from the building but manages only a few steps before she too is stabbed through the heart and killed.

Back at the dining table, the students are excitedly discussing the arrival of their anticipated visitors at midnight. They pour scorn on Nancy's insistence that she had seen something happening out on the courtyard through one of the hall windows. Leia is momentarily startled when, upon briefly leaving the room, she encounters slow-witted handyman Ralph Kramer (Buck West), who is tending the plants. In spite of the fact that he is wielding a large pair of sharp secateurs which would easily have the capacity to wound, the students callously mock Ralph for his lumbering appearance and dense manner.

In the kitchen, Mrs Jensen is entertaining her sharp-tongued friend Mrs Tina Ransoni (Judy Hess) – a widow who is waiting to be admitted to hospital for a heart bypass. Leia interrupts their conversation to inform Mrs Jensen that she and her fellow students have decided, given that it is the festive season, that they will do the washing up after the meal, meaning that she can retire early to bed. The housekeeper is taken aback at their apparent selflessness, little realising the true reason behind their helpful offer. Mrs Ransoni suspects a ruse however, deriding the students as being over-privileged and self-satisfied.

Having dropped off her gift of cannoli, Mrs Ransoni departs the campus, leaving Mrs Jensen to head for her room. The girls elect the virtuous Nancy to deliver her a glass of warm milk, reasoning that she is the one student who will never be suspected of deceit. Just as the seemingly-unwary housekeeper is getting to work on her sewing machine, the anticipated private jet is arriving on the school's landing strip. The students race to meet the visitors, leaving the hapless Nancy trailing in their wake. Tripping over in the darkness, she encounters Ralph who courteously offers her his flashlight so that she can stay safe in the dark.

Privileged playboy T.J. jumps from the plane with his revelling cohorts, all of whom soon find themselves pairing up with willing new partners. As he embraces Leia, he orders the plane's pilot (Dan Stryker) to stay with the aircraft until it is time to depart – a command which does not go down well with the beleaguered employee, especially when Leia had offered him a place to stay at the school only for T.J. to rebuff the offer on the pilot's behalf. Nancy arrives on the scene just as everyone is heading back to the school, but the other students make it plain that her wholesome presence is unwelcome.

The partying students and their guests socialise in one of the school's common areas, where conversation is accompanied by a guitar serenade. None of them suspect that a certain secretive figure, sporting what looks (on closer inspection) like a Santa Claus costume, is sharpening a knife in a nearby workshop. As medical student Alex (Forrest Swanson) regales the party with a stultifyingly dull account of modern surgical techniques, the sharp-tongued Trisha (Angela Bath) retreats to the kitchen to retrieve a few beers. As she rifles in the fridge, the lights go out – she suspects this to be the work of her amorous companion Tom (Solomon Trager). However, she becomes confused when, in the darkness, she is only just able to discern a figure dressed in a fur-trimmed Santa Claus outfit. She has barely enough time to admonish the new arrival for their dramatic flourish before her throat is cut, silencing her forever.

Elsewhere in the school, Nancy has broken away from the gathering but soon bumps into the concerned Ralph again. He warns her that she should be in bed at such a late hour, and insists that she lock her door – he feels that evil is in the air. Reluctantly, Nancy tells the shambling handyman that a party is underway, but he remains persistent about his counsel of immediate danger. Though confused at Ralph's assertion, the earnestness of his warning leads Nancy to assure him that she will do as he says.

Back at the party, Trisha's absence is beginning to raise suspicions as to her whereabouts. Tom decides to go in search of her, making his way through the school's darkened corridors, but soon grows frustrated when his new partner is nowhere to be found. Stumbling outside, he is shocked when he discovers what looks like the outline of a body. However, he has little time to process this information before the murderous figure of Santa Claus assaults him. Managing to escape the unconventional attacker's clutches by a hair's breadth, Tom races off into the darkness. His flight doesn't last long, as the enigmatic assailant is in close pursuit. When Tom stumbles in the undergrowth, the murderous figure in the Santa Claus costume quickly takes the initiative and smashes the visitor's head with a heavy rock, shattering his skull in the process.

Shortly afterwards, the shadowy Santa can be seen burying the victims in shallow graves on the campus grounds – a safe distance from the main school building. Back at the party, the dwindling number of students question where the others have gone, but quickly reason that they must have simply decided to seek out more private surroundings. The remaining couples then set off to seek more secluded places of their own. But the partnerless Nancy, oblivious to the recent murders, is wandering outside in the night as she contemplates her reluctant singleton status. She encounters another student on her way to get some milk from the kitchen, but is puzzled by a puddle of blood on the floor; unaware of Trisha's demise, they assume that Ralph has cut himself on his garden shears by accident. As Nancy mops up, she is startled by the arrival of the socially awkward Alex, who has come to get himself a drink. Though he seems to truly notice her for the first time, Alex promptly departs after Nancy helps him to find some refreshments, once again leaving the young woman alone in the near-darkness.

Back outside, Nancy finds it impossible to find somewhere to think due to the indiscreet sounds coming from the couples nearby. This makes her feel more unwanted than ever. While she continues to roam, unaware of any danger, a nearby romantic tryst is being interrupted when the partners are beheaded by an axe and shot by a crossbow respectively. The ethereal culprit once again remains in the shadows. Finally, Nancy decides to retreat to her room, the smattering of illuminated Christmas lights doing nothing to cheer her mood. She is interrupted by the unexpected (and not entirely welcome) arrival of Ralph, who repeats his warning that dark deeds are afoot. Nancy is unsettled by his uninvited presence, but the handyman remains resolute – he insists that she take his copy of the Bible and pray with all her heart to ward off demonic forces. It is clear that Nancy doesn't know what to think of his continued protestations, which are becoming increasingly arcane, but he emphasises that – of all the students at the school – she is the one person whose safety actually matters to him. Promising to take care of her, he leaves the room as swiftly as he had arrived.

As the festively-attired killer digs more graves on the school grounds nearby, the bookish Alex is uneasily fending off the advances of beautiful student Melody (Linda Gentile). Sensing Alex's obvious inexperience, she becomes all the more determined to find out the true extent of the medical graduate's knowledge of anatomy. As he fumbles his way into her embrace, neither suspects that the sinister figure in the Santa Claus costume is now filling in the latest round of fresh resting places on the campus, their victim total still mounting.

The next morning, the students and their visitors enjoy a breakfast served by Mrs Jensen. The housekeeper is suspicious of T.J.'s story that his private plane had developed technical problems, causing its 'unexpected' landing at the school. She informs them that it will be for the best if they depart before school superintendent Mrs Calvin returns to the campus the next day, but reacts strangely when she is asked if she had slept well the previous night. Melody reflects on their diminished numbers, wondering where the other couples have gone, but the group brush off her concerns by reasoning that they are all probably still in bed. T.J. suggests that the remaining couples take advantage of the unseasonably good weather and go on a picnic. Nancy, who remains brusquely shunned by the others, offers to go and find the various missing students and their partners. As the group react with lukewarm assent, the apprehensive Ralph watches developments from nearby.

Nancy is confused when her search for the absent classmates turns up nothing – especially as their rooms appear to have been abruptly abandoned to the point that they still have their Christmas lights switched on. At the picnic later, she remains anxious towards the vanished students even as the frolicking couples around her remain satisfied that they must simply be enjoying themselves elsewhere. Unconvinced by their glib reasoning and general lack of concern, Nancy goes for a stroll around the grounds and encounters Alex, who becomes playfully flirtatious even though his advances are gently rebuffed. Stumbling through the undergrowth as the medical student playfully runs after her, Nancy is horrified when she trips over the fresh corpse of Ralph; a gaping wound on his head suggests that he has been fatally struck by a heavy object.

The police are called to look into Ralph's murder, with investigating detective Chief Polansky (Sam Shamshak) determined to get to the bottom of the seemingly-inexplicable killing. While the students and their guests are puzzled at the question of who would want to slay the simple-minded handyman, they are considerably more bothered about the prospect of their parents discovering the truth about their party the previous night. Mrs Jensen implores them to let

Polansky know if they have any information that might aid his enquiries – not least as the policeman is deeply suspicious about the fact that so many of the students appear to be missing without a trace. Nancy tearfully recounts Ralph's agitated, religiously-fevered conversation from the previous night and holds herself responsible for not telling someone sooner, but Polansky insists that she is free from blame. Sympathetically, he tells her that Ralph had previously been a patient at a mental hospital and had a violent past which had left him with a lengthy criminal record, so the most likely explanation is that an old acquaintance may have held a grudge against him.

Polansky tells the assembled group to call him if they should find any additional information that may be of use to his enquiries. Though he is leaving two of his officers on the premises, he encourages them to keep the school securely locked and remain inside at all times until the murderer can be identified. Trying to raise their spirits, Mrs Jensen offers a home-cooked meal, but no-one appears to have much of an appetite. Paranoia starts to grip a few within the gathering, as they begin to question if the unfathomable disappearance of the other students and guests may be linked to Ralph's murder. There is sharp disagreement between those who believe that there is no cause for worry, and others who are grudgingly beginning to think that something sinister is afoot.

As Polansky impresses upon his two detectives the importance of keeping the students safe (knowing that their parents have considerable social influence, he is concerned for his professional reputation if anything goes wrong), Alex and Nancy approach Mrs Jensen about the events surrounding Ralph's demise. The housekeeper seems genuinely shocked at the likelihood that they may all be in danger, having thought that the murder of Ralph had been specifically targeted. However, she believes that the policemen guarding the school will be enough to deter any further foul play, adding that – in any event – she always keeps a sturdy rolling pin close by to defend herself the event of an assault.

As night falls again, the detectives arrange a shift system to watch over the jittery students. They assure the increasingly nervous group that in all probability the person who murdered Ralph is likely to have taken flight directly after the killing. But although logic would suggest that the criminal is now many miles away, the officers guarantee that they will remain at their post on the campus until Ralph's assassin has been placed in custody. One of the detectives is taken to a nearby room to have a nap while his colleague remains on duty.

Mrs Jensen heads off to bed, leaving the rest of the students on tenterhooks downstairs. Melody suggests that T.J. should bring his plane's pilot into the school building for his own safety, given that the older man has remained with the plane since its arrival. But in spite of Alex's reasoning that there is safety in numbers, T.J. angrily refuses, asserting that he has always strongly disliked the pilot... and, in any case, he is probably now too soporific with soft drugs to be of much use in keeping them safe. T.J. then heads for the kitchen to retrieve some beer from the refrigerator. He spots something through the kitchen door, but can find nobody outside when he goes to have a look. On the way back, he is irked when he finds Leia having a romantic encounter with one of the detectives in her room.

T.J. returns to the common area just as Alex and Nancy decide to search the surroundings in order to check for anything unexpected. None of them suspect that, in a location not far from their own, the figure in the Santa Claus costume is picking up a heavy axe with sinister intent. While Nancy and Alex stalk through dimly-lit corridors, the other detective is keeping watch on the grounds outside. He is confused when he spots a stranger in a Santa Claus outfit striding towards him, but barely has time to ask what the interloper is doing there before an axe is buried between his eyes, killing him in an instant.

Still peeved at Leia's flirtation with the police officer, T.J. tries to persuade Melody to join him in a romantic tête-à-tête outside the building. He brushes off her worries about safety by pointing out that not only does he hold a black belt in karate, but the police are keeping an eye on the entire area, meaning that no-one would reasonably try to commit a crime while they are present. Meanwhile, the lethal Santa Claus impersonator is now inside the building, heavy costume boots creaking along the floorboards with every step. Alex and Nancy continue to check that the school's doors and windows are securely locked, creeping upstairs into a gloomy attic area as the festively-clad murderer watches them from a distance. Though their investigations turn up nothing, Nancy becomes increasingly jumpy given the number of unexplained noises she can hear around her. Little do they realise that the killer is now mere feet away from them.

Back in the common area, Nancy is disturbed to find that T.J. and Melody are both absent, oblivious to the fact that the pair are currently taking a romantic walk in the grounds outside. Alex bemoans the fact that he is even present at the school (he had only joined Alex's party because his parents were holidaying in Europe), while Nancy similarly regrets that there is a distinct lack of festive cheer this Christmas. She cannot imagine the unseasonal scene of carnage currently taking place upstairs, however, where Polansky's other detective is being stabbed to death by the killer in the Santa Claus suit. Moving on into an adjacent bathroom, the murderer confronts the hysterical Leia, who has just discovered a decapitated head in her shower cubicle. Pulling away an abundant white beard, the costumed assassin reveals their true identity to Leia (though unseen by the audience), causing her to become even more panic-stricken.

As T.J. declares his romantic interest in Melody, neither of them seeming overly concerned by the unexplained absence of the detective who is supposed to be on patrol outside the building, Alex continues to grow closer to Nancy by inviting her to dance in the common area. These tender embraces are soon torn asunder, however, as T.J. is garrotted with a length of piano wire by the costumed killer, leading Melody to flee the murder scene and hammer desperately on one of the school's doors. Nancy and Alex come racing to her aid. Once back inside, the distraught Melody relates the circumstances of T.J.'s demise, warning that none of them are now safe. Deciding to track down the others, the remaining trio head for Leia's room... only to discover the detective's corpse and the decapitated head hanging in her shower. Now desperate, Alex declares that they must find help at any cost. He races to the nearest telephone, only to discover that the line is dead – the connection has been cut by the killer, using the late Ralph's garden secateurs.

To their surprise, Melody and Nancy hear a now-unstable Leia singing nearby. Rushing to her aid, they find her on the landing in a state of deep shock; she appears oblivious even to their presence. Realising that an escape on T.J.'s private plane is likely to be their last chance of staying alive, they dash to the door only to be intercepted by the murderer as they try to escape. As the Santa Claus impersonator lunges with a knife, only narrowly missing the intended target, Melody makes a break for safety. Leia and Nancy are stunned as the killer pulls back their mask to reveal their true identity at last – none other than Mrs Jensen. Seemingly deranged, she rants furiously that Nancy was responsible for drugging her daughter and letting her fall to her death from one of the building's balconies (the events shown in the film's pre-title sequence), only growing more incensed when Nancy – who is only in her first year at the school – denies even knowing the woman in question. As Mrs Jensen springs forward with the knife again, Nancy only barely manages to deflect the blade, seemingly incapacitating the older woman as she does so.

While Nancy desperately looks for a hiding place in the school, a rather worse-for-the-wear Santa Claus figure is emerging from one of the building's doors. This time the killer is in hot pursuit of the fleeing Melody, who is tearing through the grounds towards the private plane. In spite of repeated missteps, she finally reaches the aircraft and explains to the pilot – barely coherently – that they need to leave immediately or else face being the latest of the killer's victims. While the pilot has difficulty believing her frenetic tale, he begins pre-flight checks on the plane's propellers... only for the two of them to be torn apart when the blades are suddenly set in motion. Above them, in the cockpit, a now-very-familiar figure in a Santa Claus costume can be seen at the controls having engineered their dismemberment.

Back in the school building, Mrs Jensen is back on her feet and continuing to stalk Nancy. Leia, now increasingly unhinged as a result of extreme shock, sings to herself as he pirouettes along the hallways. Nancy manages to reach a supply room and arms herself with a large knife. As she stealthily creeps around the shadowy corridors, Nancy is once again attacked by Mrs Jensen, but narrowly manages to evade the assault – much to the incandescent rage of the psychotic older woman. The sinister game of cat-and-mouse continues until Nancy discovers that she has inadvertently reached a dead end – the very balcony where Mrs Jensen's daughter had plummeted to her demise two years earlier. Seeing her opportunity, and still clad in the Santa Claus costume, the murderer creeps out onto the balcony in pursuit of her twisted justice... only to be pushed over the edge by Nancy, thus causing history to repeat itself.

Outside the school, Mrs Jensen writhes around in agony on the ground; after her fall, she is now close to death. Nancy speeds off the balcony to the safety of a nearby room and starts to cry hysterically, believing that the nightmare is finally over. But she is interrupted only a few moments later when a dejected figure in a Santa Claus outfit arrives – carrying another person who is similarly dressed in a Santa Claus costume. Much to Nancy's consternation, the second stranger removes his beard to reveal that he is none other than Chief Polansky. Consumed by grief, he explains bitterly that he is actually Mrs Jensen's husband, voicing the erroneous belief that Nancy has not only killed their daughter but his wife as well. Raging that Nancy should have been their first victim, he begins to furiously strangle her. In his frenzy, Polansky doesn't spot the return of Alex, who enters the fray wielding a crossbow with intent. Sensing his one chance, Alex takes a shot at the murderous detective, only just managing to save Nancy in the nick of time. As Polansky collapses dead onto the corpse of his late wife, Alex comforts Nancy and apologises for having panicked, retreating when she needed him the most. Together, they sprint off into the night in search of safety, leaving the now-totally unbalanced Leia singing beatifically on the balcony in their wake.

Of all horror features to deal with the festive season in the 1980s, *To All a Goodnight* is among the least engaged with recognisable yuletide conventions. In spite of the occasional selection of muted Christmas decorations thrown into the mix, such as the fir tree in the school's communal area and some garlands and various illuminated displays placed around some of the rooms, there is very little to connect the film's events to the holidays. Interestingly, given the fact that *To All a Goodnight* first appeared when the slasher horror subgenre was still in its infancy, its approach ends up appearing more hackneyed than pioneering; tropes which would epitomise many later entries in the field are here dragged out, dutifully employed and then abandoned – or, in some cases, rehashed to diminishing effect. *8os Horror Central,* for example, has been representative of this line of criticism in their review of the film:

> This film came at the start of the 8os slasher cycle but still manages to be clichéd and repetitive. There's the red herring (a Crazy Ralph type gardener), the twist ending, the tour of the dead, the deadly preamble, and of course, the useless authority. These are some common traits of slashers and they feel downright beat to death here. There is no suspense, no originality, and no creativity. The filmmakers really dropped the ball with the Christmas theme. There isn't [sic] any Christmas oriented gags or deaths in the film. We get a couple Christmas lights but no decorations, no Christmas songs, and we barely see the killer Santa. The good news is the film moves a solid pace.[1]

While *Christmas Evil* had been deeply rooted in yuletide traditions and trappings, focusing as it did upon the protagonist's fixation with the figure of Santa Claus and all the customs that entailed, quite the opposite was the case of *To All a Goodnight...* and yet this was, in many ways, amongst the least of the film's problems. Though now a fairly obscure feature in the history of Christmas cinema, the movie has become infamous for being plagued with technical shortcomings including highly variable sound quality (mostly noticeable in the often muddy dialogue), cheap-looking and massively unconvincing murders, night shots that have quite clearly been filmed in broad daylight and treated with ineffective processing, and a characterless score which singularly fails to be either ominously threatening or suspense-inducing at any point. Yet although this catalogue of inadequacies would spell critical doom for most films, when taken together they actually help to make *To All a Goodnight* something of a guilty pleasure – a film which epitomises the expression 'so bad it's good', and is unabashedly rough-and-ready to the degree that it can prove to be enormous fun if the viewer is in the right mood.

Alongside its many production flaws, the movie also suffers from various other drawbacks ranging from continuity errors to narrative illogicalities. The dialogue is staggeringly stilted and corny throughout, often making next to no sense, while the usual slasher horror titillation is at a bare minimum (the occasional gratuitous shots of attractive women in skimpy underwear notwithstanding). Further undermining the festive flavour, the weather seems uncannily warm for a Christmas film – the students dine outside in summer clothing such as T-shirts, which may well be the case throughout December in some regions of the USA but is not generally a convention of holiday season cinema. Likewise, the characters appear overly willing to explain away the growing number of mysterious absences a little too glibly to be even remotely credible. Dave Kaye has not been alone in noting the way in which the shallowness of the main characters' depiction is both to the film's detriment and (paradoxically enough) its benefit:

> The characters are also rather stupid even for slasher flick standards. When all their friends end up missing nobody seems to be very concerned, chalking it up to they just went home, and even after a dead body is found they still have no concerns about their friends or themselves for that matter. [...] Slasher flicks often feature idiotic characters, but this bunch are just total idiots. With that said, the screenplay does serve its purpose and while the characters might be shallow idiots they are also a bit fun.[2]

Alex Rebar's screenplay was not entirely without its innovative flourishes, however. In introducing the rather off-putting character of Ralph (Buck West's creepy handyman, with a disconcerting line in portentous pronouncements) only to have him executed halfway through the narrative, Rebar attempts to throw the viewer off the scent of the real killer. Ralph is so archetypally unnerving that it is hard to believe any director or screenwriter would deploy such an obviously unsettling figure as the real killer, given the conspicuousness of his strange proclamations and shared antipathy with most of the student body, but his relatively early departure is significant nonetheless as it removes him from any potential bait-and-switch function at the film's denouement. Likewise, although detecting Mrs Jensen's involvement in the murders would not likely have required the deductive powers of Sherlock Holmes, the surprise introduction of a second culprit in the form of Chief Polansky is remarkably effective (even if the actual reveal is rather ham-fistedly executed). Largely this is due to the character's brief screen time making him seem like an improbable candidate for the role of murderer – though Sam Shamshak's likeably hammy performance does make Polansky stand out as one of the film's more memorable figures, despite repeatedly tripping over his dialogue. As Nathaniel Thompson has asserted, the film works best when considered in the spirit in which it was produced: 'Famously incompetent on many technical levels, *To All a Goodnight* will never be cited as anyone's idea of good cinema; however, it's loaded to the gills with that naive charm found in so many slasher films before the ground rules had really been set. Eccentric dialogue, bizarre hairstyles, a surplus of varied kill scenes, a baffling cameo by porn legend Harry Reems [credited as Dan Stryker] as an airplane pilot [...], wildly random lighting and day-for-night shifts make it a great party film if you're with the right crowd, and any killer Santa film by definition has to be tons of fun around Christmas time'.[3]

Though most of the cast are instantly forgettable (with the possible exception of Jennifer Runyon, several years before her brief appearance in Ivan Reitman's hugely successful *Ghostbusters* in 1984), their very anonymity aids the film's efficacy simply because the order of the slayings is in no way obvious from the start. Whereas some films of this type would see characters portrayed by better-known actors surviving until the climax while those of lesser-recognised performers were more likely to be mowed down in earlier sequences, in *To All a Goodnight* everyone is a potential victim from the get-go – a fact underscored by the fact that the murder spree commences so briskly. Peripheral characters such as Judy Hess's waspish Mrs Ransoni come and go in seemingly-baffling fashion, whereas the treatment of others is simply mystifying (such as the pilot of T.J.'s private plane, who the audience are expected to believe has been sleeping beneath the stationary aircraft for more than a day without once questioning what is going on).

Given its well-documented range of weaknesses, it is intriguing to consider just how much cult longevity *To All a Goodnight* has continued to exhibit in the years since its initial release. Though its profile has never been particularly high, and its cult qualifications are probably more due to its early place in the development of the slasher horror subgenre than its status within the canon of Christmas cinema, the film has still managed to gather a respectable number of fans over the decades. As James Jay Edwards has observed, Hess's movie has retained a subdued significance which has been recognised amongst cineastes with a taste for popular genres:

> Even with its killer Santa motif, *To All a Goodnight* was outdone by *Christmas Evil* and the *Silent Night, Deadly Night* franchise. However, instead of simply dropping off of the slasher movie map, *To All a Goodnight* has built a fairly healthy cult following. Looking back on the film 35 years later, it's easy to see how influential it really was. Viewed through modern eyes, *To All a Goodnight* appears to be a standard slasher movie, maybe even a cheap knockoff of a superior film. It's only when one is reminded that it was released in 1980, before the golden age of the slasher was in full swing, that it can be appreciated for being so ahead of its time.[4]

Yet if the film has retained a measure of recognition amongst horror movie aficionados, it has fared less well in the annals of Christmas movies. Many reference guides reduce *To*

All a Goodnight to a mere footnote, if it isn't omitted from their pages altogether; a reflection on the film's strange reluctance to engage with the customs and practices of the festive season in anything but the most superficial of ways. This is particularly jarring when considering the numerous stylistic similarities between the film's setting and Bob Clark's infinitely more effective take on the festively-themed slasher horror, *Black Christmas*. As Keith Bailey explains, a comparison between the two films' respective qualities is striking: 'If you want a Christmas slasher movie that takes place on a university campus, then I suggest that you rent [...] *Black Christmas*. It uses the university setting to great effect, showing it darkened and frozen by the cold and snow. There's suspense, horror, and an unexpected ending. [...] There is then no reason to rent *To All a Good Night*, for it is devoid of suspense, horror, good plot twists, good gore, good nudity, and sleaze. And it's boring and slow to boot'.[5] Not all appraisals of the film have been quite as excoriating, but when considering the powerfully understated efficiency of Clark's movie – which had been one of the most important and popular of all 1970s cinematic Christmas features – it is plain that *To All a Goodnight* suffers greatly by comparison. Adam Rockoff, for instance, has highlighted the fact that contrasting the two films' merits inevitably stresses the manifest illogicalities of the latter movie in ways which are often deeply unflattering:

> [Hess's] lone directorial effort, while not a blatant rip-off of *Black Christmas*, owes quite a bit to Clark's film, right down to the muted lighting and Yuletide set dressings. [...] One would have to ascertain that in *To All a Goodnight* murder is the ultimate aphrodisiac, for the characters barely have time to dodge the next errant

crossbow arrow before hopping into bed with each other. The film attempts a 'twist' ending with little effect; there are actually two killer Santas - a cook and the investigating officer - whose daughter was killed in a prank two years before when her classmates backed her over a balcony, from whose height it would seem that a sprained ankle, not a broken neck, would most likely result.[6]

Part of the reason for the film's regular critical drubbing, quite aside from its technical inadequacies, has been the way in which it presents some tantalisingly intriguing situations only to singularly fail in following them through. Perhaps most obviously, the themes of parental loss and the irrational nature of extreme grief are sadly underdeveloped – a missed opportunity, given the potential for a poignant examination of the emotional cost of irresolvable heartache. Because the killers' respective identities are not revealed until the very end of the film, there is no real chance to flesh out anything more than the fundamental nature of their lethal motivations, or to explore what emotional factors have driven grieving parents – over the course of two years – to become vengeful murderers. The situation that is presented does, however, lead the audience to apply themselves to rather more immediate quandaries, such as how the students could all have been oblivious to the fact that the school housekeeper was married to the chief of the local police force, or why the long-term residents at the school were unaware of the connection between Mrs Jensen and the young woman who had died in tragic circumstances not too long beforehand. (Similarly, why does Mrs Jensen try to persuade T.J. and his friends to expedite their departure from the school by warning of the superintendent's imminent return when she is obviously planning to murder them all before they have the chance to leave?) Here, too, there is a certain subversive appeal in the film's heavy-handedness; Hess's sheer breeziness in explaining away convoluted issues of continuity in order to keep the momentum going, even when stretching plausibility beyond breaking point, is undeniably admirable in its tenacity, even if the end result is far removed from anyone's definition of a cinematic classic. That being said, *To All a Goodnight* does fit comfortably into a wider tradition of horror features which were emerging at the time of its production; Patrick Bromley has commented that 'there's little to differentiate *To All a Goodnight* from the glut of slashers released in the wake of the success of John Carpenter's *Halloween*. That's both its curse and its blessing; as a student and fan of horror from that period, the movie plays like a time capsule of what was happening in the genre at that point. Though uninspired, there's a charm in the way it hits familiar beats. To be fair, there is some novelty in the climax, but by the time those scenes arrive it's difficult to still be invested or actually care'.[7]

Another reason why the film remains of interest to horror enthusiasts is the fact that it would be the only full-length motion picture to be directed by David Hess; a true cult figure, both as an actor and musician. While Hess's creative involvement alone would have made the film of interest to admirers of his wider artistic work, the singular nature of this side-step into the director's chair has meant that the film came to be regarded with greater curiosity than might have otherwise been the case. Of course, in the eyes of many critics *To All a Goodnight* has lingered in the collective memory for the wrong reasons, as Dave Wain explains:

> David Hess was undoubtedly an icon of cinema. Primarily known for his genre defining role in *The Last*

House on the Left, he also starred in a number of excellent horror films that included Ruggero Deodato's controversial *House on the Edge of the Park* (1980), the stunning (and currently deleted) *Hitch-Hike* (1977), and Wes Craven's *Swamp Thing* (1982). Despite an incredibly creative life that included an impressive song-writing career, he only felt compelled to move behind the camera once, which was for [*To All a Goodnight*]. [...] Judging by his disdain for it in interviews, it seems the chore of shooting this film put David Hess off the directorial vocation for life. It was an arduous shoot on a meagre budget, with very little room for error due to the amount of film they had to shoot on. The cast was made up of out of work actors (and at times it's easy to see why they were out of work), although some of the technical guys were very proficient such as Mark Shostrom whose make-up work can be seen in a slew of genre pictures after this.[8]

If there was any one factor which contributed to a lack of audience awareness of *To All a Goodnight* when it first emerged into cinemas, it was the fact that its seemingly-disputatious premise never quite seems to pay off in the same way as would be the case with the more thematically complex *Christmas Evil* or the more contentious *Silent Night, Deadly Night*. Whether as a sadistic murderer or a jolly old elf, the figure of Santa Claus seemed strangely out of place in a film which had such a tenuous link to the festive season; with Christmas decorations so relatively thin on the ground and yuletide dialogue references all but non-existent, the audience could be forgiven for overlooking the fact that the film was supposed to be set over the holiday period at all, and thus when a character appears in a Santa Claus costume (killer or otherwise) the effect cannot help but appear somewhat jarring. Ian Jane notes that there are 'some okay murder set pieces here but no real scares or suspense, even if the basic idea of a killer in a Santa Claus suit is eerie enough in its own right. The premise works on the same level that something like *Maniac Cop* works on, in that it takes something that we're taught to trust and see as a positive and twists it around to instantly play against social expectations. Santa Claus is a good guy, right?"[9] Yet while the same trope would be employed more effectively elsewhere – and much more memorably, in many cases – here the homicidal Jolly Old Saint Nick appears oddly out of place within the film's central setting, and even superfluous at times. There is an undeniable sense that if the killers had assumed any guise other than Santa Claus, the trappings of Christmas are so fragile and unconvincing that there would have been little necessary change to the narrative, making the film's scares somewhat less effective within the context of festive cinema. As *Oh, The Horror*'s commentator Wes R. observes:

> For horror filmmakers, the challenge of making a movie set around Christmas is often 'how can we make the holiday scary?' The answer is often to corrupt Christmas and have the film go against everything Christmas stands for. A meaningful, peaceful holiday like Christmas is then filled with images of bloodshed and carnage. The easiest and most common target in Christmas horror... the killer Santa Claus. [...] Hess' direction isn't bad. In fact, it's quite competent. It's just not particularly memorable or flashy. Take his name off the film, and you could've substituted it with any other director of slasher movie ripoffs of the time and no one would be any the wiser.[10]

Thus although *To All a Goodnight* is largely ineffective as a Christmas film, and is far from the most terrifying horror movie ever to be committed to celluloid, it does at least have its heart in the right place. As a seemingly-limitless supply of unsympathetic characters – oversexed and overindulged – are gradually picked off one by one (to the point that the viewer may actually start to feel some sympathy with the endlessly patronised housekeeper who is mowing them down), the viewer may discern a dark reflection of Harry Stadling's deadly moral crusade in *Christmas Evil*: the impartial figure of Santa Claus judges ethical shortcomings at the festive season and doles out restorative justice accordingly. Sadly, however, *To All a Goodnight* could never come close to reaching the same level of devious subversion as the Lewis Jackson film, as *Horror Talk*'s reviewer ZigZag explains: '*To All a Good Night* is the result of two actors getting behind the camera and trying to make a horror film. David Hess (*The Last House on the Left*) directs this early slasher flick from a script by Alex Rebar (*The Incredible Melting Man*) equipped with a solid premise and many elements that would become routine in the coming decade. [...] Victims are strangled, stabbed, decapitated or bludgeoned until Santa can convey the true meaning of Christmas to these thankless spoiled toads'.[11]

While *To All a Goodnight* was largely ignored by critics at the time of its initial release, over time its cheap-and-cheerful charm has ensured that it has preserved some level of interest amongst cult film buffs. While it will never be mistaken for a classic of either Christmas cinema or the horror genre, it has slowly come to be regarded with a greater level of affection in recent years. Kaye's views are representative of this thaw in critical opinion, asserting that the film warrants a greater degree of attention than has been the case in years past: 'Quite honestly I wouldn't rate *To All a Goodnight* as one of the best slasher flicks of the 80s, but I think the movie deserves more recognition than it gets. If anything this movie owes a little more to *Black Christmas* than *Halloween* and, while this movie is very much your standard 80s slasher flick again, it came out prior to many of the more well-known slasher flicks of the 80s'.[12]

Although *To All a Goodnight* appears fated to forever languish in the shadows of other, more prominent Christmas-themed horror films which appeared in the early-to-mid 1980s, a recent high-definition home entertainment release on Blu-Ray disc has helped in some way to rehabilitate the movie's reputation, gaining it a new audience some three and a half decades after its production. Only time will tell whether Hess's feature will grow in prominence alongside its contemporaries, but as it stands *To All a Goodnight* remains an interesting curio in Christmas cinema; a film which exhibits so many different narrative defects and unabashed technical discrepancies that its unrealised good intentions, sheer ineptitude and overall goofy charm ultimately combine to make it very difficult for all but the most hard-nosed cinemagoer to develop a true antipathy towards.

REFERENCES

1. Anon., ' *To All a Goodnight*', in *80s Horror Central*, 2012. <http://80shorrorcentral.webs.com/toallagoodnight1980.htm>

2. Dave Kaye, 'Santa Claus, Sorority Girls, and Serious Slashing: *To All a Good Night* Review', in *Slasher Studios*, 24 March 2012. *<http://www.slasherstudios.com/2012/03/24/santa-claus-sorority-girls-and-serious-slashing-to-all-a-good-night-review/>*

3. Nathaniel Thompson, ' *To All a Goodnight*', in *Mondo Digital*, 12 December 2014. *<http://mondo-digital.com/allgoodnight.html>*

4. James Jay Edwards, 'Cinema Fearité Presents *To All a Goodnight*: A Killer Santa Movie From a Time Before Killer Santa Movies Were a Real Thing', in *FilmFracture*, 25 December 2014. *<http://www.filmfracture.com/frame_of_mind/cinema_fearit_presents_to_all_a_goodnight__a_killer_santa_movie_from_a_time_before_killer_santa_movies_were_a_real_thing>*

5. Keith Bailey, ' *To All a Goodnight*', in *The Unknown Movies*, September 2014. *<http://www.the-unknown-movies.com/unknownmovies/reviews/rev63.html>*

6. Adam Rockoff, *Going to Pieces: The Rise and Fall of the Slasher Film, 1978-1986* (Jefferson: McFarland and Company, 2002), pp.98-99.

7.   Patrick Bromley, '*To All a Goodnight*', in *DVD Verdict*, 6 December 2014.
<*http://www.dvdverdict.com/reviews/toallgoodnightbluray.php*>

8.   Dave Wain, '*To All a Goodnight*', in *UK Horror Scene*, 14 November 2013.
<*http://www.ukhorrorscene.com/tales-that-witness-crapness-2-to-all-a-goodnight-1980/*>

9.   Ian Jane, '*To All a Goodnight*', in *DVD Talk*, 21 October 2014.
<*http://www.dvdtalk.com/reviews/65711/to-all-a-goodnight/*>

10.   Wes R., '*To All a Good Night*', in *Oh, The Horror*, 14 December 2008.
<*http://www.oh-the-horror.com/page.php?id=449*>

11.   ZigZag, '*To All a Good Night* Movie Review', in *Horror Talk*, 14 December 2009.
<*http://www.horrortalk.com/index.php/reviews/719-to-all-a-good-night*>

12.   Kaye, 2012.

3

Trading Places (1983)

Paramount Pictures/Cinema Group Ventures

Director: John Landis
Producer: Aaron Russo
Screenwriters: Timothy Harris and Herschel Weingrod

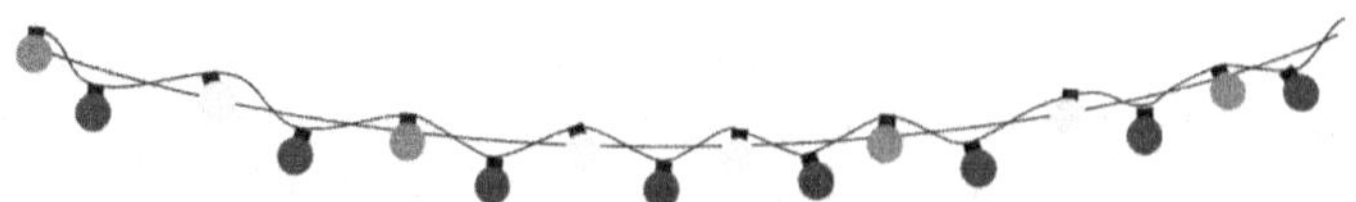

If the earliest years of the 1980s had witnessed a concern with subverting and remoulding the conventions of Christmas cinema to make new points about modern sensibilities relating to the festive season, *Trading Places* would exchange the horror of films such as *Christmas Evil* and *To All a Goodnight* in favour of a darkly humorous take on social attitudes and human nature: one which would eventually come to be regarded as one of the most original, ingenious entries in the genre over the course of the eighties. As Gary J. Svehla and Susan Svehla have attested in their acclaimed 1998 survey of festive cinema, *It's Christmas Time at the Movies*, *Trading Places* offers 'thoughtful insights about human nature, while at the same time making its audience laugh. It just happens to be one of the most inventive Christmas movies of the last two decades'.[1]

Trading Places was also noteworthy for the careful restraint with which the film engaged with the festive season. Its central plotline has often been considered as having more in common with Mark Twain's novel *The Prince and the Pauper* (1881) than it has with any form of conventional Christmas narrative. And yet, with its underplayed yuletide trappings, the film is nonetheless imbued with a distinctly festive spirit of humanity and fair play, where kindness and philanthropy win out against covetousness and malice thanks to a potent mix of scheming ingenuity and the exultantly restorative essence of the holiday season.

A gifted screenwriter, producer and actor as well as an internationally-recognised director, *Trading Places*'s John Landis began his film-making career with the comedic horror *Schlock* (1973), a well-received feature which he was also to write and appear in as a performer. His filmography then went from strength to strength as he helmed chaotic comedies *The Kentucky Fried Movie* (1977) and the monumentally successful *National Lampoon's Animal House* (1978), before directing one of the most acclaimed of all his films, *The Blues Brothers* (1980), an action-packed musical comedy which would prove to be a lasting contribution to eighties popular culture. He followed this up with the atmospheric horror *An American Werewolf in London* (1981), cinema documentary *Coming Soon* (1982), a segment of the anthology film *Twilight Zone: The Movie* (1983), and one of the best-known music videos of all time, the thirteen-minute epic *Thriller* (1983) which accompanied Michael Jackson's record-breaking song of the same name. Thus with his high profile, expectations of Landis were high at the time of *Trading Places*'s emergence into cinemas, and the stage was set for one of the 1980s most appealing Christmas comedies.

Trading Places begins, replete with a stirring performance of Mozart's famous *Marriage of Figaro* overture, in downtown Philadelphia. A montage of shots, showing everything from historical landmarks to busy shoppers, indicates that Thanksgiving is passing and that Christmas is now well on its way. Focusing on an upmarket town house, dapper butler Coleman (Denholm Elliott) is retrieving a freshly-delivered newspaper from the front step, the shot juxtaposed with a homeless man who is sheltering under an old newspaper in a vain attempt to retain some of his body heat. Coleman is preparing a sumptuous breakfast on a silver tray for his employer, Louis Winthorpe III (Dan Aykroyd), a wealthy stockbroker. After assisting him to prepare for work, Coleman chauffeurs Winthorpe to his place of employ: prosperous commodities brokerage Duke and Duke. There, he makes his way past similarly expensively-suited colleagues to reach his oak-panelled private office, where he discovers with satisfaction that an earlier hunch on the price of pork bellies has paid off. Winthorpe clearly has a keen instinct for the market, even although he appears detached and aloof when interacting with other people.

Moving to an opulent mansion house situated in expansive, snow-covered grounds, brothers Randolph and Mortimer Duke (Ralph Bellamy and Don Ameche), the elderly owners of Duke and Duke, are also leaving home – in their case, in a chauffeur-driven Rolls Royce. Watching the stock market from their car's on-board computer, they are impressed to discover that Winthorpe's tip for pork belly shares has paid off, netting them a tidy sum. They telephone Winthorpe to congratulate him, and arrange to meet him later at the exclusive Heritage Club.

As their car arrives at the club, the Dukes are appalled when they are accosted by penniless beggar Billy Ray Valentine (Eddie Murphy). Claiming to be a Vietnam War veteran with no use of his legs due to a combat injury,

Valentine pleads with Randolph and Mortimer for anything they are willing to give, but soon ends up being dragged away by the club's doorman (P. Jay Sidney). Once inside, Mortimer reads with enthusiasm a newspaper report which appears to bode well for Duke and Duke's forthcoming trading in orange juice. But Randolph seems indifferent to the news, being more concerned with an article on the subject of natural selection. Randolph is convinced that an individual's environment shapes their character and potential, while Mortimer is equally certain that one's capabilities and aptitudes are entirely a matter of genetics. As they debate, Winthorpe arrives with the monthly paycheques for the Dukes to sign. He is puzzled by one cheque, made out to a certain Clarence Beeks, when no employee is listed under that name. However, Mortimer is alarmed at Winthorpe's attention having been attracted to the matter, assuring him that Beeks has been contracted purely in a research consultancy capacity and thus should be considered off the record. To get him off the subject, the Dukes ask Winthorpe how preparations are going for his impending marriage to their grand-niece, Penelope Witherspoon (Kristin Holby). But they have no real interest in his personal affairs, and dismiss him curtly as soon as their business is complete. After Winthorpe's departure, Mortimer reflects that they are fortunate to have the younger man as a steady hand on their company's tiller. Randolph responds that his competence comes as no real surprise, given Winthorpe's expensive Ivy League education, but Mortimer retorts that with Winthorpe's impeccable breeding he would have been certain to succeed irrespective of his social background.

Outside in a snowy park, Valentine is approached by two police officers (Robert E. Lee and Peter Hock) who are suspicious of his purported blindness and inability to walk.

Being Vietnam War veterans themselves, they know after a few questions that his cover story is bogus, and when they rumble his scam he affects amazement, claiming that his sudden 'recovery' is a miracle from God. Keen to put as much distance as he can between himself and the policemen, he hurriedly moves away from them only to accidentally bump into Winthorpe, who is in the process of leaving the club. Unintentionally knocking Winthorpe's briefcase out of his hand, Valentine quickly attempts to return it, but Winthorpe believes he is being mugged and calls the police. Panicking, Valentine races into the club hoping to escape custody but, as he is still holding the briefcase, Winthorpe becomes increasingly convinced that the younger man is attempting to abscond with the company payroll. The police need little time to catch Valentine, and Winthorpe – believing nothing of Valentine's account that the whole encounter has been an unfortunate accident – presses full charges. Before Valentine is taken into custody, Randolph asks him a few questions about his background and determines that he is the product of his deficient upbringing and an impoverished environment. But the unabashedly racist Mortimer disagrees, believing that genetics is the key issue.

The scheming Duke brothers hatch a plan which will prove once and for all whether nature or nurture is the deciding factor in life. They propose that they should ruin Winthorpe – stripping him of his wealth, influence and prestige – in the belief that he will then immediately turn to a life of crime. In order to do this, however, they believe that he will have to lose everything: his home, his job, his fiancée, and his friends. After all, the Dukes reflect, they have utterly destroyed enemies in the past for the sake of expediency in business, so it makes little difference to them if they decide to do the same thing to an innocent man in the name of intellectual curiosity. That night, while Winthorpe is having a romantic evening with Penelope, the Dukes telephone Coleman and explain their plans to him. Being in their employ (Winthorpe's lavish home is owned by the brothers), the reluctant butler has no choice but to agree to make the necessary arrangements.

The next morning, Valentine is entertaining the other incumbents of his jail cell with hilariously overblown tall tales of his purported attack on Winthorpe. He is amazed to discover that he has been bailed, and has barely left the confines of the police station before the Dukes' Rolls Royce pulls up alongside him. Explaining that they were responsible for putting up his bail money, Randolph and Mortimer tell Valentine that they operate a philanthropic organisation which assists people in need. Although the penniless Valentine is deeply suspicious of their ambiguous motivations, they assure him that their concern for his wellbeing is genuine. They will provide him with an $80,000-a-year post at their firm, a car, a house, and anything else that he requires. Valentine decides to play along, but is clearly uneasy about the indistinct basis of their generosity. The Dukes waste no time in moving Valentine into Winthorpe's home, introducing him to Coleman and assuring him repeatedly that the house, and everything that is in it, is now Valentine's own private property. But once he is out of earshot, Mortimer makes it clear to Randolph that as soon as their bet has been settled – one way or another – Valentine will be thrown back out onto the streets again at the earliest possible opportunity.

Soon after, a blissfully-unaware Winthorpe is making his way to the Heritage Club as normal. He is oblivious to the fact that he is being tailed by Clarence Beeks (Paul Gleason), the Dukes' private operative. The club's members have been summoned by its president (Gwyllum Evans) due to an accusation of theft. Beeks is called as a security expert and pinpoints Winthorpe as the perpetrator; his wallet is shown to contain three marked $50 bills which have allegedly been stolen from a jacket in the club's cloakroom. In reality, Beeks has planted them on the stunned Winthorpe, who is forcibly removed from the club and taken to a nearby police station. Unknown to Winthorpe, Beeks follows him and has a word with a corrupt cop named Clements (Frank Oz), who 'discovers' an illegal bag of phencyclidine that has been stashed in Winthorpe's suit, meaning that he is charged with narcotics offences above and beyond the original accusations that have been levelled against him.

Still somewhat in awe of the good fortune that has been bestowed upon him, Valentine hooks up with some old acquaintances and takes them back to his house for a raucous party. However, he soon tires of their company, belatedly realising that they have no respect for either him or his new home. Dismayed by the contempt with which they are treating the opulent house, he orders them to leave. Coleman, noticing a change in Valentine's attitude already (he is starting to appear increasingly protective of his property and belongings), suggests that he have an early night before starting his new job in the morning; he will take care of the mess that is left behind.

A mess is exactly what Winthorpe finds himself in; now thoroughly roughed up by his fellow inmates, he is released from his police cell when Penelope arrives to bail him out. Disgusted by his unkempt appearance, she tells him that he has been fired by Duke and Duke following allegations of embezzlement. Winthorpe is shocked, knowing that this new revelation is as untrue as all the other accusations that have been made against him. Penelope is convinced that Winthorpe has been leading a double-life as a drugs dealer, a claim that he strenuously denies. But just as Penelope appears to be on the cusp of believing him, Ophelia (Jamie Lee Curtis), a prostitute who has been bribed by Beeks, arrives and begs Winthorpe for a quick fix of angel dust. Now certain that Winthorpe has been dealing in narcotics, Penelope rounds on him furiously, telling him that she never wants to see him again before swiftly departing in her expensive car.

Bewildered by this latest mystifying incident, Winthorpe asks Ophelia why she had interjected when she is clearly a stranger to him. Ophelia replies that she had been paid by one of Winthorpe's friends to play a part in an elaborate practical joke on him, but Beeks has already disappeared when she points in his general direction, leaving both of them baffled. Now desperate, he persuades her to pay for a taxi to his house on the proviso that he will repay her in full when they get there. However, the locks on the doors have all been changed, and Coleman pretends not to recognise him. The butler, though looking rather guilty at his employers' subterfuge, threatens to call the police if Winthorpe doesn't depart from the doorstep immediately. Growing ever more mystified, Winthorpe's next stop is at the bank, where he tries to make a cash withdrawal only to be told that tax inspectors have frozen his account. He is forcibly ejected from the premises before he can attempt to negotiate.

Winthorpe is now left with literally nowhere to turn. Realising that he is telling the truth about his fall from grace, as improbable as it seems, Ophelia takes pity on him and agrees to take him home with her until he can get back on his feet. As their taxi departs, Winthorpe is staggered when he sees Valentine passing in his own private limousine, particularly when he notices that it is being driven by Coleman. Valentine is equally shocked when he sees the bedraggled Winthorpe, remembering him from his earlier encounter, and becomes apprehensive when an uncomfortable Coleman awkwardly evades the subject. The limousine arrives at the headquarters of Duke and Duke, where Valentine is arriving for his first day in Randolph and Mortimer's employ. There, he is treated to an absurdly patronising explanation of commodities brokerage by the brothers, but it is clear that the savvy Valentine is already taking to the business like a duck to water.

Ophelia arrives with Winthorpe at her apartment in a rough area of the city. Still enraged by Coleman's betrayal and unable to deduce exactly what has caused his downfall, Winthorpe vows revenge. But the level-headed Ophelia explains that he has no time to plot retribution; there is the far more pressing issue of making ends meet. Winthorpe is speechless when she reveals to him the details of her line of work in prostitution, but she is entirely too rationally-minded to bother engaging with his apparent disapproval. Instead, Ophelia explains that her willingness to put a roof over his head comes at a price: she plans to retire from the sex trade within the next few years, and will be expecting a five-figure sum from Winthorpe in return for her current benevolence.

Back at Duke and Duke, Valentine impresses Randolph when he shows a clear aptitude for reading the market, making the Dukes a substantial profit when he correctly predicts the falling price of pork bellies (thus mirroring Winthorpe's earlier predictive talents). This development irritates Mortimer, who can see that Randolph is gleeful over early evidence that his theory of the pre-eminence of environment over genetic factors is a valid one: Valentine may lack Winthorpe's expensive education and privileged upbringing, but he has a keen insight into the behaviour of the general public that is entirely alien to the elitist Duke brothers. Mortimer secretly deposits Randolph's money clip on the ground in an obvious attempt to test Valentine's loyalty as they depart. However, the younger man immediately returns it to its owner as soon as he notices it, lending further credence to Randolph's premise of nurture triumphing over nature. Mortimer, who clearly expected Valentine to steal the money, is not happy.

Winthorpe makes an unexpected – and deeply unwelcome – appearance at an exclusive sports club, where he remains a member. He approaches a group of his old friends, including Penelope, in the hope that they will support him as character witnesses when he fights the charges that have been brought against him. Aghast, the snobbish acquaintances are clearly embarrassed by his presence and demand that he leave, leading Winthorpe to realise how insubstantial their bonds of friendship really were. Next, he heads for a pawnbroker's store in an attempt to trade in his expensive watch. Unimpressed, the shop's owner (Bo Diddley) believes the item to be stolen and offers Winthorpe a comparatively paltry $50 in return for it. Winthorpe is dismayed, but realises that he has little choice but to consent. As he is in the process of transacting with the pawnbroker, he notices a handgun on sale in the shop and appears to take a keen interest in it.

On the way back to Ophelia's apartment, Winthorpe passes the window of a high-class restaurant and is flabbergasted to discover the Duke Brothers and a collection of upper class business associates enjoying dinner with Valentine. The whole room appears to be hanging on the charismatic Valentine's every word, leading Winthorpe into an even greater state of puzzlement. As he stands outside the window in the pouring rain, watching his former employers lionising a total stranger while he becomes drenched, Winthorpe cannot seem to believe how far he has fallen so quickly. By the time he returns to the apartment, he is running a fever. Ophelia puts him to bed, cancelling an appointment with one of her clients in order to give Winthorpe a decent night's sleep.

The next morning is Christmas Eve. In spite of Winthorpe's protestations that he is becoming a nuisance, Ophelia tells him to stay in bed until he is fully recovered. Heading out for some Christmas shopping, she promises that she will return later to cook him a quiet dinner. Before she leaves, she gives him a copy of the day's *Financial Journal,* leading Winthorpe to boggle at a front-page headline which states that the Dukes' surprise appointment of Valentine is thrilling the market. Furious, Winthorpe declares that he will have vengeance before the festive season has passed.

A bountifully-supplied Christmas party is being held at the headquarters of Duke and Duke. The brothers are presiding over a punchbowl while their employees mill around, but no-one appears to realise that Winthorpe is also present in the room, heavily disguised in a decidedly tatty Santa Claus outfit. As Winthorpe helps himself to the extravagant buffet, covertly stuffing his pockets with expensive hors d'oeuvres, Valentine is in his office puzzling over the monthly payroll. In particular, he is confused by a $10,000 cheque made out to none other than Clarence Beeks. He approaches the Dukes to ask for an explanation, but Mortimer hurriedly pockets the cheque and fobs him off by telling him that Beeks has recently left the firm. Valentine becomes suspicious when Mortimer lets slip some vague information about his bet with Randolph.

On returning to his office, Valentine discovers Winthorpe desperately concealing a range of narcotics in one of his desk drawers. Winthorpe, believing that Valentine was responsible for the drugs which had been planted on him earlier, is keen to repay the favour and calls the Dukes into the office with the hope of framing Valentine. But the brothers are quick to take Valentine's side, leading Winthorpe to produce the handgun that he had procured from the pawn shop as soon as Valentine calls security. Suddenly worried for their safety, the Dukes try to persuade Winthorpe to put the gun away, but are interrupted by the arrival of a security officer. Shouting threats of reprisal, Winthorpe manages to escape the building, but the incident has left Valentine mystified. Mortimer and Randolph tell Valentine the cover story of Winthorpe's alleged misdemeanours, but their astute new employee is clearly beginning to smell a rat.

Later, Valentine is in a stall in the company's gents' toilets when the Dukes enter the washroom. Unaware that Valentine is either present or within earshot, Mortimer tells his brother that he now accepts the fact that environment has proven to be a more potent motivator than genetics where Winthorpe and Valentine have been concerned. Admitting defeat, he grudgingly hands over a $1 bill to Randolph – their agreed bet. Valentine is appalled as he overhears the conversation, particularly when he learns that Winthorpe's personal and professional reputation has been destroyed solely for the Dukes' private amusement. Mortimer is unwilling to rehire Winthorpe after his recent conduct, and they also clearly plan to unceremoniously return Valentine to an itinerant life on the streets after the New Year. However, they agree to wait until the Secretary of Agriculture releases the annual crop reports at the beginning of January – providing that Beeks fulfils a mysterious task that they claim to have set him.

Deeply inebriated and clutching a bottle of whisky, Winthorpe is staggering out of the Duke and Duke building. Valentine, also leaving, catches sight of the bedraggled figure and tries to speak with him, but Winthorpe assumes that the other man has an ulterior motive and hurries off, quickly catching a bus to Ophelia's side of town. On arrival, he believes that he has reached his lowest ebb when a dog urinates against his leg mere moments before a torrential thunderstorm. Withdrawing his gun, he tries to blow his brains out only to discover that the empty chamber is clicking harmlessly. Expressionless, he throws the gun away only for it to discharge into a shop window as soon as it hits the sidewalk. Shortly afterwards, Valentine arrives by taxi and follows Winthorpe to Ophelia's apartment, where he finds that the soggy Santa has passed out in the bathtub.

Winthorpe awakes in his old bed on Christmas Day, back in his opulent town house and believing that his whole predicament has simply been a bad dream. He becomes outraged by Valentine's presence when he discovers it, but the Dukes' treachery is soon explained to him in detail and corroborated by Coleman, who was privy to their bet from the start. Winthorpe immediately plans to assault Randolph and Mortimer with a shotgun, ending their duplicity once and for all, but Valentine suggests instead that they give the brothers a taste of their own medicine and ruin their fortunes. A chance news bulletin on television shows Clarence Beeks, an operative for a private security firm, ferrying the crop reports on behalf of the government prior to their announcement in January. Immediately recognising the name, Winthorpe and Valentine both realise that the Dukes plan to intercept the reports prior to their official release, illegally gaining inside knowledge which would allow them to gain supremacy in the lucrative frozen orange juice market.

Back at the Duke and Duke building, Valentine intercepts a phone call between Beeks and the Duke brothers where the security man arranges a rendezvous in a high-class New York hotel so that he can relay his top-secret information. Sure enough, on New Year's Eve Beeks is boarding a train from Washington D.C. en-route to Philadelphia. The train is packed with costumed revellers; among the many passengers are Harvey (James Belushi), a party-loving man in a gorilla suit, and – implausibly enough – an actual gorilla (Don McLeod) which is being transported to the city in a cage. Much to Beeks's irritation, Valentine appears unexpectedly in his train compartment impersonating a Cameroonian student, followed shortly after by Coleman, dressed as a priest and sporting a highly variable Irish accent. Next comes Ophelia, affecting a Swedish accent but dressed in a traditional Austrian national costume (including lederhosen). While Beeks is – at Ophelia's request – storing her heavy backpack on a luggage shelf, Valentine swipes his briefcase and substitutes it for an identical replacement. He then smuggles the case out of the compartment and passes it to Winthorpe, who is hiding further along the carriage.

Just when things look as though they can't possibly become any more convoluted, Winthorpe himself arrives in the compartment – dressed as a Rastafarian and affecting a charmingly flamboyant attitude. With some further subterfuge, he attempts to return Beeks's case without him noticing. But the canny security agent reveals that he is only too aware what has been going on, pulling a gun on Ophelia and threatening to shoot if they don't do exactly as he says. Beeks orders them to leave the compartment, and the group weaves through a drunken party in the buffet carriage before ending up in a cargo container next to the caged gorilla. It is clear that Beeks plans to execute Winthorpe, Valentine and their associates, but he is momentarily distracted by the sudden appearance of the costumed Harvey. Sidetracked, he is then knocked unconscious by the nearby gorilla when he strays too close to his cage. Wasting no time, the group strip Beeks of his clothing and put him into the gorilla suit, then lock him in the cage with the real primate while they make their getaway.

In a darkened multi-storey hotel car park, Mortimer and Randolph are awaiting the arrival of Beeks with their advance copy of the crop report. Sure enough, a shadowy figure in a hat and trench-coat appears, seemingly out of nowhere, and accepts from the brothers a briefcase packed with banknotes. In return, he throws them a manila envelope; its contents delight the Dukes no end. They thank Beeks for a job well done, but the shady individual has already departed. At no point to the brothers realise that the man they have been dealing with was actually Valentine, disguised in Beeks's stolen clothing.

Armed with the predictions of the real crop reports, Valentine and Winthorpe head for the New York Stock Exchange with every penny they have, together with the collective life savings of Coleman and Ophelia. Believing, from the false report that they have been given, that orange production has been adversely affected by the harsh winter, the Dukes attempt to corner the market, driving up the price. But once this figure has peaked, Winthorpe begins to sell instead, sending the price back down again. Bewildered, Mortimer and Randolph realise to their horror that the crop reports they obtained have been falsified. They frantically head down to the trading floor in a vain attempt to reverse the instructions they had given for their dealings. They are interrupted by the scheduled statement from the U.S. Secretary of Agriculture (Maurice D. Copeland), which confirms that the winter weather has had no discernible effect on orange production. Stunned, the Dukes have no alternative but to look on as they are financially ruined. They seem totally amazed at the resourceful way in which Winthorpe has betrayed them, though Valentine reveals that he had made his own $1 bet with Winthorpe – that the two of them could ruin the Duke brothers and make a fortune in the process. Winthorpe and Valentine leave the stock exchange wealthier than in their wildest dreams, while Randolph and Mortimer – who had thrown every penny they owned into their scheme – face insolvency and humiliation. Thus Winthorpe, Valentine, Ophelia and Coleman enjoy their new-found riches from the comfort of a paradisiacal Caribbean hideaway, knowing that the vindictive Dukes will no longer be in a position to ruin the lives of anyone else.

As many commentators have noted, *Trading Places* is a film which very much wears its heart upon its sleeve in terms of the moral point that it seeks to convey. As Larry Elliott and Dan Atkinson have succinctly put it, '*Trading Places* contained the explicit message that not only was greed bad, but that it ultimately led to ruination'.[2] Landis presents a film where altruism is clearly the victor over self-interest, unambiguously marking out the boundary lines between Randolph and Mortimer Duke (cold, distant, snobbish, uncaring, racist and egocentric) and the majority of the less wealthy characters (who are generally selfless, inventive, warm and inclusive). Yet the film does contain some surprisingly mixed messages in this regard. The film's opening shots, cutting between scenes of luxurious opulence and grinding poverty, are suggestive of a much starker depiction of free market excesses than those featuring in the central scenario which Landis actually sets up. Clearly we are shown that unfettered capitalism has an ugly side which contains the potential to create grotesques such as the Duke brothers, but it is that same system of capitalistic freedom which gives Valentine and Winthorpe the capability to turn the tables on their adversaries in the most devastatingly effective of ways. So it is perhaps more correct to say that the film's primary concern is not capitalistic inequity at all, but rather cultural attitudes towards wealth and the way that society had come to regard economic prosperity as an end in itself. The standoffish Winthorpe comes to realise that his wealth was no guarantor of a satisfying life, and finds that poverty has a humanising effect – he has no choice but to engage with wider society when his personal circumstances change, forcing him to deal with people directly rather than through proxies such as Coleman or his subordinates at Duke and Duke. Likewise, Valentine clearly finds within himself hitherto-undiscovered reserves of business acumen, but he retains the ability to realise that cash is far from the all-encompassing panacea that he had so long presumed it to be when he was impoverished and homeless. Winthorpe is faced with the unpalatable realisation that money attracts fair-weather friends who exhibit no lasting loyalty (even his engagement is shown to be little more than a social imperative, his fiancée being even more obsessed with prestige and position than he initially was), while Valentine becomes increasingly aware that the

Dukes are treating him as little more than one of the commodities that they trade in, lifting him out of poverty with every intention of plunging him back into it again just to satisfy their perverse whims – and never once with any regard for him as a human being.

And yet, for all its slyly multifaceted engagement with socio-economic issues – Western society's relationship with free market capitalism was, after all, one of the key topics of eighties American film-making in general – *Trading Places* is also indisputably a Christmas movie at heart. While the film's key premise would have been potent enough at any time of the year, Winthorpe's suffering appears particularly poignant when reflected against the cosy light of tinsel and festive decorations, while the snowy Philadelphia streets provide an atmospheric backdrop to events. There is an interesting visual contrast between Ophelia's homely but endearingly low-key Christmas tree and the magnificent but singularly characterless corporate celebrations taking place at Duke and Duke, and yet most remarkable is the way in which the festive season weaves its transformational powers upon the film's characters, improving the lives of Winthorpe and Valentine (albeit through respective baptisms of fire) while eventually consigning Mortimer and Randolph to a deserving fate. If Winthorpe is the Scrooge of the tale, an avaricious snob turned responsive egalitarian, then the Duke brothers are surely the latter-day corporeal incarnations of Jacob Marley, unavoidably destined for ruin due to the short-sightedness of their own unthinking materialism.

However, if we consider the central issue of *Trading Places* to be the corrupting influence of excessive wealth then it is interesting to see how Timothy Harris and Herschel Weingrod's screenplay deals with the topic in a broader context. There is no doubt that the Duke brothers are the villains of the piece, their 'old money' background and towering social influence shielding them from censure to such an extent that they seem thoroughly jaded with their all-encompassing ability to buy and sell whatever (and whomever) they please. Yet in some ways there seems to be precious little of the Christmas spirit in evidence throughout the film's final act, for Winthorpe and Valentine find that they can only succeed by countering the Dukes' dishonest scheme in a manner which suits their own interests – not by reporting Beeks' duplicity to the authorities, but by using the very same chicanery to benefit them financially. Alan Nadel makes the point that 'at the end of *Trading Places*, the ultra-rich, ultra-WASP Winthorpe (Dan Aykroyd) and the black street hustler Valentine (Eddie Murphy) combine not to right the injustices perpetuated by the corrupt commodities dealers, the Duke brothers, but to get rich by employing the Dukes' dishonest tactics against them'.[3] This was an audacious narrative strategy, but one which does raise the rather immediate issue of whether two wrongs can make a right: the money raised from Valentine and Winthorpe's frantic dealing at the New York Stock Exchange not only assures their own long-term wealth, but also that of the hard-working Coleman and Ophelia into the bargain, while the Dukes are jointly condemned to ruination. So while it does seem clear that it is the greed and excess which can thrive in the shadow of unchecked capitalism that are being criticised here, rather than the mechanics of the free market system itself, the long-term fate of the protagonists remains unclear at the film's conclusion. When all is said and done, it is left to the viewer to ascertain whether the characters' new-found riches will truly be able to secure happiness for any of them in the future

(Ophelia's love for Winthorpe is, after all, something that was born in poverty and remains beyond price), or whether any of the beneficiaries of Randolph and Mortimer's misfortune will be fated to tread the same road of detached ennui that had tainted the Duke brothers so thoroughly, thus repeating the same entropic cycle. As David Denby perceptively observes:

> In John Landis's *Trading Places*, the wealthy and comfortable characters – the capitalists – are cold-eyed bastards, while the poor are generous and kind. Yet, Landis and his screenwriters must have decided that in Ronald Reagan's America no one really wants to identify with the poor; at the last minute, they turn the heroes into big winners, leaving them on a Caribbean beach with luxurious ladies in tow. Since the movie, up to this point, insists that money corrupts, we might expect success to corrupt the heroes too. But *Trading Places* isn't the kind of movie that resolves its conflicting fantasies; it just ends.[4]

The film's appeal is due in large part to the quality of the persuasive performances delivered by its lead performers. Dan Aykroyd impresses as the priggish Louis Winthorpe, a man who is forced to go from riches to rags (and then back to riches again) in the course of less than a month. From Winthorpe's pampered preening and smug self-satisfaction through to his slow-motion meltdown as his life collapses around him, Aykroyd takes his time to gradually build an impression of likeability around Winthorpe as the film progresses, allowing audience sympathy to grow in a way that lends a very palpable sense of the character's complicated emotional journey. (His whisky-soaked, suicidal variation on Jolly Old Saint Nick also must rank as one of the most melancholic appearances of Santa Claus in living memory.) At the time of *Trading Places*'s release, Dan Aykroyd was well-known for being one of the writing staff on television's popular *Saturday Night Live* between 1976 and 1979. He and his co-writers won the Emmy Award for Outstanding Writing in a Comedy/Variety or Music Series in 1977, and were nominated for Emmys again in 1978 and 1979. In terms of performance, Aykroyd was active in television from the mid-seventies, making his big-screen debut in romantic comedy *Love at First Sight* (Rex Bromfield, 1977). He appeared in a number of memorable TV features at the time, including Eric Idle and Gary Weis's *The Rutles: All You Need Is Cash* (1978) and Gary Weis's *Things We Did Last Summer* (1978), before hitting the big time as Sergeant Frank Tree in Steven Spielberg's *1941* (1979) and, most especially, as Elwood Blues in *The Blues Brothers* (John Landis, 1980), which featured a screenplay written by both Aykroyd and Landis. Aykroyd continued to appear in comedies such as *Neighbors* (John G. Avildsen, 1981) and *Doctor Detroit* (Michael Pressman, 1983) before being cast as Louis Winthorpe and, the following year, would deliver what was perhaps his best-remembered performance of the decade as Dr Ray Stantz in Ivan Reitman's *Ghostbusters* (1984), a film which he co-wrote with Harold Ramis. In 1990, Aykroyd was nominated for the Academy Award for Best Actor in a Supporting Role in recognition of his performance as Boolie Werthan in Bruce Beresford's *Driving Miss Daisy* (1989).

Aykroyd is matched step for step by Eddie Murphy's barnstorming performance as the cunning Billy Ray Valentine. Murphy throws his all into the role, producing an intelligent, high-energy rendering of a very distinctive and shrewd character. Valentine's development curve is every bit as dramatic as Winthorpe's proves to be, allowing Murphy's innate charm and skill for character development to shine through from every scene. Like Aykroyd, Murphy was a writer for *Saturday Night Live* – in his case, between 1982 and 1984 – as well as making appearances as a performer on the show from 1980 until 1984. Also a talented and often controversial stand-up comedian, and later a producer and screenwriter, he made an explosive cinematic debut as Reggie Hammond in Walter Hill's *48 Hrs* (1982) (a role which he would later reprise in Hill's sequel, *Another 48 Hrs*, in 1990). Murphy's acting career continued to be highly successful throughout the eighties, with lead performances in films such as *Beverly Hills Cop* (Martin Brest, 1984), *The Golden Child* (Michael Ritchie, 1986) and *Coming to America* (John Landis, 1988). In more recent years, Murphy was nominated for the Best Performance by an Actor in a Supporting Role Academy Award for his appearance in Bill Condon's well-received musical drama *Dreamgirls* (2006).

Trading Places was not to be the last time that these two creatively industrious actors would collaborate with director John Landis. Aykroyd and Landis worked together again on *Spies Like Us* (1985) and *Susan's Plan* (1998), as well as the prologue of fantasy thriller *Twilight Zone: The Movie* (1983), which was also helmed by Landis. Murphy and Landis would join forces in later years when Murphy was headlining *Coming to America*, and also when he reprised his famous role as Axel Foley in Landis's *Beverly Hills Cop III* (1994).

Screen veterans Don Ameche and Ralph Bellamy lead an excellent supporting cast with their scene-stealing performances as the two Machiavellian Duke brothers. The film also benefits from the always-classy Denholm Elliott at his most reserved as the compassionate butler Coleman, and Paul Gleason's enjoyably sleazy turn as the larger-than-life Clarence

Beeks (channelling something of the demanding authoritarianism that he would so memorably bring to the role of Principal Richard Vernon in John Hughes's iconic 1985 comedy drama *The Breakfast Club* a few years later). Jamie Lee Curtis impresses in an early role as the streetwise, gum-chewing Ophelia. Curtis had made appearances in many successful horror films from the time of her cinematic debut in John Carpenter's cult classic *Halloween* (1978), including *The Fog* (John Carpenter, 1980), *Prom Night* (Paul Lynch, 1980), *Terror Train* (Roger Spottiswoode, 1980) and *Halloween II* (Rick Rosenthal, 1981), but her award-winning performance in *Trading Places* marked a shift in gear for her acting career which would see her attain an even higher profile as the decade continued.

Trading Places also features an interesting range of unusual cameo appearances from actors and performers such as Alfred Drake, Bo Diddley, Al Franken, Tom Davis, Frank Oz and, perhaps most notably, James Belushi, the brother of Dan Ackroyd's co-star John Belushi in Landis's *The Blues Brothers*. Indeed, this latter connection was just one association which existed between *Trading Places* and Landis's earlier film. The prison number which is assigned to Winthorpe is exactly the same number that is given to Jake Blues, played by John Belushi, in *The Blues Brothers*. Landis would repeatedly prove himself to be no stranger to clever in-jokes: Don Ameche and Ralph Bellamy would later reprise their roles in a cameo as a (now destitute) Randolph and Mortimer Duke in Landis's later film *Coming to America*, also starring Eddie Murphy, where an uncanny twist of fate allows the ageing brothers to discover that they have been presented with one last chance at redemption.

Trading Places did well at the box-office, and also met with a generally warm reception from reviewers. Critics took particular note of the fact that the film works hard to present an engaging (rather than preachy) social message; Roger Ebert, for example, commented that:

> [*Trading Places*] wants to be funny, but it also wants to tell us something about human nature and there are whole stretches when we forget it's a comedy and get involved in the story. [...] This is good comedy. It's especially good because it doesn't stop with sitcom manipulations of its idea, and it doesn't go only for the obvious points about racial prejudice in America. Instead, it develops the quirks and peculiarities of its characters, so that they're funny because of who they are. This takes a whole additional level of writing on top of the plot-manipulation we usually get in popular comedies, and it takes good direction, too.[5]

If the relative restraint of Landis's approach, and that of Weingrod and Harris's screenplay, was worthy of praise, so too was the carefully-pitched humour. While the film did, of course, employ many over-the-top situations and the occasional sight gag to entertain audiences, it never strives for laughs to the point that the dramatic content is entirely subsumed. Thus biting wit is generated by Winthorpe's rapid decline into poverty and Valentine's fish-out-of-water improvement in fortunes, but never to the extent that the characters appear to be excessively patronised or demeaned as a result (in spite of the Dukes' best efforts to the contrary) on account of their surprising resilience and adaptable natures. Jay Carr noted that the film's deftly-employed comedy was allowed to develop organically rather than ever appearing forced or stilted: 'It's easily the best of the movies I've seen by the various *Saturday Night Live* alumni, and part of the reason it's funny and satisfying is that it doesn't strain'.[6]

The film was also considered by many commentators of the time to have been not only a successful comedy in its own right, but also a hugely fruitful star vehicle for Eddie Murphy – very much an eighties icon in the making at the time. A number of commentators were fulsome in their approval of Murphy's energetic performance as Billy Ray Valentine, which they perceived as being vital to the film's success. (Matthew Fraser was far from alone in his concise summation that '*Trading Places*, which is wildly funny at times, is Murphy's film'.[7]) More recent appraisals of the film have come to consider *Trading Places* as being one of the early catalysts which would propel Murphy into the upper echelons of the Hollywood A-list, eventually making him one of the most successful actors in eighties cinema. Martin Flanagan describes *Trading Places* as 'a lively and beautifully cast riff on the theme of nature versus nurture imbued with a message concerning the inhumanity of the Reagan era. As a vehicle for Murphy the movie delivered, and the star, one of the biggest of the 1980s, would return to Landis for *Coming to America*'.[8]

While *Trading Places* has, in the years since its release, come to be regarded more in terms of a socially-aware comedy than a Christmas film, its subdued festive trimmings and message of positive transformation (taking place alongside, rather than because of, the holiday season) have nonetheless meant that Landis's movie has securely earned itself a place within the genre. That being said, the film is less overtly concerned with paying homage to the predominant themes of Christmas cinema than it is with distorting the iconography of the holiday season for comedic ends. As Tyler Foster has explained:

> First and foremost, *Trading Places* is a performance piece. Anyone who says *Trading Places'* story is paper-thin is right, but that's beside the point. Aykroyd's Louis starts out as an unlikable caricature of high society, but once he's been tossed out on his ear, Louis' insistent innocence slowly turns from grating to funny until Louis is stuffing entire salmon into the worst Santa outfit that's ever existed (it looks like it was unwashed before it was even manufactured). [...] *Trading Places* holds up. Hell, it even seems vaguely relevant, thanks to the montage of lower-class people struggling to make ends meet that makes up half the opening credits. It's a focused, well-performed, modestly scaled comedy that remains consistently funny.[9]

Thus if there is a predominant Christmas theme at play within the film, it is that of the responsibility of the individual to show moral concern for others – including society at large. The Duke brothers may have the material resources to enact any aspersive scheme they desire, but it is the ingenuity of people they consider to be distant social inferiors which ultimately wins the day. While Winthorpe and Valentine turn the tables on the Dukes, the fact that they ensure that Coleman and Ophelia join them – all of their life savings are necessary to provide sufficient capital to enact revenge at the stock exchange – ensures that this particular team effort is the very epitome of a David versus Goliath clash between unfeeling financial titans and quick-thinking, hard-working individuals. While the economic downfall of ethically warped antagonists may not seem to be too closely in tune with the general ethos of a Christmas morality tale, in truth *Trading Places* did not stray too far from accepted conventions of festive cinema – even going so far as to borrow from earlier generic precedents in pleasingly effective ways. As Nathan Rabin has remarked:

> [*Trading Places*] cleaned up at the box office during Murphy's Reagan-era heyday, and [...] let director John Landis channel Frank Capra. *Trading Places* taps into the farcical prankster side of Capra's persona – Landis describes it as his version of a '30s-style 'social comedy' – in its irreverent tale of a small-time con man (Murphy) who trades places with stuffy über-WASP Dan Aykroyd at the whim of playfully perverse tycoon brothers Ralph Bellamy and Don Ameche. [...] Elmer Bernstein's Oscar-nominated score and Robert Paynter's cinematography give the film a retro grandeur that's part Charles Dickens, part screwball comedy.[10]

Although *Trading Places* has come to be regarded as one of the eighties' most winningly-crafted comedies, it has not been entirely without its detractors. Much of this criticism has been aimed at the perceived success – or otherwise – of the delicate balancing act which accompanies its treatment of the polarising issues of prosperity and poverty as effectively forming two sides of the same coin (that is, characters who are materially wealthy but morally bankrupt, and vice versa). Janet Maslin, at the time of the film's release, noted that 'it's a big, lavishly staged farce that aims to please even those who favor sophisticated screwball comedy, a genre to which it is greatly indebted. Indeed, Preston Sturges might have made a movie like *Trading Places* – if he'd had a little less inspiration and a lot more money. [...] This extravagant-looking film is itself too obviously enamored of wealth and prosperity to rail at the establishment with any real conviction. Everyone in the film aspires to the prosperity that is also so cleverly mocked here'.[11] Others were instead to draw attention to the tonal qualities of the film, taking exception to its status as a classic of eighties comedy due to its frequent digressions into more profound dramatic territory. Mike Long is representative of this line of criticism, observing that *Trading Places* 'has some classic comedic moments, but on the whole, the movie is too much of a downer to be considered a comedy. While the plight of Louis does contain some black humor, there's also a very desperate and eventually violent side to it. The last act of the film has some laughs, but it becomes more of a suspense thriller'.[12]

On the whole, however, *Trading Places* has retained a healthy popularity within eighties comedy, Christmas cinema, and especially as part of John Landis's wider, eclectic filmography. Whereas many other comedy films of the decade have suffered as a result of dated styles of humour or being overly reliant on the cultural references of the time, the universality of *Trading Places*'s central theme has allowed it to remain accessible to modern audiences, prompting numerous home entertainment releases on various different formats over the years. As Scott Weinberg has remarked, the film's structural refinement and narrative finesse have helped to make it a truly memorable feature: 'John Landis strikes a perfect tone between old-school storytelling and decidedly modern vulgarity. And although it clocks in at just under two hours in length, *Trading Places* breezes by, thanks to a tight and clever screenplay, a solid stable of comedic actors, and a director who was at the very top of his game'.[13] However, in the eyes of many critics the success of the movie was first and foremost secured by the captivating quality of its stars' compelling performances, ensuring that the film was elevated from polished proficiency into the realms of truly memorable cinema. It was this appealing combination of elements which, as David Nusair argues, has made *Trading Places* such a classic of eighties comedy:

> Armed with standout performances from stars Dan Aykroyd and Eddie Murphy, *Trading Places* undoubtedly (and effortlessly) lives up to its reputation as one of the most impressive comedies to emerge out of the 1980s. [...] It's an unabashedly high concept premise that's employed to positive effect by director John Landis, although it does go without saying that the lion's share of praise for the film's success belongs to both Aykroyd and Murphy - as the actors' exceedingly engaging work ultimately proves instrumental in smoothing over some of the more questionable elements within the narrative.[14]

Trading Places performed well at awards ceremonies, being nominated for the Best Music: Original Song Score Oscar at the Academy Awards in 1984 for Elmer Bernstein's stirring soundtrack. Eddie Murphy was nominated for a Golden Globe Award in the Best Performance by an Actor in a Motion Picture (Comedy/Musical) category, while the film itself was nominated for the Best Motion Picture (Comedy/Musical) award at the same ceremony. At the BAFTA Awards, Denholm Elliott won the Best Supporting Actor Award and Jamie Lee Curtis was awarded Best Supporting Actress, while Timothy Harris and Herschel Weingrod's script was nominated in the Best Screenplay: Original category.

With its overarching message of individual empowerment and its upbeat central message of common humanity overcoming dishonourable greed, *Trading Places* had set the prevailing agenda for many later Christmas films of the eighties. Although the movie is situated largely within the hard-faced world of finance, there is a genuine sense of benign warmth at its heart, and Landis's inventively progressive approach to the festive season leaves a lasting impression that Christmas miracles still had a place in the modern world – even one that was filled with divisive politics and widespread fiscal woes. *Trading Places* was right at the vanguard of the Christmas film's return to prominence – and relevance – among cinematic audiences after the genre's long period of relative creative neglect throughout the sixties and seventies, and its success with the critics and at the box-office augured well for the fortunes of this ever-versatile category of film in the years to come. But besides all this, there are very few movies which can claim to have quite as direct an impact upon the very world that they had depicted in the same way as *Trading Places* did; as Robert Smith has noted, Landis's film was to become such a robust fixture in popular culture that even the financial services industry could not ignore the prominence of its reputation: 'Trading commodities on inside information obtained from the government wasn't actually illegal when the movie came out, but it's illegal now. It was banned in the 2010 finance-overhaul law, under a special provision often referred to as the Eddie Murphy Rule'.[15]

REFERENCES

1. Gary J. Svehla and Susan Svehla, *It's Christmas Time at the Movies* (Baltimore: Midnight Marquee Press, 1998), p.112.

2. Larry Elliott and Dan Atkinson, *The Age of Insecurity* (London: Verso, 1999) [1998], pp.147-48.

3. Alan Nadel, 'Movies and Reaganism', in *American Cinema of the 1980s: Themes and Variations*, ed. by Stephen Prince (Chapel Hill: Rutgers University Press, 2007), pp.84-86.

4. David Denby, 'Supply-Side Hero', in *New York Magazine*, 22 August 1983, pp.62-63.

5. Roger Ebert, '*Trading Places*', in *The Chicago Sun-Times*, 9 June 1983.

6. Jay Carr, '*Trading Places*', in *The Boston Globe*, 9 June 1983.

7. Matthew Fraser, '*Trading Places*', in *The Toronto Globe and Mail*, 10 June 1983.

8. Martin Flanagan, 'John Landis', in *Contemporary North American Film Directors: A Wallflower Critical Guide*, ed. by Yoram Allon, Del Cullen and Hannah Patterson (London: Wallflower Press, 2002), pp.310-12.

9. Tyler Foster, '*Trading Places*: Special Collector's Edition', in *DVD Talk*, 24 August 2010.

<http://www.dvdtalk.com/reviews/47288/trading-places-special-collectors-edition/>

10.   Nathan Rabin, ' *Trading Places/ Coming to America*', in *The Onion A. V. Club*, 13 June 2007.
<http://www.avclub.com/review/trading-places-coming-to-america-7767>

11.   Janet Maslin, 'Ackroyd in *Trading Places*', in *The New York Times*, 8 June 1983.

12.   Mike Long, ' *Trading Places*', in *DVD Sleuth*, 13 June 2007.
<http://www.dvdsleuth.com/TradingPlacesReview/>

13.   Scott Weinberg, ' *Trading Places*', in *JoBlo*, 5 June 2007.
<http://www.joblo.com/blu-rays-dvds/reviews/trading-places-se>

14.   David Nusair, 'The Films of John Landis', in *ReelFilm*, 1 July 2009.
<http://reelfilm.com/jlandis.htm#trading>

15.   Robert Smith, 'What Actually Happens at the End of *Trading Places?*', in *Planet Money: The Economy Explained*, National Public Radio, 12 July 2013.
<http://www.npr.org/sections/money/2013/07/19/201430727/what-actually-happens-at-the-end-of-trading-places>

4

A Christmas Story (1983)

Metro-Goldwyn-Meyer/Christmas Tree Films

Director: Bob Clark
Producers: Bob Clark and René Dupont
Screenwriters: Jean Shepherd, Leigh Brown and Bob Clark,
from a novel by Jean Shepherd

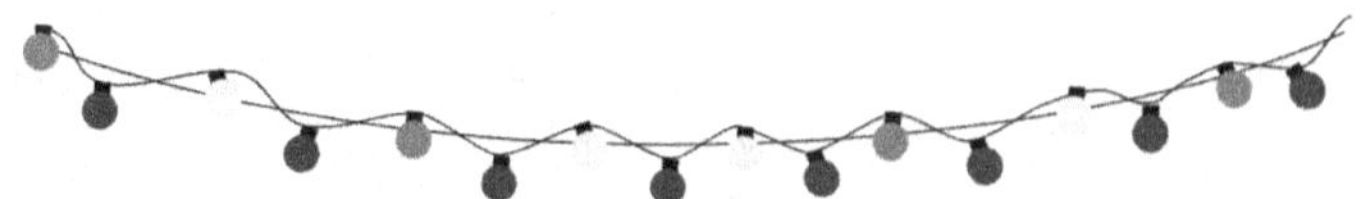

Trading Places had underscored the fact that the world of the 1980s was changing rapidly, and the public perception of Christmas with it. Following in a similar vein, *A Christmas Story* was to juxtapose the mores of modern society with that of America's then-recent historical past, an affectionate cross-generational love letter to a bygone age of the festive season. The eighties, after all, were to see social and cultural attitudes shifting in a number of ways, and the Christmas movie was just one genre which was to be challenged and reconfigured in the light of this new age of cynicism and aggressive individuality. Thus while *A Christmas Story* was warmly nostalgic with regard to its subject matter, it stopped short of idealising the era of its setting any more than it sentimentalised Christmas itself. Playing out like a diametric opposite of the twisted events of *Christmas Evil*'s prologue, where the holiday season is this time the source of heartfelt reminiscence rather than lifelong trauma, *A Christmas Story* was part of a broader re-examination of the festive season which was taking place throughout the 1980s, contrasting sympathetically-rendered yuletide recollections with some of the stark emotional realities of growing from childhood into adolescence.

A Christmas Story was adapted from the novels of actor and writer Jean Shepherd, with primary reference to *In God We Trust, Others Pay Cash* (1966) though with other incidents from the film having appeared in his later work *Wanda Hickey's Night of Golden Memories and Other Disasters* (1971). Popular for his wry observations and down-to-earth humour, he was a recognisable name to audiences thanks to well-received features such as his TV documentary series *Jean Shepherd's America* (1971) and his many radio broadcasts over the years. His long career established him as one of the most prominent American humourists of the late twentieth century, and he was renowned as a true multimedia personality before the term had even been popularised. Shepherd was to act as the narrator of *A Christmas Story* in addition to collaborating on its screenplay, and he also appeared in a number of different roles throughout the film – some of them quite unforeseen.

It seemed slightly ironic that this cheerful slice of wistful nostalgia should have been brought to the big screen by Bob Clark, the same man who had been responsible for presenting one of the darkest, most edgy depictions of the festive season in the form of the previous decade's *Black Christmas* (1974). Yet *A Christmas Story* has come to be regarded as one of Clark's best-known features, and the vast stylistic disparities between it and his earlier film were to fit surprisingly contentedly into what was an increasingly versatile filmography. Following *Black Christmas*'s appearance in 1974, Clark had gone on to direct tense thriller *Breaking Point* (1976), Sherlock Holmes mystery *Murder by Decree* (1979) and the moving theatre-based drama *Tribute* (1980) before he released one of his most commercially successful films, the infamous teen comedy *Porky's* (1982). This was followed soon after by the equally raucous *Porky's II: The Next Day* (1983), collectively establishing him as a productive director who was unafraid to experiment with wildly different genres and approaches to his craft. With *A Christmas Story*, however, he was to engage with a type of film which was quite different in tone and content from any of his previous movies. The end result would ultimately be one of the most enduringly successful of all eighties Christmas films.

December has arrived in the snowy Indianan town of Hammond. It's the 1940s and, in a house in Cleveland Street, nine-year-old Ralphie Parker (Peter Billingsley) is eagerly awaiting the approach of the festive season. Having recently been transfixed by the annual window display in one of the town's department stores, he has become singularly obsessed with the prospect of receiving a Red Ryder BB gun for Christmas. Coming to the swift conclusion that this is the dream gift that he has always wanted, Ralphie becomes totally focused on convincing his parents to buy one for him before it is too late.

Ralphie's initial efforts to gain the attention of his mother (Melinda Dillon) and father (Darren McGavin) are far from successful. Trying desperately to drop hints wherever possible, he is crushed when his mother tells him that there is no way that she will consider buying him a gift that will run the risk of him losing an eye. Ralphie can see no easy way of circumventing her parental concern, but remains absolutely fixated on having a BB gun of his own. He crafts a fanciful daydream where he defends his home from a pack of nefarious burglars, but is soon brought down to earth when his father enters one of his regular battles with the house's temperamental furnace.

Once his mother has bundled up Ralphie's younger brother Randy (Ian Petrella) to face the winter cold, the two boys head for school. After an English lesson, two of Ralphie's friends – who have been having a protracted argument about whether someone's tongue will stick to ice-frosted metal – enter an elaborate exchange of dares and double-dares until Flick (Scott Schwartz) accedes to Schwartz's (R.D. Robb) taunting and plants his tongue on the school's frozen flagpole. Unfortunately for Flick, who had long ridiculed Schwartz's warnings, he soon finds himself stuck fast to the frigid metal pole, leading soon after to an embarrassing visit from the police and fire brigade. The boys' teacher, Miss Shields (Tedde Moore) is dismayed by Flick's fate, but Ralphie's amusement at his headstrong friend's fortunes soon turns to joy when he discovers that the class has been set an essay-writing assignment, the topic being what gift the students would most like to receive for Christmas. Surely, he reasons, this may present him with another opportunity to emphasise his desire for the much-wanted BB gun.

On their way home after school, Ralphie, Randy, Schwartz and Flick (now vehemently attesting that he'd felt no pain at all during his encounter with the flagpole in a hopeless attempt to save face) are accosted by school bully Skut Farkus (Zack Ward) and his dim-witted sidekick Grover Dill (Yano Anaya). They manage to escape with only their pride damaged, racing in the opposite direction as Farkus and Dill sneer at their retreat. Once he is safely ensconced in the warmth of his home, Ralphie quickly puts pencil to paper as he scribbles out an impassioned treatise on the essential nature of BB guns and why they make such uniquely good Christmas presents. As he marvels at his finished work, his father arrives back from work with exciting news – he has received a telegram with the announcement that he will soon be the recipient of a major prize that he has won in a competition. Mr Parker is convinced that this ambiguous treasure will be delivered later that evening, and much speculation takes place over what it might actually turn out to be.

Sure enough, as the family eat dinner there is a knock at their front door. A delivery man (Jim Hunter) has arrived with a mysterious wooden crate. Mr Parker can barely contain his excitement as it is wheeled into the living room, and he wastes no time in opening it with a crowbar and hammer... only to reveal, through seemingly endless piles of sawdust, a lamp-stand in the shape of a woman's leg, complete with stocking and high-heeled shoe. Mr Parker is delighted by his new acquisition, but his wife is appalled and Ralphie is just plain confused. Yet nobody will be allowed to dampen Mr Parker's spirits: he is so delighted by this unexpected bounty that he proudly displays it right in the centre of his living-room window, then rushes outside to see what it looks like from the street. Mrs Parker is mortified as many of her neighbours and other passers-by stop on the sidewalk to peer with curiosity at the peculiar lamp. However, she manages to distract any awkward questions from Ralphie by directing him and his brother with their favourite radio programme (*Radio Orphan Annie*) which, as luck would have it, is just starting its broadcast.

The next day, Ralphie and his friends race to school, keen to avoid another confrontation with Farkus and Dill.

Ralphie hands over his assignment to Miss Shields, confident that his literary genius will be richly rewarded by a good grade. After he has returned home, his father takes the whole family to a rather shabby Christmas tree emporium, where a silver-tongued salesman (Les Carlson) tries to convince him of the virtues of his stock. It quickly becomes apparent that many of the trees have seen better days, but Mr Parker nevertheless strikes a bargain and has one of the better specimens tied to his car. On the drive home, however, a flat tyre forces him to pull over and affect repairs. Mrs Parker suggests that Ralphie go out and help his father, but following a mishap the boy is heard swearing, causing his parents to later punish him by sucking on a bar of soap until he confesses the source of the profanity. Ralphie knows full well that he had heard it from his father, who is no stranger to a curse-word, but believing discretion to be the better part of valour he blames his friend Schwartz instead. Mrs Parker calls Schwartz's mother to complain (resulting in a quick clip round the ear for Ralphie's hapless acquaintance), following which she promptly sends Ralphie to bed, where he dreams of his family's remorse when they discover that he has gone blind – not from an accident with a BB gun, but from soap poisoning.

Morning brings a flotilla of Christmas gifts for Mrs Shields as her students await the grades from their essays. Many of the children have brought her trinkets or little potted plants, but – not to be outdone – Ralphie presents her with an ostentatious wicker basket filled with fruit, hoping to unsubtly entice her into giving him a favourable mark for his essay. He gets home after school to the exciting discovery that his *Radio Orphan Annie* decoder pin has arrived in the mail – his long-awaited reward for collecting countless tokens from malted beverage jars. Ralphie's exhilaration continues until the radio programme broadcasts its secret message and, armed with his decoder, he avidly decrypts the series of numbers only to be faced with an advertisement for the self-same malted drink which sponsors the show. Feeling betrayed by this blatant marketing ploy, Ralphie's disappointment is tangible.

Later, his father is once again fighting the house's furnace down in the basement when the infamous leg lamp is unexpectedly and accidentally shattered... while, by total coincidence, Mrs Parker is watering plants nearby. Mr Parker is distraught at the loss of his beloved prize, blaming his wife for deliberately breaking it just to get it away from the living room window. He accuses her of being envious of his affection for his hard-won reward, but Mrs Parker denies having been responsible for damaging it, eventually blurting out that it was the most egregiously-designed lamp that she'd ever had the misfortune to set eyes upon. Undeterred, Mr Parker tries desperately to repair it with glue, but fails miserably. Still fuming, though appearing genuinely saddened by the loss of his treasured trophy, he silently takes the remains of the lamp into the garden and buries them like the body of a much-loved pet. Ralphie seems nonplussed at the loss of his father's 'major award', though the new sense of ill-feeling that now permeates the house doesn't bode well for his increasingly desperate attempts at hinting for his perfect gift.

Narrowly avoiding another skirmish with Farkus and Dill (the hapless Flick is not so lucky), Ralphie makes it back to school with high hopes of achieving a top grade for his BB gun essay. But he is crushed when Miss Shields returns his exercise book with a mark of C+, adding as an afterthought that he is sure to shoot out his eye if he ever gets his hands on the aforementioned air rifle. Any hope Ralphie has of presenting his parents with a top-graded piece of writing, thus advancing his aim of impressing the virtues of the Red Ryder BB gun in the process, has been cruelly dashed. Disenchanted by his bad fortune, he makes his way home only to be snowballed by Farkus, which – combined with the sense of injustice resulting from his earlier disappointment – finally tips him over into an incoherent rage. He furiously barrels into the mocking bully, walloping him for all that he is worth. Farkus's sidekick Dill is likewise no match for the outpouring of Ralphie's pent-up wrath, and is reduced to running for his father while the onslaught continues. Only the arrival of Mrs Parker, summoned by the anxious Randy, can break up the fight – a tearful Ralphie is led away as the stupefied Farkus, now thoroughly bloodied, shakes himself out of his dazed disbelief.

Back home, Ralphie is full of apprehension over his father's reaction to the news of the fight. However, Mrs Parker tactfully skirts around the issue and skilfully manages to get her husband onto his favourite subject of baseball instead, saving Ralphie from near-certain punishment. Ralphie is grateful to his mother for her thoughtfulness, and later – once the air has cleared – wonders what his next step should be on the path to the BB gun. He decides to ask Santa Claus to provide the gift, in the hope that Jolly Old Saint Nick will intercede on his behalf. Fortunately for Ralphie, Santa is currently to be found not at the North Pole, but at the rather more conveniently-located Higbees Department Store in town. Following the family's visit to the annual Christmas parade, and after much cajoling, Mr and Mrs Parker finally relent and allow Ralphie and Randy the chance to visit Santa with their requests for presents. But the queue is impossibly long, meaning that by the time the boys finally reach Santa the store is almost ready to close. Frogmarched over by some rather belligerent elves, Ralphie is overawed when he meets Santa (Jeff Gillen, voice of Jean Shepherd) and is then too tongue-tied to ask for the BB gun. But the store is operating a kind of high-pressure production line for the grotto, meaning that each individual child's time on Santa's knee is at a premium. Just as he is being whisked away by one of Santa's surly helpers, Ralphie suddenly recovers his voice and makes clear his plea to Father Christmas, only to be told – to his despair – that if he received the BB gun he would be in danger of taking his eye out. By the time his parents return, Ralphie is thoroughly miserable.

On the night of Christmas Eve, Mr Parker is struggling gamely with the family's decorated tree – nothing is allowed to deter his enthusiasm for his impressive array of electric fairy-lights, including the occasional blown fuse. Soon it is time for the brothers to turn in for the evening, hastened by their mother's warning that Santa will soon be delivering their presents. Sure enough, the next morning has brought the freshly-fallen snow of a white Christmas, though Ralphie and Randy scarcely have time to notice before thundering downstairs to their presents. Alongside patterned socks and a toy zeppelin, Ralphie is aghast to discover that his Aunt Clara has gifted him a bright pink bunny costume which his mother forces him – despite his vocal protestations – to try on. But as luck would have it, this indignity is only prelude to a last-minute Christmas surprise for Ralphie; after all of the gifts have been opened, his father casually draws his attention to a solitary, unopened and thus-far unnoticed box... which contains none other than a Red Ryder BB gun.

Utterly euphoric, Ralphie can barely suppress his excitement as he races outdoors to make full use of his treasured new possession. But underestimating the recoil of the air rifle, he accidentally knocks his glasses from his face. In a fevered attempt to find them, Ralphie tramples over the spectacles, shattering both lenses. He rapidly concocts a tall story to avoid antagonising his mother, but neither of them notices that the house's back door has been left open, allowing their neighbour's dogs into the kitchen. The intruding hounds quickly wreak havoc, toppling the kitchen table and devouring the family's Christmas turkey. Mrs Parker is distraught at the scene of canine carnage, but her husband – practical as ever – decides that the family need not go hungry because of this unexpected disaster. He drags everyone across town to the Chop Suey Palace, where the manager (John Wong) and his team of waiters (Johan Sebastian Wong, Fred Lee and Dan Ma) serenade the Parkers with an upbeat selection of Christmas carols as they get ready for their meal. Quite in spite of all the stumbling blocks that have faced them, the family find themselves in high spirits and – knowing that the most important thing is that they are safe, well and together – are fully able to enjoy their meal.

Later that night, Mr and Mrs Parker toast the passing of another Christmas by the electric light of their tree, watching a new fall of snow from the living room window. Tucked up in bed, his BB gun lovingly nestled in his arms, Ralphie reflects on the ultimate success of his efforts to receive this most valued of gifts, knowing somehow that there would never be another Christmas present quite like it ever again.

It would take a hard heart indeed not to be touched in some way by the invitingly nostalgic whimsicality of *A Christmas Story*. From Ralphie's daydreaming flights of fancy to the low-key, mildly bizarre family conflicts which surface throughout the film (quarrels so surreal that they will inevitably strike a chord with almost any real-life family), Bob Clark weaves a skilful narrative tapestry which quickly builds emotional sympathy between the audience and his range of likeable characters. His use of period detail is impeccable throughout, from the vintage automobiles on the streets of Hammond through to the wonderful array of forties-era toys on display under the Parkers' Christmas tree. So too does Clark exhibit a keen eye for the rituals and traditions of childhood, from the now-legendary frozen flagpole incident to the ongoing territorial skirmishes between Ralphie and his younger brother Randy. Even Ralphie's encounters with paper-tiger bully Skut Farkus are transformed into a clash of the titans, the mundanity of this everyday schoolyard conflict seeming like a monumental struggle from the viewpoint of guileless youth. Jean Shepherd's voice drips with reminiscent zeal as he very effectively narrates the film's action from the point of view of an adult Ralphie, who is affectionately looking back upon his bygone childhood with the benefit of wistful hindsight (an analogous approach, similarly combined with colourful daydream scenarios, was later used to great effect in ABC's highly successful TV series *The Wonder Years*, 1988-93). Yet perhaps the most immediate impression of all is the tangible sense that everyone involved in the film seems to be having a lot of fun, most especially in the delightfully fanciful range of fantasy sequences.

Clark appears intent on presenting the flipside of the festive season that he had brought to audiences in the darkly threatening *Black Christmas*, and indeed the fond collection of memories presented in *A Christmas Story* is deeply evocative of a time and a place that contemporary audiences were all too aware had passed into memory, albeit that of the collective national consciousness. He is careful never to allow the film to sink into a quagmire of cloying sentimentalism, peppering the narrative with bittersweet reminders that for young Ralphie, childhood is on the cusp of passing (as we see in his bitter disillusionment over the decoder key which can be used only to decrypt commercial advertisements, and the realisation that his much-sought-after BB gun is the absolute pinnacle of Christmas gifts, as though acknowledging that his youth is likely to be all downhill from hereon in). This kind of rapidfire but welcomingly cheerful nostalgia was the perfect antidote for audiences who had been facing the grim realities of resurgent Cold War tensions and the economic turbulence of the early eighties. Like *Trading Places*, released in the same year, *A Christmas Story* faced the difficulty of appearing in cinemas at a time when Christmas films had been largely out of vogue in cinemas for over two decades, and thus Clark works hard to articulate a kind of national longing for a departed golden age in much the same way that *Trading Places* had succeeded in presenting a timely commentary on the nature and distribution of wealth in a modern context. The two films exhibited radically different themes and approaches, and yet both are acutely concerned with making the Christmas film relevant for contemporary cinemagoing audiences.

Another topic which was raised by *A Christmas Story*, and one that would be revisited by other films later in the decade, was that of the commoditisation of the festive season. Although this had become a staple theme of many films in the genre since the late forties, *A Christmas Story* seems intent on emphasising that the commercialisation of the festive season had been a long and still-ongoing process, stressing that it was unfair to situate any criticism that Christmas was being subverted into a protracted marketing campaign solely upon the doorstep of the 1980s. As had been the case with *Trading Places* (and, to a lesser extent, *Christmas Evil*), Clark chooses to do this not by criticising the mechanics of the free market, but rather by highlighting the ambivalence of its social effects upon cultural attitudes. While it is true that Ralphie's desires seem entirely fixated upon a mass-marketed toy, its commercial value is less relevant to him than is the intrinsic need to possess what is, in his eyes, the very acme of gifts. Whether his parents or Santa Claus (or even the Easter Bunny) are ultimately responsible for its acquisition is neither here nor there: his intense yet innocent focus on his goal is what is paramount. And yet the audience is left in no doubt that the love and approval of Ralphie's family appears to matter at least as much to him as any materialistic desire: his gratitude and firm acknowledgement that there would never be another present quite like it seems to accentuate the fact that the adored BB gun would not be casually cast aside in favour of the next year's favoured craze, but his affection for his parents and brother – with all of their many foibles – is expressed more or less all the way throughout the film. Likewise, the commercial sector is depicted as more than simply an arbiter of skilfully-marketed Christmas goods; it is portrayed as something which typifies convenience just as much as it symbolises acquisitiveness or materialism. Whereas on one hand we see the encroachment of corporate insincerity towards the meaning of Christmas in the form of the cheerless department store Santa's grotto (staffed by stroppy employees who are working strictly to rule, and without much in the way of festive cheer), the other extreme is that of the expediency of service provision: when the Parkers' turkey dinner is ruined, a trip to a nearby restaurant quickly resolves the problem. In this sense, screenwriters Clark, Brown and Shepherd adroitly make the point that in spite of whatever warm glow may be reflected from the memories of our respective childhoods, there never really was a true golden age of Christmas – the festive season is, and always has been, exactly what each of us chooses to make it. As Greg Metcalf has put it, '*A Christmas Story* approaches the nostalgic image of Christmas from a different angle, recollecting Jean Shepherd's childhood Christmas and the travails it entailed. Santa Claus is a fearsome individual, the child's parents oppose his desired Christmas rifle, and the family Christmas dinner takes place in a Chinese restaurant. While appealing, Christmas isn't as good as it used to be and it never was'.[1]

Peter Billingsley makes for an agreeable Ralphie Parker, never allowing his performance to stray into mawkishness or excess. His admirable restraint in the role is a key factor in the film's success, for he creates an affable and accessible character who was relevant to child audiences watching in the eighties just as much as he was relatable to mature audiences who were more closely acquainted with the historical period depicted throughout the film's narrative. Billingsley would have been familiar to audiences at the time due to his portrayal of Messy Marvin, the star of Hershey's Chocolate Syrup advertisements throughout the early eighties; as David J. Mansour explains, 'seen in televised commercials airing in the mid-1980s, the accident-prone lad (played by Peter Billingsley) would spill everything he touched except for Hershey's Chocolate Syrup'.[2] He had made his cinematic debut in Joseph Brooks's romantic drama *If Ever I See You Again* (1978), and continued to build an impressive early filmography with appearances in films such as *Honky Tonk Freeway* (John Schlesinger, 1981), *Paternity* (David Steinberg,

1981) and *Death Valley* (Dick Richards, 1982) before his
appearance in *A Christmas Story*. Billingsley was nominated
no less than four times for Young Artist Awards, winning in
1987 for his starring role in Hoite C. Caston's *The Dirt Bike
Kid* (1985). In later years, he has been a successful
screenwriter, director and producer in addition to continuing
his acting career.

Just as important to the effectiveness of *A Christmas
Story* was the depiction of Ralphie's appealingly offbeat
parents. As Mrs Parker, Melinda Dillon creates an engaging
and eminently practical home-maker, someone who cares for
her young family just as much as she despairs of her husband's
oddball schemes. Dillon, who had been active on American
television since the early 1960s, was perhaps best-known for
playing Jillian Guiler in Steven Spielberg's *Close Encounters
of the Third Kind* (1977), although she had also appeared in a
diverse range of other movies which included *The April Fools*
(Stuart Rosenberg, 1969), *Bound for Glory* (Hal Ashby,
1976) and *Slap Shot* (George Roy Hill, 1977). She was
nominated for the Best Actress in a Supporting Role
Academy Award for her appearance in *Close Encounters of
the Third Kind*, and also for her performance in Sydney
Pollack's *Absence of Malice* (1981). Additionally, in terms of
her connection with Christmas features, she would play Dulcy
in Michael Ray Rhodes's modernised television version of
The Juggler of Notre Dame (1982), a remake of Milton H.
Lehr's 1970 cinematic original. Dillon's down-to-earth
approach throughout *A Christmas Story* contrasts perfectly
with Darren McGavin's pleasingly eccentric turn as Ralphie's
father. A mass of preposterous ideas cloaked beneath a cloud
of mild profanity, Mr Parker is one of the most remarkable
characters in the film. A gruff but devoted family man with a

heart of gold, even his ongoing battle with his wife over the infamous 'leg lamp' does little to dampen his insatiable enthusiasm for the approaching Christmas celebrations. McGavin had been active in film and on television since the mid-1940s. Perhaps best-known to viewers as investigator Carl Kolchak in ABC's memorable but short-lived TV series *Kolchak: The Night Stalker* (1974-75) and its two preceding TV movies in 1972 and 1973, he had a prolific career as an actor which saw him appearing in episodes from dozens of well-known television series including *Alfred Hitchcock Presents* (1955), *Rawhide* (1961), *Dr Kildare* (1965), *Police Story* (1974), *The Martian Chronicles* (1980), and in the title role of all 78 episodes of Revue Productions's *Mike Hammer* (1958-59), a series based upon Mickey Spillane's detective novels. In 1990 he was nominated for an Emmy Award for Outstanding Guest Actor in a Comedy Series for his appearance as Bill Brown in TV series *Murphy Brown* (1988).

A *Christmas Story* also features many enjoyable supporting performances, including *Black Christmas*'s Les Carlson as the shady Christmas tree salesman and Tedde Moore as Ralphie's slightly strait-laced schoolteacher, Miss Shields. There is a cameo appearance from Jean Shepherd who, along with the voice of the narrator (the adult Ralphie) and the department store Santa Claus, also appears as a well-dressed man waiting in the queue for Santa's grotto. Bob Clark makes his own appearance in an entertaining cameo as Mr Swede, the Parkers' pleasant but rather obtuse neighbour, who is in awe of Mr Parker's overblown account of his 'major award' as the staggeringly tacky novelty lamp shines proudly from the family's living room window.

A somewhat mixed response from the reviewers of the time awaited *A Christmas Story* on its release. Some praised the film for its skilful evocation of nostalgia surrounding its forties setting, drawing attention to the admirable way in which Clark generated wistfulness without overtly romanticising the period. As Roger Ebert observed, 'in a poignant way, *A Christmas Story* records a world that no longer quite exists in America. Kids are no longer left unattended in the line for Santa. The innocence of kids' radio programs has been replaced by slick, ironic children's programming on TV. The new Daisy BB guns have a muzzle velocity higher than that of some police revolvers, and are not to be sold to anyone under 16'.[3] Yet on the other hand, some critics considered Clark's direction to be somewhat leaden in places, believing that it struggled to convey the subtle intricacies of Shepherd's shrewd sense of humour. This was reflected in Vincent Canby's appraisal of the film, which stated that 'Mr Clark, the director of *Porky's* and *Tribute*, does not have a light touch. However, his heavy touch is not quite the same thing as Mr Shepherd's habit of finding humor through the exaggeration of language. The movie's big comic pieces tend only to be exceedingly busy'.[4]

Nevertheless, the film's critical reputation has been greatly enhanced over time as its cult status has continued to grow. More recent appraisals have commended the universality of the film's appeal, which have enabled it to reach out to new audiences of all ages. This has even reached beyond cinematic studies of Christmas movies; David A. Cook, in his well-received study of festive traditions and customs *The Inspirational Christmas Almanac* (2006), succinctly describes *A Christmas Story* as 'warm nostalgia for all who were children during the late 1940s – and delightful chuckles for everyone else'.[5] Some have remarked upon the charming way in which the film examines how the Christmas spirit is able to reveal itself in everyday life, and often in ingenious but unanticipated ways; the various domestic practices and rituals leading up to the festive season are charted with care, but the affection within the family unit and the anticipation amongst the child characters towards the coming festivities seem just as prominent. Yet it is precisely the film's lack of sentimentalism which has contributed to its lasting appeal, as Noel Murray has argued: 'Though it's fundamentally a light comedy, *A Christmas Story* contains plenty of hurt and anger, all drawn directly from the stories and monologues of radio raconteur Jean Shepherd, who narrates his reminiscences of growing up in Middle America in the '40s, applying elevated language to the politics of profanity and schoolyard "triple-dog" dares. [...] Clark took his moment of Hollywood clout and ran with it, developing a piece true to Shepherd's finely detailed recollections and good-natured cynicism. *A Christmas Story* grasps the full scope of childhood injustice and obsession'.[6]

Many commentators have singled out Clark's skill in presenting a level-headed depiction of his chosen period, venerating the cultural charm of the time without viewing either youth or the festive season through rose-tinted glasses. At a time when, in TV movies in particular, there had been a tendency to lapse into sickly corniness when addressing the holiday season of years past, Clark – aided to no small degree by the screenplay he co-wrote with Shepherd and Brown – manages to avoid this pitfall entirely, and much to the resulting film's benefit. As Brian W. Fairbanks suggests:

> Perhaps because it so superbly applied a modern sensibility to the innocence associated with an earlier

era, *A Christmas Story* transcended its generic title and its distributor's indifference to become a modern classic following its release to television and home video. [...] *A Christmas Story* succeeds because it's sweet but never cloying. It's grounded in reality yet avoids the cynicism that film-makers usually favor when attempting to avoid sentimentality. Despite scenes reminiscent of one of Norman Rockwell's *Saturday Evening Post* covers, the film never idealizes childhood or Christmas, and yet it positively glows with nostagia.[7]

To examine exactly why *A Christmas Story* has come to fit so contentedly into the canon of festive cinema, it is necessary to consider the particular qualities which marked it out from other entries emerging in the field at the time. Today, the film is considered one of the most memorable and enduring of all 1980s Christmas films, and part of the reason why it has remained so popular amongst audiences of different generations is the wide-ranging accessibility of its comedy. James Berardinelli, for example, observes that 'the movie is short on sentiment and long on humor, but it's not over-the-top humor. [[...]] The movie understands what's funny in being human: how our foibles and frailties can provide the fodder for laughter. Add to that the sardonic observations of the narrator (Ralphie as an adult, voiced by Jean Shepherd), and you have the mixture for a motion picture that never ceases to be enjoyable'.[8] Others have considered Clark's keen eye for detail to be a major factor in the film's distinctiveness, singling out his ability to delineate childhood observation within a framework that was relevant both to younger viewers and adults alike. From a commercial standpoint, this highly inclusive approach would pay dividends not just at the box-office, but with later audiences who would first encounter the film via means other than its initial cinematic screening.

Likewise, the abundant moments of appealing weirdness which crop up throughout *A Christmas Story* have lent it a lasting cult appeal. As Glenn Erickson has sagaciously noted, 'Clark knows when to play things straight, as in the unbroken long-shot of the final Chop Suey Christmas Dinner. He also knows when he can be clever, as shown in Ralphie's disastrous visit to Santa. Clark's wide-angle Santa-boot-in-the-face shot expresses the trauma of childhood powerlessness as well as anything in David Lean's *Great Expectations*. Even better, Clark knows that childhood can be downright icky. None of Ralphie's friends are candidates for prize citizenship and others seem like budding psychos. Before video games and Children's Rights, childhood was mysterious, magical and largely invented from one's own imagination'.[9] Overall, however, in the opinion of many commentators the lasting success of the movie – and the niche it has so indelibly carved itself in popular culture – can be explained by the careful equilibrium that Clark achieves in presenting both the occasional farcicalities of family life and the longing for a past age that can no longer be regained. For ultimately, *A Christmas Story*'s sense of wistfulness is achieved not only by emphasising that the innocence of childhood is a fragile thing that cannot ever be reclaimed once lost, but also by its faithful evocation of the historical era of the 1940s – a difficult time for many, due to economic hardships and the grim realities of war, yet also a period which is presented as simpler and more straightforward in terms of cultural attitudes. It is this judicious combination of factors which has assured the film's long-term reputation amongst audiences, aiding in the continuation of its popularity even in the present day. As Mike Long has stated:

A Christmas Story has truly become a classic. The film works because of the balance it shows between an idealistic view of life and a very realistic look at the everyday ups and downs of family life. The movie takes a look at a simpler time in American life when things were more innocent. [...] What makes *A Christmas Story* great is its skewed, and often very frank, view of everyday life. From Randy's refusal to eat, to Ralphie's humiliation in receiving a present which is not age-appropriate to the crazed finale, *A Christmas Story* truly clicks when it's reflecting just how odd the average family can truly be. This is where the inspired narration, provided by Jean Shepherd himself, really kicks in. While *A Christmas Story* has many memorable moments, it's the lines from the narration which will stick in your head.[10]

Although *A Christmas Story* was only a moderate box-office success at the time of its cinematic release, it soon followed the likes of *It's a Wonderful Life* (1946) and the Alastair Sim version of *Scrooge* (1951) onto cable television channels where it rapidly developed a rock-solid cult following. The film's heady mix of humour and nostalgia has proven to be a lasting success with audiences ever since, and it has become so immortalised in festive lore that it is now something of a tradition for it to be broadcast on American cable TV in 24-hour marathons during December. As Diane Werts has explained, 'it wasn't until cable TV started playing this family-suitable film endlessly a decade [[after its release]] that viewers realized what they'd missed. Suddenly, TNT or TBS was airing *A Christmas Story* for 24 hours every Christmas, starting a new screening every two hours. Then everyone came to root for Depression-era 10-year-old Ralph Parker and his wide-eyed quest for a Red Ryder Carbine-

Action Two-Hundred-Shot Range Model Air Rifle'.[11] Yet *A Christmas Story* follows in the footsteps of those earlier, timeless festive features not just in its phoenix-like resurrection from obscurity, but also in the masterful treatment of its subject matter. Today the film is, as Dennis Prince describes, generally regarded as a modern classic that is very much in keeping with the prevailing themes of Christmas cinema's golden age: 'A picture that exists as a very "tradition" in its own right, Bob Clark's 1983 sleeper hit *A Christmas Story* has been cited by most as the perennial holiday favorite. While 1946's *It's a Wonderful Life* and the subsequent year's *Miracle on 34th Street* are properly regarded as seasonal "classics", it's fitting that this latter-day low-budget affair has similarly warmed viewers' hearts by revisiting the same postwar era that produced Capra's and Seaton's respective pictures. Credit both director Clark and novelist/humorist/lecturer Jean Shepherd for their unrelenting attention to detail that faithfully paints a picture of 1940s working-class America with brush strokes that even Rockwell would have admired'.[12]

While the endlessly-shifting march of modern sensibilities has meant that many eighties entries in the canon of festive film-making have fallen by the wayside of the cultural consciousness in recent years, the engagingly reflective reminiscence of *A Christmas Story* has meant that Clark's movie continues to attract new audiences both on home entertainment formats and via its annual television screenings. As Kevin Matthews has stated, this ongoing recognition amongst the public is largely due to the way that the film captures so accurately the artless pleasures of youth in ways that transcend both its 1940s setting and its 1980s time of production:

The movie is full of the stuff of legend, as long as all of your legends were created in your childhood when everything was bigger and better. [...] What the movie does so well, arguably better than any other Christmas movie (and possibly why it remains a solid seasonal favourite in America every year), is show Christmas and the run up to Christmas Day from both perspectives. You get the unbridled enthusiasm and yearning from the kids as they wait to find out what gifts they're getting and if all of their daydreams will come true, and you also get the parents struggling to get everything good while keeping their kids in line. And you also get to see that these divisions aren't always so clear. There's a pleasant blurring of the boundaries and a shared joy here that shows the parents thrilled by how happy that their children can be.[13]

It is, quite possibly, the way in which Clark manages to ameliorate a melancholic longing for lost youth with the sheer exuberance of re-enacting the fun and expectancy of a childhood Christmas which has ultimately cemented *A Christmas Story* so prominently into the annals of festive cinema. The film has become fondly remembered for its many humorous, often gleefully absurd sequences (the flagpole incident, bunny suit and leg lamp 'major award' among them), and yet it could be convincingly argued that it is its evocation of an age of national and youthful innocence – which inevitably invites comparison to the conditions of our uncompromisingly reductive and often pessimistic modern age, both in the eighties as much as in the present day – that has come to be regarded as its most significant achievement. As Stephanie Star Smith suggests:

Perhaps the most important thing about *A Christmas Story* is that it doesn't forget it's a funny film about kids and families. Real kids, not precocious prodigies that act like adults, but kids. Kids who have to deal with adults who, to their minds, don't know what it's like to be eight years old and have to deal with all the trials and tribulations of life in the schoolyard. Kids who are concerned about avoiding the local bully so they can get home and hear their favorite radio show, about finding just the right way to ask for their heart's desire so that come Christmas morning, the present of their dreams is under the tree. Kids who plan and dream and play and exist in a world where adults no longer belong, but that we all recognize as a place we once were.[14]

A Christmas Story performed strongly at the awards ceremonies of the time. This was particularly true of the Genie Awards, where the film won the Best Achievement in Direction award for Bob Clark (the accolade was tied with David Cronenberg, who additionally won that year for his film *Videodrome*, 1983), and also the Best Screenplay award. Furthermore, at the same ceremony *A Christmas Story* was nominated for awards in no less than seven other areas: Best Motion Picture, Best Performance by an Actress in a Supporting Role (for Tedde Moore), Best Achievement in Cinematography, Best Achievement in Film Editing, Best Achievement in Costume Design, Best Achievement in Overall Sound, and Best Achievement in Sound Editing. The film's screenplay was nominated for a Writers' Guild of America Award for Best Comedy Adapted from Another Medium, while at the Young Artist Awards there were nominations for Peter Billingsley (Best Young Actor in a Motion Picture: Musical, Comedy, Adventure or Drama) and Ian Petrella (Best Young Supporting Actor in a Motion Picture: Musical, Comedy, Adventure or Drama).

Beyond the film's perennial appeal with audiences, a stage adaptation of *A Christmas Story* was written by Philip Grecian in 2000 and immediately became popular with theatregoers, being performed annually in a variety of venues since its debut. Moreover, Bob Clark was to revisit the same characters in 1994 with his film *It Runs in the Family* (also occasionally known by the alternative title *My Summer Story*). Starring Charles Grodin as Mr Parker, Mary Steenburgen as Mrs Parker and Kieran Culkin as Ralphie, the sequel retained only Tedde Moore from the original cast (again playing Miss Shields) along with the voice of Jean Shepherd, narrating once more in the guise of an adult Ralphie. Although the belated follow-up has some degree of similarity to the original film, not least in its poignant recollections of childhood experiences, it performed poorly at the box-office and was not a critical success. Donato Totaro is largely representative of the opinion of reviewers when bluntly remarking that 'Clark failed [...] with an attempt to recapture the past glory of *A Christmas Story*, with the limp sequel *It Runs in [the] Family*'.[15]

With *A Christmas Story*, Bob Clark had presented eighties cinema with one of its most unique, heart-warming depictions of the festive season and, although the scale of his achievement was not immediately obvious at the time of its release, it has remained one of the most unfailingly successful films in the genre to have been produced in that decade. Because of the sheer immutability of the movie's backwards-looking fascination with the customs of yesteryear, albeit cast within the subtle light of wistful modernity, it is still regularly entertaining audiences more than three decades after its cinematic debut. At a time when the very thematic apparatus of the Christmas film was being examined and reconsidered,

A Christmas Story was a breath of fresh air, its blend of the traditional and the innovative ultimately helping to pave the way for the gradual re-emergence of festive movie-making as a means of commercial and critical interest amongst commentators and audiences.

REFERENCES

1.   Greg Metcalf, '"It's (Christmas) Morning in America":
     Christmas Conventions of American Films in the 1980s', in
     *Beyond the Stars: Plot Conventions in American Popular
     Film*, ed. by Paul Loukides and Linda K. Fuller (Bowling
     Green: Bowling Green State University Popular Press, 1991),
     100-13, p.105.

2.   David J. Mansour, *From Abba to Zoom: A Pop Culture
     Encyclopedia of the Late 20th Century* (Kansas City:
     Andrews McMeel Publishing, 2005), p.310.

3.   Roger Ebert, '*A Christmas Story*', in *The Chicago Sun-
     Times*, 24 December 2000.

4.   Vincent Canby, '*Christmas Story*: Indiana Tale', in *The
     New York Times*, 18 November 1983.

5.   David C. Cook, *The Inspirational Christmas Almanac:
     Heartwarming Traditions, Trivia, Stories, and Recipes for
     the Holidays* (Colorado Springs: Honor Books, 2006), p.103.

6.   Noel Murray, '*A Christmas Story*', in *The Onion A.V.
     Club*, 9 December 2003.

7.   Brian W. Fairbanks, *I Saw That Movie, Too: Selected Film
     Reviews*, 3rd edn (Morrisville: Lulu.com, 2010), pp.87-88.

8.   James Berardinelli, '*A Christmas Story*', in *ReelViews*, 24
     April 2016.
     <http://www.reelviews.net/reelviews/christmas-story-a>

9.   Glenn Erickson, 'A Christmas Story', in DVD Savant, 2
        November 2008.
        <http://www.dvdtalk.com/dvdsavant/s2736stor.html>

10.   Mike Long, 'A Christmas Story', in DVD Sleuth, 2
        November 2008.
        <http://www.dvdsleuth.com/AChristmasStoryReview/>

11.   Diane Werts, Christmas On Television (Westport:
        Greenwood Press, 2006), pp.15-16.

12.   Dennis Prince, 'A Christmas Story', in DVD Verdict, 8
        January 2007.
        <http://www.dvdverdict.com/reviews/christmasstoryhddv
        d.php>

13.   Kevin Matthews, 'A Christmas Story', in FlickFeast, 20
        December 2011.
        <http://flickfeast.co.uk/reviews/film-reviews/christmas-
        story-1983/>

14.   Stephanie Star Smith, 'Classic Film Review: A Christmas
        Story', in Box Office Prophets, 25 December 2002.
        <http://www.boxofficeprophets.com/moviereviews/christm
        asstory.asp>

15.   Donato Totaro, 'Bob Clark', in Guide to the Cinema(s) of
        Canada, ed. by Peter Harry Rist (Westport: Greenwood
        Press, 2001), pp.38-39.

5

Merry Christmas, Mr Lawrence
(1983)

National Film Trustees/Jeremy Thomas Productions

Director: Nagisa Ôshima
Producer: Jeremy Thomas
Screenwriters: Nagisa Ôshima and Paul Mayersberg,
based on *The Seed and The Sower* by Laurens van der Post

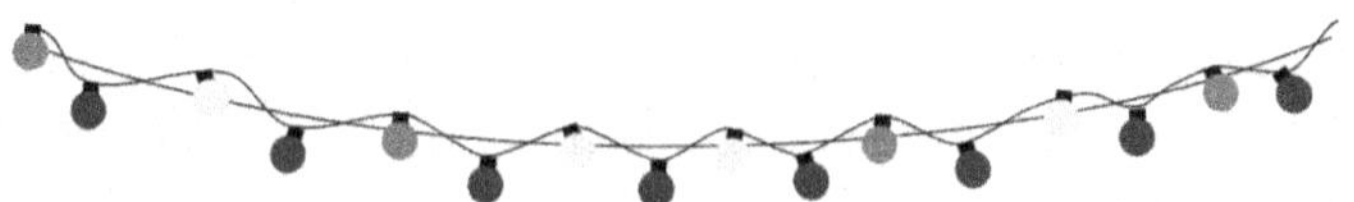

Quite in spite of its deceptively festive-sounding title, *Merry Christmas, Mr Lawrence* is possibly the least likely of all 1980s Christmas films to be considered a traditional favourite of the holiday season. Lauded by critics and widely praised for its relentlessly harrowing portrayal of life in a World War II prison camp, the movie is often overlooked in studies of Christmas cinema; as Gary J. Svehla and Susan Svehla have noted, this 'critically respected prisoner of war film is not something you'd look to for jolly holiday viewing'.[1] And yet, regardless of its unrelentingly grim content and fleeting engagement with the festive season, *Merry Christmas, Mr Lawrence* nevertheless contains at its heart a sentiment which would be very much in keeping with the very best of yuletide film-making, paving the way for many later films that would explore the complicated effects that Christmas can bring about during times of warfare.

Part of the reason why *Merry Christmas, Mr Lawrence* is generally omitted from most surveys of festive cinema is that the film's content contains one of the most unconventional of all Christmas-themed narratives – and while the events taking place in December are pivotal to the story in many ways, for many commentators the brief engagement with the holiday season is so subsumed by the many other themes being explored that it is often disregarded entirely. Numerous other films, such as *The Bells of St Mary's* (Leo McCarey, 1945) or *Bell, Book and Candle* (Richard Quine, 1958) have, over the years, come to be regarded as comfortably sheltering under the umbrella of the Christmas film genre, perhaps due to their December release dates, even though their engagement with the holiday season is at best transitory. With its oppressively humid setting in the Pacific Theatre of World War II, *Merry Christmas, Mr Lawrence* was considerably further removed from a traditional festive environment than the aforementioned features, and yet in its exploration of the transformative and cross-cultural appeal of Christmas it would be disingenuous to discount the film's significance simply because of its somewhat incongruous fit within the wider canon of yuletide cinema.

Merry Christmas, Mr Lawrence was helmed by famed Japanese director and screenwriter Nagisa Ôshima, who had earned the respect of critics both nationally and internationally for films such as the satirical *The Ceremony* (*Gishiki*) (1971), the hugely controversial *In the Realm of the Senses* (*Ai no Corrida*) (1976), and *Empire of Passion* (*Ai no Bōrē*) (1978), which was to win him the Best Director Award at the 1978 Cannes Film Festival. With a prolific career spanning the 1950s to the late 1990s, Ôshima remained a revered and often provocative talent in his native Japan as well as in world cinema until his death in 2013, and his films continue to fascinate and absorb audiences in the present day. *Merry Christmas, Mr Lawrence* remains one of his most instantly recognisable features amongst Western audiences, and the film's profound emotional content has become just as memorable as its unbearably sultry tropical locale. The events of the movie were adapted from *The Seed and the Sower,* a 1963 novel by South African author Laurens van der Post which focuses mainly upon his characters' experiences within a Japanese prisoner of war camp during the Second World War. (Some incidents from van der Post's 1970 text *The Night of the New Moon* were also included in the film's narrative.) Standing in for the Javanese backdrop depicted in the feature was an Australasian filming location; as Yoshiharu Tezuka notes, '*Merry Christmas, Mr Lawrence* was shot in New Zealand to utilize the generous tax shelter fund there'.[2]

Another reason for the heightened audience anticipation surrounding the film was the inspired casting of two hugely charismatic musical legends in the form of David Bowie and Ryûichi Sakamoto. Bowie, one of the most pioneering and successful figures in British music since the 1960s, was one of the world's best-selling recording artists; a master of reinvention, his record sales were estimated at around 140 million worldwide at the time of his death in 2016. A prolific artist known for his many chart-topping albums, which at the time included *Hunky Dory* (1971), *The Rise and Fall of Ziggy Stardust and the Spiders from Mars* (1972), *Aladdin Sane* (1973) and *Let's Dance* (1973), amongst many others, Bowie commenced a cinematic acting career in 1976 in the role of Thomas Jerome Newton in Nicolas Roeg's *The*

Man Who Fell to Earth (though he previously had made brief appearances on television and in short features), moving on to a range of further challenging characters in films such as *Christiane F.* (Uli Edel, 1981) and *The Hunger* (Tony Scott, 1983). He combined theatrical performances with an acting career on stage, perhaps most notably in a famous Broadway run of Bernard Pomerance's *The Elephant Man* between 1980 and 1981. *Merry Christmas, Mr Lawrence* has come to be regarded as one of Bowie's most critically-acclaimed performances, and this was similarly to be the case for his cast-mate Ryûichi Sakamoto. Making his cinematic debut in the film, Sakamoto had achieved fame both as a solo performing artist and as a member of electronic music group Yellow Magic Orchestra – a band which had achieved worldwide popularity in the late seventies due to a string of successful releases including 'Computer Game' (1978), and 'Behind the Mask' (1978). *Merry Christmas, Mr Lawrence* was to mark the beginning of Sakamoto's long-running association with film composition; his career achievements would eventually see him becoming a multiple award-winner in later years, securing an Academy Award, Grammy Award, BAFTA Award, and two Golden Globe Awards. His haunting original soundtrack has become one of his most renowned works, with the brooding main theme achieving particular popularity. As Gordon S. Miller has observed, 'Ryuichi Sakamoto was a well-known musician in Japan not an actor when he signed on, [[and]] also composed the film's score, which is synthesizer based and offers bell-like sounds. When first heard during the opening credits, the music contrasts harshly with the historical setting. However, the incongruity evokes the film's theme, and over the course of the film, it proves to be a good fit'.[3]

It is 1942, and in a prisoner of war camp situated on the island of Java during the height of the Second World War, Lieutenant Colonel John Lawrence (Tom Conti) – a captured British Army officer – is awakened from sleep in the middle of the night by a forthright Japanese military guard named Sergeant Gengo Hara (Takeshi Kitano). The prisoners' leader and spokesperson, Royal Air Force Group Captain Hicksley (Jack Thompson), stridently informs Lawrence that he is under no obligation to accompany the guard at this unsociable hour, but Hara is insistent – and, as Lawrence speaks fluent Japanese, he is aware that the sergeant's request is one of importance. Flanked by guards, the colonel is marched from the makeshift dormitory through the prison camp which is based in a lush, humid stretch of Pacific jungle.

The liaison officer between the Japanese military and the Allied prisoners, Lawrence is led to an unusual scene: a Dutch captive and a Korean soldier are being held in a remote area of the camp's grounds, surrounded by a circle of guards. Hara explains that the Dutch detainee, Karl de Jong (Alistair Browning), had been imprisoned in a cell for stealing bananas, only to subsequently suffer a sexual assault at the hands of the Korean combatant, Kanemoto (Johnny Ohkura). Disgusted by this attack, Hara goads the culprit into repeating his crime; if he accedes to the demand, the sergeant will allow him to commit suicide in payment for his crime. Lawrence is appalled at the savagery of the scene, not only at the notion of the self-inflicted death penalty for Kanemoto but also the fact that de Jong will be forced to suffer a second intimate assault. Hara is oddly unconcerned about the Dutchman's wellbeing, reasoning that he seemed to have done too little to fend off the attack that had occurred in his cell, but Lawrence intervenes and asks the young man directly what had happened. De Jong replies that the Korean guard had been responsible for dressing one of his wounds in the prison cell over several days, but his initially compassionate interest had suddenly and unexpectedly turned more personal.

The Dutch inmate's account is interrupted by the arrival of the prison camp's youthful commander, Captain Yonoi (Ryûichi Sakamoto). Lawrence cries out to Yonoi in the hope of interrupting the disturbing scene that is set to unfold, but is violently silenced by Hara. In the altercation that follows, Kanemoto attempts to escape but is wounded in the attempt by another of the guards. The sergeant offers Kanemoto a straightforward option: suicide or execution. However, the Korean has already stabbed himself in the abdomen by the time Yonoi arrives at the scene. His desperate efforts have been in vain though, as the wound does not appear fatal. The captain demands an explanation for the puzzling spectacle before him, and Hara clarifies the situation by stating that if they should report Kanemoto's death as having occurred in an accident (even a self-inflicted one), his family will be given a pension after he is deceased. Yonoi seems discomfited by the act that has taken place, especially as Hara is so reluctant to give details of the true nature of the Korean soldier's crimes, but has no time to discuss the matter further; he is expected at a military trial that is taking place in nearby Batavia.

Later, Yonoi arrives at a military-commandeered building and meets with Colonel Fujimura (Ryûnosuke Kaneda), the court president, who informs him that the defendant they are about to judge is likely to be a difficult case. The captured officer in question is Major Jack 'Strafer' Celliers (David Bowie), a New Zealander serving in the British Army who has been apprehended during special forces operations in the Banten Valley. Accused of carrying out guerrilla warfare along with other paratroopers, the defendant is alleged to have attacked a Japanese transport, looted it, and murdered one of the soldiers on board while wounding several others. Though his assigned interpreter (Rokkô Toura) makes plain the seriousness of the charges, including the near-certain recommendation of the death penalty, Celliers has no time for court protocol and responds insolently to the questions that are asked of him. The Major denies the charges, explaining that he had surrendered himself to the Imperial Japanese Army willingly because they had threatened to execute innocent villagers unless he ended his campaign of attritional warfare. He has since been incarcerated in solitary confinement, but has singularly refused to supply any details about himself beyond his name and military rank. Colonel Fujimura is unconvinced by Celliers's assurance that his subordinates had all been killed in action, and insists that he must also have been leading native soldiers into his offensive operations – a charge which Celliers also denies.

Yonoi taunts Celliers for having allowed himself to be captured when a Japanese officer would sooner have killed themselves, but he appears to be developing a strange, unspoken fixation with the uncooperative major. After a short period of questioning, Yonoi determines that Celliers had been under the orders of British Imperial Command in India rather than the military commander in Java (who had been taken prisoner some months earlier), meaning that the officer was not acting independently but rather in a legitimate wartime capacity. Due to international law, this means that he should be spared execution and instead be made a prisoner of war. Celliers also reveals that he had been beaten in captivity when it became clear that his guerrilla operations were not the vanguard of an invasion by Allied forces, showing the bruising and scars that he had suffered. His military judges are unimpressed by the display.

The court retires to make their decision, and Celliers finds himself facing a lengthy delay until word reaches him that his verdict has been postponed. Back in captivity, he continues to baffle his jailers by miming the basic necessities he is being denied, such as clean drinking water and the ability to shave. Eventually he is brought back before the military tribunal and informed that, having been found guilty on all charges, he is to be sentenced to immediate execution. Chained in place before a firing squad, Celliers seems almost disappointed when he discovers that he is not to meet his demise at all: the soldiers' rifles are only firing blanks, but the sadistic mind games of his captors do not appear to have the required impact.

At the prison camp, Lawrence attempts to intercede on de Jong's behalf with Sergeant Hara. The colonel explains that word has started to spread of the sexual assault on the young prisoner, and that he will now require protection in case a further attempt is made to attack him. Hara is contemptuous of the request, explaining that no Japanese soldier would ever ask a favour of an enemy combatant, but before Lawrence can attempt any further diplomacy they are interrupted by the arrival of a new prisoner – Jack Celliers. Undernourished and thoroughly exhausted by his transportation from the military camp in Batavia, Celliers collapses to the ground shortly after being transferred into the custody of the camp. Lawrence immediately recognises the major, piquing the curiosity of Yonoi who demands further information. When Lawrence explains that he and Celliers had fought the Nazis in Libya during the North Africa campaign, Yonoi grants Celliers access to the camp's medical facilities.

While the new arrival rests, the prison commander questions Lawrence about Celliers in more detail, asking about his military conduct and personal qualities. The colonel is confused about Yonoi's focused interest in Celliers, but the Japanese commander responds only that he considers it to be a matter of top priority that the major is returned to full health as quickly as possible. Before Lawrence can discuss the issue any further, the blustering Group Captain Hicksley arrives at Yonoi's office to answer the commander's summons. Yonoi demands to know which of the prisoners have expertise in munitions and artillery. When Hicksley flatly refuses to answer, Yonoi angrily reminds him that no inmate at the camp is protected by the tenets of the Geneva Convention, and thus he will uncover the truth one way or another. He warns Hicksley that any further lack of compliance will lead to his replacement by another officer, but the group captain is not swayed by the commander's threats. As he departs, however, it becomes increasingly obvious that Hicksley suspects Lawrence of getting too close to the enemy.

Later, as a bedraggled work party of Allied prisoners staggers back into the camp, Hicksley approaches Lawrence in private and enigmatically explains that they should be able to keep up their munitions plan for some time before their Japanese overseers suspect the nature of their scheme. (He does not elaborate on this strategy in any detail; it is unclear whether he refers to strategic brinkmanship with Yonoi, or an actual plot against their captors.) When Lawrence pleads with Hicksley to listen to his advice regarding interaction with the camp's staff, emphasising his knowledge of Japanese culture and the soldiers' complex social practices, Hicksley arrogantly cuts him off, reminding him not just of his rank but also that the group captain attended a better quality of public school back in England – a factor which he believes has lent him an innate element of social superiority over his fellow countrymen. Lawrence understands that the military force running the camp are shrewd and experienced, but the condescending Hicksley believes that Japan is losing the war and expects the Pacific conflict to be over within months.

Lawrence pays a visit to Celliers in the camp sickbay and receives a report from the prisoner overseeing the major's health. He is told that Celliers has managed to survive an ordeal that would have killed most other people, but that he is now recuperating remarkably well and thus is likely to be back to health within a few weeks. Lawrence temporarily transfers his bunk to the sickbay in order to keep a closer eye on his old comrade's recovery. Shortly afterwards, in the dead of night, Hara arrives and wakes the colonel from his sleep, informing him that Celliers is now on the point of regaining consciousness. The Japanese sergeant is confounded when Lawrence explains that the new arrival had willingly surrendered; he believes the capitulation to have been a deeply shameful act. However, Lawrence replies that the British believe quite the opposite: suicide would have been the dishonourable choice in this instance, as the prisoners believe that if they remain alive there is still a chance that they may survive their captivity and eventually overcome their enemies. Hara finds the argument unconvincing, and is also wary of Yonoi's determination to supplant Hicksley with Celliers as the prisoners' leader.

Celliers eventually awakens and, though clearly feverish and in pain, wonders aloud why Yonoi had decided to spare his life when he could so easily have been executed for war crimes. His survival seems to vex him even more than having regained consciousness in his current, new location. Before the matter can be discussed further, Yonoi arrives with a guard detail, causing Lawrence and Hara to duck out of sight. Seeming preoccupied with Celliers's wellbeing to the point of obsession, the prison commander again emphasises how essential it is that the major be returned to full health without delay.

The next morning, the violent sound of samurai sword training echoes through the sickbay; Yonoi and one of his subordinates is exercising with katanas nearby. Celliers, now making a recovery, confides in Lawrence that he finds Yonoi's fascination with him to be mystifying. They speculate whether the commander's frantic swordplay practice may be an attempt to vent his frustration towards recent events. On a nearby bed, de Jong snaps into agitated wakefulness at the sound of combat, his manner suggesting the after-effects of shock. Concerned for the young man's health, as well as that of the other prisoners, Lawrence sends an official request to Yonoi asking him to refrain from the shouting involved in his traditional combat training. When the commander asks him if the noise is affecting Celliers's recuperation, and Lawrence responds that it is, Yonoi agrees to tone down the volume of his sword-fighting during future seassion. In conversation, Lawrence reveals that he had been present in Tokyo during the violent Japanese uprising of 26th February 1936. Yonoi bitterly explains that he had been posted to Manchuria during the revolution six years earlier, and feels profound guilt that his comrades-in-arms had been executed while he had remained alive.

Later, Yonoi stages the execution of the rapist Kanemoto. The commander is unhappy that Celliers is not present for the event, but Lawrence calmly tells him that the major is still too weak to leave his hospital bed. Yonoi ensures that de Jong has a clear view of his attacker's demise, but Hicksley angrily informs him that the Allied soldiers should not be forced to watch a scene of capital punishment. Ignoring him, Yonoi orders the execution to go ahead; Kanemoto accepts ritual suicide, and after stabbing himself is beheaded by the guards. De Jong, traumatised by the bloodshed that ensues, bites part of his tongue off; even the swift intervention of his fellow captives cannot save him from choking to death. Hicksley is incandescent at the events that have unfolded, but Yonoi warns everyone present to say nothing of what has occurred. Yonoi rounds on Lawrence, asking him in front of the other prisoners if he believes that the execution was performed correctly. Thoroughly drained by what he has seen, Lawrence responds that not only is the prison commander wrong, but so is everyone else that was present at the chaotic scene. Livid at the perceived criticism of his decisions, Yonoi confines all of the prisoners to their bunkhouses for the next 48 hours, commanding that no food or water be accessible to them for the entirety of that period.

With the enforced fasting affecting even the patients in the sickbay tent, tensions run high. The guards become particularly disgruntled when the prisoners refuse to go along with the façade (for official purposes) that De Jong is still alive when the man has clearly died. The tense situation seems set to boil over when Celliers is discovered to be missing from the daily roll call, but is suddenly defused when the major – now apparently in better spirits – arrives carrying a basket of recently-picked flowers, a gesture which he says has been performed in memory of their fallen comrade. Starving, the ravenous prisoners eat the unusual red plants while Lawrence recites the Lord's Prayer in tribute to the late de Jong. Hicksley arrives, and is wryly amused by Celliers's subversive behaviour. He demands that Lawrence explain why he hasn't been more forthright about Yonoi's intention to install Celliers at the new prisoners' spokesperson – an issue of intense concern to the group captain – and gives a stern warning that he will never voluntarily relinquish his position.

Shortly afterwards, a flash inspection of the sickbay by prison guards unearths some contraband food, though the soldiers are confused by the presence of so many flowers. In defiance, Celliers makes it clear that the detainees have been eating the flowers in order to stay alive, causing him to be dragged out of the sickbay by the Japanese soldiers. Yonoi arrives on the scene and, wondering aloud whether Celliers is the human embodiment of an evil spirit, commands that the rebellious major be taken to a cell. Hara asks Lawrence why the prisoners are singing hymns – another obvious sign of defiance – to which the colonel replies that they are practicing in preparation for Christmas, as the festive season is fast approaching. Believing Lawrence to be insolent in his response, Hara savagely beats him. Another of the guards produces a concealed radio, found during the search of the sickbay. Yonoi determines that Lawrence will be taken into custody; as the colonel had recently transferred to the medical tent to watch over Celliers, he will likely have knowledge of the crime that can be extracted by his captors.

Some time later, Celliers is being held in solitary confinement. One of the Japanese soldiers attempts to gain access to his cell and, when it becomes clear that he is acting independently of official orders, he overcomes the guard posted to the holding area and takes the key by force.

Creeping into the cell, the invader attempts to stab Celliers to death, but the major anticipates the attack and overcomes the assassin. Celliers then escapes through the now-open door and desperately searches the surrounding area for Lawrence, who is also being held nearby. He discovers the colonel hanging from a tree, bound by rope into a standing position, and quickly frees him with the knife of his intended killer. Lawrence is delirious, pleading with Celliers to leave him where he is, but the major is determined to make good their escape from captivity. Carrying his prone comrade towards the camp perimeter, Celliers runs straight into Yonoi and appears to challenge him to armed combat. The prison commander draws his sword, but in response Celliers drops the recently-procured knife and surrenders. Yonoi is puzzled by his behaviour, pointing out that Celliers could have been free if he was able to overcome the commander, but their exchange is interrupted by the arrival of Hara and his soldiers. Once Lawrence and Celliers are back in their respective cells, Yonoi interrogates the would-be assassin. The soldier offers his life in exchange for exceeding his authority. Curious about his motives, Yonoi asks the man why he had tried to murder Celliers in the first place, to which he replies that he believes the British officer to be a demonic spirit who is trying to taint the commander's soul. He then performs ritual suicide with Yonoi's consent.

A maltreated Lawrence is invited to the funeral of the dead man, who Yonoi reveals to have been his batman; a soldier functioning as the officer's personal servant. The commander explains that as a recorded suicide would mean that the soldier's widow would not receive a pension, the death will be reported as accidental. When he suggests that the same will be true of Lawrence, the usually-placid colonel is outraged – even in his greatly weakened state, having been repeatedly beaten by guards since entering solitary confinement. Yonoi unemotionally reveals that someone must be executed for the fact that a radio was present in the camp; although he knows that Lawrence is almost certainly telling the truth when he proclaims his innocence, the commander is also aware that someone must be seen to be punished for the crime. The colonel is furious at the injustice of facing an execution for someone else's misconduct, but Yonoi informs him that he is only waiting for the official papers to arrive in order to set the death sentence in motion. Now openly enraged, Lawrence rages against the unfeeling doctrines of the commander's religion and topples the funeral altar before being restrained by a guard. As he is being led away, he goads Yonoi by pointing out that the commander would never have willingly sacrificed Celliers in the same way, given the value that the commander seems to place on the British captive. Seeming discomfited by the observation, Yonoi offers Lawrence one last chance to speak with Celliers before the colonel faces execution.

Unceremoniously thrown into a grimy holding area, Lawrence finds that Celliers is able to converse with him from an adjacent cell. He describes the discussion with Yonoi at the funeral, and reflects bitterly that his life is set to come to an end over something so trivial as the presence of a radio set. Though separated by a wall between their cells, Celliers senses that his comrade is exhausted, undernourished and badly battered, and resolves to do his best to improve Lawrence's spirits. Lawrence reminisces about being present at the fall of Singapore, reflecting sadly on the ensuing bedlam of the Japanese invasion. Celliers reveals that he too is haunted by the past, though in his case the pain is considerably more personal. Through a flashback, Celliers contemplates the events of his childhood – specifically, the interactions between his twelve-year-old self (Chris Broun) and his brother (James Malcolm). Celliers's younger sibling had a physical deformity and was terrified of humiliation while at boarding school; though he knew of the brutal initiation rites there, Celliers did nothing to ameliorate his brother's suffering at the hands of his peers for fear that it would reflect badly on his own reputation. He was never able to forgive himself for the distance that subsequently grew between his brother and himself as a result, and though Celliers would later become a successful lawyer he threw himself headlong into his wartime role in the hope that the suffering he experienced in combat might alleviate his own sense of personal shame.

Unexpectedly, Lawrence and Celliers are removed from their cells and taken to Hara, who has taken up temporary residence in the commander's office. The sergeant is heavily drunk and, giggling uncontrollably, announces that he has decided to play Santa Claus: as it is Christmas, the two British officers are now free from solitary confinement and have clearance to return to their fellow prisoners. Celliers and Lawrence can barely believe their luck as Hicksley arrives to take them back to the camp; Lawrence is so severely fatigued that he has to rely on the other two inmates to carry him out of the office. The inebriated Hara wishes them all a heartfelt 'Merry Christmas' as they depart.

Upon his return, Yonoi summons the senior-ranking prisoners to his office and is amazed to find Lawrence present. Demanding an answer from Hara, now sober, the sergeant explains that he had interrogated a Chinese prisoner and discovered that it was he who had been responsible for having trafficked the radio into the sickbay. Realising his error in blaming Lawrence, he had him released immediately – along with Celliers, fearing that the two men may have become martyrs if they had died in captivity without good reason. Yonoi is angered that Hara had exceeded his authority, ordering prisoner releases without having first consulted the commander, but the exchange is interrupted by the supremely undiplomatic Hicksley who makes the rash decision to interject. He demands to know why Yonoi intends to replace him with Celliers as the prisoners' leader. Lawrence despairs at Hicksley's lack of discretion, having forced the issue at the worst possible point. Frustrated by the group captain's constant refusal to provide intelligence on the prisoners' activities, Yonoi orders an immediate parade of the entire camp – all six hundred inmates are to be present. The commander also confines Hara to quarters for the next 72 hours; following this disciplinary period of suspension, the sergeant is to be deployed to Haruka to oversee a work team constructing a new airstrip there.

Every prisoner, whether able-bodied or wounded, rushes onto the parade ground. The assembly is surrounded by armed Japanese soldiers. Yonoi arrives by jeep and immediately demands to know why several of the sick inmates from the infirmary are not on parade. Hicksley and several of his fellow officers protest, but the commander is insistent that the invalids are fetched immediately. Most are so severely ill that they are unable to walk without help from other prisoners; some even have to be stretchered. Yonoi stipulates that they walk unaided, arguing that it is their spirits which are sick rather than their bodies. His argument is weakened somewhat when one of the inmates collapses, and Hicksley proclaims that the man has died due to the strain of the journey from the sickbay. The commander assembles Hicksley and several of the other senior officers and again asks which of the prisoners have armaments experience. When Hicksley once more replies falsely that no-one in the camp has any such specialist knowledge, Yonoi has him prepared for an immediate beheading. As Yonoi withdraws his sword, however, Celliers breaks rank, casually approaching the commander and gently kissing him on both cheeks. Yonoi is so overwhelmed by the unforeseen gesture that he faints, causing the guards to furiously attack Celliers in retaliation.

In response to the major's actions, the camp's newly-assigned commander (Hideo Murota) sentences Celliers to death – he is to be buried alive for his affront to Yonoi's authority. Held in an upright position by soldiers while he is slowly submerged in a pit of loose earth, only Celliers's head is allowed to remain above the surface while he is left to a slow and tortuous death by exposure. The new commander explains that Yonoi has been reassigned, and that he will not prove to be as easily manipulated as his predecessor had been. Lawrence, Hicksley and the others watch from a perimeter fence, knowing that they are powerless to intervene. As the prisoners' work party departs the camp, Hicksley pours scorn on Lawrence's knowledge of Japanese culture, considering his diplomatic efforts to be impotent and recommending that the colonel should consider trying the practice of ritual suicide himself. But the contemplative Lawrence seems quietly resistant to the haranguing group captain's insults.

While the prisoners sing hymns at night, echoing Celliers's earlier defiance of camp protocol, the iconoclastic major is close to death and imagines a startling vision of reconciliation with his estranged younger brother. In Celliers's final moments, Yonoi approaches the severely sunburned prisoner in the middle of the night, cutting off a lock of his hair to retain as a keepsake. The former prison commander then offers the major a final salute as they part for the last time.

Four years later, the geopolitical situation has changed dramatically. Imperial Japan has been defeated by Allied forces, and Lieutenant Colonel Lawrence is now a free man. Late one night, he finds himself visiting another prison camp, and a familiar inmate – none other than Sergeant Hara. The incarcerated Japanese soldier had sent a message to Lawrence, requesting his urgent presence at the camp. Hara has now learned some English, and welcomes Lawrence into his cell with the news that he is set to face execution for war crimes the following day; the colonel has arrived just in time for one final conversation. Regretfully but with sincere forgiveness, Lawrence informs Hara that he would personally have pardoned him and sent him home to his family, but the decision lies with others – people who believe themselves to be as right in their choices as Yonoi and Hara once did with their own judgements. But of course, the colonel adds, the truth is that nobody is ever truly right in their determinations. The pair share memories about the long-dead Jack Celliers, and Lawrence reveals that before Yonoi left the prison camp he had asked him to take the lock of Celliers's hair to his home village in Japan and consecrate it in a shrine. Hara voices his own regret that Yonoi had himself been executed in the aftermath of the war. The sergeant then grins, remembering the events of that fateful Christmas in 1942, and offers his thanks to Lawrence – by agreeing to Hara's call for an audience when he could so easily have ignored it, this time it is the colonel's turn to be Father Christmas. As Lawrence turns to leave, taking no satisfaction whatsoever in his erstwhile adversary's fate, the smiling Sergeant Hara barks out his parting words – 'Merry Christmas, Mr Lawrence' – echoing his expression of goodwill from the momentous Christmas Eve of four years ago.

While *Merry Christmas, Mr Lawrence* is unlikely to ever be considered the most traditional of cinematic festive fare, Ôshima's film has some remarkable observations to make about the capacity for personal transformation which lies within individual people; a key characteristic of many Christmas movies. From Celliers's dramatic and multifaceted effect on Yonoi's mindset through to the eventual role-switch that is carried out between Lawrence and Hara (where captive becomes captor), the film is full of fascinating character observations. The meaningful events of Christmas Eve are, of course, crucial in acting as a catalyst for the outcomes of the third act; if not for Hara's uncharacteristic decision to take up the altruistic mantle of Santa Claus, Lawrence would not have been pardoned and Celliers would not have been at liberty to disrupt parade protocol (and social etiquette) so thoroughly that he inadvertently secures Yonoi's replacement. As his fond recollection of the event demonstrates, Hara is himself fully aware of the positive effects of his drunken behaviour; in a sense, he implicitly admits that saving Lawrence's life was one aspect of his wartime military conduct for which he has no regret.

It is interesting to note that while some overseas markets used an alternative Japanese title for the film – *Furyo*, literally meaning 'Prisoner of War' – in Japan itself Ôshima's feature retained its festive-sounding designation in the form of *Senjô no Merī Kurisumasu*, which translates as 'Merry Christmas on the Battlefield'. And indeed, the latter designation is entirely appropriate, as *Merry Christmas, Mr*

Lawrence could not have been more drastically removed from the snowy locales or warm family scenes which had typified so many festive movies up until this point. No-one would easily confuse a blood-soaked prison camp in the clammy Javanese jungle for a traditional yuletide setting, and yet – strangely enough – it is the uncompromising depiction of unyielding brutal violence, severe illness and endless physical hardship which ultimately emphasises the values of human camaraderie, grace under fire and indeed the indomitability of the Christmas spirit even in the most unbearable of circumstances.

Just as the film juxtaposes the time-honoured kind-heartedness of Christmas with the pitiless cruelty of warfare, so too does it offer various opposing qualities through the characters' diverse range of interactions. The arrogant, racist Hicksley clashes with the compassionate pragmatist Lawrence, the superstitious but inexperienced officer Yonoi is frequently at variance with the practically-minded veteran soldier Hara, and of course the freethinking, rebellious Celliers is completely at odds with the prisoners' unspoken social protocols as well as the official regulations of his Japanese captors. Yet just as salient as the oppositions between these central figures are the unusual familiarities which emerge between them; while this is most noteworthy in the multiply-layered acquaintance which grows between Hara and Lawrence, each struggling to identify with the alien culture of the other, the same effect emerges elsewhere in the narrative. A.D. Barker has described the unusual bond which develops between the characters as being at the heart of the film's message: 'The Lawrence/Hara dialogues civilize and generalize the relationship of wartime enemies. Hara is no pacifist but he has rough charm and an evident humanity; the contingent nature of power and justice is wonderfully brought home when years later he is the prisoner, Celliers and Yonai [sic] are long dead and Lawrence is the prison liaison officer'.[4] The very delicate yet crucially important line of demarcation which lies between comrade and adversary is one which the film repeatedly examines and re-examines, challenging audience presumption as well as causing the viewer to think carefully about the nature of the relationships that they are watching unfold. Maureen Turim, for instance, observes that 'those moments in which the enemy is perceived as potential friend and the friend as potential enemy are most disconcerting as they trouble the boundaries of the oppositions. In *Merry Christmas, Mr Lawrence* the lines of friendship are complex and challenge these boundaries. The two main Japanese characters, Captain Yanoi [sic] and Sergeant Hara, are juxtaposed with the British soldiers, [Group Captain] Hicksley, Colonel Lawrence, and Major Celliers, a confrontation of enemies. Yet the lines of friendship cross these groupings and do not necessarily prevail within them. Sexual attraction and political repulsion each in different ways color the formation of friendships'.[5]

Ôshima's screenplay was written in collaboration with Paul Mayersberg (who had prior experience of writing for Bowie in the 1970s pop culture classic *The Man Who Fell to Earth*), and consistently demonstrates considerable depth throughout. Such is the subtlety of the film's highly nuanced approach to the cultural struggle taking place between the main characters, it is left largely to each audience member's personal judgement as to whether Yonoi is fascinated by Celliers on an individual level, or is instead enraptured by what the independently-minded major represents in opposition to the prison camp commander's own inflexible personal philosophy. In a sense, it is never entirely clear

whether Yonoi craves Celliers's personal approval or rather if
he simply seeks (consciously or unconsciously) to emulate and
even assume for himself the indefinable qualities which this
inscrutable captive represents. When Celliers's unabashed
disobedience makes it gradually more difficult for Yonoi to
avoid subjecting him to severe punishment, it is Hara's sense
of humanity (albeit exacerbated through inebriation) and the
pretext of Christmas benevolence which allows the major to
be pardoned at a point where official procedure would have
made it difficult (if not impossible) to do so. Here too, of
course, festive goodwill is cast through the prism of complex
cultural interaction, as Slawomir Magala notes: 'Captain
Yunoi [sic] is out of the camp, and Sergeant Hara is drunk
because it is Christmas. "Merry Christmas, Mr Lawrence",
says Hara, "get back to your fellow inmates". He pardons
them, saying that he is "Father Christmas". When Yunoi [sic]
returns, he metes out a disciplinary punishment to Hara, but
is obviously relieved that Celliers and Lawrence survived
thanks to Hara's ingenious cross-cultural trick'.[6]

Though the film has become famous for its insight into
the complexities of the intersections which lie between male
friendship, identity and sexuality (not a single female
character is featured throughout), Ôshima takes great care to
explore interpersonal issues with consideration and sensitivity,
ensuring that the full spectrum of human psychology is
properly acknowledged. Although the issue of male
relationships and sexuality within a prisoner of war camp
setting had been candidly explored in a handful of earlier
features, most prominently *The McKenzie Break* (Lamont
Johnson, 1970), rarely had the topic been deliberated with
such searching contemplation. As Miller has reflected, '*Merry
Christmas Mr Lawrence* is very engaging in that it confounds

the expectations derived from its war setting by delivering a meditation on cultural differences. Instead of the stereotypical plot about prisoners trying to escape their confines, the film presents a completely different and much more believable story about the men's interpersonal relationships and the resulting acts of cruelty and kindness performed between the four main characters'.[7] Yet for all the significance of sexual character and behaviour, Ôshima never employs the topic gratuitously; we are clearly shown that while sexual attitudes are an important characteristic of human existence, they are also complicated and are frequently multiply-layered. As Svet Atanasov has posited, many aspects of the film defy straightforward interpretation, and what appears to be clear-cut might in fact be more intricate than face value may suggest: 'In one of the most memorable scenes from *Merry Christmas Mr Lawrence* – which has given many Western critics the confidence to incorrectly conclude that the film houses homosexual overtones – Celliers publicly kisses Yonoi in order to humiliate him. It is the most efficient way for him to hurt his enemy – exposing his disappointment with the fact that he is forced by international law to treat the prisoners in the camp in a way that contradicts his beliefs'.[8]

Although *Merry Christmas, Mr Lawrence* featured uniformly excellent performances from its cast – most especially the quartet of lead actors – it has become especially well-known for David Bowie's captivating turn as 'Strafer' Jack Celliers. (The nickname 'strafer' was, in wartime, an appropriation of the German term 'strafe' – literally to 'punish' – though it would also be used to refer to a method of attacking ground targets with automatic gunfire from an aircraft. Lawrence has some difficulty explaining the expression to Yonoi when the commander enquires about it.)

While Bowie was to enjoy many successful roles throughout the eighties and beyond, the freethinking Major Celliers remains one of his most outstanding cinematic appearances of the decade, with numerous commentators considering it to be the breakthrough development in his acting career. Janet Maslin was far from alone in her praise for the film when she noted at the time of its release: 'David Bowie plays a born leader [...] and he plays him like a born film star. Mr Bowie's screen presence here is mercurial and arresting, and he seems to arrive at this effortlessly, though he manages to do something slyly different in every scene. The demands of his role may sometimes be improbable and elaborate, but Mr Bowie fills them in a remarkably plain and direct way. Little else in the film is so unaffected or clear. [...] *Merry Christmas, Mr Lawrence* is closer to a curiosity than to a triumph, though its conception is certainly ambitious. Mr Oshima has staged the film in a spacious tropical setting and filled it with a great number of extras. Even so, Mr Bowie always stands out from the crowd'.[9] Depicting with great aplomb Celliers's lifetime of guilt and remorse over the character's neglect of his fearful younger brother, Bowie always casts a restrained but revealing light on the unpredictable major's motivations. Part of the reason for the lasting sense of fascination behind this enigmatic protagonist's struggle with his personal demons is Bowie's incredibly confident performance, at all times self-assured yet undeniably off-kilter in its application. Few actors could so boldly carry off the simple deed of eating flowers or delivering an unexpected kiss as an act of acute civil defiance, and yet there is no denying the profundity of Bowie's impact in rendering these exploits as logical and convincing. Marcus Dodge has observed that 'the curve ball here is always Bowie. He's just been allowed to play really. At first it's a little odd but there's a scene early on where he mimes having a shave and some food in front of his guards and there's something unexplainably mesmerizing about his performance. This continues throughout the film and all of his segments, whether it be his flashback story or his neck deep burial in a sand pit, this character feels a whole lot more exciting than the film around him. Bowie's performance really is delightfully off beat and everything compelling about this story revolves around him for most of the run time'.[10] Commentators such as Chuck Stephens have also remarked upon the interesting artistic fusion which resulted from Bowie's collaboration with Ôshima; a unique synthesis which helped to cement the film within the popular culture of the decade:

> Rarely, and appropriately for a film in which every culture is examined with an alienating reserve, have the topiary realities of Britain seemed farther away. Adding to these alienations, Bowie – fresh from the physically demanding contortions he'd found success with on Broadway as *The Elephant Man*, and now working with what the self-proclaimed 'novice actor' described as 'the least stylized role' of his career – seems, for much of his performance, to have been left largely alone by Oshima (allowing the singer to indulge in a momentary return to his midsixties roots as a mime). Oshima's approach to filmmaking, Bowie would tell the press corps at Cannes later that year, was much like his own 'behaviorist' approach to acting, based on 'expression, not impression… I felt that we possibly understood one another better than I've understood some Western directors'.[11]

While Bowie's central performance was to dominate the film, in the opinion of many reviewers at least, this was not to detract from the uniformly excellent selection of lead actors which surround him. Ryûichi Sakamoto brings a wealth of repressed emotion to Captain Yonoi, emphasising the character's depth of conflict as well as his sense of military duty. Though much critical discourse has focused on Yonoi's complicated relationship with Celliers, just as intriguing is his interaction with Tom Conti's Lawrence and Takeshi Kitano's Hara. Both actors were well-known in their respective homelands. Scots-born actor Conti enjoyed a high profile throughout the eighties, having won a Tony Award for his performance in Brian Clark's *Whose Life is it Anyway?* in 1979 and later being nominated for an Academy Award in the Best Actor category for his performance in *Reuben, Reuben* (Robert Ellis Miller, 1983). In later years, he has found additional success as a novelist and theatre director. Kitano, who has come to be better recognised by his stage name 'Beat' Takeshi, had risen to prominence through the huge success of his comedy career throughout the 1970s, moving into acting and eventually directing in the 1980s. (A true 'renaissance man', Kitano has also been active as a screenwriter, singer, poet, author, artist and video game designer over the years.) With two such exceptional talents, it comes as no surprise that the strange companionship which develops between Hara and Lawrence is one of the highlights of the film; while both characters have a problematic relationship with Yonoi, who assumes a position of authority over the two of them in different ways, they come to view each other with a kind of shared cultural curiosity. Though the association never quite develops into a friendship, neither too is it merely a shared antipathy based upon mutual distrust. As Atanasov has suggested:

> While the war rages on far away from Java, a strange
> bond forms between Celliers, Lawrence, Yonoi, and

Hara. Even though they remain enemies, the men begin to admire each other – Yonoi admires Celliers and his spirit while Hara is impressed with Lawrence's tact and diplomatic skills. The more time the men spend together, however, the less they understand what motivates them. What confuses them the most is the fact that neither side is particularly supportive of the war. Eventually, some of their mutual admiration evolves into frustration. [...] It is scripted as a war film but it is in fact a very complex examination of Japanese spirituality, and in particular [the] Japanese attitude towards violence and death. The film's morality is deeply rooted into the Japanese belief that, like life and death, love and violence are interconnected. Unsurprisingly, the admiration and respect Yonoi and Hara gradually develop for Celliers and Lawrence are expressed through acts of violence.[12]

Because of the magnetic qualities of the film's predominant quartet of actors, Jack Thompson's Group Captain Hicksley is often somewhat overlooked – and unjustly so, as Thompson delivers an excellent portrayal of the loud-mouthed, conceited RAF officer; a man still desperately clinging to the subtle social cruelties of the British class system while living in tortuous captivity thousands of miles from home. A figure of significant stature in Australian film, Thompson had been active on television and most notably in cinema since the late 1960s, appearing in many features such as *Breaker Morant* (Bruce Beresford, 1980) and *The Man from Snowy River* (George T. Miller, 1982). With Hicksley he creates a memorable grotesque; a swaggering, self-important elitist who seems more preoccupied with preserving his standing amongst the other prisoners than he does with the convoluted politics of survival. Gregory Desilet makes the important point that 'although the major conflict portrayed in the film occurs between the Japanese and the prisoners, the greater contrast in character exists between Lawrence and Celliers and the ranking British officer, Hicksley-Ellis. He never falters from intense hatred of the Japanese and shows no inclination or capacity to discover what manner of person the enemy is. The dehumanization of the Japanese makes it possible for him to keep the conflict clearly polarized. For Lawrence, this surrender to hatred is too easy and constitutes too great a dehumanization of oneself'.[13] Here we become aware of the gulf which exists between the straightforward bipolarity of Hicksley's view of the war and Lawrence's practicality in attempting to find areas of commonality between the prisoners' situation and their captors' cultural imperatives. The conceptual chasm could not be more profound, not least as Hicksley has no intention of even attempting to bridge it – nor would he even see the point in embarking on such a course of action. As Roger Ebert has noted, this lends the film an interesting dynamic which set it apart from the crowd: 'Here's a movie that is even stranger than it was intended to be. *Merry Christmas, Mr Lawrence* is about a clash between two cultures (British and Japanese) and two styles of military service (patriotic and pragmatic). That would be enough for any movie, and there are scenes when it is enough, and the movie works pretty well. [...] This is interesting material, especially since Oshima plunges a little more deeply into the psychology of his characters than your average prisoner-of-war movie is likely to'.[14] This conflict – and the endeavours of various characters to overcome or circumvent it in different ways – is, of course, at the very heart of the film's concerns; behaviour which is pivotal to the Japanese code of honour is anathema to the British prisoners, and in many ways the inmates' attitudes are similarly baffling to their captors. The regular application of brutal violence, usually as a means of control but sometimes simply to humiliate or undermine, further obscures the clarity of any potential areas of commonality, making Lawrence's attempts at diplomacy all the more difficult. Desilet expands on this issue, explaining that 'when pressed by Hara for an explanation of the British "cowardliness" in surrender, Lawrence answers that the British do not commit suicide because they want to keep on fighting. Even as a prisoner, he keeps on fighting by attempting to bridge the conflict and cultural chasm between them. For Lawrence, this is how the war is really fought – not by trying merely to overcome the enemy by force'.[15]

While the degree of mediation achieved by Lawrence proves to be modest in its reach, at least in tangible terms, he undeniably manages to earn the respect of his jailers in ways that would have been inconceivable – and largely undesirable – to the supercilious Hicksley. Yet of course, Ôshima takes great care to outline the sheer impenetrability and brutality of the situation, never intimating that either side is able to occupy the moral high ground. Hara may grow to appreciate Lawrence's viewpoint, but he never quite reaches a point where he can overlook their relationship as captor and detainee – a fact which makes the film's conclusion in the post-War 1946 all the more poignantly fitting. Clark Douglas has commented that *Merry Christmas, Mr Lawrence* 'makes a genuine attempt at presenting a level-headed look at both sides of the conflict, though obviously most viewers will bring a certain level of personal feeling to the proceedings that skew it one way or the other. It isn't so interested in examining the specifics of the war as in the general differences between the two cultures. [...] Over the course of the film, Lawrence and

Hara do not manage to convert each other but rather develop a sense of mutual understanding and respect. Their scenes together are some of the film's most curiously touching, with Conti's subtle reserve playing beautifully against Hara's raw emotion'.[16]

Merry Christmas, Mr Lawrence is a film which has resisted easy categorisation since its initial release. Though it may ostensibly seem like a war movie, its emphasis on interpersonal and intercultural communication – as well as its oblique interest to Christmas cinema enthusiasts – has introduced an element of generic complication. Ôshima's highly distinct stylistic approach and Bowie's unusual leading performance have combined to blur generic boundaries still further, while the complexities of the film's thematic concerns have introduced other impediments to straightforward classification. Wimal Dissanayake details the fact that '*Merry Christmas, Mr Lawrence* thematizes a number of intersecting issues such as Self and Other, repressed homosexuality, brutalities of war, cultural difference and the nature of desire. [...] All this takes place against a backdrop of war and cultural difference. Although *Merry Christmas, Mr Lawrence* can be broadly defined as a war film, it is very different in intent and texture, from a film like [David Lean's *The*] *Bridge on the River Kwai* with which one might be initially tempted to compare. Unlike the latter film, which is decisively focused on suspense, the former deals with the complexities of character, motivation and background'.[17] The contrast with Lean's hugely influential 1957 World War II film, based upon Pierre Boulle's novel *Le Pont de la Rivière Kwai* (1952), has been made by other critics, and yet (beyond discussion of the films' respective situations within Japanese prisoner of war work camps during the Pacific campaign) the comparisons have largely centred on the marked narrative dissimilarity which exists between the two films rather than attempts to identify thematic parallels. Discussing the issue of cross-cultural understanding between the Imperial Japanese forces and Allied prisoners, Dave Lancaster has ventured the opinion that 'this theme has been successfully mounted before by David Lean with his masterpiece *The Bridge on the River Kwai,* but if anything Oshima's film is more intellectually stimulating. Very little in the way of traditional action is visible and yet characters become both maimed and valiant. [...] It also jolts back to childhood flashbacks which could be the film's only real problem – they could've been handled better by being more brief and less obvious. As they stand, they distract and break the momentum. However, by the brilliant closing scene that sees a reversal of sorts, the film's minor cracks have been smoothed'.[18]

With its pivotal theme of cultural turbulence, contrasting areas of mutual connection with irreconcilable differences, at the very core of *Merry Christmas, Mr Lawrence* is a powerful argument for common humanity: a motif that would not be lost on any enthusiast of festive cinema. Yet rarely would a Christmas movie delve quite so deeply into the psychological underpinnings of such commonalities, nor dwell to quite the same extent upon the polarity of cultural territory as expounded through the anomalous relationship which develops between Sakamoto and Bowie's respective characters. Douglas notes that 'the core of the film lies in the electric relationship between Celliers and Yonoi. It was something of a stroke of genius casting Bowie and Sakamoto in those respective roles – Bowie had established himself as one of the rock gods of Britain (and many other places, for that matter) while Sakamoto was arguably the biggest rock star in Japan at the time. So here they are, these two cultural icons, representing their respective cultures in strikingly theatrical form: Celliers is the epitome of strong-willed rebellion and non-conformity, while Yonoi strives valiantly for order and control'.[19] Thus the essence of the shared humanity for which the film strives can be found in the disputed terrain explored through interactions between the main characters, but most especially in the Celliers/Yonoi pairing which drives the narrative most decisively. And it is this sense of moral ambiguity, suggestive of the cruelty not just of war but of life itself, which resonates through the film so intensely; the notion that irrespective of attempts to overcome differences, circumstances sometimes act unexpectedly against even the noblest of intentions. As Jamie S. Rich has stated:

> *Merry Christmas, Mr Lawrence* has an impressive final act. The fate of Celliers is macabre, and despite the panting earnestness of the early scenes, Oshima knows that repressed emotions are more effective in this case than any sweaty relief would ever be. *Mr Lawrence* is a sad film, one where there is no clear line between right and wrong, and thus no satisfaction for anyone. The melancholy denouement neatly encapsulates all the things the rest of the film touches on: war is destructive, and it causes men to act in ways that are against their nature. The cultures that have been clashing finally get a moment's peace, and they eventually understand each other in some fashion – even if it is only two men, they represent some part of the whole.[20]

Merry Christmas, Mr Lawrence performed strongly at awards ceremonies, being nominated for the Palme d'Or

Award at the 1983 Cannes Film Festival and winning Ryûichi Sakamoto the Best Score Award at the BAFTA Awards in 1984. However, the film received even greater acclamation in Japan, winning the Most Popular Film Award at the Awards of the Japanese Academy and being nominated in the categories of Best Film, Best Director, Best Art Direction, Best Music Score, and Best Supporting Actor (for Takeshi Kitano). *Merry Christmas, Mr Lawrence* also won the Reader's Choice Award at the Kinema Junpo Awards, and was conferred prizes for Best Film, Best Director, Best Screenplay, Best Film Score, and Best Supporting Actor (again, for Kitano's performance) at the Mainichi Film Concours.

The critical success of *Merry Christmas, Mr Lawrence* laid the groundwork for the release of later, more explicitly Christmas-oriented war movies such as *A Midnight Clear* (Keith Gordon, 1992) and most especially *Joyeux Noël* (Christian Carion, 2005), the acclaimed dramatization of the events surrounding the famous Christmas Armistice of December 1914 during World War I. While Ôshima's film may not have been the epitome of festive cheer, to put it mildly, its overarching themes of seeking peace and goodwill even in the midst of horror and bloodshed nonetheless mark it out as being one of the most powerful – and exceptional – entries in the wartime subgenre of Christmas cinema. Though it was never a film that was ever likely to become a comforting mainstay of the holiday season, *Merry Christmas, Mr Lawrence* is nonetheless a commanding clarion call to overcome cultural disparity and discover areas of commonality in the pursuit of mutual good.

REFERENCES

1. Gary J. Svehla and Susan Svehla, *It's Christmas Time at the Movies* (Baltimore: Midnight Marquee Press, 1998), p.112.

2. Yoshiharu Tezuka, *Japanese Cinema Goes Global: Filmworkers' Journeys* (Hong Kong: Hong Kong University Press, 2012), p.88.

3. Gordon S. Miller, '*Merry Christmas, Mr Lawrence*', in *High Def Digest*, 18 November 2010.
    <http://bluray.highdefdigest.com/3589/christmas_lawrence.html>

4. A.D. Barker, '*Bridge on the River Kwai* and the Japanese Prisoner of War Camp Movie: A Multiculturalism Too Far?', in *Multicultural Dilemmas: Identity, Difference, Otherness*, ed. by Wojciech H. Kalaga and Marzena Kubisz (Frankfurt am Main: Peter Lang, 2008), 93-106, p.100.

5. Maureen Turim, *The Films of Oshima Nagisa: Images of a Japanese Iconoclast* (Berkeley: University of California Press, 1998), p.173.

6. Slawomir Magala, *Cross-Cultural Competence* (Abingdon: Routledge, 2005), p.186.

7. Miller, 2010.

8. Svet Atanasov, '*Merry Christmas, Mr Lawrence* Blu-Ray Review', in Blu-Ray.com, 28 September 2010.
    <http://www.blu-ray.com/movies/Merry-Christmas-Mr-Lawrence-Blu-ray/12777/#Review>

9.   Janet Maslin, 'David Bowie in *Merry Christmas*', in *The New York Times*, 26 August 1983.

10.   Marcus Dodge, '*Merry Christmas, Mr Lawrence*', in *DVD Active*, 2011.
        <*http://www.dvdactive.com/reviews/dvd/merry-christmas-mr-lawrence.html*>

11.   Chuck Stephens, 'Lawrence of Shinjuku: *Merry Christmas, Mr Lawrence*' in *The Criterion Collection*, 28 September 2010.
        <*https://www.criterion.com/current/posts/1605-lawrence-of-shinjuku-merry-christmas-mr-lawrence*>

12.   Atanasov, 2010.

13.   Gregory Desilet, *Screens of Blood: A Critical Approach to Film and Television Violence* (Jefferson: McFarland and Company, 2014), pp.89-90.

14.   Roger Ebert, '*Merry Christmas, Mr Lawrence*', in *The Chicago Sun-Times*, 16 September 1983.

15.   Desilet, 2014, p.90.

16.   Clark Douglas, '*Merry Christmas, Mr Lawrence* (Blu-Ray) Criterion Collection', in *DVD Verdict*, 28 September 2010.
        <*http://www.dvdverdict.com/reviews/mrlawrencebluray.php*>

17.   Wimal Dissanayake, 'Habermas' Concept of Public Sphere and the Cinema of Oshima Nagisa', in *Across the Oceans: Studies from East to West in Honor of Richard K. Seymour*, ed. by Irmengard Rauch and Cornelia Moore (Honolulu: University of Hawaii, 1995), 61-76, p.72.

18.   Dave Lancaster, '*Merry Christmas, Mr Lawrence*', in Cinemas Online, 2011. <*http://www.cinemas-online.co.uk/film-reviews/merry-christmas-mr-lawrence-a101751.html*>

19.   Douglas, 2010.

20.   Jamie S. Rich, '*Merry Christmas, Mr Lawrence.* Criterion Collection (Blu-Ray)', in *DVD Talk*, 28 September 2010. <*http://www.dvdtalk.com/reviews/44638/merry-christmas-mr-lawrence/*>

6

Don't Open Till Christmas (1984)

Spectacular Trading International

Director: Edmund Purdom
Producers: Steve Minasian and Dick Randall
Screenwriters: Derek Ford with Al McGoohan

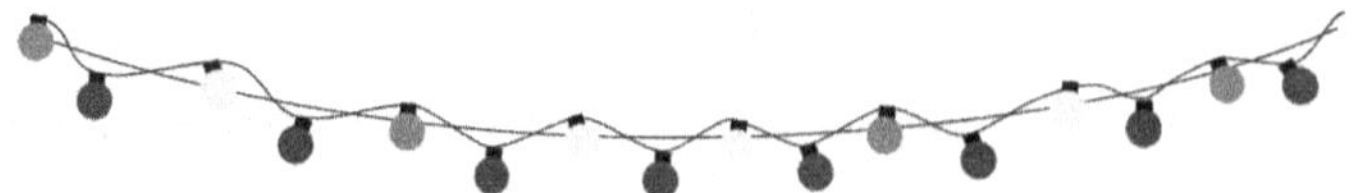

While the early eighties had witnessed a boom in horror cinema, not least those which featured a festive setting, *Don't Open Till Christmas* was to stand apart from the crowd for a variety of reasons – and not all of them positive. Firstly, unlike the other prominent Christmas horror films of the period the movie was filmed and produced in the United Kingdom, featuring British actors and locations which were mainly situated around the London area. Similarly, even at this relatively early stage in the development of the slasher horror, the premise of the murderer in Santa Claus guise was deftly turned on its head: in this feature, the figure of Jolly Old Saint Nick would be the target of a killing spree rather than its homicidal instigator. However, this stylistic innovation and the country of production would likely prove to be the areas of greatest interest to admirers of Christmas horror, as *Don't Open Till Christmas* would eventually become infamous as one of the most singularly chaotic and unconvincing films ever to emerge in the entire subgenre. As Jeremy Wheeler has incisively explained: 'Now here's a twist to the Christmas horror genre – have the serial killer be killing Santa Clauses instead of the other way around. Sadly, that's just about the best thing *Don't Open Till Christmas* has going for it'.[1]

Don't Open Till Christmas was to be the sole directorial credit of actor Edmund Purdom, a British actor on stage and screen who had established himself in theatrical performances (including at the Royal Shakespeare Theatre as well as in numerous Broadway appearances) before becoming active in film. His plentiful screen roles included Prince Karl in *The Student Prince* (Richard Thorpe, 1954), the physician Sinuhe in *The Egyptian* (Michael Curtiz, 1954), and soldier Michael Dermott in *The King's Thief* (Robert Z. Leonard, 1955). Though his appearances as an actor during the fifties and sixties were especially prolific, he later became similarly active in Italian cinema and television up until the time of his death in 2009, also establishing himself as a capable music recording specialist. A versatile talent who became especially well-known in later years for his varied voice-over work, Purdom's decision to engage with film directing would prove to be a short-lived career choice; *Don't Open Till Christmas* was to be riven with production difficulties, ultimately leading to a movie that is often remembered for all the wrong reasons.

One frosty winter's evening, a man dressed in a Santa Claus costume (John Aston) meets with his girlfriend (Maria Eldridge) for a romantic encounter. As they retreat to his car, which is parked nearby, neither is aware that a stalker is watching their every move. While the couple's embrace becomes more amorous, the unseen prowler moves closer to their position, eventually attracting their attention. When the man angrily orders the unwelcome interloper to leave, the response is immediate and deadly – he is stabbed in the chest and left to die in the alleyway. Terrified, his partner attempts to flee the scene, but the mysterious killer quickly intercepts her and ensures that she, too, meets her demise at the end of his blade.

Later, festive revellers are celebrating at a fancy dress party elsewhere in the city. Kate Briosky (Belinda Mayne) and her boyfriend Cliff Boyd (Gerry Sundquist) playfully tease Kate's genial father (Lawrence Harrington), who feels self-conscious about dressing up as Santa Claus to distribute gifts at the party. The ebullient Cliff bounds into the heart of the gathering and announces that Santa is about to join the merrymakers to spread some festive cheer. But only moments after Kate's father has made his way into the applauding crowd, one of the costumed partygoers impales the head of the luckless Santa Claus with a spear. While everyone watches in shock as he falls dead to the ground, Cliff jumps into action and confronts the killer... only to discover that the murderer has left a decoy in their wake, and has used the distraction to escape from the area unseen.

At New Scotland Yard, the headquarters of the London's Metropolitan Police, Detective Chief Inspector Ian Harris (Edmund Purdom) reacts with a mixture of dry amusement and weary dejection at a lurid newspaper article reporting on the recent killings. He grimly explains to his departmental assistant, Detective Sergeant Powell (Mark Jones), that they are coming under greater pressure from their superiors to bring the murderer to justice before he or she can commit any further bloodshed. Harris suggests that they interview Kate and Cliff about the death of her father in the hope of uncovering some new leads, but Powell informs him that Kate is too distraught by recent events to come in for an interview. Instead, he has arranged for them to visit her at home later that day. Kate's father was wealthy and popular, meaning that there are no obvious suspects who would have sought his demise. However, as Kate now stands to inherit the family fortune Harris and Powell consider that Cliff may be the most obvious beneficiary; if he had somehow been able to engineer the older man's death, they conjecture, then Cliff would be well placed to defraud the money from his grieving girlfriend.

The two detectives arrive at Kate's high-rise apartment and explain that they are no closer to tracking down the killer. Harris mentions that the murderer has left no trace thus far; when Cliff asks about the sinister disguise that the assassin had worn while carrying out the lethal attack on Kate's father, the inspector responds that so far the clues to the killer's identity have all proven to be red herrings. It seems that no-one throughout the capital wearing a Santa Claus costume as Christmas approaches can be considered safe. Almost as if to illustrate his point, that night another murder is carried out when a street corner Santa Claus (George Pierce) is garrotted and roasted on a grill he had been using to roast chestnuts. As the victim's body bursts into flames, the enigmatic killer is revealed to be wearing a translucent plastic mask with a maniacal grin spread unsettlingly across its face.

The next morning, a helmeted motorcycle courier speeds through the busy streets of London; their destination is the home of Inspector Harris. His housekeeper (Wendy Danvers) announces that the courier has delivered a festively-wrapped box bearing a label which reads 'don't open till Christmas'. Harris casually responds that he intends to follow the box's instructions and keep its contents a surprise until Christmas Day arrives later in the week. He then leaves for work, telling the housekeeper that he will next see her on Christmas Eve – a date which is now only a few days away.

Back at his office at New Scotland Yard, Harris and Powell discuss the latest death. Powell explains that, according to police records, the most recent victim had links to London's gangland and thus his death may have been coincidental – the murder may have been caused by a rival gang rather than the serial killer who is suspected of the other Santa Claus slayings. The sergeant asks whether they should now be searching for a psychopath, given the mounting body count, and Harris tells him that the police top brass now suspect that this is indeed the case; any assumption that the last murder was motivated by an underworld territorial dispute seems wholly unconvincing in the light of the events which have taken place over the past few days.

Powell tells Harris that Kate has been in touch by telephone, and the inspector promptly returns her call to clarify that there have been no further developments in the police enquiry. At her apartment, Kate is concerned by the death of the chestnut vendor Santa Claus, but Cliff assures her that there is no need to worry; the police are looking into the case with ever greater urgency. Instead, he seems more insistent that she return a phone call from a solicitor who has telephoned the apartment; while Kate protests that she needs time to grieve her father's untimely death, Cliff suggests that this will be the perfect opportunity to get things back to normal. However, when Kate tells him that the police wanted to know if she and Cliff had any immediate plans to marry, he seems to find the tone of the question somewhat discomfiting.

Elsewhere in London, a reporter named Giles Harrison (Alan Lake) contacts Powell from a public telephone box. He explains that he works for the *Daily News*, and is enquiring if there have been any further leads in the serial killer investigation. As Powell is derisive about the sensationalist headlines concerning the case that have appeared in the tabloid newspaper, he curtly refuses to give Harrison any detailed information and instead tells him to attend Harris's forthcoming news conference if he wants to ask any questions. However, Harrison hints that he has useful information, and tells Powell that his promotion prospects within the police force will be greatly improved if he was to solve the case without the involvement of his superior officer. When Powell presses him for further information, Harrison only responds that he will be back in touch later, hanging up the phone without preamble.

In a dark alleyway, a drunken man in a Santa Claus outfit (Ashley Dransfield) is staggering along in a manner which suggests that he is somewhat the worse for wear. Inebriation proves to be the least of his worries, however, when he unexpectedly encounters the shadowy murderer, who wastes no time in shooting the intoxicated man in the face. The costumed victim is killed instantly, slumping to the ground in a bloodied heap.

In the morning, a dejected Kate is wandering the streets when she is unexpectedly approached by Harrison. He introduces himself as a *Daily News* journalist and enquires whether he might be allowed to ask her a few questions about her recent ordeal. Suspicious of his motives, Kate replies that Inspector Harris has instructed her not to discuss any aspect of the case with the press, but Harrison is insistent – he tells her that his interest is with her personal response to the situation, rather than the details of the police investigation. Disdainfully, she replies that anyone who has lost a family member under such tragic circumstances would never be so tactless as to ask such a question. But as she rushes away, telling him to direct any further enquiries to the police, Harrison reveals that he has indeed lost a close relative unexpectedly and thus can understand her feelings better than she realises.

As night falls, Harris leaves New Scotland Yard to the sound of a police band playing upbeat music in celebration of Christmas. However, his mood is anything but jubilant. At an Underground station elsewhere in London, Cliff is busking with a flute when he encounters an old friend named Gerry (Kevin Lloyd). They go for a drink together, and Gerry reveals that he has started working as a photographer of adult material. He invites Cliff to visit his studio, and suggests that it may be a lucrative side-line for him if they should work together – especially if he can persuade the grieving Kate to consider doing some modelling. Cliff reluctantly agrees to the suggestion, though only by asserting that any photoshoot involving Kate should not be too explicit under the circumstances.

That evening, Cliff hoodwinks Kate into visiting the studio under the misconception that Gerry has invited them out to dinner. The couple arrive to discover that, rather than a professional photography workspace, the 'studio' is in fact a cramped area in the corner of Gerry's dingy flat. Kate in unimpressed when they enter to discover Gerry taking snapshots of the personable, scantily-clad Sharon (Pat Astley), but is furious when she discovers that the two men expect her to appear in a photoshoot herself. Just when she feels that her upset can get no worse, Gerry produces a skimpy Santa Claus outfit which he expects her to wear for the photographs; appalled by their insensitivity, she bursts out of the apartment. Cliff heads off in pursuit of her, but Gerry suggests that he stay for the rest of the shoot and think about spending the night with Sharon rather than his mourning girlfriend.

Some time later that night, Cliff and Sharon head outside the flat to prepare for some outdoor shots. Before Gerry can arrive with the equipment, two police constables arrive on the scene, leading Cliff to panic that they might be charged with a public indecency offence (as Sharon's Santa Claus 'costume' is little more than a red, fur-trimmed cloak with little underneath). Unnerved, and with the apartment door accidentally locked shut behind them, he bolts away into the night leaving Sharon to fend for herself. Realising that she must evade the notice of the police in order to avoid arrest, she turns down an alleyway only to encounter the masked killer. She screams in terror as he wields a razor in her direction, but inexplicably the murderer seems to change his mind when he discovers her gender. Without a word, he races away from the alley, leaving her unharmed. Now thoroughly shocked by the confrontation, Sharon stumbles back towards the flat and is intercepted by the two police officers who soon sense her distress and take her to safety.

In the morning, Sharon is paid a visit at home by Harris and Powell. She has little time for their questioning, but the inspector points out that she should be more co-operative – given that she had been arrested for indecent exposure, the only reason she was released from the police station so quickly had been on account of her brush with the serial killer. Pushing ahead with the interview, Harris asks what had happened to Cliff when he had fled the area after spotting the two police constables, but Sharon admits that she has no idea – he simply seemed to have vanished. However, she also points out that the murderer's mask made it impossible to determine any aspect of his or her identity, though they did appear to have very distinctive eyes. Harris then dashes from the apartment without warning, leaving Powell to continue the questioning on his own. But it quickly becomes apparent that Sharon has little else of use to add to their enquiries, given the fleeting nature of her encounter with the killer.

Elsewhere, another man dressed as Santa Claus (Wilfred Corlett) is attending a peep show at a sex club. He reveals to the private dancer (Kelly Baker), safely behind the dividing wall of a glass booth, that his seasonal attire can be explained by the fact that he is working as a Santa Claus at a nearby department store. But the man becomes so engrossed in his conversation with the affable young dancer that he is taken completely by surprise when the murderer emerges into the darkened room and fatally stabs him in the back of the head. The dancer screams in terror at the bloodshed of the unprovoked attack.

Back at Kate's apartment, Cliff is relating the (somewhat selectively-chosen) events of the previous evening to his enraged girlfriend. Kate is deeply contemptuous of Cliff's claim that he had left the vulnerable Sharon to fend for herself so that he could track down Gerry and get his revenge. Their argument is interrupted by the arrival of Harris, who pointedly begins to question Cliff over his whereabouts during the attack on Sharon. Cliff appears genuinely shocked when he discovers that the model had been attacked, having no idea of her safety after he had left her alone the previous night. Kate is livid that Cliff and Gerry would have risked Sharon's security by asking her to appear in a public place wearing a Santa Claus costume, given the number of victims that the murderer has already clocked up. Cliff realises that as he has now been present at the site of two of the killings, he must be considered a suspect by the police. When her boyfriend is out of earshot, Kate asks Harris if she might meet with him at a private location to discuss the case further. The inspector gives her some contact details and tells her to get in touch later.

Powell enters his office at New Scotland Yard to discover Harrison rifling through Harris's desk. The sergeant demands an explanation for Harrison's presence, pointing out that his cover story as a journalist is unconvincing – nobody at the *Daily News* had ever heard of him. The reporter rationalises the situation by telling Powell that he writes for the paper under the pen name of 'Giles Morgan', hence the misunderstanding. When the sergeant asks him what kind of information he can provide that might be of use in the murder investigation, Harrison cryptically responds that Inspector Harris has been deliberately withholding information about the case from Powell and his fellow officers. His patience growing thin, Powell orders him to elucidate further about this allegation, but Harrison chooses that moment to withdraw from the office, suggesting only that the sergeant may want to consider having the inspector followed – doing so may present interesting results, he implies. However, Powell has other ideas and decides to have the untrustworthy Harrison tailed as well.

Later that night, Inspector Harris is weaving around crowds of Christmas shoppers in a busy commercial area of the city. He has no idea that Powell is following him from a safe distance. However, as the inspector meanders around pedestrians and carol singers alike, he eventually manages to inadvertently shake Powell who loses him in the multitude of passers-by. At the same time, an inebriated man in a Santa Claus outfit (Sid Wragg) emerges from a pub and drunkenly tries to ride home on a bicycle. He is attacked by a group of teenagers, who force him to flee on foot before stealing his bike. In a fumbling attempt to escape from them, the man stumbles into the London Dungeon – a macabre tourist attraction – where he hopes to find shelter. An administrative assistant (Paula Meadows) attempts to stop his entry, but fails; seconds later, the masked killer arrives and murders her before she can alert the authorities. Then, disguised as a monk from one of the Dungeon's displays, the assailant stalks the hapless Santa Claus-costumed victim deeper into the building before repeatedly stabbing him to death with one of the props from the exhibition.

Kate and Cliff are returning to their apartment following an inquest into the murders. Cliff is in an uncharacteristically contemplative mood, wondering aloud why Harris had not been present at the event given that he is the senior investigating officer in the serial killer case. But back at New Scotland Yard, the inspector is coming under renewed pressure from his superiors. His latest order is to start putting decoy 'victims' onto the streets – plain-clothes police officers dressed in Santa Claus outfits, with the singular intent of luring the killer out into the open. Harris seems suspicious when he learns that Powell has already put the plan into operation, sensing the sergeant's ambition. However, the inspector also reflects that his inability to pinpoint the killer has almost certainly heralded the end of his career in policing – that is, if he doesn't decide to pre-empt the upper echelons of the force by resigning before they have the chance to dismiss him.

Harris attends a circus later that day, where a number of costumed police officers are present in the guise of Santa Claus. One particular Father Christmas (Derek Ford) is passing out gifts to young children as part of the performance. After the event, however, there are further grisly slayings – the circus Santa Claus is killed by repeated stab-wounds when the murderer approaches him with a retractable blade in his boot, whereas the police minder (also clothed in Santa Claus garb) has his throat slashed. A further, festively-clad police officer is stabbed through the eye with a steak-knife, ensuring that he too meets a rapid demise.

At a London street market the next day, Cliff is again busking with his flute while accompanied by Kate. Harris arrives and approaches the couple, asking if Cliff may have heard anything through any unofficial connections he may have. In spite of the desperation implied in the inspector's line of questioning, his presence immediately makes Cliff suspicious that he is being followed by detectives. Harris renews his offer to Kate that he is available to talk whenever she feels the need. She responds that she hasn't ruled out the possibility.

At New Scotland Yard, the private dancer who had witnessed one of the Santa Claus slayings has been called in for questioning. Powell is frustrated when it becomes clear that the dancer is unable to provide any details about the murderer beyond that which had already been established. However, she does reiterate a warning that Sharon had given after her own encounter with the killer, saying that the assailant had 'smiling' eyes that she would recognise if she ever saw them again. Knowing that the dancer's life is most likely in danger, given that she saw the murder and could potentially identify the assassin, Powell arranges for a constable to drive her directly back to her home. He also makes preparations to have her house put under police surveillance until the killer is brought to justice. However, she gives her escort the slip and decides to leave the headquarters on her own... little realising that she is being followed. Rather than heading home, the dancer returns to work, but moments later the killer arrives and smashes through the glass of her private booth in an attempt to strangle her. Recognising the face of her assailant, she races out of the club and tears along the street, the murderer in close pursuit. Just when she thinks that she has evaded him, the killer double-backs on himself and drags her down a flight of stairs to a shabby basement apartment. Restraining his terrified victim with chains, the menacing assassin explains to the dancer that – as she can now testify to the murderer's identity – he intends to kill her as soon as he is satisfied that she has recognised 'the error of her ways'. The dancer is confused by the mysterious man's ambiguous warning that he is on a mission to challenge the very nature of the modern Christmas, where price has become more important than value.

Kate telephones Harris's home using the number he had given her, but discovers from his housekeeper that he is currently visiting somewhere named 'Parklands'. When Kate enquires further, the housekeeper replies that she shouldn't attempt to contact him there, but rather should wait until he returns to his office at New Scotland Yard. She emphasises that under no circumstances should she reveal the fact that she has said anything, which puzzles Kate even further. Some time later, Powell telephones Harris from the police office once he has got back home to give him an update on the case, only to discover that the inspector has been removed from the investigation by their superiors. With yet another Santa Claus murder to deal with, Powell decides to release Cliff, who had been remanded in custody as a precautionary measure while the police enquiries continue. As Cliff is baffled by Powell's change of heart, the sergeant responds that he doesn't believe Cliff to be responsible... but he has a hunch that he now knows who the true culprit is.

In London's theatre district, yet another heavily drunk Santa Claus (Ricky Kennedy) stumbles through the stage door of a playhouse in search of a non-existent party. He is swiftly ejected, but upon leaving the building immediately bumps into the murderer. Running as fast as he can, the man sprints back into the building and races for dear life into the lower levels in an attempt to evade his pursuer. There, he almost interrupts a musical performance by actress Caroline Munro (playing herself) as he attempts to find a way to safety that avoids crossing the killer's path. However, his luck rapidly runs out, and the unfortunate Santa Claus is raised to the stage via a trapdoor... with a machete lodged in his face.

A harried Powell visits Kate at her request, and she describes the telephone conversation with Harris's housekeeper as well as some subsequent research that she has conducted. She explains that the 'Parklands' which had been mentioned is actually a mental hospital, and that there is no record of Harris's name on any birth certificate, meaning that to all intents and purposes the inspector doesn't exist. Powell brushes off her amateur investigating, reasoning that there are any number of reasons why Harris may have been visiting Parklands and remarking that Kate's inability to find the inspector on the Register of Births and Deaths could be down to a simple clerical error. But Kate remains convinced that she is on the right track, in spite of the sergeant's doubts.

Determined to get to the bottom of the mystery over Harris's motivations, Kate decides to visit Parklands herself – albeit in disguise. She later telephones Powell to inform him that she has discovered something of interest, but finds that the sergeant is currently out of the office. Meanwhile, a department store Santa Claus (Max Roman) is brutally castrated in a public toilet by the killer; the grisly, blood-soaked sight is uncovered by a member of the cleaning staff shortly afterwards.

That night, Kate visits Harris at his home and tells him that she wants to talk further about the case. The inspector replies that he is no longer involved in the investigation, having been suspended by the force, but remains interested in its outcome. He offers to take her out to dinner at a city restaurant, and they celebrate Christmas Eve with a turkey dinner. As Kate pumps the unwitting detective for information, surreptitiously turning the tables, an increasingly paranoid Cliff appears and spots her together with Harris. Before he has the chance to interject, however, he is ejected from the building on account of not being properly attired to meet the restaurant's dress code.

Back home, Kate discovers a note which seems to be written by Cliff... but before she has the chance to read it, she is interrupted by an intruder – Giles Harrison. She is shocked by the journalist's presence and demands to know how he managed to enter her apartment, but he breezily tells her that the porter had let him in and – at any rate – he feels that he is welcome anywhere he goes. Harrison's self-assuredness soon turns to panic when Kate informs him that she is due to telephone Inspector Harris to confirm that she has returned home safely; the intruder fears that he will be taken into custody if Harris learns of his presence. Kate explains that she had been at a meeting at Parklands and, from a discussion with one of the doctors there, has deduced that Harris and Harrison are in fact brothers; the inspector changed his name when Giles was admitted to the mental hospital, hence his apparent lack of a birth certificate. Harrison explains that the inspector would visit him every month at Parklands, and often regaled him with details of his work with the police. When Kate confronts the deranged Harrison about the murder of her father, he explains that killing him was necessary because the costumed man had reminded him of Christmas. His twisted logic is lost on the increasingly horrified Kate.

Powell attempts to contact Kate from his office at New Scotland Yard, but the ringing telephone puts Harrison into a state of alarm. Now desperate for help, she pushes past him in an attempt to grab the phone receiver, but Harrison intercepts her movement and stabs her repeatedly with a knife. Draping tinsel over her corpse, he returns the receiver to its cradle.

Having heard the altercation on the other end of the line, Powell deduces that Kate is in danger and drives to her aid. Discovering her dead body on the floor of her apartment, he immediately suspects Inspector Harris's involvement and rings up the Special Squad to ask if they were aware of his whereabouts. He is informed that the inspector has never left his apartment that evening, baffling Powell as it suggests that Harris cannot have been responsible for Kate's murder in spite of his belief to the contrary. A police constable spots Harrison fleeing the scene, leading Powell to chase the murderer into a vehicle scrapyard. A game of cat and mouse then plays out, which ends only when Harrison connects a car to the electricity supply with a set of jump-leads; once the sergeant attempts to open the car's door in search of his target, he is fatally electrocuted.

Back at his basement lair, Harrison brings the imprisoned dancer some food. When she asks to be untied in order to eat it, Harrison grudgingly obliges, but he becomes visibly uncomfortable when she asks him why he isn't celebrating the early hours of Christmas Day. Noticing his anxiety about the subject, the dancer continues to jog his childhood memories of the festive season; when he is suitably distracted, she hits him over the head with a wooden beam. Her escape attempt is short-lived, however, when Harrison reveals that he has locked the room's door... and he is the only one with a key. He rages at what he perceives to be her ingratitude: he had allowed her to live until Christmas Day, a fact which he believes reflects his generosity. Confused, she asks why he hadn't killed her earlier, to which he irrationally replies that she is to be his personal sacrifice to everything negative that Christmas represents to him. Realising that her life is in greater danger than ever, she attacks him once again, this time getting access to the key and rushing out of the flat.

The dancer breathlessly ascends flight after flight of stairs in her attempt to evade Harrison, but the killer is in hot pursuit. Discerning her growing exhaustion, he steadily stalks after her, eventually attacking with a length of chain. But he underestimates the dancer's agile dexterity; dodging him several times, she steps aside as her assailant eventually entangles his chain with the stairway banister, pitching himself over the top and plummeting to the floor far below. Still in a state of terror, the dancer descends to his prone form... only to discover that Harrison has somehow managed to survive the fall. Venomously, he grabs for her throat and furiously begins to strangle her.

A flashback to Harrison's childhood then plays out, where he remembers a visit from a costumed Santa Claus – his own father – and watches in awe as the jolly figure hands out presents at a Christmas party. He appears particularly transfixed with one specific gift, a Swiss Army penknife, and wields it to the amusement of the party guests. Later, his mother sends him to bed, but the young Giles unexpectedly discovers his father (still dressed as Santa Claus) in an extramarital tryst with one of the visitors. When his mother stumbles onto the scene, Giles's father retaliates angrily and pushes her down a flight of stairs, also striking the young Harrison himself (in spite of the youth's fruitless attempts to defend himself with his new penknife). Thus the murderer's seemingly unfathomable motivations are now finally revealed.

Back in the present day, Inspector Harris finds himself unable to sleep. He gets up and blearily wanders his apartment in the early hours of Christmas morning. Spotting the festively-wrapped package that had been delivered earlier, still bearing the 'do not open till Christmas' notice, Harris discovers on closer examination that the gift is also sporting a tag which informs him that it is 'a Christmas present from your loving brother'. Curious, he unwraps the parcel to find a music box within. A tiny, revolving Santa Claus figure rotates to the sound of 'Jingle Bells'… only for the box to detonate a concealed explosive moments later, killing Harris in the process.

At least on paper, *Don't Open Till Christmas* almost appears to employ a direct inversion of *Christmas Evil*'s central premise: in this scenario, a young child is traumatised by an early encounter with a Santa Claus-costumed figure which forever alters their view of the holiday season, and the confrontion has a deleterious effect on their mental health in general. Yet whereas *Christmas Evil*'s protagonist Harry Stadling had desired to assume the mantle of Santa Claus for himself, striving to somehow correct his tainted memories of Christmas with an idealised version of the festive season that never truly existed, in *Don't Open Till Christmas* the serial killer follows the rather more logical trajectory of responding to his formative upset by seeking to eliminate the figure of Santa Claus and all that the yuletide celebrations represent. For Giles Harrison, the central themes of Christmas – such as mutual goodwill to all people, and generosity of spirit – are merely a smokescreen for the psychological damage that he believes the season is capable of, given the nature of his own adolescent distress. This is largely where the similarity ends, however, as in its execution *Don't Open Till Christmas* has much more in common with the low-budget pandemonium of *To All a Goodnight* than the thought-provoking cult classic *Christmas Evil.* From its opening point-of-view shots, complete with obligatory heavy breathing, through to the inscrutable closing sequence (why would the lead officer in a crime investigation delay opening a box containing potential key evidence just because of a cryptic gift tag?), the film is a morass of narrative illogicalities, baffling continuity inconsistencies, and prohibitively cheap production values.

Part of the reason for the disjointed nature of *Don't Open Till Christmas*'s narrative can be explained by the major behind-the-scenes difficulties which took place during the film's production. The director's chair, though initially occupied by lead actor Edmund Purdom, was vacated by its incumbent and then assumed by a variety of others before the film eventually reached the editing stage. As Alan-Bertaneisson Jones has explained, this troubled process ultimately led to a fragmentary viewing experience even in spite of the best efforts of the production team to turn the available footage into a commercially viable feature film:

> Purdom (whose only turn in the director's chair this was) didn't last the course, so the film's writer, Derek Ford (a director of mainly sexploitation movies like *The Wife Swappers*) took over the reins for a while, before

Al McGoohan [the pen name of director/screenwriter Alan Birkenshaw], on whose story Ford's script was based, took over, directing 'additional scenes' that apparently included all the gory slayings. Editor Ray Selfe, a bit of a British cheapjack exploitation movies Jack-of-all-trades, had the unenviable task of trying to bring all of this together coherently into a saleable finished product - though his success in this respect is dubious to say the least, and this film is definitely both pretty 'bad' and decidedly 'ugly'.[2]

Whether due to the film's tortuous production problems or simply the eccentricities of Derek Ford's screenplay, *Don't Open Till Christmas* presents a seemingly-endless profusion of plot discrepancies which are mystifying in their inconsistency. When London is supposedly gripped by panic at the fact that someone is indiscriminately killing anyone in a Santa Claus outfit, why don't the police simply advise people to stop wearing these costumes until after the murderer has been apprehended? If Inspector Harris is really so concerned that people will realise that he is related to his mentally ill brother, why doesn't he change his surname to something more radically different than simply his original name minus its final syllable? Given Harrison's misogynistic behaviour elsewhere in the film, why does he choose to spare Sharon's life when he has a perfect opportunity to murder her? When veteran officer Powell discovers Kate's body, why doesn't he respect police protocol and dust her apartment's telephone receiver for fingerprints, rather than contaminating the whole crime scene in the way that he so casually does? Similarly, when Powell calls his colleagues to ask about Harris's whereabouts, why do they report that the inspector has never left his apartment all evening when Harris had accompanied Kate to a restaurant only a few hours earlier?

These contradictions are merely the tip of the iceberg in a film where a character inexplicably attempts to comfort his grieving girlfriend by tricking her into attending a glamour photoshoot wearing the same style of costume that her father had been murdered in only days earlier, and indeed the viewer's time may be better spent trying to identify what elements of the plot actually do make sense rather than the abundance of incidences that don't.

The highly erratic continuity is only one aspect of the film that has come in for criticism, however. The many gruesome Santa Claus slayings frequently play next to no part in the main plot, hardly ever being mentioned in any real detail by the main characters after the hunt for the serial killer has been set in motion, which rather underscores their late-in-the-day inclusion (as 'Al McGoohan'/Alan Birkenshaw's grafted-in 'additional scenes') as well as their increasingly gratuitous nature as the narrative unfolds. In this film, we soon discover, chestnuts are far from the only things to be found roasting on an open fire, and anyone unfortunate enough to be found wearing a Santa Claus suit is fair game for Harrison's inventive taste in slaughter. Though the film's humdrum pacing and overall quality may have left horror fans unimpressed, it did at least offer plenty of variety when it came to the murders which take place throughout. As Daryl Loomis has opined, 'if there's something good to say about *Don't Open Till Christmas*, it's the creative kills. Our Santa slayer doesn't have one specific mode of offing good Saint Nick; he utilizes everything from a pedestrian stab to the gut and a spear through the mouth, to an old fashioned castration. It's truly a gruesome bit of nastiness. [Dick] Randall was one of the true kings of exploitation and here, in one of his final productions, he lets it all hang out. By no means does that make the film good; indeed, it's barely watchable. But if you like the idea of the red stuff making Santa's suits even redder, you'll get it here in spades'.[3] Yet even the creative array of executions on display has done little to impress enthusiasts of either the Christmas slasher subgenre or horror cinema in general, given the lack of both genuine suspense or plausible outcomes. For a film to truly generate a sense of fear or trepidation in its audience, it must (in most cases) present a tangible feeling of realistic credibility and/or apprehensive foreboding, leading viewers to become engaged with the unfolding events that they are witnessing. With *Don't Open Till Christmas*, as Brian W. Collins has argued, the singular lack of this capacity to scare would lead to a largely insipid viewing experience: 'Even by slasher standards, it's incredibly low on logic. I can chalk some of the blame up to the post production troubles (such as when a character is released from being a suspect, despite the fact that we never saw him being brought in for questioning in the first place), but the killer seemingly has GPS on all of London's Santas, as a couple of them are killed despite going into unexpected areas'.[4]

Don't Open Till Christmas is packed full of peculiar creative choices, including the opening title sequence (which features a burning ornament of Santa Claus, presaging not only the murders but the means of Inspector Harris's abrupt death at the conclusion), the presence of British cult favourite Caroline Munro in an inexplicable musical number, and a supremely bland original score which singularly fails to engender either portentous suspense or any kind of Christmas-oriented ambience. Similarly, the very poor lip synch makes it palpably noticeable where additional dialogue has been dubbed into the film – especially when an actor's mouth doesn't actually move when the aforementioned lines are spoken. The acting varies from the mediocre to the decidedly stilted, with Purdom's beleaguered police inspector arguably coming out on top, while the uneven plot logic (as well as the identity of the killer becoming fairly obvious from a reasonably early point in proceedings) drains any real tension from the film's attempts at calculated distractions. As John Kenneth Muir has observed, 'the slasher paradigm is a basic template, and in adhering to it, *Don't Open Till Christmas* fails to offer much by way of surprises or innovation. There are red herrings aplenty, including Inspector Harris and Kate's boyfriend, Cliff, and the film suffers from a plethora of dull, repetitive P.O.V. heavy breathing stalk shots, now *de rigueur*. [...] *Don't Open Till Christmas* is one of the dullest slasher pictures made in the 1980s, in part because it consists of almost nothing but a series of death sequences involving St Nick'.[5] Taken together, these shortcomings ultimately combine to bring about that which is perhaps the most damning of all failings which can befall a truly effective horror movie; not that the feature is simply substandard, but that it is often stultifyingly dull. Todd Martin is not alone amongst commentators in criticising the film's monotony and overall lifelessness: 'I really didn't care who the killer was or why he was doing it, and I cared even less once we get both of these questions answered as his true identity is very easy to deduce and his motive is moronic and pointless. I think that the biggest problem with the movie is that it is just boring. We go from pointless scene to pointless scene over and over again and the only thing that managed to keep my attention was the fact that we are treated to scenes of various people dressed like Santa Claus getting whacked in between (and believe it or not even those got a little redundant and old after a while)'.[6]

One further major problem with *Don't Open Till Christmas* (and a drawback which it shared with the earlier *To All a Goodnight*) is that beyond the central motif of Santa Claus-costumed victims facing their demise, the film is singularly lacking in any real sense that its events are taking place during the festive season. We see Christmas shoppers in busy London streets, a police band playing upbeat music and even a fancy-dress party to mark the coming of the holidays, and yet none of these sequences can do much to dislodge the general feeling of urban gloominess which permeates much of the production. While *To All a Goodnight* had remained reasonably likeable on account of its many cheerful moments of ineptitude, here the dreary backstreets, dimly-lit rooms and occasional (usually doomed) attempts at gritty realism mean that *Don't Open Till Christmas* has less in common with other Christmas horror movies of the time and greater similarity to the tonal quality of *Pieces* (Juan Piquer Simon, 1982), a lurid cult slasher thriller which had also been produced by Dick Randall and Steve Minasian as well as featuring Edmund Purdom in one of the main roles. Yet if the film has retained any kind of following, it has largely been on account of the curiosity value of its British location filming which has distinguished it from the better-known American entries in the Christmas horror subgenre that were emerging onto the market at the time. As Noel Murray has explained, this has lent *Don't Open Till Christmas* a rather idiosyncratic quality, meaning that the film 'combines the polite reserve of the BBC drawing-room mystery with the creative impalings of American exploitation. [...] The killer is revealed to the audience about two-thirds of the way through the film, but even that fails to drive the plot any closer to a conclusion. Instead, there's more killing, and more harrumphing by the authorities and the citizenry alike. "Are you any nearer to solving these dreadful Santa Claus crimes?" someone politely asks at one point. It's a question that remains damnably unanswered, even now'.[7]

Among the film's other oddities are the conspicuous absence of actor Nicholas Donnelly as Dr Bridle, one of the staff members at Parklands mental hospital, who – though he is listed in the film's end credits and is mentioned by Kate in the dialogue – never actually appears on camera. However, several members of the production team can be seen in a range of cameo roles throughout; screenwriter Derek Ford appears as the ill-fated Santa Claus giving out presents at the circus, composer Des Dolan was cast as a detective police constable, and producer Dick Randall makes an uncredited appearance as one of the guests at the Christmas party which culminates in Kate's father being skewered with a spear. Randall and his fellow producer Steve Minasian can also be heard as radio presenters at various points in the film.

Due to its low-budget nature, *Don't Open Till Christmas* was largely ignored by reviewers at the time of its initial release, and its reputation amongst film buffs and horror cinema fans has remained uniformly low ever since. Scott Aaron Stine's opinion of the film is essentially representative when he states that '*Don't Open Till Christmas* is drab British tripe about a masked killer doing away with every Old Saint Nick that crosses his or her path. [...] Although murders are plentiful, the killings are rote and the gore just as lame. (Stab wounds spurting H.G. Lewis-style red paint seems to be a favorite of the effects people.) [...] Don't open until Christmas? Hell, why bother taking it out of the box at all'.[8] Other appraisals have only rarely been any more favourable, with critics drawing attention to the film's numerous production deficiencies and narrative flaws. Dave Jackson, for example, notes that 'plot lines simply stop. Characters end their screen time on cliffhangers. Scenes intercut madly and seemingly without thought. The closest thing to a male lead exits through a restaurant door and never returns. More screen time is given to a rotating Scotland Yard sign than some of the main characters. The final scene is hysterical and tumbles in out of nowhere. [...] *Don't Open Till Christmas* is both mind-numbing and exhilarating. It is an incomprehensible train-wreck trapped in a frustrating dream that goes nowhere, but with all the sleaze, boobs, and bloodied Santa outfits, I forgot to care'.[9]

Today, *Don't Open Till Christmas* is largely forgotten amongst the general public, though it retains a certain amount of tacky charm for die-hard followers of slasher horrors or obscure Christmas movies. Though few would deny that the visual trappings of the holiday season are in distinctly short supply throughout the film, for any devotees of features which have plumbed the depths of quality to the point that they have reached the category of 'so bad it's good' there is plenty in *Don't Open Till Christmas* that will raise a knowing smile. As Bill Gordon observes, even given the quagmire of overly-familiar tropes and flawed attributes on display the film still offers up a few nuggets of interest: 'The whole project is shot on the cheap. The soundtrack is your simplistic 80s synth that is played even over normal conversations. The holiday theme is never fully exploited and plot points are never fully explored and/or dropped entirely (one gets the sense that the cutting room floor was very messy). [...] All is not lost. The movie sidesteps slasher conventions by featuring mostly male victims (females are threatened/killed also, but statistically they have a better chance of surviving here). There's even a shock death of a main character that I had expected to make it to the end'.[10] However, there is little doubt that in the present day, as had been the case in the year of the film's release, *Don't Open Till Christmas* has been eclipsed by other similarly-themed features which have come to be regarded more favourably by audiences – most especially the contentious and widely-reported *Silent Night, Deadly Night* which was released at around the same time. In particular, the odd deficiency of festive ambience and the antagonist's balefully deranged schemes amalgamate to produce a confused sense of threat that is never properly realised; even the conclusion makes little sense. (As Harris does not appear to be present during his brother's childhood Christmas trauma, why exactly does his younger sibling seek to damage the inspector's career – or plan to murder him outright? The discrepancy is never resolved.)

Though it was something of a miracle that *Don't Open Till Christmas* saw the light of day at all, given its well-publicised production issues, in the eyes of some commentators the behind-the-scenes difficulties have actually come to appear more interesting than the content of the film itself. As Derek Botelho has stated, while the movie may fit securely within the recognised generic framework of the slasher horror, including the subgenre dealing specifically with Christmas-oriented settings, it is its essentially uninvolving nature which has ultimately led it to be disregarded by so many: '*Don't Open Till Christmas* just isn't very good, or even interesting. It's another bandwagon film to ride the coattails of many holiday themed horrors kicked off by *Black Christmas* and *Halloween* in the 70s. [...] So let's see, we have a murderer killing men dressed as Santa Claus and a mystery about who did it. Sounds OK on paper right? Well tear that paper up and flush it in the toilet. How can you have a mystery that is so dull and uninvolving? That is the cardinal sin of this script. Nothing is really going on in terms of the investigation, you don't know much about the characters, and so in turn you can only care so much'.[11]

Though unlikely to ever sneak its way onto many cineastes' list of the finest Christmas features of the eighties, or indeed ever to be in contention for the most effective seasonally-themed horror films, *Don't Open Till Christmas* is a genuine enigma: poor on too many levels to be considered recommended viewing, and yet so entertainingly inadequate in such a plentiful range of aspects that it seems almost churlish to disregard it entirely. Perhaps most unflatteringly of all, some reviews – such as the detailed commentary offered by the *Anything Horror* website – have claimed that any aspects of the film which have come to be regarded with a positive appraisal may have actually come about less through deliberate planning on the part of the creative team, and more as a result of sheer blind luck:

> The kill setups aren't suspenseful and everything has a very bland feel to it. Some of the kills are decent [...] but there's definitely not enough here that will keep your interest. [...] *Don't Open Till Christmas* is disappointing on so many levels. The writing is lazy and was extremely repetitive; the editing is choppy and confusing; the soundtrack is terrible and in many places not synced up to people's mouth's moving; and the f/x are about as 'special' as red-coloured water flowing from a wound. Some reviewers have called this plot 'intricate and confusing', but that makes it sounds like it was done on purpose.[12]

Don't Open Till Christmas might not be Britain's greatest contribution to festive cinema, and it is difficult to argue against the fact that the overall impression left by the film is 'cheap' rather than 'cheerful'. As a cult curiosity, it just about passes muster on account of its disjointed but quirky appeal, but as an example of eighties horror it is considerably less successful. Lacking the thematic depth of *Christmas Evil,* the popular appeal of *Silent Night, Deadly Night* and the slightly askew charm of *To All a Goodnight,* over the years *Don't Open Till Christmas* has gradually become one of the lesser-known features of 1980s festive cinema, and in truth its diminishing profile has been lamented by few. Worth seeking out only by those nostalgic enough to appreciate its slightly mesmerising concoction of unintentional humour and deadly earnestness in dimly-lit locations scattered around the murkiest areas of Margaret Thatcher's London, the film presents Christmas horror at its most maladroit and wilfully surreal.

REFERENCES

1. Jeremy Wheeler, '*Don't Open Till Christmas*', in *AllMovie*, 2011.
    <http://www.allmovie.com/movie/dont-open-till-christmas-v14335/review>

2. Alan-Bertaneisson Jones, *Fright Xmas* (Milton Keynes: AuthorHouse, 2010), p.108.

3. Daryl Loomis, '*Don't Open Till Christmas*', in *DVD Verdict*, 16 December 2011.
    <http://www.dvdverdict.com/reviews/dontopentillchristmas.php>

4. Brian W. Collins, '*Don't Open 'Til Christmas*', in *Horror Movie a Day*, 3 November 2009.
    <http://horror-movie-a-day.blogspot.co.uk/2009/11/dont-open-til-christmas.html>

5. John Kenneth Muir, *Horror Films of the 1980s* (Jefferson: McFarland, 2007), p.384.

6. Todd Martin, 'Film Review: *Don't Open Till Christmas*', in *Horror News*, 24 June 2015.
    <http://horrornews.net/75698/film-review-dont-open-till-christmas-1984/>

7. Noel Murray, '*Don't Open Till Christmas*', in *The Onion A. V. Club*, 21 December 2011.
    <http://www.avclub.com/review/dont-open-till-christmas-66833>

8.   Scott Aaron Stine, *The Gorehound's Guide to Splatter Films of the 1980s* (Jefferson: McFarland, 2011), p.110.

9.   Dave Jackson, '*Don't Open Till Christmas*', in *Mondo Exploito*, 18 December 2014.
        <http://mondoexploito.com/?p=11571>

10.   Bill Gordon, '*Don't Open Till Christmas*', in *Horror Fan Zine*, 12 December 2011.
        <http://horrorfanzine.com/dont-open-till-christmas-edmund-purdom-1984/>

11.   Derek Botelho, '*Don't Open Till Christmas*', in *Daily Dead*, 26 December 2011.
        <http://dailydead.com/review-dont-open-till-christmas-dvd/>

12.   Anon., '*Don't Open Till Christmas*... Don't Open at All!', in *Anything Horror*, 22 December 2011.
        <http://anythinghorror.com/2011/12/22/holiday-horrors-dont-open-till-christmas-1984/>

7

Comfort and Joy (1984)

Kings Road Entertainment/Lake (Comfort and Joy) Ltd.

Director: Bill Forsyth
Producers: Davina Belling and Clive Parsons
Screenwriter: Bill Forsyth

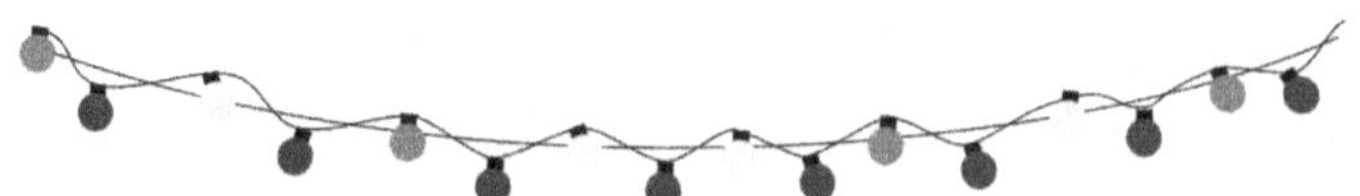

While *Don't Open Till Christmas* may not have epitomised the British film industry's finest hour when it came to producing festive cinema, the United Kingdom would be home to rather more memorable yuletide movie-making during the 1980s. Bill Forsyth's *Comfort and Joy*, an unabashedly Scottish take on Christmas, would prove to be almost as unorthodox in its approach as Edmund Purdom's film had been, albeit in very different ways. Rarely would a festive feature involve such disparate elements as relationship breakups, underworld violence or indeed the appearance of such distinctively Scottish delicacies as Barr's Irn-Bru and fish and chips. Yet precisely because of its whimsical creative peculiarities, *Comfort and Joy* has come to be regarded as one of the most noteworthy of Christmas movies to emerge from the United Kingdom during the eighties, ensuring that the film has retained a certain degree of longevity – at least in the country of its production, where it is regarded with affection thanks to its appealing central performances and inimitable rendering of inner-city Glasgow during the holidays.

Although *Comfort and Joy* is now generally acknowledged as one of the lesser-known entries in director Bill Forsyth's wider filmography, its atmospheric urban setting and conspicuously unsentimental approach to the festive season has made it something of an underrated feature of his celebrated 1980s output. At the time of its production, Forsyth had risen to public attention for his comedy-drama *That Sinking Feeling* (1979), followed by high school romantic comedy *Gregory's Girl* (1981) and his Highlands-set satire *Local Hero* (1983). The latter two films had earned him BAFTA Awards and nominations – a winning streak which would continue with *Comfort and Joy*. Although this festively-situated film would not secure him quite the same level of unanimous critical praise as that which had accompanied the release of *Gregory's Girl* and *Local Hero*, it would nonetheless still exhibit Forsyth's characteristic flair for pithy dialogue, engaging characterisation and the ability to transform seemingly-mundane environments into the settings for extraordinary events.

While British cinematic output focusing upon the festive season is considerably less plentiful than that of the United States, the country has nonetheless produced numerous features which celebrate traditional Christmas values – sometimes in contemporary ways which elevate social realism beyond the traditional fantasy aspects which exemplify so many entries in the genre. While the characters in *Comfort and Joy* share a certain amount of the domestic anxieties which had driven other British Christmas films such as, for instance, *The Holly and The Ivy* (George More O'Ferrall, 1952), it has become better known for its subversion of seemingly mundane happenings into the realms of the adventurous or even wantonly surreal, echoing the more fanciful approach of movies such as *Bush Christmas* (Ralph Smart, 1947) and arguably the UK's greatest contribution to Christmas cinema, Brian Desmond Hurst's *Scrooge* (1951). In its acute awareness of festive tropes, usually demonstrated through its adept undermining of such conventions, *Comfort and Joy* expertly creates a warm sense of goodwill through its unusual juxtaposition of light comedy and surprisingly profound commentary on human life in the postmodern age. The movie is congruent with Greg Metcalf's assertion that the festive 'films of the 1980s – and perhaps their audiences, as well – simultaneously reject as illusionary, yet lovingly embrace, the Christmas conventions'.[1] As a result, Forsyth's feature has become amongst the most prominent of all Scottish films to deal with the festive season; in combining warm-hearted seasonal geniality with a singular lack of yuletide schmaltz, it gleefully turns on its head the audience's expectations of what to anticipate from contemporary Christmas cinema. The result, as Alonso Duralde has put it, is 'one of [Forsyth's] best films; *Comfort and Joy* gives us a bleak and rainy Scotland that's nonetheless suffused with Christmas spirit, with soggy Santas everywhere. [...] Balancing laughs, sweetness, and an underlying tone of melancholy, Forsyth concocted one of the all-time great Christmas movies'.[2]

Life seems good for Glaswegian disc jockey Alan 'Dicky' Bird (Bill Paterson). He has a regular job with a popular Glasgow radio station, Metrosound (albeit in a somewhat unglamorous time slot), and a beautiful long-term girlfriend named Maddy (Eleanor David) with whom he has lived for several years. Something of a free spirit, and a kleptomaniac to boot, Maddy is a serial shoplifter; an illegal pastime which makes Alan distinctly edgy. Shortly before Christmas, he follows her around a city centre department store and watches uncomfortably as she pilfers one item after another – always evading the eyes of the shop's security team. On the drive home, he voices his disquiet at her copious thefts as she rifles through a seemingly-endless stash of purloined novelty items and clothes – not only is he worried about her breaking the law so casually, but they are more in need of basics such as food than the sundry knick-knacks she keeps procuring. But the carefree Maddy brushes off his concerns with a breezy kiss, alarming him as she comes close to burning the upholstery of his cherished BMW convertible with a lit cigarette.

Later, they enjoy a romantic evening together as they decorate their apartment's Christmas tree with some of the copious electric lights that Maddy has acquired during previous shoplifting sprees. Following dinner, Alan is perplexed to discover his girlfriend collecting together all of her possessions into a cardboard box; nonchalantly, she announces that she has decided to leave him and move out of the flat. Shocked at this sudden development, Alan asks why she has come to such an unexpected decision, but Maddy simply replies that she had made her mind up a while beforehand – she just hadn't found an appropriate juncture to bring the matter up. However, she is resistant to any discussion about her choice; a few moments later her friend George (Ron Donachie) arrives with some associates to transport her possessions elsewhere. Alan watches in stunned shock as boxes, furniture and clothes are moved out of the apartment, leaving the living area virtually stripped bare by the time Maddy has finished.

Dumbfounded at the abruptness of Maddy's departure, to say nothing of her refusal to talk about her decision to leave him, Alan is devastated at his turn of fortune. Arriving at work the next morning for his six o'clock shift, the consummate professional 'Dickie Bird' adopts his trademark upbeat radio persona, masking his heartache with a flurry of light-hearted banter. During a traffic report Alan calls up one of his close friends, hospital surgeon Colin (Patrick Malahide), and arranges to meet him in the mid-morning after his radio shift is over. Colin duly arrives at Alan's near-empty apartment and commiserates with his friend; not only has Maddy removed herself from her ex-partner's life, but it is clear that she has left him with next to nothing. Attempting to comfort Alan, Colin explains that his friend has been handed a rare opportunity: the chance to start his life anew in early middle-age. However, the distraught DJ finds it difficult to engender much enthusiasm; not only is he heartbroken, but he has little more than a random scattering of furniture and some Christmas cards to his name. Before departing on medical business, Colin gives further food for thought by pointing out that as Maddy was such a force of nature, Alan is now free to live his own life unfettered by being in thrall to such a strong personality. But all of this comes as cold comfort to the newly-single radio presenter.

Alan goes shopping for some kitchen utensils and other essentials, but finds himself emotionally stung by the sight of happy couples enjoying each other's company in the festively-decorated shopping area. Reluctant to return to his empty home, he decides instead to take a meandering drive through the city – even given its heavy congestion due to the pre-Christmas traffic. On his travels, he spots an attractive woman (C.P. Grogan) working in a 'Mr Bunny' ice-cream van. Exchanging smiles with her, Alan has the impulsive idea to follow the van: a journey which takes him deeper into the city, and then over to a suburban area. Eventually the vehicle draws into the roadside to serve customers, and Alan is there soon afterwards to order an ice-cream cone… only to be faced not by the good-looking woman, but her male co-worker Trevor (Alex Norton). Unfazed if slightly disappointed, he pays for the cone and walks back to his car. Before he can reach it, however, he spots the approach of a number of masked men who suddenly attack the Mr Bunny van. Shattering windows and slashing tyres, the assailants are only narrowly fought off by Trevor and his associate Charlotte when (implausible though it may seem) they repel their onslaught by squirting various sauces and essences at them. Alan is fearful when one of the masked attackers makes a grab for him… but soon discovers that the man has recognised him as 'Dickie Bird' and wants to make a request for the next morning's radio show. He only lets the bewildered DJ go when Alan agrees to play a song by Dean Martin or Annunzio Mantovani during his forthcoming shift at the station.

As the crowbar-wielding aggressors speed off in a car, Alan hurriedly returns to the Mr Bunny van to offer assistance. However, Trevor politely but insistently refuses any help, claiming that everything is under control. Refusing to even discuss the nature of the attack, he hurriedly drives off in the now less-than-roadworthy van, leaving Charlotte to desperately gather together its contents as confectionery spills out onto the streets as the vehicle crawls off into the sunset. Alan watches the bizarre sight with a mixture of disbelief and quiet amusement. Finally returning to his empty flat for a solitary glass of whisky as night falls, the psychologically drained DJ fantasises about Maddy's return – an outcome that he knows to be vanishingly unlikely.

The next morning, Alan is heading for work when he opens his car door to discover that the seats have been covered in upturned ice-cream cones. An anonymous note pointedly informs him to keep his silence about the previous day's events, or else face unwelcome consequences. Eventually getting to the Metrosound studios, he follows a tortuously long-winded session of recording advertising jingles with a visit to the station's jittery managing director, Hilary Sandeman (Rikki Fulton). Alan suggests a change to the format of his show, proposing that he play down the usual light entertainment content in favour of hard-hitting documentary features. He claims that there are stories taking place in Glasgow that deserve proper investigative reporting, rather than his usual blasé accounts. However, the traditionalist Hilary believes that the change of heart can be explained by a mid-life crisis triggered by Alan's split from Maddy, and is reluctant to tamper with the existing arrangement of the popular Dickie Bird show. Seeming supportive, Hilary approves the newly-motivated DJ's request for the use of a tape recorder to produce the mooted documentary. But as soon as Alan has left the office, Hilary telephones the legal department for information on when 'Dickie' Bird's employment contract is next due to be renewed... including an enquiry about whether it contains a sanity clause which can be invoked.

Alan wastes little time in making a start on his documentary, but his initial recordings are vague and directionless. After a brainstorming session at his apartment produces little that is of value, he decides to visit Colin for some much-needed emotional support. Explaining that

Maddy's departure has laid bare his own personal inadequacies, Alan tells Colin that he envies the doctor's harmonious domestic existence; everywhere he looks, he sees families in happy homes and realises all too gnawingly that he has only an empty flat and no partner to support him. Colin and his wife suggest that Alan stay with them overnight rather than return to his barren apartment; the despondent DJ is touched when Colin's young daughter requests a song on his next radio show, feeling that he still has some kind of purpose.

Following another hopelessly optimistic dream of Maddy's return, Alan finds that all he has to really look forward to the next morning is a fresh recording session for more banal promotional jingles. The radio station receptionist passes on a phone message from a mysterious Bruno Culinari, stating that he will meet Alan in the building's car park at six o'clock that evening. However, when he appears on schedule Alan discovers a 'Mr McCool' ice-cream van in the car park, which drives off as soon as he arrives. Realising that he is being prompted to follow, the puzzled DJ drives off in pursuit and finds himself drawn further into the city until they eventually arrive at a shadowy distribution depot. Though the cloak and dagger treatment has left Alan feeling more than a little nervous, he is met by the disarmingly affable Bruno (George Rossi), his brother Paolo (Peter Rossi) and associate Renato (Billy McElhaney). They usher him into the factory nearby, where he is introduced to the company's mannerly owner, Mr Luigi McCool (Roberto Bernardi). Speaking in heavily accented English, though often lapsing into Italian, Mr McCool tells Alan that the ice-cream trade in the city is highly territorial, with companies respecting unwritten rules regarding the areas that they conduct business in. 'Mr Bunny', otherwise known as Trevor, has thrown this delicate balance into disarray by trading wherever he pleases. In spite of Alan's protestations that he has no affiliation with Trevor, and has only met him briefly on one occasion, Mr McCool has decided that the hapless DJ will act as an intermediary between the two rival companies in an attempt to broker peace. Making it clear that he will not take 'no' for an answer, Mr McCool explains that Alan, being a neutral party in the dispute, will be the best hope for the ice-cream community to avoid an escalation in hostilities.

After an impromptu guided tour of the factory and an autograph request, a now-thoroughly-baffled Alan heads for home. Though distracted by these bewildering new developments, he accidentally discovers a stash of Maddy's clothes, photographs and other belongings underneath his bed, which brings a fresh wave of regret and loneliness washing over him. Nonetheless, Alan presses ahead in his efforts to respect Mr McCool's request; on his radio show the following morning, he issues an enigmatic statement requesting that Mr Bunny meet him again at the same place that they last encountered each other. The station's technical staff seem flummoxed by his cryptic declaration.

Pausing only for a quick trip to his dentist, Roderick Nisbet (Ronald McCleod Veitch), for some oral surgery after the show has concluded, Alan heads off to the suburban location where he first met Trevor and Charlotte. After searching the area, he eventually comes into contact with the Mr Bunny van more literally than he would have preferred when, taking a sharp corner, his BMW collides with it. Trevor reacts in frustration, pointing out that the van was his reserve vehicle – all of the others in his fleet are currently being repaired, meaning that he is officially out of action.

Sadly for Alan, his own car has been even more badly damaged in the crash. Trevor invites him back to his depot in the city so that they can talk in more detail.

Alan finds the Mr Bunny headquarters to be a thoroughly professional operation; mechanics are working round the clock to get Trevor's fleet of ice-cream vans back in action. Joining Charlotte in the main office, Alan explains to Trevor the basic outline of Mr McCool's offer to enter into negotiation talks. However, the owner of Mr Bunny has no interest in accepting the apparent olive branch; he tells Alan that McCool has no real intention of opening a dialogue and, in truth, has only one true aim – the complete eradication of Trevor's business. Alan is nonplussed at the deadly seriousness with which Trevor describes the hard-fought autonomy of his company, seeing the conflict as an unnecessarily violent battle over something so seemingly trivial as confectionery sales, but eventually he manages to broker a deal by which Mr Bunny and Mr McCool will come around the table for business talks over territorial claims. As he leaves, watching in pained displeasure as his beloved BMW is coarsely panel-beaten by Trevor's rough-and-ready team of mechanics, he ham-fistedly tries to ask Charlotte out on a date only to meet with a decidedly aloof response.

Though his car's appearance is now less than ideal, Alan calls Mr McCool from a public phone box and is summoned to one of the family's restaurants. There, he meets with McCool himself and discusses the result of his earlier conversation with Trevor. The ice-cream boss presses Alan for the location of the Mr Bunny depot, but he firmly refuses the request, stipulating that he wants to remain neutral in order to safeguard any future negotiations. Mr McCool divulges that Trevor is part of the Marinetti family, who are renowned in the area for their fish and chips business. The two families were once close, but a rift grew between them when Trevor decided to make an unprecedented move into ice-cream sales. When McCool discovers that Trevor had gifted Alan a tub of ice-cream during his visit to the Mr Bunny depot, he becomes elated – a taste of his competitors' product will surely reveal the origin of Trevor's supplies. But quickly surmising that they want him to take sides in their dispute, Alan decides to depart, parting with the words that he will continue to act as an intermediary for them only if he is allowed to remain strictly uninvolved with the disagreement between Mr McCool and Mr Bunny.

Unfortunately for Alan, McCool is dissatisfied with his principled attempts at impartiality. During the night, some of his operatives break into the ill-starred DJ's flat and steal the tub of Mr Bunny ice-cream from his kitchen freezer. Perturbed by Mr McCool's unexpected escalation of events, Alan issues a warning via his radio show to indirectly warn Trevor that treachery is afoot. His ambiguous message mystifies managing director Hilary, who calls Alan into his office for an explanation. Believing the presenter to be delusional, he insists that Alan begin attending consultations with psychiatrist Fergus Forrester (Arnold Brown). However, the meeting is of limited use; Forrester believes that Alan's seemingly-strange behaviour has been triggered by the sudden loss of Maddy, whereas Alan has come to realise that the breakup may actually have been beneficial in helping him discover who he really is. Later, he visits Colin during his hospital rounds and fills him in on the latest developments in the ice-cream dispute. The surgeon cautions Alan that he is using his new mediation role as a distraction from dealing with the issue at hand; his distress at Maddy's unexpected departure. Colin then buoys his friend's confidence by introducing him to long-term patient Miss Wilson (Elspet Cameron), an elderly lady who is thrilled to meet 'Dickie Bird' as she listens to his show every weekday morning. It becomes clear that although she has been in hospital for months, Alan's broadcasts help her to feel as though someone is there for her, mitigating her obvious loneliness.

At night, Alan returns to the Mr Bunny depot and warns Trevor that McCool has stolen his tub of ice-cream, allowing him to identify its source. Laughing, Trevor tells him that the knowledge will do his competitors little good; all of his ice-cream has been made using McCool's own recipe – acquired by the Mr Bunny company on account of the fact that Charlotte is actually Mr McCool's daughter. Alan becomes exasperated at the continued obfuscation, wondering aloud how he can help end the dispute when both sides are resorting to such curiously devious methods, but is interrupted when a gang of McCool's family and workers burst into the depot carrying large wooden mallets and crossbows. Trevor is livid, believing that Alan has betrayed his confidence and led his enemies right to his door. His protestations of innocence falling on deaf ears, Alan only just manages to escape the violent carnage with his health intact as the gang of McCool aggressors proceed to demolish the factory and everything in it. His car fares less well, however, as an incensed Trevor and several of his workers clobber its bodywork with iron bars in revenge for his 'treachery'. Needing no second bidding, Alan speeds away from the premises as fast as he can.

Reaching the sanctuary of Colin's home, Alan joins his friend and his family for breakfast as he recounts his narrow escape the previous evening. Stupefied by recent events, he points out that he has little hope for the world if deadly feuds can flare up over something as trifling as a family disagreement between ice-cream and fish and chip companies. One of Colin's daughters points out that she likes the sound of ice-cream and chips, but the thought of such an unlikely culinary combination seems to bring about a fresh idea in Alan. Later, while briefly visiting the radio station to request that a greeting for the hospital-bound Miss Wilson be broadcast by his weekend shift counterpart, he overhears a recipe (in a recorded segment by Hilary's wife) which mentions an unusual Chinese delicacy: ice-cream fritters. Now sparking a major new notion in Alan's mind, he calls up his bemused manager at home and requests a copy of the recipe as soon as possible.

Stopping at a Chinese supermarket in the city for some additional supplies and information (and to give an autograph to a young fan in the process), Alan returns to his now thoroughly wrecked BMW to discover a cluster of Trevor's associates standing watch over it. They tell him that their boss requests his presence, but a newly-chipper Alan replies that this is just as well because he is similarly in search of an audience with Trevor. Travelling together, he drives to what remains of the Mr Bunny headquarters: now little more than an assorted collection of wreckage. Thoroughly deflated by what has happened, Trevor informs Alan that – in the harsh light of day – he bears him no ill-will for what has happened. But Alan sees an opportunity and tells him to phone Mr McCool in order to arrange a meeting. Trevor is confused by the DJ's renewed enthusiasm, but considers that he has nothing left to lose and thus reluctantly agrees to his request.

McCool consents to a summit and chooses a temporarily-closed milk bar on the outskirts of the city as the venue. The two parties meet in the car park; Alan is amused, after all the recent violence, to discover that McCool is actually Trevor's uncle. They listen sceptically as Alan outlines his proposition: the two families can end their constant feuding by adopting the new product that he is introducing – ice-cream fritters. By using Trevor's family's fish and chip shops to supply the batter and the McCool retail operation for the ice-cream as well as the distribution of the fritters via their fleet of vans, the product – which is hugely popular in China – could end their dispute as well as potentially generating a huge profit. Alan demonstrates the technique behind the creation of the fritters at one of Mr McCool's ice-cream parlours, and although initially unconvinced the entire clan quickly become enraptured by the idea when they discover that it is a workable scheme: both hot and cold, simultaneously bitter and sweet, the fritters have the capacity for year-round sales. As the room erupts into excited activity, with the various family members discussing pricing strategies and possible different flavours, Alan decides to strike while the iron is hot and negotiates a healthy percentage of the sales – along with the costs involved in repairing his ramshackle BMW.

In an epilogue, Alan is covering an afternoon radio show on Christmas Day. The studio is deserted, with the exception of himself and a single technician. Served up with Christmas pudding, Alan explains that he has volunteered to take over the shift from a colleague in order to give them a chance to spend more time with their family. Yet the reminder of his own singleton status seems to be less painful in the light of recent events. Raising a plastic cup of Irn-Bru in a toast to his unseen listeners, Alan dedicates his broadcast to anyone who is tuning in alone – wherever they are, they are all welcome to join in his party, celebrating the holiday season in the sometimes strange but often wonderful city of Glasgow.

If *Comfort and Joy* succeeds as a Christmas film, it is largely because it so beautifully underplays its festive allusions. While audience members know that the action is taking place in the approach to the holiday season – decorations are on display, shops are full of gifts, and so on – Forsyth takes great care never to allow the Christmas trappings to distract us from the lives that are playing out irrespective of the time of year. Unexpected relationship breakups are just as painful in December as they are at any other time of the year (if not more so), lonely people are even more acutely aware of their solitary status, and life carries on irrespective of whether we want to involve ourselves in the festivities or not. But by that same token, we see the vital importance of the support of friends in action, Alan's emotionally raw but nonetheless essential decision to move on with his life post-Maddy, and many of the exquisitely-observed eccentricities of modern society which help to make life worth living. For a film which is exclusively filmed in and around an often moodily-lit urban locale, the enormous warmth and amiability of *Comfort and Joy* make the film arguably one of the most life-affirming Christmas movies to emerge from the United Kingdom; there are few other productions which could treat the festive season quite so matter-of-factly and yet emerge as such an inspirational beacon of goodwill and common humanity.

Central to the appeal of *Comfort and Joy* is Bill Paterson's assured performance as the likeable Alan 'Dickie' Bird. A local radio personality who has grown dissatisfied with his lot in life, we see – in the days following his breakup with Maddy – a gradual but sincere transformation in his character as he come to realise just how much he means to the people of Glasgow. Paterson's radio voice is pitch-perfect; whether in Alan's regular broadcasts or the monotonous recording sessions for asinine advertising jingles, it is easy to imagine waking up in the city to the sound of his mellow tones. From repeated requests for autographs and song requests through to his touching encounter with the infirm, hospital-bound Miss Wilson, we see a slowly dawning realisation taking place within Alan that his professional achievements have not been as humble as he initially feared, and that he has had an impact upon his community which is more wide-ranging than he had previously considered. As Adam Lippe has observed:

> That's one of the unique things about *Comfort and Joy,* that it comes out of a time (1984), where there weren't hundreds of radio stations and TV shows. If a DJ says something on the air, most of the locals are likely to hear it, because there isn't much else they'd be listening to. That's a key point to Alan's survival; he knows he actually reaches people. He isn't reduced to a tiny niche on the Internet, as most of us are now. Alan's level of celebrity is just as small as the town he's famous in; which is how he gets away with being a local personality, but not above being overly disrespected. He may know his place, but he's not a conformist who's just worming his way through what he's been given, just as Forsyth did with his movies. And like most Forsyth films, *Comfort and Joy* is warm and gentle without being cloying or maudlin. And it somehow avoids off-putting levels of cynicism. Like Alan, it's just the right amount of not important.[3]

Widely recognised not just across the UK but elsewhere in the world, Paterson had – by the early 1980s – firmly established himself as a talented actor both on stage and screen. Active in theatre from the late sixties, and on television from the seventies onwards, he made the transition to cinema in the early eighties: in 1984 alone he was to have roles in films as varied as Roland Joffé's *The Killing Fields* and Malcolm Mowbray's *A Private Function* alongside his lead performance in *Comfort and Joy*. Much to his credit, he manages to construct Alan into a sympathetic character without ever rendering him as mawkish or self-pitying; while the DJ's distress over his romantic split (and the resulting devastation of his domestic environment) is palpable, Alan's subsequent voyage of self-discovery becomes entertaining precisely because he is such a sociable and engaging figure. Bearing in mind that one of the key themes of Christmas cinema is its focus upon the potential for individual transformation during the festive season, Alan's situation within a contemporary urban setting and the modest nature of his epiphany mean that *Comfort and Joy* is all the more uplifting on account of its self-effacing pragmatism. As Frederic Brussat and Mary Ann Brussat note, 'in this spunky Scottish drama, filmmaker Bill Forsyth has fashioned an intimate, whimsical and engaging story that makes many deft observations about human nature. The director describes the film as "a serious comedy about a man who has one of those weeks when everything goes wrong". Alan finds a new lease on life by sheer luck and a few crucial moral decisions. *Comfort and Joy* is perfect viewing for a New Year's celebration, and will put an indelible smile on your face'.[4]

The film's central conflict was controversial at the time of release, at least in Scotland, due to the way in which it mirrored the events of Glasgow's violent 'Ice-Cream Wars' which rocked the city throughout the 1980s. This turf war between rival criminal gangs, which was alleged to have involved a trade in illegal narcotics and stolen goods which were sold via a 'front' of confectionery retail in ice-cream vans, was considerably more violent than the out-of-left-field events of *Comfort and Joy* would suggest. Forsyth's film captures the absurdity of something so seemingly innocent as ice-cream vans being used as an instrument of underworld conflict, while transposing the fictional (and somewhat more fanciful) Culinari/Marinetti family feud onto the much more brutal reality of the organised crime which had driven the true life bloodshed. In so doing, he makes good use of his inner-city Scottish setting to capture both the local flavour and the nation's trademark biting wit; as Roger Ebert has remarked:

> Bill Forsyth's *Comfort and Joy* [is] one of the happiest and most engaging movies you are likely to see this year, and it comes from a Glasgow director who has made a specialty out of characters who are as real as you and me, and nicer than me. [...] I suppose a movie could be made about American ice cream wars, but the truck drivers would all be movie stars. Forsyth finds ordinary people. The star of *Comfort and Joy* is Bill Paterson, an offhand, pleasant chap who is always polishing his car. The other actors – including the Italians who own Mr McCool – are the kind of low key caricatures that Forsyth knows how to draw so carefully that they never go over the edge.[5]

The charm of *Comfort and Joy* is further enhanced by the many astute in-jokes and humorous observations which crop up throughout the action. In pursuing the Mr Bunny van, having become beguiled by the beautiful Charlotte, Alan unwittingly follows a 'rabbit' down a (literal) tunnel to an uncertain destination in a manner similar to the protagonist of Lewis Carroll's *Alice's Adventures in Wonderland* (1865).

The radio station where Alan works, Metrosound 261, is a subtle parody of Radio Clyde 261 (a famous Glaswegian radio station which broadcast on 261MW until the end of the eighties). Throughout the film, we hear a constant stream of tedious radio news reports about a giant panda's supposed pregnancy and untimely demise, satirising the traditional slow-down of hard news commentary over the holiday season. There is even an appearance of the old Marx Brothers 'sanity clause' gag, which is dusted down and reused by Hilary in a phone conversation with his secretary. However, there is just as much pleasure to be had in the highly perceptive portrayal of the actions and interactions of the characters, whether in the incessant bickering between the McCool siblings, the Mr Bunny sound engineers (responsible for recording the vans' ethereal chimes) running for cover as the depot is invaded, Trevor sounding deadly serious as he waves a stuffed rabbit mascot around in the air with every point he makes, or indeed the slow-motion destruction of Alan's prized 1983 BMW 323i Baur TC convertible (made all the more excruciating when we see Trevor's mechanics spreading the contents of their dinner over its bonnet, including the inevitable presence of a bottle of Barr's Irn-Bru, during their 'repairs').

There are many other aspects of *Comfort and Joy* which anchor the film securely in its country of production. Mark Knopfler, who composed the atmospheric original score, was better-known at the time as the guitarist, singer and songwriter in Dire Straits, a Scottish rock band which he had co-founded in 1977 in collaboration with his brother David Knopfler. As a result, dialogue which echoes lyrics from Dire Straits songs can be heard throughout the film; at one tongue-in-cheek moment, Alan even mentions the band's name. Irn-Bru, a carbonated soft drink which originated in Scotland and which has become famous for its bright orange colouring, is often described as 'Scotland's other national drink' (second only to whisky). The beverage is widely consumed throughout Scotland and in the wider United Kingdom, and true to form we see it cropping up – in A.G. Barr's unmistakeably-styled glass bottles – at various points in the film, most notably during Alan's closing toast during his Christmas Day broadcast. *Comfort and Joy* also benefits hugely from a brief but very welcome supporting performance from Scottish comedy legend Rikki Fulton in the role of twitchy radio boss Hilary Sandeman. Widely acclaimed throughout Scotland as one half of the comedy duo Francie and Josie (along with fellow Glaswegian Jack Milroy) for many decades, throughout the 1980s and early 1990s Fulton was also well known for his starring role in *Scotch and Wry*, an irreverent BBC Scotland sketch show which became a staple of Hogmanay viewing throughout the country. All of these seemingly-disparate creative elements come together in an unusually satisfying way, constructing a patchwork of Scottish culture which is never less than entertaining. As David Denby has described, Forsyth makes full use of his native country to provide a dynamic and appealing environment in which to situate the film's action: 'The movie is muted and also (God forgive me) a bit provincial, yet there are Forsythian details that keep one involved. The courtly ice-cream mobster makes threats and ceremoniously assures Alan that he speaks "for the entire ice-cream community"; the trucks of the gangster's rival dealer (Mr Bunny) emit gently tinkling noises – aural stardust in the gray Glasgow evening'.[6]

Bill Paterson is accompanied by a uniformly impressive cast of co-stars, some of whom had worked on previous Forsyth features. Clare 'C.P.' Grogan, a former member of the

Scottish Youth Theatre, appeared in Forsyth's *Gregory's Girl* in 1981, but was perhaps more prominent within popular culture as the lead singer of new wave band Altered Images. She would later feature in the BBC's science fiction comedy series *Red Dwarf* as Kristine Z. Kochanski, before the role was assumed by Chloe Annett in later years. (She was often credited under the name 'C.P. Grogan' on account of the fact that when she joined the actors' union Equity there was already an existing member on their records with the name of 'Claire Grogan'.) Also a veteran of Forsyth productions, having appeared in his earlier film *Local Hero*, actor Alex Norton would become a familiar face to viewers in Britain and beyond; with roles in films of international significance, including *Braveheart* (Mel Gibson, 1995) and *Les Misérables* (Bille August, 1998), he also achieved great popularity as police Detective Chief Inspector Matt Burke in STV's long-running crime drama *Taggart* (1983-2010) between 2002 and 2010. Additionally, Patrick Malahide impresses as Alan's empathetic surgeon friend Colin. At this point still best-known for his many television performances (including appearances in high-profile series such as *The Professionals, Minder, The Sweeney* and *The Black Adder*), he would appear more frequently in cinematic roles from the 1990s onwards. Considered collectively, this ensemble of actors helped to make *Comfort and Joy* a memorably entertaining viewing experience, as Robert Horton has explained:

> You can sense that Forsyth and his marvelous group of actors are working with the merest wisps of plot. What they capture so beautifully are the details that make up the lives of these characters – ways of talking, of eating, of exchanging concern. Absurd elements always find their way into Forsyth's movies, but he keeps them

from being stupid by never violating the dramatic underpinnings of his situations. [...] Although the title seems to be ironic at the beginning of the film – when even the birds are mistreating Bird by bombing his car – at the end we see that a lot of people have found comfort and joy along the way. And the title is also a perfect description of the film's effect on an audience. It's not a blockbuster, it won't win Oscars, but *Comfort and Joy* is going to make you feel just fine.[7]

It is undoubtedly more on account of the film's feel-good factor, rather than its downplayed festive trappings, that it has established itself as an entry in the genre of Christmas cinema – albeit one that is too often unjustly overlooked, on account of its fairly limited release at the time of its first appearance in theatres. The legacy of *Comfort and Joy* has been further impaired by its proximity to Forsyth's earlier, highly successful comedies, which have overshadowed its reputation within his broader filmography. In some ways, this situation was exacerbated by a distinctly lukewarm reception from reviewers following its initial emergence into cinemas, as Samantha Lay explains: 'With two stories spliced together, each battles for narrative supremacy and as a consequence neither the Dickie Bird mid-life crisis strand nor the ice-cream war drama are properly developed. Considered deeply flawed by critics, the film did not do well at the box office. Forsyth claims the film was widely misunderstood, that the public expected the humour of his earlier films, and that its deeper concern, a critique of war in general, was entirely missed'.[8] While indeed the deeper nuances of the film – that conflict can sometimes become so deeply rooted that it begins to result in irrational outcomes which appear incomprehensible to those uninvolved in the nature of the feud – are often discounted in favour of the immediacy of the comedic content, its generic complexity and sheer curiosity value have made certain that Forsyth's movie continues to persist in the cultural consciousness, if even in a fairly low-key manner. As Graeme Clark notes, 'scripted by the director Bill Forsyth, *Comfort and Joy* was another in his line of gentle Scottish comedies with a line in quirky humour. Coming across like a Raymond Chandler mystery if Philip Marlowe had been a Glaswegian DJ in the eighties, [...] *Comfort and Joy* is an unlikely but warm-hearted shaggy dog story of a Christmas film that is underrated by many, and although it doesn't quite reach the heights of *Gregory's Girl* or *Local Hero*, there's no shame in that'.[9]

Though the film considers carefully and sympathetically the nature of the human condition, especially in the heightened emotional environment of the festive season, Forsyth deliberately restricts its scope to regional rather than national concerns. While *Comfort and Joy* may offer an appealing snapshot of Glasgow's abundant cultural tapestry, it is not a movie that addresses the wide-ranging socio-cultural issues affecting Scotland at the time, or attempts to explore the complexities of the Caledonian Antisyzygy; as Svet Atanasov has observed, the director's approach is as unconventional as it is stylistically distinctive:

> Whether or not one enjoys the film depends largely on one's response to this flavor. It is genuinely Scottish and it mixes comedy and drama in a very unorthodox way. There are segments in which the comedy is fairly straightforward, but elsewhere it is actually used to highlight the absurdity of a reality that people like Dicky no longer seem to recognize. So there is a unique balance between comedy and drama that may not appeal to everyone. Because Forsyth does not attempt to produce any profound observations about his

country and its unusual contrasts, the film remains light and brisk. It also helps that Forsyth does not judge the main characters and the logic behind their actions; on the contrary, he embraces them and their logic because with the type of dilemmas they face many of the clichéd rights and wrongs become absolutely irrelevant.[10]

Comfort and Joy profits immensely from Chris Menges's highly skilled cinematography, offering sweeping views of Glasgow's urban and suburban areas in ways which alternate between the familiar and the powerfully elaborate. Later to win the National Society of Film Critics Award for Best Cinematography for his work on Roland Joffé's *The Killing Fields*, Menges ensures that the visual aspects of Alan Bird's municipal travelogue around Glasgow are never less than varied. While Mark Knopfler's well-judged score adds an air of metropolitan sophistication to proceedings, it is the adroitly-realised dialogue of Forsyth's screenplay which establishes itself as one of the film's most noteworthy features. The script would win Forsyth the Best Original Screenplay award at the BAFTA Awards in 1984, and certainly the playful candour of the characterisation and the swiftness of the narrative pace were both creditable in their realisation. Yet such was the screenplay's alternative nature, not all commentators have been fully convinced of its approach; as James Wolcott remarked, 'when the movie is functioning simply as a character sketch, it's funny and original. Sadly, its plot mechanics swerve it astray. [...] At the end of *Comfort and Joy*, Alan doesn't have Maddy or the Mr Bunny girl, and yet he raises his cup in Christmas cheer, mildly lonely, mildly pleased. The movie is a little too complacent in its deary eccentricities'.[11] Indeed, the lack of a traditionally happy ending may have surprised those who were expecting the film to adhere more closely to the conventions of festive cinema's golden age, but in truth Forsyth seems more concerned with delineating the simple pleasures of human existence than he is with providing some kind of unrealistic life goal for the underdog Alan to achieve. For it is in pursuing these small but important enjoyments that every life finds worth, as is the cultivation of a desire to help and support others – a theme which recurs throughout the film in everything from Colin opening up his home to his heartbroken friend to Alan's unexpected importance to the life of Miss Wilson, who listens every morning to his show without fail as though the pair shared an active friendship. As Vincent Canby has pointed out, the film works best when Alan's emotional journey is lightened by humorous observations and unexpected happenings: 'Most of *Comfort and Joy* is about Alan's efforts to break loose, not only from his relationship with Maddy but also from his public personality as a disk [sic] jockey. He longs to become a serious radio journalist. [...] One good running gag throughout *Comfort and Joy* is the series of radio newscasts that punctuate Alan's holiday week – "No less than eight Christmas truces are in jeopardy today". There's also some very funny business about a radio station's celebrity look-alike contest in which few of the contestants look like anybody but themselves'.[12]

As Forsyth underscores the potential for radio to be simultaneously a powerful medium of news dissemination and a mouthpiece for an entire community (including its more outré elements), so too does he emphasise the capacity of the mass-media to reshape perceptual expectation and act as a kind of mirror for its listeners. Alan is only too keenly aware of the fact that in spite of achieving peace between the two warring Italian families (something that would have been impossible without his professional reputation), his own domestic situation has not changed – and yet, in his personal development over the few days since Maddy's departure, he has grown and matured in ways that he had never anticipated. There is no denying, as Michael Brooke has put it, that 'for all the appearance of success (even securing a financial stake in the new ice-cream fritters venture), at the end [Alan] is still left alone in a largely deserted radio station on Christmas Day trying to whip up a party atmosphere – presumably aimed at others in his situation'.[13] However, the truth is more complex that it may appear at face value. While it is true that Alan is forced to face Christmas alone, he chooses to do so not by wandering an empty apartment in self-absorption but rather by volunteering to cover a colleague's shift so as to allow his workmate to spend the day with his family. The altruism of this gesture aside, it could be surmised that Alan's part in resolving the ice-cream dispute – and his numerous experiences along the way – have awakened the character to a new degree of community awareness, encouraging him to play a greater part in the lives of his listeners by buoying their sense of wellbeing, and knowing reciprocally how his own self-worth is bolstered as a result. Thus he completes his journey of personal transformation over the Christmas period which, though scarcely Scrooge-like in the scope of its reconfiguration of his character, nonetheless improves his general outlook as well as his emotional state, leaving him optimistic for the life that lies ahead.

While *Comfort and Joy* is an offbeat and life-enhancing slice of British Christmas cinema, its comparatively low profile outside of the UK has led to its current reputation as something of a hidden gem of festive movie-making. Though its critical status has improved over time, the film has still to establish itself as a classic of the genre, but its recent releases on home entertainment formats and discovery by new audiences may aid in its endurance, enhancing its significance in the popular cultural consciousness. As Philip Concannon has commented, there is much to recommend a viewing of the film even in spite of uncertain critical perceptions amongst reviewers:

> Bill Forsyth's *Comfort and Joy* underwhelmed at the box-office on its release in 1984 and has subsequently been out of circulation for many years, which partly explains why it has never achieved the acclaim and cult status enjoyed by his other early '80s crowdpleasers *Gregory's Girl* and *Local Hero*. Another reason, however, might be because this comedy-drama doesn't feel as fully formed as those previous efforts, and it suffers from an underpowered narrative engine. Much of the charm and lightness of touch that defines Forsyth's work is still evident, though. [...] There are cherishable moments throughout. Paterson nails the persona of the genial but frustrated radio host whose celebrity status seems largely confined to children, the elderly and ice cream salesmen. Forsyth's ear for dialogue, meanwhile, is as finely tuned as ever, and his elegant direction gives the film a real cinematic sheen, with the scenes shot at night being particularly striking.[14]

Scotland may not be the first country to spring to mind when Christmas films are mentioned, and yet *Comfort and Joy* was to become one of the most innovative and original festive movies to emerge in the genre during the eighties. With its invigorating mixture of off-the-wall comedy and restrained domestic drama, the film has continued to impress audiences with its heartfelt message of mutual co-operation and shrewd exploration of the potential for personal improvement and transfiguration. Forsyth had created one of British cinema's most fascinating tributes to the festive season, and in the process had paid homage to a vibrant and creatively diverse Scottish city in a manner which celebrated its people as much as its culture. *Comfort and Joy* may not be the most conformist of Christmas films, but it is certainly among the most sincere in its artistic aims... and if nothing else, a movie which concludes with a character toasting his audience while holding a gently bubbling plastic cup of Irn-Bru is very difficult to actively dislike.

REFERENCES

1.   Greg Metcalf, '"It's (Christmas) Morning in America": Christmas Conventions of American Films in the 1980s', in *Beyond the Stars: Plot Conventions in American Popular Film*, ed. by Paul Loukides and Linda K. Fuller (Bowling Green: Bowling Green State University Popular Press, 1991), 100-13, p.104.

2.   Alonso Duralde, *Have Yourself a Movie Little Christmas* (Milwaukee: Limelight Editions, 2010), p.59.

3.   Adam Lippe, 'The Mob's Ice Cream Enforcer: A review of *Comfort and Joy*', in *Examiner.com*, 27 April 2012. <*http://www.examiner.com/review/the-mob-s-ice-cream-enforcer-a-review-of-comfort-and-joy*>

4.   Frederic Brussat and Mary Ann Brussat, '*Comfort and Joy*', in Spirituality and Practice, 10 July 2003. <*http://www.spiritualityandpractice.com/films/reviews/view/6087*>

5.   Roger Ebert, '*Comfort and Joy*', in *The Chicago Sun-Times*, 23 October 1984.

6.   David Denby, 'She is Woman', in *New York Magazine*, 15 October 1984, 81-83, p.83.

7.   Robert Horton, '*Comfort and Joy*', in *What a Feeling!*, 6 July 2012 [1984]. <*https://eightiesmovies.wordpress.com/2012/07/06/comfort-and-joy/*>

8.   Samantha Lay, 'Bill Forsyth', in *Contemporary British and Irish Film Directors: A Wallflower Critical Guide*, ed. by Yoram Allon, Del Cullen and Hannah Patterson (London: Wallflower Press, 2001), 97-99, p.98.

9.   Graeme Clark, '*Comfort and Joy*', in *The Spinning Image*, 2004.
<http://www.thespinningimage.co.uk/cultfilms/displaycultfilm.asp?reviewid=969>

10.   Svet Atanasov, '*Comfort and Joy* Blu-ray Review', in *Blu-Ray.com*, 29 February 2016.
<http://www.blu-ray.com/movies/Comfort-and-Joy-Blu-ray/144453/#Review>

11.   James Wolcott, 'Small Comfort', in *Texas Monthly*, December 1984, p.188.

12.   Vincent Canby, '*Comfort and Joy*: Comedy from Scotland', in *The New York Times*, 10 October 1984.

13.   Michael Brooke, '*Comfort and Joy*', in *BFI Screen Online*, 2006.
<http://www.screenonline.org.uk/film/id/514458/index.html>

14.   Philip Concannon, '*Comfort and Joy*', in *The Skinny*, 29 February 2016.
<http://www.theskinny.co.uk/film/dvd-reviews/comfort-and-joy>

8

Gremlins (1984)

Warner Brothers/Amblin Entertainment

Director: Joe Dante
Producer: Michael Finnell
Screenwriter: Chris Columbus

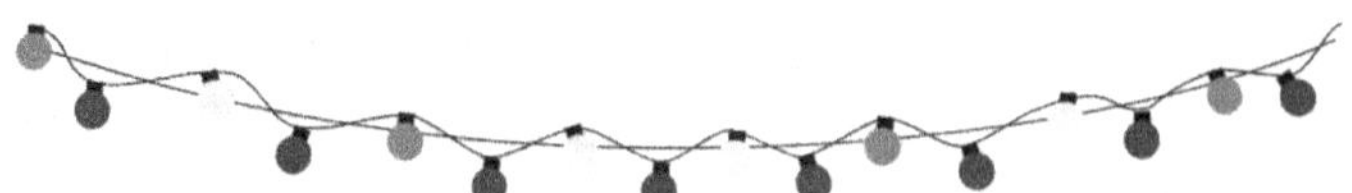

Famously one of the most anarchic films to emerge into 1980s popular culture, *Gremlins* has established a firm reputation for itself amongst the most revolutionary Christmas movies of the decade. The movie has become well-known for its high degree of profitability at the box-office, its provocative content, and indeed for the emergence of a huge wave of merchandising tie-ins which accompanied its release. But these were just some of the reasons why *Gremlins* came to be so firmly embedded within the popular culture of the eighties; along with Ivan Reitman's *Ghostbusters*, Martin Brest's *Beverly Hills Cop* and Steven Spielberg's *Indiana Jones and the Temple of Doom*, it has become immortalised as one of the blockbusters which would typify the American popular cinema of 1984.

Gremlins has also become an interesting curiosity on account of the film's efficient amalgamation of various genres, often in unpredicted but startlingly effective ways. The Christmas setting which permeates the movie's action is deliberately subverted to become a backdrop for the nefarious deeds of the rebellious title characters, while classic Christmas themes are hinted at only to be turned completely on their head later in the film – and in a way which thoroughly confounds viewers' presumptions. Aiding in this ingenious bait-and-switch strategy was the artistic combination of globally-renowned producer Steven Spielberg, widely known at the time for his evocation of small town America facing extraordinary circumstances (as seen in films such as *Close Encounters of the Third Kind*, 1977, and *E.T.: The Extra-Terrestrial*, 1982), and director Joe Dante, whose creative approach to anarchic onscreen mayhem in independent features had brought him to Spielberg's attention. Dante had already established cult credentials through helming features such as horror spoof *Piranha* (1978) and werewolf-themed thriller *The Howling* (1981). Though active in directing from the late 1960s, he would not truly emerge into the annals of popular culture until his cinematic work from the late seventies onwards; in later years he would solidify his position as a cult director, most especially in the 1980s through the release of films such as *Explorers* (1985), *Innerspace* (1987) and *The 'Burbs* (1989). All of these films would toy dexterously (albeit in wildly dissimilar ways) with the genre boundaries separating science fiction, fantasy, comedy and horror. Also the director of a section of the speculative fiction anthology *Twilight Zone: The Movie*, produced by Spielberg and John Landis in 1984, Dante would direct numerous features for television over the years, including several episodes of popular TV series.

The collaboration of Spielberg and Dante would prove to be a productive and creatively fruitful one, and a partnership which was to produce one of the darkest

Christmas comedies ever to surface in mainstream cinema. Popular with audiences and attracting a wide range of critical responses from reviewers (both at the time of release and in the present day), *Gremlins* would go on to become one of the most commercially successful films of the year, and raised the bar with regard to what could be expected from the increasingly flexible genre of Christmas cinema. As Adam Tyner has stated:

> *Gremlins* was Dante's first feature-length film for a major studio, with his closest brush in the studio framework up to that point being his 'It's a Good Life' segment in *Twilight Zone: The Movie*. With a budget barely breaking the $10 million mark, *Gremlins* wasn't a particularly pricey gamble even by the standards of the day. It opened on the same day as *Ghostbusters* and, despite not having a nearly comparable amount of hype behind it, managed to tally nearly $150 million domestically. That's before taking into account video sales and rentals, re-releases, foreign box office, and the extensive amount of merchandising and promotional tie-ins.[1]

One Christmas, amiable inventor Randall Peltzer (Hoyt Axton) is wandering a big city Chinatown district as he attempts to sell his goods to traders. Randall has a secondary objective to his visit, which is to find an unusual Christmas gift for his son, so he is intrigued when a young boy (John Louie) invites him to browse his family's store. Descending a flight of stairs to a dimly-lit basement shop, he discovers a treasure trove of unusual ephemera which is diligently watched over by the boy's elderly grandfather, Mr Wing (Keye Luke). After making an inept sales pitch for one of his own products, Randall finds himself entranced by a cuddly little creature named a Mogwai which is huddled away in the farthest reaches of the shop. Realising that the tiny being would make the perfect present for his son, Randall attempts to pay Mr Wing for the Mogwai. However, the elderly man refuses to part with it at any cost, stating that taking care of the creature would require great responsibility. Mr Wing's mind on the matter is made up, but his grandson knows that the family cannot afford to refuse Randall's offer of a cash payment and privately arranges to sell the Mogwai to him later. Receiving the little creature in a sturdy travelling case, Randall is given three vital instructions from the young boy which are crucial to the Mogwai's wellbeing: never expose it to sunlight or other bright lights, keep it away from water, and never allow it to be fed after midnight.

Back at Randall's home, the small town of Kingston Falls, snow has fallen and the municipal Christmas decorations are being hung around the neighbourhood. Randall's son Billy (Zach Galligan) finds his day has started with little in the way of festive cheer: his unreliable car is refusing to start, leading him to walk to work in order to avoid being late for his shift at the local Savings and Loan. Arriving just in time, he gets to his desk mere moments before his girlfriend, Kate Beringer (Phoebe Cates) – another clerk who works in the building – appears at his side with a petition. She is attempting to stop Ruby Deagle, a property rental agent and the town's most formidable busybody, from taking the lease away from a popular local bar on the grounds that it is a public nuisance. Shortly after, the intimidating Mrs Deagle (Polly Holliday) arrives in person, shoving her way through the queue of customers to accuse Billy's dog Barney of having destroyed one of her expensive imported Christmas garden ornaments. When Billy offers to pay for a replacement,

Mrs Deagle replies that money will not be necessary – what she really wants is Barney, who she intends to have euthanised. Billy is aghast at her cruelty, but Mrs Deagle doesn't realise that the young clerk has secretly brought his dog to work with him. Infuriated by Mrs Deagle's callousness, Barney springs out of his hiding place under Billy's desk and attacks his adversary, knocking her off her feet in the process. Though seemingly unharmed, Mrs Deagle plays up the assault to a farcical degree, bringing the branch's manager Mr Corben (Edward Andrews) and his bumptious assistant Gerald Hopkins (Judge Reinhold) racing to her aid. Billy is apologetic about Barney's actions, but his employer doesn't see the funny side of the situation – and nor does Mrs Deagle, who vows revenge on both the hapless worker and his dog.

Later, Hopkins approaches Billy in a local bar and tells him that he had only narrowly managed to avoid being fired on account of the day's earlier events; only Mr Corben's reluctance to dismiss a member of staff at Christmas had saved his job. Swaggering and self-important, Hopkins berates Billy for his lack of ambition, warning him that he expects to be manager within a few years and will be less tolerant than the job's current incumbent. He also points out that Billy has little chance of getting ahead when his modest post at the Savings and Loan is more or less all that is supporting his entire family, given the low sales generated by his father's unsuccessful inventions business. Billy is surprised to spot Kate serving tables, and she explains that she has taken on a second job at the bar. The arrogant Hopkins tries in vain to ask her out for dinner, but she is unimpressed by his audacity and leaves him in no doubt of her total disinterest in his pretensions.

Heading home, Billy arrives just in time to help his mother Lynn (Frances Lee McCain) with dinner... though it turns out that his father's time-saving kitchen gadgets have just the opposite effect than intended. Realising that Lynn seems upset, Billy enquires why she has become so unhappy – especially as the holiday season is fast approaching. She responds that Mrs Deagle had paid her a visit with some bad news. But her tearful story is interrupted when Randall arrives home, full of festive spirit. Billy's father brings the positive news that he may have sold supplies of one of his new inventions to a retailer (leading to a highly sceptical expression from his wife), and presents his son with a large, familiar-looking wrapped box. Cryptically, he explains that this is one gift that won't wait until Christmas to be opened. Billy finds his curiosity piqued by the strange present and gratefully receives it... though he is puzzled by his father's insistence that the lights be dimmed before the box is unwrapped. Randall is delighted by Billy's thrilled response to his new companion, and tells him that the little Mogwai has the name of 'Gizmo'. Lynn takes a photo of the family with Gizmo, but is alarmed when the little creature reacts in terror at the light of the camera's flash. Jogging his memory, Randall recounts the three vital rules necessary for the appropriate care of the Mogwai.

Billy finds his new friend to be responsive and sociable, and is especially fascinated by Gizmo's musical abilities – the diminutive creature trills along to music as well as singing of his own volition. The next morning, while doing battle with another of Randall's inventions (a fruit peeler/juicer, which sprays the entire kitchen with a liquidised orange), Billy receives the family Christmas tree from delivery boy Pete Fountaine (Corey Feldman). As Pete has become tired of wearing an unwieldy plastic Christmas tree costume while carrying out his duties, Billy offers to stash it in his room. Noticing Gizmo, Pete is enchanted by the little creature and asks Billy if he can hold him for a moment. However, when reaching for the Mogwai he accidentally topples a jar of water onto him, causing Gizmo to convulse in agony. Pete and Billy watch in fascination as a series of five furballs pop out of Gizmo's back... only to rapidly grow into other fully-formed Mogwai. Pete asks if he can have one of the newly-born group of creatures, but changes his mind when the Mogwai he chooses – which, unlike Gizmo, has a stripe on its head – tries to bite him. Billy is amazed at the little beings' ability to reproduce so instantly, but is disconcerted when he sees that Gizmo is crying in distress.

Telling Randall about this development, Billy notes that the newly-generated batch of Mogwai do not behave like Gizmo; they are more mischievous, and seem to have nominated the striped Mogwai as their leader. Though Billy worries about the fact that the younger creatures do not share Gizmo's docile, friendly nature, all that Randall can see is their commercial potential; if new Mogwai can be created simply by exposing one of them to water, they will have unprecedented capacity for mass-production, perhaps leading to a new merchandising craze for Christmas and beyond.

During the night, Billy hears the sound of whimpering from outside the house and is horrified to see his beloved dog Barney hanging from the porch on a string of decorative lights. The family are bamboozled at the question of who could have caused such cruelty – not least as Randall is certain that he had securely locked the front door before going to bed. Billy is certain that Mrs Deagle is behind Barney's mistreatment, given the way that she had threatened him previously, but Lynn is unconvinced. However, to ensure the distressed dog's safety Randall offers to temporarily take him to his mother's house on his way to an out-of-town inventors' convention, returning Barney only when Christmas has arrived.

The next morning, Billy takes one of the Mogwai to the laboratory of Roy Hanson (Glynn Turman), his old high school science teacher. There, he exposes the little creature to a minute amount of water, ensuring that yet more Mogwai are produced within a few seconds. Baffled by the tiny beings' amazing reproductive capacity, the analytical Mr Hanson asks if he can keep one of the Mogwai in the laboratory to enable him to run some tests.

Later, Billy meets up with Kate just as she is ending her shift at the bar. Together, they persuade an oddball, unemployed plough driver named Murray Futterman (Dick Miller) to leave the premises; spouting inebriated warnings about 'gremlins' turning machinery faulty, he eventually heads for home, but Kate convinces him to walk rather than drive when he is so clearly drunk. Accompanying Kate back to her own house, Billy is a little startled when she emphasises just how much she hates Christmas. Given her generally effervescent personality, the declaration takes him somewhat aback, but she recounts the loneliness and sadness which accompanies the festive season for too many people in society. Though confounded by her downbeat train of thought, Billy arranges to take her out on a date in a few days' time.

That evening, Billy notices that the new batch of Mogwai are behaving discontentedly and, checking that the time has not yet reached midnight, he heads for the kitchen to get them something to eat. When he feeds them some chicken, they devour it ravenously, but Gizmo refuses the offer of food.

Over at Mr Hanson's lab, the teacher is tying up his research work on the caged Mogwai in the early hours of the morning. But as he departs, he doesn't notice the creature reaching through the bars for a half-eaten sandwich nearby.

The following morning, which is Christmas Eve, Billy awakes to discover that each of the Mogwai (except Gizmo) have become encased in cocoons. When his mother asks if he has fed them after midnight, thus breaking the rules of their care, he replies that he had made sure not to do so… before discovering that his bedside clock has been unplugged from the wall-socket, meaning that he had incorrectly judged the time when he had fed them. The Mogwai under observation at Mr Hanson's lab has also become swathed in a cocoon, which is now completely filling its cage. The teacher conjectures that the creatures have entered a pupal stage, and are undergoing a change in form which will only become clear when they emerge from their cocoons.

Later in the day, Gizmo watches in horror as the other Mogwai begin to burst free from their cocoons in Billy's room. Meanwhile, the same thing happens in Mr Hanson's lab while he is taking a science class. Unseen, the transformed creature goes into hiding, which leads Mr Hanson to attempt to lure it out into the open with a bar of chocolate. By the time Billy arrives at the school, responding to an earlier phone call from Mr Hanson, he discovers the teacher lying dead on the floor with a hypodermic syringe lodged in his posterior (presumably in revenge for him having taken blood tests on the Mogwai the day beforehand). When Billy attempts to call for help, he is unexpectedly scratched when he reaches for the telephone on Mr Hanson's desk; the mutated creature escapes into the building's ventilation system before Billy can even catch sight of it. Retreating to the school's medical room to bandage the wound on his hand, he is again assaulted by the former Mogwai, which it seems has become altered into a vicious, malevolent imp – a Gremlin.

Back at the Peltzer household, Lynn becomes alarmed when she hears loud noises coming from Billy's room. Knowing that everyone else is out of the house, she realises that the only thing causing the disturbance is likely to be whatever has left the cocoons. Stopping to grab a kitchen knife, she quietly makes her way upstairs only to discover the remnants of the Mogwais' pupal shells. Billy calls home, but – before Lynn can hear his warning to leave the house immediately for safety's sake – the Gremlins cut the telephone line. When she returns to the kitchen, she is assailed by the malignant creatures from all quarters, forcing her to dispatch the invaders by resorting to shredding them in a blender, stabbing them with her knife, and even cooking one of them to death in her microwave oven. Another mutated Mogwai hides in the family Christmas tree until Lynn ventures close enough, then attempts to strangle her with a length of decorative garland. Only Billy's timely arrival saves her, as he is able to catch the Gremlin unawares and send it flailing into the room's roaring fireplace, where it burns to death. 'Stripe', the Mogwai with the distinctive facial streak, has been watching the demise of his followers from a distance; keen to avoid being next in line, he smashes through the living room window and races away.

Pausing only to drop his mother off with neighbour Dr Molinaro (John C. Becher) to have her wounds treated, Billy returns to the kitchen in search for any clues to Stripe's intended destination. While weaving through the carnage, he discovers Gizmo trapped in a laundry chute – having been thrown there by his vindictive offspring. Taking the upset

Mogwai with him in a canvas bag, Billy follows Stripe's footsteps in the snow, unaware that his father is trying to call home from the convention he is attending in another town. Billy's pursuit eventually leads to the town's YMCA, where he discovers that the main door has been smashed. Venturing further into the building, a game of cat and mouse ensues which eventually results in Stripe falling into the centre's swimming pool. The effect is immediate: smoke and flashes of light emerge from the water as Stripe begins to generate an entire army of Gremlins.

Billy attempts to warn the police of the danger that the town is now in, but Kingston Falls's Sheriff (Scott Brady) refuses to take his fantastic tale seriously. While he tries in vain to convince them of the truth, the Gremlins go on the rampage, inflicting havoc on the town and its citizens. Two early victims are Murray Futterman and his wife Sheila (Jackie Joseph), whose house is partially demolished when the Gremlins drive Murray's prized snow plough directly through the front door and into the Futtermans' living room. Others, such as the genial Mr Anderson (Harry Carey Jr) are attacked when the Gremlins lie in wait in unexpected places, such as inside mailboxes or electricity substations.

Eventually, with telephone calls coming in to the Sheriff's office from concerned residents, the grudging lawman and his deputy (Jonathan Banks) are forced to respond. They are unaware, however, that Stripe has pinpointed his next victim: Mrs Deagle. Tricking her into thinking that she is being visited by Christmas carollers, only to scare her senseless when the truth of their appearance is revealed, Mrs Deagle retreats into her house and bolts the door. She has no idea that the Gremlins have tampered with her assisted mobility stair-lift, and thus when she attempts to get upstairs she is unprepared for an uncontrollable lurch of acceleration which eventually sends her flying out of a window in the top floor of her house. The Sheriff's patrol car is passing just as the hapless Mrs Deagle plummets to the ground, dying on impact from the impact. While they try to digest this unanticipated sight, local man Dave Meyers (Joe Brooks), who performs as Santa Claus every Christmas Eve, is spotted being viciously attacked by a group of Gremlins. Unable to fully process the chaos that is breaking out all around his squad car, the Sheriff speeds off back to the station. However, he is unaware that a Gremlin has cut his brakes, causing a violent collision a few moments later.

Billy discovers to his amazement that, just for once, his dilapidated car is actually working. Driving off with Gizmo still in his bag, he turns on the car's radio just in time to hear the town's local broadcast station being wrecked by Gremlins during a phone-in show. Meanwhile, Kate is fending off an attack of the mutated Mogwais at the bar where she works; dozens and dozens of the savage little creatures are reducing the place to wreckage. As they drink, gamble and generally engage in an orgy of destruction, Kate accidentally discovers that they hate bright lights and uses the flash of a Polaroid camera to cut a path through the bar in order to make an escape. Billy arrives just as she runs free from the building, but when his car's ignition refuses to fire up the engine again they are forced to make a getaway on foot. Retreating to the Savings and Loan building where the pair work, they discover another scene of pandemonium: the entire place has been ruined by the Gremlins, with heavy damage evident everywhere. Kate dejectedly points out that she now has more than one reason to hate the festive season. When Billy asks what she means, she replies that when she was a child her father had died when trying to climb down through their home's chimney stack on Christmas Eve dressed as Santa Claus. Breaking his neck as he made the descent, his body had to be extracted by firemen, who discovered him still in costume with his arms full of holiday gifts.

As Randall heads home from his inventors' convention with Barney the family dog, Kate and Billy are stepping out onto Kingston Falls's eerily deserted main street. Fires and wreckage can be seen all around, along with many crashed and abandoned cars. The pair soon discover that the Gremlins have congregated in the town's cinema, where they are collectively engrossed in a screening of the Walt Disney Company's animated film *Snow White and the Seven Dwarfs* (1937). The usually-uncontrollable creatures are transfixed by the movie, even singing along to the musical numbers. While the Gremlins are temporarily distracted, Billy heads to the boiler room and deliberately starts a gas leak, then ignites a fire on the main floor of the cinema. He, Kate and Gizmo only just manage to escape the building before the gas ignites, killing all of the Gremlins inside as a result of the ensuing explosion.

Unfortunately for Billy and Kate, Stripe has narrowly managed to evade the blast as well; he had ventured over the road to a department store during the movie in order to raid its supplies of candy. Breaking into the store in pursuit, the pair soon discover the errant Gremlin making a getaway on a skateboard. Splitting up, Kate and Gizmo head off in search of the building's lighting controls while Billy remains on the trail of Stripe. Only just managing to avoid death when the malevolent sprite begins firing circular saw-blades and crossbow bolts at him, Billy looks on in horror as Stripe then attacks with a chainsaw. But as Kate has now broken into the electricity control panel in the store's offices, she brings the building's lights up to full intensity, forcing Stripe to retreat further into the shop.

Randall is just arriving back in the town, aghast at the widespread turmoil which meets him, when Barney jumps out of the car and runs at full speed into the department store in search of Billy. Stripe, meanwhile, is heading for a garden display containing a decorative water fountain. Knowing that the Gremlin intends to create yet another army of its fellow creatures, the injured Billy continues to give chase but is halted when he faces a hail of bullets; Stripe has acquired a handgun from one of the store displays. As the Gremlin covers himself in water, ready to generate a new wave of mutated Mogwai, Gizmo arrives in a toy car and throws open the shop's ceiling shutters just as dawn is breaking. Randall and Kate arrive as sunlight streams into the room, melting the agonised Stripe as he is exposed to the bright radiance.

Later on Christmas Day, with all trace of the Gremlins now gone the television news are reporting that mass hysteria and rioting have been the cause of the vast amount of damage that has engulfed Kingston Falls. Self-delusion is the order of the day as the malevolent creatures are quickly forgotten, chalked up to the public imagination. Now safe in the Peltzers' living room, the family and Kate are surprised by the sudden arrival of Mr Wing. Disparaging at the carnage that has been wrought by the Mogwai, he has come to collect Gizmo and return him to the safety of his shop. Admonishing Randall, he says that it is clear to him that Western society is not yet capable of providing the responsibility required to care for these creatures, but – when it becomes clear that Gizmo has become fond of Billy – he softens his tone and adds that perhaps some day Randall's son may be ready to provide the guardianship which is needed. As Mr Wing heads off into the night, with Gizmo in one hand and a gift from Randall in the other (another of his useless inventions: the 'smokeless ashtray'), the audience is reminded that the next time something goes wrong with any of their appliances, it may be an idea to check for Gremlins before thinking about calling for a repairman.

One of the most immediate things to emerge from a viewing of *Gremlins* is just how dexterously Dante manipulates audience expectation with regard to the film's highly inventive narrative. From the opening shots of a mysterious junk-shop and a wholesome, snow-covered American town, viewers are led to expect a backward-looking celebration of past Christmas cinema, complete with copious allusions to films such as Frank Capra's *It's a Wonderful Life* (1946). Early scenes incline us to connect characters to specific roles from Capra's famous movie, such as Mrs Deagle being correlated with Lionel Barrymore's miserly Mr Potter, Randall as Thomas Mitchell's eccentric Uncle Billy, Mr Wing as Henry Travers's spiritually-evolved Clarence, and of course Billy himself in the role of James Stewart's kind-hearted, community-oriented George Bailey. But as we soon discover, these anticipations are soon thoroughly turned on their head, situating the film's concerns firmly in the realms of modern fantasy rather than the matters of bygone years. Whole situations are set up early in the narrative only to become ignored entirely, such as Billy's enmity with pretentious undermanager Gerald Hopkins and Mrs Deagle's aggressive land-grab which is threatening the town. This approach may have been exacerbated by the amount of the film which was left on the cutting room floor during the editing stage; the rough cut was substantially longer than the finished product, and showed Hopkins locking himself into the Savings and Loan's vault for safety during the Gremlins' onslaught on the premises. Similarly, Mrs Deagle's plan to force local people out of their homes and businesses was explained as being on account of a plan to establish a huge shopping mall at the centre of town, thus destroying its appealingly traditional character. Nonetheless, the disconnection between a careful setup and non-existent payoff works well simply because of the way in which it disrupts the audience's prediction of forthcoming events, leaving them slightly off-balance throughout the film's running time. Chris Columbus's screenplay presents engaging characters who prove (in the main) to be enjoyable company, and the central premise that he depicts is suitably original in nature to maintain the attention of viewers. Having penned scripts throughout the eighties for films such as *Reckless* (James Foley, 1984), *The Goonies* (Richard Donner, 1985) and *Young Sherlock Holmes* (Barry Levinson, 1985) before moving into directing with features which would include *Adventures in Babysitting* (1987) and *Home Alone* (1990), *Gremlins* was to be a screenwriting highlight of Columbus's early career; the movie's fast pace and anarchic streak was to win it a place in the hearts of many a cineaste. Yet as Michael Stailey has observed, the content of Columbus's screenplay was initially far darker than the version of the film which eventually reached theatres might suggest:

> Interestingly enough, Columbus' original script was far more menacing than what ultimately wound up on screen. For as memorable as it is to see Barney the dog hung with Christmas lights, Mrs Peltzer strangled with a Christmas tree garland, Mrs Deagle catapulted from her motorized stair-chair, not to mention gremlin death

by blender, microwave, and fireplace, it could have been much worse. The dog was supposed to have been brutally murdered. Billy was to have walked into the house to see his mother's decapitated head rolling down the stairs. And little Gizmo was the first to mutate into the creature that became the malevolent Stripe. You can thank Spielberg's firsthand experience with *E.T.* to recognize when a character will become a fan favorite and open a world to profitable merchandising. That particular change was made well into production, causing Dante and company to scramble and find ways to make Gizmo the hero without having the budget or the technology for him to be seen traveling anywhere without the help of Billy's trusty backpack. In the end, he became an iconic figure worldwide.[2]

As though anyone would possibly be able to miss the creative team's thematic intentions in presenting the audience with the picture-perfect small town serenity of Kingston Falls, Dante treats us to a clip from the climax of *It's a Wonderful Life* on a television set in the Peltzer residence, ensuring that we all know that we are in comfortable and recognisable cinematic surroundings... before all hell breaks loose. As a contrasting clip later appears on Billy's television, drawn from Irvin Yeaworth's sci-fi horror *The Blob* (1958), we start to become aware of a determined shift in tone as the true nature of the Mogwais' metamorphosis begins to make itself clear. (An example of Columbus's fastidious attention to detail, the word 'mogwai' is actually a Cantonese term which can be loosely translated as 'monster', 'demon' or indeed 'gremlin'.) Likewise, just as Dante juxtaposes the traditional holiday season sequences at the beginning of the film (the Sheriff trying to light-heartedly scrounge a free Christmas tree from a local trader, for instance) with the wholesale carnage that later ensues, so too is this transition mirrored in Jerry Goldsmith's inspired original score – shifting adroitly from ever-so-slightly discordant Christmas-inspired themes to the hectic melody which accompanies the rampaging Gremlins on their wrecking spree throughout the town. It is in the act of so carefully engineering this headlong lurch from the cosily familiar to the lawlessly chaotic that, as Vincent Canby remarks, Dante and Columbus had sought to maximise the entertainment value delivered to their audience:

> Kingston Falls, U.S.A. [is] a perfect movie set of a town, where the plastic snow never melts and where, you can be sure, they start playing Christmas carols the day after the Fourth of July. In this comically idealized setting, it's just a matter of time before each of the mogwai prohibitions has been broken, with grotesque results that nearly destroy Kingston Falls as well as the movie. [...] Both Mr Dante and Chris Columbus, who wrote the screenplay, have antic senses of humor, but they are unreliable. They attack their young audience as mercilessly as the creatures attack the characters. One minute they're fondly recalling Frank Capra's sentimental classic, *It's a Wonderful Life*, and the next minute they're subjecting this Capraesque Smalltown, U.S.A., to a devastation that makes the original *Invasion of the Body Snatchers* look benign.[3]

Like many of Dante's other features, *Gremlins* is unquestionably a film which is brimming with affection for cinema past and present. There are many Spielbergian in-jokes (including a model E.T. in the department store toy section, and Rockin' Ricky Rialto's advertising billboard being an obvious homage to 1981's *Raiders of the Lost Ark*), while the Kingston Falls set itself not only visually resembles the small town America of years past but would also reused as the famous Hill Valley town square in Robert Zemeckis's *Back to the Future* (1985) the following year – both would be shot on the Universal Studios backlot. There are some shrewdly-considered cameo appearances from the likes of Steven Spielberg as the driver of an experimental mobility scooter at the inventors' convention attended by Randall, composer Jerry Goldsmith playing a man in a phone booth, and Warner Brothers animation legend Chuck Jones in the role of the cordial 'Mr Jones', a mature gent who passes favourable comment on Billy's sketching skills at the local bar. Pop culture allusions abound at the inventors' convention attended by Randall (everything from Fred M. Wilcox's *Forbidden Planet*, 1956, to George Pal's *The Time Machine*, 1960, receives a visual nod) and – most especially – during the Gremlins' incumbency at Dorry's Bar, which parodies everything from Adrian Lyne's *Flashdance* (1983) to Atari's immensely popular 1983 *Star Wars* wireframe vector arcade game. These craftily-realised references capture perfectly the film's strategy of blending the nostalgic and the modern to striking effect. As Roger Ebert sagely points out, 'the whole movie is a sly series of send-ups, inspired by movie scenes so basic they reside permanently in our subconscious. [...] *Gremlins* was hailed as another *E.T.* It's not. It's in a different tradition. At the level of Serious Film Criticism, it's a meditation on the myths in our movies: Christmas, families, monsters, retail stores, movies, boogeymen. At the level of Pop Movie-going, it's a sophisticated, witty B-movie, in which the monsters are devouring not only the defenseless town, but decades of defenseless clichés'.[4]

There is an immense amount to enjoy in *Gremlins*'s offhand humour and inspired characterisation, from the avaricious Mrs Deagle naming all of her cats after units of currency (such as Rouble, Kopeck, Drachma and Dollar Bill), and Randall's endless range of wacky inventions – each one appearing slightly more hopeless than the last. The tolerance of modern audiences may vary with regard to the xenophobic Murray Futterman and his nationalistic obsession with imported foreign technology; his pathological need to put the blame for (usually imagined) faults in non-American machinery on proverbial 'Gremlins', of course, presages the arrival of the real thing in the form of the mutated Mogwai and their genuine destructiveness. Such is the film's infectious sense of likeability that the relentless good humour and high-octane action does make it easier to overlook the occasional illogicality in the plot. For instance, no-one addresses the fact that the warning about never feeding a Mogwai after midnight seems particularly pointless given that it is always midnight somewhere on the planet at any given time, while during the climactic battle Billy's wooden baseball bat seems to survive for an inordinately long time against the unrelenting force of Stripe's chainsaw. In all, though, any inconsistencies seem largely inconsequential given Dante's juggernaut-style approach towards keeping the entertainment coming thick and fast; as Naomi Barnwell notes, 'instead of driving toward an overly moralistic conclusion, the film is allowed to instead enjoy its riotous ensemble. [...] *Gremlins* gloriously reeks of the Spielberg-era in which it was made (no doubt helped by Spielberg's producing credit in the film) and contains everything that makes 80s films great. The mixture of non-CGI creatures, recognisable stock characters (the town drunk and evil older woman being examples), creative sound effects and innocently ingenious soundtrack that suitably captures Gizmo's recognisable whistle all amount to an hugely enjoyable film'.[5]

Perhaps the epitome of the film's creative approach of clashing dark humour with a tranquil festive setting comes in the form of Kate's famously morbid Christmas Eve tale – a monologue which, for many commentators, summed up the sophistication of Dante's satirical methodology in microcosm. Delivered by an admirably deadpan Phoebe Cates, Kate's account of her father's demise in Santa Claus garb as an innocent holiday season surprise goes horribly wrong is magnificently pitched, in the sense that many members of the audience will genuinely be in two minds over whether they should be laughing at the ghoulish humour or commiserating with this obviously-traumatised character's plight. Dante was forced to fight for the scene's inclusion against profound studio scepticism, but for more than a few critics its distinctively mordant bite has come to define the film. As Glenn Erickson remarks, 'Dante saves his sharpest instance of cinematic disquiet for a much-discussed macabre Christmas story scene, told by Phoebe Cates's Kate. An anticipated belly-laugh suddenly turns into a grim little moment worthy of the black humorist Charles Addams. In one of his comments Dante mentions having to choose between this verbal creep-out or another scene in which Judge Reinhold is discovered locked in the bank vault. He kept the Downer Christmas Story'.[6]

If Kate's warnings of the potential dangers lurking beneath the surface of Christmas's apparent joy and goodwill were not cautionary enough, Mr Wing's scathing indictment of Western consumerism drives the point home with unwavering accuracy. Though more critical of the superficiality of the throwaway society than he is of late monopoly capitalism generally, Mr Wing gives voice to the view that not every natural resource is suitable for mainstream exploitation or mass audiences. This admonition has remained relevant even to modern viewers, as Ben Rawson-Jones argues: 'The central message of humanity's greed is perhaps more pertinent now than ever and epitomised by the oriental shop owner's words when he takes Gizmo back at the end: "You do with mogwai what society has done with all of nature's gifts. You do not understand. You are not ready"'.[7] Interestingly, of course, Columbus and Dante cannot resist the temptation to lampoon even the timeless wisdom of Mr Wing; while the elderly man is appalled at the notion of Gizmo's worldview being contaminated by mass-media like television he still gratefully receives Randall's gift of the smokeless ashtray invention, thus proving that even he is not beyond the allure of commercial convenience or tacky gadgetry. As John Kenneth Muir has commented, while there is a variety of different available interpretations of the film's underlying fundamental message, it seems clear that the primary objective of Dante and Columbus was to provide the greatest possible amount of sheer entertainment for their audience: 'Whatever the Gremlins represent (foreign machinery infecting America, a natural resource misused, or a new commodity in the culture of conspicuous consumption), Joe Dante's is a brilliantly unsentimental and horrific film. The scene in which a suburban mother battles a Gremlin in her suburban kitchen with every tool at her disposal (including the microwave oven) is brilliantly mephitic, and the film only goes off the rails when it stops to feature Gremlin antics and carousing at a local bar. The scene, involving a Gremlin break dance and doing a *Flashdance*-style routine (replete with leg warmer), is hysterical, but stops the film's momentum'.[8]

Beyond the exploration of the incompatibility between the altruistic tendencies of Christmas and the self-indulgent materialism of modern consumer culture, which of course was a perennial theme of eighties festive cinema, *Gremlins* also contained a certain degree of postmodern sensibility in the way that it appeared to indirectly hold its own audience to account for the scale of the havoc that is wreaked by the eponymous creatures. By the viewer's apprehension of violent carnage once the Gremlins are unleashed, antedated by the production team at the exact point when all vestiges of cosy Christmas tropes have been swept aside in favour of pugnacity and commotion, they play a part in spurring on the very havoc that they subsequently witness. In this assessment, as Calum Marsh explains:

> *Gremlins* becomes a very different kind of satire: one targeted at its own audience. The audience, after all, is the morally suspect group indirectly responsible for the havoc and mischief the gremlins cause, because it's the audience that loves to consume violence and destruction and misbehavior of all kinds. Here the spectacle collapses in on itself. [...] People are notoriously averse to criticism, and *Gremlins* goes out of its way to reassure us that its entertainments are safe to enjoy. Keeping its satire ambiguous is an effective strategy for deflecting our concerns that we're being admonished. Lapping up the spectacle of violence, it's usually assumed, is acceptable as long as there's a cogent point to be understood, and 'consumer culture corrupts' will do just fine in a pinch.[9]

Controversy also accompanied the cinematic release of *Gremlins* on account of the sometimes graphic nature of the mayhem wrought by the malicious sprites, perhaps best illustrated in the graphic attack on Joe Brooks's Dave Meyers character while dressed as Santa Claus (somewhat laying bare the film's strategy of aggressively challenging the comforting conventions of the festive season). Although the movie did not contain the type of graphic gore or adult situations that would have made it suitable for an 'R' rating, there was considerable criticism over the tense level of suspense and general comic violence which was depicted, leading to much media coverage at the time. In particular, parents who had expected family-friendly fare were, in many cases, displeased by the rebellious humour and more macabre elements of the film. This led, as Bruce G. Hallenbeck describes, to the creation of a new classification for cinemas which would be more appropriate for movies of this type: 'Joe Dante's *Gremlins* [[was]] a movie that took comedy-horror to new heights of screams and laughter, and one of the two films (the other being Steven Spielberg's *Indiana Jones and the Temple of Doom*) released that summer that led to a new movie rating: PG-13, for films that were too dark or violent for a PG rating but not quite nasty enough for an R. [[...]] *Gremlins* was the recipient of [[...]] criticism for a scene in which one of the title creatures is thrown into a microwave oven, whereupon it explodes in a welter of blood and viscera. But that's part of the brilliance of Dante's approach: Although *Gremlins* is essentially a mainstream, family film, there is a dark and subversive undercurrent that keeps the viewer off guard, wondering in which direction it will veer next'.[10]

While the film has undoubtedly become highly reputed for the darkly humorous pandemonium caused by the titular Gremlins, Dante and Columbus pack far more into its running time than simply a series of movie homages, sight gags and scenes of gleeful destruction. *Gremlins* is a feature which was made with obvious affection for its subject matter, and one which reflects a warm fondness for the very kind of phenomena – Christmas cinema, small town life, clichéd romances – that it ultimately sets out to demolish. Strangely, this strategy has the odd effect of actually reinforcing these themes; the Gremlins' anarchy doesn't quite manage to snuff out the flame of Christmas, Kingston Falls is inadvertently saved from Mrs Deagle's nefarious commercial plans, and Billy and Kate manage to stay together (and alive) in spite of all the odds. As Mike Long has stated, the generic complexity of the movie is just one of the reasons why it has come to be so influential: '*Gremlins* is one of those films which has become such a part of the cultural landscape that it's difficult to forget the impact that it had upon its initial release. The movie was a very unique blend of funny, scary, and cool, and this reflected those working behind the cameras. [...] An avid film fan and a lover of old movies, Dante packs the film with movie references, as well as an interesting mixture of slapstick comedy, gross-out moments, and genuine creepiness. But, he also gives the movie heart and you can't help but fall in love with Gizmo'.[11] This fevered cross-pollination of genre characteristics has not convinced every critic of the film's efficacy, however. Given the intentional clash between the opening scenes' idealised depiction of provincial life and the major disruption of audience supposition that soon follows it, the mismatch of styles proved to be too much for some commentators to find entirely palatable. David Sterritt, for instance, remarks that *Gremlins* is 'a bubbling stew of movie styles and memories. Think of *A Christmas Carol* visited by *The Birds*. Think of *The Muppet Movie* run amok. Imagine a berserk film editor splicing *It's a Wonderful Life* to *Invasion of the Body Snatchers*, with quoting from *Snow White* and a nod to *The Texas Chainsaw Massacre.* [...] This isn't complicated, but it calls for real filmmaking skill, especially when it comes to striking an emotional balance. Dante and his cronies don't quite succeed. The movie is best when dousing us with Spielberg sentiment and whimsy. It's weaker when the more demonic sensibility of director Dante takes over'.[12]

When considered as a Christmas film, *Gremlins* is no less complicated in terms of categorisation. Because the rampaging creatures are unable to destroy Kingston Falls, albeit that many casualties are felled in their attempt, the festive season somehow manages to survive because the town itself (and a majority of its community) has endured the barrage loosed upon it. But when balanced against Kate's tragi-comic account of her father's untimely Christmas Eve demise and Mr Wing's stony-faced warnings of the potential destructiveness of unchecked materialism, the audience is faced with a rather more multifaceted realisation. During the climax in the department store, Stripe's desperate attempts to remain alive cause predictably vast amounts of damage to the festively-decorated commercial displays: a commentary on the excess of the busy Christmas shopping season, where thousands of dollars' worth of stock is consumed (or, in this case, ruined) in the moments before the sun comes up on Christmas Day. Yet as the news reports leave us in no doubt, with the Gremlins' demise the media find that they have no reasonable alternative but to announce that the damage has been caused by human hysteria, ensuring that society is able to deceive itself back into a state of comfortable obliviousness. Human behaviour is implied to be the real menace at large, suggesting a variance between its predictability (avaricious acquisitiveness) and unpredictability (the savageness of the 'riots', which unexpectedly challenge notions of social stability). In a sense, the film celebrates the overall resilience of Christmas's positive effect on communities while simultaneously shining a spotlight on just how precarious these seemingly-resilient festive conventions can sometimes prove to be. As David M. Keyes argues, '*Gremlins* may have once been about the charming possibilities of movie creatures with big hearts, but as an adult it fashions a reality that plays like the worst of Norman Rockwell's nightmares: a world in which all the conventional undertones of holiday spirit are destroyed under the influence of a beastly host of monsters that do everything in their power to inspire chaos and disorder. How delightfully oblivious I must have been not to detect the gloominess of this fantasy. And yet there is satire here: a sense of silly but thoughtful consideration on the Christmas traditions and how easily all the relatable façades crumble as a consequence of simple illusions being so easily shattered'.[13] In the final analysis, however, because Kingston Falls represents the ideal of the traditional American community, the tenacious persistence of its Christmas trappings – even when under inexorable attack by the Gremlins – speaks of a wider adaptability of the festive season both in practical and generic terms. Just as the Christmas film was being forced to develop and adjust in order to remain relevant in the rapidly-changing socio-cultural environment of the eighties, Dante's movie issues both a warning and a note of reassurance: that the central themes of the genre's golden age were still pertinent, but that they would need to justify themselves anew in a world that was becoming increasingly cynical and grounded in material self-determination. Yet the catalyst for this meditation on the tropes of the holiday season lies squarely with the widespread mischief of the Gremlins and their subsequent destructiveness, and – as Colin Jacobson has observed – it is for the warped ingenuity of their waywardness that the film has become so well-known: 'Modern movies span genres more readily than they did even back in the Eighties, so *Gremlins* offered something genuinely unusual. Neither straight horror flick nor simple comedy, the movie fused those elements neatly and created a lively and amusing piece of work. None of this would have worked without the compelling attributes of the gremlins themselves. Of course, Gizmo's cuteness instantly attracts us – who wouldn't want a pet like that? – but it's the wild gremlins that make the film succeed'.[14]

While Zach Galligan and Phoebe Cates both make for appealing leads, Dante's film owes at least as much to the infectious charm of its many supporting players – Hoyt Axton as the ham-fisted but endearing inventor Randall, Keye Luke's delightfully knowing turn as the mystic sage, Corey Feldman as gutsy teenager Pete Fountaine, Dick Miller's irascible but earnestly patriotic Murray Futterman, and most especially Polly Holliday as the exultantly malevolent Ruby Deagle. Yet for all the allure of its human actors' performances, it is for the endless hordes of sneering green monsters unleashed by Dante onto his unsuspecting audience that *Gremlins* continues to be recalled so fondly. While their reign of terror is eventually brought to an abrupt end, some writers – such as Barry Langford – have suggested a further allegory for the creatures' devastating rampage; that the rapidly-multiplying Gremlins were symbolic of changes in cinematic exhibition which were threatening to sweep away long-established norms:

> In *Gremlins*, when the affectionate mogwai Gizmo (something like a cross between a koala bear and one of *Star Wars'* Ewoks) comes into contact with water, numerous smaller, and decidedly less benign, mogwais -

the eponymous Gremlins – are parthogenetically generated from his own squirming body. These small but vicious creatures proceed to put the film's perfectly confected small town (a briefly glimpsed TV clip invokes the Bedford Falls of Frank Capra's *It's a Wonderful Life*) to the sword. From the mid-1980s, motion picture exhibition in all its forms – theatrical and domestic – [...] in the US generally, was also a story of the rapid, and apparently endless, multiplication of small entities that seemed to find their way into every corner of a movie market itself growing rapidly in every direction. These new, fast-evolving market presences may not have launched the same cannibalistic assault as the Gremlins; their advent, nonetheless, spelled doom for at least some of their older competitors.[15]

While the artistic objectives of Dante's film can be interpreted in a number of ways, there was no doubting its commercial success. One of the most profitable films of 1984, *Gremlins* was produced on an estimated budget of $11,000,000,[16] and went on to achieve an impressive domestic lifetime gross of $153,083,102.[17] In addition to its significant performance at the box-office, *Gremlins* is also well-remembered for its wide-ranging merchandising campaign at the time of its release – somewhat ironically, given its warnings about the danger of unfettered commercialism. The film inspired a wave of tie-in products which included stuffed toys and action figures, various computer games (both in the interactive fiction and arcade adventure genres), trading cards, audio adaptations, a breakfast cereal, and a novelisation written by George Gipe (who would also adapt the screenplay of *Back to the Future* into prose for a mass-market paperback release the following year). Additionally, *Gremlins* performed well at a number of award ceremonies, winning a Golden

Screen Award in Germany and picking up a Young Artist Award for Best Family Motion Picture (Adventure), in addition to seeing Corey Feldman nominated for the Best Young Supporting Actor in a Motion Picture Award at the same ceremony. The film did especially well at the Academy of Science Fiction, Fantasy and Horror Films Awards, winning Saturn Awards in the categories of Best Director, Best Special Effects, Best Music and Best Supporting Actress (for Polly Holliday) as well as nominations for Best Writing, Best Make-Up, Best Supporting Actor (for Dick Miller) and Best Performance by a Younger Actor (for Corey Feldman).

Given its success with audiences and critics alike, *Gremlins* would receive a sequel some years later. Once again directed by Joe Dante, *Gremlins 2: The New Batch* featured a screenplay by Charles S. Haas and was released by Warner Brothers in 1990. Though the film retained lead performers Zach Galligan and Phoebe Cates from the original (with Dick Miller and Keye Luke also returning in supporting roles), *Gremlins 2* dispensed with the Christmas setting and transferred the action from the provincial environment of Kingston Falls to the urban metropolis of New York City. With a considerably lighter tone and even more emphasis on film and pop culture parodies than before, the sequel included numerous entertaining cameos (including one from Dante himself) and built confidently upon the original's postmodern credentials; film critic Leonard Maltin, who had been disparaging of *Gremlins* in 1984, is personally called to account for his scepticism of the film's virtues in the sequel, while the events of the first movie are also artfully lampooned.

Gremlins may have featured more chaotic action than most Christmas films that were released in the 1980s, but it would also prove to be one of the most thought-provoking.

Both defying and celebrating the tropes of festive cinema, the film was to concurrently applaud the traditional values of community life while cautioning audiences about the fragility of long-held cultural conventions in uncertain and fast-moving times. While Dante and Columbus present a movie which is equally timely and nostalgic, there is little doubt that the overall ethos behind its production is one of exuberance and entertainment. The Gremlins may drive Kingston Falls to the brink of total disaster, but they clearly enjoy themselves while doing so – and by extension, there will be few in the audience who don't find themselves revelling in the sheer amusement generated by the creatures' disreputable misadventures at one point or another. While *Gremlins* was a film which rebelled against many traditional conventions of Christmas cinema, it also concisely made the point that these tropes were themselves shifting as a result of changing audience appreciation regarding intermingling genres and challenges to orthodox creative approaches. In so doing, Dante was among the first to establish the foundation for an assertive reassessment, deconstruction and reconfiguration of long-established thematic characteristics of the Christmas film – a process which would continue throughout the decade and beyond.

REFERENCES

1. Adam Tyner, '*Gremlins*: Special Edition', in *DVD Talk*, 20 August 2009.
    <http://www.dvdtalk.com/reviews/4426/gremlins-special-edition/>

2. Michael Stailey, '*Gremlins*', in *DVD Verdict*, 1 June 2012.
    <http://www.dvdverdict.com/reviews/gremlinsbluray.php>

3. Vincent Canby, '*Gremlins*: Kiddie Gore', in *The New York Times*, 8 June 1984.

4. Roger Ebert, '*Gremlins*', in *The Chicago Sun-Times*, 8 June 1984.

5. Naomi Barnwell, '*Gremlins*', in *Roobla*, 7 December 2010.
    <https://roobla.com/2010/12/07/gremlins-1984/>

6. Glenn Erickson, '*Gremlins*', in *DVD Savant*, 4 December 2009.
    <http://www.dvdtalk.com/dvdsavant/s3081grem.html>

7. Ben Rawson-Jones, '*Gremlins* Review: Fiendishly Funny Classic Re-released for Christmas', in *Digital Spy*, 6 December 2016.
    <http://www.digitalspy.com/movies/review/a443304/gremlins-review-fiendishly-funny-classic-re-released-for-christmas/>

8. John Kenneth Muir, *Horror Films of the 1980s* (Jefferson: McFarland, 2007), p.394.

9.   Calum Marsh, '*Gremlins*', in *Slant*, 11 May 2012.
        <http://www.slantmagazine.com/dvd/review/gremlins>

10.   Bruce G. Hallenbeck, *Comedy-Horror Films: A Chronological History, 1914-2008* (Jefferson: McFarland and Company, 2009), p.131.

11.   Mike Long, 'Gremlins', in *DVD Sleuth*, 1 December 2009.
        <http://www.dvdsleuth.com/GremlinsReview/>

12.   David Sterritt, 'Dante's *Gremlins* Mixes Humor and Horror', in *The Christian Science Monitor*, 7 June 1984.
        <http://www.csmonitor.com/1984/0607/060707.html>

13.   David M. Keyes, '*Gremlins*', in *Cinemaphile*, 7 December 2014.
        <http://www.thecinemaphileblog.com/2014/12/gremlins-1984.html>

14.   Colin Jacobson, '*Gremlins*', in *DVD Movie Guide*, 18 December 2009.
        <http://www.dvdmg.com/gremlinsbr.shtml>

15.   Barry Langford, *Post-Classical Hollywood: Film Industry, Style and Ideology Since 1945* (Edinburgh: Edinburgh University Press, 2010), p.183.

16.   Budgetary data drawn from the *Internet Movie Database*.
        <http://www.imdb.com/title/tt0087363/business>

17.   Box-office data drawn from *BoxOfficeMojo.com*.
        <http://www.boxofficemojo.com/movies/?id=gremlins.html>

9

Silent Night, Deadly Night (1984)

TriStar Pictures/Slayride

Director: Charles E. Sellier Jr.
Producer: Ira Richard Barmak
Screenwriter: Michael Hickey, from a story by Paul Caimi

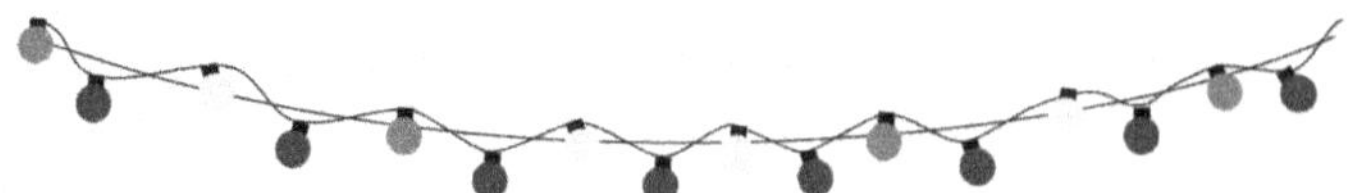

Perhaps the most overtly prominent of all Christmas horror films to be released in the 1980s, *Silent Night, Deadly Night* was unquestionably one of the most controversial films ever to emerge in the genre. Lambasted by public groups who were deeply offended by its core concept of Christmas-themed slaughter, and largely derided by the critics of the time, the movie appeared doomed to obscurity from the outset. And yet – precisely because of the widespread contention which accompanied its 1984 release – in due course *Silent Night, Deadly Night* was to become something of a cult classic, extending its longevity far beyond the level that it would likely otherwise have enjoyed.

As Don Sumner has observed, '*Silent Night, Deadly Night* suffered from several forms of banning. In Britain, the banning was direct and to the point – essentially release was prohibited even without the classification as a video nasty. In the United States, however, the banning was driven by community outrage. The Parent-Teacher Association staged huge protests immediately upon the release of this film, fueled by the fact that it was released right around Christmas time. [[...]] *Silent Night, Deadly Night* is not necessarily a good film in its own right, but the controversy surrounding it certainly adds points on the cult classic meter'.[1] In a fateful twist, for all of these early attempts to have the movie removed from public consumption the storm of fevered debate which followed its advertising campaign and subsequent cinema release would eventually lead to a surge in interest from cult movie buffs; coupled with the growing availability of home entertainment formats, *Silent Night, Deadly Night* would eventually become the definitive Christmas horror film of the 1980s for many aficionados of the genre.

The film bears no relation to the obscure but similarly-titled *Silent Night, Bloody Night* (Theodore Gershuny, 1972), a little-seen, low-budget holiday season thriller starring Patrick O'Neal, Mary Woronov and John Carradine. (Nor indeed did it share much in the way of stylistic similarity with Bob Clark's chillingly atmospheric *Black Christmas*, 1974, which is sometimes known by its alternative title *Silent Night, Evil Night*.) The fictional incidents depicted in *Silent Night, Deadly Night* were, however, very loosely inspired by Paul Caimi's short script treatment *Slayride*, which was optioned by executive producer Scott Schneid and developed into a full-length screenplay by Michael Hickey. As Schneid later related in an interview, Caimi's artistic influence over the finished product was ultimately to be minimal: 'I want to be clear, there is NOTHING we took from that script other than one sentence – not even a sentence, a three word idea! "A killer Santa". We took that and developed an entirely new treatment'.[2] Hickey would face an interesting challenge in taking the premise of a murderer in a Santa Claus costume, a concept which had already been widely explored throughout the early eighties, and finding an original way of presenting the increasingly-familiar festive slaughter scenario innovatively enough to establish pertinence with audiences. The end result, however, would prove significantly more volatile than anyone on the creative team had ever dared to anticipate.

Silent Night, Deadly Night marked a relatively rare stint in the director's chair for veteran producer Charles E. Sellier Jr. With a long-running career which spanned dozens of feature films and over two hundred television shows, he was especially well-known for producing *The Life and Times of Grizzly Adams* (1974) – a feature based upon his own 1972 novel of the same name, and which would inspire a short-lived television series (1978-79) as well as a TV movie entitled *The Capture of Grizzly Adams* (1982). His prolific output spanned popular genre television, religious documentaries, classic literary adaptations and even science fiction features, but by contrast his directorial career was limited to just four motion pictures. These included documentary film *Encounter with Disaster* (1979), ribald teen comedy *Snowballing* (1984), and vigilante thriller *The Annihilators* (1985). However, of all his directorial efforts *Silent Night, Deadly Night* was to emerge as easily the most notorious.

On Christmas Eve 1971, the Chapman family – Jim (Jeff Hansen), Ellie (Tara Buckman) and their sons Billy (Jonathan Best) and Ricky (Melissa [sic] Best) – are headed to visit Jim's elderly father at the Utah Mental Facility. The five-year-old Billy is eagerly awaiting the arrival of Santa Claus that night, though his infant brother is too young to know the significance of the date. Arriving at the care institution, the Chapmans find Billy's grandfather (Will Hare) to be in an unresponsive state of near-catatonia. However, when Jim and Ellie momentarily leave the room to review a medical report on Grandpa's health, the elderly man abruptly becomes more active. Clearly mentally disturbed, he tells Billy that Christmas is not the time of joy and peace that everyone supposes, but rather a period of terror and punishment. Furthermore, he points out, while Santa Claus only brings presents to children who have been well-behaved throughout the year, he will actively seek to reprimand those who have ever misbehaved. Billy is unnerved by the older man's words of warning, but upon the return of his parents he finds that Grandpa has returned to his earlier semi-comatose state.

Night falls during the long drive home, and Billy's parents are concerned when their son relates his grandfather's cautionary advice that Santa Claus will be coming to punish him for earlier misdeeds. Puzzled at how the seemingly-withdrawn old man could have issued such a strange threat, Ellie tries to calm Billy's nerves, only for her son to warn that in questioning Grandpa's judgement she too has done something naughty. They are unaware that, at a nearby general store, festive cheer is very far from the agenda; a homicidal criminal dressed as Santa Claus (Charles Dierkop) holds up the shop, shooting dead the sales clerk when the man tries to resist. Livid that the cash register contains only a paltry amount of money, the felon speeds away from the scene in his car.

Some time later that night, the Chapmans discover an unexpected sight on the road – the store robber's car has broken down, and they now appear to be getting flagged down by none other than Jolly Old Saint Nick himself. Not realising the man's true identity, Jim is amused by the unusual sight and wakes up Billy. However, his son is petrified by the presence of Santa Claus and, fearing retribution for his behaviour throughout the year, begs his father not to stop the car. But keen to offer the stranger some assistance, especially on Christmas Eve, Jim nevertheless decides to park alongside the criminal's damaged vehicle. This soon proves to be his undoing, as the psychotic felon pulls a gun, fatally shooting Jim. He then subjects Ellie to violent sexual abuse before cutting her throat. Billy escapes from the car and watches the whole blood-soaked scene from a hiding spot at the roadside. The criminal rages at his inability to hunt Billy down, though he ultimately has no choice but to leave both the young boy and his infant brother alive.

Three years later, the parentless Billy and Ricky are now resident at St Mary's Home for Orphaned Children, a care institution operated by nuns. As Christmas approaches once again, Sister Ellen (A. Madeline Smith) has encouraged her class to draw festive pictures celebrating the holiday season. However, she his horrified when Billy (Danny Wagner), now eight years old, produces a graphic depiction of Rudolph the red-nosed reindeer being decapitated and Santa Claus suffering multiple stab wounds. Sister Ellen sends Billy to the orphanage's Mother Superior (Lilyan Chauvin) for disciplining. The overbearing senior nun scolds Billy and demands that he go to his room, warning him that he will soon learn regret for his actions, but – once the boy has left the office – the kindly Sister Margaret (Gilmer McCormick) reflects that the drawing is a manifestation of the trauma that still haunts Billy over the violent death of his parents. Thus, she reasons, he must receive help to overcome his demons if he is to have any hope of living a normal life, noting that his struggle appears to become greater with every passing Christmas. However, Mother Superior has absolutely no intention of considering the psychological underpinnings of

Billy's behaviour; as far as she is concerned, repeated punishment will be the only way to ensure that his wrongful impulses are corrected appropriately – especially as she believes that he would have been too young to fully comprehend the nature of his parents' grisly fate.

Later, Billy watches despondently from the window of his room as the other children enjoy themselves playing in the snow. Realising his isolation, Sister Margaret visits and encourages him to join them in building a snowman outside. Billy is reluctant, given Mother Superior's stern instructions, but eventually responds to her friendly encouragement. On his way out of the building, however, he hears unexpected sounds from further along the corridor and decides to investigate. Peering through a keyhole, he discovers a young couple (Barbara Stafford and Paul Mulder) in a passionate embrace... but the sight reminds him painfully of his mother's semi-clothed state when she was killed three years earlier. Mother Superior abruptly arrives and throws Billy aside, marching into the room and proceeding to repeatedly belt the pair as a penalty for their sin of fornication.

Afterwards, as the children continue to enjoy games in the snow Mother Superior marches out into the playground and reprimands Billy for having left his room. Questioning him about what he saw earlier, she emphasises that punishment for all transgressive actions is not only necessary but beneficial, as it makes amends for wrongdoing. Ignoring protestations from Sister Margaret and Ricky (Max Broadhead), now four years of age, Mother Superior takes Billy back to his room and belts him over and over again in penance for his disobedience. She then sends him to bed, though he is tormented by vivid nightmares recalling the night of his parents' murder. Terrified, he races from his room, but Mother Superior catches him and forcibly restrains him to his bunk. Sister Margaret is appalled by the brutishness of this cruel treatment, but feels powerless to stop it.

Christmas Day arrives, and the children react with excitement and joy as they unwrap their gifts. However, Mother Superior is disdainful of the jubilant display, considering it a mockery of the true meaning of Christmas. Billy is returned to his fellow classmates and seems much calmer, which Mother Superior considers to be proof that her uncompromising methods are proving effective. Sister Margaret is deeply unconvinced, knowing that the holiday season is at the root of Billy's anxieties, but the senior nun is determined to show that he has been 'cured' by insisting that Billy sit on Santa Claus's knee during the orphanage's annual visit. Predictably, Billy is terrified when he sees the jovial red-suited figure (Spencer Ashby), but Mother Superior literally drags him into the room and deposits the hysterical boy onto Santa's lap. She insists that he express heartfelt gratitude to Santa for the gifts he has received, but this leads Billy into a frenzy of panic; now frantically unbalanced, he punches the costumed man with all his might, knocking the shocked St Nicholas impersonator off his chair. Before anyone can catch him, Billy races to the relative safety of his room and cowers in the corner, feverishly muttering regret for his actions. However, the incensed Mother Superior soon arrives to carry out fresh punishment in retaliation for his misbehaviour.

Ten years later, it is December 1984 and Sister Margaret is pleading with local toy shop owner Mr Sims (Britt Leach) to consider Billy for employment. Every other store in the area has refused to give him a job, and Mr Sims seems less than enthusiastic about the prospect of having the young man on his payroll. However, he has one opening in his stockroom, and when he realises that the eighteen-year-old Billy (Robert Brian Wilson) looks strong enough to shift heavy goods around the store he eventually relents and offers him the post.

Billy takes to his new job like a duck to water, and his diligence is noted by Mr Sims. However, his highly moral conduct – refusing to drink alcohol and disapproving of profanity – goes down less than well with his underhanded supervisor Andy (Randy Stumpf), who despises Billy's clean-living attitudes. Things change for the worse when Christmas approaches and the shop is decorated for the festive season; Billy becomes introverted and irritable, and is especially disturbed when the store hires a Santa Claus (J. Paul Broadhead) to welcome children over the holidays. His mental upset is noticed by his empathetic co-worker Pamela (Toni Nero), who Billy has developed feelings for. However, due to his strict disciplining at the orphanage he is profoundly conflicted, believing that his attraction to her is somehow sinful; an internal tension which is further exacerbated when he begins to fantasise about Santa Claus stabbing him in punishment for his attraction to Pamela.

On Christmas Eve, news reaches the toy store that the seasonal employee playing Santa has broken his ankle in an ice-skating accident, forcing Mr Sims to ask Billy to step into the role instead. Realising that his future at the company depends on his compliance, Billy dutifully dresses up in the vacant costume... but almost immediately, the unresolved trauma of his childhood experiences begins to revisit him anew. Though he winds up disconcerting the children who come to visit his grotto, warning them of dire punishment if they should behave badly, he appears to the parents and other employees to be a model Santa Claus. However, when Sister Margaret telephones the store to speak with Billy, she fears the worst when she learns about his new role for the holidays.

At closing time, a jubilant Mr Sims declares that party season has started; producing bottle after bottle of liquor, he and his employees start to celebrate the end of the busy shopping season. But Billy seems acutely uneasy, reluctant to drink alcohol or to join in with the fun. As his colleagues slowly become gradually more inebriated, he watches dejectedly as Andy makes a drunken move on Pamela. But when the party begins to wind down, Billy starts to become concerned when Pamela is taken further into the stockroom by Andy, and – upon quietly investigating – discovers that the repellent undermanager is in the midst of sexually assaulting her. The combination of seeing the woman he desires being attacked and memories of his own mother's fate on the night of her death finally pushes Billy over the edge. Still dressed in the Santa Claus suit, he grabs a nearby string of Christmas lights and strangles Andy with them. Stunned by the unexpected violence of his actions, Pamela turns on Billy, which leads him to stab her to death as a 'punishment' for her apparent defiance. Shortly afterwards, a highly intoxicated Mr Sims lurches into the stockroom in search of the others, but his incursion is met by deadly force from Billy who fatally bludgeons him with a hammer. Finally, the only other person who remains in the building – administrator Mrs Randall (Nancy Borgenicht) – stumbles upon the scene of slaughter and tries to flee, only to be pursued by an axe-wielding Billy. After a frenetic chase through the darkened store, she manages to grab the axe and attempts to smash open the locked main doors, only to be felled by a crossbow bolt fired by her costumed foe. Little does

Billy realise that moments after he has left the scene of his crimes, Sister Margaret arrives at the store and witnesses the bloodshed in all its horror.

Close by, a babysitter named Denise (Linnea Quigley) is enjoying a romantic encounter with her boyfriend Tommy (Leo Geter) while desperately trying to keep Cindy (Amy Stuyvesant) – the little girl she is caring for – out of the room. Denise warns Cindy that Santa won't bring presents for naughty children, and thus she should get back to sleep as quickly as possible. But none of them expect the sudden arrival of the deranged Billy, who spots Cindy's barely-clothed form from the street and inexplicably decides that she deserves disciplining. Smashing through the house's front door with his axe, he proceeds to 'punish' Denise and her partner for their intimate tryst. Overcoming her attempts to fight him off, Billy impales Denise on the antlers of a mounted reindeer's head, then interrupts Tommy's attempt to call the police by throwing him out of a window to his demise. As he leaves, he encounters Cindy, who is delighted to see the celebrated festive figure in her house. Enquiring whether 'Santa' has left her a present, Billy sombrely asks whether she has been naughty or nice. When she replies that she has done nothing bad, Billy gifts her the blood-stained box-cutter that he had earlier used to murder Pamela – much to the little girl's profound puzzlement.

Meanwhile, the police have been tipped off about the toy store murders by Sister Margaret and are actively looking for a killer in a Santa Claus costume. Officers Miller (Richard D. Clark) and Murphy (Tip Boxell) are bemused by their captain's orders, but are forced to take the matter seriously when they discover a man in a Santa suit climbing a ladder to gain entry through a house's first-floor window. However, their subsequent arrest proves to be in vain when the man turns out to be a father attempting to surprise his children. In a wooded area nearby, Billy notices patrol cars speeding by with their sirens blazing and begins to realise that the police are in pursuit of him. Still clutching his axe, he accidentally encounters a pair of teenagers named Doug (Vince Massa) and Jim (John Michael Alvarez), whose night-time sledging session has been interrupted by bullies Bob (John Bishop) and Mac (Richard C. Terry). Stealing the younger boys' sledges and forcing them to flee, the interlopers have little time to enjoy their illicit fun: Billy makes his presence known and promptly decapitates one of them, compelling the other to race off in terror.

The next morning is Christmas Day, and Sister Margaret is at the local police station helping Captain Richards (H.E.D. Redford) with his enquiries. She is horrified by the news of Billy's latest murders, reasoning that all of his homicidal actions have been triggered by the pent-up distress relating to his parents' demise. Richards suggests that if his behaviour is adhering to some kind of perverse logic, there must be some way of predicting his next move – which leads the aghast Sister Margaret to realise that Billy must be heading back to the orphanage. But at St Mary's, the staff are busy watching over the children as they open their presents; one little girl leaves the office's telephone off the hook, meaning that the police are unable to warn the nuns of the danger that faces them.

Before heading out to the orphanage in person, the captain sends a dispatch to all patrol cars in the area to watch out for the Santa Claus-garbed killer. One policeman who receives the message, Officer Barnes (Max Robinson), heads directly to St Mary's and is alarmed to see a man in a Santa

Claus costume approaching some children in the schoolyard. When the man does not respond to repeated warnings to surrender, Barnes feels he has no option but to shoot him dead. But as paramedics arrive to remove the corpse, it becomes clear that this particular Santa Claus was actually Father O'Brien, a local priest who was profoundly deaf – hence his inability to hear the officer's orders.

Mother Superior, now confined to a wheelchair, harshly berates Barnes for shooting Father O'Brien – even as a disastrous result of mistaken identity. While adamant that the children in her care must come to no harm, she is obviously sceptical about the police warning that has been issued regarding a killer on the loose. Barnes scouts the building's perimeter for safety's sake, but is soon murdered by Billy when searching an outhouse. One of the children spots 'Santa Claus' outside the main doors of the orphanage and, enraptured by his presence, lets him into the building – much to the horror of Mother Superior. The elderly nun closes her eyes in resignation as Billy raises his axe, having pronounced her 'naughty', but is saved at the last second when Captain Richards arrives and shoots the murderer repeatedly. With his last breath, a strangely serene Billy assures the children that they are safe at last: 'Santa Claus' is gone. But as Sister Margaret cradles the serial killer's prone form, his brother Ricky (Alex Burton) – now fourteen – glares in cold fury at Mother Superior, chillingly echoing his brother's fateful moral declaration that she has been 'naughty'.

Silent Night, Deadly Night was an atypical film in the increasingly well-populated field of Christmas-themed horror cinema, in the sense that it unveils the identity of its killer early in the narrative and thus relies on the suspense generated by the uncertainty of Billy's subsequent actions.

More than most festively-situated slasher horrors, there is a definite focus upon the damaged psychology which is responsible for the mounting bloodshed; with the exception of the sadistic murderer who kills Billy's parents in the first act, this is a film with few clearly-defined villains. Mother Superior's depiction is rarely allowed to stray into the realms of caricature; the authoritarian nun is depicted not as straightforwardly malevolent but instead dangerously misguided. Her austere manner and severe discipline is ameliorated by her occasional (if rare) scenes of understated compassion towards the children in her care, and there is little question that her actions – while demonstrably abusive and damaging in nature – are intended to shape the moral character of those in her charge rather than to intentionally impair them. But of course, we see in Billy's actions the endpoint of her absolute refusal to consider the emotional basis of his mental disturbance, and thus even after his homicidal rampage he appears something of a tragic figure – almost as much of a victim as those he has so brutally murdered. As Jim Harper has suggested, the gradual and deliberate development of Billy's breakdown – while triggered by highly engineered means – marks the film out as being slightly more contemplative than many of its contemporaries: ‘*Silent Night, Deadly Night* presents the most complex psychological picture of all the slasher movie killers. Billy watches his father killed and his mother raped by a man dressed as Santa Claus. Later on the nuns at school teach him that sex is evil, and he soon manages to combine sex, death and Father Christmas into one highly unstable mixture. A day spent dressed as the jolly fat man pushes him over the edge, and before long Billy is impaling naked women on the antlers of a stuffed moose. The first twenty minutes of the film are spent charting his descent into madness, considerably longer than any other slasher movie'.[3]

For all the deliberately considered psychological groundwork that it lays, *Silent Night, Deadly Night* demonstrates many tropes which were familiar to the subgenre; the scantily-clad victims, the novelty value of its inventive range of murders, the less-than-subtle in-jokes (Mr Sims's toy store, 'Ira's Toys', is a very obvious tip of the hat to producer Ira Richard Barmak), and some genuinely creepy moments. The latter is perhaps most amply demonstrated by Will Hare's awe-inspiringly sinister grandfather, whose avuncular outward appearance defies the baleful delivery of his dialogue – the kind of nightmarish character that presents the very antithesis of warm festive sentiment. Yet it is for the Santa Claus-costumed Billy that the film remains most famous; the unbalanced serial killer, with a glazed expression and deranged trademark call of 'Punish!' for anyone unfortunate enough to cross his path, is an undeniably disconcerting presence. Jack Santino considers the fact that 'at least one writer has speculated that the twisted, evil Santas of [Christmas horror] films are a nod towards the pagan underpinnings of Christmas itself, a reflection of some of the supernatural elements of that festival that seem to have been sanitized out of recognition by the modern sentimentalization of it. Whatever the case, Christmas was probably chosen more for the shock value of a usually joyous, comforting occasion and introducing an element of the horrible into it, than capitalizing on imagery intrinsic to the occasion, as in *Halloween*'.[4] There are numerous reasons why, in plumbing the darkest depths of the holiday season for traumatic content, Sellier's film is regularly at its most effective: the awkward, inebriated party at Mr Sims's toy shop which lays bare the staff's near-total lack of genuine camaraderie, the short-lived 1970s store clerk's cynicism towards the avarice eroding the true sentiment of Christmas, and most especially the contrast between the euphoric children opening their presents at the orphanage and Mother Superior's joyless, puritanical condemnation of the festive season's carnival attitude (one which she feels to be at odds with the religious foundations of the holiday). This strategy reaches its apex with Billy's breakdown, a mental collapse that is prompted – at least in part – by the irreconcilable conflict between a natural attraction to a member of the opposite sex and his deep-seated moral indoctrination which warns that any motivation towards intimacy is somehow sinful and worthy only of penance. Combined with his dangerously repressed (thus never properly resolved) trauma regarding his parents' death, and his phobia of Santa Claus elicited by his disturbed grandfather's fevered warnings, the audience is presented with a wretched and misunderstood figure who is never fully able to disengage from the source of his inner torment – not least during December, when the iconography of the festive season is naturally at its height. This certainly situates the film closer to the thoughtful narrative approach of *Christmas Evil* than the more straightforward formulations of *To All a Goodnight* or *Don't Open Till Christmas*, while no-one would reasonably mistake *Silent Night, Deadly Night* for high art, it contains enough complexity to stand apart from many other contemporary horror features of the early to mid-eighties. As Rosie Gibbs has observed, 'perhaps what elevates it a little above a flat-line cheap-thrills watermark is that rather than follow the *Scooby-Doo* route of "who's the maniac?", we know from the start who's undertaking the killings and have the full case history as to why he's wound up the way he has.

We don't exactly see the events through his eyes as such, but we're walking alongside him throughout his spree and whilst we may not approve of Billy's actions, I think the viewer sympathises with the terrible childhood he's endured and the film suggests to us in bittersweet fashion, during the montage of him settling into his work as a toy store clerk, that he may have turned out okay in the end, if only it were possible to escape the spectre of Santa Claus in [the] modern USA'.[5]

Part of the reason for *Silent Night, Deadly Night*'s slightly abnormal status within Christmas horror lore can be traced to its nonconformist approach to the apparatus of the genre. While it does, of course, stay true to many tropes that would be expected of a Christmas horror movie, the intent by Sellier and screenwriter Michael Hickey to flesh out the film's characters and explore the emotional significance of the events which are depicted has caused it to occupy a problematic position within this category of film: too psychologically complex to be considered a straightforward slasher feature, it is not quite profound enough to function at the level of serious drama. The legacy of the film's critical reputation, as *Oh, The Horror*'s commentator Josh G. has considered, remains somewhat chequered: 'Here it is. The ultimate killer Santa movie. Sleazy, cheesy, and for some, a queasy experience. It's hard to say if *Silent Night, Deadly Night* is actually a standard slasher film, or whether it's what you'd have expected. [...] It can be argued that *Silent Night, Deadly Night* shouldn't work as a slasher because it doesn't focus around a group of teenagers or adults, but a bunch of individuals and couples. Somehow, *Silent Night* keeps its story and main cast at the viewer's thoughts. Even though this is purely a "just for fun" outing, a lot of characters are being developed without us realising that it's happening'.[6]

There is also an unobtrusive political dimension to the film, in the sense that Mother Superior's Manichean sense of ethicality and deeply repressed approach to natural sexual responses was presumably intended to mirror (and quite possibly lampoon) the oppressiveness of the early eighties' prevailing ideological milieu of moral puritanism. And while the narrative rarely operates at this level of refined thematic sophistication, there are flashes of satire evident in Billy's inability to reconcile his impossibly suppressed physical and emotional urges with the cruelly strict (and at times bizarrely burdensome) moral code which has been inculcated into his mindset over his many years at the orphanage. This, as Henry Stewart has noted, has exemplified a parodic edge exhibited by the film which has often been neglected by reviewers: 'This midnight classic is wittier, with more flashes of visual sophistication, than your typical disposable slasher, [...] infusing Jesus' birthday with a taste of the Old Testament made mortal. [...] As such, [Billy Chapman] embodies Reagan-era conservatism, then at its peak, mocking the strict discipline of compassionless, law-and-order, moral-policing reactionaries every time he hollers his tagline, whenever he finds a woman with her top off or an adolescent bully throwing his weight around: "PUNISH!" If [Billy] was post-Carter America's Santa Claus, he was also its Krampus'.[7]

While *Silent Night, Deadly Night* contains some surprisingly perceptive characterisation, such as the subtle but well-drawn conflict between Mother Superior and Sister Margaret over the best way to ensure Billy's rehabilitation or indeed the delicate hints of marital disharmony sketched out between Billy's ill-fated parents, there is ultimately no denying the fact that the plot is more or less entirely orchestrated with the singular aim of tipping the unhinged foundling completely over the edge and putting him on the path of wanton carnage. The disparity between this simple narrative strategy and its less-than-straightforward execution has lent the film elements of both strength and weakness, but certainly has not hindered its cult reputation. As reviewer Devon B. of *Digital Retribution* has described it:

> While no one can deny *Silent Night, Deadly Night* is a slasher, there is something odd about it too. The film really, really delves into the psychological factors that cause its killer, making Billy the most sympathetic slasher I've seen. Even more unusual is that secondary characters are also developed! Not since Nurse Ratched have I so loathed a character like the Mother Superior (brilliantly played by Lilyan Chauvin), but she's also not just a total bitch. She clearly wants what's best for the children at the orphanage, and also holds herself to her own strict rules, much like Inspector Javert from *Les Misérables.* A much nicer, empathetic nun is also given some depth, which makes for three somewhat rounded characters in this 'gratuitous slasher'. The film's well built characters also lead to its downfall, as the only ones that are of interest are 1) the killer, who you know isn't going to be doing so well by film's end, 2) the Mother Superior, who you want to not be doing so well by film's end and 3) the nice nun, who is safe and secure out of Billy's path until the film's end. So while the film builds and builds, it loses tension once Billy snaps, and sadly turns into exactly what everyone criticizes it for being: a mindless slasher.[8]

While *Silent Night, Deadly Night* is widely recognised with the Christmas horror subgenre, it has conversely never quite reached the level of appreciation enjoyed by other horror franchises of the 1980s, appearing considerably less culturally significant than the likes of the *Friday the 13th* films. But it is nevertheless important to remember that *Silent Night, Deadly Night* was actually released at the same time as Wes Craven's 1980s colossus of the genre, the franchise-spawning *A Nightmare on Elm Street*. Furthermore, the Sellier film actually compared rather favourably at the box-office with Craven's pop culture titan, at least initially, as Andrew Parker describes: '*Silent Night, Deadly Night* out grossed *Nightmare on Elm Street* in its opening weekend, but [...] [it was] the controversy and success on home video of *Silent Night, Deadly Night* [which] ensured the film's status as a potential franchise'.[9] As Parker suggests, the overwhelming notoriety which heralded the release of *Silent Night, Deadly Night* in cinemas was to eclipse any discussion of the film's contribution to the genre, with the debate firmly centring on its alleged debasement of Christmas symbolism in the furtherance of its artistic aims. The notion that the film was somehow anti-Christmas in its sentiment was to dog its financial performance in cinemas from an early stage, and the media furore which met its theatrical release swiftly curtailed any chance of lasting box-office success. Andrew Schanie remarks that '*Silent Night, Deadly Night* opened in limited release on the East Coast [on] November 9, 1984. Three weeks later it closed, though not due to slumping ticket sales. Parents began writing letters of complaint to the media, calling the movie "an intrusion of children's dreams and fantasies". [...] *Silent Night, Deadly Night* was pulled from theaters. Director Charles Sellier believed executives decided to pull the movie before it had an impact on the studio's stocks. To this day Sellier states he never intended to stir any controversy. [...] No one who worked on the movie realized the anger, and free publicity, their little slasher flick would produce'.[10] While the ensuing infamy stoked up avid interest amongst some movie enthusiasts – not least devotees of horror cinema – the picketing of cinemas and TriStar's decision to withdraw the film from public exhibition ultimately meant that audiences would need to wait until it resurfaced on home video before making up their own minds about its perceived merits. Driven on by the media storm which had raged around its original release, the video version of *Silent Night, Deadly Night* was to achieve no small amount of commercial success – profitability which defied the movie's earlier critics and laid the capstone for further entries in the series. As Alan-Bertaneisson Jones observes: 'Ironically, it was the very notoriety that the protestors against the first film generated in having *Silent Night, Deadly Night* removed from cinemas in 1984 that helped lead to its success when released on video, and the mixture of that success and notoriety that all but ensured that sequels were produced exploiting both. And while other – and in some instances much better – films were being produced which married festive themes with horror, it surely helped to solidify in the public mind the concept of the Christmas Horror as a sub-genre having a "series" of films that exploited the notoriety of the original *Silent Night, Deadly Night.* [...] The 1980s saw the Christmas Horror Movie establish its identity and begin to proliferate as a recognised sub-genre'.[11]

One of the most puzzling issues surrounding *Silent Night, Deadly Night* is the fact that such a heightened degree of controversy should have surrounded the film's inclusion of a Santa Claus-costumed murderer as its central figure, given that the same motif had been employed repeatedly throughout the early 1980s and even earlier. Certainly Burt Kleeger's infamous poster artwork – which depicted Billy in his distinctive Santa Claus regalia descending a chimney complete with blood-spattered axe in hand – may have played no small part in promulgating the film's subversive theme amongst the general public in ways that had exceeded the profile of earlier Christmas horror films. Yet as Adam Rockoff has commented, the image of a serial killer in Santa Claus garb had already become so entrenched within the annals of the genre, the intense public reaction which met the film remains something of a mystery to this day:

> Many theaters stopped showing the film entirely and Tri-Star even scrapped *Silent Night, Deadly Night*'s entire West Coast run. What made this entire episode so confusing was that *Silent Night, Deadly Night* was only the latest in a fairly long line of similar films which depicted a killer Santa Claus. As early as 1972, Joan Collins was terrorized by Santa in the now-classic horror anthology *Tales from the Crypt* (1972). Although *Black Christmas* lacks the requisite jolly villain, it does set a series of disturbing murders on what is traditionally the most peaceful and joyous day of the year. *To All a Goodnight* [...] and *You Better Watch Out* [aka *Christmas Evil*] – which not only features a psychotic Santa, but attempts to explain his psychosis with a scene of his mother getting it on with a visibly aroused St Nick – were certainly as offensive as *Silent Night, Deadly Night*, but apparently were not well-known enough to rile the masses. [...] Lost in all of this righteous indignation was the film itself.[12]

As Rockoff suggests, the wave of hysteria surrounding the appearance of *Silent Night, Deadly Night* in cinemas has tended to obscure analysis of the film itself. Protests generally focused upon the film's iconography rather than its actual narrative, and in truth the conventions which it follows are no more shocking than any other entry in the genre which had preceded it. Though Sellier's feature contained a number of capable performances which set it apart from many other slasher movies of the time – among them Gilmer McCormick's empathetic Sister Margaret, Britt Leach's wittily unscrupulous evocation of the self-serving Mr Sims, and of course Lilyan Chauvin's sublimely flinty, imperious Mother Superior – the fact remained that *Silent Night, Deadly Night* was unabashedly a low-budget horror film which exhibited few pretentions beyond telling an absorbing story in an efficient manner. The extent to which it achieved this modest aim has, however, been a subject of contention amongst commentators. Jack Sommersby, for instance, notes that 'while it's not particularly scary or inventively staged, *Silent Night, Deadly Night* makes for an enjoyable slasher flick that's hardly ever nice and almost always naughty. Those with fragile sensibilities and staunch religious convictions won't likely find anything even remotely redeemable about this horror tale involving a killer Santa who wreaks merciless havoc upon a small town in Utah. But for those who harbor even a tad bit [[sic]] of resentment toward the consumer-is-king holiday season – along with an affinity for good gore and nudity – it goes down with the satisfying kick of a whiskey-spiked eggnog'.[13] Others have been less receptive to the film, drawing attention to the ways in which the larger-than-life scenarios which are depicted have a tendency to become unintentionally humorous when viewed out of the context of the horror genre. (This is no more evident than in Billy's inexplicable choice of victims following his initial quartet of toy shop murders, where he appears to randomly charge around the neighbourhood bellowing his emblematic moral battle cry – an image which becomes less effective and more prospectively comical with every repetition.) Depending on one's mood, as Paul Mavis has suggested, the end result has considerable latent comedic potential – a capacity that was presumably never intended by Sellier: 'You might find fault in Michael Hickey's script (from Paul Caimi's *Slayride* story) with the ham-fisted 1940s Freudian underpinnings that cause little Billy to eventually crack, but there's no getting around the fact that Sellier, Jr. puts the movie over with simple-yet-effective storytelling, even achieving an increasingly giddy tone for the sick-joke-loving viewer (like myself) who can't quite believe how outrageously far Billy is pushed before he snaps (by the time Sellier, Jr. shows Billy being forced to put on the Santa suit and scaring the begeesus out of the little kids sitting on his lap, you could have added a laugh track and created the *Saturday Night Live* skit to end all *SNL* holiday skits)'.[14]

Critical discord regarding perceptions of the film's artistic proficiency has continued following its re-release on modern home entertainment formats in recent years, with a number of reviewers drawing attention to the fact that at least some of its shortcomings can be traced to its era of production. Daniel Benson, for instance, has not been alone in emphasising the fact that the shock value of *Silent Night, Deadly Night* has greatly diminished in the time since its initial release: 'It was a controversial movie in the early '80s, no surprise given the subject matter, but by today's standards it's pretty tame stuff. There are some reasonably inventive kills based around the holiday season (strangulation with Christmas lights, impalement on reindeer horns) but not much to really get the excitement up. It's not that it's a bad movie *per se*, just plainly obvious that it was a cheap cash-in on the popular slasher genre of its age'.[15] However, others have drawn attention to the fact that, as the film is so very clearly a product of its time, some unedifying cultural attitudes are on display which would have no place alongside more enlightened, modern sensibilities. This is best exemplified in the rather distasteful hint of misogyny which surfaces in Billy's violent attacks on women, given his mental correlation between nudity and sinfulness, leading to distinctly unsavoury sexist connotations. Eric Henderson perceptively observes that 'as it was made in the locked-down '80s, the controversy was not too surprising. (Also indicative of the conservative times it was created in: the violence is kept to a bare minimum.) But lost in the controversy is the film's unmistakably savage (and sadly archetypal) presentation of women's death scenes, which are distressingly juxtaposed with the exposure of their breasts in a manner that implicates their sexuality with their "naughtiness," or original sin as it were. This was obviously not new territory for the slasher genre, mind you, but *Silent Night, Deadly Night* brought the idea to new levels of cold sleaziness'.[16] Henderson correctly concludes that this form of chauvinism was by no means unusual within the slasher horror at this point in the genre's development, but – on account of the very deliberate way in which Billy's murderous actions reflect the ascetic moral teachings that have been instilled in him – the implication seems all the more distastefully prominent in *Silent Night, Deadly Night.* For instance, the fact that Billy fatally assaults the babysitter Denise on the night of Christmas Eve – for no obvious motivation beyond spotting her in a doorway wearing very little in the way of clothing – underscores his deeply ingrained psychological association between the female form and sexual temptation, leading him to suppress his personal urges in the most violent way possible. Denise herself has, of course, committed no actual transgressive misconduct; her 'punishment' at Billy's hands is solely the result of his desire to subdue his own internal disquiet – a process which he somehow erroneously mistakes as some sort of perverse justice. While this premise is undoubtedly intended to be disturbing or even tragic in its reflection of a profoundly damaged psyche, the objectionable nature of its sexist connotations is difficult to ignore in the more progressive and free-thinking present day.

Not all critical appraisals of *Silent Night, Deadly Night* have been entirely negative; commentators who are willing to evaluate the film based solely on its fidelity to long-held conventions of the horror genre have found that its technical aspects often prove proficient, and many have concluded that Sellier and Hickey's creative strategy of juxtaposing Christmas imagery with horror tropes generally succeeds in producing an unsettling atmosphere. Representative of this line of analysis, Jay Alan remarks that 'the death scenes are awesome for its time of release. The Gore Score is around a ten. The Special Effects, done by Rick Josephson, were ahead of most that came out around this time. There is a surprise decapitation, with a full view of the headless body as the head rolls down a hill behind it. [...] The music score, composed by Perry Botkin is creepy and almost sounds as if it were made to take the spirit right out of the holiday, which is a plus in my eyes. Especially during the title card of the film. The score blasts at you with a splat of blood to prepare you for the slay ride that lies ahead'.[17] But when all is said and done, while *Silent Night, Deadly Night* may well have laid claim to the title of the most recognisable of 1980s Christmas horror films, the legacy of its widespread notoriety

has often dwarfed the fact that – at its heart – Sellier's movie
is a fairly modest affair which is far more inclined towards
providing entertainment and expected scares than it is in
encouraging its audience to ponder over issues of ideological
or philosophical import. As Mike Long observes:

> Once you get past the 'gimmick' – a killer dressed as
> Santa Claus – *Silent Night, Deadly Night* has nothing
> else to offer us. When viewed as a straight horror
> film, the movie is just another slasher movie from the
> early 80s. (Actually, it was a little late to the party, as
> the slasher craze had been going on for over 5 years at
> that point.) Director Charles Sellier, Jr. and Writer
> Michael Hickey bring us the basic trauma from the
> past creates a killer in the present plot. The only
> difference from the other films of this particular era is
> that *Silent Night, Deadly Night* isn't a murder-
> mystery. We know that Billy is the killer and we
> spend most of the first half of the movie waiting for
> him to snap. Once he does (in a contrived manner),
> then the movie simply turns into a few scenes of Billy
> attacking random people and then the inevitable
> finale occurs.[18]

Though it may have seemed inconceivable at the time
of *Silent Night, Deadly Night*'s release, given the wave of
heightened public protest which had accompanied its initial
appearance in cinemas, Sellier's film was to be followed by no
fewer than four sequels over the years ahead. *Silent Night,
Deadly Night Part 2* (Lee Harry, 1987) followed the story of
Billy's homicidal brother Ricky over the Christmas period
some years after the events of the first film, charting his
eventual retribution on the orphanage's Mother Superior.
(The critical reception towards the sequel was very poor, not
least due to the fact that a significant amount of re-edited

material from the Sellier original was employed, often confusingly, as a money-saving strategy.) A psychic twist was introduced into *Silent Night, Deadly Night 3: Better Watch Out!* (Monte Hellman, 1989), where an increasingly unhinged Ricky once again goes on the rampage over the holiday season after awakening from a coma induced by the events of the previous movie. An entirely new story began for the franchise in *Silent Night, Deadly Night 4: Initiation* (Brian Yuzna, 1990), where the murderous Santa Claus motif was dispensed with and a supernatural theme – where a Los Angeles journalist looks into a mysterious murder, only to provoke a deadly coven of witches – was introduced instead. *Silent Night, Deadly Night 5: The Toy Maker* (Martin Kitrosser, 1991) juxtaposed Christmas fantasy with technological horror, fusing philosophical concerns about individual identity with the anxieties surrounding the fast-developing digital age of the early nineties. Although the fifth film was to be the last in the cycle, a remake loosely inspired by the original Sellier movie was released in 2012. Steven Miller's *Silent Night* starred Malcolm McDowell, Donal Logue and Jaime King, and focused upon a mysterious figure in a Santa Claus costume who goes on a killing spree in an urban area, rapidly leading to him becoming the target of a frantic police manhunt. The film's dark humour and the novelty value of its featured murders impressed some reviewers, but the overall critical reception was decidedly variable.

While *Silent Night, Deadly Night* may enjoy a reputation as the eighties' most disputatious Christmas horror film, in truth the movie is but one part of a much wider generic patchwork that was being woven at the time. Along with features such as *Black Christmas* and *Christmas Evil*, *Silent Night, Deadly Night* was to help establish the cornerstone for a lucrative and persistently popular subgenre of Christmas cinema which continues to thrive even in the present day. The Christmas horror film, with its satirising and subversion of traditional festive conventions, seemed perfectly suited to the ongoing period of reinvention which ran through the wider genre of Christmas cinema during the 1980s, and the stylistic tropes and thematic foundations which were put in place – most especially in the early eighties – would pave the way for many later features such as *Elves* (Jeffrey Mandel, 1989), *Jack Frost* (Michael Cooney, 1997), *Dead End* (Jean-Baptiste Andrea and Fabrice Canepa, 2003), *Santa's Slay* (David Steiman, 2005) and *Krampus* (Michael Dougherty, 2015). Like it or loathe it – and critics did both, in equal measure – the Christmas horror film was set to become a lasting feature for decades to come, and in no small part due to the influence of emergent entries in the genre released throughout the eighties.

REFERENCES

1. Don Sumner, *Horror Movie Freak* (Iola: Krause Publications, 2010), p.188.

2. Brian Collins, 'All is Bright: The Producers of *Silent Night, Deadly Night* on Christmas's Best Horror Film', in *Birth. Movies. Death.*, 12 December 2014.
<http://www.birthmoviesdeath.com/2014/12/12/all-is-bright-the-producers-of-silent-night-deadly-night-on-christmass-best>

3. Jim Harper, *Legacy of Blood: A Comprehensive Guide to Slasher Movies* (Manchester: Headpress/Critical Vision, 2004), p.43.

4. Jack Santino, *New Old-Fashioned Ways: Holidays and Popular Culture* (Knoxville: University of Tennessee Press, 1996), p.123.

5. Rosie Gibbs, '*Silent Night, Deadly Night*', in *UK Horror Scene*, 4 December 2015.
<http://www.ukhorrorscene.com/the-ukhs-writers-christmas-horrors-silent-night-deadly-night-1984/>

6. Josh G., '*Silent Night, Deadly Night*', in *Oh, The Horror*, 16 December 2008.
<http://www.oh-the-horror.com/page.php?id=452>

7. Henry Stewart, 'The Best Old Movies on a Big Screen This Week: NYC Repertory Cinema Picks, December 16-22', in *Brooklyn Magazine*, 16 December 2015.

<http://www.bkmag.com/2015/12/16/the-best-old-movies-on-a-big-screen-this-week-nyc-repertory-cinema-picks-december-16-22/5/>

8. Devon B., '*Silent Night Deadly Night 1&2*', in *Digital Retribution*, 25 December 2006.
<http://www.digital-retribution.com/reviews/dvd/0565.php>

9. Andrew Parker, 'Defending the Indefensible: *Silent Night Deadly Night* Parts 1&2', in *Dork Shelf*, 18 December 2012.
<http://www.dorkshelf.com/2012/12/18/defending-the-indefensible-silent-night-deadly-night-parts-1-2/>

10. Andrew Schanie, *Movie Confidential: Sex, Scandal, Murder and Mayhem in the Film Industry* (Cincinnatti: Clerisy Press, 2010), p.108.

11. Alan-Bertaneisson Jones, *Fright Xmas* (Central Milton Keynes: AuthorHouse, 2010), p.143.

12. Adam Rockoff, *Going to Pieces: The Rise and Fall of the Slasher Film, 1978-1986* (Jefferson: McFarland and Company, 2002), p.157.

13. Jack Sommersby, '*Silent Night, Deadly Night*', in *eFilmCritic*, 2 December 2003.
<http://www.efilmcritic.com/review.php?movie=3194&reviewer=327>

14. Paul Mavis, '*Silent Night, Deadly Night*: Christmas Survival Double Feature', in *DVD Talk*, 4 December 2012.
<http://www.dvdtalk.com/reviews/58650/silent-night-deadly-night-dbft/>

15.   Daniel Benson, '*Silent Night Deadly Night*', in *Horror Talk*, 20 November 2009. *<http://www.horrortalk.com/index.php/reviews/701-silent-night-deadly-night>*

16.   Eric Henderson, '*Silent Night, Deadly Night*', in *Slant Magazine*, 22 October 2003. *<http://www.slantmagazine.com/film/review/silent-night-deadly-night>*

17.   Jay Alan, '*Silent Night, Deadly Night*', in *Horror News*, 18 March 2011. *<http://horrornews.net/32216/film-review-silent-night-deadly-night-1984/>*

18.   Mike Long, '*Silent Night, Deadly Night* (1984)/*Silent Night, Deadly Night Part 2* (1987)', in *DVD Sleuth*, 4 December 2012. *<http://www.dvdsleuth.com/SilentNightDeadlyNightDoubleFeatureReview/>*

10

One Magic Christmas (1985)

Walt Disney Pictures/Northpole Picture Company of Canada

Director: Phillip Borsos
Producer: Peter O'Brian
Screenwriter: Thomas Meehan, from a story by
Phillip Borsos, Barry Healey and Thomas Meehan

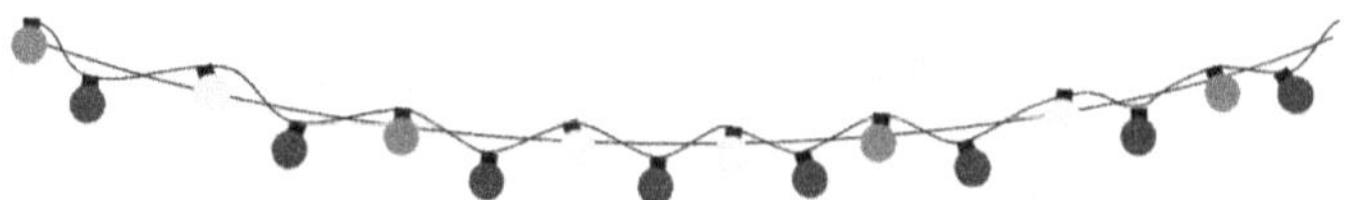

If the first half of the 1980s had been especially noted for the emergence and establishment of the Christmas horror movie into the periphery of mainstream cinema, along with a number of noteworthy experimental features, the rest of the decade would instead become known for alternating between traditional and decidedly off-kilter approaches to festive cinema. Just as features such as *Trading Places*, *Comfort and Joy* and *Gremlins* had set the stage for new and progressively more inventive iterations of the recognised conventions of festive cinema, vigorously contrasting elements of the familiar and the pioneering to produce a fresh take on the Christmas film, so too would the latter half of the 1980s bear witness to continued generic innovation. Yet as the decade reached its midway point, a deliberate return to the kind of long-established tropes most closely affiliated with the genre's forties and fifties heyday could also be identified, and few features could claim quite such an affinity with those time-honoured narrative conventions as the Walt Disney Company's *One Magic Christmas*.

With its combination of traditional Christmas thematic elements and a surprisingly hard-hitting central scenario which lent itself much more to the economically turbulent 1980s than it would likely have done to the post-austerity golden age of festive cinema in the late forties and early fifties, *One Magic Christmas* would prove to be an unusual yuletide feature in many respects. Contrasting grinding hardship and hard-edged realism with a sense of fanciful whimsy which harkened back to a considerably more light-hearted period of festive film-making, *One Magic Christmas* has come to be regarded as a divisive feature which has characterised the tendency of some eighties Christmas movies to straddle a delicate line between strident modernity, social relevance and backward-looking nostalgia.

The film was helmed by Canadian director, screenwriter and producer Phillip Borsos, a well-regarded figure in North American cinema who had achieved critical success with earlier movies such as crime drama *The Grey Fox* (1982) and thriller *The Mean Season* (1985). Following his death in 1995 at the age of only 41, the Whistler Film Festival established the Borsos Award in the director's honour, where Canadian films being screened at the annual festival may be entered into contention for a jury-awarded prize. Borsos and writer Barry Healey collaborated on the storyline of *One Magic Christmas* with Thomas Meehan, a versatile and highly experienced scriptwriter who penned the film's screenplay. Meehan has become perhaps most immediately recognisable for his collaborations with director/producer Mel Brooks on films such as *To Be or Not to Be* (1983) and *Spaceballs* (1987), as well as stage adaptations of Brooks's popular cinematic work which has included *The Producers* (2001) and *Young Frankenstein* (2007). Meehan has been conferred the Tony Award for Best Book of a Musical on three occasions, most notably for his well-received Broadway debut *Annie* (1977), and has been nominated for three Primetime Emmy Awards, winning the Outstanding Writing Achievement in Comedy, Variety or Music Award in 1970 for *Annie: The Women in the Life of a Man* (Walter C. Miller, 1970). He is also a regular contributor to *The New Yorker* magazine.

Deep in the American countryside, an angel in human form named Gideon (Harry Dean Stanton) is cheerily playing a Christmas carol on his harmonica when he is interrupted by the disembodied voice of St Nicholas (Jan Rubes). The spectral Santa Claus explains that he is allocating assignments to angels for Christmas, and this year Gideon is facing a tough case – a woman named Ginny Grainger, who is so bereft of festive cheer that she never offers anyone a yuletide greeting.

In a small town in the United States named Medford the Christmas celebrations are already well underway, with shoppers packing the streets in search of gifts for friends and loved ones. Gideon watches silently from the side-lines as Ginny (Mary Steenburgen) and her family walk by. There is obvious friction between Ginny and her husband Jack (Gary Basaraba); the latter wants to take their children Abbie (Elizabeth Harnois) and Cal (Robbie Magwood) to visit a department store Santa Claus, but Ginny refuses on the grounds that they are too low on funds to afford the admission fee. Jack is good-natured and full of Christmas cheer; he even resists the temptation to argue with Ginny when she irritably needles him over his lack of income after having been laid off by his erstwhile employers, Continental

Radio, some months beforehand. Cal and Abbie remain excited about Santa's rapidly-approaching annual visit, but Ginny pours cold water over their exhilaration by telling the kids not to expect too much from Christmas on account of their straitened financial circumstances. In spite of his wife's despondency, the persistently optimistic Jack tells his son and daughter to write down everything they want in a letter to Santa.

Making matters worse, Ginny and Jack's home is owned by Continental Radio, and the company has decided to evict them during the holiday season given that Jack is no longer in their employ. They have only ten days left to pack up their belongings, and a bad weather front has brought heavy snow to the area which is further hampering their efforts. Ginny is irked when Jack, rather than helping her to pack up their belongings, instead spends his time in the basement building bicycles from spare parts to give to the less fortunate kids of the neighbourhood. Jack reveals to his genial friend Eddie (Elias Koteas) that he would dearly love to open a bicycle shop of his own, but lacks the funds to start up an independent business. However, he and Eddie are raising cash for another worthy cause – providing electric lights for the town's community Christmas tree.

Outside, kids playing in the street look up in amazement as the snowfall suddenly comes to an abrupt halt. Gideon, still watching from a distance, seems to have called on a little supernatural help to improve the weather. He listens intently as Abbie and Cal discuss their hopes for the coming Christmas celebrations. Molly Monaghan (Sarah Polley), an impoverished little girl who lives nearby, reflects sadly that she would like nothing more than a bicycle for Christmas; the siblings exchange knowing glances, aware of their father's altruistic plans. Abbie glumly points out that her mother has no festive spirit, and is always unmoved by everyone else's Christmas cheer. Gideon hears this last observation with concern, but his musing is interrupted when kids playing on the street accidentally send a hockey puck flying towards Abbie, Cal and Molly. Using uncanny powers of telekinesis, Gideon diverts the puck in mid-air, causing it to crash through the window of a nearby house. The kids scatter desperately in an attempt to avoid the blame, but Molly and Cal watch the unlikely scene in awe.

Back at the Grainger family home, Ginny is annoyed when Continental Radio representative Frank Crump (Graham Jarvis) arrives unannounced to show the uppity Mr and Mrs Noonan (John Friesen and Debra McGrath) and their children (Julie Beaulieu and Jeremy Dingle) around their home. The Noonans are set to be the house's new occupants after the Graingers' departure, but add further indignity to the situation by openly criticising the decorative choices of the current inhabitants. Further problems later ensue when the family bathroom is accidentally flooded, and Cal unintentionally smashes the window while trying to mop up.

Things don't get any better for Ginny at work, where she is employed as a sales assistant at a local supermarket under the management of the officious Herbie Conklin (Timothy Webber). Gideon watches from a nearby aisle of the shop as Ginny faces obstreperous customers such as Harry Dickens (Wayne Robson) and the awkward sight of Molly Monaghan's mother (Joy Thompson-Allen) realising at the last moment that she has insufficient funds to pay for her shopping. The overburdened Ginny has little time for the festivities, even with only a few days to go until Christmas Day, but while the pressure at work continues to escalate

Abbie and Cal are helping their father to decorate the Medford community Christmas tree at the centre of town.

That night, as Abbie gets ready for bed she asks Jack what he will be getting Ginny for Christmas. Jack replies that he intends to gift her an amethyst ring which used to belong to his late grandmother, but swears his young daughter to secrecy. Abbie then asks if angels really exist, given that Ginny has previously asserted that they are merely imaginary. Jack tells her that it all comes down to a matter of faith; he personally believes that angels watch over the people of the earth, but that they are invisible and thus their efforts often go unseen. After the children are both in their beds, a tired Ginny reveals to Jack that she has managed to buy some Christmas gifts during her lunch break – a tea-set for Abbie and an Etch-a-Sketch for Cal. Jack is delighted at the thoughtfulness of her presents, but feels that the children deserve more... leading to another argument about their precarious situation and dwindling funds. Unknown to either of them, Cal and Abbie are listening to their disagreement from the top of the stairs. Cal is upset that their reduced circumstances will mean that they are likely to expect little if anything in the way of gifts this Christmas, but Abbie chooses instead to place her hopes in the benevolence of Santa Claus.

Later, Abbie decides to follow her father's earlier advice and writes a letter to Santa. As she does so, Ginny is apologising to Jack for her short temper, explaining that the stress of the forthcoming move, the restrictions of their fast-diminishing finances and the pressures of her job have been getting to her. Jack responds that her viewpoint would be much improved if she had any time for the magic of Christmas, but the cynical Ginny responds that she feels as though the festive season is nothing more than a combination of rampant commercialism and cloying insincerity. Meanwhile, Abbie races out in the dead of night to post her letter to Santa in the street's mailbox. Seeing her, Gideon uses his powers to magically retrieve the letter, much to Abbie's bewilderment. The little girl is sceptical of his claim to be an angel because he is not invisible, but Gideon explains that sometimes even angels have to show up for real. He tells her that one Christmas many years ago, he rescued a child from drowning in a river but ended up being unable to save himself. Because of his selflessness, he was made a Christmas angel after his human life had ended. This means, he clarifies, that every year he must help one person to embrace the Christmas spirit. When Abbie excitedly asks if he can help Ginny to become more enthusiastic about the festive season, he replies that he intends to exactly that – but that he will need Abbie's help in order to do so. Gideon tells her to take back her letter to Santa Claus and ask Ginny to mail it for her instead. This, he promises, will be her mother's first step to rediscovering the wonder of Christmas. Abbie then runs home, but only narrowly avoids being knocked down by a car when Gideon once again intervenes with his spiritual powers to save her. Ginny, who has only just discovered her daughter's absence, is less than impressed by Abbie's claims of having met an angel and angrily rebukes her for venturing outside on her own in the early hours of the morning.

The next morning, Ginny's mood appears to improve as the family take a drive together. At their kids' prompting, she and Jack reminisce about their youth, discussing Ginny's childhood days growing up at her father's motel and the romance which blossomed with Jack following a blind date. The Graingers soon arrive at the home of Jack's grandfather

Caleb (Arthur Hill), an amiable old man who captivates the children with stories of Santa Claus. While searching his attic for some Christmas lights, Caleb uncovers a snow-globe with a North Pole scene and a book of festive stories which had belonged to his mother, both of which he gifts to an enraptured Abbie and Cal.

That night, the children excitedly talk about Santa's coming arrival, though Abbie finds her enthusiasm dampened somewhat by Ginny's disinterested responses about the snow-globe and Santa's North Pole home. The little girl is particularly deflated when Ginny tells her that she hasn't had the chance to mail the letter to Santa Claus. However, once her mother has left the room Gideon appears out of nowhere. Abbie tells the angel that she fears that Ginny will never love Christmas, but Gideon replies that her antipathy towards the festive season was not always so – in years gone by, she was full of the Christmas spirit, but something changed in her that only Ginny can set right. Gideon warns Abbie that some extraordinary events will be taking place over the coming day, but that she must not be afraid by what unfolds. Before disappearing, Gideon explains that when the time comes for Abbie to find him, he will be waiting for her at the town's Christmas tree.

Downstairs, Ginny is rummaging through some correspondence when, to her irritation, she discovers Abbie's letter to Santa Claus. She is further exasperated when she finds that Jack is still playing around with financial figures as he tries to work out a way of launching his bicycle company without sufficient funds. Pointing out that he needs to expend more effort on finding a regular salaried job rather than indulging in pipe dreams about owning his own business, Ginny's glib dismissal of Jack's aspirations leads her husband to leave the house in anger. Realising his frustration, she races after him and attempts rapprochement, saying that her desperation over their escalating monetary woes is dominating her judgement. Pessimistic about their mounting worries, she asks aloud what the point of her existence has been. Jack replies that life is only purposeless when people lose sight of its simple pleasures: a starry night, and the company of each other. When Ginny's depressive viewpoint continues to grind him down, Jack decides to walk on alone in order to collect his thoughts.

Returning home, Ginny is startled when she encounters Gideon. Though she is unaware of his identity as an angel, she is confounded by his insistence that she must accept the spirit of Christmas before it's too late. Pointing out that she has little to be positive about this festive season, Gideon nonetheless tells her that it is important that she discovers the true meaning of the holidays. Curious, Ginny asks how the stranger knows her name, only to find that he has disappeared into thin air. She then watches in amazement as every electric Christmas light in the street is suddenly and inexplicably extinguished right in front of her eyes.

The next morning is Christmas Eve. With the family breakfasting around the kitchen table, Ginny tells them that she will be working at the supermarket all day until ten. Jack asks if it is really necessary that she work a double shift, but his wife replies that it is more than her job is worth if she refuses. Ginny also gets increasingly snappy at Jack's regret that she will have to miss the lighting of the community Christmas tree, and grumpily dismisses Abbie's wide-eyed enthusiasm about Santa's coming visit that night. She departs just as Eddie arrives with the portable electricity generator which will be required for lighting the tree later in the day;

Jack hushes his friend when he raises the issue of the fundraiser, telling him that Ginny is unaware of their efforts.

At a filling station on the way to work, Ginny is intrigued to see Harry Dickens – the problematic customer whom she had earlier served at the supermarket – frantically trying to sell his decrepit car to a garage mechanic (Sam Malkin). His desperation to raise funds is tangible. When he fails in his attempt, Dickens appears to be filled with a terrible resolve. Meanwhile, Jack parks outside the town's bank in order to make a withdrawal. Though he warns his kids to stay safely in the car, Abbie can't resist the temptation to visit her mother at work and tell her excitedly about the new Christmas tree that Jack has bought for the family. Ginny is outraged when she learns that her husband is planning to take money out of the bank without telling her, and storms away from her cash register. When Conklin sees her leave her post during the Christmas rush, he fires her for breaking company rules – though her ire is such that she barely breaks her stride.

Once Ginny has returned Abbie to the car, she heads to the bank in order to confront Jack... only to discover that a gun-toting Dickens is in the middle of staging a hold-up. Realising that the bank staff will not comply with his demands, he takes a hostage and edges towards the door. When Jack tries to intervene in the hope of a peaceful resolution, the agitated Dickens shoots him dead. As the distraught Ginny races to her fallen husband's side, Dickens uses the resulting chaos to make a break from the building and quickly commandeers the nearest car – which happens to be Jack's. Ginny watches in horror as Dickens speeds away, her children still in the back seat. Now utterly hysterical, Ginny jumps into Dickens's own rust-bucket of an automobile and sets off in pursuit just as the police arrive at the bank.

After a while spent trailing her family car, Ginny discovers that Dickens's vehicle is out of fuel and she is soon forced to abandon it on a remote country road. With no other choice, she gives chase on foot, but shortly afterwards a police patrol car spots her and the officers inside pick her up. Some distance ahead, another police car is blockading a bridge in an effort to impede Dickens's escape. Panicking, Dickens steps on the accelerator but clips the stationary patrol car at speed, thus causing the stolen vehicle to plunge over the side of the bridge into a fast-flowing river below. Ginny arrives just in time to watch the car containing her two children as it sinks into the icy depths.

Back at the now-empty Grainger family home, Ginny bursts into tears at the thought of having lost her entire family within a single day. She is oblivious to the fact that Gideon has saved both Abbie and Cal from their frozen fates and is returning them to shelter. Soon afterwards, Caleb arrives with the joyful news that the police have discovered both Grainger children by the roadside, reasoning that Dickens must have dropped them off before driving to his death. But on their return home, Abbie has a different account of proceedings, insisting that it was Gideon who had retrieved her and her brother from otherwise-certain death. Ginny is too overjoyed at their miraculous return to bother rejecting her daughter's explanation, though the elusive angel is watching the tearful reunion from just across the street.

Later, Ginny sorrowfully explains to the children the events that led up to Jack's death. Though both are distressed by the news, Abbie feels certain that Gideon can help, having seen his magic powers in action. Remembering his promise that he could be found at the town Christmas tree, Abbie sprints off to ask for his aid. Cal tells Ginny of his sister's plans, leading her to set off to find Abbie and bring her home to safety. She does not realise, however, that Gideon already at the rendezvous point as he had arranged. Abbie explains her desire to see Jack brought back to life, and her mother's broken heart mended in the process. Gideon says that granting this wish is beyond his own abilities, but he knows someone who might be able to help – none other than Santa Claus. By the time Ginny arrives on the scene, both her daughter and the angel have disappeared, much to her sorrow.

Eddie sees Ginny and tries to reassure her that Abbie has probably wandered home on her own. He offers to drive her back to the house, though neither of them realise that Gideon has actually transported the little girl far away to Santa's workshop at the North Pole. The angel encourages Abbie to knock on the door, where she is greeted by the kindly Mrs Claus (Rita Tuckett). She is then taken deeper into the building, where she meets Santa Claus himself. Explaining the situation, she pleads with him to bring her father back from the dead, but with genuine regret Santa tells her that some requests cannot be achieved even with his extensive powers. However, he gives her one last hope by revealing that there is a single person who still has the ability to return Jack to the living – her mother, Ginny. When Abbie enquires further, Santa says that he has something that she will need to give to Ginny in order to help her regain her Christmas spirit. He takes the girl into the heart of his workshop, where she watches in wonder at toys being made for children all around the world. The people constructing them are dressed in costumes from many different backgrounds, nationalities and time periods. At one point, Abbie spots her old school janitor who had died some time ago. Santa explains that everyone assumes that elves help to run the workshop, but in actuality his assistants are really just ordinary men and women whose lives on earth have come to an end. He greets them all by name, and in many different languages.

Eventually they reach Santa's mail room, where every letter ever sent to the workshop is stored. Santa finds a letter which had been posted to him from a little girl whose name was Ginny Hanks. Placing it in Abbie's care, he tells her to give it to her mother as soon as possible. Shortly after, Santa departs in his sleigh to take care of his Christmas deliveries while Mrs Claus summons Gideon to return Abbie to her home. As she expected, neither Ginny or Cal believe the story of her North Pole adventure, but her mother's scepticism is profoundly shaken when she discovers the letter that she had written to Santa Claus many years beforehand. Returning downstairs, Ginny realises that in the pandemonium of the past day she has forgotten to post Abbie's own letter to Santa. Heading off to the street's mailbox, she once again meets Gideon who watches in satisfaction as Ginny finally posts the envelope containing Abbie's letter. He wishes her a heartfelt Happy Christmas, and when she offers him a 'good night' in return she notices that all of the street's Christmas decorations have suddenly illuminated again. But her astonishment does not end there. Walking up the road towards her is none other than Jack, completely unharmed. Elated, she embraces him passionately, but her husband is somewhat taken aback – from his point of view, they have only just parted after their quarrel the previous evening. Ginny realises to her bewilderment that, due to Gideon's intervention, all of the troubling events of Christmas Eve have never happened.

The next day, the Graingers begin Christmas Eve anew – though only Ginny is aware of the outcomes of their previous attempt. Around the kitchen table at breakfast, she stuns her family by telling them that she plans to take the day off; if her overbearing manager decides to fire her, that is less important than spending Christmas with her loved ones. Then, right on cue, she finds Dickens at the gas station once again pleading with the garage mechanic to buy his car. Knowing what will happen next, Ginny steps in and offers to buy Dickens's old camp stove for $50. Recognising her from their earlier meeting at the supermarket, where he had been obnoxiously rude to her, Dickens is staggered by her generosity. Moved almost to tears with relief at having such desperately-needed money, he thanks her and wishes her a merry Christmas.

At the supermarket, Ginny explains to Conklin that – even in spite of the Christmas rush of customers – she needs to spend the holidays with her family. To her astonishment, the uptight manager agrees with her reasoning and gives her the day off, though with the proviso that she be back at her cash register first thing after Christmas. Later, the Graingers carry out their planned festive deliveries – including dropping off the much-wanted bicycle with Mrs Monaghan and her daughter Molly. Then the townsfolk watch with delight as Eddie kicks the generator into life and lights up the community Christmas tree. As Ginny gets into the swing of the infectious festive spirit at last, she spots Gideon watching from the shadows – his work now done.

Back home, Ginny suddenly decides on the perfect Christmas present for Jack; she signs him a cheque for $5000 – all of their remaining savings – so that he can achieve his dream and open his own bicycle shop. Her musings are soon interrupted by a loud thump from the roof of their home; Santa Claus is paying his annual visit. Ginny quietly creeps into the living room just as St Nicholas is ticking the Grainger home off of his list, his deliveries made for another year. The pair regard each other in silence for a moment, before Santa smiles and wishes Ginny a warm 'Merry Christmas'. For the first time in many years, Ginny offers him the same greeting in return, just before Santa departs in his sleigh to complete his long global task of spreading joy and goodwill.

Watching *One Magic Christmas* is a strangely disjointed experience. Though emotionally affecting in some ways, the movie treads an uneasy boundary between social commentary and imaginative fantasy, borrowing narrative elements from Frank Capra's 1946 masterpiece *It's a Wonderful Life* and Scrooge's redemption from Charles Dickens's *A Christmas Carol* whilst ultimately failing to recapture the power and effectiveness of either. The film's debt to Capra is made plain from the opening sequence, which is unabashedly inspired by *It's a Wonderful Life* (right down to the motif of an angel receiving a Christmas-themed supernatural assignment), while the town of Medford in which the action takes place is a none-too-subtle allusion to the earlier movie's Bedford Falls. Yet the similarity often proves to be skin deep, with Borsos's film pushing the envelope somewhat with regard to the tragedies endured by the Grainger family and their later resolution (or erasure, depending upon one's point of view). While Ginny's Scrooge-like transformation is heavily signposted in the grand tradition of Christmas cinema past, the combination of wistful reminiscence and hastily-reversed catastrophe never quite seems to be entirely convincing, making the film appear curiously disordered overall. The amalgamation of realism and fantasy ultimately makes for an awkward clash, with the imaginative scenes at Santa's workshop jarring uneasily with the small town authenticity of icy streets, bustling stores and seasonal community spirit.

There is, however, a rather more pressing concern beyond the issues surrounding the film's stylistic effectiveness. The reversal of Jack's death, due to Ginny's abrupt acceptance of the festive spirit and a little magic from Santa and his assistant Gideon, is arguably one of the most irresponsible narrative decisions ever made in Christmas cinema, rivalling the events of *All I Want For Christmas* (Robert Lieberman, 1991) where Leslie Nielsen's Santa Claus miraculously reverses the divorce of the protagonist's parents in response to his yuletide wish. As Matthew M. Foster astutely observes, 'George Bailey never had it this bad. It is all told without a speck of humor or joy. Ginny is miserable, her husband and children are getting to be, and you will be too while watching. [...] The end result is glib, and an insult to anyone who has really lost family members. Apparently, the best way to deal with the horrible death of a spouse and young children is to visit Santa. But then in this film, we don't see anyone dealing with death in any fashion, realistic or otherwise. Ginny retains the same level of melancholy no matter what happens around her'.[1] Even though Jack's resurrection comes about via the turning back of time rather than a more direct method of revival, making his demise seem as though it was merely a bad dream, it is a plot development which is likely to require a fair bit of explanation for some younger members of the audience.

The sheer relentlessness of the misfortune which is heaped upon the Grainger family was not lost on many reviewers, who have come to regard the endless succession of domestic calamities as excessive even in terms of the

Capraesque festive scenario that Borsos and screenwriter Meehan are reaching for. Jeffrey M. Anderson rings the changes between artistic intention and end product by calling attention to the film's inability to make good on its narrative objectives: 'The movie is a desperate remake of *It's a Wonderful Life*, which itself treads on dangerous ground. That movie is depressing for almost two hours, then redeems itself in a marvelous ending that only Frank Capra could pull off. [...] I was just sitting there, thinking I needed a dose of Christmas spirit, and this movie made me more depressed than I already was. If you have kids, don't let them see this movie'.[2] While there is little doubting the good intentions of the production team, the immediacy and overarching scale of the family's plight eventually overshadows the attempts at light-hearted quirkiness which characterise the movie's fantasy elements, and this results in diminishing the effectiveness of both. While acknowledging the social problems being encountered by many families during the 1980s was far from an untried strategy in the festive cinema of the decade, in this case the exploration of economic hardship and its effects on the individual as well as the family unit has the effect of hampering the very point that Borsos and Meehan set out to make – namely that loved ones and community are more essentially important to wellbeing than commercial endeavours, and that the act of rediscovering the Christmas spirit is intrinsically linked with appreciating and caring for the people who are around us. As Roger Ebert explains, in execution the hazardous narrative strategy implemented by the screenplay never quite manages to pull off the desired effect of delivering an adept conclusion that can act as an effective antidote to the harrowing action which precedes it:

This is very unfortunate. What we have here is a movie with an intelligent screenplay, wonderful performances and skillful direction, but it is a tactical miscalculation from beginning to end. [...] [There] is a happy ending, but, boy, do we have to sweat for it. I don't know what the filmmakers were thinking of. Couldn't they have had the Graingers face some more everyday problems, like a sick dog or overdue heating bills? Did there have to be three deaths in the family, in addition to unemployment and no toys under the tree? Aren't they laying it on a little thick? I think so, and I'll bet little kids will think so, too.[3]

For a film which was released under the Walt Disney Pictures banner, the content was considerably darker than might otherwise have been expected, with an uncompromisingly bleak central scenario and the inclusion of themes which were far removed from many children's dramas of the time. These included the challenges of maintaining a marriage under severe economic strain, the deleterious effects of long-term unemployment on personal self-esteem, and the disastrous impact of widespread industrial redundancies on entire communities. While these topics were understandably toned down to some degree in order to conform to mainstream expectations of family-friendly Christmas cinema, their very presence in such a movie was something of a peculiarity at the time, and the film does seem to fit rather inelegantly amongst the wider Disney output of the period. As Ella Donald notes, 'gone are the usual middle-class comforts of Disney families, the cushy settings, situations and twee optimism. Instead, *One Magic Christmas* is about a family that is on the brink of "going to the poor house", worrying about money in bank accounts and the quality of presents, along with many others in the neighbourhood. [...]

One Magic Christmas is a near-meaningless title of not necessarily a bad film, just an incredibly odd one. Its storyline and themes make it a hard sell, which explains the choice of the title on Disney's part'.[4] Yet in its artistic aims, the film is at least homologous with a general tendency throughout the eighties to establish congruence between traditional Christmas motifs and contemporary settings, corresponding fantasy situations with modern environments often in ways which allow for social commentary or even veiled cultural satire. Yet lacking the subversive streak of early 1980s horror cinema or the sardonic bite of some of the decade's Christmas-themed comedies, the outcome proves to be patchy and occasionally lacklustre. Andy Webb has noted the fragmented nature of the narrative, remarking that its lack of coherence is ironically highlighted by its own allusions to earlier films of the genre: 'What is for certain is that the storyline to *One Magic Christmas* has been inspired by some much greater Christmas movies as it has an angel being sent to help out a troubled family and in particular the mother who has become a total Christmas sceptic. [...] *One Magic Christmas* is a conflicted movie which doesn't know its audience. It goes from being this realistic and down beat drama of a family going through hard times into this child like fantasy and the blend of the two just doesn't work, making it feel like two movies thrown together'.[5]

In the tradition of earlier angel-themed Christmas films, such as *The Bishop's Wife* (Henry Koster, 1947), the mystical nature of Gideon is downplayed, with his paranormal powers presented only via the context of his superficially-earthly appearance. Unlike the earlier Koster or Capra films, here the angel is not a heavenly agent so much as an assistant of Santa Claus, assigned to ensure that Christmas goodwill is enjoyed by all rather than to offer moral rectification (as had been the case of the ghosts in *A Christmas Carol*). Brian Attebery points out that 'the Christmas angel Gideon in *One Magic Christmas* [...] [is] fully humanized, [...] a former human who drowned in the Snake River saving a child. Yet [he upholds the responsibility of] issuing spiritual wake-up calls to skeptical and jaded individuals'.[6] The film benefits greatly from Borsos's inspired choice of Harry Dean Stanton, cast against type as the unobtrusive, gentle-hearted angel who sets in motion Ginny's reconnection with the Christmas-loving spirit of her youth. Active in film and television since the 1950s, Stanton was a prolific actor and a well-known face to moviegoers of the eighties due to appearances in many high-profile features which included *Alien* (Ridley Scott, 1979), *Escape from New York* (John Carpenter, 1981), *Paris, Texas* (Wim Wenders, 1984) and *Repo Man* (Alex Cox, 1984). Stanton's performance is well-complemented by Jan Rubes, who makes for an appealing Santa Claus; wise, kindly and munificent, Rubes is every inch the compassionate old St Nicholas that is required to offset the film's darker moments. While admittedly, as Kim Newman has observed, 'the surprisingly dour *One Magic Christmas* [...] [has] made a fairly feeble case for [the] beloved old figure of universal benevolence and charity',[7] the fact remains that the scenes at Santa's workshop are a definite highlight of an otherwise gloomy and disconsolate film. The skilfully-rendered interior of Santa's North Pole workplace is inspired, imbued with many well-considered fine details (thanks in no small part to Rondi Johnson's virtuosic set design), while the substitution of the expected army of elves with an international cross-section of historical peoples makes for a breath of fresh air –

albeit one which is in largely in tune with the film's generally unconventional approach.

One Magic Christmas showcased many solid supporting performances, not least from talented child actors Elizabeth Harnois, Robbie Magwood and Sarah Polley who all render an accomplished portrayal of characters who – due to domestic circumstances beyond their control – find themselves trapped between weary scepticism and hopeful anticipation. Arthur Hill impresses in his brief appearance as thoughtful grandfather Caleb, while the film was also an early feature in the career of Elias Koteas who shortly afterwards would find fame as the laconic oddball Duncan in the John Hughes-scripted *Some Kind of Wonderful* (Howard Deutch, 1987). However, if *One Magic Christmas* belongs to anyone it is its star Mary Steenburgen, who excels in the unenviable task of turning the disenchanted killjoy Ginny into a rejuvenated acolyte of the festive season. Steenburgen, who had won an Academy Award and Golden Globe Award in the category of Best Supporting Actress for her appearance in *Melvin and Howard* (Jonathan Demme, 1980), was becoming an increasingly well-recognised artist in American cinema at the time thanks to performances in such varied and high-profile films as *Cross Creek* (Martin Ritt, 1983), *Romantic Comedy* (Arthur Hiller, 1983) and *Ragtime* (Milos Forman, 1981), for which she was again nominated for a Best Supporting Actress Golden Globe Award. She faced something of an uphill struggle in *One Magic Christmas*, largely because Ginny's lack of yuletide cheer is palpably understandable – there are likely to be few members of the audience who, faced with a similar barrage of hardships, would themselves be brimming with festive joy. Thus attempting to generate viewer sympathy with the character's plight is hampered by the unconvincing swiftness of Ginny's moment of epiphany, where she is able to momentarily put to one side the still-raw grief of her husband's recent death to fully embrace the Christmas spirit – simply on account of being briefly reunited with a reminder of her younger self's holiday season exuberance. Though Steenburgen's performance is never less than capable, she must constantly fight hard against the character's depressive nature and increasingly desperate predicament in order to present a figure that is in any way likely to encourage audience engagement. Blaine Allan explains that '*One Magic Christmas* [...] might be accused of structural flaws in [its script]. The apparent deaths of Jack, Cal, and Abby [sic] have no structural function except as a means to wear down Ginnie [sic] by showing her how awful life can turn in a flash. Arguably, they also stand as punishments for her ill temper. It is only because Abby [sic] makes her trip and Ginnie [sic] sees the letter reminding her of the girl she once was that she also retrieves the Christmas spirit and Gideon's mission is accomplished'.[8] Because Ginny faces such a tortuous series of dilemmas, her personal quandary appears ever more difficult to watch (especially in a family film, where they are considerably less foreseeable), and thus the result of the character's eventual conversion to optimistic festive cheer is not so much that of audience jubilation but rather a relieved sense of unexpected reprieve.

In spite of its questionable narrative choices, there are many agreeable aspects of *One Magic Christmas*'s production to enjoy which include the chilly winter atmosphere of its well-realised snowy venues (nicely depicted in Frank Tidy's efficient cinematography) and Michael Conway Baker's contemplative original score, not least in the way that the melody of popular seasonal carol *O Christmas Tree* is woven into the score at various points such as Gideon's opening harmonica recital, the chase sequence as Ginny desperately pursues Dickens, and its triumphant rendering at the film's climax. However, it is for its selection of winning performances that *One Magic Christmas* is at its most memorable, given that so many of them are strong enough to be able to stand apart from the general lop-sidedness of the plot. As Michael Walsh elucidates, not even the unyielding misery of the Grainger family's trials can entirely obscure the charming sense of whimsicality lurking beneath the film's often-grim exterior:

> 'Tis the season to be suspicious of films with cloying titles like *One Magic Christmas*. Such films seem manufactured to recall feelings from that remembered long ago when the Yuletide was a time of families and faith, not crass commercialism. Unfortunately, these feelings lose a lot in contemporary translation. 'Christmas spirit' is a quality that Thomas Meehan's screenplay never bothers to describe or define. [...] Despite its dumb premise, this [...] release manages a number of genuinely affecting moments. Under Phillip Borsos's direction, actress Harnois gives a performance designed to make Steven Spielberg envious. Borsos's picture is at its best when it focuses on this wonderfully talented child. Abbie's visit to St Nicholas (Jan Rubes) in his North Pole headquarters is a beautifully realized fantasy, the sequence that comes closest to living up to the picture's promising title.[9]

In spite of the movie's generally lukewarm critical reception, subsequent home entertainment releases have seen the hostility of commentators towards *One Magic Christmas* becoming considerably more muted over the passing years.

While admittedly the film has not become a regular staple of festive television scheduling to the same extent as many other Christmas movies of the era, limiting the scope of audience familiarity to some degree, many recent appraisals of Borsos's feature have taken their cue from the sentiment of Janet Maslin's contemporary review in *The New York Times* which stated: 'Only at Christmastime can the cautionary tale take on the kind of inspirational quality it has in Frank Capra's *It's a Wonderful Life*, in which a good man sees what the world would have been like without him. Phillip Borsos' *One Magic Christmas* doesn't have the same multi-hanky impact, but it's an affecting, well-played film in a similar vein. Mr Borsos, the director of *The Grey Fox* and *The Mean Season*, has a gravity here that at first seems decidedly un-Christmasy. But his solemnity is credible and appealing, and it ripens, slowly but surely, into a charmingly seasonal brand of childlike wonder'.[10] Sure enough, more current evaluations of the movie have gradually overlooked its cumbersome conjunction of social criticism and festive fantasy to focus with greater emphasis upon the low-key magnetism of its more fanciful sequences and the skilful evocation of the ingenuous wonderment of youth. Some reviewers, such as Daniel W. Kelly, have drawn attention to Borsos's careful meditation on childhood innocence – a factor which is often overlooked due to a wider preoccupation with the film's irregular plot dynamics: 'As if you couldn't tell from the description, *One Magic Christmas* borrows the best elements of classics such as *A Christmas Carol* and *It's a Wonderful Life* to totally pull at your heartstrings. Yet, this movie does it with the added charm of being seen through a child's eyes, adding a fairy tale quality that will have children and adults smiling and crying. [...] And visually, you experience Christmas. You feel like you are on the snow-covered streets at night, with the winter mist escaping from your lips. You are convinced you've stepped into Santa's workshop and been given a tour by the man himself. *One Magic Christmas* is everything a Christmas movie is supposed to be'.[11] Thus while it would seem improbable to expect the film to ever be featured in the annals of classic twentieth century Christmas cinema, it contains enough in the way of appealing characters and pleasing stylistic content to elevate it safely beyond the confines of mediocre banality. And while *One Magic Christmas* may never quite reach the lofty goals that its ambitious premise sets out for itself, its earnest sincerity and understated ethicality are never in question. As Dean Duncan has suggested:

> *One Magic Christmas* is an honourable updating/ commercialization of the Scrooge myth, in which a disappointed pilgrim is dragged through a therapeutic round of tribulation on the way to being wrapped in the arms of redeeming love. [...] In some small measure, *One Magic Christmas* is a bit like Carl Dreyer's magisterial masterpiece, *Ordet* (Denmark, 1955). The distribution and heft of its various small miracles – empathy, kindness, resiliency, community – almost make the big miracle unnecessary. [...] The North Pole is completely successful, especially the little mythological variation that they fashion with those elves. Finally, Harry Dean Stanton contributes one of film history's strangest performances as one of film history's strangest angels. Still, definitely, worth a watch![12]

Although many a parent will no doubt have baulked at the complex elucidation that may be required due to the film's assertion that Santa Claus has the supernatural power to restore loved ones from an early grave (a somewhat manifest indicator of Christmas cinema's gradual drift away from the conventional religiosity of the genre's 1940s infancy in favour of a more secular reinterpretation), *One Magic Christmas* was nonetheless a film which was packed with intriguing cultural observations. The notion that traditional community spirit was not dead, in spite of all the economic pressures which had come to bear on it, was a refreshing statement in a decade of increasingly hard-nosed individuality and self-determination, and Meehan's screenplay takes considerable care to emphasise the importance of family and collective aspirations over conformity and faceless corporatism. In so doing, Borsos's film not only reflected the concerns of many eighties entries in the Christmas movie genre but also foreshadowed the predominant themes of home and hearth that typified numerous festive motion pictures of the following decade. *One Magic Christmas* may never be uttered in the same breath as the genre masterpieces which inspired it, but for its meditative solemnity and heartfelt endorsement of mutual community support and shared affinity it is a surprisingly affecting – if often rather idiosyncratic – slice of 1980s yuletide film-making.

REFERENCES

1.   Matthew M. Foster, '*One Magic Christmas*', in *Foster on Film*, 2004.
      <*http://fosteronfilm.com/holidays/xmas/onemagicchristmas.htm*>

2.   Jeffrey M. Anderson, '*One Magic Christmas*', in *Combustible Celluloid*, 14 May 2007.
      <*http://www.combustiblecelluloid.com/digitalwatch/onemagxmas.shtml*>

3.   Roger Ebert, '*One Magic Christmas*', in *The Chicago Sun-Times*, 22 November 1985.

4.   Ella Donald, '*One Magic Christmas*', in *Letterboxd*, 23 December 2013.
      <*https://letterboxd.com/jchastained/film/one-magic-christmas/*>

5.   Andy Webb, '*One Magic Christmas*', in *The Movie Scene*, 2004.
      <*http://www.themoviescene.co.uk/reviews/one-magic-christmas/one-magic-christmas.html*>

6.   Brian Attebery, *Stories About Stories: Fantasy and the Remaking of Myth* (Oxford: Oxford University Press, 2014), p.150.

7.   Kim Newman, 'You Better Watch Out: Christmas in the Horror Film', in *Christmas at the Movies*, ed. by Mark Connelly (London: I.B. Tauris, 2000), 135-142, p.139.

8.   Blaine Allan, 'Directed by Phillip Borsos', in *North of Everything: English-Canadian Cinema Since 1980*, ed. by William Beard and Jerry White (Alberta: The University of Alberta Press, 2002), 106-121, p.117.

9.   Michael Walsh, 'Christmas Cheer, Or Else', in *Reeling Back*, 20 December 2013.
        <http://reelingback.com/articles/christmas_cheer_or_else>

10.   Janet Maslin, '*Magic Christmas*, with Santa and Angel', in *The New York Times*, 22 November 1985.

11.   Daniel W. Kelly, '*One Magic Christmas*', in *DVD Talk*, 29 September 2004.
        <http://www.dvdtalk.com/reviews/12490/one-magic-christmas/>

12.   Dean Duncan, '*One Magic Christmas*', in *Films in Review*, 26 March 2015.
        <https://sites.lib.byu.edu/filmsinreview/film_review/one-magic-christmas/>

Santa Claus: The Movie (1985)

TriStar Pictures/Calash Corporation/GGG/Santa Claus Ltd.

Director: Jeannot Szwarc
Producers: Ilya Salkind and Pierre Spengler
Screenwriter: David Newman,
from a story by Leslie Newman and David Newman

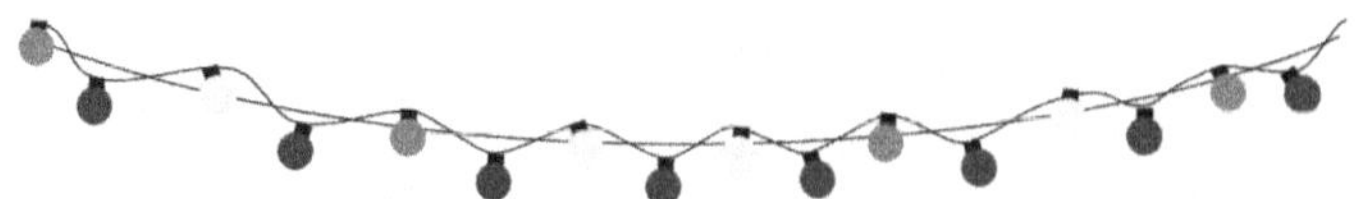

I f some Christmas movies in the early eighties had portrayed a certain degree of ambivalence between the conflict that was being established between the mass consumption of the modern age and the altruistic notions of the Christmas spirit, then *Santa Claus: The Movie* was instead to nail its colours firmly to the mast. While the pervasive commercialisation of Christmas had been a concern long before the age of cinema, dating back to at least the mid-nineteenth century, the acerbic social criticism of 1980s films such as *Trading Places, Christmas Evil* and *Gremlins* would establish the basis for a new exploration of this perennial topic throughout the decade and beyond. Many of those movies were to criticise the conspicuous consumption of the Reaganomics era at the same time as their characters paradoxically used the advantages of the free market to overcome unchecked avarice and excess; consider *Trading Places*'s use of the New York Stock Exchange to inhibit the uncontrollable acquisitiveness of the film's antagonists, or the sophisticated technological solutions required to subdue the Mogwai – the ultimate in aggressively demanding, high-maintenance consumers – throughout *Gremlins*. Yet with *Santa Claus: The Movie*, the thematic *modus operandi* was to shift in subtle but significant ways compared to those earlier films of the 1980s. A stirring clarion call imploring the audience to never forget the simple joy of giving, the film formed the most comprehensive origin story for Santa Claus that had appeared in cinemas up until that point. Ultimately, however, it would prove to be a movie that did not simply focus upon the character of Santa Claus himself, but one which would examine precisely what it was that this legendary figure has come to stand for within popular culture.

While it is true that *Santa Claus: The Movie* had one of the highest profiles of all Christmas films in the 1980s, it has also become infamous as one of the decade's costliest box-office failures – in terms of its performance in American cinemas, at least. Behind the film were the famed Paris-based producers Alexander and Ilya Salkind, the father and son team who had so successfully brought comic book hero Superman to the big screen in 1978 with Richard Donner's well-received cinematic adaptation of the same name. Thus with audience anticipation running high, the stage was set for a truly epic interpretation of the jolly festive figure's untold life story.

Santa Claus: The Movie was directed by Jeannot Szwarc, who had been active in television and film since the late 1960s. Szwarc had helmed episodes from popular TV series such as *Ironside* (1968 and 1969), *Alias Smith and Jones* (1971), *Columbo* (1973), *The Six Million Dollar Man* (1974), *Kojak* (thirteen episodes between 1973-77), and no less than nineteen episodes of *Rod Serling's Night Gallery* from 1970 until 1973. His cinematic work in the seventies had included science fiction horror *Bug* (1975) and maritime thriller sequel *Jaws 2* (1978), but it was the early eighties which were to see his profile as a film director becoming more fully established: time travel adaptation *Somewhere in Time* (1980), spy thriller *Enigma* (1983) and comic book adventure *Supergirl* (1984) had all been reasonably well-received by audiences and many critics, while these films had also featured a prominent range of star names such as Christopher Reeve, Martin Sheen and Peter O'Toole.

Santa Claus: The Movie begins on a Christmas Eve of many centuries ago, in a setting that vaguely suggests a period in the early Middle Ages. A large group of enraptured children are listening to an elderly lady (Aimée Delamain), mesmerised by her tales of mythical elves who live at the very top of the world at the North Pole. They are all huddled together in a warm log cabin, safe from the harsh blizzard that is blowing outside. Some of the older children are growing listless, however; they are awaiting the arrival of Claus (David Huddleston), a kindly woodcutter who lives nearby with his wife Anya (Judy Cornwell). Sure enough, a sleigh soon arrives outside drawn by reindeer: Claus has made his annual appearance, and is soon joyfully handing out hand-carved wooden toys to the jubilant boys and girls. The villagers are amazed that Claus can find the time to make such beautiful gifts when he works so many long hard hours at his chosen profession, but his wife explains that making Christmas special for the little ones is very important to her husband, driving him to put in as much effort as is necessary.

Claus is keen to depart, as he has made more toys for children in another village nearby. The villagers urge him to reconsider, given the harshness of the weather, but he protests that his reindeer Donner and Blitzen will be able to get through the snow to their destination. However, their warnings soon transpire to be prescient indeed; a short while after departing, the snowfall grows so heavy that Claus eventually loses his way. The reindeer, unable to draw the sleigh through such treacherous conditions, collapse from the cold. With no way of leaving on foot, Claus and Anya are trapped in the sleigh, the freezing temperatures eventually making them succumb to unconsciousness as the snow falls even heavier.

When they awake, the forest around them has disappeared. In its place are the icy plains of the North Pole, where a huge, spectral building takes form in front of their astonished eyes. They are further dumbfounded when a group of diminutive, brightly-clothed people approach their sleigh. The head of the assembly introduces himself as Dooley (John Barrard), who explains that Claus and Anya's arrival has long been expected. Dooley tells the couple that he and his colleagues are from a race known as elves – not the fanciful legend that the old storyteller had spoken of, but real, flesh-and-blood creatures. The elves introduce Claus to what is to be a new home for Anya and himself – a vast workshop at the very top of the world, which has been shrouded from the naked eye.

Inside, Claus is impressed by the elves' expansive toy-making facilities, and is given a guided tour by Dooley and another of the elf supervisors, Puffy (Anthony O'Donnell). The displaced couple watch in wonder as they witness the painstaking creation of many painted wooden toys of all shapes and sizes. Claus also becomes bemused by Patch (Dudley Moore), an elf with a seemingly unquenchable interest in science and technology who seems determined to impress the new arrivals. Eventually, the elves lead Claus and Anya to a gargantuan storeroom which is packed from floor to ceiling with immaculately-built wooden toys of all shapes and sizes. Dooley explains that Claus has been set the task of delivering all of these many gifts to children across the world. Awestruck, Claus responds that there is no way that he could possibly live long enough to perform such a task, but Dooley is amused by his doubt. Claus and Anya, he clarifies, will both live eternally – their lifespan is now as infinite as that of the elves.

Taken aback by these miraculous events, neither Claus nor Anya find that they are able to sleep at night. Claus decides to pay a visit to his reindeer, only to discover Patch talking to them kindly in an attempt to persuade them to eat. Like Claus himself, Donner and Blitzen are a little stunned by their circumstances and feel reluctant to consume much. Pleased at Patch's gentle manner, Claus asks to meet the many other reindeer in the stables and is soon introduced to Prancer and Dancer, Comet and Cupid, and so on. He is baffled as to why the workshop would require so many reindeer, but Patch remains tight-lipped on the details, instead telling Claus that all will be revealed in the fullness of time.

As time passes, Claus becomes overjoyed as he watches the creation of so many wonderful new toys for the world's children. The elves run an incredibly efficient operation which is administered with clockwork precision, and yet each and every gift is made with painstaking care and attention. Meanwhile, some elves are treating the reindeers' food with a mysterious magic dust, and Anya is enthusiastically overseeing the creation of a new fur-trimmed suit for Claus which is being created by elf tailor Goober (Melvyn Hayes).

Claus can only observe with wonder and amazement as he sees simple blocks of wood rapidly turned into beautifully crafted toys, which are then flawlessly gift-wrapped and placed into large parcel sacks.

Soon Christmas is approaching, and Claus – now decked out in his freshly-tailored red suit, and standing by a grand sleigh drawn by all of the workshop's reindeer – is addressed by the Ancient One (Burgess Meredith), the oldest and wisest of all the elves. He tells Claus that his appointment to his new role is the fulfilment of a prophecy that one day a skilled craftsman and artist, having no son or daughter of his own, would come to distribute gifts to every child on Earth. Claus is sceptical of how he will be able to visit the home of each and every boy and girl in just one night, much less have the ability to do so on an annual basis, but the elderly elf explains that time will effectively stand still for the period of Claus's travels, allowing him to take as long as is necessary to deliver presents to everyone across the globe. Elated that Claus will be taking up the mantle of distributing Christmas gifts from that point onwards, the Ancient One proudly proclaims that the jolly, red-suited toymaker will be known henceforth as Santa Claus. Taking up his seat in the majestic new sleigh, Claus watches as the elves feed the reindeer from plates of victuals treated with magical dust. The reindeers' antlers then convulse with a golden light, the animals appearing mystically energised. Before he knows it, Claus's sleigh is flying out of the workshop and into the air, leading him on his long journey.

As the centuries pass, the legend of Santa Claus rapidly begins to spread. Children all across the globe, delighted with their gifts, start writing letters to Santa, thanking him for his generosity and giving suggestions of what they would like him to bring them in the coming year. Soon the elves are inundated with correspondence – mail which is magically whisked out of the homes of each child when they aren't looking, and then sent through the skies all the way to the North Pole workshop. After many years have gone by, Claus receives a letter from a little girl who is upset at the way her brother is mistreating her beloved kitten in the lead up to Christmas. Infuriated by this cruelty, Anya suggests that Claus should only deliver presents to children who have behaved themselves throughout the year. Albeit with some reluctance, Claus agrees to her proposal and tells Dooley to compile an annual list of which children have been naughty, and which have been nice.

As the decades fly by and he eventually reaches the modern day, Claus is slowly becoming worn out by all of the requests from the children of the world. Their Christmas wishes have led to an increasingly packed schedule, making it difficult for Claus to get everything done in time for each following year. Anya recommends that he think about employing an assistant to ease his burden, but Claus is hesitant, feeling that nobody would want all of the hard work that would accompany such a position. Dooley disagrees, however: he can think of two elves who would be only too happy to be considered for the post.

Meanwhile, in a cold and snowy New York City, homeless adolescent Joe (Christian Fitzpatrick) is struggling against the freezing conditions. The fact that everyone around him is so full of the Christmas spirit does little to help his general mood of despondency, particularly as he is trying hard to keep out of view from any passing police patrols. He watches with disdain as a street corner Santa (Walter Goodman), who claims to be collecting for charity, pockets the donation money for himself. But Joe is unaware that he too is being watched; a little girl named Cornelia (Carrie Kei Heim) is looking out at him from an opulent town house across the street. They catch each other's gaze momentarily, but Cornelia is soon called away by her guardian with a warning to concentrate on her homework instead of idle distractions. It seems that in spite of her luxurious surroundings, Cornelia is almost as unhappy as the chilly, penniless Joe.

At the North Pole, Claus is unsure whether to choose the technologically-minded Patch as his assistant, or the reliable traditionalist Puffy. He tells both elves to apply themselves to their own method of toy production; the one who is able to yield the best results will be awarded the job. Patch immediately goes to work on an elaborate production-line system, which initially proves able to construct and paint complex toys with precision. However, when Patch steps up manufacturing to a hazardous rate of production, the toys quickly become unsafe – steps in the process are missed out in error, leading to the toys ending up in a dangerous condition. Claus is unaware of this fact, as is Patch, so when he sees the prodigious output of Patch's manufacturing – which appears to be much greater than the respectable amount produced by the old-school toymaker Puffy – he has no hesitation in awarding the innovative elf with the treasured assistant's role.

On Christmas Eve, a miserable Joe is forced to watch from the street as families gather together for meals in the warmth. Cornelia is not oblivious to his plight, however – when the opportunity arises, she sneaks some food and drink outside for him to collect, though the two never actually have the chance to meet. As Claus flies over the city on his annual rounds, he spots Joe warming himself near a brazier and takes pity on him. Claus decides to take the youngster for a ride on his sleigh, an experience which takes Joe aback – until that night, he had never believed that Santa Claus even existed. Claus brings Joe along on his travels as he distributes gifts to children throughout the city, and eventually they arrive at Cornelia's house. The young girl is amazed to discover Santa himself delivering presents to her home, though Claus feels a little self-conscious at having been caught in person. Joe and Cornelia recognise each other from their earlier distant encounter and quickly strike up a friendship. Cornelia offers to prepare some food for him while Claus chooses to depart, allowing the two acquaintances to get to know each other better. As he leaves via the building's chimney, he promises Joe that they will meet again.

After Christmas has passed, Dooley and Claus are dismayed when dozens of Patch's wooden tricycles and carts are returned to the North Pole as defective goods. Never in all the centuries of Claus's gift distribution has any child been compelled to return a faulty present. A deeply saddened Claus is forced to dismiss Patch from his post as assistant, but the elf is so ashamed at his lack of quality control that he saves Claus the trouble and resigns instead, handing over his cherished assistant's apron. As Puffy is awarded the position in his stead, Patch becomes so miserable that he decides to leave the workshop in search of pastures new. Stopping only to wish the reindeer a mournful farewell, Patch departs without telling anyone of his plans, taking with him only a bag of the elves' magic dust.

At the same time, in Washington D.C., a U.S. Senate hearing has been convened to investigate the unsafe toys that are being manufactured by shady businessman B.Z. (John Lithgow). The panel's chairman (Jerry Harte) is appalled when the lack of safety involved in the construction of B.Z.'s toys becomes apparent – a cheap doll made from a highly flammable material easily bursts into flame when in brief contact with a cigarette lighter, while another is shown to be stuffed with broken glass, nails and sawdust. Trying hard not to appear ruffled, B.Z. assures the investigating panel that he will look into the matter and ensure that these dangerous exhibits are simply a couple of isolated, defective units. But the chairman is wholly unconvinced by these assurances of greater quality control and demands that every B.Z. toy on the market is withdrawn from sale immediately, threatening the revocation of B.Z.'s licence to manufacture and trade if he does not comply.

Brushing his way past the press, B.Z. is clearly flustered behind his cool professional façade. His chief of staff, Dr Eric Towzer (Jeffrey Kramer), informs him that the company's sales have suffered badly as a result of the negative publicity surrounding their manufacturing issues and general business practices, and that things will need to turn around rapidly to save the company from disaster. But B.Z.'s fate takes an unexpected turn when, returning to his office, he finds Patch. The elf seems to have appeared there out of thin air, much to B.Z.'s bewilderment. On his arrival in New York, Patch has come across an elaborate shop window display showcasing B.Z.'s toys, and – believing the disreputable manufacturer to be a modern-day equivalent of Santa Claus – is keen to offer his services to him. As altruism is an entirely foreign concept to B.Z., he is suspicious of Patch's motives, but the elf explains that he has conceived of a way to deliver an exciting new toy to children through B.Z.'s production facilities, delighting the planet's youth while restoring his tarnished reputation with Claus and the other elves. B.Z. initially believes Patch to be an escaped lunatic, but soon warms to his idea when the diminutive new arrival professes to have no knowledge of money, thus making him eminently vulnerable to being swindled. Patch suggests that he uses his magic elf dust to create special lollipops which will be advertised on television all across the world, but which will be distributed for free. Scandalised by the notion of giving anything away for nothing, B.Z. eventually realises that if he does share out the lollipops at no cost, he has a unique chance to mend his company's badly-damaged standing with the public. Furthermore, if Patch's treats are as successful as he believes they will be, customers will be potentially willing to pay huge amounts to try them again. His curiosity (and business acumen) now well and truly piqued, B.Z. agrees to turn over the use of his company's factories to Patch.

Back at the elven workshop, Claus is worried about the whereabouts of his old friend. Anya and the elves are also concerned about Patch, but Claus feels particularly guilty, worrying about his own culpability in his former assistant's departure. He tries to take his mind off of things by carving a wooden figure, just as he did in the olden days, but Anya soon notices that Claus has unconsciously modelled the toy on Patch. As Christmas once again approaches, however, B.Z. airs a deeply tacky commercial which features Patch publicising his new lollipops. The elves pick up the transmission, and are dismayed to find their lost friend working for a rival organisation. Aggrieved by Patch's involvement with a mercantile toy company, Claus nonetheless voices relief that they now know that the wayward elf is safe. But he has little time to ponder the situation: Christmas Eve has arrived, and he has presents to deliver once again.

This holiday season, however, Santa's sleigh has a competitor in the skies: in New York, Patch is launching the Patchmobile, a futuristic car (albeit one which appears to be made from painted wood) which runs on magic elf dust. Launching into the air with great excitement, Patch sets to work delivering a magic lollipop into the home of every child. Claus soon discovers one of the sparkling sweetmeats under the Christmas tree of each home as he makes his rounds, making him question whether he still has relevance to the world's boys and girls. But he is soon cheered when he discovers his friend Joe and presents him with a gift of his own – the handmade wooden model of Patch. Claus seems touched that the sceptical young man has come to trust him, particularly when the rest of the planet seems to have lost all faith in his philanthropic purpose.

On Christmas morning, curious young children unwrap Patch's lollipops and discover that they have the short-lived ability to float in mid-air. Everyone is entranced by the unique gravity-defying sweets, with the exception of Cornelia: she has little time for the greedy B.Z., who has by now been revealed as her step-uncle and usually-absent guardian. But the company's magical gifts soon cause a media sensation, with journalists from press and television swarming into B.Z's boardroom seeking further details. B.Z. is deliberately evasive, but leads the reporters to believe that another, even more incredible product will soon be on the way. Rapidly making his departure when the questions start becoming more awkward, B.Z. tries to persuade Patch to manufacture a new successor to the lollipops – a candy cane which contains an even more concentrated formula of elf dust. Patch is reluctant; believing that he has now proven his worth as an innovator to Claus, he is now ready to return to his friends at the North

Pole. But B.Z. remains persistent, assuring Patch that this is just one last favour to bring lasting joy to children all around the world. Privately, he knows that the product will enable anyone who consumes it to fly rather than simply hover; an unmatchable piece of merchandise that will net him a fortune in revenue. Somewhat unenthusiastically, Patch tells him that such an item could theoretically be ready by the following December, but B.Z. is disinclined to wait for Christmas to come around again – he wants to strike while the iron is hot, and maximise on the intense media interest. To this end, he declares that the candy canes should be ready for distribution on March the 25th, exactly three months afterwards: a date which he proudly designates Christmas II.

Claus deeply despairs at the rise of B.Z.'s tawdry gimmicks, feeling certain that the world no longer has any place for him. He laments the fact that society has changed so much since he first started delivering presents that he has now become little more than a relic of a bygone age. The festive season has become so commercially-oriented, he feels, that no-one seems to take delight in the simple act of giving any longer. The elves try to cheer him up with novel new toys, but nothing seems to stir up any enthusiasm in him. For the first time in his life, Claus feels aimless in his calling.

B.Z. is awakened early in the morning by Towzer, who is the bearer of grim news. Patch's candy canes, which are based upon a very condensed recipe of magic elf dust, are proving to be extremely chemically volatile; when they are placed near a source of heat, they cause a violent explosion. But B.Z. is unconcerned with what he considers to be a trifling detail; his plan is to pocket as much as he can in advance payments for the new product, and then leave the country for Brazil before the canes' lethal nature is uncovered.

This way he will be safely free from any punishment or threat of extradition while Patch, who is blissfully unaware of the sweets' instability, will be forced to face the consequences on his behalf. B.Z. is outraged when he discovers that his conversation has been overheard; Cornelia has smuggled Joe into the basement due to him suffering a bad cold, and a random sneeze tips off the corrupt toymaker to the boy's presence. He has Joe forcibly restrained and taken to his factory, where he will be kept incarcerated in order to avoid leaking the news of the canes' explosive nature.

However, B.Z. is blissfully unaware that Cornelia has also been eavesdropping on his nefarious plans. She quickly composes a letter to Claus, which instantaneously arrives at the North Pole – much to the surprise of Dooley, who isn't expecting any Christmas requests so early in the year. On learning that Joe is in danger, Claus quickly gets his sleigh ready, but the elves inform him that two of the reindeer are ill with the flu. Knowing that he will be forced to enact his rescue with only six reindeer instead of the usual eight, Claus heads straight to New York and retrieves Cornelia from her home. Together, they rush off to rescue Joe, but discover that Patch has beaten them to it – having stumbled across the captured youth in the factory, the homesick elf has released him and offered passage to the North Pole. Once back amongst his friends, Patch intends to give his supply of candy canes to Claus. This will not only restore his tarnished reputation, he reasons, but should also give Santa the year off from making new toys. However, Patch is unconscious of the canes' instability in the presence of heat, and has stashed a huge amount of them into the storage compartment of the Patchmobile.

A tense chase ensues, where Claus and Cornelia pursue the errant Patch and his new friend Joe. As the Patchmobile races towards the Arctic, its lethal cargo begins to heat up, and Claus – seeing a plume of smoke rising from the flying car – realises that time is of the essence. Persuading his reindeer to perform an intricate 360° loop, Claus is only just able to manoeuvre his sleigh under the Patchmobile in time to retrieve Joe and Patch as the car explodes into a sensational fireball. The old friends are overjoyed to see each other safe and well once again.

Returning to the workshop, the elves are overjoyed at the return of the long-lost Patch. Amazed to see Santa's celebrated residence in person, Cornelia and Joe beg Claus to allow them to stay there until the following Christmas. Laughing, Dooley remarks that he will now need to add the title of schoolteacher to his never-ending list of duties. Cornelia seems unconcerned at what her crooked step-uncle's reaction to her apparent disappearance may be, but – unknown to her or the others – B.Z. has performed a vanishing act of his own. As the police storm his factory and take Towzer into custody, the malevolent businessman stuffs himself with Patch's candy canes, allowing him to fly out of his office and evade justice. But unfortunately for B.Z., the canes have a rather more extreme effect on his physiology than he had intended; while Claus and his friends celebrate at the North Pole, the unscrupulous industrialist is left floating in orbit around the Earth with no idea of how to return home.

Santa Claus: The Movie is very much a film of two halves. The beginning of the movie is a strikingly effective exploration of the genesis of the Santa Claus figure, charting his transformation from a selfless, kind-hearted woodcutter to the bringer of joy and happiness to all the children of the world. This presents a clear break from traditional depictions of Santa Claus as an alter ego of the Christian St Nicholas, offering instead an alternative interpretation where Claus's powers are magical rather than spiritual in origin; as Jack Santino notes, '*Santa Claus: The Movie* took great pains to establish a magical origin for [Santa Claus], conveniently overlooking the obvious derivation of *Santa* from *Saint* and *Claus* from *Nicholas*'.[1] That being said, more or less everything else which surrounds the Santa Claus mythos in modern popular culture is present and correct throughout the film – the ornate elf-run workshop at the North Pole, the cookies and milk on the mantelpiece, the 'naughty and nice' list, and even a brief airing of Clement Clark Moore's poem 'A Visit from St Nicholas' (often better known today as ''Twas the Night Before Christmas', as a result of its famous opening line).

However, the film's latter half often appears rushed in terms of action as well as resolution and, in many ways, is an uneasy fit with what has preceded it. With such a charming and elaborate setup of Claus's new home, including the affable elves' mystical motivations and the amazing scale of the North Pole workshop, the narrative's abrupt collision with the present day can't help but leave much of the second and third acts seeming a little flat by comparison. Having clearly established Claus's philanthropic kindness, the film's later sections set up the ruthless manufacturer B.Z. as the very embodiment of self-interest and monetary greed: the absolute antithesis of everything that Santa and the Christmas spirit seek to represent. The over-the-top, cigar-chewing industrialist, complete with expensive tailored suit and spats, is the scheming architect of Christmas II: a superficial corporate monstrosity which makes a mockery of the very nature of the yuletide holidays. While previous entrepreneurial nemeses of the festive season such as *It's a Wonderful Life*'s Mr Potter and the Duke Brothers of *Trading Places* may have considered Christmas to be an irrelevance at best, or a mawkish inconvenience at worst, the disreputable B.Z. wants nothing less but to stamp out Santa (and, by extension, the true meaning of Christmas) altogether, all in the name of blatant profit.

This, perhaps, best highlights one of the core thematic tensions within *Santa Claus: The Movie*, in spite of the film's strong defence of generosity and munificence, encouraging opposition to the corporate mentality and excessive individual materialism, it is clearly itself a commercial endeavour – a feature which has been carefully structured to appeal to the broadest potential demographic and thus the largest possible audience. As Nathan Rabin has so adroitly considered, '*Santa Claus: The Movie* represented a rather transparent attempt to spin a *Superman*-like franchise out of the world's most indulgent gift-giver. [...] As with so many Christmas movies the anti-materialist sermonizing can't help but feel disingenuous since *Santa Claus: The Movie* is a money-making venture first, second, third, fourth and fifth and a creative endeavor a distinct sixth'.[2] David Newman's screenplay expresses concerns about the corrosive effect of a fragmentary and unpredictable postmodern culture on long-established Christmas traditions, best articulated through Claus's soul-searching with regard to how he can possibly find a consequential role for himself in today's aggressively consumer-oriented society. Authentic meaning proves to be as elusive a concept for Santa as it is for the contemporary world in general. Yet the North Pole workshop's output is shown to be entirely isolated from any kind of market system, emphasising the virtue of the elves' generosity in stark contrast to B.Z.'s obdurate covetousness. Thus, as Daniel Miller has observed, the film's complex negotiations of both emotional and pecuniary value allows the audience to 'see a more complete version of the myth of Santa Claus, even if [it is] created by popular media rather than folk stories. We also see antipathy toward mass produced toys from factories and a removal of any association of Santa's gifts with market-place transactions. [...] As such stories refine the American Santa Claus myth, Santa continues his apotheosis'.[3] Although it presents a narrative which is generally rather cautionary in its view of modernity, the film nonetheless seems so eager to appear relevant to contemporary secular audiences that it is at pains to dissociate its protagonist from the pre-existing religious legend of St Nicholas, instead creating a more inclusive new identity for him which is based entirely around the expectations of popular culture. As Santino suggests, this greater inclusiveness allows for a wider appeal for the character in an increasingly irreligious society which leans more heavily upon material rationalism, amplifying his sense of universality: 'Films [such as *Santa Claus: The Movie*] feature adults who, like the adults in the audience, provide Christmas for youngsters, who pass on the Santa Claus legends and traditions. It is they who find, through the course of the film, that Santa really does exist'.[4] For B.Z., however, even the redemptive qualities of the festive season cannot provide him with a lifeline to deliverance – a relatively unusual variation for a Christmas movie (though he faced a fate which had befallen Mr Potter, Mrs Deagle and the Duke Brothers before him, amongst others). Having squandered any potential for goodwill during his exploitative partnership with

Patch, B.Z.'s greed eventually destroys him, underpinning the damaging nature of excessive (and insatiable) avarice. Thus the point is made that even though the desire for fervent profit-making has become synonymous with the modern age, most especially in the materialistic eighties – sometimes even at the expense of authenticity or quality (as B.Z.'s dubious goods so emphatically demonstrate) – no amount of acquisitiveness can ever replace the lasting satisfaction that comes from willing philanthropy. Mark Connelly takes note of this dichotomy, stating that 'in *Santa Claus* there is a great deal of emphasis laid on the fact that all the toys made at the North Pole workshops should be completed with the loving eye and attention to detail of a craftsman. [...] [By comparison] quality is of absolutely no interest [to B.Z.] and everything is sold for the highest possible mark-up. [...] But the overall moral is clear: modernity and profit-making go hand-in-hand and can be taken too far'.[5]

There is much to recommend the sumptuous production values of *Santa Claus: The Movie*, not least Stephanie McMillan's outstanding set decoration and Bob Ringwood's highly imaginative costume design. Szwarc and his creative team conjure up a workshop for Santa Claus which is surely the stuff of dreams for any young viewer, with a painstaking attention to detail that quickly builds a tangible sense of wonder – though principally throughout the film's first half-hour. This is especially true of the marvellously expressive Animatronic reindeer, which are so characterful that they brighten up every scene that they appear in. Henry Mancini provides a dynamic and emotionally moving score, blending many styles and supplementing the soundtrack with the music of several well-known Christmas carols as well as numerous effective contributions from recording artists such as Aled Jones, Sheena Easton and The Ambrosian Children's Chorus. The film is also aided by many pleasing supporting performances and cameo appearances from veteran character actors such as Burgess Meredith, John Barrard, Jeffrey Kramer, Don Estelle, Judy Cornwell and Melvyn Hayes.

It seems obvious to note that any film entitled *Santa Claus: The Movie* is almost certain to live or die based upon the skill of its lead actor, and in David Huddleston the role was occupied by a performer who truly looked the part, successfully embodying the humanity and compassion of the festive spirit. Huddleston's Santa was more kindly than out-and-out jolly, however, and his interpretation of the character can feel slightly ill-at-ease – warm and affable for the most part, but also oddly self-contained at times. Largely this can be blamed on the script's evocation of the existential crisis that the character faces; a somewhat atypical approach when it comes to depicting Santa Claus in a Christmas film. Yet Huddleston proves himself more than worthy of the famous red hat, and it is of little surprise that for many members of the MTV Generation who grew up with the film in the eighties, his portrayal of Santa Claus has become the definitive one – and the benchmark by which later performances of the role would be judged. Huddleston had been acting on television and in film since the early sixties, and was perhaps best known for his prolific appearances in Westerns such as Howard Hawks's *Rio Lobo* (1970), Robert Benton's *Bad Company* (1972) and Ted Kotcheff's *Billy Two Hats* (1974). He parodied his Western character actor persona magnificently in Mel Brooks's anarchic comedy *Blazing Saddles* (1974) as the patriarchal Olson Johnson. A versatile performer, he continued to be active on television throughout the seventies and eighties while also appearing in a wide variety of different film genres in the cinema – his numerous movie roles included prominent parts in crime drama *Country Blue* (Jack Conrad, 1973), police action movie *McQ* (John Sturges, 1974), science fiction conspiracy thriller *Capricorn One* (Peter Hyams, 1977), action spoof *Go For It* (Enzo Barboni, 1983), and flamboyant comedy *The Act* (Sig Shore, 1984). In 1990 he was nominated for an Emmy Award in the Outstanding Guest Actor in a Comedy Series category for his appearance as Grandpa Arnold in TV's *The Wonder Years* (1988).

Dudley Moore shines brightly in the role of Patch, the elf inventor who is so keen to assist Claus that his ambition clouds his judgement, leading him into a journey of self-discovery that defines the second and third acts of the film. One of the true masterstrokes of *Santa Claus: The Movie* lay in the casting of the charismatic Moore spectacularly against type – he was far better known to audiences of the time for his sophisticated wit and roguish charm – and he makes the most of his character's appealing naiveté to create a likeable eccentric; a kind of *idiot savant* who is simultaneously brilliant and blundering. In spite of Patch's rather overwrought punning (hardly a scene passes without mention of 'elf-confidence', 'elf-control', 'elf-awareness', etc.), some of the film's most memorable sequences feature his marvellous Heath Robinson-style inventions, breathing new life into both the timeless traditionalism of the North Pole and the bleak, impersonal B.Z.-owned factories. Moore was recognisable to a generation of British viewers for his BBC television series *Not Only... But Also* (1965-70), in collaboration with Peter Cook, and for films such as *The Wrong Box* (Bryan Forbes, 1966), *Bedazzled* (Stanley Donen, 1967) and *The Bed Sitting Room* (Richard Lester, 1969). He continued to be highly active both on television and in the cinema throughout the 1970s, appearing in films including *Alice's Adventures in Wonderland* (William Sterling, 1972), *Foul Play* (Colin Higgins, 1978) and *The Hound of the Baskervilles* (Paul Morrissey, 1978), before achieving major success in Blake Edwards's *10* (1979) and most especially Steve Gordon's *Arthur* (1981), his performance in the latter gaining him an Academy Award nomination for Best Actor in a Leading Role. He was nominated for Golden Globe Awards five times in his career, winning on two occasions – for his lead role in *Arthur*, and for his performance in Blake Edwards's *Micki + Maude* (1984).

Featuring alongside Moore in the pivotal role of B.Z. was the always-watchable John Lithgow. Making the most of his every appearance, Lithgow appears to take great delight in embellishing the disreputable character's palpable greed and moral laxity, giving a scene-stealing performance which becomes so deliberately over the top that it is one of the most entertaining aspects of the whole film. A highly successful character actor, Lithgow's cinematic career began in the early 1970s when he appeared in Paul Williams's comedy drama *Dealing: Or the Berkeley-to-Boston Forty-Brick Lost-Bag Blues* (1972). He made appearances in films such as *The Big Fix* (Jeremy Kagan, 1978), *Rich Kids* (Robert M. Young, 1979) and *All That Jazz* (Bob Fosse, 1979), before going on to even greater success in the eighties. His profile was considerably enhanced following performances in a variety of features which included *The World According to Garp* (George Roy Hill, 1982), George Miller's segment of *Twilight Zone: The Movie* (1983), *Terms of Endearment* (James L. Brooks, 1983), *Footloose* (Herbert Ross, 1984) and Peter Hyams's *2010* (1984), a belated sequel to Stanley Kubrick's influential 1968 sci-fi classic *2001: A Space Odyssey*. He has been nominated twice for Academy Awards, for his supporting performances in *The World According to Garp* and *Terms of Endearment*. Later in his career, he was to be nominated on four occasions for Golden Globe Awards for his television work, winning twice (for appearances in *3rd Rock from the Sun* in 1997 and *Dexter* in 2010), and his TV performances also led to him being nominated for an astonishing eleven Emmy Awards throughout his career, winning on four occasions to date (in 1986, 1996, 1997 and 1999).

Upon its release, *Santa Claus: The Movie* met with a critical response that could only be described as lukewarm at best. While some reviews praised the entertainment value of Lithgow's enthusiastically exaggerated performance, positive appraisals were often expressed to the detriment of the film's other actors; *New York Magazine*'s review, for instance, remarked that 'the invaluable John Lithgow shows up as a greedy capitalist, and the movie briefly shakes the tinsel out of its brains. If the uproarious and perverse Lithgow had played the white-bearded reindeer-lover himself, the picture might have amounted to something. But he didn't, and the frolicsome elves take over again'.[6] Contrastingly, others expressed an opinion that the film suffered from the fact that the antagonism generated by the boggling B.Z. was altogether too subdued and is introduced into proceedings too late, meaning that the narrative ultimately lacked the excitement that should have been generated by the tension and dispute between Claus's guileless generosity and B.Z.'s profit-driven avarice. As Roger Ebert commented:

> Lithgow is supposed to be in the great tradition of superhero villains, like Gene Hackman's Lex Luthor in *Superman*, or all of the bizarre enemies Batman had to

face. Lithgow gives a nice hateful performance, but the villain is not drawn big enough, and he doesn't have enough to do. Indeed, the central weakness of *Santa Claus: The Movie* is its lack of real conflict. The movie needs a super-Scrooge, and all it gets is the kind of bad guy Ralph Nader might have invented. The biggest crisis is when a couple of reindeer come down with runny noses.[7]

A common response amongst commentators was that the opening scenes of the film were very effectively staged, engendering a sense of awe and wonderment, but that the epic tone that these sequences suggest is soon squandered by the remainder of the narrative, which appears somewhat bland and directionless by comparison. Here, as Anthony Nield has observed, the screenplay attempts in vain to juggle too many incongruent components within an increasingly cluttered plot, meaning that any possibility of overall structural integrity was ultimately a forlorn hope: 'There *are* clearly problems at the script stage, most notably the fact that it feels as though ⟦the film has⟧ been designed by a committee. Rather than offer any kind of coherency, it instead shoehorns in various disparate elements in the most ungainly of fashions: how Santa came to be; a lovable street urchin who also happens to be an orphan; a big name star ⟦...⟧ and an evil toymaker seemingly based, albeit loosely, on Lex Luthor'.[8] This diversity of criticism has continued into the present day, with the most positive retrospective reviews choosing to focus firmly on commending the film for the beauty and grandeur of its early scenes at the North Pole, even in spite of the widespread critical disdain of its rickety structure and creaking narrative. For example, H. Paul Jeffers extols the movie's ambition, praising the way that it 'told the story of how Santa came to be and contained excellent scenes of Santa's workshop and all the other features that you'd expect to find at the North Pole, from the reindeer to Santa's sleigh'.[9] Others have been considerably more disparaging in their commentary, censuring the film for the way in which the transition between the mythic splendour of Santa's workplace and the lacklustre urban setting of the present day sequences clashes so awkwardly – not least when the subtexts of unselfishness and common humanity begin to kick in. Graeme Clark has described *Santa Claus: The Movie* thus: 'A film which ground to a halt halfway through to plug the wares of fast food and soft drink companies had a cheek trying to tell us about the true, non-commercial spirit of Christmas. [...] Being preached to by a sheer commercial enterprise such as this is galling to say the least – obviously every blockbuster wants to make major profits, but not every one had to be as hypocritical as this was'.[10]

As the above summation suggests, many recent reviews have drawn attention to the irony of the fact that *Santa Claus: The Movie*'s condemnation of unchecked commercialism was ultimately to coincide with the film becoming one of the greatest box-office calamities of the eighties – at least, amongst audiences in the United States. With lacklustre reviews at the time of its first release, Nield notes the fatefulness of the fact that the film's long-term legacy has been secured not through the memorability of its production, but by a considerably less desirable accolade: '[The antagonist B.Z.] is solely an excuse for some rather transparent digs at production line anonymity, cynicism in general and especially the twin evils of capitalism and commercialism – the last of which can't help but prompt a certain savage irony given that *Santa Claus: The Movie* is now remembered solely as that over-hyped, over-publicised multi-million disaster'.[11] Indeed, the scale of its box-office failure within the domestic market cannot be overstated: having been produced on an estimated budget of $50,000,000,[12] the film's domestic gross in the U.S. would prove to be only $23,717,291.[13] Given the copious, wide-scale publicity for *Santa Claus: The Movie* on the build-up to its release, its lack of success with American audiences couldn't possibly have been anything other than a huge disappointment to the film-makers involved. Even though its fortunes were very different in Britain and continental Europe, where *Santa Claus: The Movie* performed favourably with audiences and actually became a commercial success overall, doing much more than simply breaking even, the lack of interest in the crucially important North American market precluded the possibility of any cinematic sequels or spin-offs going into production. That said, the film has remained popular enough in recent years to have achieved releases on both DVD and Blu-Ray, and it has also become a regular staple of festive television schedules for decades.

The commercial underachievement of *Santa Claus: The Movie* has baffled commentators since the time of the film's first appearance in cinemas, and has led to much debate in the years since. Given its vast budget (almost unprecedented for the time) and the sheer scale of public expectation, the curiosity factor alone seemed likely to generate greater box-office figures than ever proved to be the case. While the critical reception was far from overflowing with praise, similarly the press reviews at the time of the film's release were not unanimously derogatory either. The mystery of its lack of profitability has been compounded by its gradually-developing cult reputation: a growing following which found its genesis almost immediately after the movie's mid-eighties release. Bill Gibron concisely places *Santa Claus: The Movie* within the wider context of the cinema of the time, considering its unevenness as well as its peculiarly patchy narrative:

> For the most part, *Santa Claus: The Movie* gets the legend part mostly right. But the minute our UK comedian gets his dwarfish tights in a bunch and heads off to commiserate with Lithgow's B.Z., the movie just sinks. Sure, we can buy the notion of an aging Santa needing 'helpers' – it plays into every parent/child department store conversation there has ever been. But things go from twee to terrible quickly. As a villain, B.Z. is too over the top, too cigar-chompingly obvious to be anything other than a buffoon, and the inclusion of two little brats – Joe and Cornelia – is just pandering PC overkill. As with many stuffed scripts films from the era, an action scene has to resolve everything, something called a 'Super Duper Looper' (and Donner's inner ear issues) needing to be established and then incessantly restated before the day can be saved.[14]

Other criticism of *Santa Claus: The Movie* has been levelled at the perceived insipidness of its execution. While the traditional Christmas themes of interpersonal co-operation and unthinking selflessness could not have been made more palpable, other movies of the period were making the same point via more strident or subversive means. Likewise, considering the film's vast budget it is a matter of regret that so many scenes from this extravagant production feel strangely forgettable as soon as the narrative departs from Santa's luxuriantly-designed workshop at the North Pole. Some commentators, such as Kevin Matthews, have levelled these shortcomings squarely at the film's director: 'Jeannot Szwarc directs with no flair. While there's plenty of magic on screen there's very little magic emanating out to the viewer. [...] It *is* nice to settle down during the Yuletide season to watch this but it's only a novelty piece and there are many other seasonal treats vying for your attention that are better deserving of your time'.[15] The deeply contradictory nature of the film has also drawn censure from some quarters, highlighting not just the stylistic lurch between the fantastical whimsicality of the elves' domain and the somewhat dingy, lifeless present day sequences but also the contrariety of its anti-covetousness message when the production was so obviously influenced by the era of high capitalism. This has led critics such as Vincent Canby to react with considerable scepticism with regard to the creative team's approach and its divergence from the ostensible disposition of the screenplay's key themes: 'Apparently the producers and Jeannot Szwarc, the director, have spared no expense on a production that manages to look both elaborate and tacky. It has the manner of a listless musical without any production numbers. From the appearance of the toys that the elves turn out, this Santa's workshop must be the world's largest purchaser of low-grade plywood. Even the sleigh-flying scenes aren't great. In the spirit of the season, the film plugs Bloomingdale's, McDonald's and Coca-Cola, the parent company of Columbia Pictures, which is part-owner of Tri-Star Pictures, this film's distributor'.[16]

In general, however, the passing years have lent a sense of growing nostalgia to viewings of Szwarc's film, which have helped to blunt the sharpness of contemporary criticism. The general inoffensiveness of the production has shielded it from any sustained contempt by reviewers, and – given its central location within a decade which was noted for colourful fantasy cinema such as *The NeverEnding Story* (Wolfgang Pietersen, 1984), *Labyrinth* (Jim Henson, 1986) and *Willow* (Ron Howard, 1988) – it has acquired a degree of warm recollection that was singularly lacking during its original run in theatres. And this, ultimately, may be the film's lasting legacy amongst the viewing public; not as a cinematic triumph or box-office catastrophe, but rather a comfortably traditional slice of festively-themed entertainment that is wistfully remembered. As Matt Edwards has sagaciously observed:

> History has reframed *Santa Claus: The Movie*, changing it from big budget failure to a bit of a curiosity and a tradition. [...] It's got less edge than a yoghurt. It all feels very old fashioned. But then, I suppose it's old. That'll do it. It's just a soft, pleasant Christmas film. I can't quite imagine what would drive someone to make a film like this, or how they apparently spent so much money doing so, but now that it's here it's hard to grumble about.[17]

In the end, it seems that the cause of the intense critical divergence surrounding *Santa Claus: The Movie* may stem not from any one particular deficiency in the film's production, nor even any combination thereof, but rather that it tries a little too hard to be all things to all audiences. On one hand, it strives to be a captivating account of how one of the most prominent emblems of the Christmas experience came into being (in terms of modern interpretation, at least), while on the other it seeks and largely fails to become a moral tale in a present-day setting that has relevance to audiences. Although the film's decidedly askew plot structure and string of strangely disjointed narrative incidents hinder the production team's attempts to fulfil every aspiration that the screenplay sets itself, its atypical mix of fable and contemporaneity – along with the lavish quality and intricacy of much of the production – combine to make *Santa Claus: The Movie* a dazzling but maddeningly inconsistent curiosity which, in an admittedly understated way, still seems oddly arresting amongst other Christmas cinema of the time.

REFERENCES

1. Jack Santino, *All Around the Year: Holidays and Celebrations in American Life* (Champaign: University of Illinois Press, 1994) [1985], pp.189-90.

2. Nathan Rabin, 'My Year of Flops: Case File #96: *Santa Claus: The Movie*', in *The Onion A. V. Club*, 25 December 2007. *<http://www.avclub.com/articles/my-year-of-flops-case-file-96-santa-claus-the-movi,10128/>*

3. Daniel Miller, *Consumption: Critical Concepts in the Social Sciences, Volume IV: Objects, Subjects and Mediations in Consumption* (London: Routledge, 2001), pp.325.

4. Jack Santino, *New Old-Fashioned Ways: Holidays and Popular Culture* (Knoxville: University of Tennessee Press, 1996), p.144.

5. Mark Connelly, 'Santa Claus: The Movie', in *Christmas at the Movies*, ed. by Mark Connelly (London: I.B. Tauris, 2000), 115-34, p.123.

6. Anon, 'Brief Movie Reviews: *Santa Claus: The Movie*', in *New York Magazine*, 16 December 1985.

7. Roger Ebert, '*Santa Claus: The Movie*', in *The Chicago Sun-Times*, 27 November 1985.

8. Anthony Nield, '*Santa Claus: The Movie*', in *The Digital Fix*, 16 November 2005.

<http://film.thedigitalfix.com/content.php?contentid=592
46>

9.   H. Paul Jeffers, *Legends of Santa Claus* (Minneapolis:
      Lerner Publishing Group, 2001), p.88-89.

10.   Graeme Clark, '*Santa Claus*', in *The Spinning Image*, 2005.
      <http://www.thespinningimage.co.uk/cultfilms/displaycul
      displ.asp?reviewid=6566>

11.   Nield, 2005.

12.   Budgetary data from the Internet Movie Database.
      <http://uk.imdb.com/title/tt0089961/business>

13.   Box-office data from BoxOfficeMojo.com.
      <http://www.boxofficemojo.com/movies/?id=santaclaust
      hemovie.htm>

14.   Bill Gibron, '*Santa Claus: The Movie*', in *DVD Talk*, 26
      October 2010.
      <http://www.dvdtalk.com/reviews/45152/santa-claus-
      movie-25th-anniversary-edition/>

15.   Kevin Matthews, '*Santa Claus*', in *FlickFeast*, 21 December
      2011.
      <http://flickfeast.co.uk/reviews/film-reviews/santa-claus-
      1985/>

16.   Vincent Canby, '*Santa Claus*, with Moore and Lithgow',
      in *The New York Times*, 27 November 1985.

17.   Matt Edwards, 'Revisiting *Santa Claus: The Movie*', in
      Den of Geek, 22 December 2015.
      <http://www.denofgeek.com/movies/santa-claus-the-
      movie/revisiting-santa-claus-the-movie>

12

Better Off Dead (1985)

CBS Theatrical Films/A&M Films

Director: Savage Steve Holland
Producer: Michael Jaffe
Screenwriter: Savage Steve Holland

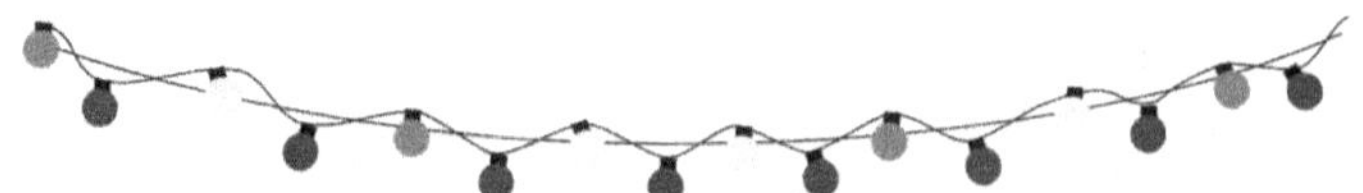

The 1980s have come to be considered something of a qualitative zenith for the teen movie genre, with film-makers such as John Hughes, Joel Schumacher, Herbert Ross, Howard Deutch and Cameron Crowe all exhibiting a lasting impact upon popular culture throughout the decade. The eighties marked an era where the teen movie evolved dramatically, with sensitive characterisation, relatable themes and cultural relevance supplanting the predictably formulaic dramas and ribald comedies of earlier decades. Often less recognised is the fact that the genre also influenced the development of Christmas movie during this period, albeit in a somewhat modest and unobtrusive way.

While the romantic comedy-drama had a long history of generic cross-pollination with festive cinema, with such hybridisation manifesting itself in films such as *Holiday Affair* (Don Hartman, 1949), *White Christmas* (Michael Curtiz, 1954) and *The Apartment* (Billy Wilder, 1960), plots featuring teenage and student romance were comparatively less common. This would change in the 1980s, with the topic becoming more readily addressed throughout the decade – though the romantic comedy genre often proved to be a more tenuous fit for eighties yuletide settings than other categories of film. Whereas the tropes of the Christmas horror film had, more often than not, been intrinsically linked to the traditional themes of the festive season (such as *Christmas Evil* and *Silent Night, Deadly Night*, both of which had employed the figure of Santa Claus and public suppositions of the modern holiday season as the activator of their grisly action), the Christmas romantic comedy often proved to be much less directly involved with the conventions that underpinned their festively-oriented situations, and were usually restrained in their implementation of yuletide themes. Films such as *The Sure Thing* (Rob Reiner, 1985) featured a road trip which took place over the Christmas period, though its focus was geared more towards the clash of strong personalities between two obstinate but likeable students than it was with themes deriving from the festive season. Similarly, *Some Girls* (Michael Hoffman, 1988) was a fish-out-of-water comedy which would draw on the conflicts and peculiarities which flare up during a student's slightly unnerving visit to the home of his former girlfriend's bohemian family during the holidays. Like these two other comedies, *Better Off Dead* uses a Christmas setting as an inspired backdrop for its action; the protagonist's often acute embarrassment and discomposure is magnified by the fact that his personal crisis takes place during a period of the year that is expected to be uplifting and life-enhancing. In this sense, this yuletide-situated romantic teen comedy fits amicably into Greg Metcalf's wider observation about festive cinema, that 'the most dominant use of Christmas in the 1980s films is to heighten the isolation of an individual protagonist, underlining his separation from the pleasures of family or community. Most of the time the protagonist is eventually reintegrated into a romantic couple or some sort of family group. In fact, the reintegration often begins during the holiday season, but at Christmas itself the individual's alienation is generally at its peak'.[1]

Better Off Dead was the brainchild of Savage Steve Holland, an animator, writer and director for both television and cinema. Although he had made his start in the industry providing the on-screen animations for popular CBS TV game show *Press Your Luck* (1983-86), *Better Off Dead* marked the beginning of a directorial career which would see Holland helming movies such as *One Crazy Summer* (1986), *How I Got Into College* (1989), *Legally Blondes* (2009), *Big Time Movie* (2011) and the festively-themed *A Fairly Odd Christmas* (2012) and *Santa Hunters* (2014). Active also as a producer and voice actor, Holland has had a prolific career – most especially in the field of television animation, where his talents have been in continuous demand since the late eighties.

During the period just before Christmas, things could be going better for teenager Lane Meyer (John Cusack) and his family in the American town of Greendale. His father Al (David Ogden Stiers), a local lawyer, is obsessed with the damage being caused to his home by a paperboy named Johnny Gasparini (Demian Slade), who regularly manages to smash the windows of Meyers' property by throwing newspapers through them without even leaving his bicycle. Lane's mother Jenny (Kim Darby) constantly tries out experimental recipes for family meals, though her good intentions cannot disguise the fact that she almost always renders the food inedible due to her outlandish concoctions. Both parents are increasingly concerned about Lane's single-minded fixation with his beautiful girlfriend Beth Truss (Amanda Wyss); his bedroom is festooned with photographs of her, and even his wardrobe has a picture of Beth's face leering over every coat-hanger. They are also slightly troubled by Lane's younger brother Badger (Scooter Stevens), a young boy of nearly eight years old who always remains silent but is given to strangely compulsive behaviour and sporadic bursts of technical genius.

Lane leaves early for some skiing trials, pausing only to argue with Al about the sporty 1967 Camaro that he had bought some months earlier – an inoperative car which now lies derelict on the family's front lawn due to the fact that Lane has been unable to restore it to a workable condition. As he departs in his rickety station wagon (a rather more conventional but nominally reliable mode of transport), he is unaware that he is being watched from across the street by Monique Junot (Diane Franklin), an exchange student from France who is staying with Lane's neighbours. The householder, Mrs Smith (Laura Waterbury), is delighted to have Monique staying with her – largely because she hopes to engineer a romance between the student and her overweight, socially awkward son Ricky (Daniel Schneider). Unfortunately for Mrs Smith, Ricky's curious behavioural quirks and general indifference towards the attractive Monique do not exactly bode well for any prospective relationship blossoming between them.

As he drives to the town's nearby ski slopes, Lane encounters drag racers Yee Sook Ree (Yuji Okumoto) and Chen Ree (Brian Imada) – the former of which has the uncanny ability to imitate popular TV sports commentator Howard Cosell after learning English from having watched *Wide World of Sports* (1961-98). They challenge Lane to a race, but he accidentally reverses at the same time as his opponents accelerate away, causing him to collide with the vehicle behind him. As Lane picks up his girlfriend, he is blissfully unaware that Beth has decided to end their six-month relationship in favour of a new romance with Roy Stalin (Aaron Dozier), the expert captain of the ski team who has mastered the perilous K-12 ski slope. Binning Lane's photo in favour of Roy's, she decides not to break the news to her erstwhile boyfriend until after the trials have taken place.

Later, Lane and Beth watch Roy make a skilful descent of the aforementioned K-12 slope; Beth notes adoringly that he is the only skier to have negotiated the entirety of the steep incline with success, while others have actually died trying. Lane is considerably less impressed by the achievement, as is his top-hatted best friend Charles de Mar (Curtis Armstrong) who is also spectating. Back at the base of the slope, Roy announces the entry requirements for prospective new members of the ski team, but soon proves to be a vain and self-obsessed individual, revelling in the female attention that is showered on him. Roy detects the fact that Lane is in a relationship with Beth and immediately seeks to humiliate him at every possible turn. The attraction between Beth and Roy is mutual, much to Lane's annoyance. When Lane later undergoes the ski trials, he puts on an excellent display but is failed by Roy on a time penalty solely because he wants to get rid of him at the earliest opportunity.

After the trials are over, Beth breaks the news to Lane that she has decided to end their relationship as she feels that she owes it to herself to have a boyfriend who is more popular, better looking, and who drives a more upmarket style of car. Lane is devastated by the news, not least because he has nothing but contempt for the good-looking but morally bankrupt Roy. As though things couldn't get any worse, the drag racers appear at a road junction and once again challenge Lane to a chase... only for him to accelerate into a truck in front of him, which contains the same angry driver that he had collided with earlier the same day.

Lane somehow manages to make it home alive, but finds that his family are apathetic towards his heartache. He proceeds to hang himself in order to end his emotional torment, but changes his mind when he reflects on his lack of life experience... just as his mother opens the door while vacuuming and sends him flying into the air on the end of a noose. Later, Charles rebukes Lane for his fatalism and tells him that suicide is not the answer to his problems. He tries to comfort his friend by telling him that, as they live in Greendale – a place located far from civilisation – Lane must accept the fact that Roy is a small town hero simply because his first-class skiing abilities cannot be matched by other denizens of the community. Lane suggests that if he too is able to descend the K-12 slope safely, he may have a chance of winning back Beth's affections. But when Charles points out what an unlikely outcome this would be, even given Lane's own proficiency on skis, the dejected teen decides that – if there is truly no chance of reigniting his relationship with Beth – he will redouble his efforts to end his life.

At dinner, Al again raises the issue of the broken-down Camaro with Lane – something of a sore point, as Lane had borrowed $200 from his father to purchase the car only to consequently leave it in the driveway for months. Al points out that Lane had only bought the car to impress Beth, who had found it visually appealing, further rubbing salt in the wound of his emotionally distraught son. Jenny suggests that Lane should visit the Smiths' house and welcome the new arrival Monique to the neighbourhood. Al derisively comments that Mrs Smith had presumably arranged to provide hospitality for Monique only on the grounds that her reclusive crochet-fixated son Ricky may never have encountered a woman of his own age otherwise, cannily underscoring the fact that Lane has a chance of new romance. But as Lane is still deeply wounded by Beth's rejection of him, he doesn't take his mother's suggestion seriously and decides to withdraw to his room.

On his way from the dining room, Lane passes Badger's bedroom and notices that his younger brother is working on a plastic laser gun. Lane asks his sibling why he insists on playing with toys when he is rapidly approaching adolescence, but Badger responds by revealing that he has converted the toy into an actual laser weapon, demonstrating its capabilities by blasting a hole through some cardboard packaging. He decides to leave his brother to his experiments, and continues to his room where he again tortures himself over Beth's decision to abandon him in favour of Roy. Drifting off to sleep, he dreams about the first time they met during the summer – an ill-starred introduction where tries to impress her with his footballing talents in a park, only to end up running through a family's picnic lunch. However, from the mutual clumsiness of their first conversation it seems obvious to everyone but Lane that the relationship was more or less doomed from the start.

Lane awakens to find a Post-It note stuck to his forehead which explains that the rest of the family have gone out. He prepares himself breakfast, his stunned incredulity at Beth's behaviour now turning to angry resentment. While he grumbles to himself about the injustice of the breakup, the doorbell rings. Answering the front door, he is met by the belligerent paperboy Johnny, who informs him that payment for daily newspaper deliveries is now overdue and demands two dollars in recompense. As Lane has no money to hand, he concocts a tall tale about a family crisis and promises to pay Johnny back as soon as he can.

Heading for high school in his car, Lane is exasperated to discover that every radio channel is broadcasting sad songs about romantic disappointment or the pain of breakups, which eventually leads him to tear out the car's radio and throw it out of the window in frustration. Things don't improve when he arrives for a mathematics class led by the cerebral Mr Kerber (Vincent Schiavelli), who launches into an abstruse and long-winded explanation of obscure geometry before inviting the class to present their solutions to an incomprehensible problem he has set. Unfortunately for Lane, he has forgotten to do the required homework – and even more nightmarishly, the teacher decides to call him to the front of the class to explain in detail how the geometric conundrum can be answered. As he watches Beth confidently sketching out the solution in chalk, Lane has another unpleasant flashback to a disastrous romantic encounter with her a few months earlier, where his car's tyres were stolen during what should have been an amorous evening together parked in the woods. To his embarrassment, he discovers that his memories have bled rather explicitly into his hastily-improvised answer on the chalkboard – much to the bewilderment of the class.

Pained to see Beth kissing Roy on the way out of class, Lane feels as miserable as ever. However, his friend Charles promises to help him win his old love back by any means necessary – even though this may involve some out-of-the-box thinking. They are interrupted when Mr Kerber makes a rather unorthodox request of Lane – clearly uncomfortable about the question, he self-consciously asks if he may have Lane's permission to take Beth out on a date now that their relationship is over... much to the younger man's confusion. Later in the school cafeteria, Monique watches in puzzlement at the odd behaviour on display; the corpulent Ricky, his tray piled high with food, eats Jell-O through a straw, while Charles is snorting his own Jell-O as though it was some kind of narcotic substance. Nearby, Lane sketches a parodic cartoon of Roy serenading Beth on his guitar. He is alarmed when the drawing comes to life, and the animated Beth berates him for his general hopelessness and perceived inferiority to the macho ski captain. Lane fires back at the cartoon Beth by saying that any woman in the school would love to go out with him, and sets his sights on the glamorous cheerleader Chris Cummins (Tina Littlewood). The animated Beth points out that Chris is impossibly out of his league, and that she dates members of the entire school basketball team which means that any romantic ambitions on Lane's part would lead to him being torn limb from limb. Now fuming at the cartoon's continual humiliation of him, Lane has an angry outburst at the sketch-pad... leading to the entire room looking at him in open confusion. Desperate to win back some shred of credibility, Lane attempts to engage the roller-skating Chris in conversation but is soundly rebuffed. Borrowing some roller-skates to wear in an ill-fated attempt to suggest some commonality between them, he trips over and accidentally tears her dress off, leading to a sound (and somewhat predictable) thrashing from the musclebound basketball team.

Limping painfully back to his car, Lane spots the smiling Mr Kerber driving away from the school with Beth in his passenger seat, adding further insult to injury. His indignity now at its apex, Lane heads for a road bridge and stands on its outer ledge, ready to jump to his death. Charles arrives and tries to deter his old pal from his latest suicide bid, promising that he will lend any help he can to aid Lane in beating the K-12 slope and winning Beth back. Parting with a supportive slap on the back, he accidentally overbalances his friend, sending Lane plummeting into a passing garbage truck.

Christmas Eve arrives, and Lane decides that the time to conquer K-12 has come at last. Charles comes along for moral support, though his advice is of nominal use at best. After hours of second-guessing himself, Lane finally plucks up the courage to jump over the edge of the incline... but ends up lying in a painful heap shortly afterwards. Back home, Al is ornamenting the family home with brightly-coloured Christmas decorations, including a huge ribbon and bow for the recently re-glazed garage door. As he continues his embellishments, Lane is on the phone to Beth in the hope that he can deliver her a Christmas gift by way of rapprochement. Unfortunately for him, she reveals that Roy has just bought her a gigantic teddy bear which is taller than she is; a disappointing revelation given that Lane was intending to give her a dinky teddy bear in a gift box as a present. Realising that he is fighting a losing battle, he hangs up abruptly.

Opening Christmas presents proves to be a rather joyless experience in the Myer household; Jenny has bought Lane an endless succession of frozen microwaveable meals as gifts, whereas Badger has been gifted a dazzling selection of high-tech equipment. The holidays are faring little better in the Smith household, where the increasingly desperate Mrs Smith attempts to kindle even the feeblest spark of romance between Monique and Ricky by encouraging her son to give the exchange student a gift... which turns out to be a framed photograph of himself. Mrs Smith hopes that the French woman will find the present to be a welcome memento of her time in the United States, but Monique seems less than thrilled at the prospect.

As Jenny unveils her special gift for Al – a festively-decorated but supremely tasteless overcoat made from aardvark fur – Lane is in the garage attempting to poison himself with carbon monoxide by filling the enclosed area with fumes from the exhaust of his stationary car. A jubilant Al reveals to Jenny that he has finally got round to replacing all of the windows in the garage door that had been smashed by Johnny's newspaper deliveries, much to his wife's happiness. While they marvel at the new glass, a semi-conscious Lane – once again regretting his suicide attempt – slumps onto the car's gearstick, causing it to reverse through the garage door at speed and wrecking it in the process. Monique, who is laughing in incredulity at the framed photo of Ricky, watches with interest from over the road at Lane's impromptu semi-conscious emergence from the Myers' garage.

The first postal delivery after Christmas brings a book on how to successfully attract women for Badger, and an unheeded request to Lane from the mailman (Taylor Negron) to take Beth out for a get-together now that her relationship with the hapless teenager has concluded. Al tells Lane that he has arranged a date for him with Joanne Greenwald (Rima Delane), the daughter of one of his legal partners at work. Lane is deeply uninspired by the notion, as he is only interested in winning Beth back, but relents in the face of Al's persistence – not least as his father is repeatedly cribbing from a book on teenage argot in the hopes of making his appeal sound more relevant.

Lane reluctantly makes his way to the Greenwalds' home, believing that Joanne will be enthusiastic about dating such an eligible singleton, but is surprised when she appears to be pushily forthright and won't let him get a word in edgeways. Somewhat clinically, she informs him that she has no desire to go out with him and is only appearing to do so as a favour to her father (who in turn has arranged the date as a favour to Al). She works out the average price of a dinner for two in town, splits the total in half, and tells Lane to pay her $13.67 so that they can skip the evening altogether. Lane is bemused, but finds her logic impeccable and thus decides to pay up.

At the school's annual New Year's Eve party, Lane and Charles sit on the side-lines free of any interest from the opposite sex. Roy and his entourage mock the pair's single status, but are left confused when Charles (slightly the worse for wear) reacts to their taunting with raucous laughter. Not receiving the response they expected from their provocation, the group departs just as the oafish Ricky enters the school hall dragging his date for the night – the supremely reluctant Monique – behind him. As Lane watches despondently as Beth dances lovingly with Roy, Ricky is throwing Monique around the floor with supreme inelegance, treating her more like a prop than a dance partner. Lane dejectedly wanders away from the school, too miserable to see in the New Year, but Monique spots his departure and heads off after him.

In her eagerness to get acquainted with Lane, Monique accidentally trips him up, though this inauspicious introduction does little to jeopardise the instant attraction between them. Lane recognises her as the student visitor staying with the Smiths, but discovers that she appears to speak no English which makes conversation difficult. Their meeting is soon interrupted by a now-jealous Ricky, who breaks up the exchange and insists that Monique accompany him to the school entrance so that his mother can pick them up. But even yet another insult from a passing Roy can do little to cheapen the flourishing sense of allure between Lane and the young French woman. He is, however, somewhat ruffled on the way back to his car when he is accosted by Johnny and a seemingly-endless band of reinforcement paperboys, all of them demanding that he pay the overdue two dollars.

Lane gets home by the skin of his teeth, only to fall foul of Al's suspicions; as his father is reading a book on drug-taking in youth culture, he believes that Lane's perceived state of paranoia can be explained by narcotic abuse rather than a morose pack of pursuing paperboys. Then, heading upstairs, Lane discovers that Badger is hosting a private party of his own – surrounded by a multitude of adult women whom he has attracted as a result of his recently-arrived book. Wishing them the compliments of the season, he wearily withdraws.

Fresh opportunities arrive with the New Year, and Al reveals that he has been instrumental in landing a new job for Lane. As his son has been out early on the slopes with Charles continuing to hone his skiing skills, he is barely on time for his first day... which turns out to be at a fast food eatery named Pig Burgers. This proves to be unfortunate for Lane, as the no-nonsense manager – Rocko (Chuck Mitchell) – is the owner of the truck that he regularly crashes into with his car. Though he shows no obvious recognition, the overbearing (and supremely unsanitary) manager reels off the various responsibilities of the job to an obviously jaded Lane before insisting that he wear a humiliating uniform which combines a chef's hat with a pig's snout. Due to his boredom at the repetitive labour, Lane soon drifts into a daydream where he fantasises about reanimating the burgers, Frankenstein-style, in an obvious tribute to James Whale. A lengthy stop-motion sequence follows, featuring dancing burgers and French fries, before the manager returns to the kitchen and sees the reality of the situation – burned food as far as the eye can see. Incensed, he fires Lane and throws him out of the kitchen... where he meets Beth and Roy, who are currently at the restaurant on a date. Roy can't resist yet another sideswipe at the pig-hat-wearing Lane, thus bringing his embarrassment to another crescendo.

A while later, Lane has yet another attempt at safely descending the K-12 slope only to fail miserably once more. Returning home, he spots a recently-arrived package for Badger – a guide to his latest project, a space shuttle which can be constructed entirely from household items. He also finds a copy of the day's newspaper, which contains a headline featuring a man who has committed suicide by deliberately starting a fire. The article appears to give him an idea, but his thoughts are interrupted when Barney Rubble – a character from Hanna-Barbera's vintage cartoon series *The Flintstones* (1960-66) – speaks to him from the living room television set and politely enquires if he has Lane's permission to take Beth out on a date. Lane's reaction to the request is as swift as it is foreseeable.

Heading for his room, Lane grabs a selection of blankets and sheets, swathing himself in bed linen before heading to the garage in search of some petrol. Unable to find any, he has to settle for a jar of primer instead, but when he heads back into the house to find a box of matches his mother grabs him and guides him into the dining room – it turns out that the Myers are entertaining guests. Somewhat self-conscious in his garb of bedclothes, Lane simmers in mortification as he realises that Monique is there along with Ricky and his brash mother. Jenny has produced a French-themed dinner which includes French fries with French dressing, along with Perrier water – much to Monique's bafflement. Al is confused when Monique does not respond to questions in English, reasoning that she must have acquired some proficiency in the language to have qualified for the student exchange. However, dinner comes to an abrupt halt when Mrs Smith confuses Lane's jar of primer with an exotic cocktail. Flicking her cigarette lighter, she accidentally ignites the primer, causing an explosion.

The next day, Lane is driving Monique and Ricky to school. He expresses regret for Mrs Smith's fate, though he does add by way of consolation that she is expected to make a full recovery from the blast. The two drag racers appear once again, and Ricky begs Lane not to take their bait and agree to a potentially dangerous race. Monique has other ideas, however, and jams her foot onto the accelerator. A chaotic chase then ensues which sees Lane initially take the lead. But while attempting to avoid knocking down a group of nuns who are crossing the road, he immediately slams the car into reverse and winds up speeding into a nearby construction site where the battered automobile lands in a pool of water. Ricky is dumbfounded by his brush with disaster, but the thrill-chasing Monique bursts into paroxysms of laughter.

Lane eventually nurses his ailing station wagon to school, and he regales Monique with tales of how he could beat the drag racers hands-down if only he could get his Camaro up and running. Roy and his entourage appear and demean him once again, bringing his fervour to an abrupt end, but the French student seems thoughtful about Lane's idea. Later at the cafeteria, Lane continues to engage Monique in conversation (despite the mistrustful Ricky's attempts to watch her every move), but Roy decides to barge in and shower her with slimy chat-up lines. Unimpressed with the chauvinist bully, Monique drenches him with a can of cola, feigning innocence and claiming that it was a mistake. When Roy starts to turn belligerent, Lane interjects and challenges him to a skiing contest on the hazardous K-12 slope. Too narcissistic to back down, and knowing that his standing at the school rests on maintaining his sporting reputation, Roy agrees to the challenge. Lane hopes to keep the contest quiet in order to avoid further humiliation if he should lose, but a school-wide announcement over the public address system soon puts paid to that idea.

The end of the week soon comes, and an apprehensive Lane begins to worry that near-certain defeat awaits him. Monique asks about the tarpaulin-covered Camaro in the front garden, remembering their earlier conversation, but Lane promises to tell her about it when he returns. She appears contemplative as he drives off to pick up a new set of skis from local sports supplier Smitty (Rick Rosenthal), who has suffered numerous bone breakages and abrasions as a result of having attempted to ski down the K-12 himself. Knowing that this does not augur well for his own hopes of success, Lane drives off only to discover that Johnny has climbed onto his station wagon and is still angrily demanding that two dollars be paid immediately in order to settle his newspaper account. After much erratic driving in order to dislodge the argumentative paperboy, he eventually manages to give him the slip by manoeuvring through a car wash.

Returning home, Lane finds an angry Monique on the Smiths' front lawn and is startled to discover that she speaks excellent English. It transpires that she has been pretending to have no language skills outside of her native French simply as an attempt to evade the boorish Ricky, but now her temper with the lecherous slob has finally frayed to breaking point. Pleading with Lane not to reveal that she is bilingual, she tells him that she will no longer endure Mrs Smith's doomed attempts at contriving a romance between her and Ricky, who she finds repellent. Lane agrees to her request, and they bond over a love of baseball and their shared contempt of the aggravating Smiths.

Early the next morning, Lane is surprised to find Monique hard at work on the restoration of the Camaro. She reveals that she is a talented motor mechanic, and has already managed to get the engine running – though there is still a long way to go before it is roadworthy. Pushing the car into the garage, the pair continue working on it together, with Monique proving to be patient of Lane's mechanical ineptitude. As they grow closer, Monique asks why Lane continually attempts to commit suicide only to change his mind at the last moment. He explains the situation with Beth, and tells her that life without his former girlfriend isn't worth living. The Frenchwoman is puzzled; as she sees it, Lane killing himself to gain Beth's attention would be a waste of time. In her opinion, his efforts would be better expended in trying to beat Roy at his own game. Lane is frantic at the fact that the skiing contest is only a day away, but Monique is more certain of his potential than he is, ensuring him that all he needs is to have greater confidence in himself. To bolster his sense of self-assurance, she encourages him to take the now-fully-restored Camaro out on the road, where he catches the drag racers unawares and embarrasses them in front of their girlfriends. In a celebratory mood, Lane then takes an unsuspecting Monique to Pig Burgers to enjoy a romantic meal for two. She is, however, a little nonplussed with his choice of food – a processed Christmas dinner on a metal tray which includes turkey, mashed potato and cranberry sauce. But Lane saves the day with a proficient recital on his saxophone, impressing her with both his talent and thoughtfulness.

The day of reckoning is finally at hand, and Lane stands at the summit of the K-12 slope in anxious astonishment; he has no idea of how he can even hope to beat Roy's spotless record. Monique tells him to believe in himself, demonstrating that the slope is conquerable by jumping off its apex and effortlessly skiing down the incline herself. Attempting to follow her, however, Lane's performance follows its customary path and he painfully tumbles downward in an unedifying spectacle. But Monique refuses to give up so easily, and insists on further practice until Lane becomes more capable. Soon they are performing increasingly dangerous manoeuvres together, leading Lane to have far greater confidence in his chances, but their training session is brought to a halt when Charles arrives and informs them that everyone has now gathered and is waiting for the contest to begin. But as his friend departs, he accidentally runs over one of Lane's skis, breaking it in the process. Then things go from bad to worse when, improbably enough, Johnny arrives on a specially adapted ski-bike and doggedly pursues Lane for his unpaid two dollars.

Forced to make his getaway on only one ski, Lane arrives at the apex of K-12 just as Roy is beginning to doubt that his rival will even bother showing up. Still being tailed by the pugnacious paperboy, Lane wastes no time in hurtling down the deadly slope, the contest now of secondary importance. Roy is stunned at Lane's apparent bravery, and the crowd watch in awe as the pair race down the steep incline with Jonathan in close pursuit. Bemused at the paperboy's presence, Roy attacks Jonathan and sends him plummeting into a crevasse – a lengthy fall which he barely survives.

Roy is livid as the race reaches its conclusion and Lane is declared the winner. The crowd goes wild, and Beth – immediately sensing that Roy's star is now in its descent – kisses the triumphant Lane. As the two drag racers appear from nowhere and give a post-contest commentary, Lane watches in concern as Ricky and a heavily bandaged Mrs Smith arrive to drag Monique away. Racing after them, he engages in a spontaneous duel to win the hesitant Frenchwoman from Ricky; eventually succeeding in liberating her, the pair race away in the Camaro. But not all is lost for the loutish Ricky, as it turns out that he has a genuine admirer waiting in the wings – much to the disdain of his abrasive mother.

Lane drives Monique to the one place in America that she has always wanted to visit – Dodger Stadium in Los Angeles. He parks the Camaro in the centre of the famous baseball park, and the couple kiss tenderly. This moment of passion is regrettably short-lived, however, when the indefatigable Johnny arrives on the scene on his bike, still in hot pursuit of his as-yet-unpaid two dollars.

On the face of it, *Better Off Dead* may seem like a typical underdog story of a put-upon everyman who, in the face of overwhelming odds, somehow manages to win the day. Yet in the hands of Savage Steve Holland, this ostensibly straightforward story is transformed into one of the most nonconformist and visually creative teen movies of the eighties, blending established generic tropes and pure surrealism to highly successful effect. The free-wheeling mix of animation, stop-motion techniques and live action footage made the film stylistically striking in ways which helped it stand apart from many others in a crowded genre at the time of production, its plot straying unapologetically into absurdity at a moment's notice. Though the film's Christmas connections are fairly subdued for the most part, the audience are never allowed to entirely forget that it takes place during the holiday season – the bizarre gifts, jaunty range of decorations and Lane's ham-fisted attempt at a romantic Christmas dinner all help to situate the narrative within a yuletide framework, even if the central premise is not exactly overflowing with festive cheer.

There is little doubt that the humour surrounding the film's central premise is likely to be divisive: enjoyable for aficionados of dark comedy, but potentially upsetting for anybody who has lost someone (most especially as a result of suicide) during the holiday season. Though Lane's attempts to end his life are invariably half-hearted and wildly unsuccessful, there are some who will no doubt find them to be difficult viewing, even though the general oddness of *Better Off Dead*'s range of incidents does admittedly blunt the emotional edge of the character's existential woes. Treating such a controversial subject as the key aspect of a festively-situated teen comedy was symptomatic of a wider tendency within the Christmas cinema of the 1980s to embrace a somewhat darker take on a season which had traditionally been associated with benevolence, exultation and light-heartedness. Thus although we are eventually offered a happy ending, the protagonist must scale a veritable mountain of misfortune before he can reach his moment of glory.

While it has achieved success as a cult classic rather than as a mainstream hit, *Better Off Dead* owes much of its longevity to the endless stream of over-the-top situations that writer/director Holland serves up. The film is packed with entertainingly inscrutible character moments such as the soft-spoken Jenny's inedible culinary 'delights' (which include boiled bacon, live octopus and a strangely mobile jelly with raisins), Charles's inexplicable pickled animal foetus that he carries around school in a jar, Joanne Greenwald's unusually exotic dental brace, and the fact that Lane showers while wearing (mismatched) socks, only to dry them out later with an electric hairdryer. However, the film has become affectionately remembered amongst eighties cineastes for a handful of standout set-ups which include the always-silent Badger's implausible inventions, the supremely tongue-in-cheek Japanese-American drag racers, Al's gift of the truly hideous festive aardvark-skin coat, and most especially Johnny's obsessive demands for the two dollar newspaper fee – a repeated motif which builds in intensity (and farcicality) as the film continues. (There is never any explanation as to why Johnny keeps insisting so adamantly that the two dollars be paid, when he is presumably never asked to reimburse the Myers for the criminal damage that he repeatedly causes to their home when delivering the papers in the first place.)

Also of note is the way in which Holland uses the film to lampoon the conventions of the teen movie even at the same time as he occasionally mirrors or adapts to them. In spite of its central theme, *Better Off Dead* is not a satire on the topic of youth suicide in the manner of Michael Lehmann's acclaimed *Heathers* (1988), but rather a meditation on teenage life and the complex social structures which govern it. A comedy of embarrassment which inevitably sees Lane mortified, undermined and generally demeaned in every way possible, we see his humiliation in microcosm via the running gag that everyone and anyone seems capable of dating Beth apart from Lane himself. Much to his chagrin, she appears to make herself accessible to everyone from her mathematics teacher to the local postman to the Hanna-Barbera cartoon character Barney Rubble, while her doting former beau is left speechless at her casual emotional cruelty. As Ryan Cracknell observes, 'Steve Holland plays with so many clichés in *Better Off Dead* you'd think that he's well aware of the fact. But he takes several of them that all-important step further to give the film a familiar but different feel. [...] The entire plot has a feeling of *déjà vu* to it, combining elements of teen comedy, underdog romance and even the sports movie. Even with its feeling of oddball familiarity, *Better Off Dead*'s charm stems from its imagination and attitude'.[2] Indeed, while the film is arguably at its best when distorting the clichés of youth cinema (consider the weirdly enthralled reaction that the mathematics class demonstrates for Mr Kerber's incomprehensible lessons in geometry), it also succeeds when amplifying the genre's truisms to preposterously intensified levels: the nerdish Ricky's spectacular social ineptitude (greeting a beautiful woman by clearing his sinuses with a nasal spray) or the growling, über-macho basketball team.

In spite of its subversive qualities and innovative meandering into animated sequences or stop-motion scenes, at heart the film's central narrative remains strangely traditional in its nature, corresponding to the conventions of the genre in many key ways. The protagonist, having lost the supposed love of his life, undergoes a journey of self-discovery in an attempt to win her back, only to eventually realise that his true affections lie elsewhere. Yet in Holland's hands, the film becomes rather more than the sum of its parts, drifting blithely between gleeful ludicrousness and subtle profundity. As Richard Crouse has remarked, 'much of [the film] is typical teen underdog fare – Lane is in love with Ms Wrong, but ends up with the right girl by the time the credits roll – but there is an irreverence on display that sets it apart from the average kid flick. Holland seems to really understand the sense of isolation and displacement typical of the difficult teen years, but more importantly, also knows how to lampoon it. Everything about this movie has an off-kilter feel, as if reality has been tilted 45 degrees, creating a crazy world that is both unique and delightful'.[3]

Although the film is set over the holidays, beginning just before Christmas and concluding just after the New Year has begun, its snowy locale tends to lend it more seasonal association than its otherwise alternative engagement with the festivities in general. The ski resort-based teen movie was an oft-visited subgenre throughout the eighties, with the inevitable climactic head-to-head skiing competition later satirised by films such as Steve Pink's parodic *Hot Tub Time Machine* (2010), which incidentally also starred a (much older) John Cusack. Paradoxically, although *Better Off Dead*'s general stylistic approach was largely set in opposition to the orthodox tropes of youth cinema at the time, its cult permanence has led to it becoming a singular example of the genre within its eighties context; as Keith Staskiewicz has argued, the film 'is a wonderfully off-kilter iteration of the typical coming-of-age-and-getting-the-girl movie. [...] Genuinely funny, surprisingly cohesive, and more quotable than the Bible, *Better Off Dead* is definitely a time capsule, but its appeal hasn't gotten old'.[4] While Holland's movie may have lacked the public popularity that has accompanied the films of John Hughes, Rob Reiner and others, it has nonetheless endured amongst cult movie fans and devotees of eighties cinema, meaning that its endurance has never truly eroded over the years. Andrew Gilstrap explains that:

> From haircuts to music, the 1985 film has elements that are purely of its era, but it also boasts moments of surreal humor that were unlike anything else going on in teen comedies at the time. [...] *Better Off Dead* finds its comfort zone not in the established clichés of '80s teen comedies, but in the loopy little avenues discovered by its unique sense of humor. A menacing paperboy in search of two dollars ('plus tip!'), a mother whose cooking more closely resembles genetic tampering than food, a pair of yellow-blazered drag-racing brothers whose only English comes from vintage *Wild World of Sports* [sic] and Howard Cosell: these and other little oddball moments pop up throughout *Better Off Dead,* producing quotes and scenes that are cherished by the film's devoted cult audience. How devoted and cult? Well, even the Camaro has its own website.[5]

While the yuletide trimmings do assist in making Lane's ordeal all the more keenly felt, he eschews the traditional approach of emphasising the festive season's ability to transform worldviews and reform the nature of individuals, instead using Christmas as a means of illuminating his characters' personalities through their reaction to holiday customs. The considerate but peculiar Jenny puts obvious thought into her Christmas gifts, for instance, taking great care to purchase microwaveable TV meals for Lane that will suit his tastes without ever considering whether this choice necessarily constitutes a suitable present. Meanwhile, the vain but socially ham-fisted Ricky gifts Monique a framed photograph of himself – surely the ultimate in self-important conceit – which not only reveals his own lack of humility but also the hopelessness of his romantic ambitions (made clear when Monique bursts into uncontrollable laughter as soon as he is out of earshot). Just as the predictable beats of teen movies past are twisted and reconfigured by Holland's off-the-wall approach, so too are the long-established conventions of Christmas cinema shrewdly reshaped by his idiosyncratic style. This can often be detected in the calculated disruption of expectation; for instance, Al unconvincingly feigns gratitude for the gift of his unsightly aardvark overcoat, brushing off his wife's unconvincing assurance that it is the height of fashion and everyone in the area will be wearing coats like it, only to later discover that his cranky neighbour is clad in identical attire. Nor indeed would it be easy to reconcile the cosy fireside scenes of opening presents (the roaring fire in question being broadcast on television rather than situated in a real hearth) with a miserable Lane's Christmas Day attempt to poison himself with carbon monoxide in the family garage. This was a bravura juxtaposition of the film's insouciance and its underlying moments of perceptive insight, as Holland cunningly shines a light on the magnified emotional difficulties which can manifest themselves for many people over the holidays.

Better Off Dead is hugely benefited by John Cusack's affably engaging performance as the beleaguered Lane Myer. Taking place early in his career, which at that point had included appearances in teen movies such as *Class* (Lewis John Carlino, 1983), *Sixteen Candles* (John Hughes, 1984) and *The Sure Thing* (Rob Reiner, 1985), Cusack would later go on to several roles in other youth-centric eighties features which included *Stand by Me* (Rob Reiner, 1986), *One Crazy Summer* (Savage Steve Holland, 1986) and *Say Anything* (Cameron Crowe, 1989). Developing a successful filmography as a highly versatile actor in many dramatic and comedic roles, Cusack was nominated for a Golden Globe Award in the Best Performance by an Actor in a Motion Picture (Comedy or Musical) category for his performance in Stephen Frears's *High Fidelity* (2000), and also shared a BAFTA Award nomination for penning the screenplay for *High Fidelity* with co-writers D.V. DeVincentis, Steve Pink and Scott Rosenberg. In addition to acting and screenwriting, he has also been active as a producer. With Lane, Cusack makes the most of Holland's adroitly-constructed dialogue, crafting a likeable character whose numerous discomfitures elicit audience sympathy and ensure that the protagonist's many trials throughout the film maintain interest. His excellent grasp of comic timing and amicable onscreen charisma meant that, as James Kendrick has noted, Cusack adds a great deal to the film's appeal: 'As a director, Holland isn't particularly inventive, although he knows just how to stage each joke at Lane's expense for maximum embarrassment. [...] After so many interchangeable teen comedies, *Better Off Dead* is an amusing example of how old material can be renewed with a unique slant. It doesn't hurt that John Cusack was cast in the lead role – he brings to the character of Lane Myer a charming credibility that continues to define his career. Even when Lane is at his lowest, it's impossible not to like him and feel for him'.[6]

Cusack receives sterling support from stage veteran David Ogden Stiers, instantly recognisable to a generation of television viewers as the aristocratic Bostonian Dr Charles Emerson Winchester III in CBS's long-running sitcom

*M*A*S*H* (1972-83) between 1977 and its finale in 1983. As Al, Lane's caring but out-of-touch father, Stiers brings a wonderfully observed line in bruised dignity to this caring family man – not least in his extensive range of pained expressions and tangible sense of helplessness at the events which rage around him. (His doomed attempts at gaining credibility with his son by implementing slang terms from an already-out-of-date book on teenage vernacular are a particular joy to behold.) Similarly impressive is the beautifully understated performance by Kim Darby, a long-time veteran of TV and cinema who was perhaps best-known to audiences for her performance as Mattie Ross in *True Grit* (Henry Hathaway, 1969). The gentle-mannered but oddly perplexing Jenny – with her variety of anomalous gastronomic specialities – makes for an effective foil to Al's anxieties, often seeming like the eye of the storm within her personal bubble of perpetual eerie calm as chaos regularly thunders around the confines of her home.

Better Off Dead is chock full of pleasingly unconventional performances, ranging from Diane Franklin's spirited exchange student Monique to Curtis Armstrong's permanently spaced-out Charles, by way of Aaron Dozier's Roy Stalin – a masterclass in sneering arrogance and high school social primacy (though in spite of the antagonist's surname, its Russian translation being 'man of steel', this condescending bully eventually proved to be more of a paper tiger). As Scott Tobias has suggested, these winningly-rendered oddball characters have played a significant part in the film's cult success: 'It would be a stretch to call 1985's *Better Off Dead* [...] anything greater than a broad, shambling, hit-or-miss piece of comic craftsmanship. What it has in its favor is affability – some owed to Cusack's gawky young charisma, some to Holland's goofy tone and lightly surreal sense of humor, and still more to a cast where even the villains are mostly likeable'.[7] There is much to enjoy about the film's production values, including Isidore Mankofsky's capable cinematography – contrasting wintry ski slopes with a cosy mountain town atmosphere to good effect – and Gary Moreno's inspired set design. Rupert Hine's original score is energetic and enjoyable, complemented by an virtuosic range of songs which included the bitingly acerbic 'One Way Love (Better Off Dead)', performed by Elizabeth Daily at the school's New Year's Eve party. (Other well-judged music choices included Neil Sedaka's 'Breaking Up is Hard to Do' and Paul Simon's 'Fifty Ways to Leave Your Lover', heard on Lane's car radio as he desperately tries and fails to put his recent romantic split out of his mind.)

Perhaps exactly because of Holland's avowedly out-of-the-ordinary approach, *Better Off Dead* has split critical opinion since the time of its original release in 1985, with commentators divided regarding the film's merits and overall effectiveness. Janet Maslin, for instance, opined that 'sustained humor doesn't seem to be what interests Mr Holland; his style could better be described as hit and run. But some of the gags in *Better Off Dead* have a lot more cleverness than the material – just another silly story about a lovesick high school boy and the cute, annoying habits of his friends and family – might warrant. [...] The film doesn't seem to have much of a focus. But it doesn't seem to want one, either. It simply piles on the jokes about suburban family life'.[8] Similarly, the movie's deliberately scattershot narrative strategy – which has long been considered part of its charm by many of its fans – did not win it unanimous praise, especially amongst reviewers who disapproved of the unabashed haphazardness of Holland's methodology. This, as Robert Horton has remarked, can make *Better Off Dead* something of an acquired taste: 'Many of his ideas, while bizarre, have a certain structure to them, and he does know how to exploit a running gag. But the overall concept of the movie is so foolish, you can't do much more than sit back and say, "Well, yes, that's amusing," without getting much drawn into the proceedings. Holland gives us no reason to care about any of this and I, for one, didn't'.[9]

Although the film's illogicalities do occasionally stray a little too far from sound plot coherence (for instance, when Lane arranges a romantic dinner for Monique why does he take her to the very same restaurant where he had been humiliatingly fired only days earlier?), the combination of Holland's offbeat narrative and Cusack's easy-going charm almost always succeeds in papering over the cracks of discrepancy in even the most implausible scenarios that are presented. And yet the moments of triumphant weirdness and plethora of peculiar character traits conceal a much more reflective stratum of emotional commentary which was sometimes overlooked; while the audience are laughing at Lane's seemingly endless catalogue of misfortunes, they are also encouraged to commiserate and identify with his predicament. As Martin Liebman takes note, 'the ebbs and flows of love and emotion are depicted to the extreme in *Better Off Dead*, a movie that gleefully demonstrates the seriousness of the romantic matters at hand but juxtaposes them against all of the drama that comes with being a teenager. [...] The movie doesn't really make a whole lot of sense – though the plot is easy to follow – because it's so minute-by-minute and always changing, but that's why it works so well as a depiction of teenage life and love. There's no rhyme or reason to it, very little structure, and not much purpose. That sounds an awful lot like love and life and the teenage years, hence the movie must be doing *something* right'.[10]

While *Better Off Dead* may not have earned a place for itself in the annals of all-time classic youth cinema of the 1980s, its cult credentials and subsequent home entertainment releases have ensured that it has never dropped out of the view of popular culture altogether. Although it is less likely to feature in top ten lists of most-watched eighties teen movies alongside landmark features such as *The Breakfast Club* (John Hughes, 1985), *St Elmo's Fire* (Joel Schumacher, 1985) and *Pretty in Pink* (Howard Deutch, 1986), the arresting quality of *Better Off Dead*'s sheer audacity in presenting such a wantonly unfathomable cinematic environment has continued to win the film admirers even in recent years. Arguably it is this infectiously amiable quality which has contributed to the film's surprising durability, as M. Enois Duarte has observed: '*Better Off Dead*, a favorite 1980s teen comedy, is not an entirely well-made movie. It often feels somewhat unfocused, choppy, and randomly slapped together. Some characters can be a bit uninteresting and seem to lack motivation while first-time director Savage Steve Holland delivers a very workmanlike pace. I can admit the movie has issues worth considering for first-time viewers and part of my enjoyment is very likely due to nostalgia. But like the script's main character, the film's various drawbacks are compensated with a charming and wittily amusing personality. It's a quirky, offbeat look at the pressures of being a teenager in love'.[11]

Similarly, although it is one of the less well-remembered entries in the canon of 1980s festive cinema *Better Off Dead* remains an entertaining and visually diverting film which never outstays its welcome. Though almost certainly better regarded for its audacious experimentation than for its often-oblique Christmas-related content, the film is nonetheless an enjoyable slice of escapist reminiscence from a decade that was heavily populated by teen movies and yuletide features alike. Demonstrating enough imaginative caprice to give pause to even the most sceptical festive movie fan, *Better Off Dead* may not have been standard holiday season fare, but – as Kevin Matthews has expounded – the feature holds up precisely because of its artful departure from the conventions of both the teen movie and Christmas film genres:

> [*Better Off Dead*] is one of the most deliriously off-kilter teen movies to ever make use of the well-worn template. The fact that it's so surreal and unique, while also providing some solid laughs and a likable main character (played by John Cusack) to root for allows it to hold up well, even almost thirty years after it was first released. [...] The fact remains, however, that this film is so good not because of the characters, or not JUST because of the characters (and who can forget that malicious paperboy wanting the money due to him?), but also because of the way it refuses to stay within the parameters of any standard teen movie. There's some fun animation, a dancing hamburger, some strange moments around the dinner table and some impressive skiing. And that's not even the half of it.[12]

Better Off Dead is never likely to be considered amongst the most prominent of 1980s Christmas films, but it certainly deserves to be remembered as one of the most stylistically ingenious. Both very much a product of its era and yet strangely ahead of its time, Holland's motion picture debut remains agreeable, relatable and resolutely outré – a heady combination that has delighted fans as much as it has confounded many critics. Certainly it is difficult not to admire the boldness of a feature boasting an end credits reel which concludes with the playful line 'The movie's over... you can go home now' – a similar motif to that which would be used a year later when John Hughes famously employed a similar, celebrated fourth-wall-breaking conceit with his legendarily self-assured protagonist in *Ferris Bueller's Day Off* (1986).

REFERENCES

1.   Greg Metcalf, '"It's (Christmas) Morning in America": Christmas Conventions of American Films in the 1980s', in *Beyond the Stars: Plot Conventions in American Popular Film*, ed. by Paul Loukides and Linda K. Fuller (Bowling Green: Bowling Green State University Popular Press, 1991), 100-13, pp.101-02.

2.   Ryan Cracknell, '*Better Off Dead*', in *Movie Views*, 6 July 2003.
   <http://movieviews.ca/better-off-dead>

3.   Richard Crouse, *The 100 Best Movies You've Never Seen* (Toronto: BCW Press, 2003), pp.17-18.

4.   Keith Staskiewicz, '*Better Off Dead*', in *Entertainment Weekly*, 12 July 2011.
   <http://www.ew.com/article/2011/07/12/better-dead-review-john-cusack>

5.   Andrew Gilstrap, '*Better Off Dead* Boasts Moments of Surreal Humor', in *Pop Matters*, 2 August 2011.
   <http://www.popmatters.com/review/145582-better-off-dead-blu-ray/>

6.   James Kendrick, '*Better Off Dead*', in *QNetwork.com*, 1998.
   <http://www.qnetwork.com/index.php?page=review&id=976>

7.   Scott Tobias, '*Better Off Dead* (Blu-Ray)', in *The Onion A.V. Club*, 3 August 2011.
   <http://www.avclub.com/review/better-off-dead-blu-ray-59871>

8.   Janet Maslin, '*Better Off Dead*', in *The New York Times*, 11
        October 1985.

9.   Robert Horton, '*Better Off Dead*', in *What a Feeling!*, 7
        April 2011 [1985].
        <*https://eightiesmovies.wordpress.com/2011/04/07/better-
        off-dead/*>

10.   Martin Liebman, '*Better Off Dead* Blu-ray Review', in *Blu-
        Ray.com*, 22 July 2011.
        <*http://www.blu-ray.com/movies/Better-Off-Dead-Blu-
        ray/24222/#Review*>

11.   M. Enois Duarte, '*Better Off Dead*', in *High Def Digest*, 25
        July 2011.
        <*http://bluray.highdefdigest.com/5253/better_dead.html*>

12.   Kevin Matthews, '*Better Off Dead*', in *FlickFeast*, 31
        December 2013.
        <*http://flickfeast.co.uk/reviews/film-reviews/dead-1985/*>

13

Scrooged (1988)

Paramount Pictures/Mirage Productions

Director: Richard Donner
Producers: Richard Donner and Art Linson
Screenwriters: Mitch Glazer and Michael O'Donoghue

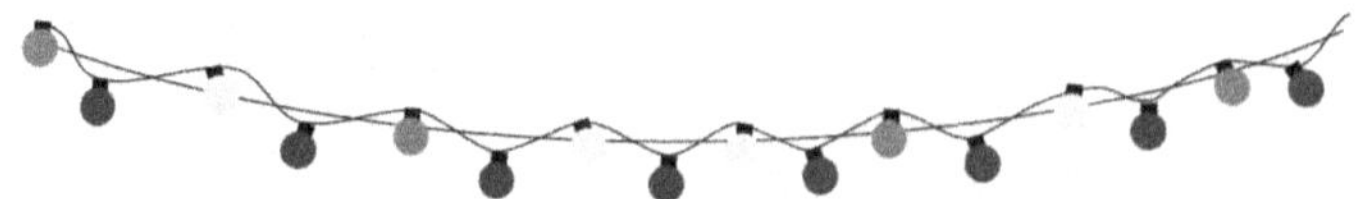

By the time of the late 1980s, the predominant themes of Christmas cinema as the decade neared its conclusion – that is, that the corporate over-commercialisation of Christmas was actively presenting itself as threat to the meaning and spirit of the season, and that modern sensibilities were often at odds with long-established holiday traditions – had become so well-established in the public consciousness that it was almost in danger of reaching a point of over-familiarity. Films such as *Trading Places*, *Santa Claus: The Movie* and *One Magic Christmas* had all emphasised the need to value and protect the Christmas spirit at all costs, promoting altruism and mutual cooperation lest their central significance to the festive season risked becoming lost in a never-ending torrent of economic commoditisation and toy advertisements.

Scrooged, however, was to follow a slightly different trajectory. Whereas other festive films of the eighties had presented a stream of contemporary corporate villains as their antagonists – characters who exhibited neither conscience nor virtue, such as the Duke Brothers, Mrs Deagle and the acquisitive B.Z. – *Scrooged* was instead to turn the tables by examining in detail the nature and motivations of just such an over-ambitious, business-obsessed scoundrel during the holiday season. With its entertainingly venal protagonist Frank Cross, *Scrooged* would not only follow the traditional path of moral transformation that had been typical of so many earlier Christmas films, but – in the process of his redemption – also illuminated something of the merchandise-focused and marketing-obsessed culture of consumption that was perceived to have taken root throughout the course of the 1980s.

Although an updating of *A Christmas Carol* had been attempted before (most notably in the case of Eric Till's Depression-era *An American Christmas Carol*, which had been broadcast on television by ABC in 1979), *Scrooged*'s finely tuned sense of contemporary cultural anxiety and the scathing bite of the screenplay's supremely sardonic wit meant that the film seemed tailor-made for the time of its production. The intense aura of raw cynicism which is evoked was to lend *Scrooged* a different kind of relevance to audiences than the other, much more traditional adaptation of Dickens's tale that had been produced earlier in the decade. Clive Donner's *A Christmas Carol* (1984) had aired on the CBS television network in the United States, but had later gone on to receive a cinematic release in the UK. With a starry cast that had included George C. Scott as Ebenezer Scrooge, David Warner as Bob Cratchit and Frank Finlay as the Ghost of Jacob Marley, this atmospheric but entirely orthodox period adaptation had received an amenable reception from critics on both sides of the Atlantic. Yet *Scrooged*, with its relentless sense of world-weary modernity and complex but effective metanarrative structure, was in no danger of being mistaken for the customary Victoriana established in most filmic variations of Dickens's tale.

Responsible for bringing the project to the big screen was industry veteran Richard Donner. A long-time stalwart of film and television, Donner had helmed episodes of some of America's best-known TV series throughout the 1960s and 70s. His directorial work read like a veritable who's-who of classic American TV: Donner's early career had included helming episodes of such popular series such as *Have Gun, Will Travel* (1961-62), *The Twilight Zone* (1963-64), *The Man from U.N.C.L.E.* (1964), *Gilligan's Island* (1964-65), *Get Smart* (1965), *The Fugitive* (1966), *The Wild Wild West* (1966), *Ironside* (1972), *Kojak* (1973-74) and *The Streets of San Francisco* (1974), amongst a great many others. He had also directed films for the cinema at that time, such as crime farce *Salt and Pepper* (1968) and romantic comedy-drama *Lola* (1970), but he shot to prominence soon afterwards with supernatural horror *The Omen* (1976) and then the vastly successful, all-star comic book adaptation *Superman: The Movie* (1978). Throughout the early eighties, he directed features in a wide variety of genres including emotional drama (*Inside Moves*, 1980), provocative comedy (*The Toy*, 1982), romantic fantasy (*Ladyhawke*, 1985), family adventure (*The Goonies*, 1985) and crime thriller (*Lethal Weapon*, 1987). Also a producer and occasional screenwriter, Donner has additionally become known for the many cameo appearances that he has made in his films. In 2000 he was conferred the Hollywood Film Award for Outstanding Achievement in Directing at the Hollywood Film Festival.

It's the lead-up to Christmas in the New York City of the late eighties, and hard-nosed TV network president Frank

Cross (Bill Murray) is far from the epitome of festive cheer. He seems to have little enthusiasm for the festive line-up that has been presented by his panel of production executives, which includes promos for *The Night the Reindeer Died,* an action thriller which sees Santa's workshop stormed by terrorists only to be defended by a machine-gun-toting Lee Majors, and *Bob Goulet's Cajun Christmas,* where singer-actor Robert Goulet sings a cheerful selection of carols aboard a rowing boat while simultaneously attempting to dodge a pursuing alligator. Unimpressed, Cross asks to see the promo for the network's forthcoming flagship TV movie *Scrooge,* an international production of *A Christmas Carol* which is due to be broadcast live-to-air on Christmas Eve. *Scrooge* has cost his network (the fictional IBC) an eye-watering $40million to produce, and Cross is livid when he discovers that the promo reel presents a rather cosy, traditional showcase for the feature which includes its wide range of stars (such as Buddy Hackett as Scrooge, John Houseman as the narrator and gymnast Mary Lou Retton as Tiny Tim).

The assembled executives are either too sycophantic or too spineless to disagree with Cross's acidic derision towards their efforts, but one of them – Eliot Loudermilk (Bobcat Goldthwait) – reluctantly decides to buck the trend. He bravely tells Cross that, in spite of whatever personal misgivings the irascible president may have about the promo, the feedback from the public has generally been good. But Cross is not satisfied, saying that it isn't enough that the audience *want* to see the programme: they need to be filled with terror at the very prospect of missing it. He then runs an alternative promo that he has produced himself, full of unsettling imagery and ending on an apocalyptic note that suggests that *Scrooge* is essential viewing: neglecting to watch the broadcast could put the viewer's very life at risk, according to the closing slogan. The executives are stunned at Cross's single-mindedly merciless pursuit of ratings, and most of them can't leave the room fast enough as soon as the meeting is over. But Loudermilk feels that he has a moral responsibility to speak out, and approaches Cross quietly to recommend that his substituted promo should not be screened due to its inappropriately distressing nature. Cross is outraged that his judgement is being questioned, and promptly has Loudermilk fired from his post before ordering that the ill-starred subordinate is immediately ejected from the building for good measure.

Watching with ill-disguised glee from his palatial office as, many floors below, Loudermilk is handed the contents of his desk and is thrown off the premises, Cross begins dictating a list of Christmas presents to his secretary Grace Cooley (Alfre Woodard). It soon becomes apparent that almost everyone he knows is being gifted a bath towel monogrammed with the company emblem for the holidays, with the exception of the handful of people that he wants to impress or keep on-side (who will be receiving a state-of-the-art VHS videotape recorder instead). His distinctly grudging roll-call of festive offerings is interrupted by the unexpected arrival of the network's chairman, the powerful but rather capricious Preston Rhinelander (Robert Mitchum). Rhinelander has discovered some newly-conducted research which claims that dogs and cats are beginning to take an interest in television programming, and suggests that IBC should start to include gimmicks which will appeal to any household pets who may be watching. Knowing how much expectation has been placed on *Scrooge*'s potential for success among the viewing public, Rhinelander suggests that dormice should be featured as a part of the production to attract the feline viewership. Cross is staggered at the bizarre nature of Rhinelander's request, but – as he is one of the very few people in the company that he has no authority to dismiss – he has no alternative but to acquiesce to the older man's peculiar suggestions.

As Rhinelander returns to the upper echelons of the building, Cross becomes disconcerted when he meets the ambitious, smooth-talking Brice Cummings (John Glover), an impeccably-groomed young Californian who tells Cross that he had gone to school with Rhinelander's son (and is clearly on good terms with the company's top-brass). Anxious at the prospect of his lofty position as the network president coming under threat, Cross quickly retreats back to his office and demands that Grace dig up every piece of available information about Cummings so that he can formulate a defence against being usurped. Grace has a long-standing appointment to take her ill son to a medical specialist (an engagement which had to be booked some months previously), but the hard-hearted Cross couldn't care less about her family's predicaments; he tells her in no uncertain terms that his professional necessities supersede any personal arrangements of her own.

Cross's brother James (John Murray) has been waiting patiently in the network president's office for his sibling's arrival. They head out onto the street after work, and James tries in vain to persuade Cross to join him and his family for Christmas dinner. However, it becomes clear to James that his brother hates the festive season almost as much as he hates people in general. Cross quickly precludes any further discussion of the matter by deftly stealing a taxi from under the nose of an elderly lady... although, ironically, his intended destination is the annual Humanitarian of the Year Awards ceremony. There, he receives the ornamental statue which accompanies the prestigious prize with insincerely-delivered platitudes and barely disguised contempt. But the total disdain that Cross holds for the award is made even more evident when he carelessly leaves it in the back seat of a cab after returning to the IBC headquarters.

Working late in his office, Cross is surprised to hear a knock at the door. A quick examination of the hallway outside reveals nothing, but he has scarcely had time to get back to his desk before the insistent thumping begins again. The heavy doors to his office splintering apart, Cross is greeted with an otherworldly site: the gruesome ghost of his old boss Lew Hayward (John Forsythe), his body now badly decomposed and still wearing a decayed golf outfit from when he had died of a heart attack on the fairway seven years earlier. Frank, who has retrieved a revolver from his desk drawer, fires several rounds into Hayward, but firearms prove to have little effect on a target who is already dead. Unimpressed by his old protégé's attempts at bravado, Hayward explains to Cross that he is now suffering in the great hereafter as a result of his pitiless, cold-hearted actions in life. He beseeches Cross to reform his ways and become considerate of his fellow human beings before time runs out for him, too. Believing the whole encounter to be hallucinatory, Cross is dismissive of Hayward's warning, pointing out that his now-deceased predecessor was a legend in the world of TV during his lifetime... and that he didn't get to the top of the tree as a result of playing by the rules. But Hayward is insistent. Picking Cross up by the throat, he thrusts him through the glass of his office window, leaving him to dangle in mid-air many storeys above street level. Warning Cross that he will be visited by three spirits – the first to arrive at noon the next day – Hayward laughs as his rotting arm shears off at the elbow, leaving Cross to plunge to his apparent death. Just before he can make impact on the ground, however, Cross realises that he is back in his office. As he struggles to come to terms with what he has just witnessed, the telephone on his desk autonomously – and rather mysteriously – calls up his old girlfriend Claire Phillips (Karen Allen), who he hasn't seen or spoken to in fifteen years. That the keypad should do this entirely of its own accord is deeply bewildering to Cross. Leaving a hastily-improvised (and thus confusing) message on her answering machine, Cross begs for Claire to get in touch as soon as possible. With Hayward now gone and no evidence of his explosive visit in sight (even the office doors are back to normal), Cross seems to momentarily question whether the encounter had been a figment of his imagination after all. But he is forced to put his doubts aside when he takes a swig from a shot-glass and discovers a golf ball in his mouth.

Across town, Grace and her family are discussing the curious condition of her young son Calvin (Nicholas Phillips). Unable to speak, Calvin has baffled the various doctors that Grace has consulted, but the medical bills are piling up and she is concerned about how to meet the rising costs – not least as her 'Christmas bonus' from Cross has taken the form of an IBC bath-towel. A single mother of several children, it is clear that Grace is concerned that the meagre salary she receives from the network is presenting her with major difficulty in making ends meet. She is momentarily shaken from her worries when she discovers that, as the family (Damon Hines, Tamika McCollum, Koren McCollum and Reina King) lack the money for a Christmas tree, they have taken the initiative and decorated little Calvin instead, complete with electric fairy-lights.

The next morning, Cross can barely contain his merriment when he discovers that an eighty-year-old TV viewer has died while watching his disturbing *Scrooge* promo. Clearly believing that there is no such thing as bad publicity, Cross is elated that the network's advertising has raised the profile of the broadcast to a point where it has become front-page news. His gloating is interrupted when he is needed on the set of *Scrooge*, where frantic preparatory work is still ongoing. A television censor (Kate McGregor-Stewart) is protesting at the revealing costumes that are being worn by some of the dancers, but Cross is unwilling to take her concerns seriously – he is happy to court controversy amongst the general public, and sees no reason to downplay risqué elements of the production given his obsession with chasing ratings. A stage-hand accidentally knocks the censor unconscious with a prop from the set, requiring medical attention to be sought, but before help can arrive he is surprised by an entirely unexpected appearance – his old girlfriend Claire. He seems amazed to see her, the previous evening's fevered events seeming little more than a blur. Now the director of a charitable organisation that provides support for the homeless, Claire seems dismayed to discover how irritable and bitter her one-time sweetheart has become. She watches in quiet contemplation as he roughly manhandles the injured censor around so that she can see the dancers in action (the dazed woman is now too stupefied to argue), and then argues with one of the production's animal handlers (Ralph Gervais) who is refusing – on animal cruelty grounds – to staple a set of fake antlers onto a mouse for dramatic effect. Claire is astonished by Cross's callousness and general insensitivity, but he is flippant towards her concerns and sneers at her compassion. When she asks why he decided to call her out of the blue the previous night, he dodges the question, but there remains an obvious spark of attraction between the two – not least when he discovers that, like himself, she is currently single. However, their unexpected reunion is derailed following Cross's ill-tempered discovery of the silent Calvin on the set (Grace has brought him to work as a special pre-Christmas treat to see the opulently-decorated set) and then a construction disaster occurs with the elaborate backdrop of Victorian building exteriors. Watching his growing sense of furious exasperation with quiet pity, the gentle Claire withdraws before her old beau can notice her absence.

Soon after, Cross meets with Rhinelander for a pre-arranged business lunch at an upmarket city restaurant. As Cross explains some of the extravagant events that will be taking place during the transmission of *Scrooge*, including live footage of a mural being painted on the Berlin Wall, Rhinelander drops the bombshell that he has hired a consultant to collaborate with Cross to avoid any chance of him becoming unable to cope with his current weighty workload. Cross, naturally, is livid – particularly when he discovers that the consultant in question is none other than the ultra-ambitious Cummings, who has also been invited to the lunch by Rhinelander. As the unbearably smug Cummings tells Cross (in a staggering display of insincerity) not to consider him a threat to his position at the network, the clock strikes twelve. Now that noon has arrived, the events foretold by Hayward start to spring into action. Cross becomes increasingly hysterical, discovering an eyeball in his glass of water and then witnessing a waiter being set on fire.

None of the others are witnessing these hallucinations, however, and Rhinelander assumes that Cross's inexplicable delirium has been brought on by stress and overwork.

Unable to cope with the rapid succession of nightmare visions, Cross excuses himself from the table and staggers out of the restaurant. He hails a taxi, but upon entering finds that the driver is unwilling to accept his directions. Worse still, he discovers that he is trapped inside, both doors of the cab securely trapped shut. Cackling sinisterly, the unkempt driver reveals himself to be the Ghost of Christmas Past (David Johansen). Slowing down only to steal a bottle of liquor from the hapless Loudermilk (now destitute and already looking rather threadbare), the Ghost speeds into a dense mist.

When the taxi emerges from the fog, the year is 1955. Cross is baffled at the apparent shift in time, not least as a head-on collision with a truck soon proves that the cab and its inhabitants are now both invisible and incorporeal. The Ghost drives to the grim-looking house that the young Cross had grown up in, which – given that it is Christmas Eve – shows no trace of any festive cheer whatsoever. Cross is scornful, telling the Ghost that he has no intention of being affected by the apparitions of times long past. Moving inside, they discover a four-year-old Frank (Ryan Todd) sitting in front of a black-and-white television set, totally engrossed in the programming. Cross's heavily pregnant mother Doris (Lisa Mende) sits quietly nearby, but peace is soon shattered by the appearance of his gruff father Earl (Brian Doyle Murray). Young Frank soon discovers that his self-centred dad, a foreman at a meat-packing factory, has an unexpected Christmas surprise for him – five pounds of veal. When he responds that he had asked Santa Claus for a toy train, the bitter Earl responds that if he isn't happy with his festive fare, he should get a job and earn enough money to buy a train set for himself, reasoning that his son needs to learn that life is inherently unfair. As his mother heads out of the room with the parting words that Frank should be careful of spending too much time with the TV, the adult Cross is crying in despondency over the events of years gone by.

After leaving the house, Cross tries to conceal the depth of his regret, but the Ghost presses him on his wasted childhood – Frank was to spend all of his adolescence and teenage years glued to a television screen. Cross retorts that he had many enriching experiences in his youth, but the Ghost quickly notices that all of them have been pilfered from the popular programming of the time, including *Little House on the Prairie*. Frustrated, Cross asks to be returned to the IBC office, and the Ghost is happy to oblige. When they arrive, however, Cross discovers that it is 1968. A boisterous Christmas party is being held by the network executives (a tradition that Cross soon put a stop to once he had become president), but a youthful Frank – still a junior employee at the time – is stubbornly refusing to take part in the frivolities. The present-day Cross is dismayed to note how his younger self seems totally oblivious to the affections of the bubbly Tina (Rebeca Arthur), an attractive colleague with whom he was acquainted back in the sixties. But the Ghost is more concerned with another acquaintance that he made that Christmas – Claire, who he shows meeting Cross for the first time outside a convenience store. The pair immediately fall in love, and a year later they are living in an inner-city apartment together. The Ghost conjures up scenes from a happy Christmas Eve that they spent in each other's company, where the ever-romantic Cross proudly presents Claire with a gift of kitchen knives, and receives an illustrated copy of the

Kama Sutra in return – much to his appreciation. Fast-forwarding a couple of years, the young Frank is now in his early-to-mid twenties and in costume for the *Frisbee the Dog* show. Having impressed the president of the network, Hayward (still very much alive at this point) invites him and Claire to dinner during a short recess in the show's filming. Cross knows that this is the big break that his career has been waiting for. But when Claire arrives soon after, she is unhappy with the idea of dining out with Hayward – they already have a long-standing arrangement to visit friends that night. Cross is staggered by her refusal, knowing that pleasing Hayward is essential to his chances of progress in the company. Claire is upset at how cold and distant Cross is becoming towards her, and – as she starts to become aware that he now values his career more than his relationship with her – she suggests that they separate. Still totally focused on the opportunity to dine with the network president, Cross tacitly agrees, thus ending their relationship. The Ghost is stunned at Cross's foolhardiness at having put his professional life ahead of the love of his soul-mate. He berates Cross for having such a skewed idea of his priorities in life, but Cross tries hard to laugh off the criticism.

Disappearing as rapidly as he had first manifested himself, the Ghost leaves Frank back in the present day – on the set of *Scrooge*. Still shaken by his recent experiences, Frank causes a minor disturbance during the dress rehearsal before heading off to find Claire. Using the business card that she had left him during their previous meeting, he soon tracks her down at Operation Outreach, the homeless shelter that she runs on 9th Street. After initially being mistaken for Richard Burton (far-fetched though it may sound), Cross is reunited with Claire and tells her how much he regrets the choices he had made in his earlier life. She is delighted at his apparent change of heart, leading Cross to suggest that they go out to dinner there and then – just like the meal they shared on the Christmas Eve of their first meeting back in '68. But a couple of administrative hitches at the shelter lead to some unexpected setbacks; Claire asks Cross to wait momentarily until she can resolve the problems, but Cross becomes angry, adamant that Claire's assistants should iron out the issues instead. When she refuses to comply with his demands, he insists that she fires them on the spot... but cannot seem to comprehend the fact that volunteers can't be struck from a payroll that doesn't exist. Confused by his near-constant irritation, Claire tells Cross that she will gladly accompany him if he will just wait momentarily, but by now he has had enough. Storming off, Cross tells her that he has made a mistake and – in a parting shot – suggests that she should concentrate on her own self-interest for a change, rather than constantly looking out for the wellbeing of others.

Arriving back at the final rehearsal for *Scrooge*, Cross's mood doesn't improve when he discovers that Cummings has stepped in to assume directorial duties in his absence. Worse still, he is effortlessly charming the cast and crew, much to Cross's vexation. Feigning concern for the inexplicably-missing president, Cummings makes clear his willingness to take the reins of the high-profile broadcast on his behalf, swiftly departing before Cross has the chance to discuss the matter at any length.

Left alone on the empty set, Cross is more than taken aback when he discovers a life-sized fairy – the Ghost of Christmas Present (Carol Kane). Realising that her apparently sweet nature is a façade which conceals abrupt outbursts of baffling physical violence, Cross is swept across the city by the fairy and soon finds himself at Grace's home in Harlem just as she arrives home from work. Her family are excited that Christmas Eve has arrived and, in spite of their relative poverty, they are determined to make the most of the holiday season. While his siblings laugh and joke around, little Calvin remains taciturn and detached from all the festive merriment. The fairy explains that Calvin hasn't spoken a word since he witnessed the death of his father in a shooting some five years beforehand. This comes as a surprise to Cross, who is so self-obsessed that he hadn't even noticed that Grace's husband had died.

Leaving the Cooley family to their Christmas, the fairy next whisks Cross downtown to the home of James and his wife Wendie (Wendie Malick). Cross discovers that his brother is also enjoying an atmosphere of festive cheer; a group of friends have been invited round for drinks and a game of *Trivial Pursuit*. Wendie remembers that James still hasn't opened Cross's Christmas present, and with a mixture of eagerness and trepidation brings over a large wrapped box. Mindful that their gift the previous year had been a shower curtain, James tears open the decorative paper to reveal a top-quality video recorder... and promptly reasons that Cross must've accidentally mixed it up with something else. True enough, Cross fumes at the fact that Grace has obviously decided to put James's name down for the VCR instead of his intended bath-towel, but mellows slightly when he remembers that the gifts are all tax-deductible anyway. He feels chastened somewhat when James voices regret that Cross never joins them for Christmas dinner, especially when his brother resolves to keep asking every year until he finally concedes.

The next stop is a freezing cold recess beneath the streets of the city. As pedestrians walk on the metal grille overhead, Cross finds one of the regulars of Claire's homeless shelter in the underground space – a man named Herman (Michael J. Pollard), now dead from hypothermia. He rages at the pointlessness of the man's unfair demise, but knows that his regret is ultimately pointless; nothing can be done to help this dispossessed acquaintance now. Breaking down a door in an attempt to get out of the claustrophobic space, Cross inexplicably finds himself back on the set of *Scrooge* once again. This time, however, the production is mere minutes away from broadcast. Cummings is initially angered by the appearance of what he believes to be a practical joker but, on discovering that the intruder is Cross, quickly suggests that the seemingly-unhinged network president retire to his office and oversee things from a safe distance. Cross appears to be on the verge of an all-out nervous breakdown when he discovers the Ghost of Christmas Future in the elevator, but feels foolish when he discovers that it is only an actor in a disturbing costume (Chaz Conner Jr.).

Minutes later, the broadcast is in full swing. Cummings oversees the production with clockwork precision, while Cross remains in his office with considerable trepidation about what he knows is yet to come. While Rhinelander watches at home with great satisfaction as his pet cats take an interest in the antler-wearing dormice which belong to Scrooge's nephew Fred (a hastily-inserted addition to Dickens's story, made at his earlier suggestion), Cross opens a Christmas gift from his brother – a framed photograph of the two of them taken in childhood. For once he seems genuinely moved due to James's obvious fraternal affection. As the narrative of IBC's *Scrooge* reaches the encounter with the Ghost of Christmas Yet to Come, a gigantic skeletal hand reaches out of a bank of television monitors behind Cross's back. Before it can tap him on the shoulder, however, Loudermilk bursts into the office without warning and starts firing indiscriminately at Cross with a shotgun. The furious former employee explains to Cross that since losing his job, his wife has left him – taking his infant daughter – and since then he has been roughed up, robbed, and has spent much of his remaining time blind drunk. But Cross has now reached a point where virtually nothing can surprise him, and thus he is able to evade the gunfire long enough to reach the safety of an elevator.

Sadly for Cross, however, this particular elevator is far from secure. Inside is a horrific, Grim Reaper-esque being which holds the screaming husks of tortured souls beneath the folds of its dark cloak. The Ghost of Christmas Future has no discernible face: only a television screen where its head should be, which continually shows a disjointed series of rapid-fire, incomprehensible imagery. The elevator plunges downward, and the doors slide open to reveal a corridor with an observation window. Cross looks through it to discover a padded cell with an adolescent Calvin (Raphael Harris) inside. He learns that even in the future, Calvin will never speak, and subsequently he is eventually admitted to a mental institution. The young man looks up at Cross accusatorily.

Next, the Ghost takes Cross to a chic society restaurant in the future, where an expensively-dressed Claire is dining with a couple of similarly well-to-do friends (Susan Barnes and Lynne Randall). Upon noticing a group of penniless urchins begging near their table, a newly-snobbish Claire orders the waiter (Gilles Savard) to chase them from the establishment. At her acquaintances' protests, Claire snaps back that she had once wasted her time with the penniless and the destitute, but that she had reconsidered her generosity of spirit after Frank had advised her to put her own interests first. Now she has no time for the underprivileged, determined instead to look out for herself.

Finally, the elevator hits the bottom of the shaft... and the final destination. Literally. Cross is now in an austere crematorium, watching in horror as his own funeral is taking place. Only his brother and sister-in-law have bothered to attend the service; the rest of the hall is empty. As a priest (Michael O'Donoghue) recites from the Book of Psalms, a middle-aged James and Wendie watch impassively as Cross's coffin edges towards the crematorium's furnace. Desperately hanging on to the coffin's handles in a doomed attempt to halt its motion, Cross suddenly finds himself inside it just as the wooden exterior begins to catch fire. Screaming frenziedly as the flames begin to lick around him, Cross knows that he has reached the end of his life...

...Only to find himself back in the IBC headquarters again. Racing around his office with jubilation, knowing that he has only escaped death by a whisker, Cross finds himself once again at the end of Loudermilk's shotgun. But rather than choosing to run this time, Cross decides that his new approach to life will start there and then. He promises to rehire Loudermilk at twice his original rate of salary, and to promote him to the position of vice-president of programming at IBC. Loudermilk is amazed at this complete change of character in Cross, but the transformed network president has no time to debate the finer points of his redemption. He races for the elevator with a new purpose in his step.

As the broadcast of *Scrooge* nears its end, Cross bursts onto the set unexpectedly – interrupting the actors – and addresses the camera directly. Suddenly his face is on millions of TV screens across America. He apologises for having been such an inconsiderate character, arranging for a huge live show to be produced on Christmas Eve when most of the people involved would much rather have been doing anything other than working. In the control room, Cummings is ecstatic, knowing that Cross's unscripted appearance has almost certainly ended his career. But his glee is short-lived; Loudermilk bursts into the room, still armed with his shotgun, to ensure that Cross's transmission isn't taken off the air. A furious Rhinelander calls up with the singular purpose of firing Cross, but Loudermilk answers the phone and places the blame for Frank's TV appearance squarely on the now-bound and gagged Cummings, ensuring that the pushy careerist will take the flak for having put Cross on live television. But as Cummings is a little tied up by now, there is little that he can do except sit back and watch in resignation.

Cross soon whips up a party atmosphere on the set, expressing his regret for the way he has treated his brother and his colleagues over the years. He also declares his undying love for Claire, causing her to race out of the shelter on 9th Street and catch a taxi to the studio. As Cross's monologue to camera continues, other executives and members of the crew begin to creep into shot, as do many of the actors. He extols the virtues of kindness and generosity, and tells the world that if people really put their faith in the Christmas spirit, they can change everything for the better. All they need to do is believe, and the planet can become a much-improved place for everyone. Cross is awestruck when little Calvin wanders up to him and utters his first words in years ('God bless us, everyone', in the grand tradition of Tiny Tim), much to the joyful amazement of his mother who is watching nearby. As Claire joins him for a celebratory kiss, their love rekindled at last, Cross notices his old boss – the still-decomposing Hayward, on the edge of the set but unseen by the others –

who now appears to be satisfied that his work of reforming Cross's character is complete.

Scrooged is quite possibly the least conventional version of *A Christmas Carol* ever committed to film. Not only is it a thoroughly contemporised take on Dickens's story (though there is admittedly a scattering of cultural references which have badly dated it), but it manages to successfully employ a risky strategy of planting a fictional production of *A Christmas Carol* at the very heart of its narrative, which is itself – of course – a loose adaptation of the very same novella. It is much to the credit of screenwriters Mitch Glazer and Michael O'Donoghue that they are able to pull off this potentially hazardous approach so ably; the Dickens tale is so familiar to Cross that he immediately recognises the *modus operandi* of the Ghosts of Christmas, for instance, but he still remains unable to resist the allure of their transformative power. The network's cheesy production of *Scrooge* is the source of much of the film's best satire, not least in its outrageous gimmicks (such as the hilariously crowbarred-in appearance of the antlered dormice, obviously added by the IBC production team at the very last minute) and improbable casting which includes Buddy Hackett as a somewhat unlikely Ebenezer Scrooge, the charismatic Jamie Farr as the ghost of Jacob Marley, and gymnast Mary Lou Retton as a surprisingly acrobatic Tiny Tim Cratchit.

Some commentators have argued that the protagonist's obstinately cynical outlook – and the film's flippant sense of irony in general – does lend its purpose more readily to parodying the extremes of the modern Christmas (and the media's embellished interpretation of it) than it does to promoting Dickens's original theme of extolling the values of Christmas throughout the year. Thomas M. Leitch, for instance, notes that 'given its barrage of references to and excerpts from earlier adaptations of the story, *Scrooged* [...] is more clearly successful as both a satire and an example of the misdirected excess of the bad Christmas than as an exhortation to keep the good Christmas in which [it] eventually holler[s its] faith. By establishing [its] worldly, ironic skepticism about pervasive heresies of Christmas – mercantilism, commercialism, self-absorption, a determination to follow the prescriptions of popular entertainment – so much more powerfully than [its] call to conversion, [*Scrooged*] faithfully register[s] the faithlessness of the modern world, or at least its resistance to traditional expressions of faith'.[1] Indeed, others such as Murray Baumgarten have raised the important point that because the film spends so long lampooning the oft-clichéd redemptive ethos of *A Christmas Carol* in the form of IBC's televised production of *Scrooge*, it becomes difficult to consider its own closing scenes of a rehabilitated Cross with quite the desired degree of genuine earnestness:

> *Scrooged* stages a doubled psychological reading of Dickens's tale. Not only does the film include sections of film-within-a-film dramatization of *A Christmas Carol*, it also parallels the dramatization with Cross's experiences, which adapts Scrooge's. At the film's climax Cross, having discovered a new way of seeing, knowing, and understanding, enters the televised dramatization of Dickens's tale and speaks for its values of generosity, kindness, and connection. Now he acts out all those values and meanings he has consistently undermined thorough the violence of his earlier behavior. What he has previously manipulated, through his illusion-making power, turns upon him and transforms his understanding of illusion. And Cross's

intervention and entrance into the television dramatization of Dickens's tale breaks the boundary between life and art.[2]

The careful balance that the film strikes between showcasing Cross's deep suspicion of Christmas conventions and revealing the transformative power that the festive season nevertheless contains was the source of much debate amongst commentators, leading to considerable contention regarding the film's effectiveness which has endured to the present day. James Chapman, for instance, has not been alone in claiming that *Scrooged* is situated within the very same category and niche of media convention as the kind of productions that it aims to send up, leading to an inescapable internal contradiction that it is never quite able to transcend: '*Scrooged* is a very hit-and-miss affair. It borrows from different traditions of comedy, mixing satire and slapstick in a haphazard manner. [...] It might be suggested that *Scrooged* itself belongs to the same crass tradition of popular culture which it sets out to satirize'.[3] Interestingly, other critical observers have noted that the journey of redemption that Frank Cross undergoes, coupled with the film's combination of ethical concerns and modern anxieties, closely mirrored the moral struggle articulated in Bill Murray's later role as TV presenter Phil Connors in Harold Ramis's well-received fantasy film *Groundhog Day* (1993); Jim Whalley, for instance, remarks that 'in narrative and theme, *Groundhog Day* most resembles *Scrooged*, Murray plays a cynical, career-orientated member of the television industry who is forced through an unexplained supernatural manipulation of time to reassess his values and become a "better" person. Where the films differ is that in *Groundhog Day*, he plays a Pittsburgh weatherman forced to relive the same day over and over again'.[4] Whereas *Groundhog Day* has become firmly established as one of the best-received comedies of the 1990s, however, the critical reputation of *Scrooged* has been considerably more chequered.

Richard Donner creates a memorable evocation of a chilly New York throughout *Scrooged,* capturing not only the icy ambience but also the city's distinctively dynamic visual character and fast-moving environment. He ensures that the film works well in harmonising its satirical criticism of network television (most noticeable in Rhinelander's crackpot schemes to chase ratings, and the smiling ruthlessness of Cross and Cummings's brinkmanship) with rather less subtle wit such as the perpetually-injured censor and the ongoing tribulations of the hapless Loudermilk. Wayne Finkelman's costume design is noteworthy, not just in relation to the eye-catchingly attired Ghosts of Christmas but most particularly in the flashback sequences set in the late sixties and early seventies, where some seriously groovy fashion styles are in evidence. Danny Elfman's score also aids the production, lending both energy and atmosphere, and there is a great deal to enjoy in the triumphant rendition of Jackie De Shannon, Randy Myers and Jimmy Holiday's 'Put a Little Love in Your Heart', the film's climactic song which is performed to good effect by Annie Lennox and Al Green.

The term 'star vehicle' is often overused when discussing movies, especially in the thriving celebrity culture of the eighties, but there is no question that *Scrooged* is a film which is absolutely dominated by Bill Murray's laconic, no-holds-barred central performance. While this prompted some critics to note that the film's success with individuals would likely depend on the degree to which they appreciated Murray's acting style, there is no doubting that he throws everything – up to and including the kitchen sink – into the role of Frank Cross. The film's overall efficacy, therefore, hinged on ensuring enjoyment of the presentation of its principal figure, as David Denby observes: '*Scrooged* is too much a one-man show. [...] Other comics clamor for space, but the picture remains all Bill Murray. Faced with a vision of his own death, he shrieks and hollers and pops his eyes – anything to keep the movie going. What happens to him at the end, however, is worse than death. [...] Swaying and waving his arms, he's like Jerry Lewis in the final, emotionally debauched stages of an 18-hour telethon'.[5] From the character's snarling, subordinate-persecuting tyranny to his underplayed, affecting moments of emotional awakening (all the more powerful due to his admirable dramatic restraint), every frame of *Scrooged* seems centred entirely on Murray from start to finish. Whether Cross is terrorising production staff or haranguing charity volunteers, Murray seems to be having the time of his life – and when the cantankerous network executive offhandedly leaves his Humanitarian of the Year Award on a New York taxi, it acts as a surprisingly potent metaphor for his concern for people in general. Well-known to American audiences for his appearances on TV's *Saturday Night Live* between 1975 and 1980, Murray quickly established himself as a prominent performance talent in eighties cinema due to appearances in films such as Harold Ramis's *Caddyshack* (1980), and Ivan Reitman's *Meatballs* (1979) and *Stripes* (1981). His star was to climb even higher after his roles in *Tootsie* (Sydney Pollack, 1982) and most especially Ivan Reitman's massively successful *Ghostbusters* (1984), though he had also appeared to less public fanfare in films such as fantasy *Nothing Lasts Forever* (Tom Schiller, 1984) and romantic drama *The Razor's Edge* (John Byrum,

1984), an adaptation of the W. Somerset Maugham novel. Additionally, he made a short but memorable cameo appearance as masochistic dental patient Arthur Denton in musical comedy remake *Little Shop of Horrors* (Frank Oz, 1986). (There is a nifty, fourth-wall-breaking reference to this film in *Scrooged* where, right at the film's conclusion, Cross can be heard shouting Audrey II's famous catchphrase 'Feed me, Seymour!') Murray was nominated for the Golden Globe Award for Performance by an Actor in a Motion Picture for his performance as Dr Peter Venkman in *Ghostbusters* and, later in his career, for his appearance in Wes Anderson's satire *Rushmore* (1998). He won a Golden Globe (again, in the Best Performance by an Actor in a Motion Picture: Comedy/Musical category) for his standout performance in acclaimed romantic comedy-drama *Lost in Translation* (Sofia Coppola, 2003), and was also to be nominated for an Academy Award for the same role.

Balancing the misanthropic excesses of Cross's bullying, self-centred persona is his first and only true love, the beautiful Claire Phillips. Clearly fulfilling Belle's function from *A Christmas Carol* just as plainly as Lew Hayward is a substitute for Jacob Marley, Claire's natural compassion and generosity of spirit is very ably articulated by Karen Allen, who enjoys an excellent on-screen chemistry with Bill Murray while presenting a memorably sanguine, breezy foil to Cross's unyielding scorn and pessimism. (Unlike Dickens's Belle, however, Claire discovers that she and Cross have one last chance at reconciliation – an opportunity that was forever denied to Scrooge.) Allen's cinematic career started on a high note thanks to an impressive and likeable performance in John Landis's hugely successful *National Lampoon's Animal House* (1978). After a small role in Woody Allen's *Manhattan*

(1979), she went on to higher-profile appearances in films such as *The Wanderers* (Philip Kaufman, 1979), *Cruising* (William Friedkin, 1980) and *A Small Circle of Friends* (Rob Cohen, 1980). Much greater fame came in 1981 with the role of feisty adventurer Marion Ravenwood in Steven Spielberg's *Raiders of the Lost Ark* (a role which she would reprise many years later in Spielberg's *Indiana Jones and the Kingdom of the Crystal Skull*, 2008). In the years leading up to *Scrooged*, she continued to build her reputation as a performer through a diverse range of roles in films including domestic drama *Shoot the Moon* (Alan Parker, 1982), mind control thriller *Split Image* (Ted Kotcheff, 1982), science fiction adventure *Starman* (John Carpenter, 1984), and murder mystery *Backfire* (Gilbert Cates, 1988). She was also nominated for an Independent Spirit Award for her supporting performance in Paul Newman's *The Glass Menagerie* (1987), adapted from the perennially popular drama by Tennessee Williams.

Scrooged was remarkable in its idiosyncratic but highly effective (and wide-ranging) ensemble of supporting actors. Hollywood legend Robert Mitchum is exceptional as the addlepated network chief Preston Rhinelander, while actor and stand-up comedian Bobcat Goldthwait also impresses, cast against type as the meek but independently-minded junior executive Eliot Loudermilk. John Forsythe, Alfre Woodard and David Johansen all deliver solid performances, as does John Glover as the joyfully slimy Brice Cummings. Nicholas Phillips makes an affecting appearance as Calvin Cooley, Grace's wordless son (a character whose name was presumably a wry reference to US President Calvin Coolidge – the original 'man of few words'), but perhaps the standout supporting appearance comes from Carol Kane as the Ghost of Christmas Present – almost certainly the most brazenly pugilistic fairy ever to appear in any Christmas film. There are, additionally, many cameo appearances throughout *Scrooged*, including several of Bill Murray's brothers who also worked in the acting profession: John Murray features as Cross's despairing brother James, Brian Doyle Murray as his crotchety father Earl, and Joel Murray as a guest at James's Christmas Eve party. There were also brief appearances by the film's screenwriters, both veterans of *Saturday Night Live* (as Murray himself had been). Michael O'Donoghue features as the priest who presides over Cross's future funeral, while Mitch Glazer can be seen as another of the family friends who are attending the party of James and Wendie.

To say that *Scrooged* split the opinions of reviewers at the time of its release would be a gross understatement; it proved to be perhaps the most critically divisive Christmas film of the entire decade, provoking some strong reactions on both sides. Some commentators, such as Vincent Canby, favoured the high-quality production values and the humorous, carefully selected cameos, voicing the opinion that 'no expense has been spared in the film's physical production and casting. The movie looks as if it cost a lot even when it's not necessary; the classiness of the supporting cast, however, is. [...] *Scrooged* is nothing if not contemporary'.[6] Yet countering the positivity of this view was the opinion of other critics, such as Roger Ebert, who felt that the film's cynicism became so all-encompassing that it permeated the whole production, somewhat deadening the comedy and rendering the conclusion ineffective: 'Murray's ill humor affects the chemistry of scene after scene, introducing a kind of undertow. When he shouts at people, he doesn't add a little spin of self-mocking exaggeration, so that we know to laugh. He seems to be really shouting. And the other actors look as if they really feel shouted at. [[...]] You can't bad-mouth *A Christmas Carol* all the way through and then expect us to believe the good cheer at the end. In his studies of Dickens in preparation for this role, Murray seems to have read only as far as "Bah! Humbug!"'.[7]

Other major press reviews of *Scrooge* at the time of its release differed widely; a few critics praised the movie for its genuine embrace of the festive spirit as it nears its climax ('*Scrooged* is that rarest of contemporary Hollywood phenomena – a Christmas movie with Christmas spirit',[8] noted *The Boston Globe*'s Jay Carr) and lauded its distinctively biting humour: as *The Chicago Tribune*'s Gene Siskel observed, 'the film works very well, providing lots of laughs, in its first half, setting up the Bill Murray character and his callousness'.[9] Others found a note of balance between the extremes of opinion; Mick LaSalle, for example, points out that '*Scrooged* doesn't pack the wallop of *A Christmas Carol* – you won't cry or walk out resolving to become a better person – but it's a funny and imaginative high-class effort. Best of all, it stars Bill Murray, who has only to raise an eyebrow to get laughs'.[10]

Negative arguments were also abundant, however; proving the point that there are few things quite so subjective as humour, *Variety* magazine did not pull its punches, stating that '*Scrooged* is an appallingly unfunny comedy, and a vivid illustration of the fact that money can't buy you laughs. [[...]] Unfortunately for the film, things ring false from the start because Bill Murray's cruelty seems very arbitrary, unfunny and ultimately unconvincing'.[11] There was also criticism of the film's perceived lack of emotional impact, as well as censure of the engineered stage-management of the audience's psychological response to the film. As Hal Hinson has discussed, *Scrooged* can be seen as something of a curate's egg; startlingly effective in some aspects and yet seeming strangely contrived in others:

> The screenwriting team of Mitch Glazer and Michael O'Donoghue have created a nifty, self-reflecting contraption out of the Dickens tale, but though the structure is inventive and full of possibilities, scene by scene it plays out as hopelessly old hat. Here and there, an image might strike us as perversely inspired [...] or a performance might give us a jolt, but overall, the context is stiflingly impersonal. [...] *Scrooged* is a mixture of populism and disdain, but the populism isn't convincing. It's like *It's a Wonderful Life* told from the Lionel Barrymore character's point of view and made by people who secretly liked him best.[12]

For all its critical divisiveness, in recent years the film's stature amongst audiences has grown substantially, with its unapologetically eighties urban milieu and entertainingly misanthropic central character inducing considerable reminiscence value – particularly since the turn of the century. Jeffrey M. Anderson has ventured the controversial but by no means solitary opinion that 'Bill Murray is the one of the greatest screen Scrooges in this 1980s updating, which features the funniest and most callous Christmas Special spoof ever filmed ("The Night the Reindeer Died"). [...] [It is] one of his finest comic performances. Regardless of the sheer excess, it's hard not to be moved by his final transformation'.[13] Perhaps precisely because of *Scrooged*'s ability to encourage nostalgia for a particular time and place – as well as a very distinct strain of comedy – many modern commentators have been inclined to overlook many of the criticisms levelled at the film during its initial theatrical run in favour of appraising

Donner's movie more specifically within its chronological and socio-cultural context. As Gary Panton states, 'among the best of the adaptations [of *A Christmas Carol*] is *Scrooged*, which plays with the story by dumping it in a modern day setting and casting the marvellous Bill Murray in the lead role. [...] At its most satirical it's a commentary on the pressures of corporate life in the 80s, with a nod and a wink in the direction of yuppies everywhere. At its funniest, it's a loudmouth comedy with some extremely funny moments and a gooey centre'.[14]

Intriguingly, *Scrooged* has become immortalised just as much as an eighties comedy experience as a Christmas film, and the movie fits comfortably into the pantheon of Bill Murray's wider popular cinema of the decade such as *Caddyshack*, *Stripes* and *Ghostbusters*. Rob Gonsalves suggests that the retrospective wistfulness of the feature's knowingly-rendered late-1980s climate is what has subsequently moored it within the annals of pop culture: '*Scrooged* represents the *ne plus ultra* of the big-comedy style – it looks and sounds like *Die Hard*. Michael Chapman's icy cinematography casts a gleaming blue pall over everything, and Danny Elfman's typical robustly morbid score makes the movie feel like a Tim Burton film. The milieu, a network building on Christmas Eve and the teeming confines of the mind of network president Frank Cross (Bill Murray), justifies what Pauline Kael called the movie's heartless beauty. [...] It's also a throwback to a time when serious money and resources could be thrown at a movie like this, a problematic movie that lurches tonally this way and that, but which makes an unembarrassed case for weirdness and humanity'.[15]

With its combination of underplayed pathos and mordant humour, *Scrooged* was to adapt its take on the old

Dickens fable for audiences jaded by the eighties' culture of conspicuous consumption and acutely familiar with the moral mechanics of *A Christmas Carol.* To this end, the screenplay's restraint with regard to messages of personal principle and heightened emphasis towards satirising materialistic culture has led to many audiences (especially in the present day) being attracted to its persistently unsentimental approach. Regarding the film's inimitable drollness, Andy Webb has remarked that '*Scrooged* works because pretty much every scene has something funny going on, be it a cleverly worded joke which will make adults laugh or some visual gag which will have children laughing. [...] *Scrooged* is a wonderful Christmas movie full of humour which updates the classic Charles Dickens *A Christmas Carol* to a much more modern setting without losing the moral message. Whilst it will probably be appreciated more by those who watched it in their younger days it is still as much fun for all the family today as it was when originally released even if certain aspects of it are now dated'.[16] Even in a decade where festive cinema had experienced a significant darkening of tonality in comparison to previous eras of the genre, the efforts by Donner and his production team to produce a very particular type of remorselessly moody stylistic tendency has paid dividends over the years. With its amalgam of no-nonsense incisiveness and shrewdly-employed whimsy, the clash of urban realism and outlandish fantasy has continued to charm and fascinate viewers – largely because of the film's blatant determination to forge its own path through very well-trodden territory. This strangely intangible but unique quality, as M. Enois Duarte has commented, is likely the reason for its longevity: 'Revisiting the film every time, it remains just as funny as ever, with a pithy, succinct pace that's engaging and energetic. Wildly imaginative and magical, *Scrooged* comes with a winning cast which allows Bill Murray to shine in a memorable performance as a modern-day Ebenezer Scrooge. Over the years, it has attained a devoted following, making it a favorite watch during the Christmas season. Admittedly, there are probably finer, more polished choices for celebrating the yuletide, but Donner's darkly edgier take offers much-needed relief when surrounded by the overwhelming cheer while still delivering the same merry message'.[17]

In its lampooning of a consumer culture obsessed with image and social status, *Scrooged* may have flirted with familiar tropes of the decade, but it is the film's gleeful eccentricity and resolute refusal to resort to mawkish emotionalism which has established it as a lasting 1980s classic of Christmas cinema. When the audience witnesses Cross's emergence at the conclusion of the film as a reformed character, the transfiguration of a previously self-interested and at times sadistic individual into a caring and supportive member of society is not the manufactured contrivance of lesser adaptations of *A Christmas Carol*, but rather a heartfelt engagement with values which – as other festive films of the decade had similarly emphasised – were in danger of being swept away by the unrelenting tide of modernity. Not every critic agreed that Donner succeeded in pulling off this delicate sleight of hand, but in his determination to avoid truisms and celebrate the absurdities of fast-paced modern urban life, particularly with regard to the dysfunctions of the corporate sector, the film did undeniably stand out from the pack. As Mike Long has suggested, this adept deviation from formulaic genre conventions marks *Scrooged* out as a brave experiment:

Scrooged is a weird movie. It seemed strange in 1988 and it seems even weirder today. You look at this movie and think, 'This was a tentpole holiday movie?' Yes, it was, and that's a testament to the star power of Bill Murray. But, what makes this movie strange? Well, at its core, it is a pretty straight-forward adaptation of *A Christmas Carol*, and placing the 'Scrooge' character in entertainment, as opposed to money lending is a genius move. From there, things get odd. [...] Sure, we get plenty of wacky movies today, but *Scrooged* comes across as an odd collision of a clever idea, a big star, and a corporate push to make a hit movie. It swings for the fences, but comes up short in many ways. Still, you can't go wrong with a Bill Murray comedy and even when the movie is baffling, it's still humorous.[18]

Scrooged was not forgotten at awards ceremonies following its release. Thomas R. Burman and Bari Dreiband-Burman were nominated for the Academy Award for Best Makeup in 1989, and Eric Brevig and Allen Hall's special effects work was nominated for a Saturn Award in 1990. Also at the Saturn Awards, the film was nominated in the Best Fantasy Film category, while Bill Murray was nominated for Best Actor. *Scrooged* additionally fared well at the BMI Film Music Awards, where Danny Elfman's original score was to win a coveted BMI Award.

Scrooged was a significant entry in the canon of eighties Christmas films: while its satirical corporate scenario laid emphasis on the corrosiveness of power upon high-ranking individuals who lacked a responsible ethical mindset, the movie also highlighted the redemptive ability of the Christmas spirit to turn around the attitudes of even the most ruthless and self-infatuated of individuals. *Scrooged*'s tacit suggestion appears to be that even if an organisation is driven purely by unchecked commercial gain, liberation from self-interest and subsequent moral redemption still remained an attainable prospect for individual people working within such companies: a freedom which is not just desirable, but actually essential to their long-term wellbeing both as social creatures and principled individuals. The redemptive apprehension of reaching beyond selfishness and egocentricity in order to improve the lives of others is a compelling motivation, and though far from original within festive cinema it was one which would remain relevant to Christmas film-making in the late eighties and beyond.

REFERENCES

1. Thomas M. Leitch, *Film Adaptation and Its Discontents: From* Gone with the Wind *to* The Passion of the Christ (Baltimore: Johns Hopkins University Press, 2007), pp.85-86.

2. Murray Baumgarten, 'Bill Murray's Christmas Carols', in *Dickens on Screen*, ed. by John Glavin (Cambridge: Cambridge University Press, 2003), pp.62-63.

3. James Chapman, 'God Bless Us, Every One: Movie Adaptations of *A Christmas Carol*', in *Christmas at the Movies: Images of Christmas in American, British and European Cinema*, ed. by Mark Connelly (London: I.B. Tauris, 2000), pp.29-30.

4. Jim Whalley, *Saturday Night Live, Hollywood Comedy, and American Culture: From Chevy Chase to Tina Fey* (New York: Palgrave MacMillan, 2010), p.106

5. David Denby, 'Holiday Horror', in *New York Magazine*, 5 December 1988, pp.178-80.

6. Vincent Canby, 'Bill Murray in *Scrooged:* Meanness's Outer Limits', in *The New York Times*, 23 November 1988.

7. Roger Ebert, '*Scrooged*', in *The Chicago Sun-Times*, 23 November 1998.

8. Jay Carr, '*Scrooged*', in *The Boston Globe*, 23 November 1988, p.21.

9. Gene Siskel, '*Scrooged*', in *The Chicago Tribune*, 25 November 1988.

10.   Mick LaSalle, '*Scrooged*', in *The San Francisco Chronicle*, 23 November 1988.

11.   *Variety* Staff, '*Scrooged*', in *Variety*, 25 November 1988.

12.   Hal Hinson, '*Scrooged*', in *The Washington Post*, 23 November 1988.

13.   Jeffrey M. Anderson, '*Scrooged*', in *Combustible Celluloid*, 10 December 2008.
<*http://www.combustiblecelluloid.com/archive/scrooged.shtml*>

14.   Gary Panton, '*Scrooged*', in *Movie Gazette*, 23 December 2003.
<*http://www.movie-gazette.com/572*>

15.   Rob Gonsalves, '*Scrooged*', in *eFilmCritic.com*, 29 December 2015.
<*http://www.filmcritic.com/reviews/1988/scrooged/?OpenDocument*>

16.   Andy Webb, '*Scrooged*', in *The Movie Scene*, 2000.
<*http://www.themoviescene.co.uk/reviews/scrooged/scrooged.html*>

17.   M. Enois Duarte, '*Scrooged*', in *High Def Digest*, 28 October 2011.
<*http://bluray.highdefdigest.com/5767/scrooged.html*>

18.   Mike Long, '*Scrooged*', in *DVD Sleuth*, 8 November 2011.
<*http://www.dvdsleuth.com/ScroogedReview/*>

14

Ernest Saves Christmas (1988)

Touchstone Pictures/Emshell Producers Group

Director: John Cherry
Producers: Stacy Williams and Doug Claybourne
Screenwriter: Ed Turner and B. Kline,
from a story by Ed Turner

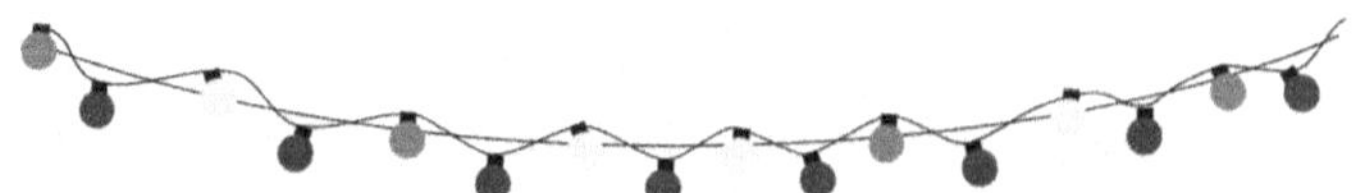

While the 1980s have arguably become best-known for the original and experimental festive cinema to emerge throughout the decade, the period was not entirely without its own range of more recognisable family fare, and *Ernest Saves Christmas* was one of the quintessential child-friendly holiday movies to emerge into theatres during this particular era of the genre's history. Riffing unashamedly on fantasy tropes established in classic yuletide movies ranging from *Babes in Toyland* (Charles Rogers and Gus Meins, 1934) to *Miracle on 34th Street* (George Seaton, 1947), *Ernest Saves Christmas* was a film with no real pretensions beyond telling a humorous, solidly entertaining story which would appeal to youngsters. However, amongst its copious slapstick and sight gags the feature has a number of surprisingly insightful observations to make about eighties cultural mores, and the trajectory of festive cinema in particular.

Ernest Saves Christmas was not the first motion picture to feature Jim Varney's famous comic character Ernest P. Worrell (his middle initial was eventually revealed to stand for 'Powertools'). Created by advertising agency Carden and Cherry in 1980, Ernest was a good-natured but accident-prone Kentuckian who was usually seen wearing denim as well as his trademark baseball cap. He appeared in literally hundreds of television commercials, advertising products ranging from car dealerships to hardware to food and drink, which were broadcast in local areas often as part of wider promotional campaigns. Over time, the character achieved greater notoriety as a result of advertising national products such as Taco John's and Coca-Cola. Generally to be seen addressing his long-suffering friend and neighbour Vern (who was never actually depicted on camera in the commercials), Ernest would give a flattering appraisal of whatever product he was advertising, sometimes followed by some form of cartoon-style indignity or calamity befalling him and usually ending with his catchphrase 'Knowhutimean?'. The character's increasing popularity led to a number of direct-to-video specials before he made the jump into cinema with a cameo appearance in *Dr Otto and the Riddle of the Gloom Beam* (John R. Cherry III, 1986), a sci-fi comedy which saw Varney assuming a number of different roles. Ernest became the central figure of *Ernest Goes to Camp* (John R. Cherry III, 1987), an amusing but scattershot farce set at a summer camp, and the character would later appear in films such as *Ernest Goes to Jail* (John R. Cherry III, 1990), *Ernest Scared Stupid* (John R. Cherry III, 1991) and *Ernest Rides Again* (John R. Cherry III, 1993), before later starring in a range of direct-to-video movies between 1994 and 1998. Endlessly parodied, referenced and imitated in the pop culture of the eighties and nineties, Ernest was a pervasive if rather divisive comic phenomenon, and *Ernest Saves Christmas* has the distinction of being the most commercially profitable entry in the cycle; as Jason Gross notes, '*Ernest Saves Christmas* was the most successful of the entire series at the box office. The film made over $28 million over its 8-week run on an estimated $6 million budget'.[1]

The *Ernest* movies were directed by John R. Cherry III, often credited simply as John Cherry. Executive vice-president of Carden and Cherry, an advertising agency based in Nashville, Tennessee, Cherry was also the founder of the National Fine Arts Title Registry. Beyond the many features that he directed (both for cinema and the home entertainment market) which involved the Ernest character, Cherry has also helmed classic comedy tribute *The All New Adventures of Laurel and Hardy in For Love or Mummy* (1999) and fantasy adventure *Pirates of the Plain* (1999). He has additionally been the producer and screenwriter of numerous independent features.

Christmas has reached the Sunshine State of Florida, and on the 23rd of December a most unexpected visitor arrives on a flight landing at Orlando International Airport – a man whose passport identifies him as none other than Mr Santa Claus (Douglas Seale). Making polite conversation with a fellow traveller (Jack Swanson), even though the other man is unaware of the stranger's identity, Santa explains that his advancing years are catching up with him and that it is time for him to appoint a replacement. With a failing memory making it difficult to recall who has been naughty and nice, Santa feels that the time for retirement is near – but as he points out, finding a suitable successor is a tricky proposition.

Nearby, Ernest P. Worrell (Jim Varney) is working as a taxi driver. In his festively decorated cab, he is speeding towards the airport in order to deliver his current passenger (Barry Brazell) in good time for the man's flight. Unfortunately for this hapless customer, however, Ernest's zeal to get to his destination leads to some high-octane manoeuvring, meaning that the stunned businessman is in a state of shock by the time the taxi eventually arrives. As he deposits both the stunned commuter and his now-ruined luggage onto the airport's baggage carousel, Ernest only narrowly avoids being caught by a crowd of angry travellers who were unfortunate enough to be entangled in the destructive path of his racing taxi. Deftly evading his pursuers, Ernest spots the recently-disembarked Santa – now holding his famous sack of toys – and bundles the puzzled St Nicholas into his taxi, speeding off before the disgruntled mob can catch up with him.

Santa's intended destination is the Orlando Children's Museum, so Ernest sets off at top speed. Remarking that his new passenger looks a little like Santa Claus, Ernest is astonished to learn that his new fare is actually the genuine article. Stopping briefly (after yet more breakneck manoeuvres) to pick up an errant Christmas tree that has fallen off the back of a truck, the wacky taxi driver is commended by Santa for his obvious devotion to the festive spirit. Santa reveals that the reason for his presence in Orlando is that he intends to meet with Joe Carruthers, the host of a recently-cancelled children's show on local TV entitled *Uncle Joey's Treehouse*. Ernest reacts with surprise and recognition, having watched the programme himself in his youth, and comments on its constant emphasis on good conduct and personal honour. Santa approvingly responds that this is why he needs to contact Joe.

The taxi journey is further interrupted by the sudden arrival of Harmony Starr (Noelle Parker), a spiky teenager who is evading the pursuit of an angry waiter (Bill Christie) after leaving the restaurant where he works without having paid her bill. Jumping into Ernest's taxi without warning, she spins a tall tale of being made to work in the restaurant over Christmas by her uncle, but her implausible reasoning seems to satisfy Ernest and his other passenger. Shortly afterwards, the trio finally arrive at their destination – the Orlando Children's Museum. When Ernest asks Santa to pay his fare, he discovers that the jolly old gentleman only carries play money; it turns out that he has mislaid any real currency that he may have had. In the spirit of the holiday season Ernest decides to waive the fee, much to Santa's gratitude.

Santa soon finds Joe Carruthers (Oliver Clark) at the museum – a genial, bearded man, Joe clearly places great importance on his job as an entertaining children's educator. Before Santa can explain why he has come all the way from the North Pole to meet with Joe, the latter's fast-talking theatrical agent Marty Brock (Robert Lesser) arrives and interrupts the conversation. A prominent role has just become available in a festively-themed horror movie named *Christmas Slay*, and Marty believes that this is the perfect opportunity for Joe to revive his career in show-business. Santa begs Joe to turn down the part and listen to his proposition, but he is treated dismissively by Marty. Before he can argue any further, however, Santa suddenly remembers that he has left his magic sack of toys in the back of Ernest's taxi. Racing outside, he discovers that the cab is long gone and berates himself for his growing inability to remember even the most important of facts.

Back at the taxi depot, Ernest is being berated by his boss Mr Dillis (George Kaplan). It becomes clear that Santa's recent free ride is far from the only time that Ernest has refused to collect a fare; he has a long history of helping out homeless people and others who cannot afford to pay. Angrily pointing out that charitable actions rarely lead to profitable results, Dillis fires Ernest. Ejecting him from the building, the irate manager throws his former employee's rescued Christmas tree after him, along with Santa's toy sack. Harmony is confused at her new friend's guilelessness, believing that he could easily have avoided losing his job if he had simply chosen to lie to Dillis, but the honest Ernest refuses to resort to deceit in order to achieve his aims.

Back at the museum, Joe and front-of-house manager Mary Morrissey (Billie Bird) are trying to help an increasingly desperate Santa to get back in contact with Ernest so that he can be reunited with his magic sack of toys. Marty is peeved that Joe is in danger of missing a decent career opportunity by holding things up to assist Santa, and insists that he drive to the studio immediately to audition for the part. Joe only agrees when Marty tells him that he will remain at the museum to support Santa, and stresses that he will join him again later. However, when Santa reveals his true identity Marty has more than a little difficulty accepting the veracity of his account.

As night falls, Ernest and Harmony are heading (in an old pick-up truck) for the home of Ernest's best friend Vern. He explains that Vern has been his closest acquaintance for many years, and that he personally taught him everything he knows about nuclear physics. However, his 'best buddy' appears less than enthusiastic to see Ernest when he forces his way in through the front door and accidentally demolishes many expensive decorations as he attempts to set up the salvaged Christmas tree in Vern's sumptuously-furnished living room. He then proceeds (albeit entirely unintentionally) to bulldoze his way through Vern's home in a disastrous attempt at fitting the oversized tree into the room, while Harmony helps herself to the opulent feast of yuletide goodies that have been left out for a forthcoming party.

Meanwhile, Santa is being taken into police custody – Marty has reported him as mentally unstable. Santa is distraught, knowing that the happiness of millions of children will hinge on the success of his mission. Marty is convinced that the elderly gent is delusional, but the kind-hearted Mary is not nearly so sure. The police fingerprint Santa and discover that each finger and thumb has the impression of a snowflake on it, baffling them. But they take no heed of his far-fetched tale of having come from the North Pole to find a successor, believing that he is suffering from a psychological disorder.

At the movie studio, Joe impresses the director of *Christmas Slay*, Carl (Bill Cordell), with the skilful interaction that he demonstrates with the film's capable cast of child actors. Marty is elated that Joe's proficient performance talents have put him in good stead for landing the part, but the morally-upright actor is more concerned about the befuddled Santa back at the museum and whether he was reunited with Ernest and his magic sack. Keen to avoid discussing the old man's fate, Marty briskly dodges the issue.

Back at Vern's house, Ernest's attempts at DIY have led to some disastrous results with the electrics in his friend's home. Heading out to his truck in search of some bolt-cutters to 'repair' an expensive chandelier, Ernest is amazed when he takes a peek inside Santa's sack of toys and discovers a bright light emanating from within. Flabbergasted by what he sees,

Ernest realises that although he took Santa's word about his identity at face value, he now has absolutely no doubt that his erstwhile taxi passenger was the real St Nicholas. Harmony remains completely unconvinced, and wonders why – if indeed the kindly old gentleman is the true Santa Claus – he has no sleigh or reindeer with him. She is completely unaware, however, that this is not quite true: all of Santa's flying reindeer have been flown to Florida in wooden cargo crates, and are currently baffling storage agents Chuck (Gailard Sartain) and Bobby (Bill Byrge) with their otherworldly presence.

Ernest returns to the museum in search of Santa, but – as it is now the middle of the night – all of the staff have gone home. He reaches into Santa's magic sack and retrieves a mysterious glowing ball, which abruptly transforms into a kitschy model flamingo. He gives it to Harmony, believing it to be what she wanted for Christmas, but the young woman is unimpressed. Now seeing the out-of-the-ordinary potential of the toy sack, she asks him to try again, and out of thin air he produces one novelty item after another. As the gifts become ever more outrageous, Harmony eventually gets Ernest to admit that he simply does not have Santa's power to magically create the gifts that are required.

At the police station, Santa is told that if he starts to give plausible answers to the questions that are being asked of him, he may well be allowed to go free before Christmas. However, even though the elderly man knows that his responses are truthful, the police are unable to believe that he is 151 years of age. Unsure of his true intentions or his mental stability, they soon wind up depositing him in a cell. But he is unaware that Ernest and Harmony, knowing that Christmas will be ruined unless Santa is reunited with his magic sack, are already working to track him down.

The next morning is Christmas Eve, and as the airport storage staff continue to marvel at the abilities of Santa's flying reindeer, Ernest and Harmony set out with a renewed sense of purpose as they seek to locate Jolly Old St Nick. None of them can guess that the aforementioned Father Christmas has somehow managed to persuade a cell full of hardened criminals to take part in an impromptu carol concert. Ernest returns to the museum and learns from Mary that Santa was taken by the police the day beforehand. Fortunately for the incarcerated St Nicholas, however, Ernest has a plan.

At the police station, Chief Spenks (Bob Norris) is informed that a representative of the State Governor's office has arrived on business. The chief is less than enthusiastic about having to deal with a bureaucrat on Christmas Eve, but it soon transpires that the government representative is none other than Ernest – disguised as a weaselly, bow-tie-wearing administrative alter-ego named Astor Clement. Harmony has also tagged along in the guise of the Governor's supercilious niece Mindy. Ernest talks his way into a snap inspection of the facility, and manages to engineer the subsequent tour so that he visits Santa's cell. Thanks to a bravura display of surreptitiousness, he convinces Spenks that Santa's delusional mindset risks spreading to the other prisoners, telling the mystified police chief that he (with apparent governmental authority) will personally remove him from the building in order to have him admitted to a secure mental facility.

Once they have safely escaped from the police station, the trio celebrate Santa's new-found freedom. Harmony remains unconvinced of Santa's magical powers, but he leaves her speechless when he reveals that her real name is Pamela Trenton and that he knows she started to become jaded with Christmas some years ago when she received a doll instead of a baseball mitt. Santa also explains that he took up his current post in 1889, and has thus been in the job for nearly a century. He tells his travelling companions that the magic of Christmas is running low because he has occupied the role of Santa Claus for too long; only by passing his responsibilities on to the next incumbent can the festive season's enchanted power be re-energised. Thus, he clarifies, Joe will need to have assumed his place as the new Santa Claus before 7pm that night, lest the true spirit of Christmas risks being lost forever.

Ernest visits Marty's talent agency in the guise of the man's waspish mother and demands a meeting. As he attempts to determine Joe's whereabouts from Marty's beleaguered personal assistant (Miriam P. Saunders), Santa speaks with Harmony and exposes the truth about her presence. Disclosing the fact that he knows that she has run away from home due to her warring parents, who had been so deeply involved in their own disagreements that they had neglected their daughter, the old man clearly hits a raw nerve. However, Harmony flatly (if unconvincingly) denies Santa's account of her personal circumstances.

Harmony decides to be dropped off back at Ernest's home while her two friends go on to the movie studio. Now in the guise of a snake handler, Ernest manages to trick his way onto the studio lot by persuading the guards that his pick-up truck contains poisonous snakes for use in a horror film that is in production (the effect actually being achieved by Santa frantically shaking a rattle and wrestling with plastic hoses beneath a dust sheet). Making his way onto the set of *Christmas Slay*, Santa is appalled by the concept of the film –

a low-budget horror movie where an idyllic family Christmas is interrupted by an alien invasion. Carl the director is displeased when Joe refuses to follow the script and use profanity in front of the child actors. However, Santa is outraged by the notion of children being terrorised at Christmas (even in a fictional setting), and is so affronted by the concept that he wallops the director, inadvertently jeopardising Joe's role in the process.

Finally worn down by Santa's persistence, Joe decides that it is time for the two of them to talk – much to the disdain of Marty. In the studio's refectory Santa outlines his request to the perplexed actor, who has some difficulty dealing with the enormity of the job's responsibilities. Santa assures him that not every child's cultural beliefs incorporate a trust in Santa Claus's existence, meaning that the number of children to whom he would have to deliver gifts in one night would be well under two billion. Joe asks why Santa doesn't simply remain in the role for longer, but the old man sadly replies that – between his diminishing Christmas magic and the fact that his memory is no longer what it was – this is not an option.

Joe appears conflicted after hearing Santa's account, but St Nicholas himself feels confident that his successor will eventually make the right decision. As Ernest's truck has been mistaken for that of a real snake handler, he and Santa head for the backwoods so that the reptiles can be safely released into their natural habitat. They then return home, where Ernest picks up Harmony before they head for the airport (where, Santa explains, he has had his sleigh and reindeer delivered for his assistants to pick up later). Harmony feels guilty, having emptied Santa's toy sack in search of goodies, but is amazed to discover that it has been mysteriously refilled when it is collected by its rightful owner. After she is asked to put the sack into Ernest's truck, however, she hides the genuine article for her own use and replaces it with a decoy. She then tells the pair that she will not accompany them due to other responsibilities, instead promising to return later.

Ernest decides to drive on to the airport and give support to Santa's mysterious helpers; they will need to get the sleigh and reindeer through the rush hour traffic in time for the Christmas deliveries. Ernest drops Santa off at Joe's home on the way to his destination, but the old man is dismayed when he finds out that the actor has now shaved off his beard and lacks any faith in the idea that he could be a worthy successor in the Santa Claus role – indeed, he seems to lack belief in the festive season in general. Joe's scepticism is not helped by the revelation that Santa's magic sack is simply a bag stuffed with feathers, the real item having been stolen by Harmony. Downcast, Santa leaves the house with the parting words that if Joe should change his mind, he still has a chance to meet with him at the museum later.

Now feeling increasingly guilty at her duplicity, Harmony heads for the nearest railway station and buys a ticket for the furthest destination she can afford, which is Miami. But being Christmas Eve, the trains are running on a reduced service and the next isn't set to depart for several hours. Settling down in the waiting area, her sense of culpability reaches new heights when she overhears some children excitedly awaiting Santa's arrival, knowing that there will be no presents this year because of her dishonest actions.

At the airport, Ernest emerges from a delivery van and enters the storage depot only to discover that Santa's flying reindeer are walking around on the ceiling. He tries to enlist the help of storage agents Chuck and Bobby, but they refuse to allow him to remove the reindeer as they are being held under the name of a Mr 'Helper Elms'. However, this turns out to be a clerical error which is quickly corrected – as two diminutive characters soon point out, the label should actually read 'Helper Elves'. Two of Santa's elf assistants, Pyramus (Buddy Douglas) and Thisbe (Patty Maloney), have just arrived on a flight with the aim of getting ready for the fast-approaching Christmas deliveries. Fortunately for Ernest, the reindeer are trained to obey the elves' commands and soon prove willing to fly into the back of his van for transportation.

Knowing that the roads will be heavily congested with holiday season traffic, Ernest decides to take a short cut through an airport runway and inadvertently winds up blowing the van's tyres on a stinger. As the elves harangue him and he chastises himself for his carelessness, an idea presents itself: there is no need for his stationary vehicle to be an impediment to their travel plans when he is carrying a cargo of flying reindeer. With some help from the elves, he manages to get Santa's sleigh into the air just in time to avoid a collision with a landing plane and a fleet of pursuing police cars which are responding to his unauthorised presence. Unfortunately for Ernest, flying the sleigh turns out to be much more difficult than it looks, leading to some swift manoeuvres which are so rapid that even air traffic control can't keep up with him.

Santa has reached the museum just as the staff are closing the building for Christmas. Mary spots the disheartened man sitting on a nearby bench and asks if he had any success in retrieving his magic sack. Santa tells her of Harmony's betrayal, and hopes that somehow she will have enough integrity to see the error of her ways. Meanwhile, the head of the Diamond World Pictures studio (Larry Francer) has drawn up a contract for Joe, aiming to sign him up for *Christmas Slay* and any subsequent sequels. Marty urges him to sign, but Joe is reluctant, requesting that the film's violence and profanity be cut back in order to better appeal to a family audience. The executive is outraged at Joe's boldness and tells him to accept the contract as it stands or not at all. The hesitant actor finds himself deeply at odds with the ultimatum, but his thoughts are interrupted when he sees Ernest on Santa's sleigh as the out-of-control vehicle speeds past the boardroom's window. Realising with joy that everything Santa had told him was the truth, Joe wishes the baffled production execs a Merry Christmas before dashing out of the building – much to Marty's exasperation.

Ernest's unintentional daredevil flying has now caught the attention of the U.S. military; two radar controllers (Bob Barnes and D. Christian Gottshall) scramble jet fighters to intercept the unknown craft and neutralise it before it can get too close to any sites of significance. This necessitates some even more erratic flying in order to shake the pursuing aircraft, much to the elves' alarm, as Ernest tries in vain to get the speeding sleigh in hand.

Joe is hurrying to the museum in his car, watching pensively as the minutes tick down to Santa's stated 7pm deadline. He is unaware that Harmony has also had a moment of epiphany and, following an attack of conscience, has decided to abandon her journey to Miami in favour of returning Santa's magic sack to him. She arrives at the museum with only moments to spare, and has a tearful reunion with Santa who forgives her for her earlier deceit. Still upset but comforted by his compassion, Harmony reveals that she has been in touch with her mother and has arranged to return home.

Next, Joe arrives and tells Santa that he has decided to accept his offer. The pair shake hands, and Santa transfers the magic of Christmas over to Joe just as the former actor discovers that he is now wearing a full Santa Claus costume – as well as having sprouted a bushy white beard. Joe also discovers that he has somehow developed all of Santa's knowledge of the children of the world (naughty and nice), but only one thing is missing: his famous sleigh. None of them realise that Ernest is currently speeding around the Earth in low orbit at a faster-than-light velocity, with no idea of how to arrive at his intended destination.

As Joe uses his new powers to create the rare sight of a snowstorm in Orlando, Ernest finally manages to get the sleigh under some semblance of control and joins his friends outside the museum just in the nick of time. Handing over the magic vehicle to Joe, its new rightful owner, Ernest says an emotional goodbye to Harmony who tells him of her intention to go back to her mother in Indiana. But Joe has a better idea; for his first Christmas as Santa Claus, he nominates Ernest as the official driver of his sleigh and Harmony as an honorary elf. Much to the distress of the real elves, Ernest gratefully accepts the offer and the sleigh once again lurches into the night as the year's gift deliveries begin. Left alone outside the museum, the erstwhile Santa reveals to Mary that he can now revert back to his real name of Seth Applegate – the first time he has gone by that appellation in a century. She asks him if he has any plans for the evening of Christmas Eve, and he replies – with much relief – that for once he doesn't have a single thing arranged for the holidays.

At first glance, *Ernest Saves Christmas* seems like the kind of inoffensive family feature that has come to form the backbone of the festive cinematic genre; with the abundant slapstick of its rubber-faced central figure, a strong moral message and a focus on the family unit, the film certainly conforms to many long-held expectations of the Christmas movie. Yet being filmed almost entirely in Florida's sunny city of Orlando, any anticipation of a snowy winter setting is abrogated almost entirely in favour of a less conventional festive environment (making Joe's magically-created blizzard at the conclusion all the more striking). This is an interesting contrast to the famous Haddon Sundblom depictions of Santa Claus in the opening credits which are accompanied by a range of time-honoured Christmas carols, suggesting a much more traditional approach before immediately challenging that conjecture. The idea of Santa Claus being an honorary role which has had many different incumbents, rather than taking the form of a single immortal figure, was fresh and innovative; the concept would later be explored in more detail in the following decade's *The Santa Clause* (John Pasquin, 1994), but this original take on the duties and function of Jolly Old Saint Nick certainly helped to make the film stand apart from the comparatively orthodox approach of other similarly-themed features of the time such as *Santa Claus: The Movie*. The screenplay by Ed Turner and B. Kline takes particular care to delineate the responsibilities of Santa's weighty professional obligation, outlining various theories about his ability to travel the entire globe in one night while also emphasising that not all cultural traditions accommodate the legend of St Nicholas. This secular updating of the Santa Claus figure was certainly in line with many other films of the decade, not least *One Magic Christmas*, though the absence of any scenes at the North Pole help to ground the Santa of *Ernest Saves Christmas* within a much more earthly context.

Perhaps surprisingly, given its ostensible guise as light entertainment for children, at times John Cherry's film acts as an unexpectedly incisive satire of the world of movie production. While the ultra-moral Joe is inevitably cast in opposition to the box-office-chasing executives at the fictional 'Diamond World Pictures', whose concerns extend only as far as ensuring the commercial viability of their products at any cost, the sensationalist nature of the low-budget *Christmas Slay* can be seen as acknowledgement of the lucrative market in festive season-focused horror movies throughout the eighties. However, Cherry not only recognises the increasing popularity of the Christmas horror subgenre but also parodies the shabby production values of many economical entries in this category of film; a point made all the more obvious with the emergence of Mike Hutchinson's rather sad-looking alien monster (a low-key triumph of Peter Mitchell's light-hearted costume design, caricaturing the B-movies of decades past). There are many other sly digs at major studio film production, from the gaggle of faceless clone executives on the studio lot to the glare of suspicion that is shared between Santa and a costumed 'impostor' on the movie set. Though the film lacks a clear antagonist, it is nonetheless critical of the uncompromisingly ruthless world of film production, making clear that Joe's concerns about the moral impact of cinematic narratives are brushed aside by the studio executives just as vigorously as any other factor which may interfere with their pursuit of profit. Every representative of the industry, from the hectoring, smooth-talking talent agent Marty Brock to the smarmy director Carl, is cast only in the light of their determination to keep the cogs of the industry turning as efficiently as possible. This was, of course, broadly in tune with the scepticism of unchecked commercialism depicted in many other Christmas movies of the eighties, and yet the approach seemed somewhat ironic given that Cherry – himself a highly successful advertising executive – employs a considerable amount of conspicuous product placement throughout his own film, underscoring its own mercantile nature. As Rita Kempley observed, '*Ernest Saves Christmas* seems benign, but underlying the facade is shameless brand-name dropping – a Bic display on Ernest's cab, FTD billboards prominently panned, Bud Light signs and so on. It's *Ernest Sells Christmas*, helping us fill out our subliminal gift lists. It's directed by adman John Cherry of *Ernest* TV commercials and *Ernest Goes to Camp*. Earnestly'.[2]

Cherry was clearly not oblivious to the audience's awareness of Ernest's commercial origins; the brief sequence at the unseen Vern's palatial home, where Ernest involuntarily causes vast amounts of damage, is an obvious tip of the hat to the style of the fourth-wall-smashing advertising campaigns which had made the character's name. Yet beyond the occasional self-consciousness made evident by its protagonist's genesis as an essentially promotional figure, *Ernest Saves Christmas* is at heart a film which adheres to the recognised tropes of festive cinema. In essence, Cherry offers up a kind of fusion of the Christmas movie and an *Ernest* film which largely preserves the conventions of the former while ensuring that audience expectations of the latter are accommodated as widely as possible. Alan Johnson remarks that 'this movie is rather meandering, with Santa Claus needing to find a replacement, and Ernest helping him out (and going through various alter-egos in the process). [...] [*Ernest Saves Christmas* is]] pretty much packed to the brim with Christmas themes and tropes, albeit with Ernest's brand of comedy'.[3] The emphasis on the family unit was also broadly reflective of thematic tendencies of the time within festive film-making, as two different approaches to the subject are taken – the restoration of the traditional family reflected in Harmony/Pamela's rapprochement with her estranged mother, and also a celebration of the unconventional or surrogate family which is brought about as a result of the close teamwork between Ernest, Santa and Harmony throughout the film. Even Joe, who seems largely alienated from the prevailing compromises of mainstream society's values due to his unbending dedication to personal uprightness and good manners, finds a new family in the form of elves Pyramus and Thisbe, along with a new purpose for himself as Santa Claus – a role more congruent to his individual attributes than anything that the entertainment industry could have offered him. In a sense, the film suggests an endorsement of traditionalism over a fleeting or superficial modernity, emphasised most clearly through Joe's worthiness to provide continuity from the outgoing Santa Claus: a result of his fervent belief in old-fashioned common courtesy and the importance of children's wellbeing. While the contemporary is acknowledged throughout the film, and even applauded in places, positive aspects of the present day are reflected through a prism which reflects them in the light of recognised qualities of affirmative traditional virtues. Mark Connelly makes the point that in the earlier *Santa Claus: The Movie*, 'the origins of Santa, and his problems in dealing with the cut and thrust of the modern world, are explored. Much the same theme fills *Ernest Saves Christmas* and seems to reflect the criticism of the "yuppy culture" of the 80s'.[4] Thus the persistence of Santa Claus's unselfishness and humanity win out over the ostentatious triviality of the ephemeral fantasies which are being peddled by the film studio, ensuring that the magic of Christmas is preserved for future generations. Thus *Ernest Saves Christmas* fits into a tradition of festive cinema that extends back to the genre's golden age, as Ryan Cracknell explains: '*Ernest Saves Christmas* shares many similarities with *Miracle on 34th Street*. In particular, both question the existence of Santa Claus as a living, breathing biological being with magical powers as opposed to a heart-warming myth that spurns on commercialism in November and December. Ironically, in the process of exploring this issue, both films are looking to reveal the spirit of Christmas as a time of giving, sharing and loving. *Ernest Saves Christmas* is an innocent enough film that will likely appeal more to the children than their parents'.[5]

It goes without saying that central to the success of *Ernest Saves Christmas* is the unstintingly energetic performance of Jim Varney in the title role. An accomplished stage actor prior to his career in commercial advertising, Varney was a highly recognisable face in the United States of the late eighties as a result of his prolific performances as Ernest which had been widely broadcast across the country. Alongside his appearances in many hundreds of commercials, Varney appeared in numerous television roles before focusing on cinema from the early 1990s onwards. Portraying characters in films as varied as *The Beverly Hillbillies* (Penelope Spheeris, 1993), *Wilder Napalm* (Glenn Gordon Caron, 1993) and *The Expert* (Rick Avery, 1995), he demonstrated a broad range which often defied his audience's presumptions, becoming especially well-known as the voice of Slinky Dog in Pixar's *Toy Story* (John Lasseter, 1995) and *Toy Story II* (John Lasseter, 1999). In 1989 he was conferred a Daytime Emmy Award in the Outstanding Performer in a Children's Series category for his starring role in CBS's

Saturday morning television show *Hey Vern, It's Ernest* (1988). Varney remained active in acting, his voice-over work being particularly well regarded, until his death from lung cancer in 2000.

Amongst the pratfalls, malapropisms and frenzied mugging to camera, Varney succeeds in adding an extra dimension to Ernest as the film proceeds; building upon the character's likeability, he emphasises a tendency towards generosity of spirit and lends a commendable degree of pathos to his stalwart defence of his temporary band of friends. In so doing, he crafts a figure which transcends its humble beginnings as a mouthpiece for TV advertising; rarely was the Ernest character quite so engagingly rendered as he was in this film, as G. Noel Gross has commented: 'After successfully taking a 30-second commercial pitchman to the big screen, here's where the lasting charm of Ernest P. Worrell really manifests. [...] It's basically nonstop, riotous pandemonium from there, punctuated by some genuinely, gulp, *sweet* moments during the final reel'.[6] Although the subjective nature of comedy has meant that Ernest's admirers and detractors have been equally vocal over the years, recognition of the character's endearing and/or annoying qualities is likely to forever be a matter of individual opinion. While there is no doubting that Varney completely immerses himself in the character, working relentlessly to wring every possible ounce of comic potential out of each scenario that Ernest finds himself landed in, it is also true that enjoyment of the film will depend on the audience's receptivity not only towards Ernest's comic appeal but also on the effectiveness of its other production qualities. As Gary J. Svehla and Susan Svehla have suggested:

The love of the Ernest character is an acquired taste, and it is a taste most appreciated by younger audiences who enjoy visual gags and broad, visual humor. Jim Varney is only as good as his material, and while he is master of his character Ernest, *Ernest Saves Christmas* succeeds by virtue of its clever script, interesting characterizations and sentimental tone. [...] Douglas Seal [sic] presents a sensitive portrayal of an old-fashioned Santa in a modern world who never once doubts that the spirit of Santa Claus may be becoming passé. Since he never doubts himself, neither do we. [...] Somehow, Jim Varney makes believers of us all, charming his audience to laugh at all the stupidity and shed a tear at the more poignant moments.[7]

Varney receives proficient support from his co-stars, not least Douglas Seale who delivers a heartfelt and multifaceted performance as the outgoing Santa Claus. Seale invests the character not just with great congeniality but also a sense of slight weariness which never quite taints his continuing sense of wonder at the transformative power of Christmas. With an acting career dating back to the 1940s, both on television and in cinema, Seale was a Tony Award-winning stage performer whose roles throughout the eighties included parts in *Amadeus* (Milos Forman, 1984) and *Heaven Help Us* (Michael Dinner, 1985) as well as an appearance in Steven Spielberg's celebrated NBC television anthology series *Amazing Stories* (1985-87), where he was to portray Santa Claus several years before taking up the mantle again for Cherry's film. *Ernest Saves Christmas* was to mark a new phase in Seale's cinema career which would see him appearing in films such as fantasy blockbuster sequel *Ghostbusters II* (Ivan Reitman, 1989), romantic comedy *Mr Destiny* (James Orr, 1990), supernatural comic drama *Almost an Angel* (John

Cornell, 1990) and – in one of his most fondly-remembered roles – the voice of the Sultan in Disney's *Aladdin* (Ron Clements and John Musker, 1992).

Also satisfyingly high-spirited is Noelle Parker in the role of the runaway Harmony Starr, who at the time was perhaps best-known for appearances in teen drama *Seven Minutes in Heaven* (Linda Feferman, 1985), tense thriller *Twisted* (Adam Holender, 1986) and crime drama *At Close Range* (James Foley, 1986). Parker portrays the sassy character with just the right degree of emotional vulnerability to make Harmony's later redemption (following her betrayal of trust) convincing enough to satisfy audience anticipation. *Ernest Saves Christmas* features several other rewarding performances from the supporting cast, including Oliver Clark as the decent but jaded Joe Carruthers, Robert Lesser as his devious agent, and most especially the Laurel and Hardy-esque storage agents Chuck and Bobby, played with admirable gusto by Gailard Sartain and Bill Byrge. Perhaps appropriately, Sartain would later go on to portray Oliver Hardy in John Cherry's 1999 film *The All New Adventures of Laurel and Hardy in For Love or Mummy*, with Bronson Pinchot in the role of Stan Laurel.

While many of the performances in *Ernest Saves Christmas* demonstrated considerable charm, the production team proved to be equally capable. The film's energetic score was composed by Mark Snow, who would later find worldwide fame for the original music he created for the Fox Network's *The X-Files* (1993-2002) and *Millennium* (1996-99). Chris August's set decoration is often inspired, not least in the case of Ernest's ramshackle house which is filled to the gunnels with exactingly-observed small details, whereas the costume design of Peter Mitchell is also neatly judged –

revealed most especially in Ernest's inspired range of eyebrow-raising disguises. Peter Stein's cinematography and Ian Thomas's art direction both make the most of a restrictive budget to ensure that the movie presents an ample degree of visual fantasy, while Cherry complements the action with many pleasingly quirky embellishments such as the small details which appear on Santa Claus's passport as it is stamped (showing that Seth Applegate was born in Prussia, but is currently resident at the North Pole). As Richard Scheib has commented, Cherry and screenwriters Turner and Kline add just enough knowing fancifulness to proceedings to ensure that the film's comedy is not entirely reliant on the mishaps of its famous protagonist:

> The film is filled with delightfully incongruous images – Santa's sleigh pursued by Air Force fighters; Santa manoeuvring a jail cell of hardened criminals into a carol-singing session; a scene where Santa passes through Customs, where the official looks at his passport and, after a glance up at a line of punks and Hare Krishnas, resignedly shrugs and passes him through. Or Santa's conversation with an exec passing through the airport where all his ideas are interpreted in business-speak. The offbeat humour is traded in for traditional twee sentimentality by the end, but heck, this is a whole lot more fun than sitting through *Santa Claus: The Movie*.[8]

The critical reception of *Ernest Saves Christmas* was decidedly uneven at the time of its release, with few areas of consensus amongst the reviewers of the late eighties. Michael Wilmington was approving of the subtle stylistic departure from the rest of the *Ernest* cycle, pointing out that 'Cherry and Varney's comedy often suggests Jerry Lewis filtered through "Hee Haw" and smothered in corn. But when this one begins, you almost breathe a sigh of relief. Ah, Christmas, season of charity and joy! Perhaps it hath charms to soothe the savage Ernest, or at least get him to mug a little less'.[9] Jay Boyar perceived an increase in production values and narrative coherence in comparison to Cherry's earlier directorial efforts, noting that 'though no *Gone with the Wind* (or even *Parenthood*), *Ernest Saves Christmas* is a step up from the insipid *Ernest Goes to Camp*. Director John Cherry has put together an amiable, thoroughly innocuous little picture. His earlier *Ernest* film was tacky, but the new one is more polished. And there's something adolescently engaging about the screenplay (by Ed Turner and B. Kline)'.[10] Dave Kehr hinted at the astute collocation of the foolhardy central character and the scale of his mystic quest, highlighting the unlikely amalgamation of the two: 'Though Ernest barely exists apart from his trademark catch phrase ("Kno-whut-I-mean?") and his propensity for waggling his nose in wide-angle lenses, Varney's energetic mugging is good for a few mild laughs. [...] *Ernest Saves Christmas* casts him as the human go-between (tribal priest? grail knight?) who must bring the natural and supernatural orders into alignment'.[11] Also representative of critical opinion at the time was Caryn James's commentary, which merged scepticism over the protagonist's original primary function as an advertising device with an acknowledgement of his divisiveness amongst reviewers and audiences alike:

> The strategy seems to be that you'll buy whatever soft drink or car or hardware Ernest is selling – anything just to get rid of him. [...] The best that can be said for the film is that it leaves Ernest behind now and then to focus on Santa, who is played by Douglas Seale with

sweetness, sincerity and an amazing amount of dignity, considering his surroundings. Ernest also appears in disguises, proving he's even more irritating when gotten up as a snake rancher or an old woman, or when he's doing his John Wayne impersonation. The film's production notes say that on the set Jim Varney, who plays Ernest, would recite scenes from Shakespeare or Harold Pinter. You might want to pay money to see Ernest do Pinter, but not his John Wayne.[12]

Certainly it is true that there was significant doubt amongst commentators with regard to the film's artistic merits, with Robert Horton being amongst the most damning voices at the time of the film's emergence into cinemas: 'The fact that *Ernest Saves Christmas* has opened a couple of weeks before Thanksgiving means either a) Touchstone Pictures is confident the film will play well though the holiday season, or b) Touchstone Pictures hopes the movie will make some quick money before people realize what a stinker it is, and then disappear so screens will be left open for more promising movies. I don't know which of these possibilities is true, but I'm leaning toward the latter'.[13] Interestingly, whereas many festive films of the 1980s have been re-evaluated more positively in the light of the passing decades, *Ernest Saves Christmas* remains a contentious title even in the present day, with critics continuing to remain dubious of the feature's virtues in their retrospective assessments. Will Brownridge, for example, emphasises that although the film was not entirely lacking in comedic charm, its effective qualities were not entirely able to offset its perceived deficiencies: 'There are a few moments that shine, and most of them involve Douglas Seale, who is an amazing Santa Claus. When Ernest and Harmony disguise themselves to break Santa out of prison, it's hilarious, but the laughs really end there. Even Jim Varney seems tired out here, even though this is only the second *Ernest* film. It's not exactly Varney's fault though, as the characters around him just aren't funny at all. Seale, Noelle Parker, and Oliver Clark are all rather serious characters, so there's nobody for Varney to work with. This makes his rubber faced antics stick out, and not in a good way'.[14] Perhaps the most ubiquitous criticism amongst contemporary commentators has been that while *Ernest Saves Christmas* may have been an passable enough entry in the wider canon of *Ernest* movies, it lacked sufficient originality and intrinsic appeal to pass muster as noteworthy festive cinema in its own right. As Andy Webb has suggested:

> Unless you are a huge fan you will find the fun quickly running thin with the majority of the movie relying on the clowning around of Jim Varney as Ernest. In truth it is what you expect and if it wasn't dominated by the silly voiced, rubber faced antics of Varney then his fans would feel short changed. So what happens if you take Varney out of the equation? Well what you have left with is a weak storyline surrounding Santa trying to find his replacement leading to a spot of bother when confusion abounds over who he is. And on top of that there is a subplot surrounding the young Harmony who tries to use Santa's sack. But none of this is that entertaining and certainly nowhere near enough for those who are not major Ernest fans.[15]

Ernest Saves Christmas is something of an enigma: an old-fashioned yuletide caper with copious modern trimmings. Though the scenario surrounding Santa Claus's search for a successor may have been a break from more traditional approaches, as was the surprisingly high-tech take on Santa's sleigh, other aspects such as the runaway Harmony's reconciliation with her parents and Ernest's temporary adoption of a surrogate family over the holiday season could easily have fitted into many Christmas-situated family comedies of years past. Certainly there is also a telling evolutionary note in the passing of the Christmas baton from the arch-traditionalist Seth Applegate to the media-savvy Joe Carruthers, suggesting that new technology need not be an isolating or alienating development but rather a fresh means of continuing and enhancing the propagation of the Christmas spirit. As with so much of the movie's approach, the positivity of present-day trappings – from digital advancements to cultural attitudes – is invariably filtered through an appreciation of the customs and principles of a more innocent time. Cherry's film was a textbook example of the way in which 1980s festive cinema exhibited both conventional and ground-breaking approaches to Christmas themes, combining long-held tropes and contemporary twists to ensure both familiarity and relatability. Though the overall success of Cherry's film does tend to hinge in the main on viewer appreciation of Jim Varney's comedic talents, enough festive season charm is on display in this far-out Christmas setting to evoke some level of enjoyment, while the convolutions of the narrative's madcap internal logic are always entertaining. Though in the final analysis, we never do find out why anyone would choose to send a herd of airborne reindeer as air freight when they are perfectly capable of flying to Orlando on their own.

REFERENCES

1. Jason Gross, '14 Air-Braking Facts About *Ernest Saves Christmas*', in *Rediscover the 80s*, December 2015. <*http://www.rediscoverthe80s.com/2015/12/14-facts-about-ernest-saves-christmas.html*>

2. Rita Kempley, '*Ernest Saves Christmas*', in *The Washington Post*, 11 November 1988.

3. Alan Johnson, '*Ernest Saves Christmas*', in *Letterboxd*, 6 December 2015. <*https://letterboxd.com/alpal/film/ernest-saves-christmas/*>

4. Mark Connelly, 'Santa Claus: The Movie', in *Christmas at the Movies*, ed. by Mark Connelly (London: I.B. Tauris, 2000), 115-34, p.115.

5. Ryan Cracknell, '*Ernest Saves Christmas*', in *Movie Views*, 14 December 2003. <*http://movieviews.ca/ernest-saves-christmas*>

6. G. Noel Gross, 'Jim Varney: A Legacy of Laughter', in *DVD Talk*, 2000. <*http://www.dvdtalk.com/cineschlock/ernest/index.html*>

7. Gary J. Svehla and Susan Svehla, *It's Christmas Time at the Movies* (Baltimore: Midnight Marquee Press, 1998), p.227.

8. Richard Scheib, '*Ernest Saves Christmas*', in *Moria: Science Fiction, Horror and Fantasy Film Review*, 2012. <*http://moria.co.nz/fantasy/ernestsaveschristmas.htm*>

9.   Michael Wilmington, 'Not Even Christmas Can Save the New *Ernest*', in *The Los Angeles Times*, 15 November 1988.

10. Jay Boyar, '*Ernest* Saves the Day When Santa Needs Help', in *The Orlando Sentinel*, 3 November 1989.

11. Dave Kehr, '*Ernest Saves Christmas* is No Real Holiday', in *The Chicago Tribune*, 14 November 1988.

12. Caryn James, '*Ernest Saves Christmas*', in *The New York Times*, 11 November 1988.

13. Robert Horton, '*Ernest Saves Christmas*', in *What a Feeling!*, 22 December 2010 [1988].
     <https://eightiesmovies.wordpress.com/2010/12/22/ernest-saves-christmas>

14. Will Brownridge, '*Ernest Saves Christmas*, or *Watch Out Vern*', in *The Film Reel*, 18 December 2013.
     <http://www.the-filmreel.com/2013/12/18/review-ernest-saves-christmas-1988-watch-vern/>

15. Andy Webb, '*Ernest Saves Christmas*', in *The Movie Scene*, 2012.
     <http://www.themoviescene.co.uk/reviews/ernest-daves-christmas-1988/ernest-daves-christmas-1988.html>

15

Die Hard (1988)

*Twentieth Century Fox Film Corporation/
Gordon Company/Silver Pictures*

Director: John McTiernan
Producers: Lawrence Gordon and Joel Silver
Screenwriter: Jeb Stuart and Steven E. de Souza,
from a novel by Roderick Thorp

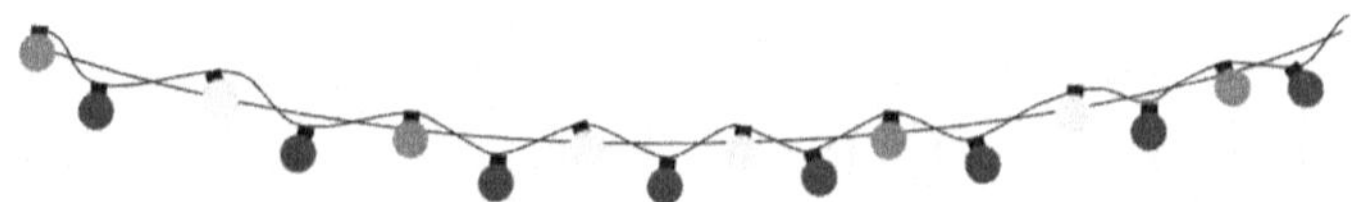

A watershed decade for the action movie, the 1980s saw stars such as Sylvester Stallone and Arnold Schwarzenegger appearing in popular and often hugely profitable films which combined public appeal with larger-than-life displays of on-screen violence. Witness to the release of films such as *First Blood* (Ted Kotcheff, 1982), *Commando* (Mark L. Lester, 1985), *Cobra* (George P. Cosmatos, 1986), *Raw Deal* (John Irvin, 1986), *Red Heat* (Walter Hill, 1988) and many others, the eighties were host to a veritable explosion in the genre, with characters such as John Rambo, Marion 'Cobra' Cobretti, John Matrix and Ivan Danko all becoming virtually synonymous with the decade. Given the booming demand for action movies throughout the eighties, it was perhaps of little surprise that a number of entries in the genre would exhibit a degree of hybridisation with the tropes of the increasingly prevalent Christmas cinema of the time. Many action-oriented films of the eighties which demonstrated this kind of cross-pollination with festive situations tended to advance their yuletide settings only sparingly; unlike the very specific holiday season environments of the decade's Christmas horror cinema, movies such as *Deal of the Century* (William Friedkin, 1983), *The Package* (Andrew Davis, 1989) and *Dead Bang* (John Frankenheimer, 1989) would generally employ the December festivities as a loose background for the narrative's proceedings rather than as an integral part of the plot. This was not always the case, however; well-received cop buddy movie *Lethal Weapon* (Richard Donner, 1987) mixed an atmospheric Christmas setting and frenetic action to great effect, with the film proving popular enough to spawn several similarly-successful sequels (though none beyond the original would be directly concerned with the holiday season). However, in years past *Die Hard* has come to be regarded by many as the definitive festive season action movie, and – though debate has raged amongst commentators over whether it can (or should) be considered a Christmas film in its own right – the movie's stylistic refinement and continuing audience appeal has ensured that it is in no danger of disappearing from popular culture at any time in the immediate future.

While it is certainly true that *Die Hard* must be deemed amongst the most ill-fitting of Christmas movies to feature within the genre, if we are to accept that it belongs within the confines of festive cinema at all, Greg Metcalf nonetheless makes the important point that '"non-traditionality" has become a convention – if not a tradition – of Christmas movies in the 1980s'.[1] Thus in a decade where films featuring the holiday season had undergone unprecedented experimentation and cross-generic synthesis,

Die Hard was certainly not unprecedented in pushing the boundaries of the genre's recognised tropes. While many commentators have expressed scepticism over the movie's credentials as a Christmas film, others such as Dirk Libbey are much more convinced of its relevance to the customs of the genre: 'So, what's required to make a Christmas movie? The first item is obvious and *Die Hard* obviously succeeds: it takes place during Christmas. This much we can all agree on. Beyond that, however, the fact that it takes place at Christmas is important to the plot. Alan Rickman and his band of thieves take a Christmas party hostage. John McClain [sic] is visiting his wife because it's Christmas. There is Christmas music on the soundtrack. These are unequivocal facts. Christmas isn't simply a backdrop, it's the reason that a number of the different plot points occur'.[2] And indeed, while *Die Hard* unquestionably concerns itself more acutely with the customs of the festive season than the vast majority of other action films of the time, its prevailing themes are also largely in tune with many of the premises which predominate within Christmas cinema. As Alonso Duralde observes, 'in its own way, *Die Hard* is as perfect a movie as *Casablanca*, blessed with a standout cast (including such stellar character actors as Reginald VelJohnson, William Atherton, Paul Gleason, James Shigeta, and Robert Davi) and one of the smartest action-movie scripts ever written. [...] Even the Christmas setting isn't a throwaway – in the classic tradition of Christmas-movie leading men, John McClane undergoes a sort of redemption, learning to appreciate his wife and to see her in a new light. Oh, and the climactic shootout involves gift wrap'.[3]

Though now widely considered to be one of the best-regarded action movies of the 1980s, *Die Hard* had an unusually convoluted genesis. Its screenplay was based upon Roderick Thorp's 1979 novel *Nothing Lasts Forever*, a thriller which acted as a sequel to Thorp's earlier 1966 book *The Detective*. A mature, moody and often tense police procedural crime novel, *The Detective* was adapted into Gordon Douglas's acclaimed 1968 film of the same name which was to star Frank Sinatra in the lead role of Detective Joe Leland. The film led to commercial and critical success, and when 20th Century Fox expressed an interest in adapting the sequel twenty years after the time of the first film's release, they were contractually obliged to approach Sinatra in order to give him first refusal over reprising his role as Leland. In his early seventies by that point, Sinatra declined to participate, and thus the film which would eventually become *Die Hard* was adapted from Thorp's novel as a self-contained narrative with no reference to *The Detective* in either its prose or cinematic form. Several actors were considered for the role of the protagonist before Bruce Willis was eventually cast as John McClane, receiving a salary of five million dollars for his performance – a virtually unprecedented figure given that Willis was not a particularly prominent movie star at the time. Such was the film's success, however, it would greatly elevate Willis's professional profile and cemented his bankability as a Hollywood leading man for decades to come.

Die Hard* was directed by John McTiernan, who at that early stage in his career was recognised for his horror thriller *Nomads* (1986) and most especially for science fiction action movie *Predator* (1987), which starred Arnold Schwarzenegger and would be responsible for the birth of a successful multimedia franchise. Later to direct films including Tom Clancy novel adaptation *The Hunt for Red October* (1991), romantic adventure *Medicine Man* (1992) and fantasy action movie *Last Action Hero* (1993), McTiernan was conferred the Franklin J. Schaffner Award by the American Film Institute in 1997 and has received wins and nominations for numerous other industry plaudits including the Saturn Awards of the Academy of Science Fiction Fantasy and Horror Films, the Blue Ribbon Awards and the Hugo Awards.

During the late afternoon of Christmas Eve, New York police detective John McClane (Bruce Willis) is travelling by plane to Los Angeles. McClane is somewhat discomfited by air travel; a businessman (Robert Lesser) in the seat next to him recommends that when he gets to his destination, he should remove his shoes and socks and try to make fists with his bare feet. This unusual technique, he promises, will help him deal with the pent-up stress of flying, but McClane is unconvinced. The businessman is alarmed when he notices that McClane is carrying a firearm, but his fellow passenger reassures him that he is a police officer with eleven years' experience in the job.

At the Nakatomi Tower, the American headquarters of the Nakatomi Corporation, top executive Joseph Yoshinobu Takagi (James Shigeta) is hosting an extravagant Christmas party to mark a highly successful year of business. As he gives a short speech, Holly Gennaro (Bonnie Bedelia) – another of the company's leading executives – is fending off the unwelcome advances of her unctuous colleague Harry Ellis (Hart Bochner). Finally sending him packing, Holly telephones her home and checks in with her daughter Lucy (Taylor Fry) and John Junior (Noah Land). The kids are excited at the prospect of seeing their father again; a shot of a framed photo on Holly's desk reveals that she is John McClane's estranged wife. Holly then speaks with her housekeeper Paulina (Betty Carvalho) and checks to see if McClane has been in touch by phone. When Paulina explains that this is not the case, Holly asks her to make sure that her home's spare bedroom is ready to receive him if he should join them. Frustrated at his lack of communication, she quietly upturns the framed family photo.

Back at the airport, McClane has collected his luggage and is met by fresh-faced limousine chauffeur Argyle (De'voreaux White) who has instructions to drive the detective to the Nakatomi Tower. The rather self-conscious young man explains that he is new to the job, but McClane reveals that he is similarly new to riding in limousines which means that they should get along perfectly. Argyle eventually loosens up and, as he is a former taxi driver, they soon start conversing during the journey. McClane reveals that he is currently separated from his wife, as Holly's thriving corporate career had led her to the Nakatomi HQ in California while he felt obliged to remain in New York City due to a large backlog of unresolved criminal cases which still have to be resolved. Dropping McClane off at the Tower's expansive plaza, Argyle offers to drive into the building's parking garage and wait for further instructions; if Holly should prefer McClane not to stay with her, Argyle will arrange for hotel accommodation instead. He passes McClane a business card so that they can stay in contact via phone.

Entering the building, McClane discovers that almost all of the Nakatomi staff have gone home for the holidays with the exception of those attending the Christmas party which is taking place on the 30th floor. When checking the employee directory he also learns that his wife has reverted to her original pre-marital surname, much to his irritation. Taking the express elevator, he soon arrives at the upmarket party and feels impossibly out of place amongst the white-collar managers and executives quaffing champagne all around him. He soon encounters Takagi, who he finds to be convivial and genuinely hospitable; the top exec reveals that he was responsible for providing the limousine, and shows McClane into Holly's office to wait for her arrival. Though Holly is currently occupied elsewhere, their entry interrupts Ellis, who is presently snorting cocaine from the surface of her highly polished desk. Takagi mentions pointedly that McClane is a policeman, and Ellis attempts to deflect attention from his illicit activities by mentioning that the ongoing party is a celebration not only of Christmas but also a major deal that has just been brokered in favour of the company – a development which has largely come about thanks to the expert negotiations of Holly. As if on cue, Holly returns to her office and appears to have mixed emotions at the presence of her husband, though she is relieved that he has made the journey to California as planned. Ellis goads McClane by explaining that the corporation has just gifted Holly an authentic Rolex watch in acknowledgement of her recent profitable actions, but the others are unimpressed by the transparent motivations of his blatant posturing.

McClane asks to be taken somewhere to freshen up after his long journey. Holly accompanies him to a private washroom and asks where he plans to stay during his visit. When he reveals that he is to live with an old colleague who has retired to the West Coast, she instead offers to let him sleep in the spare room of her own home instead. Holly admits that she has missed McClane during their separation, but he is irate that she appears to be behaving as though already divorced and sparks an argument between them. Their dispute is only interrupted when a personal assistant arrives to tell Holly that her presence is requested by Takagi; she has been asked to say a few words at the party to rally the troops. Once she has gone, McClane berates himself for his hot-headedness and lack of diplomacy.

As the party continues, no-one on the 30th floor is aware that a large courier truck has just arrived unannounced in the building's parking garage. Just as the truck comes to a halt, a car arrives separately at the Tower's entrance bearing two men: computer expert Theo (Clarence Gilyard Jr.) and skilled assassin Karl (Alexander Godunov). The talkative Theo provides a momentary distraction while Karl produces a gun and shoots dead the building's security guard. Word is then passed to the truck that the Tower has been infiltrated. As Karl finds and kills the only other security guard still on duty, their colleagues are disgorged from the vehicle in the garage: Franco (Bruno Doyon), Tony (Andreas Wisniewski), Alexander (Joey Plewa), Marco (Lorenzo Caccialanza), Kristoff (Gerard Bonn), Eddie (Dennis Hayden), Uli (Al Leong), Heinrich (Gary Roberts), Fritz (Hans Buhringer), James (Wilhelm von Homburg), and the impeccably-tailored leader of this heavily-armed international group, Hans Gruber (Alan Rickman). With adept precision, Theo locks down the building, shutting down all but a couple of the elevators and sealing off all the entrances. He then damages the Tower's computer server, ensuring that his commands cannot be countermanded. Eddie, wearing one of the company's security uniforms, takes over at the building's front desk to evade suspicion from any passers-by while Tony and Karl proficiently cut all communications with the outside world.

Up on the 30th floor, McClane is taking the advice of his fellow plane traveller and is trying to flex his bare feet into fists as a means of relieving stress. He tries to telephone

Argyle to give him an update on his progress with Holly, but is puzzled when his call is abruptly cut off – a result of the invaders on the floors below. Moments later, the deadly interlopers arrive at the party and start firing submachine guns, causing mass panic. As the Nakatomi staff are dragged out of offices and roughly assembled in the central atrium by the terrorists, McClane makes a break for it and races unseen to a nearby stairwell. In his haste to depart, he has no time to recover his recently-discarded footwear.

McClane makes a feverish ascent of the skyscraper, though much of the building remains incomplete and under construction. Bursting onto one of the empty floors, he attempts to telephone for help but realises that – just as had been the case earlier – the line has been cut. Continuing his ascent, McClane is alarmed when he spots more terrorists ferrying heavy weapons, including guided missiles. Gruber, meanwhile, has now identified Takagi as the senior executive in the building and has taken him to another part of the building while the hostages remain in the atrium. Making vague comments about teaching the Nakatomi Corporation a lesson due to its greed, Gruber ferries the puzzled senior official into a computer room where Theo appears intent on breaking into the company's network. Takagi informs him that he does not have the authorisation code required to break into the system, but that in any respect any information obtained from the system will be amended by its administrators in Tokyo soon afterwards. Yet blackmail or industrial espionage is not Gruber's concern: he reveals that he intends to steal 640 million dollars' worth of negotiable bearer bonds which are currently stored in the skyscraper's electronically-sealed vault, and that entry can only be assured via the computer system.

None of the invaders are aware that McClane has quietly infiltrated the floor that Takagi is on, and is listening intently to the conversation from a hidden position. Gruber explains that losing the money will be at best a minor inconvenience to the corporation, but insists that he must have whatever information Takagi can offer to break the code. The executive is aghast, realising that the terrorists' aim is singularly acquisitive: this is not a straightforward hostage crisis but rather a carefully-orchestrated heist. He continues to insist that only the company chairperson has access to the required code, and as he is based in Japan he is unlikely to comply. Gruber loses patience with the other man's stalling and impassively blows his brains out. Responsibility for breaking the vault code now lies with Theo, but even with his extensive expertise of computer systems he warns that the process will take hours – and even then, the last of the seven locks will be beyond his capability to disarm. The final mechanism is electromagnetically sealed, meaning that it cannot be deactivated from within the building. Strangely, Gruber does not seem particularly concerned at his colleague's grim assessment of the situation.

McClane only narrowly avoids the terrorist group in his haste to escape their clutches. As Gruber sends several of his associates to the top of the building, where they set to work rigging the roof with plastic explosives, McClane races onto the 32nd floor and triggers a fire alarm. Unfortunately for him, this is easily countered by Gruber, who informs his accomplice at the front desk to use the one remaining line out of the building to phone the fire department and cancel the alarm. Nonetheless, McClane's efforts tip off the terrorists to the fact that the hostages are not the only people left in the building, so Tony is sent to investigate. After a short but brutal fight, McClane and Tony fall down a flight of stairs and the latter's neck is broken in the melee. McClane takes anything of worth from the terrorist before sending the body down to the 30th floor in an elevator. When Gruber is met by the gruesome sight, he notes that a Santa Claus hat has been placed on the corpse and 'Now I Have a Machine Gun – Ho-Ho-Ho' is written on the deceased Tony's sweater. This somewhat undermines the terrorist's immediately-preceding speech to the hostages where he tells them that his group has every possible contingency under control.

McClane is hidden in the elevator shaft, making silent notes of the terrorists' names as they argue beneath him. He retreats into a service conduit and makes his way to the roof, where he uses a radio handset stolen from Tony to transmit a distress signal to the LAPD. The police dispatchers are sceptical of his claims, but the transmission is also picked up by the terrorists; this leads Gruber to send a team to the roof with the aim of intercepting McClane. Led by an enraged Karl, keen to avenge the death of his brother Tony, the group opens fire on McClane and the deafening hail of bullets is picked up by the police over the radio. This finally convinces them to dispatch an officer to investigate the situation.

Forced from the roof into the building's air conditioning system, McClane is closely pursued by the machine gun-toting terrorists. He escapes back into the elevator shafts, where Gruber tells Karl to seal him in (reasoning that as all of the elevator carriages are locked down, he will effectively be trapped). However, McClane manages to abscond through a conduit into the skyscraper's air ducts; Karl spots his getaway and pursues, firing indiscriminately into the ducts from beneath. More by luck than design, the beleaguered cop manages to avoid being hit.

Many floors below, LAPD Sergeant Al Powell (Reginald Veljohnson) has arrived in a patrol car in response to the distress call. He is nonplussed by a lack of any obvious signs of disturbance, and speaks with Eddie at the front desk who claims that the call-out is a false alarm. McClane, who has emerged onto the 34th floor, breaks a window in order to signal to the policeman far below, but the sound is overheard from the roof and two terrorists head down to execute him. With some quick thinking McClane is able to neutralise them both, but is aghast when he sees Powell attempting to leave the scene. Realising that the desk sergeant believes that the mayday call has simply been a prank, McClane flings one of the terrorists' bodies out of the window where it shatters the windscreen of Powell's patrol car many storeys below.

As the agitated LAPD officer radios in a report of the situation, his transmission is picked up by TV news reporter Richard Thornburg (William Atherton). Sensing a potentially major story, Thornburg manages to convince his producer to allow him to take a team to the Nakatomi Tower to investigate. However, he has been preceded by a fleet of police cars who are already taking up position in and around the plaza nearby. Hans tries to calm his remaining associates, telling them that police intervention was an unavoidable aspect of their scheme, but even he grows alarmed when he discovers that one of the recently-killed terrorists was Marco, who was responsible for carrying the group's detonators. He correctly suspects that McClane has stolen Marco's bag, which also contains a quantity of plastic explosives. After a tense exchange with McClane over the radio, Hans clarifies that the interloper and even the LAPD are little more than a diversion from his plans – he knows that his strategy will not enter its endgame until the FBI become involved.

McClane also briefly speaks over the radio with Powell, with whom he quickly establishes a rapport due to their shared professional experiences. Following their discussion, as LAPD ground reinforcements continue to escalate, the situation comes under the control of blustering Deputy Police Chief Dwayne T. Robinson (Paul Gleason). However, Robinson is unconvinced of Powell's report of proceedings and wonders whether McClane may in fact be one of the terrorists himself. Before they can debate the scenario further, Thornburg arrives and begins broadcasting live from the plaza – much to the irritation of the police.

Holly approaches Gruber and negotiates for basic amenities such as access to toilet facilities, impressing him with her forthright attitude. Meanwhile, a police SWAT team begins to assemble in an attempt to storm the building. The unfolding scene is watched with alarm by Argyle, who has picked up Thornburg's news report on his limousine's portable TV set. As he had been completely unaware of proceedings from his location in the skyscraper's parking garage, news of the terrorists' plan comes as a total shock to him, and he grows even more anxious when he realises that all exits from the car park are sealed. Powell protests at Robinson's sledgehammer tactics in invading the building, fearing that the hostages may be put at risk, but the condescending deputy chief brushes off his concerns. In spite of McClane's own warnings, the police begin their assault. None of them realise that their actions are being carefully tracked from within the skyscraper by Theo, who is watching their every move and relaying information to Uli and Eddie on the ground floor. The terrorists knock out the police spotlights and machine gun the tactical squad who are trying to gain entry through the main doorway. The police then retaliate by sending in an armoured vehicle. However, anticipating the assault Alexander and James use rocket launchers to destroy the RV before it can even reach the skyscraper.

In a desperate attempt to prevent any further police casualties, McClane retrieves the block of C-4 explosive that he had taken from Marco's bag and arms it with some detonators. Strapping the makeshift bomb between a computer CRT monitor and an office chair, he hurls it down a lift shaft and causes a major explosion, killing James and Marco while also causing extensive damage to the skyscraper's lower floors. His efforts succeed in interrupting the terrorists' defence of the building. Robinson has an angry exchange with McClane over the radio, but the latter makes it clear that he does not take the increasingly out-of-his-depth deputy chief's authority seriously.

Growing impatient at the continuing hostage crisis, Ellis talks to Gruber and pretends that he is an old friend of McClane. He gives the terrorist leader the name of his previously-unknown nemesis and also furnishes him with details of McClane's job in the NYPD. Ellis speaks with McClane over the radio and ineptly tries to negotiate for the return of Gruber's detonators, but the experienced cop immediately senses that the supercilious executive has put his own life is in danger and fervently denies that they know each other. Gruber cares little in any respect; killing Ellis, he warns McClane over the radio that he will continue murdering hostages unless his detonators are returned immediately.

Once again misinterpreting the situation, Robinson blames McClane's inaction for the death of Ellis, but his ruminations are interrupted by a transmission from Gruber. Over the radio, he issues demands for the release of various incarcerated terrorists belonging to subversive groups around the world. Gruber then explains that once he has received assurance that these prisoners have been released, he will move the hostages to the helipad on the Nakatomi Tower's roof. He stresses that the police must provide helicopters to ferry both the hostages and their terrorist captors to Los Angeles International Airport, where further instructions will be given. Robinson is unnerved, knowing that he lacks the authority to offer these assurances, but once the broadcast has ended (though unknown to the oblivious police force outside) it becomes clear that these negotiations are simply another of Gruber's diversionary tactics.

On the ground, Robinson finds that his preparations to meet Gruber's demands have been usurped by the arrival of self-important FBI Special Agents 'Big' Johnson (Robert Davi) and 'Little' Johnson (Grand L. Bush), who waste no time in taking over the situation from the clueless deputy police chief. Meanwhile, with the terrorists' numbers running low Gruber sends Karl to hunt down McClane once and for all while he heads to the Tower's roof to personally inspect the explosives which have been planted around it. Temporarily leaving his gun and flashlight near the helipad in order to check the handiwork of his associates more closely, he is startled when he jumps back down to the gangway only to come face to face with the desperate New York cop himself. Bargaining on the fact that McClane will not recognise him, given that they have only heard each other's voices thus far, the desperate Gruber immediately affects a highly convincing American accent and tries to convince McClane that he is a hostage who has managed to escape the 30th floor while his captors were momentarily distracted. Descending from the roof to the building's computer centre, the pair discuss the situation;

Gruber notes that in McClane's flight from the terrorists' initial incursion he had no time to put on his shoes. Seeming keen that the newcomer has the chance to defend himself, McClane offers him the use of his handgun. Gruber takes it, not quite believing his luck, and immediately reverts back to his native German. Grabbing his radio, he commands the others to join him in his current location. Gruber attempts to shoot McClane, but realises too late that the savvy detective has seen through the ruse and removed the bullets from the gun in advance. Karl, Fritz and Franco arrive by elevator, and in his frantic retreat McClane eventually manages to kill Franco and Fritz but is forced to leave the bag of detonators behind. Sensing a chance to further hamper the efforts of their opponent, Gruber orders Karl to shoot all of the glass partitions in the office, showering the room with jagged shards and tearing McClane's bare feet to shreds.

Gruber returns to the 30th floor, jubilant that his plans are back on track with the recovery of the detonators, but Karl is incensed that McClane is still alive in spite of all his efforts. While McClane drags himself into a washroom and agonisingly digs endless fragments of glass out of his feet, Theo is triumphantly declaring that six of the vault's seven safeguards have now been disarmed; only the electromagnetic lock remains to be circumvented. This problem is soon overcome, however, when Gruber's predictions play out exactly as he had anticipated: the FBI, following anti-terrorist procedures to the letter, cut all external electricity to the building. This forces the Tower's systems onto an emergency power supply, inadvertently disabling the final lock of the vault. The two Agents Johnson gloat that the terrorists have probably been thrown into disarray by the cut in power, but in truth quite the opposite is the case: Gruber and Theo enter the vault, which is crammed full of priceless paintings and *objets d'art*, and ecstatically begin to gather up the target of their endeavours: the millions of dollars' worth of negotiable bearer bonds.

Gruber radios the FBI, who inform him that they have arranged for the release of the terrorist captives he had requested and are now preparing to send helicopter transports to the skyscraper's roof as per the group's instructions. In reality, the FBI are actually planning to send helicopter gunships to massacre the terrorists, but Gruber – who is well aware of the linearity of their tactics – has no intention of being anywhere near the helipad, having made other arrangements for departure. Neither side has bargained on the intervention of McClane, who has now torn up his undershirt in order to bandage his feet and is gearing up to investigate the final piece of the convoluted puzzle that Gruber has set the authorities. Painfully limping back up to the roof of the Tower, McClane is horrified to discover a vast cache of plastic explosives around the helipad – now rigged up with the recovered detonators. He tries to radio information about the double-cross to Powell, but is violently attacked by Karl who has managed to catch him unawares. The terrorist separates McClane from his handset, and a vicious fight breaks out between them.

Holly is aghast when the unscrupulous Thornburg, who has used dishonest means to identify and bully his way into her family home, begins broadcasting a live interview with her daughter Lucy. Seeing the transmission, Gruber recognises the girl from photos on her mother's desk and picks up the framed image that Holly had upturned earlier, revealing a family photo of the entire McClane family. Now realising her worth as a pawn in his brinkmanship with

McClane, Gruber keeps her in his custody while sending the rest of the hostages up to the roof. He warns the accompanying terrorists to lock the doors on their way back down, trapping the captives on the helipad.

The two Agents Johnson are presently on route to the helipad themselves, armed to the teeth and casually resigned to the fact that their coarse tactics will probably cost the lives of many hostages as well as their abductors. The terrorists forcibly herd all of the remaining captives (with the exception of Holly) onto the roof, but in the nick of time McClane manages to subdue Karl by entangling him in cargo chains, then bursts onto the helipad and guides the hostages back down into the building. Searching for Holly, he is told that Gruber has taken her to the Tower's vault. The FBI Agents mistake the armed McClane for a terrorist and open fire on him with a sniper rifle, but he narrowly evades their bullets. Anxiously trying to find a way to escape with his life, McClane ties a fire defence hosepipe around his waist and uses it to jump from the roof, shooting a window a few storeys below in order to re-enter the building. At the same time, Gruber learns that the hostages are heading back down into the skyscraper and – taking no chances – ignites the detonators. An enormous explosion occurs under the helipad, lighting up the area for blocks around the Nakatomi Tower and destroying both of the FBI's helicopter gunships in the resulting fireball.

Now free of their dwindling captors, the hostages race down one of the skyscraper's stairwells as they head for safety below. At the vault, Gruber is desperately packing bearer bonds into holdalls. These bags are to be ferried down to the basement where Theo – now wearing a paramedic uniform – is driving an ambulance out of the courier van that the terrorists had arrived in. The plan is clearly that while all eyes are on the rooftop explosion, Gruber and his remaining associates will abscond with their stolen riches in the ambulance where they will blend in with all of the other emergency service vehicles in and around the plaza. However, Theo's plan is thwarted when Argyle – his limousine still trapped in the parking garage – collides at speed with the ambulance, knocking Theo unconscious and rendering the vehicle immobile.

Back at the Tower's vault, McClane is almost out of ammunition as he makes his final approach to Gruber and his accomplices Eddie and Kristoff. Knocking the latter unconscious, McClane confronts the final two terrorists and expresses his disbelief that after everything that has transpired, greed was Gruber's only real motivation. Gruber responds that the explosion on the roof was a necessary distraction; if the authorities believe that the terrorists were a group of fanatics who had died in the pursuit of a cause, they will not suspect the truth until the group has long gone – along with all of the funds that they had stolen. Knowing that the confrontation pitches two against one, McClane has no choice but to surrender his machine gun – not least as Gruber has a pistol aimed directly at Holly's head. However, the veteran cop has the last laugh: having spotted Christmas wrapping tape in the corridor outside, he has secured a pistol to his back, and uses its final two bullets to kill Eddie and wound Gruber in the shoulder. Pitching backwards into one of the skyscraper's windows, Gruber grabs Holly as he plunges through the glass. Holding onto his spouse for dear life, McClane unfastens her expensive Rolex watch – a motion which breaks Gruber's grip, causing him to plummet to his death many storeys below.

As a fortune in bearer bonds rain down onto the plaza below, the emergency services move in to provide support to the surviving hostages. Between McClane's detonation of the building's lower floors and the explosion on the roof, the scene is one of total disarray. Painfully emerging from the Tower, a dazed McClane finally meets Powell in person. Before he can thank the sergeant for all of the encouragement he has given over the radio, they are interrupted by Robinson who angrily (and mistakenly) blames McClane for having made the terrorist situation much worse than it needed to be. The deputy chief is, in turn, stopped in his tracks by the improbable appearance of Karl, still bloodied from the fight on the rooftop, who makes one final attempt to gain revenge for his brother's death. But the terrorist is at last eliminated when Powell – in an incongruous development, given his usual desk job – empties his service revolver into him, decisively bringing the nightmare to an end. As though on cue, Argyle bursts through the parking garage's doorway, his battered limousine having now seen better days. McClane and Holly head for the car, keen to return home, but are again intercepted – this time by Thornburg, pressing for a TV news interview. Knowing that his unethical practices had put their lives in jeopardy, Holly punches him in the face live on air, much to his embarrassment. At long last heading away from the scene, Argyle notes with incredulity that if this was McClane's idea of a Christmas celebration, he can't wait to see what New Year's Eve will bring.

While including *Die Hard* in a discussion about Christmas films may well seem like a contrarian choice to some, in truth the real question may not necessarily be whether McTiernan's movie deserves a place within the genre but rather whether its action instead operates as a sophisticated satire of the established conventions of festive cinema. Certainly there is something supremely ironic in watching a blizzard of the Nakatomi Corporation's bearer bonds falling onto the ruined plaza outside to the cheerful sound of Vaughn Monroe's rendition of 'Let It Snow! Let It Snow! Let It Snow!', or the understated range of Christmas decorations scattered around places like the Tower's computer centre which jar marvellously with the carnage that subsequently plays out there. As Tom Ward has remarked, *Die Hard* is a feature which toys with audience expectation and relies to a degree on subverting anticipation, meaning that its awkward fit within festive cinema is simply one part of its novel strategy: 'Action might not be what some people are used to in a Christmas film, but the whole point of *Die Hard* is to challenge the perception of Christmas. Even John McClane finds himself out of his Christmas comfort zone, in sunny LA where snow never visits. Argyle's choice of Christmas music is also strange to John who asks "Haven't you got any Christmas music?" when the limo driver blasts Run DMC's "Christmas In Hollis". It might not be what John's used to but as Argyle says, "This is Christmas music!" So, for those accustomed to snowy vistas, warm fires, Wham and Paul McCartney, *Die Hard* will already have you on the back-foot. This is Christmas, but not as we know it'.[4]

Given its prominent Christmas Eve setting, the film contains many references to the holiday season – some more obvious than others. Theo quotes (albeit rather loosely) from Clement Clark Moore as he gets ready to co-ordinate the terrorists' violent repulsion of the SWAT team, ensuring that this particular Christmas Eve is one that the LAPD are never likely to forget, while McClane's decision to put a decorative Santa Claus hat on Tony's corpse before sending it down to

Gruber with 'Ho-Ho-Ho!' written on the dead man's sweater is perhaps the least festive use of this famous yuletide attire that is humanly possible. While the above examples may suggest an approach that is closer to the Christmas horror movie in its judicious evocation of recognisable motifs which are later turned on their head (to either humorous or gruesome effect), there are other considerably more subtle nods toward the festive season which are to be found throughout the film. The name of the terrorist leader, Hans Gruber, is arguably an allusion to Franz Gruber, the Austrian composer responsible for the famous 1818 Christmas carol 'Stille Nacht' ('Silent Night'). The juxtaposition is a somewhat trenchant one, as the events at the Nakatomi Tower prove to be anything but peaceful; as Peter Hoare comments, 'German terrorist Hans Gruber is a far more evil antagonist than The Grinch! There's not even an argument, really. That furry green creep was just trying to steal Christmas. Gruber, on the other hand, was trying to steal $640 million dollars in bonds, as well as the lives of a large portion of the Nakatomi Company. The Grinch snatched presents and Christmas trees. Hans Gruber murdered several innocent partygoers, not to mention a large chunk of the [[...]] LAPD. Any great movie, holiday-themed or otherwise, has high stakes. And in *Die Hard,* Hans Gruber drove those stakes through the roof. You're a mean one, Mr. Gruber'.[5] Just as the unmistakeable strains of 'Winter Wonderland' can be heard weaving throughout Michael Kamen's commanding soundtrack, most notably following the terrorists' arrival at the Tower, and Gruber offers tongue-in-cheek assurance of Christmas miracles in the form of the FBI's staggering predictability when responding to his multifarious ploys, it seems increasingly clear that director McTiernan is setting up the audience for a very different kind of Christmas Eve experience than one that might more readily be expected from a more orthodox slice of holiday season cinema. In this sense, as Eliana Dockterman suggests, there is enjoyment to be gained precisely because of the film's determined lack of convention: 'Action movie fans will be delighted to learn that *Die Hard* qualifies as a Christmas movie. Sure, the Christmas joy ends quickly once the terrorists start taking hostages, but is there a better present than John McLean [sic] jumping off exploding buildings?'[6]

Beyond the various Christmas references which are shrewdly dispersed throughout *Die Hard,* there are other connections which anchor the film within the broader tradition of festive cinema. Certainly the familiar trope of combating excess greed with altruistic intentions, so prominent throughout the Christmas movies of the 1980s, was quite conspicuously on display – with the ingenious caveat that the acquisitive company whose headquarters form the focus of the action is actually matched for covetousness by the materialistic Gruber and his audacious scheme to relieve them of vast sums of wealth. As James Hibberd sagaciously indicates, '*Die Hard* takes on the familiar consumerism vs. family values trope, though with a bit of twist as the supposedly greedy Nakatomi corporation is one of the über-Grinch's victims. Still, it's suggested that the company has somehow corrupted the family unit. [...] You clearly have sacrifice for the community and family'.[7] Here, too, we can observe some aspect of the transformative effect of Christmas at work in the way that McClane is compelled – due to forces beyond his control – to discover new dimensions to his character, eventually putting aside the masculine posturing of his early meeting with Holly to face a stark realisation of how much his family really means to him. (This new comprehension is fortified still further when McClane leaves an emotional, potentially posthumous message for his wife prior to the climactic action of the third act, which he entrusts via radio to his new comrade Al Powell.) As Drew Taylor suggests, this development helps to situate the film more firmly within the wider confines of the genre: '*Die Hard* might be the greatest Christmas movie ever. It basically has all of the greatest bits of your favorite Christmas movie, all rolled into one. [...] In a weird way, it's just as moralistic and uplifting as *It's a Wonderful Life*. In that film, a man, despondent and morally conflicted, is shown the beauty of life (and what his life would be like if he was no longer in it), and is reborn, literally and spiritually, at the film's close. He's reconnected with the things that are really important in life. So is John McClane'.[8]

While certainly it seems that the reflective ethicality which was manifested throughout many other Christmas films of the 1980s is shared by *Die Hard*, these themes are perceptively employed and never allowed to overwhelm the action. Just as its traditional yuletide trimmings are pared down to suit the occasion of the film's corporate environment (and the consequent bloodbath that arises), so too are the moral principles of the narrative rendered in an admirably restrained way. As Molly Freeman remarks, 'think about those typical holiday films, what makes them Christmas-y? A Christmas soundtrack and/or holiday decorations? Check. The morals of Christmas: peace on earth and goodwill toward men? Check. The importance of family? Check. A romance plot? Check. Sure, the fact that John is fighting greedy Christmas-ruining burglars with machine guns and C-4 might be a bit ostentatious for a holiday flick, but the message of the movie is that good will triumph over evil. Besides, Hans Gruber (Alan Rickman) is like a scarier version of Scrooge, who also has a gun'.[9] Thus with its combination of deftly-subverted Christmas iconography and downplayed but affecting emotional content, *Die Hard* was certainly something quite different from a run-of-the-mill eighties action film, and ultimately only the individual viewer can decide whether its festive content is indicative of a place within the wider confines of Christmas cinema or is instead a purposely droll caricature of the genre's tropes. But as Danny Gallagher has considered, although the film's generic classification has been hotly disputed, most especially in recent years, there has been growing accord amongst many commentators of its qualification as an example (albeit somewhat alternative in nature) of eighties festive cinema: 'Opening and closing my own belief with an emphatic fact, *Die Hard* IS a Christmas movie and it's perhaps one of the greatest Christmas movies of all time. The fact that the events of the 1988 film take place on Christmas Eve isn't the only qualifier. *Die Hard* is about one man trying to save a group of hostages, including his estranged wife, who are trapped in a Los Angeles skyscraper by a group of violent terrorists. McClane risks his life to save his fellow man. Is there anything more noble that anyone can do at Christmas time than stop to help a complete stranger trapped in a dire situation?'.[10]

Die Hard's complex generic fusion was not solely defined by its association with Christmas cinema, however. In its similarity to what has become almost certainly the definitive skyscraper-bound disaster movie, *The Towering Inferno* (John Guillermin, 1974), the film also dexterously teased audience predictions to generate suspense – a fact delineated all the more starkly when the plastic explosives start to detonate midway through the narrative, undoubtedly leading some to question whether a taut hostage drama had suddenly turned into a battle for survival akin to the many catastrophe-oriented features of the previous decade. As Yvonne Tasker has argued, 'the movie's producers specifically acknowledge their debt to the 1970s disaster movie. [...] The film exemplifies both classic and post-Hollywood techniques. In its narrative and stylistic construction the film is astonishingly tight. [...] *Die Hard* is also held together by a range of generic and other references, both visual and verbal. Like classic Hollywood productions, the film depends for its intelligibility on genre. Yet at the same time the film, as other generic hybrids, operates in a sense beyond the categories to which the genre refers. Hybridity, that is, allows films to both draw on and redefine a range of genres, through the forging of new associations between them'.[11] Interestingly, this amalgamation of various characteristics across different genres does not necessarily dilute its claim to a place within Christmas cinema, but may actually strengthen it. This is due to the fact, as Fred Topel has contended, that films dealing with the festive season had already established a long history with just such a methodology of generic cross-pollination:

> If *Die Hard* is first and foremost an action movie, the terrorists actually add to the Christmas story rather than subtract from it. You may wish to qualify it as a 'Christmas Action Movie' but that still plants it firmly in the Christmas category. [...] Genres can be backdrops. 'Post-apocalyptic movie' refers to any movie that takes place in a wasteland after social collapse. [...] There's even precedent in the Christmas genre. Not all traditional Christmas movies are about the holiday any more specifically than *Die Hard* is. *A Christmas Carol* is a time travel movie first and foremost. It just happens

that the destination for the time travel is the date of Christmas in the past, present and future. *It's a Wonderful Life* is an alternate reality movie, one that just happens to take place at Christmas.[12]

It is interesting to note that the film's screenplay, by Jeb Stuart and Steven E. de Souza, remains remarkably faithful to the Roderick Thorp source material in many key ways. The novel *Nothing Lasts Forever* concerns a retired New York police officer (Joe Leland, the central figure of Thorp's earlier *The Detective*) visiting Los Angeles on Christmas Eve to spend time with his daughter Stephanie Gennaro. Stephanie is in the employ of the Klaxon Oil Corporation, a company whose headquarters are based within a multi-storey skyscraper in the city. During a Christmas party, the building is stormed by a group of terrorists led by a German radical named Anton Gruber (often known by his nickname 'Little Tony'). Leland and Gruber have previous history, having been adversaries during World War II. Caught unawares by the invaders, Leland escapes barefoot into the building and is forced to plan a desperate strategy to thwart the terrorists' plans and save the lives of the hostages. Aided over the radio by LAPD Sergeant Al Powell, a young officer who offers assistance from outside the tower, Leland eventually succeeds in frustrating Gruber's efforts to expose Klaxon's unethical business dealings and tip millions of dollars' worth of cash out of the skyscraper's windows. The novel introduces many characters who would later appear in *Die Hard*, including Dwayne Robinson, Harry Ellis and the psychotic Karl, though some relationships are subtly different; Leland is a paranoid and world-weary police veteran with extensive experience of terrorist situations, which he uses (along with prior knowledge of Gruber's psychology) to defeat his enemies, whereas his familial bond with his daughter Stephanie is badly strained due to the aftermath of her parents' bitter divorce some years earlier. On account of the Leland character being much older than the thirtysomething John McClane, he draws upon wartime experience which the cinematic character lacks, though many of the tactics later used by McClane (such as dropping plastic explosives down one of the skyscraper's elevator shafts, and using a fire hose to escape the rooftop explosion) have their genesis in the novel. However, *Nothing Lasts Forever* ends on a considerably darker note, with Stephanie dead as a result of Gruber's vindictiveness and Leland seemingly in danger of perishing as result of the many injuries he sustains during the terrorist attack. By contrast, the novel indirectly suggests that Leland's intervention actually costs more lives than it saves, inferring that if Little Tony's scheme had played out according to plan then it is possible that no-one would have been killed in the first place. In *Die Hard*, however, Gruber's intention had patently always been to murder the hostages as a smokescreen to allow him to escape undetected with his associates.

Another controversial issue regarding *Die Hard* is whether to consider Gruber's gang as terrorists or simply as highly-organised thieves. One of the TV news reports in the film uncovers Gruber's past history with the militant radical (and fictional) *Volksfrei* movement, but also emphasises that he had been expelled from the organisation for unknown reasons. While Gruber boasts that he purchases his suits from the same tailor as Palestinian Liberation Organisation leader Yasser Arafat, glibly trying to convince Takagi of his revolutionary leanings, he offers little conceptual proof of any genuine correspondence to anarchistic or extremist philosophies. Thus in spite of his apparent fanatical ideological posturing, Gruber manifestly has no concern for the release of the incarcerated terrorists that he uses as a negotiation tool (employing the tactic merely as subterfuge to throw the FBI off the scent of his true intentions), and seems content to use international terrorism as a façade to keep the authorities assuming that his aims are driven by political motivations. However, given the jaw-dropping amount of military-grade armaments that the group have access to, ranging from rocket launchers to C-4 explosives, it would not be unreasonable to assume that Gruber and his associates are genuine terrorists who have chosen to go rogue in order to increase their individual wealth, rather than intending to use the capital assets stolen from the corporation to fund dissident causes (presumably a more conventional approach for an organised extremist group to take with regard to a high-stakes heist operation such as that which is unleashed on the Nakatomi Tower).

An uncommon action movie requires an extraordinary hero, and in John McClane the 1980s found one of its defining figures – far from an invincible killing machine, McClane was simply an off-duty cop with an unexpected objective; a family man who was, at heart, just desperate to stay alive. Bruce Willis was cast against type at the time, better recognised amongst audiences for his comedic talents in television roles, but he invests the character with affecting vulnerability, mounting anxiety, and an appealing line in wisecracks. Though at the time of *Die Hard*'s release Willis's cinematic career had consisted of two leading performances in Blake Edwards films – romantic comedy *Blind Date* (1987) and period mystery *Sunset* (1988) – he was considerably better recognised for his role as private detective David Addison in

ABC's postmodern comedy drama *Moonlighting* (1986-89), a cleverly-scripted TV series which garnered many prizes and industry nominations including Golden Globe Awards and Emmy Awards. *Die Hard* convinced the world of Willis's star quality, and its box-office success would see him embarking upon a prolific and high-profile acting career which included major roles in films as diverse as *Bonfire of the Vanities* (Brian De Palma, 1990), *Death Becomes Her* (Robert Zemeckis, 1992), *Pulp Fiction* (Quentin Tarantino, 1994), *12 Monkeys* (Terry Gilliam, 1995), *Armageddon* (Michael Bay, 1998) and *The Sixth Sense* (M. Night Shyamalan, 1999). He has been the recipient of many international awards, ranging from Emmy Award and Golden Globe Award wins and nominations, being appointed Officer (2006) and later Commander (2013) of the French *Ordre des Arts et des Lettres*, Harvard University's prestigious Hasty Pudding Man of the Year Award in 2002, and a star on the Hollywood Walk of Fame in 2006.

Willis is given exceptional support from the film's multiplicity of excellent actors, amongst them Bonnie Bedelia as the astute, no-nonsense business negotiator Holly Gennaro, Reginald Veljohnson's sympathetic but world-weary Al Powell, and James Shigeta as the permanently unruffled Joe Takagi. Special mention is due to Paul Gleason – forever remembered as the autocratic Principal Richard Vernon in John Hughes's *The Breakfast Club* (1985) – as the deeply oblivious Deputy Police Chief Dwayne T. Robinson, as well as William Atherton in the role of pushy TV reporter Richard Thornburg, reprising the kind of presumptuous brashness that had made his performance as the officious Environment Protection Agency representative Walter Peck so enjoyable in Ivan Reitman's *Ghostbusters* (1984). The terrorist group also makes for an interesting alliance of individuals, sinister and clearly deadly yet with the odd flicker of humanity visible within their litany of cold-blooded brutality. While Clarence Gilyard Jr.'s chatterbox computer genius Theo and Alexander Godunov's glowering, lethal Karl stand out as particularly arresting performances, if anyone comes close to stealing the film from Willis it is Alan Rickman as the composed, sharply-suited criminal mastermind Hans Gruber. Rickman brings a fatal charm to this fast-thinking villain; Gruber is as polished and sophisticated as McClane is practical and grounded, leading to a memorable battle of wits between a diametrically opposed protagonist and antagonist. Amazingly, given his incredible assuredness in the role, *Die Hard* marked Rickman's cinematic debut. Having worked extensively in theatre and on British television throughout the seventies and eighties, the significant accomplishment of McTiernan's film helped to propel Rickman into a highly diverse and successful career in the movie business which saw him appearing in features such as *Robin Hood: Prince of Thieves* (Kevin Reynolds, 1991), *Sense and Sensibility* (Ang Lee, 1995), *Galaxy Quest* (Dean Parisot, 1999), and in later years in the recurring role of Severus Snape in the blockbuster *Harry Potter* film franchise, beginning with *Harry Potter and the Philosopher's Stone* (Chris Columbus, 2001). Rickman was the recipient of many awards in his lifetime, including a BAFTA Award, Golden Globe Award, Emmy Award and many other industry plaudits and nominations.

While *Die Hard* is aided greatly by the uniformly high standard of its performances, the film was also lauded at the time of its release for the excellence of its technical qualities. McTiernan, aided by some outstanding cinematography from Jan de Bont, genuinely manages to turn a soulless corporate office setting into one of the eighties' most unforgettable movie battlegrounds, cleverly using visual cues to characterise the skyscraper's various upper levels (such as the plush atrium where the hostages are held, the computer centre, and sections which are still under construction). Strangely enough, as Dave Kehr and others have pointed out, the exterior of the fictional Nakatomi Tower was actually the semi-complete headquarters of 20th Century Fox, the studio that would eventually distribute the film in theatres: 'McTiernan, who directed last summer's *Predator*, composes the action cleanly and logically, making good use of Jackson DeGovia's elaborate post-modernist set – the building becomes something of a character in itself (the exterior belongs to the Fox Plaza, located just a few steps from the 20th Century Fox studio). The picture acquires a sense of scale that, while wildly disproportionate to its actual content, can't help but impress'.[13] For an action movie so focused on its elaborate setup that almost twenty minutes pass before the first gunshots are fired, McTiernan certainly leaves no stone unturned when the conflict does start in earnest; the C-4 explosion caused by McClane to disrupt the terrorists' violent repulsion of LAPD forces is a particularly standout sequence, skilfully brought to life by the use of a vast number of camera flashbulbs attached to the real building and a cleverly-realised explosion carried out on a scale miniature. The overall effect is seamless, and certainly put an awe-inspiring visual focus on the scale of McTiernan's creative ambition. Yet as Kevin Thomas has observed, in spite of the film's overwhelming technical sophistication its overall success still lies in the underlying contemporary relevance of its central scenario: 'The commandeering of the skyscraper is a textbook study of the ⟦action movie⟧ process, as terrifyingly persuasive as it is swift. It's a formidable introduction to the visual virtuosity of director John McTiernan and cinematographer Jan De Bont, who are backed spectacularly well by ingenious production designer Jackson DeGovia and a raft of special effects magicians. [...] The film makers never lose sight of the lowest common denominator at one end of the scale and the yuppie mentality at the other. *Die Hard* plugs into the populist myth that in the crunch both the local police and FBI brass (Paul Gleason and Robert Davi, respectively) will act reflexively like egotistical jerks and that, if the day is to be saved, it will be by canny, resourceful lower-echelon types like McClane'.[14]

While the film's pop culture references help to reinforce its debt to numerous identifiable totems of the American entertainment world – there are mentions of Roy Rogers, John Wayne, Gary Cooper, Grace Kelly and even Sylvester Stallone's John Rambo – further allusions are less readily discernible. Michael Kamen's authoritative musical score for the film punctuates the mounting tension with some neatly-calculated motifs, among them a repeated evocation of 'Ode to Joy' from Beethoven's Ninth Symphony; the same piece was used to accompany the 'ultra-violence' caused by Malcolm McDowell's delinquent character Alex DeLarge in Stanley Kubrick's infamous *A Clockwork Orange* (1971). This covert implication is further reinforced by a subtle suggestion of Arthur Freed and Nacio Herb Brown's 'Singin' in the Rain' (1929), subversively employed with devastating panache in Kubrick's film.

Die Hard made major waves in the critical community when it first hit cinemas in 1988, engendering a wide range of commentary – most of it positive. Chris Chase was among the many reviewers who praised the film's tightly-controlled spectacle, commending it for its sheer entertainment value: 'In

Die Hard, Bruce Willis is your basic little guy up against a gang of international terrorists, and they've got chain saws and machine guns and plastic explosives and he has just the one measly handgun. But he's brave as Rambo and taller than Mel Gibson, so don't you worry that he's going to come to grief. ⟦...⟧ I can't begin to tell you how much carnage is wrought, how many fires are started, how many bodies go crashing out of windows, how many armored cars and helicopters and villains are destroyed. There are good performances from everyone in this long, often funny, very violent but exciting melodrama'.[15] Chase's approval was mirrored in the views of Caryn James, who acknowledged *Die Hard*'s technical proficiency while also recognising its role as larger-than-life entertainment: 'Partly an interracial buddy movie, partly the sentimental tale of a ruptured marriage, the film is largely a special-effects carnival full of machine-gun fire, roaring helicopters and an exploding tank. It also has a villain fresh from the Royal Shakespeare Company, a thug from the Bolshoi Ballet and a hero who carries with him the smirks and wisecracks that helped make *Moonlighting* a television hit. The strange thing is, it works: *Die Hard* is exceedingly stupid, but escapist fun'.[16] However, not all responses to the film proved to be quite so favourable. Hal Hinson, for example, considered the melange of high-octane action and glossy professionalism to be so carefully choreographed that the overall effect almost seemed unabashedly manipulative: '*Die Hard* is a logistical wonder, a marvel of engineering, and relentlessly, mercilessly thrilling. It has masterfully executed effects, a pile-driver steady pace and a sleek, nonporous design. Add a percussive, big-star performance to the state-of-the-art mechanics, turn up all the knobs, and you've got a sure-fire, big-bucks, major-studio-style summer attraction. All that's left is to light the fuse. So why am I not having fun? *Die Hard* is all these things, but it's not a movie to like. It gets your heart pounding, then makes you hate yourself for it'.[17] Perhaps the most prominent of all dissenting interpretations was that of Roger Ebert, who (in a review which was much discussed at the time) famously identified one perceived mis-step that he felt damaged the film's overall effectiveness:

> On a technical level, there's a lot to be said for *Die Hard*. It's when we get to some of the unnecessary adornments of the script that the movie shoots itself in the foot. Willis remains in constant radio contact with a police officer on the ground (Reginald VelJohnson) who tries to keep his morale up. But then the filmmakers introduce a gratuitous and unnecessary additional character: the deputy police chief (Paul Gleason), who doubts that the guy on the other end of the radio is really a New York cop at all. As nearly as I can tell, the deputy chief is in the movie for only one purpose: to be consistently wrong at every step of the way and to provide a phony counterpoint to Willis' progress. The character is so willfully useless, so dumb, so much a product of the Idiot Plot Syndrome, that all by himself he successfully undermines the last half of the movie. Thrillers like this need to be well-oiled machines, with not a single wasted moment. Inappropriate and wrongheaded interruptions reveal the fragile nature of the plot and prevent it from working.[18]

While the general critical consensus surrounding *Die Hard*'s release was largely favourable, the film's continued popularity with audiences – not least through television screenings, home entertainment releases and now streaming via on-demand Internet video services – has led to even greater approval of its merits. From the nostalgia value of its unmistakeable 1980s fashions and yuppie environment through to the meticulous engineering of its plot, *Die Hard* has sustained its place in popular culture: not least on account of the huge influence that it would have on later action movies following its release. As Tyler Foster has stated, 'the original *Die Hard,* which introduced audiences to infinitely resilient NYC cop John McClane (Bruce Willis), did in fact change everything when it was released in 1988, shifting the idea of action movies away from gritty, cheap Arnold Schwarzenegger vehicles and more in the direction of stylish, big-budget productions with a likable, emotionally vulnerable hero with a snappy comeback for everything. The influence of *Die Hard* on Hollywood action pictures was so enormous that it became a movie executive shorthand: every action movie was described as "*Die Hard* on a..." It's impossible to point to a single thing that makes the original *Die Hard* so successful. The film is a perfect storm of savvy decisions that seem logical and innocuous but pay off in incredible dividends when watching the finished film'.[19] Foster's appraisal was far from isolated; other critics have also drawn attention to the vast impact of McTiernan's movie in the decades following its emergence into cinemas. Amy Flower, for instance, remarks upon the way in which the film has come to reshape expectations of the action movie, raising the bar of audience anticipation in ways which continue to reverberate even in the present day: '*Die Hard* is essentially the benchmark for all action films that followed in its wake. [...] Some actually rather gruesome bits are entwined with genuinely suspenseful moments and over-the-top cartoon-styled action, more clichés abound than you can poke a stick at [...], memorable one-liners are thick on the ground and, of course, it all wraps up with a suitably happy ending. Combine all this with John

McTiernan's snappy direction and Jan De Bont's stylish photography and you could scarcely ask for more. That *Die Hard* is still an absolute thrill ride of a flick today [...] and with a remarkable amount of attempts to emulate its runaway success in its wake, is simple testament to just how brilliant, engrossing and downright entertaining this film is'.[20]

Due to the huge commercial success of *Die Hard*, the film has received four sequels to date. The first, *Die Hard 2: Die Harder* (Renny Harlin, 1990), was set exactly one year after the events of the original movie, and concerned McClane being forced to deal with a team of mercenaries who are holding Dulles International Airport in Washington D.C. to ransom as part of an intricate plan to free an imprisoned South American dictator. Though *Die Hard 2* retained the Christmas Eve setting of the initial entry in the series, the references to the holiday season were considerably toned down by comparison – as was the film's sense of claustrophobia. Later sequels included *Die Hard with a Vengeance* (John McTiernan, 1995), *Live Free or Die Hard* (Len Wiseman, 2007) and *A Good Day to Die Hard* (John Moore, 2013), though none of them would engage with yuletide tropes as part of their respective narratives. The franchise has also inspired a coin-operated arcade game and several tie-in videogames, as well as BOOM! Studios' comic series *Die Hard: Year One* (2009-10), a prequel which explores McClane's early years in the NYPD during the United States Bicentennial celebrations in the summer of 1976.

Die Hard was not overlooked at industry award ceremonies in the eighties, gaining nominations for four Academy Awards in the categories of Best Film Editing, Best Sound, Best Effects: Sound Effects Editing, and Best Effects: Visual Effects. It was also nominated for an Edgar Allan Poe

Award for Best Motion Picture, and won Michael Kamen a BMI Film Music Award as well as gaining sound editor Richard Shorr a Golden Reel Award at the Motion Picture Sound Editors Awards. *Die Hard* also performed well at international film ceremonies, winning Best Foreign Language Film prizes at the Blue Ribbon Awards, Hochi Film Awards and Kinema Junpo Awards.

While *Die Hard* may not be the first movie that occurs to people when discussing Christmas cinema, there is little doubt that it has carved a niche for itself within the genre as a somewhat iconoclastic entry in the wider canon of festive filmmaking. Though plastic explosives, terrified hostages and murderous terrorists may not necessarily suggest the kind of heart-warming yuletide fare that tends to be more readily associated with films of the holiday season, *Die Hard* offered audiences a startlingly different type of Christmas Eve – one which was as powerfully distinctive as any to have been presented throughout the 1980s. John McClane may not have been the festive hero that many might have expected, but the character certainly left an indelible impression on Christmas cinema which continues to be debated and celebrated today.

REFERENCES

1. Greg Metcalf, '"It's (Christmas) Morning in America": Christmas Conventions of American Films in the 1980s', in *Beyond the Stars: Plot Conventions in American Popular Film*, ed. by Paul Loukides and Linda K. Fuller (Bowling Green: Bowling Green State University Popular Press, 1991), 100-13, p.104.

2. Dirk Libbey, 'New Poll Asks if *Die Hard* is a Christmas Movie, Majority Pick Wrong Answer', in *CinemaBlend*, January 2016.
    <http://www.cinemablend.com/new/Poll-Asks-Die-Hard-Christmas-Movie-Majority-Pick-Wrong-Answer-102117.html>

3. Alonso Duralde, *Have Yourself a Movie Little Christmas* (Milwaukee: Limelight Editions, 2010), pp.106-07.

4. Tom Ward, 'Why *Die Hard* is the Best Christmas Movie of All Time', in *The Huffington Post*, 22 February 2013.
    <http://www.huffingtonpost.co.uk/tom-ward/why-die-hard-is-the-best-christmas-movie-of-all-time_b_2339117.html>

5. Peter Hoare, '10 Reasons why *Die Hard* is the Greatest Christmas Movie Ever', in *BroBible*, 23 December 2015.
    <http://brobible.com/entertainment/article/why-die-hard-is-christmas-movie/>

6. Eliana Dockterman, '11 Christmas Movies You Didn't Know Were Christmas Movies', in *Time Online*, 22 December 2014.
    <http://time.com/3634524/christmas-movies-unconventional/>

7. James Hibberd, '10 Reasons *Die Hard* is a Perfect Christmas Movie', in *Entertainment Weekly*, 24 December 2015. <*http://www.ew.com/article/2015/12/24/die-hard-christmas-movie*>

8. Drew Taylor, 'Why *Die Hard* is the Greatest Christmas Movie Ever Made', in *MovieFone*, 23 December 2013. <*http://www.moviefone.com/2013/12/23/die-hard-greatest-christmas-movie-ever/*>

9. Molly Freeman, 'Why is *Die Hard* a Christmas Movie?', in *Hollywood.com*, 2015. <*http://www.hollywood.com/movies/die-hard-christmas-movie-57258229/*>

10. Danny Gallagher, 'Is *Die Hard* a Christmas movie?: Poll Takes Pulse on Key Issue of Our Time', in *CNet*, 23 December 2015. <*http://www.cnet.com/uk/news/is-die-hard-a-christmas-movie-poll-takes-pulse-on-key-issue-of-our-time/*>

11. Yvonne Tasker, *Spectacular Bodies: Gender, Genre and the Action Cinema* (London: Routledge, 1993), p.61.

12. Fred Topel, 'No, Seriously... *Die Hard* is a Real Christmas Movie', in Crave Online, 5 December 2014. <*http://www.craveonline.com/site/796777-seriously-die-hard-christmas-movie*>

13. Dave Kehr, 'Sleek *Die Hard* Tools Action Film to Perfection', in *The Chicago Tribute*, 15 July 1988.

14. Kevin Thomas, '*Die Hard* a Slick Flick for Bruce Willis', in *The Los Angeles Times*, 15 July 1988.

15.	Chris Chase, '*Die Hard:* Cop Fights Gang of Terrorists', in *The New York Daily News*, 15 July 1988.

16.	Caryn James, 'The Police, Terrorists and a Captive Audience', in *The New York Times*, 15 July 1988.

17.	Hal Hinson, '*Die Hard*', in *The Washington Post*, 15 July 1988.

18.	Roger Ebert, '*Die Hard*', in *The Chicago Sun-Times*, 15 July 1988.

19.	Tyler Foster, '*Die Hard:* 25th Anniversary Collection', in *DVD Talk*, 29 January 2013.
	<http://www.dvdtalk.com/reviews/59327/die-hard-25th-anniversary-collection/>

20.	Amy Flower, '*Die Hard*', in *DVD.net*, 2006.
	<http://www.dvd.net.au/review.cgi?review_id=1415>

16

Prancer (1989)

Cineplex-Odeon Films/Nelson Entertainment/
Raffaella Productions

Director: John Hancock
Producers: Raffaella De Laurentiis
Screenwriter: Greg Taylor

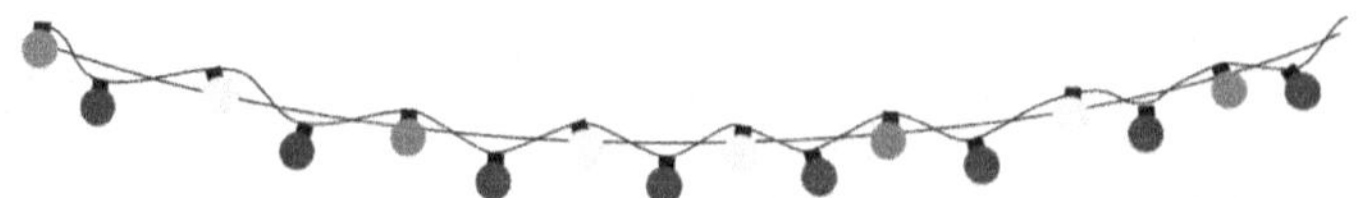

In a decade which has become noted for the innovative and often challenging qualities of its festive cinema, *Prancer* was a traditional slice of Christmas film-making which bucked the prevailing trend of its era of production. While other family features of the time, such as *Santa Claus: The Movie* and *Ernest Saves Christmas*, had steadfastly focused upon the production of entertainment which was suitable for a younger audience, the overall style had been very clearly attuned to the kind of engagingly fanciful central scenario that had typified so many earlier movies in the genre. *Prancer*, on the other hand, would exhibit a creative approach which had less in common with diverting Christmas whimsies of the field's golden age such as *The Bishop's Wife* (Henry Koster, 1947) or *Holiday Affair* (Don Hartman, 1949), instead demonstrating a greater overlap of methodology with darker-toned fantasies of the eighties such as *The Dark Crystal* (Jim Henson and Frank Oz, 1982), *The Black Cauldron* (Ted

Berman and Richard Rich, 1985), or *Return to Oz* (Walter Murch, 1985). The result was a distinctive but somewhat polarising feature which blended the harsh economic realism of life in 1980s rural America with a low-key but emotionally affecting tale of community cohesion and personal transformation during the holiday season. While *Prancer* may not have been the upbeat, saccharine yuletide chronicle that many might reasonably have expected from the film's seemingly-uplifting premise, its uncommon but contemplative consideration of Christmas tropes has made it something of a oddity – not least in the way in which the unforgiving pragmatism of the everyday encroaches upon the territory which had more traditionally been occupied by the quirkily imaginative.

Prancer was a collaboration between veteran TV screenwriter Greg Taylor (whose later prolific output would include the screenplay for Joe Johnston's 1995 fantasy film *Jumanji,* adapted from the 1981 Chris Van Allsburg novel) and director John D. Hancock. A film-maker with an eclectic back-catalogue, Hancock has directed for stage and screen as well as having also worked as a producer and writer. Though his theatrical career has included the direction of plays ranging from classical drama through to contemporary works, his work for the cinema has been similarly wide-ranging. His debut for the big screen, short film *Sticky My Fingers, Fleet My Feet* (1970), won him critical praise as well as an Academy Award nomination for Best Short Film and an Outstanding Achievement Critics Choice award from the American Film Institute. Later films would include psychological horror *Let's Scare Jessica to Death* (1971), moving baseball drama *Bang the Drum Slowly* (1973), meditative romance *California Dreaming* (1979), and poignant prison-based drama *Weeds* (1987). Hancock has additionally been active on television, helming episodes for television series as diverse as NBC's *Hill Street Blues* (1981-87) and CBS's *Cover Up* (1984-85) as well as the mid-eighties revival of *The Twilight Zone* (1985-89).

The holiday season is fast approaching in the rural town of Three Oaks, Michigan, and Jessica Riggs (Rebecca Harrell) is getting into the spirit of things at the elementary school she attends. Christmas carols are rehearsed, and soon afterwards a Nativity play is performed for the families of the students. While returning home, Jessica and her friend Carol Wetherby (Ariana Richards) spot a large Christmas decoration of Santa's sleigh and its eight reindeer being put up in a nearby street. Much to her concern, one of the model reindeer falls from the decoration and smashes into pieces on the road below; a driver has to swerve to avoid the debris hitting his car. Jessica is troubled as council workers carry the broken pieces of the model away; counting through the reindeer in the order from Clement Clark Moore's poem 'A Visit from St Nicholas', she determines that the shattered reindeer represented Prancer. Carol reassures her that the model was not one of Santa's real reindeer, but Jessica worries that only seven reindeer will not be enough to pull the sleigh.

Heading back to her home, Jessica relates the experiences of the Nativity play to her gruff father John (Sam Elliott). However, John has more pressing issues to attend to – the apple farm that he operates is facing tough times, and the winter snow is doing little to improve their prospects. He attempts to sell his three-year-old tractor to some potential buyers, but changes his mind when they deliberately low-ball him with a desultory offer. Heading indoors, Jessica greets her aunt Sarah (Rutanya Alda) – John's sister-in-law, who is currently helping out at the farm. She also speaks with her older brother Steve (John Joseph Duda) and asks if he will consider repairing her broken sled, but in the time-honoured tradition of sibling skirmishes he flatly refuses.

Although the family are facing a difficult financial situation, Jessica is determined not to allow their problems to dampen her Christmas spirit. At dinner, she asks if there is due to be a full moon on Christmas Eve, as one of her teachers had suggested that the sign augurs well for a magical festive season. Steve pokes fun at her, but their mutual aggravation is curtly shut down by the stern John. Later, while considering a photograph of her late mother, Jessica overhears part of a conversation between John and Sarah. Her father bitterly regrets his inability to properly provide for his family, even though the underlying economic situation is out of his control. Sarah urges him to break some particular news to Jessica, though she does not say what. However, John is clearly reluctant to do so.

The next day, Jessica discusses this new development with Carol and voices her confusion. In particular, Jessica cannot understand why her aunt is spending so much more time at the family's house when she has a husband back at her own home. Trying to take her friend's mind off the issue, Carol challenges her to a sled race. They enjoy their dash through the snow, even though it is unexpectedly punctuated by a detour through the property of the peculiar Mrs McFarland (Cloris Leachman), a local eccentric who becomes hysterical when Jessica accidentally runs over a few of her exotic flowers. Making her way through a forest as she heads back to the farm afterwards, Jessica is startled when she meets a reindeer on her travels. She is amazed that it shows no apprehension at her presence, though it soon dashes off into the shadows, leaving the baffled young girl in its wake.

Jessica tracks down her father in the family's barn and excitedly tells him about her encounter with the reindeer. However, he is even more irritable than usual due to a phone call from Mrs McFarland. As she had been complaining about the damage to her flowers caused by Jessica's collision with her sled, John has offered her financial recompense – money that he can ill afford to part with. Angrily, he warns her to steer clear of Mrs McFarland's property in future, but Jessica is indignant that he has shown no interest in her tale. The story of the reindeer similarly has little impact on Carol, who believes that Jessica met the reindeer as described but has difficulty with her friend's assertion that it was not simply a wild animal but actually Prancer, one of Santa's personal reindeer. She considers that the falling town decoration had been an omen of Prancer's true presence, and that the forthcoming full moon on Christmas Eve is proof of magic this holiday season. Deeply sceptical, Carol tells her that she no longer believes that Santa is capable of travelling around the world delivering all of his gifts in one night, but Jessica – aghast at her friend's doubt – then reflects that if Santa is considered to be not real, surely this means that the Judeo-Christian belief in life after death can also be considered questionable. When Carol suggests that there is no straightforward answer one way or the other, Jessica is upset and tells her that their friendship is over: after all, if she ceases to believe in heaven then how can she be sure that her mother's soul continues to live after her death? Realising how hurt Jessica is, Carol tries to placate her, but she also finds that personal beliefs cannot simply be changed to suit a given situation.

On the way home from school, Jessica discovers some reindeer tracks leading into a woodland area. Following the hoof-prints, she is alarmed when she hears the sound of gunshots nearby. She continues to wander the forest until after nightfall, when John spots her at the roadside while driving his pickup truck. He is angry that she had gone wandering in the woods in the winter, having repeatedly warned her of the danger of being accidentally shot by hunters. While John drives, Jessica asks about his earlier conversation with Sarah. Reluctantly, her father explains that he has agreed that Jessica should move in with her aunt and uncle – who live thirty miles away – because he lacks the financial resources to adequately provide for her needs. Jessica is distressed; although her father is brusque and often impatient, she loves him and does not want their family to be parted. Though he assures her that he will not be far away, and that the move will be for her benefit, Jessica warns that she will run away rather than consent to his wishes. As they argue, John narrowly avoids a collision with an unexpected obstacle in the road: the reindeer that Jessica had met previously. Noticing that the animal's leg is badly wounded, John retrieves his rifle from the truck; he explains that shooting it will be a kindness, as it will bring an end to its suffering. Jessica becomes furious at her father's intentions, no matter how well-meaning they may be. However, their conflict turns to amazement when they discover that the maimed reindeer has disappeared into thin air.

Later that night, Jessica has a vivid dream of the reindeer ornament falling from the town's Christmas street decorations. Awakening with a start, she hears a commotion outside and discovers that the doors of the farm's barn have blown open. Heading out to investigate, Jessica is astonished to discover that the injured reindeer has taken shelter inside the barn alongside the other farmyard animals. Now more sure than ever that the reindeer is Prancer, she decides to move him elsewhere on the farm to avoid any chance of John deciding to shoot him. Though obviously pained from the gash in his leg, Prancer follows Jessica's lead and limps to the comparative safety of a rarely-used outhouse where he should be secure from her father.

The next morning, as Jessica awaits the school bus, John notes with some suspicion that some of his tree saplings have been eaten; he spotted deer droppings nearby, making him even more confounded. When the bus eventually arrives, Jessica feigns having left her homework in her room and instead heads to the outhouse to check on Prancer. Realising that the reindeer is ailing, she decides that professional help is needed and tracks down the town's crotchety veterinary surgeon Dr Orel Benton (Abe Vigoda). Believing that one of the farmyard animals has been injured, Benton drives out to the Riggs homestead but is less than impressed when he discovers that the wound belongs to a reindeer instead. He decides to leave, but eventually relents in the face of Jessica's persistence and removes a bullet from Prancer's leg. Bandaging the laceration, he is puzzled that the reindeer has ventured so far south; its presence is something of a rarity in the area. Coming to the conclusion that it must have escaped from a nearby Christmas show, Benton feels a professional obligation to call the owners and enquire if they are missing any animals. However, Jessica persuades him to give her a couple of days to tell John herself before Benton contacts the show's organisers. But much to Benton's surprise, when he does make the promised phone call he is told that all of the animals in the display are accounted for, further convincing Jessica that the reindeer has come from the North Pole.

John is irate when he discovers that Jessica has missed the school bus, and grows even more indignant when she brushes off the incident as unimportant. As he is heading away on business later in the day, he worries that he is unable to trust her to behave herself. His fears turn out to be well founded; leaving Jessica in the care of Steve, she sneaks out of the house when he is making a phone call and spends the evening reading to the convalescing Prancer while feeding him in an attempt to help him regain his strength.

Realising that Santa Claus may be worrying about his reindeer's whereabouts, Jessica takes a Polaroid photo of Prancer and heads off to the town's mall. There, jovial local man Mr Stewart (Michael Constantine) is operating a Santa's Grotto for the children of busy shoppers. Jessica explains that although she is aware that Stewart is not the genuine Santa Claus, she would like him to pass on a letter to the real thing – along with the photo of Prancer. Touched by her sincerity, Stewart agrees to do his best to bring the issue to Santa's attention. He asks if there is anything she would like for Christmas, and she replies that she wants to avoid her family being broken up in the way that her father is intending. Before she can explain further, Stewart is rushed on by his manager due to a lengthening queue waiting to see the mall Santa. Unknown to Jessica, once his shift is finished Stewart heads for the offices of the local newspaper. Heartened by the girl's sincerity, he relates her fantastical story to the somewhat perplexed editor.

A while later, Jessica and Carol have patched up their differences. Swearing her to secrecy, Jessica takes her friend to the outhouse to see its temporary resident, though Carol is somewhat nonplussed to see the reindeer on the farm. Both are surprised by the unexpected presence of Steve, who has accidentally happened upon Prancer during his farmyard duties. He threatens to tell John about Jessica's secret, but she manages to change his mind when she offers to wash the household dishes for the next six months. Steve warns her that she will need to find an alternative source of nourishment for Prancer; the amount of feed that she is taking from the barn is starting to become noticeable, meaning that she risks being found out.

As night falls, John tells Jessica that her aunt Sarah will be coming to stay with them for a few days, and that she has offered to take her on a Christmas shopping trip. He is surprised when, rather than being delighted by this unanticipated treat, Jessica becomes flustered – she doesn't want to leave Prancer alone and thus tells her father that unexplained business is keeping her at the farm. Interpreting her reluctance as an indirect rebuff to his domestic plans, he sternly insists that she do as he says. But Jessica has a strategy of her own. The next morning she sneaks away from home while her father is absent from the farm, evading Sarah's notice, and heads for the home of Mrs McFarland. Initially Jessica apologises to the short-tempered widow for having earlier trespassed on her property, but then tells her that she is collecting money for an animal shelter and is offering to do household chores to this end. Mrs McFarland reluctantly agrees, and shows her into a dimly-lit room that is filled from floor to ceiling with clutter. In spite of the enormity of the job, Jessica obligingly does as she is asked, and over the hours that follow the room is returned to some semblance of order. While clearing some of the jumbled items into the house's attic, Jessica discovers a chest full of decorative electric lights and sets them up as a surprise for Mrs McFarland. Given that the cranky homeowner had previously won awards for her Christmas decorations, Jessica is puzzled when she becomes distressed at the sight of them illuminated once again. Clearly the lights bring back memories that she is keen not to exhume. However, at Jessica's urging the exterior of the house is redecorated once again, with lights bedecking the rooftop and a huge Christmas star shining brightly at its apex. Because the young girl has worked so assiduously throughout the day, Mrs McFarland trebles the agreed cleaning fee and awards Jessica with $15 for her efforts.

Jessica heads off quickly to buy a bag of oats for Prancer before the store closes. She is delighted that her animal friend starts tucking into the freshly-delivered food. John, however, is distinctly less pleased when he discovers that his daughter has absconded from the house without having told Sarah of her intended whereabouts. He goes to her room to scold her for her recklessness, but finds her sound asleep – completely tired out after her day of activity. Meanwhile, the editor of the local newspaper is looking over a depressing slate of stories for the next issue, with topics ranging from Cold War tensions to drug-related crime. Remembering the uplifting story about Prancer submitted by Mr Stewart, he reads Jessica's letter to Santa and discovers that she is looking after an injured reindeer (as the Polaroid photo attests). The correspondence makes clear that Jessica has arranged a rendezvous with Santa on the 23rd of December, intending to return Prancer to him at the remote location of Antler Ridge so that the flying reindeer will be back in action in time for Christmas Eve. Charmed by the girl's heartfelt account, the editor decides to run an article about the reindeer.

Soon after, the next edition of the paper is being delivered around the neighbourhood. Jessica has no time to read the editorial, however; she is dismayed when she finds that Steve has invited his friends over to visit the outhouse and see the reindeer for themselves. Believing that her secret has been betrayed by Carol, she shoos the young boys from Prancer's hiding place. Sarah takes Jessica and Steve to a Christmas church service, where the minister (Walter Charles) and schoolteacher Mrs Fairburn (Marcia Porter) both congratulate Jessica for the inspirational nature of her recent actions. The girl is a little bewildered by all the goodwill that she is generating, being oblivious to the newspaper article. She is also surprised to see Mrs McFarland attending the service, given her rather reclusive reputation. In her rush to get ready for church, however, Jessica has failed to properly secure the door to the outhouse, allowing the now-recovered Prancer to escape. John, who is not attending church, relaxes at home as snow piles on outside; he does not realise that the reindeer is freely prowling the farm. Eventually he hears a commotion from the barn, but Prancer hides from sight which leads John to suspect that nothing is out of place.

At the church, the minister concludes his sermon by praising Jessica for her selflessness and single-minded dedication to encouraging the Christmas spirit in others. She is completely overawed by his words, unsuspecting of the fact that anyone other than herself, Carol and Steve knew about Prancer's presence at the farm. Once the service is over, Jessica rushes off to buy a copy of the paper for herself, lamenting the fact that her secret will now be known to John. She doesn't realise that her father has other problems to deal with; Prancer has let the other animals loose from the barn, and – while John is forced to track them all down and return them to safety – the reindeer takes the opportunity to head into the warmth of the farmhouse. The bemused apple farmer watches in confusion as carload after carload of local residents begin to descend *en-masse* onto his property. When he finds out that the rogue reindeer has caused untold damage to his household contents, John grabs his rifle, but local butcher Herb Drier (Mark Rolston) persuades him at the last minute to sell Prancer rather than shoot him.

Once the townspeople have returned to their homes, John angrily confronts Jessica and berates her for having deceived him. Knowing that his sister had only the best of intentions, Steve tries to emphasise the goodwill of her actions, but John reprimands him too. Heatedly, he tells Jessica that Prancer is not one of Santa's reindeer and is nothing more than a random wild animal, wounding her feelings. Once John reveals Prancer's current whereabouts, Jessica races to Drier's butcher shop and discovers that rather than slaughtering the reindeer he has constructed an enclosure near his premises where he is using Prancer as a promotional gimmick to boost his Christmas sales.

Feeling that she has failed in her task to keep Prancer safe, Jessica voices contrition for her actions during the family meal that night. John is tired of constant enquiries from the townsfolk regarding his sale of the reindeer, which is being considered somewhat out of keeping with the festive season. Once everyone has gone to bed, Jessica leaves a note for John and sneaks out of the house with some tools and supplies. She is surprised when Steve intercepts her departure and offers to help; realising that she intends to run away from home, her brother tries to change her mind but she is insistent. Distraught at her father's constant grumpiness and the thought of moving away from home to live with her aunt, Jessica has decided to take matters into her own hands instead. Worried for his sister's safety, Steve tags along to aid in her attempt to free Prancer from captivity.

Sure enough, the pair find the reindeer unguarded outside the butcher's shop. Steve sets to work breaking the lock while Jessica stands guard. However, Jessica thinks outside of the box and decides to open the roof of the enclosure instead – if Prancer really is one of Santa's reindeer, she realises that he will be able to fly to freedom. Their efforts are interrupted by the unexpected arrival of kindly town sheriff Bert (Michael Luciano), who has come to offer comforting words to the captive animal and promises to bring him some food later in the evening. Once he has departed, Jessica falls from the tree where she has been hiding, losing consciousness with the impact. As Steve runs off to find help, Prancer breaks free from his enclosure and shows concern for the fallen Jessica, choosing to stay with her rather than leave the town to return to the wilderness.

The next day, Jessica has been returned to the safety of her own bed. John reveals to a well-wisher over the phone that she has been checked over at the hospital but all tests indicate that she is unharmed. However, Jessica is not suffering from damage to her physical health but rather her personal faith; as Prancer was unwilling to fly to freedom from his captivity, she has come to the conclusion that John and Carol must have been correct in their scepticism, meaning that he is simply a wild reindeer. Sarah tries to rally her optimism, telling her that as it is Christmas Eve there is every possibility that Santa will return to collect Prancer that very night before he goes on his long global journey for the year.

But Jessica now believes that her trust in the reindeer's origins has been sorely misplaced.

The unfolding of recent events has had a profound effect on John's own outlook, however. He pays a contemplative visit to Drier's shop so that he can check on Prancer's wellbeing now that the reindeer has been returned to his enclosure. While there he encounters a concerned Bert, who lets slip that the townspeople have arranged a secret Christmas party for Jessica. They plan to hold the event at John's farm, given that his daughter is still unwell and in bed. The farmer is taken aback by the outpouring of benevolence from the local community that Jessica's generosity of spirit has engendered.

Sure enough, a large gathering of local people assembles to sing Christmas carols outside Jessica's window; she is amazed to see so many familiar faces bearing gifts – Mrs McFarland, Dr Benton, Herb Drier and Sheriff Bert among them. As Sarah invites the carollers into the comfort of the house, Jessica watches uncertainly as John enters her room, his expression grim. Expecting further cynicism, she is surprised when he seems unusually reflective. Her father voices his disappointment that he has little to offer her in the way of Christmas presents this year, but he promises to try to return a little of the old magic to their holiday season to make the festivities more like they had been when Jessica's mother had still been alive. John reveals that he has recently discovered an old Christmas book that had been enjoyed by the family in years past, and Jessica asks him to read the closing paragraphs of 'Yes Virginia, There is a Santa Claus' – the famous editorial from an 1897 issue of New York newspaper *The Sun*, penned by Francis Pharcellus Church and extolling the virtues of the festive season. The wholehearted evocation of childhood wonder and belief in the mystery of magic deeply moves John, shaking his usual snappish façade. After Jessica's attempt to run away from home the previous night, John realises that he could not bear life without his daughter around and tells her that although he could deal with the thought of losing his farm, he can't cope with the prospect of being parted from his children.

John reveals that he has bought Prancer back from Drier and intends to take Jessica to Antler Ridge to fulfil her promise to Santa. Sadly, she tells him that she now realises that the reindeer is simply a woodland animal that has gone astray, but John tells her that the gathered townsfolk all believe him to belong to Santa and thus she should as well. Driving out into the backwoods, they soon reach their destination and John sets the reindeer free. Jessica parts tearfully with her friend, knowing that they may never see one another again. The reindeer happily races away into the forest, with Jessica following some distance behind. Tracing his hoof-prints, she and John pursue Prancer to the edge of a ravine, where the tracks mysteriously stop. Jessica is upset, worrying that the reindeer has fallen to its death from the steep precipice, but John tells her not to worry – it is Christmas Eve, there is a full moon, and this would be the perfect spot for Santa to reunite with his missing friend. Sure enough, Jessica hears the sound of sleigh-bells moments later, and looks up to see Prancer flying up to join Santa as he passes by overhead. Weepily calling out to the departing reindeer and asking him to never forget their time together, Jessica watches in wonder as Santa's sleigh heads towards Three Oaks as his Christmas deliveries for the year begin.

With its muted palette and moody lighting, *Prancer* was far removed from the kind of primary coloured extravaganza that is more readily expected from a family Christmas film. Featuring a narrative which presents far-reaching questions about personal faith in the intangible and deals more directly with emotion than many other movies of a similar type, *Prancer* was most definitely atypical festive fare for the time, and much critical attention was focused upon director Hancock's uncommon reliance upon realism given the film's enchanted central figure. While earlier films of the 1980s such as *One Magic Christmas* had addressed the issue of dealing with poverty over the holiday season, *Prancer* took the subject one step further; John makes plain the fact that his chosen vocation means that his income is at the mercy of many factors, natural and fiscal, and that while their economic situation may improve there are no guarantees that it will not worsen. There is no quick fix for the Riggs family's financial difficulties, though as a result of Jessica's wide-eyed sense of wonder at the power of the Christmas spirit we see an entire community rallying to support her belief in the intangible; in other words, the mutual amity that Prancer symbolises becomes significantly more important than the plausibility of him belonging to Santa Claus.

Due to the heightened social realism of *Prancer* (by the standard of many family Christmas films of the time, at any rate), Taylor's screenplay often exhibits a satisfying amount of character depth. The movie's nominal antagonists do not simply behave in a hostile or unfriendly fashion for the sake of it, as had been the case with *Gremlins's* wantonly belligerent Mrs Deagle, but rather have understandable reasons for their irritability. Dr Benton is irascible after the rigors of an all-night professional call-out, Mrs McFarland clearly struggles to cope following a spousal bereavement, and of course much emphasis is placed on John's difficulty in raising a young family while also facing the hard work of keeping his beleaguered business operating in trying economic times. By the end of the film, of course, these curmudgeonly characters find their worldview altered by Jessica and her single-minded promotion of festive magnanimity – a conversion expressed most manifestly in the literal transfiguration of Mrs McFarland. Naturally this was far from a ground-breaking approach for a Christmas film, especially one with a family focus, and yet Hancock injects enough stark pragmatism into proceedings to make this tale of seasonal transformation genuinely touching rather than laboriously conforming to stylistic expectation. As Kevin Thomas notes, the film's themes suited the director's ability to render emotional issues in a candid and authentic manner: '[*Prancer*] is the perfect Christmas gift for the whole family. [...] Director John Hancock is ideally cast for this material, for in films from *Bang the Drum Slowly* to the recent *Weeds* he has revealed an ability to deal with highly charged emotions with directness and without apology. Of course, *Prancer* [...] is a sentimental Christmas season heart-tugger, but it's not ashamed to be so, and it is not unduly manipulative'.[1]

Prancer was also somewhat unusual in its prominent discussion of personal faith – a topic which had been in general decline within Christmas cinema since at least the 1950s, largely due to a greater move towards secularisation in Western culture and a determination by film-makers to provide a greater sense of inclusiveness. Although, as was the case in many other Christmas films, the focus of belief in *Prancer* is Santa Claus and the existence of his reindeer, sleigh and North Pole workshop, Taylor's screenplay is surprising in its willingness (however subtle) to question why it is considered unusual to believe in the annual journey of St

Nicholas when billions of people worldwide ascribe to one form of religious faith or another. Carol explicitly voices the secularist view that every opinion has its own inherent worth, whether in favour of belief in the intangible or opposing it, yet Jessica feels threatened by her friend's agnosticism towards Santa and his herd of flying reindeer; her reasoning is that if the traditional Western Christmas legendarium can in any way be considered false then similarly her entire worldview is in danger of becoming tenuous and malleable. John makes plain the fact that festive iconography and the underlying ethos of the Christmas spirit is so important to Jessica that she continues to play yuletide music throughout the entire year – the inference being that as the holiday season was important to her late mother, honouring the tenets of Christmas has become Jessica's way of keeping her memory alive. When the film's emotional climax plays out, therefore, we witness more than simply the success of her mission to save Prancer but also the dissolution of her insecurities when she receives confirmation of her convictions. This provocative connection between the mechanics of religious belief and faith in the spirit of Christmas was certainly atypical for the time, though it would be examined again during the following decade in films such as *The Preacher's Wife* (Penny Marshall, 1996) and most especially the conclusion of Les Mayfield's John Hughes-scripted remake of *Miracle on 34*th *Street* (1994).

Misha Suslov's accomplished cinematography brings to life the film's snow-covered environs, accentuating their forbidding bleakness as well as the cosiness of the town's community-orientated atmosphere. Filming on location in the real Three Oaks, Michigan (though also featuring sequences shot in rural areas of Indiana and Illinois), Hancock particularly succeeds in articulating a child's wonder at

Christmas, and indeed at the world in general. From Mrs Fairburn's appealingly welcoming schoolroom to the frosty calm of the forest, Hancock conjures up an unmistakeable impression of commendably wide-eyed awe at even the more mundane aspects of small town life. There is no denying, however, that the overall visual tone of the film is often strikingly dark – a fact which lent it a distinctively melancholic quality, but similarly was not to the taste of many reviewers. Ralph Novak, for instance, was not alone in venturing the opinion that 'for most of this film, the audience is kept in the dark as to whether the title character is *the* Prancer, from Santa's team, out to see if he can cut it as a solo act the way Rudolph did. In fact the audience is kept in the dark in general, since almost every scene – whether it's in a dimly illuminated barn, a blizzard, a forest at night, an attic, a shed or the cab of a truck – is so badly lighted it's hard to see the actors' faces. It's a tribute to veteran TV writer Greg Taylor's script and, especially, to the acting of 9-year-old Ms Harrell that the movie remains engaging and palatably sweet – even when you can't see it very well'.[2] Not all appraisals of the film's shadowy visuals were negative in nature, however. Other commentators, such as Jay Boyar, would consider the ethereal tonality to ultimately prove beneficial to the effectiveness of Hancock's artistic aims: 'One of the least-merry Christmas movies ever made, *Prancer* casts a dark, potent spell. Though this film is too uneven to qualify as a seasonal classic, it finds its own wintry way to your heart. [...] Working from a simple (*E.T.*-influenced?) script by Greg Taylor, Hancock creates a haunting ambiance which, like the atmosphere of Dickens' *A Christmas Carol*, owes at least as much to Halloween as it does to Christmas'.[3]

Prancer also featured a restrained and often brooding original score by Maurice Jarre, which skilfully conveyed the narrative's divergence between naïve childhood innocence and the inflexibility of cynicism. In his lifetime Jarre was one of the film industry's most sought-after composers; the winner of three Academy Awards, he was nominated for Oscars on nine separate occasions for his achievements in film music. The prolific composer of scores for films as diverse as *Lawrence of Arabia* (David Lean, 1962), *Doctor Zhivago* (David Lean, 1965), *Topaz* (Alfred Hitchcock, 1969) and *Ryan's Daughter* (David Lean, 1970), he remained a formidable force throughout 1980s cinema by producing numerous well-received soundtracks including those for films such as *Top Secret* (Jim Abrahams, David Zucker and Jerry Zucker, 1984), *A Passage to India* (David Lean, 1984), *Witness* (Peter Weir, 1985), *Mad Max Beyond Thunderdome* (George Miller and George Ogilvie, 1985), *Fatal Attraction* (Adrian Lyne, 1987), and *Gorillas in the Mist* (Michael Apted, 1988). With *Prancer,* he excels in contrasting the moody strains of youthful dejection with themes evoking the eruption of miraculous phenomena into a cold and hitherto hard-edged world, and – in a manner similar to Hancock's style of direction – he never overplays his hand, thus preventing the score from straying into sickly sentimentality.

Key to the film's success is the talent of its young cast, most notably Rebecca Harrell and Ariana Richards as Jessica and Carol. Harrell would later become a producer and director as well as a high-profile environmental activist, whereas Richards would achieve worldwide fame a few years later in the role of 'Lex' Murphy in Steven Spielberg's *Jurassic Park* (1993). Both provide remarkable maturity within their performances; with Jessica's head permanently in the clouds while Carol attempts to keep her grounded, Harrell and Richards provide a realistic and balanced friendship which provides considerable charm. Both performers were nominated for Young Artist Awards (in the categories of Best Young Actress Starring in a Motion Picture and Best Young Actress Supporting Role in a Motion Picture respectively) for their appearance in *Prancer*, though Harrell was to receive the lion's share of critical praise. As Roger Ebert observed:

> This sounds like a cloying fantasy designed to paralyze anyone over the age of 9, but not the way it's told by director John Hancock and writer Greg Taylor. They give the film an unsentimental, almost realistic edge by making the father (Sam Elliott) into a tough, no-nonsense farmer who's having trouble raising his kids alone, and keeps laying down the law. And what really redeems the movie, taking it out of the category of kiddie picture and giving it a heart and gumption, is the performance by a young actress named Rebecca Harrell, as Jessica. She's something. She has a troublemaker's look in her eye, and a round, pixie face that's filled with mischief. And she's smart – a plucky schemer who figures out things for herself and isn't afraid to act on her convictions.[4]

Prancer's adult cast is similarly capable, headed by Sam Elliott as the abrupt family man John Riggs. Elliott had, by the late eighties, established himself as a charismatic actor with considerable range. His performances had included *The Games* (Michael Winner, 1970), *Lifeguard* (Daniel Petrie, 1976), *The Legacy* (Richard Marquand, 1978), *Fatal Beauty* (Tom Holland, 1987) and *Road House* (Rowdy Herrington, 1989), alongside many feature-length TV features. In later years he has won praise for his appearances in films such as

The Big Lebowski (Joel Coen and Ethan Coen, 1998), *We Were Soldiers* (Randall Wallace, 2002), and most especially in the role of Major General John Buford in *Gettysburg* (Ronald F. Maxwell, 1993). With John Riggs, Elliott produces a flawed but nevertheless relatable character who tries to conceal his hurt and vulnerabilities beneath a tetchy veneer. Fighting an uphill battle to care for his unruly children while also propping up a failing business, Elliott renders this luckless figure in a laudably sympathetic way, ensuring that even at his most disciplinarian extreme he never appears entirely unlikeable.

Though they share only brief screen time together, Elliott's performance is matched for distinctiveness by Cloris Leachman as the spiky, emotionally fragile Mrs McFarland. With a long-running career on stage, film and television that has spanned decades, Leachman has performed in many high-profile cinematic features which have included *Butch Cassidy and the Sundance Kid* (George Roy Hill, 1969), *The Last Picture Show* (Peter Bogdanovich, 1971), *Young Frankenstein* (Mel Brooks, 1974), *High Anxiety* (Mel Brooks, 1977) and *The Muppet Movie* (James Frawley, 1979), amongst dozens of others. A winner of an Academy Award and BAFTA Award, Leachman has also won a Daytime Emmy Award, Golden Globe Award and numerous Primetime Emmy Awards, alongside nominations for several more. Though *Prancer* was to be one of her lesser-known films, Leachman provides a fully engaged performance which is as fascinating as it is idiosyncratic. While Mrs McFarland essentially occupies the now-customary role of a character whose outlook is transformed (and her life subsequently improved) by the encroachment of the spirit of Christmas, the dramatic alteration of her temperament acts as a kind of counterpoint to the slowly-dawning realisation that is undergone by John; whereas the lonely widow's re-engagement with the community marks an unmistakeable social evolution, the wistful apple farmer undergoes an internal shift which is all the more profound for its subtlety.

While the human cast of *Prancer* received their fair share of critical approval, there was no such consensus when it came to the performance of Boo – the reindeer who portrayed the eponymous hero of the film. In an industry which famously sports the long-held adage 'never work with children or animals', *Prancer* may have featured an exemplary line-up of youth acting talent, but commentators were deeply divided with regards to the aptitude of its reindeer star. While some found the animal to exhibit the right kind of appeal to suitably epitomise the festive spirit, others such as Carrie Rickey were less convinced of Boo's acting abilities: '*Prancer*, a hodgepodge of *Heidi* and *Meet Me in St Louis*, takes as its premise that [a] broken reindeer ornament is magically brought to life. [...] As *Prancer*, Boo might be the least charismatic animal ever to make a major motion picture. Like a petting-zoo horse that has a horn pasted to its forehead so that it resembles a unicorn, Boo gives the impression of being a cow with one of mad King Ludwig's antler candelabra Krazy-Glued to her head. Surely it will be as disillusioning for youngsters as it is for adults that whenever Boo interacts with a human, the reindeer is being fed. This is an animal decidedly without magnetism'.[5]

Largely because of its unconventional style and narrative choices, *Prancer* split the critical community on its initial release. Some reviewers, such as Dave Kehr, felt that the blend of stark realism and uplifting quirkiness never quite melded in a satisfactory way, claiming that 'John Hancock's film does harbor a dark sensibility beneath its often excessive tinsel. Hancock is hard to classify. As a filmmaker, he seems compulsively drawn to sentimental material (*Weeds, Bang the Drum Slowly*) that can't help but contradict his unmistakable gifts for social realism and complex character psychology. *Prancer* is a typically perverse Hancock project. It's drawn from a screenplay (by Greg Taylor) that's meant to be slick and heartwarming in the Spielbergian mode, but rendered in a gritty, joyless style that sabotages most of the screenplay's themes'.[6] This scepticism was echoed by Caryn James, who expressed doubt that the film's contemplative deliberation of the transformative essence of Christmas would maintain the interest of the younger viewers who were likely to be its core audience: '*Prancer* tries so hard to scatter magic Christmas dust over the ordinary lives of a small farm community that it ends up shoveling it on; even the silver sprinkles on Christmas cookies glitter in the moonlight. *Prancer* is thoughtful, sincere and so laborious that adults can see the gears churning out Capraesque themes. For children, that creaky overload may translate into a mild case of the fidgets. [...] Its plodding competence can't provide that effortless magical touch that Christmas classics are made of'.[7]

A number of reviewers struggled with the issue of exactly where the incongruous *Prancer* should fit within the wider canon of festive cinema, noting its debt to the classics of the genre while remaining doubtful of the film's ability to attain the stature of the giants of past decades. Roger Hurlburt suggested that 'although never destined to take a place among such classic Christmas films as *It's a Wonderful Life, Miracle on 34th Street* and the Alistair [sic] Sim version of *A Christmas Carol,* John Hancock's *Prancer* undoubtedly will become a yuletide TV standby in years to come. [...]

[Sam] Elliott, sparkling snow scenes and the wonderful live reindeer are the saving graces for a film that might have become a classic. Less attention from the cranky Harrell and more on the film's notion of faith and the spirit of Christmas would have helped greatly'.[8] Still others, such as Rita Kempley, acknowledged the film's place within the wider confines of Christmas cinema while similarly conceding that it did not always quite measure up to the benchmark motion pictures which had inspired it: 'The pace, like Prancer, tends to limp, but by story's end, surely the cynics in both the town and the audience are convinced that reindeer can fly, given little girls' faith and a sprinkling of fairy dust. Oh, occasionally it's maudlin, which is also traditional, and the broken hearts of innocents bring sniffles. However, Harrell's brash debut, the use of animism and the story's sincerity add interest'.[9]

As *Prancer* has not achieved quite the same level of sustained interest as many other Christmas films of the eighties, its discussion amongst more recent commentators has been comparatively subdued. In the light of modern sensibilities, *Prancer*'s moodier qualities have become re-evaluated more positively by some reviewers; Richard Scheib, for example, remarks that 'you go in expecting the usual round of Yuletide nausea and a pandering to the sentiments and humour of family entertainment. Films of this ilk are usually drowned in sugary sentiment but contrarily *Prancer*'s sweetness is countered by a downbeat realism. It is nice, for once, to see a kiddie film that seats itself among some of the starker economic realities of the modern world'.[10] A few, conversely, have criticised the running time as seeming overlong by current standards, making the action appear ponderous as a result. David Nusair comments that *Prancer*'s duration may aid in the rendering of its characters, but counts against it in terms of momentum: 'Though the film could've easily been trimmed by a good 45-minutes and not lost a thing, the overlong running time does effectively ensure that the various characters become figures that we want to root for. [...] If it weren't for the almost interminable first hour, it seems likely that *Prancer* would be considered a mild Christmas classic. Still, it's hard to deny the film's uplifting conclusion, making it worth a look around the holidays'.[11]

While the gloomy rural vistas and forlorn reflections of bygone family Christmases would win praise from those reviewers who approved of *Prancer*'s singular lack of cloying slushiness, others felt that Hancock's creative choices took the avoidance of yuletide sentiment a little too far. Representative of this viewpoint was Andy Webb, who considered that '*Prancer* is one of the most depressing Christmas movies I have ever watched and I can't see what child would be able to sit through it, it is that depressing. It almost feels to me like that *Prancer* is a movie really for adults with its focus on a family with problems but as an adult I still found it depressing. [...] What this all boils down to is that if you like your Christmas movies bubbly and cheerful then give *Prancer* a wide birth as it is a depressing movie with a grim reality about it which makes me question whether it really is a children's movie. But if you like realism then *Prancer* might just be your sort of thing'.[12] By no means were all analyses to be quite so dubious of the film's merits, however. Though its profile may not be on par with the most popular Christmas movies of the 1980s, *Prancer* still has staunch defenders who continue to voice full-throated approval for its perceived virtues. Amongst the most vocal of these proponents is D.B. Bates, who in recent years has highlighted *Prancer*'s identified critical strengths while similarly recognising the film's status as something of an acquired taste:

> *Prancer* is a staggeringly great film on its own merits, but it's impossible to imagine happy families gathering together to watch it. It's not really a film that exists to be enjoyed so much as endured. [...] *Prancer* is a wonderful film, but it's not for anyone who wants to spend Christmas happy. 'Less miserable' is the best it can do for the already-miserable, and it'll just bring happy folks down. Nevertheless, if you want to feel an authentic emotional experience and a renewed sense of faith, you won't do any better than this film. Even the venerable masterpiece *It's a Wonderful Life* – itself incredibly downbeat until its last few minutes – doesn't plunder such dark depths or explore weighty themes with such subtlety and grace.[13]

More than a decade after the release of *Prancer*, a direct-to-video sequel was produced which continued the story of Santa's errant reindeer. *Prancer Returns* (Joshua Butler, 2001), which retained screenwriter Greg Taylor from the original, would feature an entirely new cast of characters and transferred the action to a different rural town in the United States. Featuring the reappearance of Prancer and introducing his young son (also named Prancer), even a supporting performance by celebrated actor Jack Palance was unable to assist the sequel in matching the modest critical standing of its predecessor.

Today, *Prancer* remains a genuine curio – a film which seems too introspective and downcast to take a place amongst the best festive cinema of the 1980s, and yet in its admirable exploration of personal belief, friendship and families under financial and emotional strain at Christmas it cannot help but seem highly individual amongst the more straightforward yuletide family fare of the time. While it is true that the film places surprising pressures on the audience's suppositions and endurance, those who bear with its sometimes-demanding narrative may well find themselves rewarded by an emotionally fulfilling experience. *Prancer* may only rarely be found in lists of favourite Christmas films, but those who are seeking a slightly offbeat festive experience which rejoices in community and companionship are likely to discover much to appreciate.

REFERENCES

1. Kevin Thomas, '*Prancer* an Unapologetic Christmas Heart-Tugger', in *The Los Angeles Times*, 17 November 1989.

2. Ralph Novak, '*Prancer*', in *People*, Vol. 32, No. 24, 11 December 1989.

3. Jay Boyar, '*Prancer* Puts Winter Solstice Back in Christmas', in *The Orlando Sentinel*, 17 November 1989.

4. Roger Ebert, '*Prancer*', in *The Chicago Sun-Times*, 17 November 1989.

5. Carrie Rickey, 'Girl Helps Out Santa's *Prancer*', in *The Philadelphia Enquirer*, 20 November 1989.

6. Dave Kehr, '*Prancer* a Contradictory Christmas Card', in *The Chicago Tribune*, 17 November 1989.

7. Caryn James, 'A Girl, a Reindeer and the Christmas Spirit', in *The New York Times*, 17 November 1989.

8. Roger Hurlburt, 'A Yuletide Standby Though Not a Classic', in *The South Florida Sun-Sentinel*, 18 November 1989.

9. Rita Kempley, '*Prancer*', in *The Washington Post*, 17 November 1989.

10. Richard Scheib, '*Prancer*', in *Moria: The Science Fiction, Horror and Fantasy Film Review*, 2013. *<http://moria.co.nz/fantasy/prancer-1989.htm>*

11.   David Nusair, '*Prancer*', in *ReelFilm*, 19 December 2004.
      <*http://www.reelfilm.com/prancer.htm*>

12.   Andy Webb, '*Prancer*', in *The Movie Scene*, 2003.
      <*http://www.themoviescene.co.uk/reviews/prancer-1989/prancer-1989.html*>

13.   D.B. Bates, '*Prancer*', in *The Parallax Review*, 24 December
      2010.
      <*http://www.theparallaxreview.com/on_cable/prancer.html*>

17

National Lampoon's Christmas Vacation (1989)

Hughes Entertainment/Warner Brothers

Director: Jeremiah Chechik
Producers: John Hughes and Tom Jacobson
Screenwriter: John Hughes

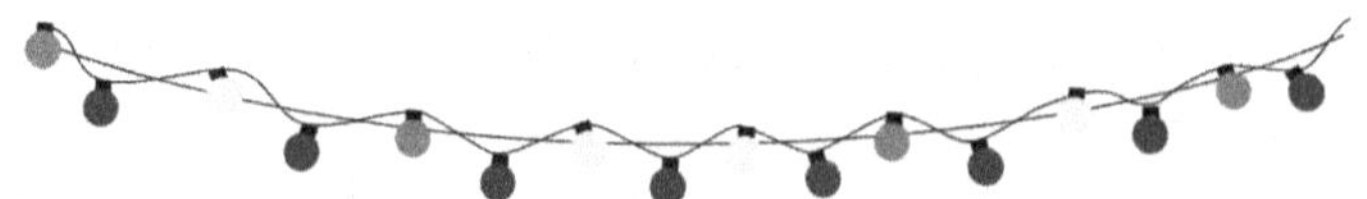

As one of the final festively-situated motion pictures to be released during the 1980s, *National Lampoon's Christmas Vacation* was to perform a surprisingly significant transitional function for Christmas cinema. While the film engages with the customary eighties theme of the philanthropic nature of the festive spirit conflicting with commercial self-interest, it also quite conspicuously laid the foundations for what would become one of the predominant concerns of Christmas movies in the nineties: namely the unchanging value of the family unit. Although family had been a topic addressed repeatedly throughout the 1980s – whether traditional, as in *A Christmas Story, Better Off Dead* or *One Magic Christmas*, or atypical, such as those of *Comfort and Joy, Santa Claus: The Movie* or even *Trading Places* – rarely was the conventional nuclear family to be quite so enthusiastically celebrated within a yuletide setting as it was in *National Lampoon's Christmas Vacation*.

The film was the third instalment in the popular *National Lampoon's Vacation* series, which had started in 1983 with Harold Ramis's hugely popular *National Lampoon's Vacation* and continued with Amy Heckerling's *National Lampoon's European Vacation* in 1985. Featuring Chevy Chase as the well-meaning but disastrously accident-prone Clark W. Griswold and Beverly D'Angelo as his long-suffering wife Ellen, the cycle had followed the Griswolds' holiday travels with their teenage son and daughter, and quickly attained a cult following amongst audiences. In *National Lampoon's Christmas Vacation*, however, the Griswolds would not be causing havoc across the United States or in continental Europe while on vacation, but (in a unique exception for the series) would instead be bringing the holiday season into their home as they enjoyed festive celebrations with their many eccentric relations. While the film marked a more family-oriented turn for the *Vacation* series in comparison to the first two ribald entries in the cycle, obvious care is taken to ensure that the yuletide theme and staunch emphasis on domestic merriment would not compromise laughs for the sake of emotional sentiment.

In the eyes of many commentators, the lasting success of the *National Lampoon's Vacation* series amongst audiences is largely accredited to the knowing, well-structured screenplays which were penned for the first three films in the cycle by acclaimed writer-director John Hughes. Achieving widespread success throughout the eighties for the cycle of teen movies that he directed (including *Sixteen Candles*, 1984; *Weird Science*, 1985; *The Breakfast Club*, 1985, and *Ferris Bueller's Day Off*, 1986) and those for which he had provided the screenplay (*Pretty in Pink*, 1986, and *Some Kind of Wonderful*, 1987), the original 1983 *National Lampoon's Vacation* was one of Hughes's earliest scripts for the cinema, and would become one of his most enduringly popular. The screenplay was based upon his short story 'Vacation '58' which had been published some years earlier in the satirical *National Lampoon* magazine, the seminal journal which went on to spawn a variety of spin-offs in many different media including films under the *National Lampoon* banner from the late seventies onwards. The darkly satirical tale of an overly enthusiastic father's determination to have the perfect holiday road trip – only to meet with catastrophe at every turn – struck a chord with many, due in large part to Chevy Chase's impeccable comic performance. This was followed a few years later by *National Lampoon's European Vacation*, which Hughes co-wrote (in a comparatively rare scripting collaboration) with screenwriter Robert Klane. That first sequel had seen the Griswolds winning a family package tour of Europe which, to put it mildly, does not go to plan. Hughes would return to solo screenwriting duties for the third *Vacation* film, as well as acting as one of the film's producers, and he appeared to take great pleasure in demonstrating that the Griswolds had no need to travel in order to cause mayhem; they were quite able to instigate utter chaos while remaining in the comfort of their own abode.

National Lampoon's Christmas Vacation was the first cinematic outing for director Jeremiah Chechik, who would later go on to direct films including *Benny and Joon* (1993), *Tall Tale* (1995) and *Diabolique* (1996) as well as a number of features for television. The film was also to see the return of not just the central cast regulars Chevy Chase and Beverly D'Angelo as Clark and Ellen Griswold, but also Randy Quaid and Miriam Flynn who were to reprise their roles as the ever-entertaining Johnson cousins (Ellen's relatives from Kansas) who had appeared to much acclaim in the original *Vacation* movie.

December has reached snowy Chicago, and devoted dad Clark W. Griswold (Chevy Chase) has taken his resigned but endlessly-patient wife Ellen (Beverly D'Angelo) and kids Audrey (Juliette Lewis) and Rusty (Johnny Galecki) on a long drive out of the suburbs to find their family Christmas tree – a vital element in marking the start of the year's festivities. Clark is absolutely determined to make the most of Christmas, whereas his long-suffering family seem reconciled to the notion of simply trying to survive it.

After a few close shaves with other drivers on the way into the wilderness, Clark eventually discovers the one flawless tree that he knows that will look perfect in the family's living room. There's only one problem: it's absolutely gargantuan. Having forgotten to take his saw with him on the journey, Clark and company are forced to dig out the huge tree (roots and all) and bring it home atop their car. Upon their return the outsized tree's massive scale leads to smug derision from Clark's stuck-up yuppie neighbours, Todd and Margo Chester (Nicholas Guest and Julia Louis-Dreyfus), though he wastes no time in giving as good as he gets in response. Ultimately, however, Todd and Margo's reservations may not have been entirely misplaced, which Clark discovers to his detriment when he unties the tree only to watch its unfettered branches shoot out and shatter his living room windows.

In bed at night, Ellen voices her concern about Clark's determination to host a large family gathering over the Christmas period, which will include her parents as well as his own. She points out that they all inevitably end up bickering over the most meaningless of small details whenever they meet, which cannot fail to put a strain on the festivities. Clark nevertheless assures her that everything will be fine, due to the unique ability of Christmas to reconcile misunderstandings. Ellen is far from convinced by his optimistic take on the situation.

At his upmarket office in the city the next day, Clark is looking forward to the lucrative Christmas bonus that he is due to receive from the food additive design department where he works. He reveals to one of his colleagues, Bill (Sam McMurray), that he has already put down a hefty deposit on a new pool that he intends to have installed in his back yard. Even the customary cantankerousness of his irritable boss Frank Shirley (Brian Doyle Murray) does nothing to dampen his festive spirit. After work, he goes shopping for some lingerie for Ellen at a large department store, though he quickly becomes tongue-tied when he finds himself being served by a beautiful sales assistant (Nicolette Scorsese).

Later, the family are each making their own individual preparations for Christmas when an ominous doorbell sounds, signalling that their relatives have arrived: Clark's parents Nora and Clark Senior (Diane Ladd and John Randolph) and Ellen's father and mother, Arthur and Frances Smith (E.G. Marshall and Doris Roberts). Even before the front door has been opened, they have already started arguing in earnest. Audrey, on the other hand, is more concerned by the unedifying prospect of them sleeping in her room during their stay – their intrusion on her privacy being judged as more than a little unwelcome.

Clark commandeers Rusty into helping him festoon the house with external Christmas lights. As ever, he goes completely overboard and enshrines every inch of the house's exterior with cabling and bulbs, though he suffers a number of minor injuries as he does so. At one point, Clark misses his footing on the ladder and clings to the house's guttering for dear life. As he does so, a sharp-edged length of ice is fired from a now-detached segment of gutter and smashes through the Chesters' bedroom window, destroying their expensive-looking stereo system. However, as the 'evidence' quickly melts as a result of the central-heating system in their home, they have no clue on their return as to what can have caused the damage (though of course, their suspicions quickly fall in the general direction of their hapless neighbour).

His work now complete, Clark insists on his relatives joining him outside in the freezing cold – in their pyjamas and dressing gowns – as he attempts to build their collective anticipation for the activation of the lights. However, much to Clark's dismay the big switch-on proves to be a damp squib when he activates the control... and nothing happens. His relatives are far from impressed by this disappointing non-event, leaving Clark frustrated. He resolves to keep checking every single light in the system until he can uncover the source of the hitch.

Having worked late into the night to find the fault in the lighting (though ultimately to no effect), Clark is late getting up the next morning. Still in his nightclothes, he sneaks up into the attic to hide away some Christmas presents. Frances, unaware of Clark's whereabouts, sees the open loft hatch and closes it to keep out the cold air. This leaves Clark trapped in the attic while all of his relatives go out shopping for the day. Fortunately, he soon finds some warm clothing in a dusty trunk, and in the process uncovers a bundle of home movies from the fifties and sixties on old film reels. He then whiles away the rest of the day watching scenes of his childhood Christmases on a projector, though the warmth of his nostalgia is rapidly dissipated when Ellen – oblivious to his position – pulls open the loft hatch and sends both Clark and the projector clattering down onto the first floor landing.

In the evening, Clark is still fastidiously checking every bulb on the exterior of the house – though still to no avail. As his aggravation mounts, Ellen eventually realises that he hasn't properly connected the power extension, and soon remedies the situation. Clark is stunned by the spectacle before him, which draws so much electricity that the nearby power station has to switch over to auxiliary nuclear reserves just to keep the rest of the city's lights on. The family are belatedly amazed by Clark's triumph, though it goes down less well with the Chesters who find themselves momentarily blinded by the intensity of the lights (especially as they were enjoying a romantic night in at the time of the switch-on).

The exhilaration of Clark's accomplishment is short-lived, however, as he unexpectedly finds himself face-to-face with the dreaded Cousin Eddie (Randy Quaid), who has driven up from Kansas in his ancient RV to spend the festive season with him. The cheerfully crude but always sociable Eddie has brought along his wife Catherine (Miriam Flynn) and a few of his extensive family, Ruby Sue (Ellen Hamilton Latzen) and Rocky (Cody Burger), along with his somewhat overly-familiar dog Snots. Clark is both startled and dismayed to see Eddie and his brood, not least as no-one had actually invited them. However, Eddie soon makes it clear that he's planning to stick around for a while, possibly even beyond the holiday season, much to Clark's consternation.

Resigned to the fact that Eddie and his family are there to stay for Christmas, and potentially longer besides, Clark takes them along with his own kids to a night of sledging. Clark intends to make use of a secret weapon – a prototype kitchen lubricant that his company has been developing. He treats the base of his sledge with the potent lotion in the hope of reducing its friction against the ground. However, it works rather too well, and he ends up careening through the air at a worryingly fast velocity. Tearing into a forest and then along a busy road at a rate of knots, Clark is fortunate to get through the encounter in one piece.

Back at work, just before he and his colleagues leave for the Christmas season, Clark is worrying about the fact that he still hasn't received his bonus. Bill assures him that he has just heard that an envelope has been delivered to his home by courier, and that surely Clark's own notification letter can't be far behind it. Returning home afterwards, Clark stares out of the kitchen window and daydreams about his family enjoying themselves in the still-to-be-installed pool. He then lets his imagination run riot, picturing the stunning lingerie saleswoman from the department store frolicking on the springboard, before he is interrupted by Ruby Sue. His little niece is concerned that she and her brother won't be receiving any Christmas gifts – the previous year, even although they had both been on their best behaviour, no presents had been forthcoming on Christmas Day. Clark feels humbled by Ruby Sue's obvious gratitude at being allowed to stay at his family's house, and makes her a promise that he'll prove to her not only that Santa Claus is real, but also that jolly old Saint Nick will bring presents for her and Rocky.

The next morning, after Clark and Ellen watch dumbfounded as Eddie empties the contents of his motorhome's chemical toilet into the street's storm drain, they jointly decide to lend Eddie and Catherine some financial aid in order to give their children some Christmas presents. When Clark later broaches the subject with Eddie, however, he is surprised to find not only that he readily accepts the idea, but that he already has a list made out – including gifts for Catherine – which he promptly hands over to the flabbergasted Clark.

Christmas Eve arrives, and with it comes the elderly Uncle Lewis and Aunt Bethany (William Hickey and Mae Questel). Lewis is tetchy and argumentative, while Bethany is cheerful but permanently bewildered. Clark and Ellen are taken aback to discover that Lewis and Bethany have (accidentally or otherwise) wrapped up their pet cat as a Christmas gift, and discreetly let it loose. Combined with the pressures of all their other guests, the cranky Lewis's irascibility taxes even Clark's good nature to the absolute limit. Christmas dinner follows shortly after, though it quickly transpires that the turkey has been grossly overcooked and is now little more than a desiccated husk. However, as Catherine was responsible for cooking it, the family chew their way through the remnants in order to spare her feelings. In the meantime, Lewis and Bethany's cat is gnawing on the power cord of the Christmas tree's lights and inadvertently electrocutes itself underneath one of the living room chairs. Clark and Eddie circumspectly remove the evidence from the house, during which Clark notices a worrying gaseous vapour starting to emanate from the drain where Eddie had emptied his chemical toilet earlier.

Clark has barely rejoined the dinner table when he spots an unusual flash from the living room – Lewis has accidentally burnt down the Christmas tree with his omnipresent cigar, scarcely avoiding incineration himself. Just as Rusty begins to worry that Clark is heading for one of his legendary meltdowns, a knock at the door signals the late arrival of the envelope containing Clark's bonus. However, upon opening it – amongst much fevered expectation from the rest of the family – he is astonished to discover that rather than a cash windfall, the envelope actually contains an annual membership to the Jelly of the Month Club. This proves to be the final straw, causing Clark to fly into a hysterical rage. He angrily proclaims that all he wants for Christmas is his boss, Frank Shirley, brought from his affluent home to account for his blatant miserliness in depriving all of his employees of their expected cash bonus. Eddie begins to look thoughtful, and slips away soon afterwards.

Still slightly unhinged, Clark promptly goes into the garden and cuts down a conveniently-placed tree with a chainsaw in order to provide a replacement for the char-grilled original. In the process, he manages to smash the Chesters' dining room window, though he shows little sign of remorse at this (or even any awareness of it happening). As Clark embellishes the tree with hastily-sourced replacement decorations, he quickly discovers a hyperkinetic squirrel hiding amongst the branches. A panicked frenzy ensues as the family try to evade the squirrel while it races through the house, a chase which culminates when the front door is thrown open and the interloping rodent jumps onto Margo, who has arrived to confront Clark about her broken window. The squirrel is soon followed by the frantic Snots, who dives onto Margo in order to attack the fleeing animal. Now bruised and tattered, the livid neighbour eventually withdraws before she can be injured any further.

With the ground floor of the house now virtually in ruins thanks to the squirrel debacle, Clark and Ellen's parents all decide that they want to leave. But Clark, now nearing a full-fledged state of mania, is having none of it. For a quiet life, everyone settles down in front of the fire while Clark recites 'A Visit from St Nicholas' for the benefit of the younger members of the family. But before he can get too far beyond ''Twas the Night Before Christmas', Eddie returns with a surprise guest – none other than Frank Shirley, in his pyjamas, gagged and tied up with ribbon. Shirley is initially incensed, threatening to fire Clark and have Eddie jailed. However, when Clark elaborates on how cheated he feels at having been unexpectedly deprived of his bonus – which he has relied upon for years – a sheepish Shirley relents and decides to reinstate it... with a generous additional increase of 20%. Clark is stunned at this unexpected turnaround in fortune. However, his elation is merely transitory, for immediately afterwards a police SWAT team arrives – having been called by Shirley's concerned wife Helen (Natalia Nogulich) – and hold Clark and his family at gunpoint. When Helen discovers the extent of her husband's penny-pinching, however, she sides with the Griswolds – as do the police. The charges are soon dropped against Eddie and the rest of the family, much to everyone's relief. As the unexpected guests get set to depart, Clark reflects wistfully that in spite of everything that has gone wrong – and the fact that his home now looks like a warzone – he still feels fortunate to be spending Christmas with his extended family. Not even the final sight of Uncle Lewis accidentally igniting the noxious fumes caused by Eddie's misuse of the storm drain can dampen his spirits, as the resulting explosion sends his garden decoration of Santa Claus, his sleigh and reindeer flying into the air, accompanied by Aunt Bethany's impromptu rendering of 'The Star-Spangled Banner'.

With its all-encompassing festive spirit and pervasive sense of geniality, *National Lampoon's Christmas Vacation* was an effective deviation from the earlier bawdy entries in the *Vacation* series, relying on the comic strengths of Clark's infectious enthusiasm to deliver the perfect holiday season while also providing plenty of keen observational insight into the delights (and potential pitfalls) of a family Christmas. Hughes's well-judged device of a traditional Advent calendar counting down towards Christmas Eve is highly effective in leading the audience towards the apex of the festivities – and the height of Clark's ever-building hysteria. Yet in spite of the film's sense of warmth and good nature, Hughes and Chechik provide more than ample touches of the requisite *Vacation* anarchy to save the film from ever risking a headlong dive into an overly-romanticised assessment of the holiday season. Once again based on one of Hughes's short stories – in this case, 'Christmas '59', which had first appeared in the December 1980 issue of *National Lampoon* magazine – there is an undeniable departure from the darker humour of the earlier two entries in the cycle in order to make the film a more family-oriented product. Robert Horton, for example, voiced the opinion that 'there has been a decided shift toward the sentimental. Whereas the original *National Lampoon's Vacation* was cruelly funny (for instance, the family dog was tied temporarily to the rear bumper of the car, then remembered about 50 miles later), the new one, *National Lampoon's Christmas Vacation*, is soft at its center. [...] In the end, Clark discovers the true meaning of Christmas. Everything ends, amazingly, with hugs and kisses and warm yuletide feelings. [...] Some people could pull this off, but Chevy Chase was funnier as a smartass'.[1]

In spite of the perceptive lightening of the film's comedic approach in comparison to the previous movies in the series, there are still welcome flourishes of the trademark pandemonium which had made the first *Vacation* features so popular amongst audiences. Just as Clark and Eddie drink egg-nog from a pair of matching Marty Moose mugs (Marty having been the mascot of Walley World in the original *Vacation* film), the audience is provided with plenty of evidence – from Clark's manic sleigh-ride to the later slapstick of the squirrel infiltrator – that this is undisputedly Christmas the way that only a *National Lampoon* movie could depict it. Chevy Chase once again dons his Chicago Bears baseball cap, which had featured in his past appearances with the Griswold clan, while Clark's unexpected home movie show hints at the genesis of Hughes's screenplay: the label on the old film reel he uncovers reads 'Xmas '59', echoing the title of the short fiction which inspired the events of *Christmas Vacation*'s narrative.

Although the film centres upon Clark's single-minded obsession to ensure that everyone staying at his home is treated to the perfect festive holiday – whether they actually want one or not – the main source of conflict comes from the heartless Frank Shirley (a brilliantly aloof performance from Brian Doyle Murray). Like so many other corporate figures in eighties Christmas films, Shirley considers the holiday season nothing more than an inconvenience at best, and his tight-fisted betrayal of the workforce is foreshadowed just enough throughout the film that, when it is eventually revealed, the audience is aware of just how much the bonus meant to Clark... and how deceived he feels at his self-important boss's barefaced dishonesty. The treachery is compounded, of course, by the fact that Clark was relying on the expected cash injection not solely for his own ends, but – once again – to provide selflessly for his whole family. The film does not seek to make any weighty point about corporate exploitation of employees or the encroachment of commercialism into the festive season: the Griswolds were much too seasoned a family of consumers to generate much scepticism concerning the growing role of the free market in determining the way that the modern Christmas was conveniently packaged for the buying public. However, the film does firmly elevate the importance of the family unit over the expediency of business or profit. When Shirley is kidnapped, it is not just Eddie who is held accountable, but rather the whole extended family which stands united behind Clark and his benevolent (but dim-witted) cousin. Likewise, when it becomes apparent that even Shirley's own wife is appalled at his short-changing of his personnel, it is suggested that there are some things – such as the much-prized tradition of the Christmas bonus – which must be considered sacrosanct even in the face of the seemingly-unstoppable march of corporate self-interest. As Shirley is grudgingly forced to admit, the world of business may be concerned with profit and domination of the market, but this is ultimately only made possible by the individual workers – a labour force which is easy to regard as a faceless conglomeration, but much less regularly as distinct people who all have their own hopes and dreams. Thus Shirley must face up to the inescapable truth of his actions' results when it is reflected in the light of Christmas: that while his budgetary reductions may have looked appealing on the pages of a ledger, they have caused dismay for employees, their families, and anyone who was reliant on the expected December payout. Fortunately for the Griswolds and their relatives, Shirley proves capable of enlightenment with an immediacy that had so often evaded the other corporate antagonists of Christmas films in the 1980s (and, indeed, in many entries in the genre beforehand).

Chevy Chase once again slips effortlessly back into the role of the good-hearted but mania-tinged Clark Griswold. Delivering a pitch-perfect performance as the perpetually unlucky father who just wants to deliver a wonderful holiday season (no matter how ill-fated his attempts may be), Chase is on top form throughout. From the running gag with the tree sap – Clark's hands end up sticking to everyone and everything after he arranges his new Christmas tree – to his exquisitely ham-fisted delivery as he falteringly tries to buy lingerie for Ellen from an attractive department store attendant, Chase's portrayal of the character constantly impresses with a continuously witty, judicious delivery and in his endless capacity for physical comedy. Chase, who had achieved enormous popularity for his appearances and writing for NBC television's *Saturday Night Live* throughout the seventies, was well established as one of the comedy icons of 1980s American film, having appeared in films which included *Caddyshack* (Harold Ramis, 1980), *Spies Like Us* (John Landis, 1985), and Michael Ritchie's *Fletch* (1985) and *Fletch Lives* (1989). He had also been nominated for the Best Motion Picture Acting Debut (Male) Award at the Golden Globes for his performance in Colin Higgins's comedy thriller *Foul Play* (1978).

There is no weak link in the supporting cast either, starting with Beverly D'Angelo as the ever-accommodating Ellen. Having appeared in prominent roles in *Annie Hall* (Woody Allen, 1977), *Hair* (Milos Forman, 1979), *Finders*

Keepers (Richard Lester, 1984), and *High Spirits* (Neil Jordan, 1988), D'Angelo had been nominated for an Emmy Award in the Outstanding Supporting Actress category for her performance as Stella DuBois Kowalski in John Erman's television adaptation of Tennessee Williams's *A Streetcar Named Desire* (1984). She again makes the most of Ellen's laconic drollness and silent despair at Clark's well-intentioned exploits, though it could be argued that the character has less to do in this film when compared to other entries in the series. Johnny Galecki and Juliette Lewis are both effective as the long-suffering Griswold kids, articulating well the frustration of warring siblings faced with the unwelcome intrusion of older relatives. Lewis, who would later be nominated for an Academy Award, Emmy and Golden Globe, was at the time best known for appearances in *My Stepmother is an Alien* (Richard Benjamin, 1988) and *The Runnin' Kind* (Max Tash, 1989). Galecki, who had also briefly appeared in *Prancer* the same year, would go on to win a Young Artist Award in 1994 (along with three other nominations for prizes between 1992 and 1995), and has been nominated for a Primetime Emmy Award and Golden Globe Award, amongst other industry plaudits. Subsequently performing in films such as *Suicide Kings* (Peter O'Fallon, 1997), *I Know What You Did Last Summer* (Jim Gillespie, 1997) and *Vanilla Sky* (Cameron Crowe, 2001), he has become particularly well-recognised in popular culture for his recurring role as David Healy in ABC's situation comedy *Roseanne* (1988-97) between 1992 and 1997, and more recently as series regular Dr Leonard Hofstadter in CBS's science-themed sitcom *The Big Bang Theory* (2007-).

William Hickey and Mae Questel are both memorable as the crotchety, cigar-chomping uncle and affably ditzy aunt respectively; Questel had been the original voice of animated characters Betty Boop and Olive Oyl, whereas Hickey – notable as the amiable barfly in *The Producers* (Mel Brooks, 1968) – had been nominated for an Academy Award for his role as Don Corrado Prizzi in John Huston's *Prizzi's Honor* (1985). However, the film's standout performance is from Randy Quaid, who comes close to stealing the show as the inimitable Cousin Eddie Johnson. If anything, Eddie is even more unhygienically off-putting than had been the case on his appearance in the first *Vacation*, and Quaid makes full use of his character's greatly-expanded screen time, brilliantly articulating both sponging guile and ingenuous charm. Managing to tread an impossibly fine line which allows Eddie to appear both repellent and oddly endearing at the same time, Quaid encourages a smile in just about every scene that he appears in.

Although the film takes place almost exclusively in one snowy suburban locale, Chechik is skilled in making full use of every situation for well-timed comedy effect. William D. Crump observes that 'sporting a loose plot, *National Lampoon's Christmas Vacation* satirizes all of the traditional family values of the holiday',[2] and certainly there is an effort to accommodate many yuletide customs throughout the film – from Clark's high-wire stunts as he staples Christmas lights to his roof all the way through to the slow-motion demolition of the Chesters' upmarket but pretentiously-decorated home. Hughes's script also makes good use of the intermittent interludes away from the Griswold house, be they at Clark's inner-city office or the area's pleasant woodland regions, and he employs them efficiently in a way that enhances the film's festive flavour rather than diminishing it. Angelo Badalamenti provides a dynamic score which nicely accompanies *Christmas*

Vacation's sense of frenzied action, as well as providing the obligatory holiday atmosphere whenever required. (Badalamenti was later to achieve huge success with his haunting theme music for David Lynch's mystery drama *Twin Peaks*, broadcast on ABC between 1990 and 1991.) Given the static nature of the family Christmas celebrations, Lindsay Buckingham's 'Holiday Road' – a song which became so prominent in early Griswold outings – is nowhere to be heard this time around. In its place, however, is the film's lively title song, 'Christmas Vacation', which is performed by Mavis Staples.

Although *National Lampoon's Christmas Vacation* exudes seasonal charm, not all contemporary critics were convinced of the film's merits. At the time of its release, some reviewers believed that the film was not fully the sum of its parts, leading to accusations that the narrative occasionally seemed disjointed. Roger Ebert, for example, claimed that 'the parts don't fit. Maybe the movie's problem is with the director, Jeremiah S. Chechik, a first-timer at feature length, although he has won awards for his TV commercials. The screenplay was written by John Hughes, whose *Planes, Trains and Automobiles* was a masterful comedy about two travelers trying to find their way home for Thanksgiving, but with the Griswold saga he seems to set up sequences that Chechik isn't able to make pay off. You have the odd sensation, watching the movie, that it's straining to get off the ground but simply doesn't have the juice'.[3] Ebert's scepticism was not isolated; Janet Maslin also suggested that the film suffered from uneven humour and flaccid presentation: 'Fatigue is in the air. This third look at the quintessentially middle-American Griswold family, led by Clark (Mr Chase) and the very patient Ellen (Beverly D'Angelo) is only a weary shadow of the original *National Lampoon's Vacation*, which found a lot to laugh at as it followed the dopey paterfamilias Clark and his quarrelsome brood on a hellish cross-country journey in their station wagon. The new film does little more than reintroduce these familiar characters [...] and let them get on one another's nerves in earnest'.[4]

Not all appraisals at the time of release were quite so doubtful of the film's virtues, however. Some industry journals, such as *Variety* magazine, voiced greater approval of the likeable ensemble cast, pronouncing that: 'Solid family fare with plenty of yocks, *National Lampoon's Christmas Vacation* is Chevy Chase and brood doing what they do best. [...] For the most part, helmer Jeremiah Chechik makes an adept debut, injecting plenty of energy and spirit'.[5] Others, including Rita Kempley, were to praise the film's entertaining evocation of the potential drawbacks of the holiday season, commending the way that Hughes and Chechik identify the shortcomings of Christmas with the family as well as extolling its advantages: 'Chase presides amiably over this uneven but affable slapstick comedy, a decked-out domestic caper that both celebrates and debunks ye olde yuletide chestnuts. Here, loving grandparents grouse about their hemorrhoids before a roaring TV set, while a cousin's dog, Snots, spills garbage over the glistening kitchen floor. The kids fuss about sharing their rooms with the relatives. "It's Christmas. We're all miserable", says Ellen, just as Clark, having finished stringing 2,500 outdoor lights, slides off the roof. Of course, this is but a small setback in Clark's quixotic quest for the perfect Christmas, a search that becomes a chain of handyman's mishaps and neighborhood feuds, a veritable flurry of foolishness. Now and again, it will sleigh you. Now and again, it won't. But the ribaldry eventually snowballs'.[6]

With the passing years, modern commentators have generally tended towards more favourable criticism of *Christmas Vacation*. Ryan Cracknell's analysis has been among the most positive of appraisals, emphasising the enduring popularity of the film since its initial appearance: '*National Lampoon's Christmas Vacation* is the ultimate family holiday film, playing on both the heart strings and the horror to capture a genuine Christmas spirit. [...] Scene after scene, *Christmas Vacation* is so consistently hilarious, it brings a lot of otherwise decent comedies down a level when compared next to it. But the comedy wouldn't be nearly as good or memorable if it weren't for the heart of Clark Griswold'.[7] Similarly, others such as Daniel Stephens have admired the nostalgia value of the film's distinctly contemporary take on the traditional concerns of the Christmas movie, remarking that '*Christmas Vacation* is probably so well-liked because it captures the spirit of the festive period, and this is almost entirely down to the writing of John Hughes. He's proven time and time again that familial values, growing-up and the little things in life, are what he's good at pointing his magnifying glass at, and while this particular film is more lightweight than some of his work, all these things are prevalent during the period where Santa starts oiling up the sleigh, and fattening up the reindeer. It's a film easy to enjoy, and even easier to relate to, whether it's problems with the Christmas tree, Grandparents arriving but not being altogether there, the decorations, the gifts, the turkey, Hughes effortlessly encapsulates the magic of the period, and does it with sugar-coated glee'.[8]

Although the reputation of *National Lampoon's Christmas Vacation* has increased in stature within the genre of festive cinema since its release, dissenting voices remain as to the deservingness of its elevated status. A few commentators, such as Chris Hicks, have advanced the claim that the film is not fully able to endure close critical scrutiny outside of its festive context, pointing out that 'the film is at its most amusing when it is merely lampooning traditional Christmas rituals – getting a tree, decorating the house with lights, having the family in for turkey dinner, discovering that a wrapped gift contains a live cat, etc. – replete with inventive sight gags and Chase's patented mugging. [...] Weighing the good with the bad, this picture is worth a look for Chase fans, but it may not hold up to repeat viewings'.[9] Reviewers such as Andy Webb, by comparison, have shifted critical emphasis, echoing concerns about the film's longevity but pinning censure on claims of a shapeless, episodic structure to the narrative: 'The trouble is that whilst writer John Hughes tried to bring together various Christmassy events from decorating the house through to cooking the dinner they don't really link together. So *Christmas Vacation* ends up basically a series of set pieces, each focussing [sic] on one element of Christmas and whilst all of them have their humour some are definitely funnier than others. It just doesn't quite come together and so whilst a good movie to put on in the background whilst doing something Christmassy *Christmas Vacation* is not a movie which demands your attention'.[10]

Overall, however, the relentless good humour of *National Lampoon's Christmas Vacation* and its place within the wider *Vacation* cycle have continued to win it admirers, with many singling out Hughes's witty dialogue and the emotional warmth of the script for particular approval. James Berardinelli acknowledges this endurance with audiences, noting that '*Christmas Vacation* is considered by many film critics to be a "guilty pleasure" – largely because some of the set pieces are as hilarious as they are juvenile. [...] Despite its failings, it is funny. Oh, and there aren't that many non-saccharine Christmas films that are vaguely watchable. If we take away *Christmas Vacation*, what are we supposed to substitute for it? [...] For those who are tired of peace on earth and goodwill to men, the third outing of the Griswolds offers a reminder that, for some, the real meaning of the season has as much to do with annoying the neighbors and putting up with the relatives as it does with something more wholesome'.[11] This carefully-maintained balance – comedy that is never allowed to drift too far into subversiveness, and sentiment which is sparingly employed to avoid treacly mawkishness – is perhaps at the heart of the film's lasting success. Sandwiched between Hughes's knowing late-eighties comedies (such as *She's Having a Baby*, 1987, and *Uncle Buck*, 1989) and his later drift into family comedies (including the screenplays for Chris Columbus's *Home Alone*, 1990, and Peter Faiman's *Dutch*, 1991), the film marked a well-defined switch in pace for his own narrative approach as a writer-producer just as it was to straddle two very different eras of festive movie-making. As Kevin Matthews observes, there are a number of reasons why the film has come to achieve its status as a contemporary classic of the Christmas movie genre:

> While so many of the older Christmas classics (especially those from the 1940s – a goldmine for festive favourites) really manage to promote the spirit of Christmas and the values that it really centres around, many other movies have produced equally great results with very different angles. Some make a point of bursting the bubble of commercialism, some provide an adaptation or riff of the classic Charles Dickens tale, others show that Christmas is more than just one day

full of traditions and excess – it's a state of mind. *Christmas Vacation* stands as a modern classic in the subgenre of festive movies because it looks specifically at the highs and lows, the amazing rollercoaster ride, that every family goes through when trying to provide a memorable day for their loved ones. The atmosphere can be warm and loving and bright but the preparation takes hard work, the cooking can become an exercise in precision timing and stress runs under everything like lumpy underlay beneath a pretty carpet. The script by John Hughes stays in line with all that viewers already know about the Griswold family but then manages to take every common Christmas practice (picking the family tree, putting up the lights, sledding, cooking the turkey) and drain every ounce of comic eggnog it can out of each and every one.[12]

Christmas Vacation was followed by a belated made-for-television spin-off, Nick Marck's *National Lampoon's Christmas Vacation 2: Cousin Eddie's Island Adventure* (2003), written by Matty Simmons. Although Chase and D'Angelo did not feature this time around, the TV movie did star Randy Quaid and Miriam Flynn, once again reprising their roles as Eddie and Catherine Johnson, as well as Dana Barron as Audrey Griswold (who had first portrayed the character in 1983's *National Lampoon's Vacation*). There was also a fourth film in the main *Vacation* series, Stephen Kessler's *Vegas Vacation* (1997), which was an entertaining but critically under-rated return to the traditional holiday format of the original film. Although the film was not to carry the *National Lampoon* brand name, and like *Cousin Eddie's Island Adventure* it was to feature no involvement from John Hughes, it did retain key cast members of the *Vacation* series including Chevy Chase, Beverly D'Angelo, Randy Quaid and

Miriam Flynn. In more recent years the series has been revived with Jonathan Goldstein and John Francis Daley's *Vacation* (2015), a profitable sequel – and reboot of sorts – to the original cycle in which Clark and Ellen's now-adult son Rusty decides to take his own family on a road trip to California which echoes the journey of the original 1983 film. Starring Ed Helms and Christina Applegate, the film featured Beverly D'Angelo and Chevy Chase in cameo appearances as the retired Ellen and Clark.

Hughes and Chechik's wryly-observed take on the traditional family Christmas, with all of its irritations as well as its many gratifications, was an inspired one which continues to stand the test of time; the film has been released many times on VHS, on DVD both as a standalone release and as part of various compilation packs, and more recently on Blu-Ray and via Internet streaming services. With its entertaining medley of oddball relatives and chaotic comedy situations, the film's continual emphasis on the importance of the family marked a turning point for Christmas films. With a new decade dawning, so too was there to be a shift in focus for festive film-making – a change in emphasis which would have new and sweeping ramifications for the genre.

The release of *National Lampoon's Christmas Vacation* came alongside that of the last festive films to appear in cinemas in the 1980s, marking the end of a decade which had seen the Christmas movie brought back into the mainstream cultural consciousness as never before. The eighties had been a period of unprecedented experimentation and cross-generic fusion for festive cinema after the long wilderness period of the 1960s and '70s, and film-makers had risen to the challenge of making long-running Christmas customs relevant to a fast-changing multicultural society. In essence, the fresh and innovative interpretations of holiday season traditions were to build upon the groundwork laid by various thematically inventive films of the previous two decades, only in a much bolder and more persuasive way, ensuring that the Christmas cinema of the eighties was to more fully embrace the reconfiguration of the genre's tropes which had been established throughout its golden age in the forties and fifties. In many Christmas films of the 1980s, festive traditions were not simply accepted at face value but would instead be held up to scrutiny, often being appraised satirically or suspiciously. Yet more often than not, these movies wound up celebrating the very customs that they were dissecting, acknowledging their continuing significance even in a world which had changed beyond recognition from the social environment of the post-War years.

While the family unit was still of central importance to many Christmas films, not least *National Lampoon's Christmas Vacation*, there was a growing acknowledgement that the traditional nuclear family was now accompanied by many different types of domestic situations – and each of them had an equal claim to the Christmas spirit. This journey from commemorating the long-held customs of the Western household through to embracing different configurations of the family unit was crucial to the concerns of 1990s festive filmmaking, but the seed had been firmly planted in the eighties. While 1980s Christmas cinema regularly explored issues of social isolation (*Christmas Evil*, *Better Off Dead*, *Scrooged*) and triumph over adversity (*Trading Places*, *Gremlins*, *Comfort and Joy*), its core theme was arguably a renewed scepticism of unfettered consumerism and the ways in which it risked undermining the true meaning of Christmas – altruism, peace and goodwill. This strategy was inevitably to call upon the apprehensions that had been raised by many classics of the genre some decades beforehand, albeit reshaped to address the anxieties of the present day. What became more prevalent, however, was a heightened acknowledgement of the fact that the family unit itself was at risk from the dehumanising effects of unrestrained and unfeeling capital gain; films as dissimilar as *One Magic Christmas* and *Die Hard* deal with ways in which the self-serving interests of indifferent employers came into conflict with the structural integrity of the family unit, the inference being that society was becoming a less caring and more hard-hearted place as a result. The following decade would take its cue from this thematic foundation, not least in its emphasis on how cultural understanding of the family was changing and the subsequent investigation of what this gradual but fundamental shift meant for the underlying topicality and social relevance of Christmas cinema in the years ahead.

Today, while several Christmas films of the 1980s have fallen into obscurity to all but the most seasoned aficionados of the genre, many are hailed as classics and continue to be enjoyed by audiences on an annual basis. Features such as *Trading Places, A Christmas Story, Gremlins, Scrooged* and *National Lampoon's Christmas Vacation* have all regularly been held up by various commentators as gold standard examples of the decade's festive cinema, and their inviting amalgam of nostalgia, script quality, production values and the high standard of their performances has meant that they have prevailed within popular culture long after the time of their initial production. The eighties marked a unique period in film-making, and this was most certainly true for the Christmas films which were released throughout the decade. Sometimes audacious, often affecting, occasionally humorous and frequently compelling, the 1980s produced some unforgettable festive cinema; at its best, these films reflected some aspect of the pioneering originality of the genre's golden age, and the striking effect of this decade's reinvigoration of the Christmas movie would continue to have a far-reaching creative impact on productions for many years to come.

REFERENCES

1. Robert Horton, '*National Lampoon's Christmas Vacation*', in *What a Feeling!*, 23 December 2011 [1989]. <https://eightiesmovies.wordpress.com/2011/12/23/national-lampoons-christmas-vacation/>

2. William D. Crump, *The Christmas Encyclopedia*, 3rd edn (Jefferson: McFarland and Company, 2013), p.301.

3. Roger Ebert, '*National Lampoon's Christmas Vacation*', in *The Chicago Sun-Times*, 1 December 1989.

4. Janet Maslin, 'On *Vacation* Once Again', in *The New York Times*, 1 December 1989.

5. *Variety* Staff, '*National Lampoon's Christmas Vacation*', in *Variety*, 1 December 1989.

6. Rita Kempley, '*National Lampoon's Christmas Vacation*', in *The Washington Post*, 1 December 1989.

7. Ryan Cracknell, '*National Lampoon's Christmas Vacation*', in *Movie Views*, 22 December 2003. <http://movieviews.ca/national-lampoons-christmas-vacation>

8. Daniel Stephens, '*National Lampoon's Christmas Vacation*', in *DVD Times*, 17 November 2003. <http://www.dvdtimes.co.uk/content.php?contentid=6068>

9. Chris Hicks, '*National Lampoon's Christmas Vacation*', in The Deseret News, 16 December 2002.

10.   Andy Webb, 'National Lampoon's Christmas Vacation', in *The Movie Scene*, 2003.
       <http://www.themoviescene.co.uk/reviews/christmas-vacation/christmas-vacation.html>

11.   James Berardinelli, '*National Lampoon's Christmas Vacation*', in *ReelViews*, 13 February 2001.
       <http://www.reelviews.net/reelviews/national-lampoon-s-christmas-vacation>

12.   Kevin Matthews, '*Christmas Vacation*', in *FlickFeast*, 9 December 2011.
       <http://flickfeast.co.uk/reviews/film-reviews/christmas-vacation-1989/>

18

Other 1980s Christmas Films

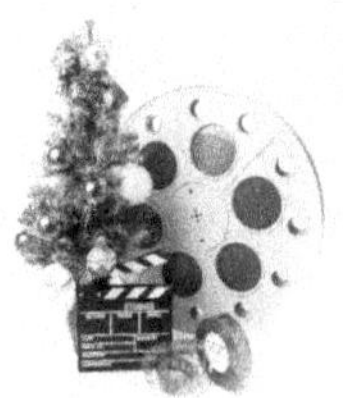

Although this book has discussed some of the most prominent Christmas features of the 1980s, many other films were produced throughout the decade which dealt with themes or scenarios related to the festive season. In this section, other eighties movies are listed which feature Christmas in one capacity or another, either as a backdrop to the action or as an integral aspect of the plot. (Motion pictures which only include very brief holiday season scenes or references are generally not included.)

Brazil (1985)
Embassy International Pictures
Director: Terry Gilliam
Starring: Jonathan Pryce, Robert De Niro, Katherine Helmond
A blistering satire on bureaucracy and totalitarianism, set during the festive season and featuring some memorably subversive Christmas imagery (often at the least appropriate of moments), this film showcases Terry Gilliam's distinctive sense of humour at its most original and gleefully twisted.

Christine (1983)
Columbia Pictures Corporation/Delphi Premier Productions/Polar Film
Director: John Carpenter
Starring: Keith Gordon, John Stockwell, Alexandra Paul
A popular film adaptation of Stephen King's horror novel of the same name, focusing on a sentient Plymouth Fury car with murderous tendencies. Scenes during the festive season feature prominently in the narrative, with the tense climax taking place on New Year's Eve.

Christmas Mountain (1981)
Christmas Mountain Productions
Director: Pierre de Moro
Starring: Mark Miller, Slim Pickens, Barbara Stanger
In this Western adventure, a cowboy rides into a small town during Christmas and discovers inequity towards some of the community's Mexican citizens. With the help of an old friend, he sets about using the festive spirit to ensure a lasting respect and understanding between the townsfolk.

Cookie (1989)
Lorimar Film Entertainment
Director: Susan Seidelman
Starring: Peter Falk, Dianne Wiest, Emily Lloyd
This organised crime-themed comedy has a subdued dalliance with the festive season, including some scenes at a Christmas party. The movie also makes good use of wintry scenes in and around New Jersey, where it was filmed, though its relationship with the holidays is otherwise fairly scant.

Dead Bang (1989)

Lorimar Film Entertainment

Director: John Frankenheimer

Starring: Don Johnson, Penelope Ann Miller, William Forsythe

A gritty and somewhat downbeat thriller which kicks off with the fatal shooting of a County Sheriff's Deputy during Christmas Eve in Los Angeles. With a plot involving illegal arms trafficking and white supremacist gangs, the film is far removed from heart-warming festive fare.

Diner (1982)

Metro-Goldwyn-Mayer/SLM Production Group

Director: Barry Levinson

Starring: Steve Guttenberg, Daniel Stern, Mickey Rourke

This celebrated coming-of-age comedy drama sees a group of old friends meeting up at their favoured hang-out spot – a diner in Baltimore, Maryland – during the period between Christmas and the New Year in 1959. Contemplative and well-performed, Levinson's screenplay for the film was nominated for an Academy Award.

DOA (1988)

Bigelow Productions/Silver Screen Partners III/Touchstone Pictures

Directors: Annabel Jankel and Rocky Morton

Starring: Dennis Quaid, Meg Ryan, Daniel Stern

A taut and thought-provoking thriller, loosely based on a (non-Christmas-situated) 1950 *film noir* of the same name. A highly respected, tenured professor of English discovers that he has been poisoned and is thus 'Dead on Arrival'. With only hours left to live, he sets out to bring his murderer to justice. Set during the holiday season, with numerous Christmas references throughout.

The Dorm that Dripped Blood (a.k.a. Pranks) (1982)
Jeff Obrow Productions
Directors: Stephen Carpenter and Jeffrey Obrow
Starring: Laurie Lapinski, Stephen Sachs, David Snow
A mysterious killer inventively dispatches a group of college students over the festive period when they decide to stay on campus to prepare a dilapidated dormitory building for a forthcoming demolition. With some imaginative twists and resourceful use of industrial tools as murder weapons, the film fits loosely into the then-emerging mould of the Christmas slasher horror movie.

Falling in Love (1984)
Paramount Pictures
Director: Ulu Grosbard
Starring: Robert De Niro, Meryl Streep, Dianne Wiest
In this romantic drama, which is bookended by Christmases, a graphic designer and an architect – both of whom are married to other people – meet during a chance encounter over the festive season. A shared attraction blossoms over the months ahead, but a bittersweet resolution is revealed the following year.

Fanny and Alexander (1982)
Cinematograph / Svenska Filminstitutet / Gaumont / Personafilm / SVT 1 / Tofisfilm
Director: Ingmar Bergman
Starring: Pernilla Allwin, Bertil Guve, Börje Ahlstedt
One of Sweden's most noteworthy Christmas-themed films, though the narrative actually spans a lengthy period between

1907 and 1910. With some pivotal scenes set during the holiday season, this multiple award-winning historical drama explores the complexities of family life including its light-hearted moments, parental love and emotional cruelties.

First Blood (1982)
Anabasis N.V./Elcajo Productions
Director: Ted Kotcheff
Starring: Sylvester Stallone, Richard Crenna, Brian Dennehy
Perhaps the least likely of all 1980s Christmas films, this first cinematic appearance of action movie icon John Rambo takes place over the Christmas period – as evidenced by the festive decorations around the town (including those bedecking the sheriff's station) in rural Washington where the former Green Beret is arrested. Based upon David Morrell's fast-paced novel, *First Blood* is not exactly a traditional yuletide staple.

Funny Farm (1988)
Cornelius Productions/Pan Arts/Warner Brothers
Director: George Roy Hill
Starring: Chevy Chase, Madolyn Smith, Joseph Maher
Taking place in autumnal Vermont, George Roy Hill's final film (adapted from Jay Cronley's comic novel) is a critically divisive comedy which featured a prominent Christmas sequence. A New York couple living in a small rural town decide, on the cusp of divorce, to bribe the local residents in order to fake an idyllic community which typifies the holiday season – all as part of a scheme to encourage the sale of their family home. All does not go to plan.

Ghostbusters II (1989)
Columbia Pictures Corporation
Director: Ivan Reitman
Starring: Bill Murray, Dan Aykroyd, Sigourney Weaver
This sequel to Ivan Reitman's 1984 pop culture colossus is set in a frosty New York City during Christmas, culminating in a spectacular action sequence amongst the New Year's Eve festivities. Centring around the titular paranormal investigators' attempts to regain the respect of the city following the explosive events of the original film, and also combating a new wave of supernatural peril which is taking shape, this commendably offbeat follow-up is full of pleasingly-drawn characters and feel-good moments.

Invasion USA (1985)
Cannon Films
Director: Joseph Zito
Starring: Chuck Norris, Richard Lynch, Melissa Prophet
An action movie set during the approach to the festive season, where a former CIA agent finds himself targeted by a bloodthirsty Soviet spy who is intent on causing mayhem by perpetrating terror attacks on American soil. Explosions and carnage abound, while one memorable sequence involves Christmas shoppers being besieged in a mall by a terrorist gang.

Jaws: The Revenge (1987)
Universal Pictures
Director: Joseph Sargent
Starring: Lorraine Gary, Mario Van Peebles, Michael Caine
The fourth instalment in the long-running shark-hunting franchise initiates its action a few days before Christmas.

Further tragedy from shark attacks leads to a desperate search before further bloodshed can erupt. Poorly-regarded by critics at the time of its release, the film is not generally considered to be a holiday season classic.

Less Than Zero (1987)

Twentieth Century Fox Film Corporation/Amercent Films/American Entertainment Partners L.P.
Director: Marek Kanievska
Starring: Andrew McCarthy, Jami Gertz, Robert Downey Jr
A college freshman gets more than he bargained for when he agrees to a former girlfriend's request to return to Los Angeles for Christmas. A somewhat bleak exploration of ennui and narcotics abuse amongst an affluent, decadent youth culture, the film was adapted from Bret Easton Ellis's 1985 novel – albeit that its characters and events profoundly departed from the book in numerous ways.

Lethal Weapon (1987)

Warner Brothers/Silver Pictures
Director: Richard Donner
Starring: Mel Gibson, Danny Glover, Gary Busey
A suicidal cop, a former soldier in a U.S. Army Special Forces division who has recently been widowed, is forced to partner with a veteran homicide officer over the festive season. Concluding with a stirring family scene at Christmas, the film features a number of pleasing yuletide trappings but is generally better known for being one of the all-time great police buddy movies.

Nutcracker: The Motion Picture (1986)

Hyperion Pictures/The Kushner-Locke Company
Director: Carroll Ballard
Starring: Vanessa Sharp, Hugh Bigney, Patricia Barker
Featuring the Pacific Northwest Ballet Company, this well-received film adaptation of Pyotr Ilyich Tchaikovsky's ballet *The Nutcracker* (1892) and E.T.A. Hoffmann's short story 'The Nutcracker and the Mouse King' (1816) retained the Christmas setting of the original source material, including the expected eye-catching iconography of toys and Christmas gifts within the dreamlike fantasy sequences. *Nutcracker: The Motion Picture* was closely based on the Maurice Sendak and Kent Stowell stage production of *The Nutcracker* which premiered in 1983.

Ordinary People (1980)

Paramount Pictures/Wildwood Enterprises
Director: Robert Redford
Starring: Donald Sutherland, Mary Tyler Moore, Judd Hirsch
Robert Redford's critically celebrated and Academy Award-winning directorial debut, this examination of the dysfunctions and eventual breakup of a well-to-do Illinois family reaches its climax at Christmas. A dark and emotionally-charged drama, this is not a film for anyone who dreads having their relatives round to visit during the holiday season.

Six Weeks (1982)

PolyGram Filmed Entertainment/Universal Pictures
Dirctor: Tony Bill
Starring: Dudley Moore, Mary Tyler Moore, Katherine Healy

Golden Globe Award-nominated tearjerker, based upon a Fred Mustard Stewart novel, which sees a wealthy businesswoman striking up an unlikely friendship with a Californian politician as she tries to find a way of realising the dream of her young daughter – who is terminally ill due to leukaemia – to take the lead role in Tchaikovsky's *The Nutcracker* ballet. The eponymous six weeks incorporate the Christmas period, including an evocative travelogue around New York City during the holiday season.

Some Girls (1988)
Metro-Goldwyn-Mayer / The Oxford Film Company / Wildwood Enterprises
Director: Michael Hoffman
Starring: Patrick Dempsey, Jennifer Connelly, Sheila Kelley
A college student is invited to spend Christmas in Quebec with his bohemian girlfriend and her family, only to face an abrupt breakup, romantic interest from unexpected quarters, and a few weeks in the company of some deeply eccentric people. The film's evocation of the festive season is just as kooky as the rest of its quirky stylistic approach.

Steel Magnolias (1989)
TriStar Pictures/Rastar Films
Director: Herbert Ross
Starring: Sally Field, Dolly Parton, Shirley MacLaine
Widely acclaimed for the performances of its star-studded cast, this moving and often highly perceptive celebration of female friendship and small town life features a pivotal Christmas scene, complete with a yuletide focus on the community depicted in the film as its members gear up to celebrate the festive season.

The Sure Thing (1985)

Embassy Films Associates/Monument Pictures
Director: Rob Reiner
Starring: John Cusack, Daphne Zuniga, Anthony Edwards
A Christmas road trip beckons for two fellow students as they both head from New England to California in order to meet up with their respective love interests. Things go not go to plan, however, and after encountering a wide range of unexpected mishaps they eventually realise that their true feelings lie with each other. A rather original take on the festive season, which is mostly depicted through the couple's ill-fated cross-country journey.

We of the Never Never (1982)

Adam Packer Film Productions/Film Corporation of Western Australia/General Television Corporation
Director: Igor Auzins
Starring: Angela Punch McGregor, Arthur Dignam, John Jarratt
A multiple nominee at the Australian Film Institute Awards (winning in the Cinematography category for its stunning vistas), this film is set in Australia at the turn of the twentieth century and explores the relationship between Caucasian socialite Jeannie Gunn and the Aboriginal community she encounters while living on a remote cattle station. Based on Gunn's autobiographical novel of the same name, the narrative culminates with a touching sequence during the festive season where the true spirit of Christmas can be seen through cross-cultural friendship and understanding.

When Harry Met Sally... (1989)

Castle Rock Entertainment/Nelson Entertainment
Director: Rob Reiner
Starring: Billy Crystal, Meg Ryan, Carrie Fisher
One of the most famous romantic comedies of the eighties, this Academy Award-nominated movie – which explores the complicated friendship and eventual love which grows between two old acquaintances – reaches its conclusion during the holiday season, with the characters' relationship finally cemented during a New Year's Eve party.

Filmography

CHRISTMAS EVIL (1980)

Production Company: Edward R. Pressman Productions.
Distributor: Pan American Pictures.
Director: Lewis Jackson.
Producers: Pete Kameron and Burt Kleiner.
Associate Producer: Michael Levine.
Executive Producer: Jerold Rubenstein.
Screenplay: Lewis Jackson.
Original Music: Don Christensen, Joel Harris and Julia Heyward.
Director of Photography: Ricardo Aronovich.
Film Editing: Linda Leeds and Corky O'Hara.
Art Direction: Roberta Neiman.
Production Design: Lorenzo Mans.
Costume Design: Deirdre Williams.
Running Time: 100 minutes.
Main Cast: Brandon Maggart (Harry Stadling), Jeffrey DeMunn (Philip Stadling), Dianne Hull (Jackie Stadling), Andy Fenwick (Dennis Stadling), Brian Neville (Marc Stadling), Joe Jamrog (Frank Stoller), Wally Moran (Philip Stadling Jr.), Gus Salud (Harry Stadling Jr.), Ellen McElduff (Harry's Mother), Brian Hartigan (Harry's Father), Peter Neuman (Moss Garcia), Lance Holcomb (Scotty Goodrich), Elizabeth Ridge (Susie Lovett), Chris Browning (Richie Sharp), Tyrone Holmes (Frankie), Patricia Richardson (Moss's Mother), Scott McKay (Mr Fletcher), Peter Friedman (Mr Grosch), Owen Hollander (Ben), Horace Bailey (Jake), John Brockman (Dr Probst), Burt Kleiner (Sol Wiseman), David Hughes (Worker), Lloyd David Hart (Tipsy Worker), Francine Dumont (Mrs Fletcher), Pamela Enz (Mrs Grosch), William Robertson (Guard), Sheila Anderson (Nurse), Robert Ari (Doctor), Philip Casnoff (Ricardo Bauma), Michael Klinger (Peter), Mark Chamberlin (Charles), Colleen Zenk (Binky), Lisa Sloan (Khaki).

TO ALL A GOODNIGHT (1980)

Production Company: Four Features Partners/ Intercontinental Releasing Corporation.
Distributor: Intercontinental Releasing Corporation.
Director: David Hess.
Producers: Sandy Cobe and Jay Rasumny.
Associate Producer: Sharyon Reis Cobe.
Executive Producers: Alex Rebar and Rick Whitfield.
Screenplay: Alex Rebar.
Cinematography: Bill Godsey.
Film Editing: William J. Waters.
Art Direction: Joe Garrity.
Production Design: Joe Garrity.
Set Decoration: Sharon West.
Running Time: 90 minutes.
Main Cast: Jennifer Runyon (Nancy), Forrest Swanson (Alex), Linda Gentile (Melody), William Lauer (T.J.), Judith Bridges (Leia), Katherine Herrington (Mrs Jensen), Buck West (Ralph), Sam Shamshak (Polansky), Angela Bath (Trisha), Denise Stearns (Sam), Solomon Trager (Tom), Jeff Butts (Blake), Bill Martins (Jim), Jay Rasumny (Dan), Dan Stryker (Pilot), Judy Hess (Mrs Ransoni), Carrie Cobb (Mrs Jensen's Daughter), Lisa Labowskie (Cynthia), Harry Sethe (Irate Father), Vivienne Kove (Sincere Mother), Alain Clenet (Clenet Driver), Dori Tressler (Girl with Cat), Michael George (Pilot).

TRADING PLACES (1983)

Production Company: Paramount Pictures/Cinema Group Ventures.
Distributor: Paramount Pictures.
Director: John Landis.
Producer: Aaron Russo.
Associate Producers: Irwin Russo and Sam Williams.
Executive Producer: George Folsey Jr.
Screenplay: Timothy Harris and Herschel Weingrod.
Original Music: Elmer Bernstein.
Director of Photography: Robert Paynter.
Film Editing: Malcolm Campbell.
Casting: Bonnie Timmermann.

Production Design. Gene Rudolf.

Set Decoration. George DeTitta and George DeTitta Jr.

Costume Design. Deborah Nadoolman.

Running Time. 118 minutes.

Main Cast. Dan Aykroyd (Louis Winthorpe III), Eddie Murphy (Billy Ray Valentine), Jamie Lee Curtis (Ophelia), Denholm Elliott (Coleman), Ralph Bellamy (Randolph Duke), Don Ameche (Mortimer Duke), Kristin Holby (Penelope Witherspoon), Paul Gleason (Clarence Beeks), Avon Long (Ezra), Tom Mardirosian (Officer Pantuzzi), Charles Brown (Officer Reynolds), Robert Curtis-Brown (Todd), Nicholas Guest (Harry), John Bedford-Lloyd (Andrew), Tony Sherer (Philip), Clint Smith (Doo Rag Lenny), Gwyllum Evans (President of Heritage Club), Jacques Sandulescu (Creepy Man), W.B. Brydon (Bank Manager), Kelly Curtis (Muffy), Tracy K. Shaffer (Constance), Susan Fallender (Bunny), Alfred Drake (President of Exchange), Lucianne Buchanan (President's Mistress), Jimmy Raitt (Ophelia's Client), James Belushi (Harvey), Deborah Reagan (Harvey's Girlfriend), Al Franken (Baggage Handler #1), Tom Davis (Baggage Handler #2), Don McLeod (Gorilla), Richard Hunt (Wilson), Maurice D. Copeland (Secretary of Agriculture), Shelly Chee Chee Hall (Monica), Donna Palmer (Gladys), Barry Dennen (Demitri).

A CHRISTMAS STORY (1983)

Production Company. Metro-Goldwyn-Mayer/Christmas Tree Films.

Distributor. MGM/UA Entertainment Company.

Director. Bob Clark.

Producers. Bob Clark and René Dupont.

Associate Producer. Gary Goch.

Screenplay. Jean Shepherd, Leigh Brown and Bob Clark, from Jean Shepherd's novel *In God We Trust, All Others Pay Cash.*

Original Music. Paul Zaza and Carl Zittrer.

Cinematography. Reginald H. Morris.

Film Editing. Stan Cole.

Casting. Jane Feinberg, Mike Fenton, Karen Hazzard and Marci Liroff.

Production Design. Reuben Freed.

Art Direction. Gavin Mitchell.

Set Decoration. Mark S. Freeborn.

Costume Design. Mary E. McLeod.

Running Time: 94 minutes.

Main Cast: Melinda Dillon (Mrs Parker), Darren McGavin (The Old Man/Mr Parker), Peter Billingsley (Ralphie Parker), Ian Petrella (Randy Parker), Scott Schwartz (Flick), R.D. Robb (Schwartz), Tedde Moore (Miss Shields), Yano Anaya (Grover Dill), Zack Ward (Scut Farkus), Jeff Gillen (Santa Claus), Les Carlson (Tree Man), Jim Hunter (Freight Man), Patty Johnson (Head Elf), Drew Hocevar (Male Elf), David Svoboda (Goggles), Dwayne McLean (Black Bart), Helen E. Kaider (Wicked Witch), John Wong (Chop Suey Palace Owner), Johan Sebastian Wong (Waiter #1), Fred Lee (Waiter #2), Dan Ma (Waiter #3), Rocco Bellusci (Street Kid), Tommy Wallace (Boy in School), Jean Shepherd (Narrator/Adult Ralphie/Man Waiting in Line for Santa/Santa Claus).

MERRY CHRISTMAS, MR LAWRENCE (1983)

Production Company: National Film Trustees/Jeremy Thomas Productions, in association with Cineventure Productions/ Recorded Picture Company/Oshima Productions/Asahi National Broadcasting Company/ Broadbank Investments.

Distributor: Shochiku Company/Palace Pictures/Universal Pictures.

Director: Nagisa Ôshima.

Producer: Jeremy Thomas.

Associate Producers: Joyce Herlihy and Larry Parr.

Executive Producers: Terry Glinwood, Masato Hara, Geoffrey Nethercott and Eiko Oshima.

Screenplay: Nagisa Ôshima and Paul Mayersberg, based on *The Seed and The Sower* by Laurens van der Post.

Original Music: Ryûichi Sakamoto.

Director of Photography: Tôichirô Narushima.

Film Editing: Tomoyo Oshima.

Casting: Shigemasa Toda.

Art Direction: Andrew Sanders.

Running Time: 123 minutes.

Main Cast: David Bowie (Major Jack 'Strafer' Celliers), Tom Conti (Lt. Colonel John Lawrence), Ryûichi Sakamoto (Captain Yonoi), Takeshi Kitano (Sergeant Gengo Hara), Jack Thompson (Group Captain Hicksley), Johnny Ohkura (Kanemoto), Alistair Browning (De Jong), James Malcolm (Celliers' Brother), Chris Broun (Celliers, aged 12),

Yûya Uchida (Commandant of Military Prison), Ryûnosuke Kaneda (President of the Court), Takashi Naitô (Lieutenant Iwata), Tamio Ishikura (Prosecutor), Rokkô Toura (Interpreter), Kan Mikami (Lieutenant Ito), Yûji Honma (Private First Class Yajima), Daisuke Iijima (Corporal Ueki), Hideo Murota (New Camp Commandant), Barry Dorking (Chief Doctor), Geoff Clendon (Australian Doctor), Grant Bridger (P.O.W. Officer), Ian Miller (English Guard), Don Stevens (Pastor).

DON'T OPEN TILL CHRISTMAS (1984)

Production Company: Spectacular Trading International.
Distributor: 21st Century Film Corporation.
Director: Edmund Purdom.
Producers: Dick Randall and Steve Minasian.
Screenplay: Derek Ford with Al McGoohan.
Original Music: Des Dolan.
Director of Photography: Alan Pudney.
Film Editing: Ray Selfe.
Running Time: 86 minutes.
Main Cast: Edmund Purdom (Inspector Ian Harris), Alan Lake (Giles
    Harrison), Belinda Mayne (Kate Briosky), Mark Jones (Detective
    Sergeant Powell), Gerry Sundquist (Cliff Boyd), Kelly Baker
    ('Experience' Girl), Kevin Lloyd (Gerry), Wendy Danvers
    (Housekeeper), Pat Astley (Sharon), Lawrence Harrington (Kate's
    Father), Ken Halliwell (Restaurant Commissionaire), Ray Marioni
    (Maitre d'hotel), Wilfred Corlett ('Experience' Santa Claus), Ricky
    Kennedy (Theatre Santa Claus), Sid Wragg (Dungeon Santa Claus),
    Max Roman (Store Santa Claus), George Pierce (Market Santa Claus),
    Ashley Dransfield (Drunken Santa Claus), Derek Ford (Circus Santa
    Claus), Adrian Black (Circus Santa), John Aston (Santa Claus in Car),
    Maria Eldridge (Girl in Car), Des Dolan (Detective Constable) Derek
    Hunt (Police Constable), Paula Meadows (Dungeon Secretary),
    Caroline Munro (Herself).

COMFORT AND JOY (1984)

Production Company: Kings Road Entertainment and Lake (Comfort and Joy) Ltd., in association with Thorn EMI Screen Entertainment and Scottish Television Plc.
Distributor: Universal Pictures/Thorn EMI.
Director: Bill Forsyth.
Producers: Davina Belling and Clive Parsons.
Associate Producer: Paddy Higson.
Screenplay: Bill Forsyth.
Original Music: Mark Knopfler.
Cinematography: Chris Menges.
Film Editing: Michael Ellis.
Casting: Susie Figgis.
Production Design: Adrienne Atkinson.
Art Direction: Andy Harris.
Costume Design: Lindy Hemming and Mary-Jane Reyner.
Running Time: 106 minutes.
Main Cast: Bill Paterson (Alan 'Dickie' Bird), Eleanor David (Maddy), C.P. Grogan (Charlotte), Alex Norton (Trevor), Patrick Malahide (Colin), Rikki Fulton (Hilary), Roberto Bernardi (Mr McCool), George Rossi (Bruno), Peter Rossi (Paolo), Billy McElhaney (Renato), Gilly Gilchrist (Rufus), Caroline Guthrie (Gloria), Ona McCracken (Nancy), Elizabeth Sinclair (Fiona), Katy Black (Sarah), Robin Black (Lily), Ron Donachie (George), Arnold Brown (Psychiatrist), Iain McColl (Archie), Billy Johnstone (Amos), Douglas Sannachan (Trevor's Workman), Billy Greenlees (Trevor's Workman), Robert Buchanan (Trevor's Workman), Alan Tall (Trevor's Workman), Bob Starrett (Trevor's Workman), David O'Hara (Engineer), Allan Wylie (Newsreader), Alistair Campbell (Keith), Charles Kearney (All-Night DJ), Elspet Cameron (Miss Wilson), Teri Lally (Shop Assistant), Pearl Deans (Maria), Ray Jeffries (Removal Man), Patrick Lewsley (Removal Man), Ronald McCleod Veitch (Dentist), Johnny Irving (Bob Hope Look-Alike), Johnny Mac (Fred Astaire Look-Alike).

GREMLINS (1984)

Production Company: Warner Brothers/Amblin Entertainment.
Distributor: Warner Brothers.

Director: Joe Dante.

Producer: Michael Finnell.

Executive Producers: Steven Spielberg, Kathleen Kennedy and Frank Marshall.

Screenplay: Chris Columbus.

Original Music: Jerry Goldsmith.

Director of Photography: John Hora.

Film Editing: Tina Hirsch.

Casting: Susan Arnold.

Production Design: James H. Spencer.

Set Decoration: Jackie Carr.

Running Time: 106 minutes.

Main Cast: Hoyt Axton (Randall Peltzer), John Louie (Chinese Boy), Keye Luke (Mr Wing/Grandfather), Don Steele (Voice of Rockin' Ricky Rialto), Susan Burgess (Little Girl), Scott Brady (Sheriff Frank), Arnie Moore (Alex), Corey Feldman (Pete Fountaine), Harry Carey Jr (Mr Anderson), Zach Galligan (Billy Peltzer), Dick Miller (Murray Futterman), Phoebe Cates (Kate Beringer), Polly Holliday (Ruby Deagle), Don Elson (Man on Street), Belinda Balaski (Mrs Joe Harris), Daniel Llewelyn (Hungry Harris Child),   Edward Andrews (Mr Corben), Judge Reinhold (Gerald Hopkins), Lois Foraker (Bank Teller), Chuck Jones (Mr Jones), Kenny Davis (Dorry), Frances Lee McCain (Lynn Peltzer), Glynn Turman (Roy Hanson), Nick Katt (Schoolchild), Tracy Wells (Schoolchild), John C. Becher (Dr Molinaro), Gwen Willson (Mrs Molinaro), Jackie Joseph (Sheila Futterman), Jonathan Banks (Deputy Brent), Joe Brooks (Dave Meyers/Santa), Jim MacKrell (Lew Landers/WDHB-TV Reporter), Frank Welker (Voice of Stripe/Mogwai/Gremlins), Howie Mandel (Voice of Gizmo).

SILENT NIGHT, DEADLY NIGHT (1984)

Production Company: TriStar Pictures/Slayride.

Distributor: TriStar Pictures.

Director: Charles E. Sellier Jr.

Producers: Ira Richard Barmak.

Executive Producers: Scott J. Schneid and Dennis Whitehead.

Screenplay: Michael Hickey, from a story by Paul Caimi.

Original Music: Perry Botkin.

Cinematography: Henning Schellerup.

Film Editing: Michael Spence.

Casting: Stanzi Stokes.

Production Design: Dian Perryman.

Art Direction: Linda Kiffe.

Set Decoration: Linda Kiffe.

Running Time: 79 minutes (theatrical cut)/85 minutes (unrated cut).

Main Cast: Lilyan Chauvin (Mother Superior), Gilmer McCormick (Sister Margaret), Toni Nero (Pamela), Robert Brian Wilson (Billy at 18), Britt Leach (Mr Sims), Nancy Borgenicht (Mrs Randall), H.E.D. Redford (Captain Richards), Danny Wagner (Billy at 8), Linnea Quigley (Denise), Leo Geter (Tommy), Randy Stumpf (Andy), Will Hare (Grandpa), Tara Buckman (Mother/Ellie), Jeff Hansen (Father/Jim), Charles Dierkop (Killer Santa), Eric Hart (Mr Levitt/Storekeeper), Jonathon Best (Billy at 5), A. Madeline Smith (Sister Ellen), Amy Stuyvesant (Cindy), Max Robinson (Officer Barnes), Vince Massa (Young Boy Sledding/Doug), Michael Alvarez (Young Boy Sledding/Jim), John Bishop (Older Boy Sledding/Bob), Richard Terry (Older Boy Sledding/Mac), Oscar Rowland (Dr Conway), Richard D. Clark (Officer Miller), Tip Boxell (Officer Murphy), Angela Montoya (Little Girl on Santa's Lap), Mollie Cameron (Girl's Mother), Jayne Luke (Other Mother in Store), Joan S. Forster (Other Mother in Store), Betsy Nagel (Other Mother in Store), Barbara Stafford (Teen Lover at Orphanage), Paul Mulder (Teen Lover at Orphanage), Spencer Ashby (Santa at Orphanage), J. Paul Broadhead (Santa in Store), Alex Burton (Brother/Ricky at 14), Max Broadhead (Brother/Ricky) at 4), Melissa Best (Infant Ricky), Dan Rogers (Dispatcher).

ONE MAGIC CHRISTMAS (1985)

Production Company: Walt Disney Pictures and Northpole Picture Company of Canada, in association with Silver Screen Partners II and Telefilm Canada.

Distributor: Buena Vista Distribution Company.

Director: Phillip Borsos.

Producer: Peter O'Brian.

Associate Producer: Michael MacDonald.

Executive Producer: Phillip Borsos.

Screenplay. Thomas Meehan, from a story by Phillip Borsos, Barry Healey and Thomas Meehan.

Original Music. Michael Conway Baker.

Director of Photography. Frank Tidy.

Film Editing. Sidney Wolinsky.

Casting. Gail Carr.

Production Design. Bill Brodie.

Art Direction. Tony Hall.

Set Decoration. Rondi Johnson.

Costume Design. Olga Dimitrov.

Running Time. 89 minutes.

Main Cast. Mary Steenburgen (Ginny Grainger), Gary Basaraba (Jack Grainger), Harry Dean Stanton (Gideon), Arthur Hill (Caleb Grainger), Elizabeth Harnois (Abbie Grainger), Robbie Magwood (Cal Grainger), Michelle Meyrink (Betty), Elias Koteas (Eddie), Wayne Robson (Harry Dickens), Jan Rubes (Santa Claus), Sarah Polley (Molly Monaghan), Graham Jarvis (Frank Crump), Timothy Webber (Herbie Conklin), Joy Thompson-Allen (Mrs Monaghan), John Friesen (Mr Noonan), Debra McGrath (Mrs Noonan), Julie Beaulieu (Noonan Child), Jeremy Dingle (Noonan Child), Jane Schoettle (Bank Teller), Damir Andrei (Bank Manager), Amah Harris (Girl in Bank), Rita Tuckett (Mrs Claus), Sam Malkin (Garage Mechanic), Garreth Bennett (Harry Dickens' Son).

SANTA CLAUS: THE MOVIE (1985)

Production Company. TriStar Pictures/Calash Corporation/ GGG/Santa Claus Ltd.

Distributor. TriStar Pictures.

Director. Jeannot Szwarc.

Producers. Ilya Salkind and Pierre Spengler.

Associate Producer. Robert Simmonds.

Screenplay. David Newman, from a story by Leslie Newman and David Newman.

Original Music. Henry Mancini.

Cinematography. Arthur Ibbetson.

Film Editing. Peter Hollywood.

Casting. Lynn Stalmaster.

Production Design. Anthony Pratt.

Supervising Art Director: Tim Hutchinson.

Art Direction: Don Dossett, John Hoesli and Malcolm Stone.

Set Decoration: Stephanie McMillan.

Costume Design: Bob Ringwood.

Running Time: 107 minutes.

Main Cast: Dudley Moore (Patch), John Lithgow (B.Z.), David Huddleston (Santa Claus), Burgess Meredith (Ancient Elf), Judy Cornwell (Anya Claus), Jeffrey Kramer (Dr Eric Towzer), Christian Fitzpatrick (Joe), Carrie Kei Heim (Cornelia), John Barrard (Dooley), Anthony O'Donnell (Puffy), Melvyn Hayes (Goober), Don Estelle (Groot), Tim Stern (Boog), Peter O'Farrell (Honka), Christopher Ryan (Vout), Dickie Arnold (Goobler), Aimée Delamain (Storyteller), Dorothea Phillips (Miss Tucker), John Hallam (Grizzard), Judith Morse (Miss Abruzzi), Jerry Harte (Senate Chairman), Paul Aspland (Reporter #1), Sally Cranfield (Reporter #2), Michael Drew (Reporter #3), John Cassady (Wino), Ronald Fernee (Policeman #1), Michael Ross (Policeman #2), Walter Goodman (Street Corner Santa).

BETTER OFF DEAD (1985)

Production Company: A&M Films / CBS Entertainment Production.

Distributor: Warner Brothers.

Director: Savage Steve Holland.

Producer: Michael Jaffe.

Associate Producer: William Strom.

Executive Producer: Gil Friesen and Andrew Meyer.

Screenplay: Savage Steve Holland.

Original Music: Rupert Hine.

Cinematography: Isidore Mankofsky.

Film Editing: Alan Balsam.

Casting: Caro Jones.

Production Design: Herman Zimmerman.

Set Decoration: Gary Moreno.

Costume Design: Brad Loman and David Roester.

Running Time: 97 minutes.

Main Cast: John Cusack (Lane Meyer), David Ogden Stiers (Al Meyer), Kim Darby (Jenny Meyer), Demian Slade (Johnny Gasparini), Scooter Stevens (Badger Meyer), Diane Franklin (Monique Junot), Laura Waterbury (Mrs Smith), Daniel Schneider (Ricky Smith), Yuji

Okumoto (Yee Sook Ree), Brian Imada (Chen Ree), Chuck Mitchell (Rocko), Amanda Wyss (Beth Truss), Curtis Armstrong (Charles De Mar), Aaron Dozier (Roy Stalin), Frank Burt Avalon (Roy's Ski Buddy #1), J. Warren David (Roy's Ski Buddy #2), Peter Ellenstein (Roy's Ski Buddy #3), Vincent Schiavelli (Mr Kerber), Edward Mehler (Buster), Thomas Rollerson (Roller Skater), Toby Iland (Nerd #1), Jonathon Charles Fox (Nerd #2), Darren Harris (Nerd #3), Randy Stoklos (Jock #1), Sam High (Jock #2), David Vaughn (Jock #3), Tina Littlewood (Chris Cummins), Steven Williams (Tree Trimmer), Stuart K. Robinson (Tree Trimmer's Helper), Taylor Negron (Mailman), Rima Delane (Joanne Greenwald), Elizabeth Daily (Herself), Rick Rosenthal (Smitty).

SCROOGED (1988)

Production Company: Paramount Pictures/Mirage Productions.
Distributor: Paramount Pictures.
Director: Richard Donner.
Producers: Richard Donner and Art Linson.
Co Producer: Ray Hartwick.
Associate Producer: Jennie Lew Tugend.
Executive Producer: Steve Roth.
Screenplay: Mitch Glazer and Michael O'Donoghue.
Original Music: Danny Elfman.
Cinematography: Michael Chapman.
Film Editing: Fredric Steinkamp and William Steinkamp.
Casting: David Rubin.
Production Design: J. Michael Riva.
Art Direction: Virginia L. Randolph.
Set Decoration: Linda DeScenna.
Costume Design: Wayne Finkelman.
Running Time: 101 minutes.
Main Cast: Bill Murray (Frank Cross), Karen Allen (Claire Phillips), John Forsythe (Lew Hayward), John Glover (Brice Cummings), Bobcat Goldthwait (Eliot Loudermilk), David Johansen (Ghost of Christmas Past), Carol Kane (Ghost of Christmas Present), Robert Mitchum (Preston Rhinelander), Nicholas Phillips (Calvin Cooley), Michael J. Pollard (Herman), Alfre Woodard (Grace Cooley), Mabel King (Gramma), John Murray (James Cross), Jamie Farr (Jacob Marley),

Robert Goulet (Himself), Buddy Hackett (Scrooge), John Houseman (Himself), Lee Majors (Himself), Pat McCormick (TV Ghost of Christmas Past), Brian Doyle Murray (Earl Cross), Mary Lou Retton (Herself), Al 'Red Dog' Weber (Santa Claus), Jean Speegle Howard (Mrs Claus), June Chandler (June Cleaver), Michael Eidam (Wally Cleaver), Mary Ellen Trainor (Ted), Bruce Jarchow (Wayne), Sanford Jensen (IBC Executive #1), Jeffrey Joseph (IBC Executive #2), Dick Blasucci (IBC Executive #3), Peter Bromilow (Archbishop), Damon Hines (Steven Cooley), Tamika McCollum (Shasta Cooley), Koren McCollum (Randee Cooley), Reina King (Lanell Cooley), Paul Tuerpé (Stage Manager), Lester Wilson (Choreographer), Ron Strang (Art Director), Kate McGregor-Stewart (Lady Censor), Ralph Gervais (Mouse Wrangler), Lisa Mende (Doris Cross), Ryan Todd (Frank as a Child), Rebeca Arthur (Tina), Roy Brocksmith (Mike the Mailman), Stella Hall (Lew Hayward's Secretary), Sachi Parker (Belle), Delores Hall (Hazel), Wendie Malick (Wendie Cross), Chaz Conner Jr (TV Ghost of Christmas Future), Maria Riva (Mrs Rhinelander), Michael O'Donoghue (Priest), Winfred Tennison (Marvin).

ERNEST SAVES CHRISTMAS (1988)

Production Company: Touchstone Pictures and Emshell Producers Group, in association with Silver Screen Partners III.
Distributor: Buena Vista Pictures Distribution.
Director: John Cherry.
Producers: Stacy Williams and Doug Claybourne.
Co-Producers: Justis Greene and Coke Sams.
Associate Producer: Ed Turner.
Executive Producer: Joseph L. Akerman Jr. and Martin Erlichman.
Screenplay: Ed Turner and B. Kline, from a story by Ed Turner.
Film Editor: Sharyn L. Ross.
Director of Photography: Peter Stein.
Original Score: Mark Snow.
Production Design: Ian D. Thomas.
Casting: Kathleen Letterie.
Art Direction: Ian Thomas.
Set Decoration: Chris August.
Costume Design: Peter Mitchell.
Running Time: 95 minutes.

Main Cast: Jim Varney (Ernest P. Worrell/Astor Clement/Auntie Nelda/The Snake Guy), Douglas Seale (Santa), Oliver Clark (Joe Carruthers), Noëlle Parker (Harmony), Gailard Sartain (Chuck), Billie Bird (Mary Morrissey), Bill Byrge (Bobby), Robert Lesser (Marty), Key Howard (Immigration Agent), Jack Swanson (Businessman), Buddy Douglas (Pyramus), Patty Maloney (Thisbe), Beecher Martin (Agent Skippy), Barry Brazell (Cab Passenger), George Kaplan (Mr Dillis), Bill Christie (Waiter), Joe Candelora (Arresting Officer), Danny Dillon (Booking Officer), Lindsey Alley (Patsy), Phran Gauci (Lacy), Bill Cordell (Carl), Larry Francer (Brad), Jackie Welch (Animal Officer), Daniel Butler (Animal Officer), Antonio Fabrizzio (Mean-Looking Man), Bob Norris (Police Chief Spenks), Carmen Alexander (Police Officer), Miriam P. Saunders (Receptionist), Cyndi Vicino (Make-up Artist), Tom Nowicki (Crew Member), Michael O. Smith (Studio Guard), Jesse Stone (Elderly Man), Angelique Walker (Girl), Zachary Bowden (Boy), Donna Phillip Miller (Mom), Paul Darby (Ticket Agent), Cynthia Ergenbright (Museum Person), Bob Barnes (Controller #1), Mike Hutchinson (Monster), Douglas Brush (Commander), D. Christian Gottshall (Controller #2), Ray Russell (Stage-Hand).

DIE HARD (1988)

Production Company: Twentieth Century Fox Film Corporation/Gordon Company/Silver Pictures.
Distributor: Twentieth Century Fox Film Corporation.
Director: John McTiernan.
Producers: Lawrence Gordon and Joel Silver.
Associate Producer: Beau E.L. Marks.
Executive Producer: Charles Gordon.
Screenplay: Jeb Stuart and Steven E. de Souza, from a novel by Roderick Thorp.
Film Editors: John F. Link and Frank J. Urioste.
Cinematography: Jan De Bont.
Original Score: Michael Kamen.
Production Design: Jackson DeGovia.
Casting: Jackie Burch.
Art Direction: John R. Jensen.
Set Decoration: Phil M. Leonard.

Costume Design: Marilyn Vance-Straker.

Running Time: 131 minutes.

Main Cast: Bruce Willis (Officer John McClane), Bonnie Bedelia (Holly Gennaro McClane), Reginald Veljohnson (Sergeant Al Powell), Paul Gleason (Deputy Police Chief Dwayne T. Robinson), William Atherton (Richard Thornburg), Hart Bochner (Harry Ellis), James Shigeta (Joseph Yoshinobu Takagi), Alan Rickman (Hans Gruber), Alexander Godunov (Karl), Bruno Doyon (Franco), De'voreaux White (Argyle), Andreas Wisniewski (Tony), Clarence Gilyard Jr. (Theo), Joey Plewa (Alexander), Lorenzo Caccialanza (Marco), Gerard Bonn (Kristoff), Dennis Hayden (Eddie), Al Leong (Uli), Gary Roberts (Heinrich), Hans Buhringer (Fritz), Wilhelm von Homburg (James), Robert Davi (FBI Special Agent Big Johnson), Grand L. Bush (FBI Agent Little Johnson), Bill Marcus (City Engineer), Rick Ducommun (Walt: City Worker), Matt Landers (Captain Mitchell), Carmine Zozzora (Rivers), Dustyn Taylor (Ginny), George Christy (Dr Hasseldorf), Anthony Peck (Young Cop), Cheryl Baker (Woman), Richard Parker (Man), David Ursin (Harvey Johnson), Mary Ellen Trainor (Gail Wallens), Diana James (Police Supervisor), Shelley Pogoda (Dispatcher), Selma Archerd (Hostage), Scot Bennett (Hostage), Rebecca Broussard (Hostage), Kate Finlayson (Hostage), Shanna Higgins (Hostage), Kym Malin (Hostage), Taylor Fry (Lucy McClane), Noah Land (John McClane Jr.), Betty Carvalho (Paulina), Kip Waldo (Convenience Store Clerk), Mark Goldstein (Station Manager), Tracy Reiner (Thornburg's Assistant), Rick Cicetti (Guard), Fred Lerner (Guard), Bill Margolin (Producer), Bob Jennings (Cameraman), Bruce P. Schultz (Cameraman), David Katz (Soundman), Robert Lesser (Businessman), Stella Hall (Stewardess), Terri Lynn Doss (Girl at Airport), Jon E. Greene (Boy at Airport), P. Randall Bowers (Kissing Man), Michele Laybourn (Girl in Window).

PRANCER (1989)

Production Company: Cineplex-Odeon Films/Nelson Entertainment/ Raffaella Productions.

Distributor: Orion Pictures.

Director: John Hancock.

Producer: Raffaella De Laurentiis.

Co-Producers: Mike Petzold and Greg Taylor.

Associate Producer. Hester Hargett.

Screenplay. Greg Taylor.

Film Editors. Dennis O'Connor and John Rosenberg.

Director of Photography. Misha Suslov.

Original Score. Maurice Jarre.

Production Design. Chester Kaczenski.

Casting. Susan Willett.

Art Direction. Marc Dabe.

Set Decoration. Judi Sandin.

Costume Design. Denny Burt.

Running Time. 103 minutes.

Main Cast. Sam Elliott (John Riggs), Cloris Leachman (Mrs McFarland), Rutanya Alda (Aunt Sarah), Abe Vigoda (Orel Benton), Michael Constantine (Mr Stewart/Santa), Rebecca Harrell (Jessica Riggs), John Joseph Duda (Steve Riggs), Ariana Richards (Carol Wetherby), Mark Rolston (Herb Drier), Johnny Galecki (Billy Quinn), Walter Charles (Minister), Victor Truro (Mr Young), Marcia Porter (Mrs Fairburn), Loren Janes (Mr Soot), Robert Zimmermann (Wagnall), Shirley Starnes (Mrs Hofsetter), Michael Luciano (Bert), Jesse Bradford (Boy #1), Eric Sardeson (Boy #2), Joseph Morano (Boy with Santa), Belinda Bremner (Miss Bedelia), Terry Jayjack (Mrs Wetherby), Steven Pressler (Hank), Dale Balsbaugh (Mr Wood), Sandra Olson (Town Woman), Dan Atherton (Town Man).

NATIONAL LAMPOON'S CHRISTMAS VACATION (1989)

Production Company. Hughes Entertainment/Warner Brothers.

Distributor. Warner Brothers.

Director. Jeremiah Chechik.

Producers. John Hughes and Tom Jacobson.

Associate Producers. William S. Beasley, Mauri Syd Gayton and Ramey E. Ward.

Executive Producer. Matty Simmons.

Screenplay. John Hughes.

Film Editor. Jerry Greenberg and Michael Stevenson.

Director of Photography. Thomas Ackerman.

Unit Production Manager. William S. Beasley.

Original Score. Angelo Badalamenti.

Production Design: Stephen Marsh.

Casting: Risa Bramon, Billy Hopkins and Heidi Levitt.

Art Direction: Beala B. Neel.

Set Decoration: Lisa Fischer.

Costume Design: Michael Kaplan.

Running Time: 97 minutes.

Main Cast: Chevy Chase (Clark Griswold), Beverly D'Angelo (Ellen Griswold), Juliette Lewis (Audrey Griswold), Johnny Galecki (Russell 'Rusty' Griswold), John Randolph (Clark Wilhelm Griswold Sr), Diane Ladd (Nora Griswold), E.G. Marshall (Art Smith), Doris Roberts (Frances Smith), Randy Quaid (Cousin Eddie Johnson), Miriam Flynn (Cousin Catherine Johnson), Cody Burger (Cousin Rocky Johnson), Ellen Hamilton Latzen (Cousin Ruby Sue Johnson), William Hickey (Uncle Lewis), Mae Questel (Aunt Bethany), Sam McMurray (Bill), Nicholas Guest (Todd Chester), Julia Louis-Dreyfus (Margo Chester), Nicolette Scorsese (Mary), Keith MacKechnie (Delivery Boy), Brian Doyle Murray (Frank Shirley), Natalia Nogulich (Helen Shirley), Michael Kaufman (Young Executive).

Bibliography

Agajanian, Rowana, '"Peace on Earth, Goodwill to All Men": The Depiction of Christmas in Modern Hollywood Films', in *Christmas at the Movies: Images of Christmas in American, British and European Cinema*, ed. by Mark Connelly (London: I.B. Tauris, 2000), pp.143-64.

Alan, Jay, '*Silent Night, Deadly Night*', in *Horror News*, 18 March 2011. <*http://horrornews.net/32216/film-review-silent-night-deadly-night-1984/*>

Albright, Brian, *Regional Horror Films, 1958-1990: A State-by-State Guide with Interviews* (Jefferson: McFarland, 2012).

Aldgate, Anthony, and Jeffrey Richards, *Best of British: Cinema and Society from 1930 to the Present* (London: I.B. Tauris, 2002).

Aldgate, Anthony, James Chapman and Arthur Marwick, eds, *Windows on the Sixties: Exploring Key Texts of Media and Culture* (London: I.B. Tauris, 2000).

Allan, Blaine, 'Directed by Phillip Borsos', in *North of Everything: English-Canadian Cinema Since 1980*, ed. by William Beard and Jerry White (Alberta: The University of Alberta Press, 2002), p.106-121.

Allon, Yoram, Del Cullen and Hannah Patterson, eds, *Contemporary British and Irish Film Directors: A Wallflower Critical Guide* (London: Wallflower Press, 2001).

—, eds, *Contemporary North American Film Directors: A Wallflower Critical Guide* (London: Wallflower Press, 2000).

Anderson, Jeffrey M., '*One Magic Christmas*', in *Combustible Celluloid*, 14 May 2007. <*http://www.combustiblecelluloid.com/digitalwatch/onemagxmas.shtml*>

—, '*Scrooged*', in *Combustible Celluloid*, 10 December 2008.
<*http://www.combustiblecelluloid.com/archive/scrooged.shtml*>

Anon., 'Brief Movie Reviews: *Santa Claus: The Movie*', in *New York Magazine*, 16 December 1985, p.115.

—, 'Don't Open Till Christmas... Don't Open at All!', in *Anything Horror*, 22 December 2011.
<*http://anythinghorror.com/2011/12/22/holiday-horrors-dont-open-till-christmas-1984/*>

—, 'Reflections', in *Masters of Imaging*, 2010.
<*http://www.mastersofimaging.net/Reflections.html*>

—, '*To All a Goodnight*', in *80s Horror Central*, 2012.
<*http://80shorrorcentral.webs.com/toallagoodnight1980.htm*>

—, 'Top 10 Classic Christmas Movies', in *The Coventry Evening Telegraph*, 23 October 2009.

Arthur, Ryan, '*National Lampoon's Christmas Vacation*', in *eFilmCritic.com*, 15 October 1998.
<*http://efilmcritic.com/review.php?movie=1116*>

Ashby, Justine, and Andrew Higson, eds., *British Cinema, Past and Present* (London: Routledge, 2000).

Atanasov, Svet, '*Comfort and Joy* Blu-ray Review', in *Blu-Ray.com*, 29 February 2016.
<*http://www.blu-ray.com/movies/Comfort-and-Joy-Blu-ray/144453/#Review*>

—, '*Merry Christmas, Mr Lawrence* Blu-Ray Review', in *Blu-Ray.com*, 28 September 2010.
<*http://www.blu-ray.com/movies/Merry-Christmas-Mr-Lawrence-Blu-ray/12777/#Review*>

Attebery, Brian, *Stories About Stories: Fantasy and the Remaking of Myth* (Oxford: Oxford University Press, 2014).

Austin, Joe, and Michael Nevin Willard, eds, *Generations of Youth: Youth Cultures and History in Twentieth-Century America* (New York: NYU Press, 1998).

B., Devon, '*Silent Night Deadly Night 1&2*', in *Digital Retribution*, 25 December 2006.
<*http://www.digital-retribution.com/reviews/dvd/0565.php*>

Babington, Bruce, and Peter William Evans, *Biblical Epics: Sacred Narrative in the Hollywood Cinema* (Manchester: Manchester University Press, 1993).

Bailey, Keith, '*To All a Goodnight*', in *The Unknown Movies*, September 2014.
<*http://www.the-unknown-movies.com/unknownmovies/reviews/rev63.html*>

Barker, A.D., '*Bridge on the River Kwai* and the Japanese Prisoner of War Camp Movie: A Multiculturalism Too Far?', in *Multicultural Dilemmas: Identity, Difference, Otherness*, ed. by Wojciech H. Kalaga and Marzena Kubisz (Frankfurt am Main: Peter Lang, 2008), pp.93-106.

Barnwell, Naomi, '*Gremlins*', in *Roobla*, 7 December 2010.
<*https://roobla.com/2010/12/07/gremlins-1984/*>

Batchelor, Bob, and Scott Stoddart, *The 1980s* (Westport: Greenwood Publishing Group, 2006).

Base, Ron, and David Haslam, *The Movies of the Eighties* (London: Portland, 1990).

Bates, D.B., '*Prancer*', in *The Parallax Review*, 24 December 2010.
<*http://www.theparallaxreview.com/on_cable/prancer.html*>

Baumgarten, Murray, 'Bill Murray's Christmas Carols', in *Dickens on Screen*, ed. by John Glavin (Cambridge: Cambridge University Press, 2003), pp.61-71.

Beard, William, and Jerry White, eds, *North of Everything: English-Canadian Cinema Since 1980* (Alberta: The University of Alberta Press, 2002).

Benson, Daniel, '*Silent Night Deadly Night*', in *Horror Talk*, 20 November 2009.
<http://www.horrortalk.com/index.php/reviews/701-silent-night-deadly-night>

Berardinelli, James, '*A Christmas Story*', in *ReelViews*, 24 April 2016.
<http://www.reelviews.net/reelviews/christmas-story-a>

—, '*National Lampoon's Christmas Vacation*', in *ReelViews*, 13 February 2001.
<http://www.reelviews.net/reelviews/national-lampoon-s-christmas-vacation>

Bohm-Duchen, Monica, *The Private Life of a Masterpiece* (Berkeley: University of California Press, 2001).

Booker, M. Keith, *Disney, Pixar, and the Hidden Messages of Children's Films* (Santa Barbara: Praeger, 2010).

Bookman, Milica, and Aleksandra S. Bookman, *Economics in Film and Fiction* (Plymouth: Rowman and Littlefield Education, 2009).

Botelho, Derek, '*Don't Open Till Christmas*', in *Daily Dead*, 26 December 2011.
<http://dailydead.com/review-dont-open-till-christmas-dvd/>

Boyar, Jay, '*Ernest* Saves the Day When Santa Needs Help', in *The Orlando Sentinel*, 3 November 1989.

—, '*Prancer* Puts Winter Solstice Back in Christmas', in *The Orlando Sentinel*, 17 November 1989.

Bromley, Patrick, '*To All a Goodnight*', in *DVD Verdict*, 6 December 2014.
<http://www.dvdverdict.com/reviews/toallgoodnightbluray.php>

Brooke, Michael, '*Comfort and Joy*', in *BFI Screen Online*, 2006. <*http://www.screenonline.org.uk/film/id/514458/index.html*>

Brown, Joe, '*Scrooged*', in *The Washington Post*, 25 November 1988.

Browne, Ray B., and Glenn J. Browne, *Laws of Our Fathers: Popular Culture and the U.S. Constitution* (Bowling Green: Bowling Green State University Popular Press, 1986).

Browne, Ray B., and Pat Browne, *The Guide to United States Popular Culture* (Madison: University of Wisconsin Press, 2001).

Brownridge, Will, '*Ernest Saves Christmas*, or *Watch Out Vern*', in *The Film Reel*, 18 December 2013. <*http://www.the-filmreel.com/2013/12/18/review-ernest-saves-christmas-1988-watch-vern/*>

Brussat, Frederic, and Mary Ann Brussat, '*Comfort and Joy*', in *Spirituality and Practice*, 10 July 2003. <*http://www.spiritualityandpractice.com/films/reviews/view/6087*>

Budd, Mike, and Max H. Kirsch, eds, *Rethinking Disney: Private Control, Public Dimensions* (Middletown: Wesleyan University Press, 2005).

Canby, Vincent, 'Bill Murray in *Scrooged*: Meanness's Outer Limits', in *The New York Times*, 23 November 1988.

—, '*Christmas Story*: Indiana Tale', in *The New York Times*, 18 November 1983.

—, '*Comfort and Joy*: Comedy from Scotland', in *The New York Times*, 10 October 1984.

—, '*Gremlins*: Kiddie Gore', in *The New York Times*, 8 June 1984.

—, '*Santa Claus*, with Moore and Lithgow', in *The New York Times*, 27 November 1985.

Carlson, Kristine Butler, '1945: Movies and the March Home', in *American Cinema of the 1940s: Themes and Variations*, ed. by Wheeler Winston Dixon (Piscataway: Rutgers University Press, 2006), pp.140-61.

Carney, Raymond, *American Vision: The Films of Frank Capra* (Cambridge: Cambridge University Press, 1986).

Carr, Jay, '*Scrooged*', in *The Boston Globe*, 23 November 1988.

—, '*Trading Places*', in *The Boston Globe*, 9 June 1983.

Chapman, James, 'God Bless Us, Every One: Movie Adaptations of *A Christmas Carol*', in *Christmas at the Movies*, ed. by Mark Connelly (London: I.B. Tauris, 2000), pp.9-38.

Chase, Chris, '*Die Hard*: Cop Fights Gang of Terrorists', in *The New York Daily News*, 15 July 1988.

Christie, Thomas A., *The Christmas Movie Book* (Maidstone: Crescent Moon Publishing, 2011).

Clark, Graeme, '*Comfort and Joy*', in *The Spinning Image*, 2004.
<http://www.thespinningimage.co.uk/cultfilms/displaycultfilm.asp?reviewid=969>

—, '*Santa Claus*', in *The Spinning Image*, 2005.
<http://www.thespinningimage.co.uk/cultfilms/displaycultfilm.asp?reviewid=6566>

Clark, Scott, '*Christmas Evil* DVD Review', in *The People's Movies*, 12 November 2012.
<http://thepeoplesmovies.com/2012/11/christmas-evil-dvd-review/>

Cohan, Steven, 'Introduction: Musicals of the Studio Era', in *Hollywood Musicals: The Film Reader*, ed. by Steven Cohan (London: Routledge, 2002), pp.1-15.

—, ed., *Hollywood Musicals: The Film Reader* (London: Routledge, 2002).

Collins, Ace, *Stories Behind the Great Traditions of Christmas* (Grand Rapids: Zondervan, 2003).

Collins, Brian, 'All is Bright: The Producers of *Silent Night, Deadly Night* on Christmas's Best Horror Film', in *Birth. Movies. Death.*, 12 December 2014.
<http://www.birthmoviesdeath.com/2014/12/12/all-is-bright-the-producers-of-silent-night-deadly-night-on-christmass-best>

Collins, Brian W., '*Don't Open 'Til Christmas*', in *Horror Movie a Day*, 3 November 2009.
<http://horror-movie-a-day.blogspot.co.uk/2009/11/dont-open-til-christmas.html>

Concannon, Philip, '*Comfort and Joy*', in *The Skinny*, 29 February 2016.
<http://www.theskinny.co.uk/film/dvd-reviews/comfort-and-joy>

Connelly, Mark, ed., *Christmas at the Movies* (London: I.B. Tauris, 2000).

—, 'Santa Claus: The Movie', in *Christmas at the Movies*, ed. by Mark Connelly (London: I.B. Tauris, 2000), pp.115-34.

Conner, Floyd, *Hollywood's Most Wanted: The Top 10 Book of Lucky Breaks, Prima Donnas, Box Office Bombs, and Other Oddities* (Virginia: Brassey's, 2002).

Connolly, Joseph, 'Personally speaking *It's a Wonderful Life* spotting all the gaffes', in *The Sunday Telegraph*, 23 December 2007.

Cook, David C., *The Inspirational Christmas Almanac: Heartwarming Traditions, Trivia, Stories, and Recipes for the Holidays* (Colorado Springs: Honor Books, 2006).

Cooper, Ian, 'Bob Clark', in *Contemporary North American Film Directors: A Wallflower Critical Guide*, ed. by Yoram Allon, Del Cullen and Hannah Patterson (London: Wallflower Press, 2000), pp.85-86.

Cracknell, Ryan, '*Better Off Dead*', in *Movie Views*, 6 July 2003.
<http://movieviews.ca/better-off-dead>

—, '*Ernest Saves Christmas*', in *Movie Views*, 14 December 2003.
<http://movieviews.ca/ernest-saves-christmas>

—, '*National Lampoon's Christmas Vacation*', in *Movie Views*, 22 December 2003.
<http://movieviews.ca/national-lampoons-christmas-vacation>

Crouse, Richard, *The 100 Best Movies You've Never Seen* (Toronto: ECW Press, 2003).

Crump, William D., *The Christmas Encyclopedia*, 3rd edn (Jefferson: McFarland and Company, 2013).

Deacy, Christopher, *Faith in Film: Religious Themes in Contemporary Cinema* (Aldershot: Ashgate Publishing, 2005).

Denby, David, 'Holiday Horror', in *New York Magazine*, 5 December 1988, pp.178-80.

—, 'She is Woman', in *New York Magazine*, 15 October 1984, pp.81-83.

—, 'Supply-Side Hero', in *New York Magazine*, 22 August 1983, pp.62-63.

Dennis, James, 'DVD Review: *Christmas Evil* Isn't Quite What You'd Expect', in *Twitch*, 25 November 2012.
<http://twitchfilm.com/2012/11/dvd-review-christmas-evil-isnt-quite-what-youd-expect.html>

Desilet, Gregory, *Screens of Blood: A Critical Approach to Film and Television Violence* (Jefferson: McFarland and Company, 2014).

Detora, Lisa M., ed., *Heroes of Film, Comics and American Culture: Essays on Real and Fictional Defenders of Home* (Jefferson: McFarland, 2009).

Dickens, Charles, *The Christmas Books* (Ware: Wordsworth Editions, 1995) [1852].

Dissanayake, Wimal, 'Habermas' Concept of Public Sphere and the Cinema of Oshima Nagisa', in *Across the Oceans: Studies from East to West in*

Honor of Richard K. Seymour, ed. by Irmengard Rauch and Cornelia Moore (Honolulu: University of Hawaii, 1995), pp.61-76.

Dixon, Wheeler Winston, ed., *American Cinema of the 1940s: Themes and Variations* (Piscataway: Rutgers University Press, 2006).

Docker, John, *Postmodernism and Popular Culture: A Cultural History* (Cambridge: Cambridge University Press, 1994).

Dockterman, Eliana, '11 Christmas Movies You Didn't Know Were Christmas Movies', in *Time Online*, 22 December 2014.
<*http://time.com/3634524/christmas-movies-unconventional/*>

Dodge, Marcus, '*Merry Christmas, Mr Lawrence*', in *DVD Active*, 2011.
<*http://www.dvdactive.com/reviews/dvd/merry-christmas-mr-lawrence.html*>

Donald, Ella, '*One Magic Christmas*', in *Letterboxd*, 23 December 2013.
<*https://letterboxd.com/jchastained/film/one-magic-christmas/*>

Douglas, Clark, '*Merry Christmas, Mr Lawrence* (Blu-Ray) Criterion Collection', in *DVD Verdict*, 28 September 2010.
<*http://www.dvdverdict.com/reviews/mrlawrencebluray.php*>

Duarte, M. Enois, '*Better Off Dead*', in *High Def Digest*, 25 July 2011.
<*http://bluray.highdefdigest.com/5253/better_dead.html*>

—, '*Scrooged*', in *High Def Digest*, 28 October 2011.
<*http://bluray.highdefdigest.com/5767/scrooged.html*>

Duncan, Dean, '*One Magic Christmas*', in *Films in Review*, 26 March 2015.
<*https://sites.lib.byu.edu/filmsinreview/film_review/one-magic-christmas/*>

Duralde, Alonso, *Have Yourself a Movie Little Christmas* (Milwaukee: Limelight Editions, 2010).

Ebert, Roger, '*A Christmas Story*', in *The Chicago Sun-Times*, 15 December 1983.

—, '*A Christmas Story*', in *The Chicago Sun-Times*, 24 December 2000.

—, '*Comfort and Joy*', in *The Chicago Sun-Times*, 23 October 1984.

—, '*Die Hard*', in *The Chicago Sun-Times*, 15 July 1988.

—, '*Gremlins*', in *The Chicago Sun-Times*, 8 June 1984.

—, '*Merry Christmas, Mr Lawrence*', in *The Chicago Sun-Times*, 16 September 1983.

—, '*National Lampoon's Christmas Vacation*', in *The Chicago Sun-Times*, 1 December 1989.

—, '*One Magic Christmas*', in *The Chicago Sun-Times*, 22 November 1985.

—, '*Prancer*', in *The Chicago Sun-Times*, 17 November 1989.

—, '*Santa Claus: The Movie*', in *The Chicago Sun-Times*, 27 November 1985.

—, '*Scrooged*', in *The Chicago Sun-Times*, 23 November 1998.

—, '*Trading Places*', in *The Chicago Sun-Times*, 9 June 1983.

Edwards, James Jay, 'Cinema Fearité Presents *To All A Goodnight*: A Killer Santa Movie From a Time Before Killer Santa Movies Were a Real Thing', in *FilmFracture*, 25 December 2014.
<http://www.filmfracture.com/frame_of_mind/cinema_fearit_presents_to _all_a_goodnight__a_killer_santa_movie_from_a_time_before_killer_sant a_movies_were_a_real_thing>

Edwards, Matt, 'Revisiting *Santa Claus: The Movie*', in *Den of Geek*, 22 December 2015.
<http://www.denofgeek.com/movies/santa-claus-the-movie/ revisiting-santa-claus-the-movie>

Elliott, Larry, and Dan Atkinson, *The Age of Insecurity* (London: Verso, 1999) [1998].

Ellis, John, *Visible Fictions: Cinema, Television, Video* (London: Routledge, 1989) [1982].

Erickson, Glenn, '*A Christmas Story*', in *DVD Savant*, 2 November 2008. <*http://www.dvdtalk.com/dvdsavant/s2736stor.html*>

—, '*Gremlins*', in *DVD Savant*, 4 December 2009. <*http://www.dvdtalk.com/dvdsavant/s3081grem.html*>

Everett, William A., and Paul R. Laird, eds., *The Cambridge Companion to the Musical* (Cambridge: Cambridge University Press, 2008).

Fairbanks, Brian W., *I Saw That Movie, Too: Selected Film Reviews*, 3rd edn (Morrisville: Lulu.com, 2010).

Fairclough, Norman, *Critical Discourse Analysis: The Critical Study of Language* (Harlow, Longman: 1995).

Felton, Bruce, *What Were They Thinking?: Really Bad Ideas Throughout History*, rev. edn. (Guilford: Lyons Press, 2007).

Fishwick, Marshall W., *Popular Culture in a New Age* (Binghampton: Haworth Press, 2002).

Flanagan, Martin, 'John Landis', in *Contemporary North American Film Directors: A Wallflower Critical Guide*, ed. by Yoram Allon, Del Cullen and Hannah Patterson (London: Wallflower Press, 2002), pp.310-12.

Flower, Amy, '*Die Hard*', in *DVD.net*, 2006. <*http://www.dvd.net.au/review.cgi?review_id=1415*>

Forbes, Bruce David, *Christmas: A Candid History* (Berkeley: University of California Press, 2007).

Foster, Matthew M., '*One Magic Christmas*', in *Foster on Film*, 2004. <*http://fosteronfilm.com/holidays/xmas/onemagicchristmas.htm*>

Foster, Tyler, '*Die Hard*: 25th Anniversary Collection', in *DVD Talk*, 29 January 2013.

<http://www.dvdtalk.com/reviews/59327/die-hard-25th-anniversary-collection/>

—, '*Trading Places*: Special Collector's Edition', in *DVD Talk*, 24 August 2010.
<http://www.dvdtalk.com/reviews/47288/trading-places-special-collectors-edition/>

Fraser, Matthew, '*Trading Places*', in *The Toronto Globe and Mail*, 10 June 1983.

Freeman, Molly, 'Why is *Die Hard* a Christmas Movie?', in *Hollywood.com*, 2015.
<http://www.hollywood.com/movies/die-hard-christmas-movie-57258229/>

Frow, John, *Genre* (London: Routledge, 2006).

G., Josh, '*Silent Night, Deadly Night*', in *Oh, The Horror*, 16 December 2008.
<http://www.oh-the-horror.com/page.php?id=452>

Gabbard, Glen O., and Krin Gabbard, *Psychiatry and the Cinema*, 2nd edn (Washington D.C.: American Psychiatric Press, 1999).

Gallagher, Danny, 'Is *Die Hard* a Christmas movie?: Poll Takes Pulse on Key Issue of Our Time', in *CNet*, 23 December 2015.
<http://www.cnet.com/uk/news/is-die-hard-a-christmas-movie-poll-takes-pulse-on-key-issue-of-our-time/>

Garrett, Eddie, *I Saw Stars in the 40's and 50's* (Victoria: Trafford Publishing, 2005).

Garrett, Greg, *The Gospel According to Hollywood* (Louisville: Westminster John Knox Press, 2007).

Gibbs, Rosie, '*Silent Night, Deadly Night*', in *UK Horror Scene*, 4 December 2015.
<http://www.ukhorrorscene.com/the-ukhs-writers-christmas-horrors-silent-night-deadly-night-1984/>

Gibron, Bill, '*Christmas Evil*', in *DVD Talk*, 14 November 2006.
<*http://www.dvdtalk.com/reviews/25047/christmas-evil/*>

—, '*Santa Claus: The Movie*', in *DVD Talk*, 26 October 2010.
<*http://www.dvdtalk.com/reviews/45152/santa-claus-movie-25th-anniversary-edition/*>

Giddings, Robert, and Erica Sheen, eds, *The Classic Novel: From Page to Screen* (Manchester: Manchester University Press, 2000).

Gilstrap, Andrew, '*Better Off Dead* Boasts Moments of Surreal Humor', in *Pop Matters*, 2 August 2011.
<*http://www.popmatters.com/review/145582-better-off-dead-blu-ray/*>

Glavin, John, ed., *Dickens on Screen* (Cambridge: Cambridge University Press, 2003).

Gonsalves, Rob, '*Scrooged*', in *eFilmCritic.com*, 29 December 2015.
<*http://www.filmcritic.com/reviews/1988/scrooged/?OpenDocument*>

Gordon, Bill, '*Don't Open Till Christmas*', in *Horror Fan Zine*, 12 December 2011.
<*http://horrorfanzine.com/dont-open-till-christmas-edmund-purdom-1984/*>

Gracey, Bill, '*Christmas Evil*', in *Behind the Couch*, 20 December 2012.
<*http://watchinghorrorfilmsfrombehindthecouch.blogspot.co.uk/2012/12/christmas-evil.html*>

Green, Stanley, *Hollywood Musicals Year by Year*, 2nd edn., rev. by Elaine Schmidt (Milwaukee: Hal Leonard, 1999).

Gross, G. Noel, 'Jim Varney: A Legacy of Laughter', in *DVD Talk*, 2000.
<*http://www.dvdtalk.com/cineschlock/ernest/index.html*>

Gross, Jason, '14 Air-Braking Facts About *Ernest Saves Christmas*', in *Rediscover the 80s*, December 2015.
<*http://www.rediscoverthe80s.com/2015/12/14-facts-about-ernest-saves-christmas.html*>

Guida, Fred, *'A Christmas Carol' and Its Adaptations: A Critical Examination of Dickens' Story and Its Productions on Stage, Screen and Television* (Jefferson: McFarland, 2000).

Hales, Stephen D., 'Putting Claus Back into Christmas', in *Christmas: Philosophy for Everyone*, ed. by Scott C. Lowe (Chichester: Blackwell, 2010), pp.161-71.

Hallenbeck, Bruce G., *Comedy-Horror Films: A Chronological History, 1914-2008* (Jefferson: McFarland and Company, 2009).

Hantke, Steffen, ed., *American Horror Film: The Genre at the Turn of the Millennium* (Jackson: University Press of Mississippi, 2010).

Hardy, Phil, ed., *The Aurum Film Encyclopedia: Science Fiction* (London: Aurum Press, 1995).

Harper, Jim, *Legacy of Blood: A Comprehensive Guide to Slasher Movies* (Manchester: Headpress/Critical Vision, 2004).

Healey, Tim, *The World's Worst Movies* (London: Octopus Books, 1986).

Henderson, Eric, '*Silent Night, Deadly Night*', in *Slant Magazine*, 22 October 2003.
<*http://www.slantmagazine.com/film/review/silent-night-deadly-night*>

Hibberd, James, '10 Reasons *Die Hard* is a Perfect Christmas Movie', in *Entertainment Weekly*, 24 December 2015.
<*http://www.ew.com/article/2015/12/24/die-hard-christmas-movie*>

Hicks, Chris, '*National Lampoon's Christmas Vacation*', in *The Deseret News*, 16 December 2002.

Hill, John, and Pamela Church Gibson, eds, *The Oxford Guide to Film Studies* (Oxford: Oxford University Press, 1998).

Hinson, Hal, '*Die Hard*', in *The Washington Post*, 15 July 1988.

—, '*Scrooged*', in *The Washington Post*, 23 November 1988.

Hjort, Mette, and Scott MacKenzie, *Cinema and Nation* (London: Routledge, 2000).

Hoare, Peter, '10 Reasons why *Die Hard* is the Greatest Christmas Movie Ever', in *BroBible*, 23 December 2015.
<http://brobible.com/entertainment/article/why-die-hard-is-christmas-movie/>

Hoffman, Robert C., *Postcards from Santa Claus: Sights and Sentiments from the Last Century* (New York: Square One Publishers, 2002).

Hollows, Joanne, and Mark Jancovich, eds, *Approaches to Popular Film* (Manchester: Manchester University Press, 1995).

Horton, Robert, '*Better Off Dead*', in *What a Feeling!*, 7 April 2011 [1985].
<https://eightiesmovies.wordpress.com/2011/04/07/better-off-dead/>

—, '*Comfort and Joy*', in *What a Feeling!*, 6 July 2012 [1984].
<https://eightiesmovies.wordpress.com/2012/07/06/comfort-and-joy/>

—, '*Ernest Saves Christmas*', in *What a Feeling!*, 22 December 2010 [1988].
<https://eightiesmovies.wordpress.com/2010/12/22/ernest-saves-christmas>

—, '*National Lampoon's Christmas Vacation*', in *What a Feeling!*, 23 December 2011 [1989].
<https://eightiesmovies.wordpress.com/2011/12/23/national-lampoons-christmas-vacation/>

Hunter, Allan, ed., *The Wordsworth Book of Movie Classics* (Ware: Wordsworth, 1996) [1992].

Hurlburt, Roger, 'A Yuletide Standby Though Not a Classic', in *The South Florida Sun-Sentinel*, 18 November 1989.

Jackson, Dave, '*Don't Open Till Christmas*', in *Mondo Exploito*, 18 December 2014.
<http://mondoexploito.com/?p=11571>

Jacobson, Colin, '*Gremlins*', in *DVD Movie Guide*, 18 December 2009. <*http://www.dvdmg.com/gremlinsbr.shtml*>

James, Caryn, 'A Girl, a Reindeer and the Christmas Spirit', in *The New York Times*, 17 November 1989.

—, '*Ernest Saves Christmas*', in *The New York Times*, 11 November 1988.

—, 'The Police, Terrorists and a Captive Audience', in *The New York Times*, 15 July 1988.

Jane, Ian, '*To All a Goodnight*', in *DVD Talk*, 21 October 2014. <*http://www.dvdtalk.com/reviews/65711/to-all-a-goodnight/*>

Jasen, David A., *Tin Pan Alley: An Encyclopedia of the Golden Age of the American Song* (New York: Routledge, 2003).

Jeffers, H. Paul, *Legends of Santa Claus* (Minneapolis: Lerner Publishing Group, 2001).

Johnson, Alan, '*Ernest Saves Christmas*', in *Letterboxd*, 6 December 2015. <*https://letterboxd.com/alpal/film/ernest-saves-christmas/*>

Johnston, Hank, and John A. Noakes, eds, *Frames of Protest: Social Movements and the Framing Perspective* (Oxford: Rowman and Littlefield, 2005).

Jones, Alan-Bertaneisson, *Fright Xmas* (Central Milton Keynes: Authorhouse, 2010).

Jones, Edward, 'Horror Clichés: Up From the Dead, and Still Fun', in *The Free Lance-Star*, 14 July 1975

Jones, Ken D., Arthur F. McClure and Alfred E. Twomey, *Character People* (New York: A.S. Barnes, 1977).

Jordan, Chris, *Movies and the Reagan Presidency: Success and Ethics* (Westport: Greenwood Publishing Group, 2003).

Kalaga, Wojciech H., and Marzena Kubisz, eds, *Multicultural Dilemmas: Identity, Difference, Otherness* (Frankfurt am Main: Peter Lang, 2008).

Kaye, Dave, 'Santa Claus, Sorority Girls, and Serious Slashing: *To All a Good Night* Review', in *Slasher Studios*, 24 March 2012.
<*http://www.slasherstudios.com/2012/03/24/santa-claus-sorority-girls-and-serious-slashing-to-all-a-good-night-review/*>

Kehr, Dave, '*Ernest Saves Christmas* is No Real Holiday', in *The Chicago Tribune*, 14 November 1988.

—, '*Prancer* a Contradictory Christmas Card', in *The Chicago Tribune*, 17 November 1989.

—, 'Sleek *Die Hard* Tools Action Film to Perfection', in *The Chicago Tribute*, 15 July 1988.

Kelly, Daniel W., '*One Magic Christmas*', in *DVD Talk*, 29 September 2004.
<*http://www.dvdtalk.com/reviews/12490/one-magic-christmas/*>

Kelly, Richard Michael, 'Introduction', in Charles Dickens, *A Christmas Carol* (Peterborough: Broadview Press, 2003).

Kempley, Rita, '*Ernest Saves Christmas*', in *The Washington Post*, 11 November 1988.

—, '*National Lampoon's Christmas Vacation*', in *The Washington Post*, 1 December 1989.

—, '*Prancer*', in *The Washington Post*, 17 November 1989.

Kendrick, James, '*Better Off Dead*', in *QNetwork.com*, 1998.
<*http://www.qnetwork.com/index.php?page=review&id=976*>

Keyes, David M., '*Gremlins*', in *Cinemaphile*, 7 December 2014.
<*http://www.thecinemaphileblog.com/2014/12/gremlins-1984.html*>

Knifpel, Jim, '*You Better Watch Out*: The *Taxi Driver* of Christmas Movies', in *Den of Geek*, 10 December 2015.

<http://www.denofgeek.us/movies/you-better-watch-out/34766/you-better-watch-out-the-taxi-driver-of-christmas-movies>

Lancaster, Dave, '*Merry Christmas, Mr Lawrence*', in *Cinemas Online*, 2011.
<http://www.cinemas-online.co.uk/film-reviews/merry-christmas-mr-lawrence-a101751.html>

Langford, Barry, *Post-Classical Hollywood: Film Industry, Style and Ideology Since 1945* (Edinburgh: Edinburgh University Press, 2010).

LaSalle, Mick, '*Scrooged*', in *The San Francisco Chronicle*, 23 November 1988.

Lay, Samantha, 'Bill Forsyth', in *Contemporary British and Irish Film Directors: A Wallflower Critical Guide*, ed. by Yoram Allon, Del Cullen and Hannah Patterson (London: Wallflower Press, 2001), pp.97-99.

Libbey, Dirk, 'New Poll Asks if *Die Hard* is a Christmas Movie, Majority Pick Wrong Answer', in *CinemaBlend*, January 2016.
<http://www.cinemablend.com/new/Poll-Asks-Die-Hard-Christmas-Movie-Majority-Pick-Wrong-Answer-102117.html>

Liebman, Martin, '*Better Off Dead* Blu-ray Review', in *Blu-Ray.com*, 22 July 2011.
<http://www.blu-ray.com/movies/Better-Off-Dead-Blu-ray/24222/#Review>

Leitch, Thomas M., *Film Adaptation and Its Discontents: From* Gone With the Wind *to* The Passion of the Christ (Baltimore: Johns Hopkins University Press, 2007).

Lester, Meera, *Why Does Santa Wear Red? ...and 100 Other Christmas Curiosities Unwrapped* (Avon: Adams Media, 2007).

Levi, Ross D., *The Celluloid Courtroom: A History of Legal Cinema* (Westport: Greenwood Publishing Group, 2005).

Lippe, Adam, 'The Mob's Ice Cream Enforcer: A review of *Comfort and Joy*', in *Examiner.com*, 27 April 2012.

<http://www.examiner.com/review/the-mob-s-ice-cream-enforcer-a-review-of-comfort-and-joy>

Long, Mike, '*A Christmas Story*', in *DVD Sleuth*, 2 November 2008. *<http://www.dvdsleuth.com/AChristmasStoryReview/>*

—, '*Gremlins*', in *DVD Sleuth*, 1 December 2009. *<http://www.dvdsleuth.com/GremlinsReview/>*

—, '*Scrooged*', in *DVD Sleuth*, 8 November 2011. *<http://www.dvdsleuth.com/ScroogedReview/>*

—, '*Silent Night, Deadly Night* (1984)/*Silent Night, Deadly Night Part 2* (1987)', in *DVD Sleuth*, 4 December 2012. *<http://www.dvdsleuth.com/SilentNightDeadlyNightDoubleFeatureReview/>*

—, '*Trading Places*', in *DVD Sleuth*, 13 June 2007. *<http://www.dvdsleuth.com/TradingPlacesReview/>*

Loomis, Daryl, '*Don't Open Till Christmas*', in *DVD Verdict*, 16 December 2011. *<http://www.dvdverdict.com/reviews/dontopentillchristmas.php>*

Loukides, Paul, and Linda K. Fuller, eds, *Beyond the Stars: Plot Conventions in American Popular Film* (Bowling Green: Bowling Green State University Popular Press, 1991).

—, eds, *Beyond the Stars: Studies in American Popular Film Volume 5: Themes and Ideologies in American Popular Film* (Madison: Popular Press, 1996).

Lowe, Scott C., ed., *Christmas: Philosophy for Everyone* (Chichester: Blackwell, 2010).

Macomber, Shawn, '*Christmas Evil* (Vinegar Syndrome Blu-Ray Review)', in *Shock Till You Drop*, 24 December 2014. *<http://www.shocktillyoudrop.com/news/371795-christmas-evil-vinegar-syndrome-blu-ray-review/>*

Magala, Slawomir, *Cross-Cultural Competence* (Abingdon: Routledge, 2005).

Mansour, David J., *From Abba to Zoom: A Pop Culture Encyclopedia of the Late 20th Century* (Kansas City: Andrews McMeel Publishing, 2005).

Marling, Karal Ann, *Merry Christmas!: Celebrating America's Greatest Holiday* (Cambridge: Harvard University Press, 2000).

Marsh, Calum, '*Gremlins*', in *Slant*, 11 May 2012.
<http://www.slantmagazine.com/dvd/review/gremlins>

Martin, Todd, 'Film Review: *Don't Open Till Christmas*', in *Horror News*, 24 June 2015.
<http://horrornews.net/75698/film-review-dont-open-till-christmas-1984/>

Maslin, Janet, 'Ackroyd in *Trading Places*', in *The New York Times*, 8 June 1983.

—, '*Better Off Dead*', in *The New York Times*, 11 October 1985.

—, 'David Bowie in *Merry Christmas*', in *The New York Times*, 26 August 1983.

—, '*Magic Christmas*, with Santa and Angel', in *The New York Times*, 22 November 1985.

—, 'On *Vacation* Once Again', in *The New York Times*, 1 December 1989.

Matthews, Kevin, '*A Christmas Story*', in *FlickFeast*, 20 December 2011.
<http://flickfeast.co.uk/reviews/film-reviews/christmas-story-1983/>

—, '*Better Off Dead*', in *FlickFeast*, 31 December 2013.
<http://flickfeast.co.uk/reviews/film-reviews/dead-1985/>

—, '*Christmas Vacation*', in *FlickFeast*, 9 December 2011.
<http://flickfeast.co.uk/reviews/film-reviews/christmas-vacation-1989/>

—, '*Santa Claus*', in *FlickFeast*, 21 December 2011.
<http://flickfeast.co.uk/reviews/film-reviews/santa-claus-1985/>

Mavis, Paul, '*Silent Night, Deadly Night: Christmas Survival Double Feature*', in *DVD Talk*, 4 December 2012.
<http://www.dvdtalk.com/reviews/58650/silent-night-deadly-night-dbft/>

McBrien, Richard, 'Angels and Spirituality: Comfort, Help of Angels May Hover Close at Hand', in *The National Catholic Reporter*, 4 March 1994.

McDannell, Colleen, ed., *Catholics in the Movies* (New York: Oxford University Press US, 2008).

McGee, Patrick, *Cinema, Theory, and Political Responsibility in Contemporary Culture* (Cambridge: Cambridge University Press, 1997).

Mechling, Jay, 'Rethinking (and Reteaching) the Civil Religion in Post-Nationalist American Studies', in *Post-Nationalist American Studies*, ed. by John Carlos Rowe (Berkeley: University of California Press, 2000), pp.63-83.

Metcalf, Greg, '"It's (Christmas) Morning in America": Christmas Conventions of American Films in the 1980s', in *Beyond the Stars: Plot Conventions in American Popular Film*, ed. by Paul Loukides and Linda K. Fuller (Bowling Green: Bowling Green State University Popular Press, 1991), pp.100-13.

Miller, Daniel, *Consumption: Critical Concepts in the Social Sciences, Volume IV: Objects, Subjects and Mediations in Consumption* (London: Routledge, 2001).

Miller, Gordon S., '*Merry Christmas, Mr Lawrence*', in *High Def Digest*, 18 November 2010.
<http://bluray.highdefdigest.com/3589/christmas_lawrence.html>

Miller, Toby, and Robert Stam, eds., *A Companion to Film Theory* (Oxford: Blackwell, 2004) [1999].

Mitchell, Jeremy, and Richard Maidment, eds., *The United States in the Twentieth Century: Culture* (London: Hodder and Stoughton, 1994).

Moore, Kenneth, *The Magic of 'Santa Claus': More Than Just a Red Suit!* (Martinez: Ken Moore Productions, 2006).

Muir, John Kenneth, *Horror Films of the 1980s* (Jefferson: McFarland, 2007).

Müller, Jürgen, *Movies of the 80s* (Köln: Taschen Books, 2002).

Murphy, Robert, ed., *The British Cinema Book*, 2nd edn (London: British Film Institute, 2001).

Murray, Noel, '*A Christmas Story*', in *The Onion A. V. Club*, 9 December 2003.
<http://www.avclub.com/articles/a-christmas-story-dvd,11656/>

—, '*Don't Open Till Christmas*', in *The Onion A. V. Club*, 21 December 2011.
<http://www.avclub.com/review/dont-open-till-christmas-66833>

Nadel, Alan, 'Movies and Reaganism', in *American Cinema of the 1980s: Themes and Variations*, ed. by Stephen Prince (Chapel Hill: Rutgers University Press, 2007), pp.82-106.

Naugle, Patrick, '*National Lampoon's Christmas Vacation: Special Edition*', in *DVD Verdict*, 16 October 2003.
<http://www.dvdverdict.com/reviews/christmasvacationse.php>

Neale, Steve, *Genre and Hollywood* (London: Routledge, 2000).

Neff, Alan, *Movies, Movie Stars, and Me* (Bloomington: AuthorHouse, 2008).

Nelson, Andrew Patrick, 'Traumatic Childhood Now Included: Todorov's Fantastic and the Uncanny Slasher Remake', in *American Horror Film: The Genre at the Turn of the Millennium*, ed. by Steffen Hantke (Jackson: University Press of Mississippi, 2010), pp.103-18.

Neuwirth, Allan, *Makin' Toons: Inside the Most Popular Animated TV Shows and Movies* (New York: Allworth Press, 2003).

Newman, Kim, 'You Better Watch Out: Christmas in the Horror Film', in *Christmas at the Movies*, ed. by Mark Connelly (London: I.B. Tauris, 2000), pp.135-142.

Nield, Anthony, '*Christmas Evil*', in *The Digital Fix*, 19 December 2012.
<http://film.thedigitalfix.com/content/id/76149/christmas-evil.html>

—, '*Santa Claus: The Movie*', in *The Digital Fix*, 16 November 2005.
<http://film.thedigitalfix.com/content.php?contentid=59246>

Normanton, Peter, *The Mammoth Book of Slasher Movies* (London: Robinson, 2012).

Novak, Ralph, '*Prancer*', in *People*, Vol. 32, No. 24, 11 December 1989.

Nowlan, Bob, and Zach Finch, *Directory of World Cinema: Scotland* (Bristol: Intellect, 2015).

Null, Christopher, '*Scrooged*', in *FilmCritic.com*, 2 January 2006.
<http://www.filmcritic.com/reviews/1988/scrooged/?OpenDocument>

Nusair, David, '*Prancer*', in *ReelFilm*, 19 December 2004.
<http://www.reelfilm.com/prancer.htm>

—, 'The Films of John Landis', in *ReelFilm*, 1 July 2009.
<http://reelfilm.com/jlandis.htm#trading>

Palmer, William J., *The Films of the Eighties: A Social History* (Carbondale: Southern Illinois University Press, 1993).

Panton, Gary, '*Scrooged*', in *Movie Gazette*, 23 December 2003.
<http://www.movie-gazette.com/572>

Parker, Andrew, 'Defending the Indefensible: *Silent Night Deadly Night Parts 1&2*', in *Dork Shelf*, 18 December 2012.
<http://www.dorkshelf.com/2012/12/18/defending-the-indefensible-silent-night-deadly-night-parts-1-2/>

Paszylk, Bartlomiej, *The Pleasure and Pain of Cult Horror Films: An Historical Survey* (Jefferson: McFarland and Company, 2009).

Patel, Sonja, *The Christmas Companion* (London: Think Books, 2008).

Paulding, Barbara, Suzanne Schwalb and Mara Conlon, *A Century of Christmas Memories 1900-1999* (New York: Peter Pauper Press, 2009).

Pontuso, James F., ed., *Political Philosophy Comes to Rick's: Casablanca and American Civic Culture* (Lanham: Lexington Books, 2005).

Prince, Dennis, '*A Christmas Story*', in *DVD Verdict*, 8 January 2007.
<*http://www.dvdverdict.com/reviews/christmasstoryhddvd.php*>

Prince, Stephen, ed., *American Cinema of the 1980s: Themes and Variations* (Chapel Hill: Rutgers University Press, 2007).

Purves, Barry J.C., *Stop Motion: Passion, Process and Performance* (Oxford: Elsevier, 2008).

Quart, Leonard, and Albert Auster, *American Film and Society Since 1945*, 3rd edn (Westport: Greenwood Publishing Group, 2002).

R., Wes, '*To All a Good Night*', in *Oh, The Horror*, 14 December 2008.
<*http://www.oh-the-horror.com/page.php?id=449*>

Rabin, Nathan, 'My Year of Flops: Case File #96: *Santa Claus: The Movie*', in *The Onion A. V. Club*, 25 December 2007.
<*http://www.avclub.com/articles/my-year-of-flops-case-file-96-santa-claus-the-movi,10128/*>

—, '*Trading Places/ Coming to America*', in *The Onion A. V. Club*, 13 June 2007.
<*http://www.avclub.com/review/trading-places-coming-to-america-7767*>

Rawson-Jones, Ben, '*Gremlins* Review: Fiendishly Funny Classic Re-released for Christmas', in *Digital Spy*, 6 December 2016.
<*http://www.digitalspy.com/movies/review/a443304/gremlins-review-fiendishly-funny-classic-re-released-for-christmas/*>

Reid, John Howard, *Hollywood Movie Musicals: Great, Good and Glamorous* (Morrisville: Lulu.com, 2006).

Rauch, Irmengard, and Cornelia Moore, eds, *Across the Oceans: Studies from East to West in Honor of Richard K. Seymour* (Honolulu: University of Hawaii, 1995).

Reid, John Howard, *Movies Magnificent: 150 Must-See Cinema Classics* (Morrisville: Lulu.com, 2005).

Rich, Jamie S., '*Merry Christmas, Mr Lawrence*. Criterion Collection (Blu-Ray)', in *DVD Talk*, 28 September 2010. *<http://www.dvdtalk.com/reviews/44638/merry-christmas-mr-lawrence/>*

Richards, Jeffrey, *Films and British National Identity: From Dickens to Dad's Army* (Manchester: Manchester University Press, 1997).

Rickey, Carrie, 'Girl Helps Out Santa's *Prancer*', in *The Philadelphia Enquirer*, 20 November 1989.

Rist, Peter Harry, ed., *Guide to the Cinema(s) of Canada* (Westport: Greenwood Press, 2001).

Rockoff, Adam, *Going to Pieces: The Rise and Fall of the Slasher Film, 1978-1986* (Jefferson: McFarland and Company, 2002).

Rose, Brian Geoffrey, *An Examination of Narrative Structure in Four Films of Frank Capra* (New York: Arno Press, 1980) [1976].

Rowe, John Carlos, ed., *Post-Nationalist American Studies* (Berkeley: University of California Press, 2000).

Ryan, Michael, and Douglas Kellner, *Camera Politica: The Politics and Ideology of Contemporary Hollywood* (Indianapolis: Indiana University Press, 1988).

Santino, Jack, *All Around the Year: Holidays and Celebrations in American Life* (Champaign: University of Illinois Press, 1994) [1985].

—, *New Old-Fashioned Ways: Holidays and Popular Culture* (Knoxville: University of Tennessee Press, 1996).

Schanie, Andrew, *Movie Confidential: Sex, Scandal, Murder and Mayhem in the Film Industry* (Cincinnatti: Clerisy Press, 2010).

Scheib, Richard, '*Ernest Saves Christmas*', in *Moria: Science Fiction, Horror and Fantasy Film Review*, 2012.
<http://moria.co.nz/fantasy/ernestsaveschristmas.htm>

—, '*Prancer*', in *Moria: The Science Fiction, Horror and Fantasy Film Review*, 2013.
<http://moria.co.nz/fantasy/prancer-1989.htm>

Schwartz, Dennis, '*You Better Watch Out* (aka *Christmas Evil*)', in *Dennis Schwartz's Movie Reviews*, 21 December 2011.
<http://homepages.sover.net/~ozus/youbetterwatchout.html>

Shail, Robert, *British Film Directors: A Critical Guide* (Edinburgh: Edinburgh University Press, 2007).

Short, Norman, '*Santa Claus: The Movie*', in *DVD Verdict*, 12 October 2000.
<http://www.dvdverdict.com/reviews/santaclaus.php>

Simpson, Paul, ed., *The Rough Guide to Cult Movies* (London: Haymarket Customer Publishing, 2001).

Siskel, Gene, '*Scrooged*', in *The Chicago Tribune*, 25 November 1988.

Slarek, Jagd, '*Christmas Evil* DVD Review', in *CineOutsider*, 22 December 2012.
<http://www.cineoutsider.com/reviews/dvd/c/christmas_evil.html>

Smith, Robert, 'What Actually Happens at the End of *Trading Places?*', in *Planet Money: The Economy Explained*, National Public Radio, 12 July 2013.
<http://www.npr.org/sections/money/2013/07/19/201430727/what-actually-happens-at-the-end-of-trading-places>

Smith, Stephanie Star, 'Classic Film Review: *A Christmas Story*', in *Box Office Prophets*, 25 December 2002.
<http://www.boxofficeprophets.com/moviereviews/christmasstory.asp>

Sommersby, Jack, '*Silent Night, Deadly Night*', in *eFilmCritic*, 2 December 2003.
<*http://www.efilmcritic.com/review.php?movie=3194&reviewer=327*>

Staiger, Janet, *Perverse Spectators: The Practices of Film Reception* (New York: New York University Press, 2000).

Stailey, Michael, '*Gremlins*', in *DVD Verdict*, 1 June 2012.
<*http://www.dvdverdict.com/reviews/gremlinsbluray.php*>

Staskiewicz, Keith, '*Better Off Dead*', in *Entertainment Weekly*, 12 July 2011.
<*http://www.ew.com/article/2011/07/12/better-dead-review-john-cusack*>

Stephens, Chuck, 'Lawrence of Shinjuku: *Merry Christmas, Mr Lawrence*' in *The Criterion Collection*, 28 September 2010.
<*https://www.criterion.com/current/posts/1605-lawrence-of-shinjuku-merry-christmas-mr-lawrence*>

Stephens, Daniel, '*National Lampoon's Christmas Vacation*', in *DVD Times*, 17 November 2003.
<*http://www.dvdtimes.co.uk/content.php?contentid=6068*>

Sterritt, David, 'Dante's *Gremlins* Mixes Humor and Horror', in *The Christian Science Monitor*, 7 June 1984.
<*http://www.csmonitor.com/1984/0607/060707.html*>

Stewart, Henry, 'The Best Old Movies on a Big Screen This Week: NYC Repertory Cinema Picks, December 16-22', in *Brooklyn Magazine*, 16 December 2015.
<*http://www.bkmag.com/2015/12/16/the-best-old-movies-on-a-big-screen-this-week-nyc-repertory-cinema-picks-december-16-22/5/*>

Stine, Scott Aaron, *The Gorehound's Guide to Splatter Films of the 1980s* (Jefferson: McFarland, 2011).

Strupp, Phyllis, *The Richest of Fare: Seeking Spiritual Security in the Sonoran Desert* (Scottsdale: Sonoran Cross Press, 2004).

Sumner, Don, *Horror Movie Freak* (Iola: Krause Publications, 2010).

Svehla, Gary J., and Susan Svehla, *It's Christmas Time at the Movies* (Baltimore: Midnight Marquee Press, 1998).

Tasker, Yvonne, *Spectacular Bodies: Gender, Genre and the Action Cinema* (London: Routledge, 1993).

Taylor, Drew, 'Why *Die Hard* is the Greatest Christmas Movie Ever Made', in *MovieFone*, 23 December 2013. <*http://www.moviefone.com/2013/12/23/die-hard-greatest-christmas-movie-ever/*>

Tezuka, Yoshiharu, *Japanese Cinema Goes Global: Filmworkers' Journeys* (Hong Kong: Hong Kong University Press, 2012).

Thomas, Kevin, '*Die Hard* a Slick Flick for Bruce Willis', in *The Los Angeles Times*, 15 July 1988.

—, '*Prancer* an Unapologetic Christmas Heart-Tugger', in *The Los Angeles Times*, 17 November 1989.

Thomas, Tony, *A Smidgeon of Religion* (Bloomington: AuthorHouse, 2007).

Thompson, Frank, *American Movie Classics' Great Christmas Movies* (Dallas: Taylor, 1998).

Thompson, Nathaniel, '*To All a Goodnight*', in *Mondo Digital*, 12 December 2014. <*http://mondo-digital.com/allgoodnight.html*>

Tobias, Scott, '*Better Off Dead* (Blu-Ray)', in *The Onion A. V. Club*, 3 August 2011. <*http://www.avclub.com/review/better-off-dead-blu-ray-59871*>

Topel, Fred, 'No, Seriously... *Die Hard* is a Real Christmas Movie', in *Crave Online*, 5 December 2014. <*http://www.craveonline.com/site/796777-seriously-die-hard-christmas-movie*>

Totaro, Donato, 'Bob Clark', in *Guide to the Cinema(s) of Canada*, ed. by Peter Harry Rist (Westport: Greenwood Press, 2001), pp.38-39.

Turim, Maureen, *The Films of Oshima Nagisa: Images of a Japanese Iconoclast* (Berkeley: University of California Press, 1998).

Turner, Graeme, *Film as Social Practice* (London: Routledge, 1999).

Tyler, Don, *Music of the Postwar Era* (Westport: Greenwood Publishing Group, 2008).

Tyner, Adam, '*Christmas Evil* (Blu-Ray)', in *DVD Talk*, 18 November 2014.
<http://www.dvdtalk.com/reviews/66272/christmas-evil/>

—, '*Gremlins*: Special Edition', in *DVD Talk*, 20 August 2009.
<http://www.dvdtalk.com/reviews/4426/gremlins-special-edition/>

Variety Staff, '*National Lampoon's Christmas Vacation*', in *Variety*, 1 December 1989.

—, '*Santa Claus: The Movie*', in *Variety*, 27 November 1985.

—, '*Scrooged*', in *Variety*, 25 November 1988.

Wain, Dave, '*To All a Goodnight*', in *UK Horror Scene*, 14 November 2013.
<http://www.ukhorrorscene.com/tales-that-witness-crapness-2-to-all-a-goodnight-1980/>

Walsh, Michael, 'Christmas Cheer, Or Else', in *Reeling Back*, 20 December 2013.
<http://reelingback.com/articles/christmas_cheer_or_else>

Ward, Tom, 'Why *Die Hard* is the Best Christmas Movie of All Time', in *The Huffington Post*, 22 February 2013.
<http://www.huffingtonpost.co.uk/tom-ward/why-die-hard-is-the-best-christmas-movie-of-all-time_b_2339117.html>

Watt, Kate Carnell, and Kathleen C. Lonsdale, 'Dickens Composed: Film and Television Adaptations 1897-2001', in *Dickens on Screen*, ed. by John Glavin (Cambridge: Cambridge University Press, 2003), pp.201-16.

Webb, Andy, '*Ernest Saves Christmas*', in *The Movie Scene*, 2012. <*http://www.themoviescene.co.uk/reviews/ernest-daves-christmas-1988/ernest-daves-christmas-1988.html*>

—, '*National Lampoon's Christmas Vacation*', in *The Movie Scene*, 2003. <*http://www.themoviescene.co.uk/reviews/christmas-vacation/christmas-vacation.html*>

—, '*One Magic Christmas*', in *The Movie Scene*, 2004. <*http://www.themoviescene.co.uk/reviews/one-magic-christmas/one-magic-christmas.html*>

—, '*Prancer*', in *The Movie Scene*, 2003. <*http://www.themoviescene.co.uk/reviews/prancer-1989/prancer-1989.html*>

—, '*Scrooged*', in *The Movie Scene*, 2000. <*http://www.themoviescene.co.uk/reviews/scrooged/scrooged.html*>

Weinberg, Scott, '*Trading Places*', in *JoBlo*, 5 June 2007. <*http://www.joblo.com/blu-rays-dvds/reviews/trading-places-se*>

Werts, Diane, *Christmas On Television* (Westport: Greenwood Press, 2006).

Whalley, Jim, *Saturday Night Live, Hollywood Comedy, and American Culture: From Chevy Chase to Tina Fey* (New York: Palgrave MacMillan, 2010).

Wheeler, Jeremy, '*Don't Open Till Christmas*', in *AllMovie*, 2011. <*http://www.allmovie.com/movie/dont-open-till-christmas-v14335/review*>

Wilson, Richard, *Scrooge's Guide to Christmas: A Survival Manual for the Festively Challenged* (London: Hodder and Stoughton, 1997).

Wilmington, Michael, 'Not Even Christmas Can Save the New *Ernest*', in *The Los Angeles Times*, 15 November 1988.

Wise, Wyndham, ed., *Take One's Essential Guide to Canadian Film* (Toronto: University of Toronto Press, 2001).

Wolcott, James, 'Small Comfort', in *Texas Monthly*, December 1984, p.188.

ZigZag, '*To All a Good Night* Movie Review', in *Horror Talk*, 14 December 2009.
<http://www.horrortalk.com/index.php/reviews/719-to-all-a-good-night>

Index

616

N

O

Q

R

U

V

W

Acknowledgements

I would like to thank each of the following people for their greatly appreciated friendship, fellowship and support during the research and writing of this book:

David and Fiona Addison, Douglas J. Allen, Dr Colin and Vivien Barron, Eddy and Dorothy Bryan, Julie Christie, Michael Donnelly, James Geekie, Denham and Stella Hardwick, The Rev. Dr Adam Hood, Dr Elspeth King, Ivy Lannon, Amy Leitch, Bryon and Allison Longbone, Rachael J. McClure, Michael McGinnes, Ian and Anne McNeish, Mary Melville, Ed Morton, Alex and Kelley Tucker, and Professor Rory Watson.

About the Author

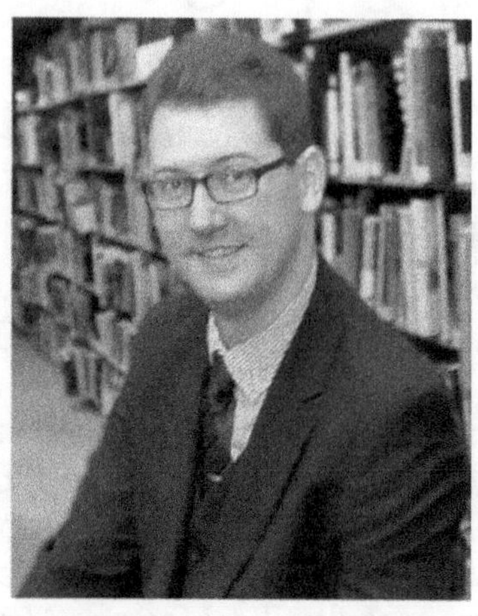

Dr Thomas Christie has many years of experience as a literary professional, working in collaboration with several publishing companies including Cambridge Scholars Publishing, Crescent Moon Publishing and Robert Greene Publishing. A passionate advocate of the written word and literary arts, over the years he has worked to develop original writing for respected organisations such as the Stirling Smith Art Gallery and Museum and the Dementia Services Development Centre, a leading independent higher education research unit based at the University of Stirling. Additionally, he is regularly involved in public speaking events and has delivered guest lectures and presentations about his work at many locations around the United Kingdom.

An elected member of the Royal Society of Literature, the Society of Authors, the Federation of Writers Scotland and the Authors' Licensing and Collecting Society, he holds a first-class Honours degree in English Literature and a Masters degree in Humanities with British Cinema History from the Open University in Milton Keynes, and a Doctorate of Philosophy in Scottish Literature awarded by the University of Stirling.

He is the author of a number of books on the subject of modern film which include *Liv Tyler: Star in Ascendance* (2007), *The Cinema of Richard Linklater* (2008), *John Hughes and Eighties Cinema: Teenage Hopes and American Dreams* (2009), *Ferris Bueller's Day Off: Pocket Movie Guide* (2010), *The Christmas Movie Book* (2011), *The James Bond Movies of the 1980s* (2013) and *Mel Brooks: Genius and Loving It!: Freedom and Liberation in the Cinema of Mel Brooks* (2015).

His other works include *Notional Identities: Ideology, Genre and National Identity in Popular Scottish Fiction Since the Seventies* (2013) and *The Spectrum of Adventure: A Brief History of Interactive Fiction on the Sinclair ZX Spectrum* (2016).

For more details about Tom and his work, please visit his website at:
www.tomchristiebooks.co.uk

For details of new and forthcoming books
from Extremis Publishing,
please visit our official website at:

www.extremispublishing.com

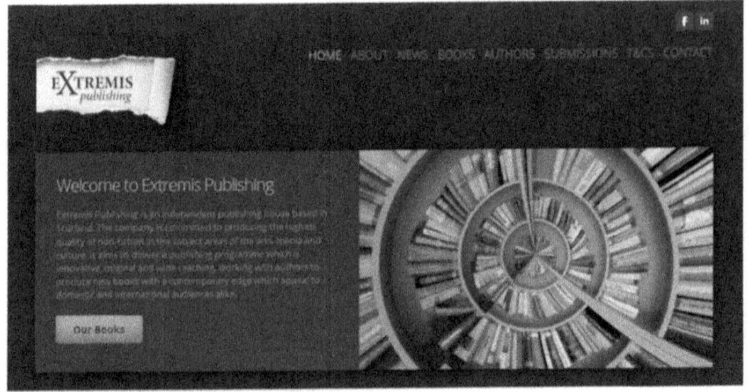

or follow us on social media at:

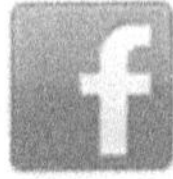

www.facebook.com/extremispublishing

www.linkedin.com/company/extremis-publishing-ltd-/